EARTH SCIENCE
THE WORLD WE LIVE IN

SAMUEL N. NAMOWITZ

with the editorial assistance of

DONALD B. STONE

AMERICAN BOOK COMPANY

earth science

THE WORLD WE LIVE IN

FIFTH EDITION

SAMUEL N. NAMOWITZ Formerly Principal, Charles Evans Hughes High School, New York City. Has been actively teaching earth science as a teacher in public high schools for over 25 years, and an instructor in geology and earth science at the college level, as well as at NSF Summer Institutes. He has written numerous articles for professional journals and the Book of Knowledge. He has also presided over or been a member of several New York City and New York State Earth Science Committees.

DONALD B. STONE Lecturer in earth science, Russell Sage College, Troy, New York. Has taught earth science at both the high school and college level for many years; has also taught earth science teaching methods at several summer institutes. He has written many articles for professional journals and co-authored other educational materials.

Cover photograph: Iceland Tourist Bureau

Cover design: A Good Thing, Inc.

Illustrations: Audrey Namowitz

Acknowledgment of Unit Photos

1. Union Pacific Railroad
2. Union Pacific Railroad
3. Icelandic National Tourist Office
4. American Airlines
5. The American Museum of Natural History
6. Mount Wilson and Palomar Observatories
7. Wide World Photo

AMERICAN BOOK COMPANY

New York   Cincinnati   Atlanta   Dallas   Millbrae

11   12   10

PREFACE

In this fifth edition of EARTH SCIENCE—THE WORLD WE LIVE IN, the emphasis on scientific inquiry has been continued and expanded. Students may begin with inquiries on their own from every chapter. Then students are introduced to the questions and problems that challenge the earth scientist. Students are made aware of the nature and limitations of scientific investigation and the extent to which answers to earth science problems may be tentative or incomplete. Students examine the hypotheses formulated by scientists and consider some of the evidence on which these hypotheses rest. Throughout the text students devise and conduct simple inquiries of their own into problems of the earth sciences.

New Features of EARTH SCIENCE—THE WORLD WE LIVE IN: Fifth Edition

1. Chapter-Opening Inquiry. A new student activity called How Do You Know That . . . ? introduces each chapter of the book. Its inclusion at the beginning of the chapter encourages students to participate in scientific inquiry on their own. Each How Do You Know That . . . ? builds such process skills as observation, comparison, measurement, control of variables, recording and interpreting data, hypothesizing and formulating models, and prediction. Each How Do You Know That . . . ? leads students from these processes of science and hands-on experiences to an awareness of the concepts to be developed in the chapter. The How Do You Know That . . . ? activity requires simple, common materials usually found in most classrooms. Each activity can be completed in one period or less time. You may want students to work individually or in small groups; or you may suggest alternating "demonstration" teams of students who do the investigation for the rest of the class.

2. Unit-Opening Inquiry. Each two-page unit opener highlights the major theme of the unit. The photograph on the right page was chosen both to illustrate a sample event or phenomenon of earth science and to elicit student inquiry. The text on the left page initiates inquiry by focusing students' attention on the photograph. Then, through questions and suggestions, it leads students to make observations and inferences about the scene illustrated. From these observations, students are then asked to make some comparisons with or inferences from their own experiences and the environment around them.

3. New Text Materials. A new chapter called "The Earth In Balance" has been added at the end of the book. Ecology is relevant to any study of the earth, its oceans, and its atmosphere. The new chapter relates environmental science to events and processes the students have already studied. Unit 3 has a new section on plate tectonics, a growing area of geology that attempts to describe the structure of the earth and the origin of the continents. This new section presents both the theories and the supporting evidence.

Unit 4 on the oceans has been revised to keep pace with oceanographic research, tools, methods, and data. Unit 6 on the universe has new materials on the solar system, exploring space, and our moon. Unit 7 contains new materials on weather and climate. The concept of microclimates is introduced, and the effects of people's activities on climate are discussed.

The Appendix contains a new set of tables on measurement and metric units based on SI—the International System of Measurement. These tables include standard units in the SI system; metric prefixes, symbols, equivalents; metric-English equivalents recommended by the SI system for length, mass, area, volume, and capacity.

Learning Aids in EARTH SCIENCE—THE WORLD WE LIVE IN: Fifth Edition

In addition to the new features just described, the fifth edition retains many of the learning tools teachers have found so helpful in previous editions. These include:

1. Illustrative Materials. Full-color and black-and-white photographs, including 72 color photos of rocks and minerals, two-color line drawings, and tables and charts are used to introduce, reinforce, and extend concepts. New line drawings and carefully selected new photographs have been added to maintain the high standard of illustration throughout the text.

2. Topic Questions. Numbered Topic Questions at the end of each chapter direct students to the main ideas covered in the same-numbered topic within the chapter. This aid simplifies the task of assigning questions to match text assignment and also highlights the major concepts in the lessons.

3. General Questions. These questions at the end of the chapter call for student application of concepts to new problems. Some questions require students to tie together the main ideas of several topics.

4. Student Activities. These activities at the end of the chapter suggest practical investigations and projects related to the work of the chapter. Great care has been taken to make the instructions clear and complete so that students may undertake the activities independently.

5. Topographic Sheets. Suggestions and references for topographic maps pertinent to chapter content are listed at the end of the chapter.

6. Vocabulary and Pronunciation Guides. Key vocabulary words are printed in boldface type within the text. The phonetic pronunciation of difficult or unfamiliar words is provided within the text following the first appearance of the word.

7. Bibliography. A bibliography, organized by unit subjects and brought up to date for this edition, now appears at the end of each unit.

8. Appendix. At the end of the book is an appendix that includes measurement tables, a table of the chemical elements, a simple key to the identification of minerals, and a table listing the properties of the common minerals.

9. Glossary and Index. At the end of the book there is a glossary of over 650 terms and an exhaustive index.

Components of EARTH SCIENCE—THE WORLD WE LIVE IN

1. THE TEACHER'S EDITION helps the teacher manage an earth science program that has both variety and appropriateness for different classrooms. A three-track Outline of Topics covered in the basic text shows how topics may be assigned for students of various ability levels. The Guide is organized by lessons, and the topics to be covered in each lesson are indicated; concepts and suggestions for each lesson are provided. Answers to all the General Questions at the end of a chapter are included. The TEACHER'S EDITION also includes sources of visual aids, specific suggestions for films and filmstrips, a list of supply houses and sources of materials, and a teacher bibliography.

Annotated Student Text Pages. This feature helps the teacher reinforce major earth science concepts, provides additional information, and suggests additional activities for the student. Overprinted references to experiments from the ACTIVITIES book and EARTH SCIENCE TRANSPARENCIES are given at appropriate places in the text.

2. ACTIVITIES IN EARTH SCIENCE is a laboratory manual providing "hands-on" learning experiences. It contains a variety of investigations for classroom, laboratory, and the field. Detailed instructions enable students to work on their own or in small groups. The *Activities* book may be used to supplement the basic earth science program, or it may be used alone to build concepts and process skills in a laboratory-oriented program.

3. TESTS FOR EARTH SCIENCE is a self-scoring booklet of chapter tests. Each chapter of the basic text is covered in a test, and answers are provided in the front of the booklet.

4. EARTH SCIENCE TRANSPARENCIES is an additional visual component of the program. This boxed set is made up of 31 full-color transparencies, with teacher information sheets, masks, clear acetate sheets, and a correlation chart keying each transparency to pages in several earth science texts. EARTH SCIENCE TRANS-PARENCIES may be used to introduce, review, compare, or extent concepts; for class or individual testing; and for individual instruction.

Acknowledgments

The authors wish to acknowledge the assistance given by a number of people at various stages in the evolution of this edition. Critical reviews of units in their areas of specialization were made by Professor Maurice Rosalsky of the Department of Geology, Professor Richard Rommer of the Department of Meteorology and Oceanography, and Dr. Robert Wolf, Chairman of the Department of Physics, all at the City College of New York. Dr. Kurt Lowe, Chairman of the Department of Geology at the City College, provided most of the specimens of rocks and minerals from which the text's color photos were made. Last, but not least, the authors wish to thank the many correspondents, both teachers and pupils, whose helpful suggestions with respect to previous editions have resulted in many subtle refinements in the language and illustrations of the text.

S.N.N., D.B.S.

CONTENTS

Unit 1   The Crust of the Earth

The photograph on the
opposite page shows one of the
worlds scenic attractions—the Grand Canyon of the Colorado River. At first glance, what
do you see in the photograph? Can you identify separate
rock layers? Do they all seem to be alike? Do they all seem
to be going in the same direction? Now look more carefully. What
evidence is there of an atmosphere? What evidence is there of water?
Is there any way to tell from the photo the shape of the earth? Why?

In this unit we explore some questions about the earth and the rock of which
it is made. How do we know the size and shape of the earth? How did the rocks
of its outer crust begin? What lies beneath the earth's crust? Some questions can
be answered by direct observation and direct measurement. Others can be
answered only by indirect methods and from indirect evidence.

Our earth is a globe of solid rock largely covered by liquid water and completely
surrounded by an atmosphere of gases. From inside the earth come geysers
and volcanoes and earthquakes. In the atmosphere there are hurricanes, tornadoes, jet streams, lightning storms, and auroras. In the ocean there are
great currents, a sea floor whose profile has until recently been almost
unknown, and deposits of strange and varied sediments. Outer space
has the moon and the planets, the sun and the stars, the Milky
Way and the galaxies, the possibility of other living worlds.

All these subjects are exciting and challenging. All fall
within the scope of the earth sciences. Despite their
separate names and separate areas of
study, the earth sciences are
all interrelated.

CHAPTER 1

The Earth We Live On

HOW DO YOU KNOW THAT . . . ?

1. Do you live near the ocean or a large lake? If so, you can verify for yourself the simple evidence of the earth's curvature shown in Fig. 1-1. Go to the shore and carefully observe a ship that is moving directly away from you out to sea. Binoculars will extend your field of vision, but your unaided eyes will do just as well. Which part of the ship disappears first? Now look for a ship that is just coming into view over the horizon. Which part appears first?

2. If you do not live near a large body of water, or prefer not to wait until you go there, try this. Get a large globe, a basketball, or any curved surface to represent the earth. Place your eye level even with the top of the globe. This is your horizon. Use a block of wood, a piece of chalk, or even your finger to represent a ship. Start the ship at an "out-of-sight" position over the horizon. Bring it up slowly until you see it all. Reverse the operation. Which part appears first? Which part disappears first? How is this different from what happens on a flat surface?

1. The Earth Is Spherical

Is the earth flat or round? This question was answered in 1522 when one of Magellan's ships completed the first circumnavigation of the earth. But long before Magellan there were evidences of the earth's spherical shape. Travelers saw the North Star rise higher in the sky as they went northward, and sink in the sky as they went southward. Stars invisible in the Northern Hemisphere appeared in the sky as ships sailed south of the Equator. Sailors also noticed that the mast of a ship was the first part to appear and the last to disappear on the horizon. (See Fig. 1-1.)

Another evidence of the earth's shape known in early times was the shape of its shadow. During eclipses of the moon it was observed that the edge of the earth's shadow as it moved across the moon was always the arc of a circle. Only a sphere always casts a circular shadow regardless of its position.

Today the earth's roundness is clearly shown in photographs taken by earth satellites and space

Fig. 1-1. The curvature of the earth is shown by the way a ship comes into view.

probes. Astronauts have seen the curvature of the surface with their own eyes. (See Fig. 1-2.)

2. The Earth Is Not a Perfect Sphere

Gravity provides further evidence that the earth is a sphere. The weight of an object is a measure of the force with which gravity pulls it toward the earth's center, and the weight depends on the object's distance from the earth's center. But a given object weighs almost the same in all parts of the earth. What does this mean? It means that all the earth's surface is almost equidistant from the earth's center. And this means that the earth is almost spherical.

Why almost? Careful measurements show that the weight of an object is *not* exactly the same all over the earth. An object that weighs 195 pounds at sea level at the earth's North Pole or South Pole loses weight as it approaches the Equator, where it weighs only 194 pounds. What does this mean? It means that the object must be nearer the earth's center at the Poles

than at the Equator. In other words, the earth is not a perfect sphere. It is flattened at the Poles and it bulges at the Equator. We call this shape an *oblate spheroid*. It is caused by the earth's rotation.

Incidentally, not all of the loss of weight at the Equator is caused by greater distance from the earth's center. Some of it, like the earth's shape, is an effect caused by the earth's rotation.

Observations by satellites have shown that the North Pole is about 80 feet farther from the earth's center than the South Pole. This has led some people to speak of the earth as "pear-shaped," but the deviation is too small to justify this adjective.

3. Eratosthenes Measured the Earth's Circumference

How does one measure the earth's circumference? In principle, the method is a simple one. Take two points a substantial distance apart on the earth, with one directly north of the other.

Fig. 1-2. Earth at crescent phase in sky above lunar surface. Photo by Lunar Orbiter I.

NASA

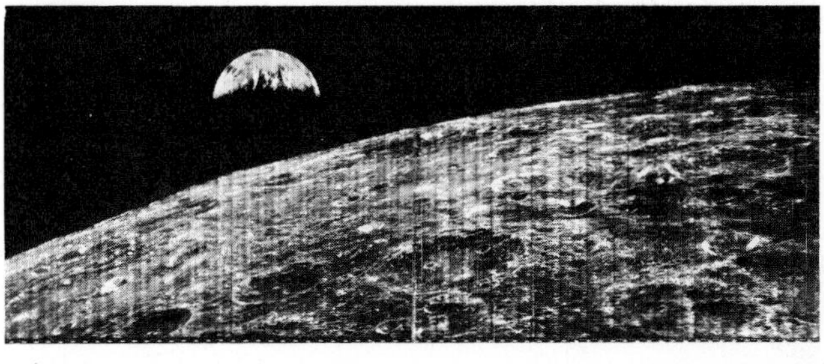

The line joining these points will then be an arc of a circle that goes around the earth through the North and South Poles. Measure the distance between the two points. Find out what part of the whole circumference the arc is (we shall see how in a moment). Then multiply the measured distance by the number of arcs needed to make the whole circle. The answer is the north-south circumference of the earth.

The first scientific measurement of the earth's circumference was probably made by the Greek astronomer Eratosthenes (er uh *tos* thuh *neez*) more than 2,000 years ago, about 200 B.C. He knew that the sun cast no shadows and therefore was directly overhead in the city of Syene (now Aswan) in southern Egypt at noon on June 21. In Alexandria, where Eratosthenes was keeper of the royal library, the sun was 7.2° below the overhead point at noon. This meant that Syene and Alexandria were separated by 7.2° on a circumference of the earth. (See Fig. 1-3.) Since 7.2° is one-fiftieth of the whole distance (360°) around the earth, Eratosthenes measured the distance between Syene and Alexandria, multiplied it by 50, and obtained an answer for the earth's circumference. Eratosthenes' measurement was made in a unit called a *stadium,* which we think was about 600 feet. Despite a number of inaccuracies in his measurements and observations, his answer is believed to have been fairly close to the real value of the earth's circumference. It was a remarkable achievement 2,000 years ago.

4. The Earth's Dimensions

The basic procedure described in Topic 3 is still used today when measurements of the earth's circumference are made. Our methods, however, give us more accurate results than were possible in Eratosthenes' time. In round numbers, the earth's equatorial circumference is about 24,900 miles. The polar circumference is about 24,860 miles. The diameter of the earth through the Poles (the polar diameter) is 7,900 miles. The diameter through the bulging Equator (the equatorial diameter) is 7,927 miles.

The total surface area of the earth is about 197,000,000 square miles. Of this, about 57,000,000 square miles stand above sea level as continents and islands. The remaining 140,000,000 square miles are covered by oceans. All the waters of the earth—oceans, inland seas, lakes, streams—are called the **hydrosphere** (water sphere). The solid earth is called the **lithosphere** (rock sphere). The gases that surround the earth are its **atmosphere.** Together, the lithosphere, the hydrosphere, and the atmosphere make up the earth.

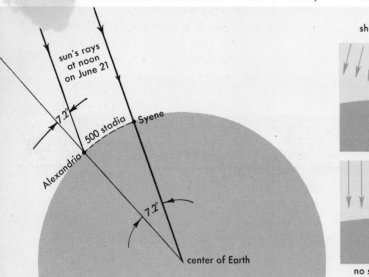

Fig. 1-3. This diagram shows the noon position of the sun's rays at Syene and Alexandria on the summer solstice.

5. From Surface to Center: What Kind of Rock?

How far is it from the earth's surface to its center? The answer, of course, is nearly 4,000 miles—half the diameter. Geologists are very much interested in these 4,000 miles. In simple terms, they want to know what kinds of "rock" make up the earth's interior. Are they in the form of solids, liquids, or even possibly gases? How hot are they? How heavy? What materials do they consist of? Do they resemble the rocks of the surface?

Such questions could be answered directly if we could obtain samples of the earth's interior at various depths. The best we are able to do in this respect, however, is not very much. Our deepest mines are only about two miles deep, and our deepest rock samples come from oil wells about five miles deep; so the geologists resort to indirect methods of study, just as astronomers must do when they study space beyond the solar system. The astronomer collects and interprets the information that comes to him in the form of light waves, heat waves, and other radiations from outer space. In somewhat similar fashion, the geologist makes special use of earthquake waves to tell him about the materials in the earth's interior through which the waves have passed. How? This is explained in Chapter 15, where we study earthquakes. He also makes use of information derived from studies of the earth's gravity, its magnetism, and the flow of heat from its interior.

6. Cross Section of the Earth

Here is a picture of the earth's interior as most geologists presently believe it to be. It represents their interpretation of the evidence now available. (See Fig. 1-4.)

At its surface the earth is covered by a comparatively thin layer or **crust** of rocks with a *specific gravity* between 2.7 and 3.0. (The spe-

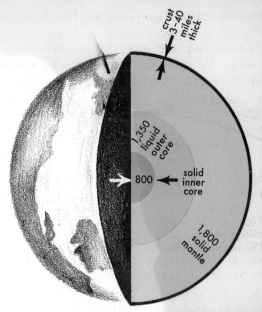

Fig. 1-4. A cross section of the earth from crust to core.

cific gravity of a material tells us how many times as heavy as water it is.) This crust is thought to be approximately 20 to 40 miles thick under the continents, but only from 3 to 20 miles thick under the ocean basins. Samples of rock from the upper crust are easily available on the continents, but not in the ocean basins.

The crust includes a great variety of rocks, many of which are described in Chapter 4. However, the principal rock of the continental crust is the common rock we call **granite** (*gran* it). The principal rock of the ocean crust is **basalt** (buh *salt*), but the basalt also continues beyond the oceans underneath the granite masses of all the continents (Fig. 1-5). Basalt is a dark gray or black rock that is appreciably heavier than granite. The specific gravity of granite is about 2.7; that of basalt is about 3.0.

A fairly abrupt change in the nature of the rock marks the end of the crust and the beginning of the *mantle*. This boundary zone between

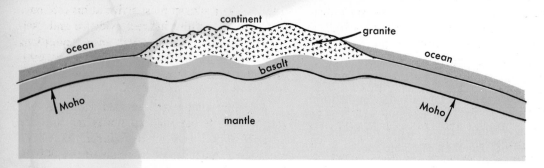

Fig. 1-5. The basalt bedrock that underlies the world's oceans forms a crust that completely encloses the earth. The continents consist largely of granite resting on the basalt. The mantle lies beneath the basalt crust.

the crust and the mantle is called the **Mohorovicic** (mo hor o *viss* ik) **discontinuity,** or more simply, the **Moho.** It was discovered in 1909 by the Yugoslavian scientist Andrija Mohorovicic. How? He studied the manner in which earthquake waves changed speed when they passed from the crust to the mantle.

The **mantle** is believed to be a region of heavy, iron-rich rock with an average specific gravity of about 5. It extends from the crust nearly 1,800 miles into the earth's interior.

At about 1,800 miles another rather abrupt change in the rock marks the end of the mantle. Here the **outer core** begins and continues about 1,350 miles into the interior. The outer core is thought to be mostly iron and nickel in a hot plastic or fluid condition. The remaining distance to the earth's center, about 800 miles, includes the **inner core.** This, too, is believed to be mostly iron and nickel, but in a solid state. Ordinarily, iron has a specific gravity of less than 8, and nickel has a specific gravity of less than 9. But the pressure on the core is so great that it has an average specific gravity of between 10 and 12. At its very center the core is almost as heavy as mercury.

7. Specific Gravity of the Earth

Sir Isaac Newton's law of gravitation makes it possible to calculate the weight of the earth from the force with which it attracts objects to its surface. The volume of the earth is easily calculated from its dimensions. Comparing the earth's weight with the weight of an equal volume of water, we get its specific gravity. This turns out to be 5.5. In other words, the earth weighs about 5.5 times as much as an all-water planet.

Does this calculated specific gravity of 5.5 support or conflict with the geologist's picture of the earth's interior? It supports it. Since the earth's crust has a specific gravity of 3.0 or less, the interior would have to have a specific gravity well above 5.5 in order to reach an *average* of 5.5. In the geologist's picture, the earth's core has a specific gravity of 10 to 12. (See Fig. 1-6.)

8. Temperatures Below the Earth's Surface

Did you ever visit limestone caverns? If your visit was in summer you know that caverns are pleasantly cool at that time. You may not know that these same caverns remain at the same temperature all year round. Neither the sun's heat nor the winter cold penetrates below a depth of about 50 feet. At this depth in the earth, the temperature usually remains equal to the average yearly temperature of the particular location.

From 50 feet downward, however, the temperature of the earth always rises. We have many observations of this rise from our excavations and borings in tunnels, mines, and oil wells. The rate of increase in temperature differs, however, from place to place. It may be as high as 1°F for every 30 feet. It may be as low as 1°F for every 200 feet. On the average, it seems to be about 1°F for every 50 to 75 feet. This may be roughly estimated as about 70°F to 100°F per mile. At this rate the rocks at a depth of two miles can easily be hot enough to boil water.

Fig. 1-6. How the rocks of the earth's interior differ in specific gravity.

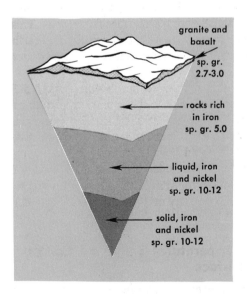

granite and basalt
sp. gr. 2.7-3.0

rocks rich in iron
sp. gr. 5.0

liquid, iron and nickel
sp. gr. 10-12

solid, iron and nickel
sp. gr. 10-12

Our direct observations of rock temperatures end only a few miles down. From there to the interior, the geologist must arrive at his estimates of temperature from indirect evidence and "scientific guesses." He must try to answer questions such as this: If the core at 3,500 miles is solid and composed of iron and nickel, how hot must it be to have a density of 12?

Why not simply assume that the "average" rate of 100°F per mile continues far into the interior? If this were so, the temperature of the mantle at 1,000 miles would be about 100,000°F. Indirect evidence makes this appear impossible. We believe the mantle to have a temperature of perhaps 5,000°F at this depth, and the core to have a temperature of not more than 10,000°F, even at the earth's center.

9. What Makes the Rocks Hot?

If the rocks get hotter as we approach the interior of the earth, there must be some source of heat in the interior. Some scientists believe that the interior still retains much of the heat which the earth had when it was a hot liquid globe. Others think that the heat comes from the radiations emitted by radioactive elements such as uranium and thorium. Still others think that at least part of the interior heat was produced by the compression of the rocks of the interior by the great weight of the rocks that lie above them.

Rocks are poor conductors of heat. This explains why the earth loses its interior heat so slowly to outer space. However, even among the rocks there are differences in their ability to conduct heat. This is probably why there are different rates of temperature change in different places.

What explains the presence of hot rock near the surface in regions of volcanoes and hot springs? We do not know, but one explanation is that the heat in such places comes from great concentrations of radioactive materials.

10. How the Crust Formed

Having described the structure of the earth, the geologist also would like to explain how this structure developed during the earth's formation. He is particularly interested in these questions: Why is the crust of the continents so different from that of the ocean basins? Why are the continents made largely of granite, whereas the ocean basins are floored by the darker and heavier rock basalt?

One hypothesis takes us back to the time billions of years ago when the earth was hot and molten, and a thin layer of relatively light liquid floated like oil on the main mass of heavy liquids. As cooling continued, the light liquid formed a thin crust of basalt over the entire surface of the earth. The heavier liquids cooled slowly to form the mantle and the core. Directly beneath the crust, however, hot liquids and gases were still escaping from the mantle. These erupted through the overlying basalt crust to form volcanic masses of granite, or of rock that later changed to granite. The volcanic masses grew through further eruption until they became our continents. According to this hypothesis, the continents are still growing in the same way, particularly along their margins, wherever volcanoes are found.

A second hypothesis suggests that the crust originally consisted of a thin layer of granite rock that completely covered a second crustal layer of basaltic rock. Then the granitic crust split up into great blocks that moved until they piled up on one another. The piled-up masses of granite became the continents. The depressions they left behind them became the basalt-floored ocean basins.

TOPIC QUESTIONS

Each topic question refers to the topic of the same number within this chapter.

1. Compare the evidences of the earth's spherical shape known in Magellan's time and before Magellan with those available to us now.

2. (*a*) Explain how gravity tells us the earth is almost spherical. (*b*) Explain how gravity tells us the earth is oblate.

3. Explain the principle involved in Eratosthenes' method of measuring the earth's circumference.

4. (*a*) How large are the equatorial and polar circumferences and diameters of the earth? (*b*) Compare the areas of ocean and land with the earth's total area.

5. (*a*) What do geologists want to know about the earth's interior? (*b*) How can the earth's interior rocks be studied?

6. (*a*) With the aid of a diagram, describe the structure and characteristics of the earth from crust to core. (*b*) Describe the Moho and its discovery.

7. (*a*) Explain how the earth's specific gravity is calculated. (*b*) Explain how the calculated figure supports the geologists' picture of the earth.

8. (*a*) What is the average rate at which temperature increases with depth in the earth? How do we know? (*b*) Why can't the rate of increase continue all the way to the earth's center?

9. (*a*) What are the probable sources of the earth's internal heat? (*b*) What causes surface rocks in volcanic regions to be hot?

10. Decribe a hypothesis that explains why the continents and ocean basins are made of different rock.

CHAPTER 2
The Nature of Minerals

HOW DO YOU KNOW THAT . . . ?

Study one or more samples of soil to see what kinds of materials you can identify. Get samples from several places—a park, empty lot, garden, field, beach, flower pot. From each place take enough soil to make a variety of observations. Spread a spoonful of each sample on a sheet of paper. Examine the materials carefully with a hand magnifying lens. Feel some of each sample. Then find out how a magnet affects each sample. Record all your observations.

What materials do you find that were once living? What materials do you find that were never living? Can you find glassy bits (quartz), shiny flakes (white mica and black mica), or black grains (magnetite)? How can you differentiate between the nonliving and the once-living materials? Which materials are you unable to identify?

1. Recognizing Bedrock

In many parts of the earth the solid outer crust is hidden by a cover of loose rock, earth, or soil. This cover may take the form of the sands of deserts and beaches, the boulders and gravels at the bases of cliffs, the soils of farm and forest, the muds and clays of a swamp, and the sediments of lake and sea floors. Beneath this loose material, however, there is always unbroken solid rock. This solid rock that seems to be firmly attached to the entire mass of the earth is called **bedrock.** It is the outer part of the earth's crust. This bedrock is not to be confused with the unattached blocks of rock known as boulders.

How deep is the loose rock or soil that covers the bedrock? In some places it may be hundreds of feet thick. In other places there may be no cover at all, and the bedrock can be seen at the surface in **outcrops** or **exposures.** Outcrops are more likely to appear in hilly and mountainous

regions than in level regions. (See Fig. 2-1.) Where road cuts pass through rocky hills, both the bedrock and its cover are likely to be visible.

2. Materials of the Bedrock

In a given locality the same bedrock is likely to extend over a considerable area. It may be granite, shale, limestone, sandstone, or any of dozens of different varieties of bedrock that form the earth's crust. But regardless of the particular variety of rock, a close inspection shows that it is composed of definite substances called **minerals.**

Minerals like quartz, mica, calcite, and magnetite range from tiny grains to pebble-size crystals, which seem to be cemented or melted together to form the rock. Some varieties of rock have only one kind of mineral in them; most varieties of rock contain two or more different

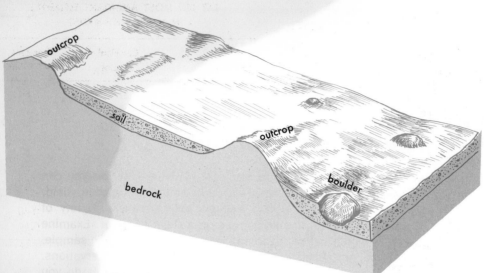

Fig. 2-1. This diagram shows how soil, boulders, outcrops, and bedrock are related.

kinds of minerals. To illustrate: limestone often consists only of the mineral calcite; granite always contains quartz, feldspar, and at least one other mineral. (See Fig. 2-2.)

Rocks may be compared to puddings, in which the minerals are like the ingredients of the pudding. The rock is the whole pudding; the minerals are the grains of rice, nuts, raisins, and other materials in the pudding. Just as raisins and nuts may be found in many different kinds of puddings, so the same minerals may be found in many different kinds of rocks.

Geologists define rocks as masses or "aggregates" of minerals. But geologists differ somewhat as to the exact definition of a mineral. According to some, minerals must be solids, not liquids, so petroleum is not classed as a mineral. Again, some geologists include as minerals all substances occurring naturally in the rocks. Others insist that minerals must be of inorganic (nonliving) origin, thereby excluding coal. In any event, the complete definition of a mineral is a rather long one, so we shall begin with a short definition, explain its meaning, and then add to it as we go along.

A mineral is a solid element or compound of inorganic origin found in nature.

3. Minerals Are Natural Inorganic Solids

This part of our definition is easy to understand. *Inorganic* means nonliving, or not derived from living things. Thus coal, petroleum, pearl, pine tree resin, and wood are not minerals, but quartz, mica, gold, diamond, and calcite are. Again, since only *solids* can be minerals, petroleum, natural gas, and the earth's waters are excluded, even though they are natural substances in the earth's crust. Ice, however, as a natural solid, is called a mineral.

4. Minerals May Be Elements

Our definition says that minerals may be **elements.** What are elements? Most of you probably know this already, but suppose we review briefly.

An element is a substance that cannot be broken down into simpler substances by ordinary

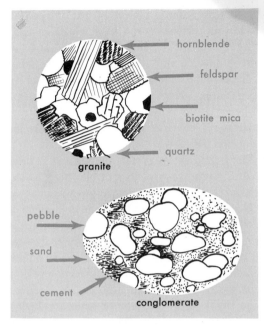

Fig. 2-2. Granite consists of interlocking crystals of different minerals. Conglomerate consists of pebbles and sand grains held by cement.

THE TEN MOST ABUNDANT ELEMENTS IN THE EARTH'S CRUST

Name	Chemical Symbol	Per cent by Weight
Oxygen	O	46.60
Silicon	Si	27.72
Aluminum	Al	8.13
Iron	Fe	5.00
Calcium	Ca	3.63
Sodium	Na	2.83
Potassium	K	2.59
Magnesium	Mg	2.09
Titanium	Ti	0.40
Hydrogen	H	0.14
Total		99.13

chemical means. (Atom smashing and atomic fission are not ordinary chemical means.) The names of many elements are familiar to all of us. Oxygen and nitrogen are important in the atmosphere; gold, silver, iron, tin, copper, lead, zinc, mercury, aluminum, and uranium are important metals; sulfur and carbon are well-known non-metals. In all the earth no more than 92 different elements occur naturally, although chemists have thus far created 12 artificial elements which are not found in the earth.

The elements that exist in nature are far from being equally plentiful. Two of the elements, oxygen and silicon, are so abundant in the substances of the earth's crust that they compose nearly 75 per cent of the total weight of the outer crust. The ten most abundant elements together make up more than 99 per cent of the weight of the outer crust.

These ten elements rarely exist in uncombined form in the minerals of the crust. Each one of them is almost always found combined with other elements. For example, oxygen and silicon are combined in the common mineral quartz; aluminum, silicon, hydrogen, and oxygen are combined in common clay.

Do any elements exist uncombined in the crust in substantial amounts? Yes—gold, silver, platinum, copper, sulfur, carbon, and a few others are in this group. (See Fig. 2-3.)

Fig. 2-3. A gold nugget. Gold is one of the few elements found uncombined in the crust.

Ward's Natural Science Establishment

5. Elements and Atoms

More than 150 years ago the English chemist John Dalton stated his belief that each element is composed of tiny particles called atoms. Today we know this to be true, and scientists have been able to determine the size of these atoms. An atom of oxygen, for example, is about ten billionths of an inch in diameter! The **atom** has long been defined as **the smallest part of an element that has all the characteristics of that element.** This definition is still true, but in the present century scientists have discovered that the atom itself consists of three kinds of still smaller particles. Furthermore, all atoms—regardless of the element—consist of the same kinds of particles! Let us see how this is possible.

6. Picture of an Atom

Atoms can be visualized as miniature solar systems, with particles of one kind whirling at high speeds in orbits, like planets, around a center or nucleus that contains two other kinds of particles (except in the case of ordinary hydrogen). Two of the three kinds of particles are charged with electricity. The third kind is neutral, or without any charge.

The particles spinning in orbits around the nucleus are called **electrons.** Each electron carries a charge of negative electricity, exactly the same amount for all electrons. In the nucleus of the atom are **protons** and **neutrons.** Each proton carries a charge of positive electricity **exactly equal to the negative charge of an electron.** The proton, however, is 1,845 times as heavy as the electron. The neutron, as its name implies (neutral), carries no electricity, but it weighs slightly more than the proton.

7. Atoms of Different Elements

The simplest and lightest of all atoms is the atom of ordinary *hydrogen,* the symbol for which

is *H.* Hydrogen has a nucleus of just one proton. Around this nucleus spins a single electron. Electrically the atom is neutral, since protons and electrons have equal but opposite charges. Scientists have found that **all atoms are, like our hydrogen atom, electrically neutral.** This means that every atom must have as many electrons outside the nucleus as it has protons in the nucleus. (See Fig. 2-4.)

The next lightest of the elements is *helium, He.* This atom has a nucleus of two protons *and two neutrons.* Balancing the two positive charges, two electrons spin around the nucleus in orbits at a fixed distance from the nucleus. The surface in which these orbits lie is called a **shell,** like the shell of an egg. Notice that the nucleus of helium contains two neutrons, which approximately double its weight but do not increase its electrical charge. **With the exception of ordinary hydrogen, all atoms contain neutrons.**

At this point you can probably "predict" the number of protons and electrons in the next lightest element, *lithium, Li.* The lithium atom has three protons in its nucleus, and three electrons spinning around the nucleus. The nucleus also includes four neutrons. Two of lithium's three electrons spin around the nucleus in a shell like

Fig. 2-4. These diagrams help us to picture the structure of atoms. Remember, however, that atoms are three-dimensional, and that electrons spin around the nucleus.

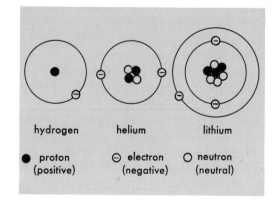

that of the helium atom, but the third electron lies beyond the first two in a shell of its own.

This scheme of atom structure seems to have been followed in nature, increasing one proton at a time for each new element, until 92 elements were formed. Each additional proton calls for an additional electron. As the number of electrons increases, new orbit shells come into existence, but **in every atom the number of electrons equals the number of protons.**

The largest number of electron shells in any atom is seven. The number of electrons differs from shell to shell, but the innermost shell never holds more than two electrons, and the **outermost shell of any atom never holds more than eight.** Other shells may hold as many as 32 electrons.

With each change in the number of protons and electrons, there is a change in the characteristics of the atom, and a new element is born. The heaviest of the natural elements, *uranium,* symbol *U,* has 92 protons in its nucleus. Its 92 electrons are distributed in its seven shells as follows: 2, 8, 18, 32, 21, 9, 2. Do they add up to 92? (See Fig. 2-5.)

8. Atomic Number and Atomic Weight

The **atomic number**—the number of protons in an atom—of hydrogen is 1; of helium, 2; of lithium, 3; of uranium, 92. Knowing the atomic number, one can easily picture or make a model of the atom of an element. For example, the atomic number of oxygen is 8. The oxygen atom therefore has 8 protons in its nucleus and 8 electrons—2 in the first shell and 6 in the second—spinning around the nucleus.

But how many neutrons are there in a nucleus? There is no simple rule relating the number of neutrons to the number of protons, although in the lighter elements they are nearly the same. However, the **atomic weight** of the ele-

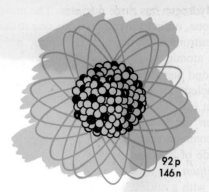

Fig. 2-5. This diagram of a uranium atom illustrates the three-dimensional nature of atoms.

ment tells us approximately the number of protons and neutrons combined in an atom. To find the number of neutrons in an atom, then, we simply subtract the atomic number (number of protons) from the atomic weight (number of protons and neutrons). For example, the atomic number of sodium is 11; its atomic weight is 23. The sodium nucleus therefore contains 11 protons and 12 (subtracting 11 from 23) neutrons. How many electrons spin around the nucleus? Since the number of electrons must equal the number of protons, the answer is 11 electrons.

One more illustration. If uranium, atomic number 92, has an atomic weight of 238, its atom must include 92 electrons, 92 protons, and 146 neutrons. Check this.

9. Nuclides

Since the identity of an atom depends only on the number of protons it has, and not on the number of neutrons, one might wonder whether a particular element could have atoms with different numbers of neutrons. Many elements do. These "different" atoms—once called isotopes—are now called **nuclides** (*nu* klides). Nuclides are **atoms of the same chemical element with different atomic weights.** Let us describe a few of the more important or more familiar nuclides.

Hydrogen has three nuclides. The most common one, ordinary hydrogen, has one proton and *no* neutrons in its nucleus. Its atomic number is 1; its atomic weight is also 1. But hydrogen has a second nuclide with 1 proton and *1* neutron in its nucleus. Its atomic number is 1, but its atomic weight is 2. This nuclide is known as "heavy hydrogen" or *deuterium* (du *teer* ee um). It is much less common than ordinary hydrogen. The third nuclide of hydrogen is very rare indeed. Known as *tritium* (*tri* tee um), it has an atomic weight of 3, with a nucleus of 1 proton and *2* neutrons. (See Fig. 2-6.)

Almost everyone has heard of "carbon 14." This is a heavy nuclide of carbon. Ordinary carbon atoms have an atomic number of 6, an atomic weight of 12. Each ordinary atom of "carbon 12," therefore, has a nucleus of 6 protons and *6* neutrons. But "carbon 14" atoms (atomic weight 14) have nuclei with 6 protons and *8* neutrons. Carbon 14 is important in the dating of events of very recent geologic time, and will be described further in Unit 5. (See Fig. 2-7.)

Uranium has a number of nuclides. Ordinary uranium, described in Topic 8, has atomic weight 238, with *146* neutrons in its nucleus. Uranium 235 (atomic weight 235), however, has only *143* neutrons in its nucleus. All nuclides of uranium must, of course, have 92 protons in the nucleus.

While all nuclides of a particular element have the same *chemical* properties, they have different weights and so can be separated from each other by a number of devices created by

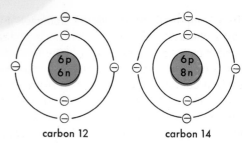

carbon 12   carbon 14

Fig. 2-7. Carbon 12 is ordinary carbon. Carbon 14 is radioactive.

scientists. Furthermore, some nuclides are radioactive, while others are not. For example, carbon 14 is radioactive, but carbon 12 is not.

10. Compounds and Mixtures

So far we have been talking about elements. But most minerals—and in fact, most substances—are compounds. **A compound is a substance consisting of two or more elements chemically combined.** Unlike a mixture, a compound has new properties entirely unlike those of the elements of which it is composed. For example, water is a compound formed from hydrogen and oxygen. Water is certainly different from a mixture of hydrogen and oxygen. Another example is salt, which is a compound of the elements sodium and chlorine. Still other examples are the mineral *quartz,* of which most sand is composed, and the mineral *galena,* an ore of lead. Quartz is a compound of the elements silicon and oxygen. Galena is a compound of lead and sulfur.

In a mixture of chemical elements the individual elements retain their own characteristics, and can usually be recognized by these characteristics—color, odor, taste, and others. The elements in a mixture may be present in any proportions, and they can usually be separated easily by "physical means"—picking them apart, separating light from heavy, dissolving the one that is soluble, using a magnet to remove magnetic elements from others, and so on.

Fig. 2-6. The three nuclides of hydrogen differ only in the number of their neutrons.

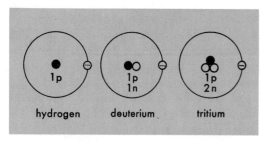

In a compound the individual elements have lost their characteristics. Each element is present in a definite proportion by weight. (This is known as the Law of Definite Proportions.) The elements in a compound can only be separated by "chemical means." For example, water and salt can be decomposed into their elements by electrolysis. The lead in galena can be separated from the sulfur by heating.

An atom is the smallest part of an element. But the smallest part of a compound consists of at least two atoms. What name do we give to this? Scientists call it a **molecule,** and define it as **the smallest part of a compound that has all the characteristics of that compound.**

11. How Elements Form Compounds: Ions

What makes the atoms of different elements unite to form the molecules of a compound? The answer lies in an electrical attraction. In its normal state each atom is electrically neutral, because it has an equal number of protons and electrons. If an atom *gains* one or more electrons, it becomes negatively charged. If an atom *loses* one or more electrons, it becomes positively charged. **An atom in a charged condition, either negative or positive, is called an ion.** (Groups of atoms may also form ions. See Topic 17.) Since opposite charges attract each other, ions of opposite charges may unite to form compounds. For example, *a positively charged sodium ion* will unite with a *negatively charged chlorine ion* to form a molecule of the compound *sodium chloride,* common salt. (See Fig. 2-8.) Two positive hydrogen ions unite with one oxygen ion (with a double negative charge) to form a molecule of H$_2$O, water.

How do atoms lose or gain electrons to become ions? This may happen in many ways. Friction between materials may rub electrons off atoms and create what we call static electricity. This happens when we rub rubber with fur. High temperatures in chemical furnaces, or in the interiors of stars, will separate electrons from atoms to form ions. The impact of cosmic rays or other high-speed particles and rays may convert atoms of oxygen and nitrogen into ions in the upper atmosphere. When mineral compounds dissolve in water, their molecules split up into ions. For example, a molecule of sodium chloride will form a positive sodium ion and a negative chlorine ion (also called a chloride ion). When the water evaporates, the ions reunite to form solid sodium chloride.

Elements that lose electrons easily and form positive ions are classed as **metals.** They include gold, silver, iron, copper, lead, aluminum, sodium, potassium, calcium, zinc, magnesium, and many others. Metals are characterized by their high luster, their ability to conduct heat and electricity, and their ability to be hammered into sheets or drawn into wire.

Elements that gain electrons easily and form negative ions are classed as **nonmetals.** They include nitrogen, oxygen, fluorine, chlorine, phosphorus, and sulfur. These elements generally lack the properties described for metals.

Some elements—such as helium, neon, and argon—never gain or lose electrons, never form ions, and so can never form compounds. They are described as **inert elements.**

Fig. 2-8. If the sodium atom loses its outermost electron, it becomes a positive ion. If the chlorine atom gains an electron, it becomes a negative ion. Sodium ions and chlorine ions can unite to form sodium chloride.

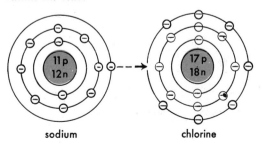

sodium   chlorine

12. Dimensions and Weight of an Atom

In Topic 5 the size of an average atom—oxygen—was given as about ten billionths of an inch in diameter. Most of the atom is empty space, however! The diameter of the nucleus is only, on the average, about one hundred thousandth of the diameter of the whole atom. Around the nucleus, at distances relatively as large as those of the planets from the sun, spin the various electrons, each no larger than a single proton.

Most of the weight of an atom is in its nucleus. As mentioned in Topic 6, a proton is 1,845 times as heavy as an electron. Neutrons are even heavier. As a result, even though the combined number of protons and neutrons is usually only two or three times as great as the number of electrons in an atom, the nucleus includes more than 99.9 per cent of the weight of the whole atom.

13. How Minerals Were Formed

Early in the earth's history, while it was still very hot and molten, all of the elements were already present as the ions of the liquids and gases of the hot earth. Because of the high temperature, these ions moved at high speeds that prevented them from combining with other ions. But as the earth cooled, many ions with opposite charges drew together to form compounds. Not all of the ions entered into combinations with other elements. The inert gases, unable to combine, remained only as elements. A small number of other elements were able to do both—some of their ions entered into combinations while others

Fig. 2-9. Some of the shapes of mineral crystals.

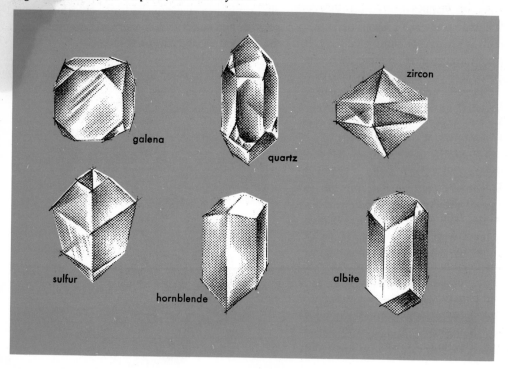

galena

quartz

zircon

sulfur

hornblende

albite

remained uncombined as elements. These included nitrogen, of which a large number of ions escaped combination, rose above the earth's surface, and formed a large part of the atmosphere. Also included were the metallic elements copper, mercury, gold, silver, platinum, and the non-metallic elements sulfur and carbon. (Where these occur as uncombined elements in the earth's crust, they are spoken of as "native gold, native copper," etc.) With few exceptions, the other elements occur in the earth's crust only as parts of compounds.

When the earth finally cooled to form a crust, its atmosphere, hydrosphere, and lithosphere came into existence. At first the atmosphere probably consisted largely of the gases nitrogen and carbon dioxide. Early in geologic time, however, primitive plants converted most of the carbon dioxide into oxygen. The hydrosphere consisted almost entirely of liquid water, formed by combination of hydrogen and oxygen ions. The lithosphere consisted mainly of *solid elements and compounds of inorganic origin* which we now call minerals.

14. Minerals Have Crystalline Structure

Minerals may be found in the form of beautiful **crystals.** These crystals have regular geometric forms featured by smooth surfaces or **crystal faces.** The crystal forms are different for different minerals, but each mineral always has the same crystal form. In quartz crystals the form is that of a regular six-sided prism. The crystals of halite (sodium chloride), pyrite (iron sulfide), and galena (lead sulfide) are cubes. Diamond crystals are eight-faced, like two four-sided pyramids fitted base to base. (See Fig. 2-9.)

Mineralogists reasoned that the crystal form of a particular mineral was probably the result of a regular geometric arrangement of its ions or atoms. In 1912 X rays were first used for studying the internal structure of crystals, and we can now take X-ray photographs that show the arrangement of the ions or atoms in crystals of the various minerals.

Figure 2-10 shows the alternating arrangement of sodium and chlorine ions in a crystal of halite. The **regular arrangement of the ions is called crystalline structure.** Most minerals have a crystalline structure. When large numbers of ions are free to arrange themselves during the growth of the mineral, large perfect crystals may be formed. More often, the conditions of growth in the earth's crust are too crowded, and crystals are hemmed in by other crystals while they are all still tiny and imperfect. The magnifying glass or microscope may, however, be able to reveal crystal faces not apparent to the unaided eye.

Not all crystals are compounds. In crystals such as those of diamond, sulfur, or gold, atoms that are all of one kind share electrons with each

Fig. 2-10. These sketches show the regular arrangement of sodium ions and chlorine ions in a crystal of halite (sodium chloride). The smaller spheres represent sodium ions; the larger spheres are chlorine ions. The lower sketch is more "realistic;" the upper sketch is diagrammatic.

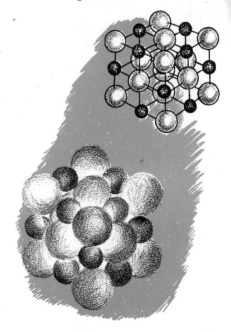

other in regular geometric arrangements. In the mineral we call diamond, for example, carbon atoms are arranged in a pattern in which each atom shares one electron with each of four other atoms.

15. Crystalline Structure and Physical Properties

The orderly arrangement of the atoms in a mineral helps to explain other properties or characteristics of the mineral in addition to its crystal shape.

A mineral is **solid** because of the close packing together of its ions or atoms, and the resulting strong electrical attractions among them. When heat weakens the bonds among these particles, solids melt into the loose groups of molecules that make up a liquid, or they evaporate into a gas in which individual molecules are far apart.

The **hardness** of a mineral seems to depend on the arrangement of its ions or atoms and the resulting electrical forces among them. A good example of this is seen in the element carbon. In one arrangement it forms diamond, hardest of all minerals. In a different arrangement it forms graphite, one of the softest minerals.

The **cleavage** of a mineral is its tendency to split easily or separate along flat surfaces. When a mineral has such tendencies in one or more directions, they seem to represent directions of weak bonds among the ions or atoms. Not all minerals exhibit the characteristic property known as cleavage.

The **specific gravity** of a mineral is the ratio of its weight to that of water. This depends on the weight of the ions or atoms of the mineral but it also depends on how closely they are packed together. For example, the specific gravity of the loosely packed mineral graphite is about 2.3, whereas that of the closely packed diamond is 3.5. Both are pure carbon.

Hardness, cleavage, specific gravity, and other *physical properties* of minerals are discussed in greater detail in the next chapter.

16. Definite Chemical Composition: Formulas

Since minerals are elements or compounds, **every mineral has a characteristic chemical composition.** If the mineral is an element, such as native copper or native gold, then of course it is composed entirely of that one substance. If it is a single compound, it follows the Law of Definite

Mineral	Chemical Name	Formula
1. quartz	silicon dioxide	SiO_2
2. magnetite	iron oxide	Fe_3O_4
3. uraninite	uranium oxide	UO_2
4. galena	lead sulfide	PbS
5. pyrite	iron sulfide	FeS_2
6. chalcocite	copper sulfide	Cu_2S
7. halite	sodium chloride (salt)	$NaCl$
8. calcite	calcium carbonate	$CaCO_3$
9. dolomite	calcium magnesium carbonate	$CaMg(CO_3)_2$
10. anhydrite	anhydrous calcium sulfate	$CaSO_4$
11. gypsum	hydrous calcium sulfate	$CaSO_4 \cdot 2H_2O$
12. orthoclase feldspar	potassium aluminum silicate	$KAlSi_3O_8$
13. kaolinite (clay)	hydrous aluminum silicate	$Al_2Si_2O_5(OH)_4$
14. muscovite (white mica)	hydrous potassium aluminum silicate	$KAl_3Si_3O_{10}(OH)_2$
15. graphite	carbon	C

Proportions mentioned in Topic 10, with each element of the compound present in a definite proportion by weight.

In Topic 10 we said that *the molecule is the smallest part of a compound that has all the characteristics of that compound.* To represent a single molecule, the chemist uses a **formula** showing the elements in the molecule and the number of atoms of each kind in it. For example, the formula for water is H_2O. This means that one molecule of water consists of two hydrogen atoms and one oxygen atom. One oxygen atom (atomic weight 16) is 16 times as heavy as one hydrogen atom. But since the water molecule includes two hydrogen atoms, the weight ratio of oxygen to hydrogen is 16:2 or 8:1. Therefore water is a compound with the *definite composition by weight* of 8 parts oxygen to 1 part hydrogen. In other words, if 9 pounds of water were to be completely decomposed by the process of electrolysis into oxygen and hydrogen, the products would be 8 pounds of oxygen and 1 pound of hydrogen.

The table on the preceding page gives the mineral name, chemical name, and formula of a few of the common minerals.

17. Families of Minerals

Minerals, like other chemical compounds, may be grouped according to the elements of which they consist. Some of the main families of minerals, according to their chemical composition, are

1. **Oxides**—compounds of oxygen and *one* other element. Examples in the preceding table include quartz, magnetite, uraninite.

2. **Sulfides**—compounds of sulfur and *one* other element. Examples: galena, chalcocite, pyrite.

3. **Chlorides**—compounds of chlorine and *one* other element. Example: halite.

4. **Carbonates**—compounds of one or more metals with the carbonate radical CO_3. (A **radical** is a group of atoms that stay together during the formation of compounds and in other chemical reactions. When a radical acquires an electric charge, it becomes an ion. When calcium carbonate dissolves in water, its molecules may form positive calcium ions and negative carbonate ions.) Examples: calcite, dolomite.

5. **Sulfates**—compounds of one or more metals with the sulfate radical SO_4. Examples: gypsum, Epsom salt ($MgSO_4 \cdot 7H_2O$), anhydrite.

6. **Silicates**—compounds of one or more metals with silicon and oxygen. Most of the common minerals of the earth's crust are silicates. Examples: the feldspars, kaolinite, the micas.

7. **Hydroxides**—"hydrous" compounds of one or more metals with the hydroxide radical (OH). Examples: muscovite, kaolinite. (The term *hydrous* also refers to the inclusion of water in the crystal, as in gypsum, $CaSO_4 \cdot 2H_2O$. This means that for every molecule of calcium sulfate, there are two molecules of "water of crystallization." *Anhydrous* means without water. The mineral *anhydrite,* for example, has the same formula as gypsum except for the water. The terms are generally used only when both hydrous and anhydrous forms of a mineral exist.)

18. Summary: What Is a Mineral?

Let us now summarize the principal characteristics of a mineral as we have described them in this chapter:

1. A mineral is a solid element or compound of inorganic origin found in nature.
2. Its ions or atoms are usually arranged in regular geometric patterns that give it a crystalline structure.
3. It has a characteristic chemical composition.
4. It has definite physical properties.

In the following two chapters many of the important minerals will be described.

TOPIC QUESTIONS

Each topic question refers to the topic of the same number within this chapter.

1. Explain the difference between boulders and bedrock.

2. (*a*) Using specific examples, explain the relation between rocks and minerals. (*b*) Define a mineral.

3. Using illustrations, explain the significance of the words *inorganic* and *solid* in our definition of a mineral.

4. (*a*) Define *element*. (*b*) Name eight familiar elements. (*c*) Give the name and approximate percentage by weight of the four most abundant earth elements. In which common minerals are they found?

5. What is an atom? Who was John Dalton?

6. Name, locate, and describe the three kinds of particles of which atoms are made.

7. (*a*) Describe the structure of the atoms of hydrogen and helium. (*b*) In what way do the 92 different elements resemble one another in atomic structure? (*c*) In what ways do they differ in atomic structure?

8. (*a*) What is the *atomic number* of an element? (*b*) What is the *atomic weight* of an element? (*c*) Explain how to determine the number of protons, neutrons, and electrons in a sodium atom.

9. (*a*) What is a nuclide? (*b*) Describe two nuclides of hydrogen, carbon, or uranium.

10. (*a*) What is a compound? a molecule? (*b*) How does a compound differ from a mixture? (*c*) What is the Law of Definite Proportions?

11. (*a*) What is an ion? (*b*) How are ions formed? (*c*) How do ions form compounds? (*d*) Define and describe metals. (*e*) Define and describe nonmetals. (*f*) Define *inert*.

12. Explain why most of the weight of an atom is in its nucleus and why most of an atom is empty space.

13. According to the hypothesis described in Topic 13, account for the origin of (*a*) the nitrogen of the atmosphere, (*b*) the oxygen of the atmosphere, (*c*) the mineral elements, (*d*) the mineral compounds.

14. (*a*) What is crystalline structure? (*b*) Explain why some mineral crystals are large and perfect, while others are small and irregular.

15. How does the crystalline structure of a mineral explain its (*a*) solid state, (*b*) hardness, (*c*) cleavage, (*d*) specific gravity.

16. (*a*) Why does a mineral have a "characteristic chemical composition"? (*b*) How does the formula H_2O tell us water is 8 parts oxygen to 1 part hydrogen by weight? (*c*) Give the chemical name and formula of three common minerals.

17. Name five mineral families, and give one example of each family.

18. Summarize the characteristics of a mineral.

CHAPTER 3

Identifying the Rock-Forming Minerals

HOW DO YOU KNOW THAT . . . ?

1. Finding out the nature of the earth's interior is like guessing the contents of a box which you cannot open. Try a "black box" experiment. This model of indirect evidence will give you an idea of the way scientists explain and predict what they cannot directly observe or measure. Put a magnet in a box. After your partner or other students infer that the box contains a magnet, have them predict what will happen to a compass needle held under the box. Make other boxes using magnetic objects, rocks of different composition and specific gravity, solids or liquids, heated and cold water. A hole can be made in the top of the box for recording temperature or sampling texture, but not for viewing directly.

2. Using Figures 1-4 and 1-6 as references, make a cutaway model of the earth with clay. How many colors will you need to show the layers? Make the depth of the layers roughly to scale. See the Measurements tables in the Appendix, p. 647, if you do metric measurements. Identify, with toothpicks and paper flags, the various rocks of different specific gravity.

1. Identifying Minerals

Over 2,000 minerals have been identified. Many of them—such as gold and diamond—are relatively rare. About 40 minerals make up so much of the rocks of the crust that they are called **rock-forming minerals.** Ten of them are so abundant that they make up more than 90 per cent of the weight of the crust.

In field work, minerals are usually identified by their physical properties, which can be determined by means of inspection and simple physical tests. Simple chemical tests may also be used.

2. Identification by Inspection

The color, luster, and sometimes the crystal shape of a mineral may be observed simply by looking at the specimen with the unaided eye.

The **color** of a mineral often helps to identify it, but very few minerals can be identified by color alone. One reason is that many different minerals have similar colors, or are entirely colorless and transparent. A second reason is that even a trace of an impurity (another element, usually a metal) in an otherwise colorless mineral such as quartz or calcite may make it pink, green, blue, violet, gray, or some other color. Amethyst, for example, is merely quartz in which a tiny amount of the metallic element *manganese* dissolved like a dye when the quartz was still liquid. A third reason is that some minerals tarnish quickly on exposure to air. Sometimes this helps to identify the mineral, as with the peacock-purple color of tarnished bornite, an ore of copper. But for most minerals one must be sure to inspect a fresh surface to determine its color. A few minerals that are easily identified because of their almost unvarying color are cinnabar, a red ore of mercury; malachite, a green ore of copper; sulfur, a bright yellow crystal or powder.

The **luster** of a mineral is the kind of "shine" —or lack of "shine"—that it has. Luster depends upon the way in which the surface of the mineral reflects light. All lusters are either *metallic* or *nonmetallic*. If a mineral sample shines like polished metal, its luster is metallic; otherwise, its luster is nonmetallic, which may be further described in a number of ways. A *vitreous* luster, shining like glass, may be seen in quartz. Mica has a *pearly* luster like that of the pearl. The mineral sphalerite, an ore of zinc, shows *resinous* or *waxy* luster, like that of yellow resin. The mineral asbestos has *silky* luster. Other common lusters are *adamantine,* like the diamond; *greasy* or *oily; dull* or *earthy.*

The **crystal shape** is sometimes helpful in identifying a mineral. (See Fig. 3-1.) If conditions were favorable when the minerals formed, their atoms or molecules arranged themselves in patterns that made flat-faced, regularly shaped solids called *crystals*. But more often the mineral grains seen in hand specimens of rocks are so small or so imperfectly crystallized that crystal faces are difficult to find.

3. Identification by Simple Tests

The streak, cleavage, and hardness of a mineral can be tested very easily. The **streak** of a mineral is the color of its powder. For many minerals it is not the same as the color of the solid lump. Iron pyrite crystals are brass-yellow, but their streak is greenish-black. Hematite is red or black, but its streak is always reddish-brown. The streak is usually obtained by rubbing the mineral on the hard, rough, white surface of an unglazed tile or piece of porcelain, called a *streak plate*. Although the color of a mineral may vary greatly, the streak rarely varies. As a general rule, the streak of a *metallic* mineral is as dark as or darker than the lump specimen. The streak of a *nonmetallic* mineral is usually colorless to white, or lighter in color than the lump specimen. Minerals that are harder than the

Fig. 3-1. Quartz crystals are six-sided prisms ending in pyramids. Perfectly symmetrical crystals are rare.

American Museum of Natural History

Fig. 3-2. The "perfect" cleavage of mica is beautifully illustrated in this photograph. This cleavage is also called basal cleavage, *because it is parallel to the base of the crystal.*

Ward's Natural Science Establishment

streak plate may have to be crushed or scraped to get the color of their powder.

The **cleavage** of a mineral is its tendency to split easily or separate along flat surfaces. Cleavage surfaces can be observed even on tiny mineral grains, making this property very useful for mineral identification. Mica splits very easily, always in the same direction, and is said to have one "perfect" cleavage. Feldspar splits readily in two different directions, at or near right angles, and is said to have two "good" cleavages. Calcite

and galena cleave in three directions. (See Figs. 3-2, 3-5, and 3-6.)

Not all minerals have cleavage. When minerals break along other than cleavage surfaces, they are said to have **fracture.** *Conchoidal* (kon *koy* dul) or shell-like fracture can be seen in the mineral flint or, better still, in the rock obsidian. (See Fig. 3-3.) The fracture surface is smoothly curved like the inside of a clam shell. *Fibrous* or *splintery* fracture leaves splinters, as in asbestos. *Hackly* fracture leaves a jagged surface with

Fig. 3-3. Conchoidal fracture, also called shell-like fracture, is well illustrated in this specimen of obsidian.

Ward's Natural Science Establishment

sharp edges, as in native copper. *Uneven* or *irregular* fracture leaves a generally rough surface, as in the mineral serpentine.

The **hardness** of a mineral may be defined as its relative resistance to being scratched. The diamond is the hardest of all minerals because *it will scratch any other mineral against which it is rubbed*. On the other hand, talc is the softest of all minerals because all other minerals scratch it. In order to give a specific measure to hardness, the mineralogist Friedrich Mohs devised a hardness scale in which ten well-known minerals were given numbers from one to ten, arranged from softest (talc) to hardest (diamond). The differences in hardness between one step and the next are about the same for all steps except the last. Diamond is very much harder than number 9, corundum.

It is easy to see that with a copper penny, a knife blade or nail file, and a small glass plate, one can determine the approximate hardness of any common mineral. If a mineral is harder than number 5 but softer than number 6 in the hardness scale, it may be said to have a hardness of about 5½. Hardness should not be confused with brittleness. Glass is a brittle substance that breaks easily when dropped, but it is much harder (resistant to scratching) than copper and many other metals.

In doing a scratch test for hardness, do not confuse the powder *rubbed off* the softer mineral with a *scratch* on the harder mineral. For example, when calcite is rubbed against glass, it may appear to have scratched it. Rub this "scratch" with your finger. If it proves to be powder that comes off and leaves the glass unscratched, the calcite is obviously softer than the glass. A real scratch can be felt with the fingernail.

4. Specific Gravity

Specific gravity is another property that is helpful in identifying a mineral. It is the ratio of the weight of a mineral to the weight of an equal volume of water. In other words, the specific gravity of a mineral tells you how many times as heavy as water it is. Nearly all minerals are heavier than water, so their specific gravities are larger than 1. Typical nonmetallic minerals—such as quartz, feldspar, calcite, and talc—have specific gravities of a little less than 3. Typical metallic minerals—such as the iron ores hematite and magnetite—have specific gravities of about 5, but others are much heavier. Gold may have a specific gravity as high as 19.3 when pure.

The specific gravity of a mineral is found as suggested by the definition. The weight of the mineral sample is found first simply by weighing it. Then the weight of an equal volume of water is found by any one of a number of methods de-

MOHS' SCALE OF HARDNESS

Mineral	Simple Test
1. Talc	1. Fingernail scratches it easily.
2. Gypsum	2. Fingernail scratches it.
3. Calcite	3. Copper penny just scratches it.
4. Fluorite	4. Steel knife scratches it easily.
5. Apatite	5. Steel knife scratches it.
6. Feldspar	6. Steel knife does not scratch it; it scratches window glass easily.
7. Quartz	7. Hardest common mineral; it scratches steel and hard glass easily.
8. Topaz	8. Harder than any common mineral.
9. Corundum	9. It scratches topaz.
10. Diamond	10. Hardest of all minerals.

scribed in physics textbooks. In one such method the mineral sample is weighed again *while the specimen is fully submerged in water.* (See Fig. 3-4.) This time it weighs less because of the buoyant effect of the water. Archimedes' Principle tells us that this *loss in weight* is equal to the weight of the displaced water. But this displaced water is equal in volume to the mineral sample that displaced it. Thus,

$$\text{Specific gravity} = \frac{\text{Weight of sample in air}}{\text{Weight of equal volume of water}}$$

$$= \frac{\text{Weight of sample}}{\text{Loss of weight in water}}$$

For example, suppose a specimen weighs 5 ounces in air and 3 ounces in water. Its loss of weight is 2 ounces. Then the specific gravity of the specimen is $\dfrac{5 \text{ ounces}}{2 \text{ ounces}} = 2.5$. In other words, the specimen is 2.5 times as heavy as water.

5. The Acid Test

Calcite, a fairly common mineral which is the principal constituent of limestone and marble, is easily identified by a simple chemical test. Calcite is calcium carbonate, $CaCO_3$. If a drop of cold dilute hydrochloric acid is placed on calcite, the drop of acid effervesces as bubbles of carbon dioxide gas are given off. (Dolomite, a carbonate of calcium and magnesium, reacts with hot acid, but not with cold acid, unless the mineral is powdered or scratched.)

$$CaCO_3 + 2\,HCl \rightarrow CaCl_2 + H_2O + CO_2$$

calcite   hydrochloric   calcium   water   carbon
       acid   chloride   dioxide

6. Special Properties of Minerals

There are many other properties of minerals which are of interest and importance to the mineralogist. Since these properties are less general than the ones treated in the preceding para-

graphs, however, they are usually reserved for special courses in mineralogy. A few particularly interesting ones will be mentioned briefly.

Some minerals are **magnetic,** and can be picked up by a magnet. The best example is magnetite, an iron ore. Lodestone, a variety of magnetite, itself acts as a magnet. Halite (rock salt) can be identified by its **taste.** A few species of minerals show **triboluminescence** by glowing (becoming luminescent) when they are scratched or crushed. **Fluorescence,** or glowing while exposed to ultraviolet light, is shown by scheelite (calcium tungstate), some calcites, and numerous other minerals. The minerals willemite (a zinc silicate), sphalerite (zinc sulfide), and others may continue to glow even after the ultraviolet light is turned off, and are then said to be **phosphorescent.** Some minerals, like the uranium minerals carnotite and uraninite, are **radioactive** and will activate a Geiger counter.

The mineral calcite splits light rays into two parts. One ray travels straight through the mineral. The other ray is bent. The result is the

Fig. 3-4. Determining the specific gravity of a mineral specimen. See Topic 4.

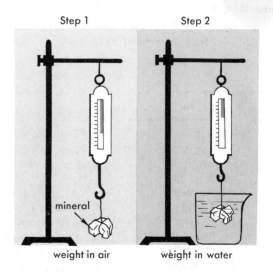

Step 1   Step 2

mineral

weight in air   weight in water

property of **double refraction,** causing two images to be seen when an object is viewed through a transparent specimen. (See color plate of calcite.)

The paragraphs that follow describe the most important of the rock-forming minerals.

DESCRIPTIONS OF ROCK-FORMING MINERALS

7. The Silica Family: Quartz, Chalcedony, and Opal

The **silica family** of minerals includes minerals composed of silicon and oxygen, with the formula SiO_2. This family is divided into three groups: quartz, chalcedony, and opal. The **quartz** group includes all visibly crystalline members of the family. The **chalcedony** (kal *sed* o nee) group includes varieties of silica with crystals so small that only X rays can detect them. The **opal** group has the formula $SiO_2 \cdot nH_2O$, and is called hydrous silica. The *n* indicates that the number of molecules of water may vary in different kinds of opal. Opal is noncrystalline, and is therefore not a true mineral, as we define the term.

Quartz is the second most abundant mineral in the earth's crust. It is an important part of granite, and forms most of the rocks sandstone and quartzite. Most sands consist largely of quartz grains. Quartz occurs in six-sided crystals, often with pyramids at the ends. It also occurs more commonly in irregular masses and grains of many sizes. Pure quartz is colorless or white, has a white or colorless streak, and has a glassy to greasy luster. Its fracture (no cleavage) is irregular or conchoidal (shell-like). Its specific gravity is 2.65. At number 7 in the scale of hardness, quartz is the hardest common mineral.

Traces of other elements dissolved in quartz act as dyes to give quartz a variety of colors. Some of the different kinds of quartz are the colorless and transparent *rock crystal* or *rhinestone,* the white *milky quartz,* pink *rose quartz,* purple *amethyst,* gray-brown to black *smoky*

Quartz Crystals in Geode

Rose Quartz

Amethyst

Opal

Orthoclase Feldspar

quartz, yellow *citrine,* and golden *tiger's eye.*

Commercially, quartz sand is used in making glass, concrete, sandpaper, and harsh scouring powders. Quartz crystals of all colors are used as semiprecious stones. Rock crystal is used to make special lenses, prisms, and acid-resistant chemical apparatus. Rock crystal is also used in radio and television transmitters to control the frequency of the transmitter's radio waves. Crystals for this use come chiefly from Brazil.

Chalcedony has no visible crystals, and occurs in irregular masses or bands of different colors. Its usual colors are white or light-gray, but traces of other elements produce such varieties as red *carnelian,* brown *sard,* green *chrysoprase,* red-spotted *bloodstone,* gray or black *flint,* tan *chert,* and yellow-brown *jasper. Agate* and *onyx* are banded varieties of chalcedony, in which some of the bands may be opal. Chalcedony has a dull to waxy luster, white streak, and conchoidal fracture. Its specific gravity is 2.6, and its hardness is 6 to 6.5.

Opal occurs in irregular masses of varied colors and patterns, often banded with chalcedony. Its appearance is often characterized by the *opalescence* or play of rainbow colors that makes opal an attractive semiprecious stone. Petrified wood is frequently composed of opal. Opal has a white streak, waxy to glassy luster, and conchoidal fracture. Its specific gravity is 2.1 to 2.3, its hardness 5 to 6.5.

8. Silicate Minerals: The Feldspars

Feldspar is the name given to a family of aluminum silicate minerals that are found in more kinds of rock than any other mineral or mineral family. There are many varieties of feldspar, but all of them have two good cleavages—at or nearly at right angles—and are about number 6 in hardness. Feldspar is a constituent of all granite rock, where it is easily identified by its color—usually white, yellow, gray, or pink—and its smooth cleavage surfaces. The feldspar family is divided into the **potassium** feldspars, with the formula $KAlSi_3O_8$, and the **soda-lime** feldspars, in which either sodium or calcium or both, take the place of the potassium.

Orthoclase (*ortho,* right; *clase,* breaking) feldspar is the most important of the potassium feldspars. Its two good cleavages meet at right angles, as its name implies. (See Fig. 3-5.) Its specific gravity is about 2.5, its luster pearly or glassy, its streak white, its colors white, gray, pink, flesh, or pale yellow. **Microcline,** less abundant than orthoclase, is also a potassium feldspar. While microcline strongly resembles orthoclase, it has a distinctive green variety called *amazonstone.*

Plagioclase (oblique breaking) feldspar is the general name given to all the varieties of soda-lime feldspars. All of these have two good cleavages that meet at an angle of 86°, which is not

Ward's Natural Science Establishment

Fig. 3-5. A crystal of orthoclase feldspar, showing its right-angled cleavage surfaces.

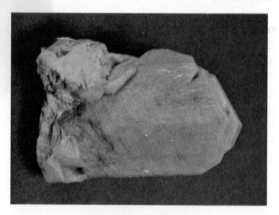

Microcline Feldspar

Labradorite Feldspar

quite a right angle. One of the cleavage surfaces usually shows fine parallel lines or *striations which distinguish plagioclase from orthoclase.* Plagioclase has approximately the same hardness, specific gravity, luster, and streak as orthoclase. The common variety *albite,* a sodium feldspar, is usually white or gray. The dark gray or bluish variety *labradorite* is noted for its *labradorescence,* a beautiful play of colors that occurs when the mineral is turned in the hand.

Orthoclase feldspar is of commercial importance in the making of porcelain, china, and scouring powder. Most clays are derived through the weathering of feldspars.

9. Silicate Minerals: The Micas

Mica, a silicate mineral with a complex formula, occurs in many different rocks. Its flat shiny flakes are easily picked out of such rocks as granite, gneiss, and schist. Mica occurs in several varieties. *Muscovite mica* or *isinglass* is usually silvery white; *phlogopite mica* is a golden brown; *biotite* mica is dark brown or black. All three micas have a white streak, pearly luster, a hardness of about 2.5, and a specific gravity of about 3. Their most striking property is the one perfect cleavage they have. Mica is often found in large flat crystals or "plates" up to several feet in diameter, and its perfect cleavage makes it possible to spilt these crystals into large, very thin transparent sheets that are both flexible and elastic—that is, they bend but return to shape.

Muscovite mica and phlogopite mica have excellent resistance to heat and electricity. This makes them useful as insulators in electrical devices—toasters, irons, motors, generators, switchboards, and many others.

10. Silicate Minerals: The Amphiboles

The amphiboles are complex silicates of calcium, iron, magnesium, and aluminum. Silicates that contain both iron and magnesium are referred to as ferromagnesian silicates. The most important member of the amphiboles is the mineral **hornblende.**

Hornblende may be dark green, brown, or black. Its luster is glassy or silky. Its streak is grayish-green or brown, its hardness 5 to 6, its specific gravity about 3.1. It has two good oblique cleavages. Its long needle-like crystals are shaped like six-sided pencils. Hornblende occurs in many rocks of the igneous and metamorphic rock groups. (Igneous rocks are rocks which at one time were in hot molten condition. Metamorphic rocks are rocks that have been changed by heat, pressure, and chemical action. See Chapter 5 for the complete explanation.)

Muscovite Mica

Biotite Mica

Phlogopite Mica

Hornblende

Augite

Olivine

11. Silicate Minerals: The Pyroxenes

The pyroxenes, like the amphiboles, are complex ferromagnesian silicates. The most important member of this family is the mineral augite (*au* jyte).

Augite is found in many igneous and metamorphic rocks. Augite strongly resembles hornblende. Like hornblende, it is dark green, brown, or black, has a hardness between 5 and 6, and has two good cleavages. Furthermore, it has a grayish-green streak and a specific gravity between 3.2 and 3.6. But it can be distinguished from hornblende by its poorer luster, its short, stout, four-sided or eight-sided crystals, and the cleavage surfaces that meet nearly at right angles.

12. Other Silicate Minerals

Olivine is an olive-green ferromagnesian silicate mineral that occurs in many dark-colored igneous rocks like those in the Palisades of the Hudson in New Jersey. It has a glassy luster, shell-like fracture, specific gravity 3.3, and hardness between 6.5 and 7. Its streak is white or yellowish. Clear specimens of the variety *peridot* (*per* ih dot) are used as gem stones. Olivine is also found in some meteorites.

Garnet

Garnet is the name of a family of minerals also common to the igneous and metamorphic rocks. Their hardness ranges from 6.5 to 7.5, their specific gravity from 3.4 to 4.2, their luster from glassy to waxy, and their color through dark red, brown, green, and black. Their streak is white. Fracture is conchoidal or irregular. Clear crystals are used as gems; poorer ones are crushed for use in such abrasives as garnet paper.

Talc, a common mineral in metamorphic rocks, is white, gray, or greenish in color. Its streak is white, its luster pearly to glassy, and it has one good cleavage. It has a marked soapy or greasy feel. Its specific gravity is 2.7. There are several varieties of talc. The most familiar one is *foliated talc,* which is white or light green in color, and is our softest mineral—hardness 1. When ground up, it is known as talcum powder, and is used in the making of cosmetics, paints, ceramics, rubber, and other products. *Soapstone* is a more massive or compact form of talc which is a darker green or gray in color, and has a hardness ranging from 1.5 to 2.5.

Chlorite is a common constituent of metamorphic rocks, being present in flaky irregular masses or sheets like those of mica. Chlorite is green, has a greenish streak, glassy to pearly luster, hardness 2 to 2.5, specific gravity 2.6 to

3.0. Like mica it has one perfect cleavage, splitting easily into flexible thin flakes. Unlike mica, however, its flakes are not elastic. When bent, they break instantly.

Serpentines are found in many metamorphic rocks. They occur either as large irregular masses or in fibrous (resembling fibers) form. The color range is usually light green to dark green. The streak is white, luster greasy or silky, and specific gravity about 2.5. Fracture is conchoidal, irregular, or splintery. Hardness ranges from about 2.5 to 5 for different varieties. The most familar variety of serpentine is the fibrous mineral *chrysotile* (*kriss* o til), better known as asbestos.

Verd antique, also known as "green marble," is a green variety of serpentine mixed with veins of calcite or dolomite.

Kaolinite or **kaolin** is a hydrous aluminum silicate formed by the weathering of feldspar and other silicate minerals. It is an important mineral in clay and in the rock called shale. Pure kaolin is white, but impurities usually color it yellow, and less often red, brown, green, or blue. It has a dull luster, white to yellow streak, earthy (crumbly) fracture, hardness between 1 and 2.5, specific gravity 2.2 to 2.6. It feels greasy, and when breathed on, it gives off a typical earthy odor.

Garnets in Schist

Talc

Serpentine

Fig. 3-6. Each one of these cleavage "rhombs" of transparent Iceland spar shows the three perfect cleavages of calcite.

Ward's Natural Science Establishment

13. Carbonate Minerals: Calcite and Dolomite

Only two carbonates are important rock-making minerals, but a number of others are important ores.

Calcite is calcium carbonate, $CaCO_3$. Though pure calcite is colorless or white, impurities dissolved in it may make it almost any color. It

has a pearly or glassy luster, a white streak, a hardness of 3, and a specific gravity of 2.7. Its three perfect cleavages at oblique angles give it a very strong tendency to break into little flat-sided rhombs (like those shown in Fig. 3-6) when dropped or struck. It is also easily identified by the acid test described in Topic 5.

Colorless, transparent calcite is called *Iceland spar.* Iceland spar's property of double

Calcite Crystals

Calcite (Iceland Spar)

refraction (see Topic 6) is used to advantage in scientific optical instruments like the polarizing microscope employed in optical analysis of minerals and rocks.

Calcite is the chief mineral—often the only one—in limestone and marble. As limestone, it is used in the smelting of iron ore, as a building stone, and in the making of important building materials like cement, mortar, concrete, and glass. As marble, it is used as a building and monumental stone.

Dolomite is calcium magnesium carbonate, $CaMg(CO_3)_2$. It is usually white, but may also be gray, green, pink, or black. Its streak is white, its luster pearly or glassy. It has a hardness of 3.5 to 4 and a specific gravity of 2.9. It cleaves like calcite. In the acid test, however, dolomite will not effervesce unless it is scratched or powdered or the hydrochloric acid is heated. This easily distinguishes dolomite from calcite. Dolomite may occur in the form of rhomb-shaped crystals, but more frequently it appears in coarse or fine grains in the "dolomitic" limestone and marble rocks of which it may be the principal mineral.

14. Ferrous Minerals: Magnetite and Pyrite

Magnetite is a magnetic iron oxide, Fe_3O_4. Both its color and streak are black. (Hematite, another iron ore which may be black, has a reddish-brown streak.) Magnetite has a metallic luster, a specific gravity of 5.2, and hardness from 5.5 to 6.5. It commonly occurs in igneous rocks in the form of small crystals. When found in large quantities, it is an important iron ore. Its name is derived from the fact that it is attracted to a magnet. *Lodestone,* a natural magnet from which the first magnetic compass needles were made, is a highly magnetic variety of magnetite.

Magnetite

Pyrite or **iron pyrites** (*pie* right *or* iron pie *right* ease) is a pale brass to golden-yellow mineral with a greenish-black streak. Its hardness is about 6. Because of its golden color and high metallic luster, it is sometimes mistaken for gold, and is known as fool's gold. It can be distinguished from gold by its greater hardness and its much lower specific gravity of about 5. The specific gravity of gold is between 15.6 and 19.3. Pyrite is iron sulfide, FeS_2. It is the commonest sulfur mineral.

Pyrite

TOPIC QUESTIONS

Each topic question refers to the topic of the same number within this chapter.

1. How are minerals usually identified in field work?

2. (*a*) Why is it difficult to identify a mineral by its color alone? (*b*) What is *luster?* Name different types of luster and give examples. (*c*) Why is crystal shape not too helpful in field identification?

3. (*a*) Explain what a mineral's *streak* is, how it is obtained, and how the streak of metallic and nonmetallic minerals differ. (*b*) Using examples, explain what is meant by the *cleavage* of a mineral. (*c*) What is mineral *fracture?* Give examples of different types of fracture. (*d*) Explain what *hardness* is. How is it determined? (*e*) Name the 10 minerals in Mohs' scale of hardness. (*f*) What precaution must be taken in observing the results of a hardness test?

4. (*a*) What is meant by specific gravity? (*b*) Compare, giving examples, the specific gravity of metallic and nonmetallic minerals in general. (*c*) Explain how to find the specific gravity of a mineral sample.

5. (*a*) Describe the acid test for calcite. (*b*) What is dolomite? How can it be "acid-tested"?

6. Describe briefly four special properties of minerals. Give examples.

7. (*a*) What is the silica family of minerals? (*b*) Give brief descriptions of the three groups in the silica family. Name some examples of each group.

8. (*a*) What is feldspar? In which rocks is it found? (*b*) What is orthoclase? Describe it. (*c*) What is plagioclase? How does it differ from orthoclase?

9. (*a*) What is mica? In which rocks is it found? (*b*) Name the three micas and describe their similarities and differences.

10. What is hornblende? In which classes of rocks is it commonly found? Name some specific examples.

11. (*a*) What is augite? In what ways does it resemble hornblende? (*b*) How can augite be distinguished from hornblende?

12. Name the minerals described in Topic 12 and tell in which rocks each one is found.

13. (*a*) Describe calcite briefly and name the two rocks in which it is abundant. (*b*) How does dolomite differ from calcite?

14. (*a*) What is magnetite? Describe it. In which rocks is it found? (*b*) What is pyrite? Describe it. (*c*) Why is pyrite called "fool's gold"? (*d*) How is pyrite distinguished from gold?

GENERAL QUESTIONS

1. Make a chart listing 10 important rock-forming minerals and giving the following information for each: formula or composition, color, streak, hardness, cleavage or fracture, specific gravity, luster.

2. In each pair, state which substance is harder and how you know: (*a*) tooth powder and tooth enamel, (*b*) chalk and slate blackboard, (*c*) diamond and glass.

3. With the minerals described in this chapter, how many half-steps can you add to Mohs' scale of hardness? (For example, mica's hardness is 2.5, placing it between gypsum and calcite in hardness.)

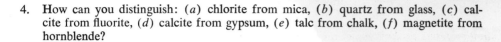

4. How can you distinguish: (*a*) chlorite from mica, (*b*) quartz from glass, (*c*) calcite from fluorite, (*d*) calcite from gypsum, (*e*) talc from chalk, (*f*) magnetite from hornblende?

STUDENT ACTIVITIES

1. Obtain the answers to General Question 4 by actual experiment.

2. Using the method described in Topic 4, find the specific gravity of talc, calcite, orthoclase, quartz, and hornblende.

3. Verify the statement made in Topic 3 with respect to the streak of metallic and nonmetallic minerals. Use at least three of each and record your results.

4. Try the acid test described in Topic 5 on as many carbonate minerals as possible; *e.g.*, calcite, dolomite, azurite, malachite, rhodochrosite, and siderite. Record your results carefully, indicating whether scratching, powdering, or heat was necessary to get a reaction.

5. Using a copper penny, a penknife, and a square of ordinary window glass, show that the hardness of each of these minerals is about as indicated: (*a*) hornblende, 6; (*b*) mica, 2½; (*c*) augite, 5½; (*d*) garnet, 7½; (*e*) kaolin, 1½; (*f*) sphalerite, 3½.

CHAPTER 4

Ores and Their Origin

HOW DO YOU KNOW THAT . . . ?

Topic 2, paragraph (6), tells you what placer deposits are and how they were related to the Forty-Niners' famous gold rush. You can make a lead "placer" by mixing approximately equal quantities (30-50 grams) of sand and gravel with about 10 tiny lead sinkers. Use the kind that pinch onto a fishing line.

The Forty-Niners separated the gold from the sand and gravel in their placers by washing out the lighter materials. Try their technique with your "placer." Put the mixture in the center of a flat or trough-shaped sheet of metal, plywood, or rigid plastic (like a sink drainboard). Tilt the sheet very slightly and place it with its lower end at the edge of a sink or large basin. Now sprinkle water gently onto the top of the sheet so that it runs through the "placer" and into the sink. Observe which materials are washed out. Continue the process until your "hydraulic mining" is finished. Why does the percentage of sand, gravel, and lead in the "placer" change under this treatment?

1. Minerals and Ores

All metals, as well as many important non-metals, are obtained from minerals in the rocks of the earth. These metals and nonmetals sometimes occur in *native* form, or uncombined with other elements, and need merely to be separated mechanically from the other minerals in the rock. Gold, copper, silver, platinum, sulfur, graphite (carbon), and diamond (carbon) are the most important native minerals. More commonly, however, elements occur combined with other elements and must be chemically extracted before they can be used. In either case, whether the desired element is found free or in combination, it usually forms only a small percentage of the rock in which it is found, and has to be separated from the rock. When the rock contains a sufficient quantity of the mineral to make the separation worth while, the rock is called an **ore.** Thus we speak of iron ore, copper ore, and sulfur ore. The valuable mineral is called the *ore mineral,* while the rest of the rock is referred to as the *gangue*

Fig. 4-1. An open-pit copper mine in Utah. The railroad cars at the lower levels of the mine help to give the scale of the photo.

Bureau of Mines U.S. Department of the Interior

(gang). Quartz, feldspar, calcite, and dolomite are common gangue minerals. The term "ore" is most often applied to metallic deposits, but it can also be used in speaking about nonmetals such as sulfur, graphite, and garnet.

2. How Ores Originated

Ores contain much greater concentrations of a particular mineral than are normally found in the rocks. Geologists are very much interested in knowing how these concentrations originated, because such knowledge can help them to find new ores and to get the most out of the deposits already known. The study of the origin of ores is complex and the following listing will simply scratch the surface of a fascinating subject. Since the term "magma" will be used, we shall define it now. **Magma is molten (liquid) rock material within the earth's crust.** Magma that flows onto the earth's surface is called **lava.** Rock formed from magma is **igneous** rock.

(1) *Heavy minerals became concentrated in cooling magma.*

In some mineral deposits, heavy minerals seem to have settled to the bottom of large bodies of magma while the magma was cooling inside the earth's crust. In this way concentrations of metallic ores of copper, chromium, iron, and nickel have occurred in igneous rocks. The diamond deposits of South Africa, found deep in the rocks of old volcanoes, are believed also to be of this origin.

(2) *Ore minerals in the form of hot liquids and gases went from cooling magmas into adjacent rocks.*

Many valuable deposits of copper, lead, iron, and zinc are found in rocks like limestone, where such rocks lie on top of large masses of igneous rocks. Geologists believe that the ore minerals were carried from the cooling magma in the form of very hot liquids and gases, which rose to the top of the magma and then entered and replaced some of the overlying rock.

(3) *Hot water carried dissolved ore minerals from cooling magma into cracks, fissures, and cavities in overlying rocks.*

This method differs from the preceding one in that the ore minerals were carried out of the magma dissolved in hot water, rather than as melted or vaporized minerals. The temperatures required for this process are not as high as those required for method 2.

As the hot water solutions cooled, the ore minerals and gangue minerals were deposited in cracks and fissures of the colder overlying rock (or sometimes in the outer zones of the cooling magma itself), to form mineral **veins.** In some rocks exceptionally thick veins or systems of veins form rich **lodes.** In other rocks thousands of tiny veins are filled with ore minerals to form **disseminated deposits.**

Some of the world's most important deposits of gold, silver, copper, lead, mercury, zinc, and tungsten originated as hot-water deposits. The geologist calls these **hydrothermal deposits** (*hydro,* water; *thermal,* of heat).

(4) *Rivers and underground waters carried minerals into seas, lakes, and swamps, where they were deposited.*

By this process, deposits of soluble minerals like gypsum, rock salt, borax, and some iron ores were formed. Valuable deposits of clay, sand, and gravel were also formed by such deposition.

(5) *Chemical weathering of some rocks removed minerals of no economic value, leaving behind higher concentrations of valuable minerals.*

The best example of this process is seen in the formation of bauxite, an ore of aluminum. Bauxite is hydrous aluminum oxide from which aluminum can be easily extracted. Geologists believe that bauxite is merely what is left of certain rocks rich in silicate minerals, after long exposure of these rocks to the chemical action of the atmosphere has removed most of the other elements in the silicate minerals.

(6) *Heavy minerals were separated from the rest of the rock by weathering, and then concentrated in one place by rivers, waves, or winds.*

Mineral deposits formed in this way are called **placer** (*plass* er) deposits. Gold, silver, platinum, cassiterite (tin oxide), and diamonds are found in placers. Placers are relatively rich deposits of heavy minerals mixed with the sands and gravels of ocean beaches or river sand bars. The famous gold rushes to California in 1849 and to the Alaskan Klondike in 1897 were caused by the discovery of very rich placer deposits of gold.

Geologists explain the formation of placers as follows: Bedrock containing a small percentage of a valuable heavy mineral—gold, for example—undergoes weathering. The rock crumbles, and the gold is washed by rains into rivers, along with other mineral fragments of sand, clay, and pebbles. As the river flows along, the heavy particles of gold tend to lag behind the other lighter mineral particles, and are concentrated in places where the river slows down and forms sand bars. Sometimes the gold is carried by the river all the way to the sea, where waves continue to wash out the lighter minerals and concentrate the heavy gold on the beaches.

Rich veins of gold and other placer minerals have been discovered by tracing the mineral-carrying river upstream to the original bedrock source called the *mother lode.* The gangue mineral in gold veins is frequently quartz.

METALLIC ORE MINERALS

3. Iron Ores

Iron is obtained chiefly from the minerals magnetite, hematite, and limonite, all of which are compounds of iron and oxygen.

Magnetite, Fe_3O_4, is a heavy black mineral, which has already been described under rock-making minerals. Great magnetite deposits occur in Brazil, Canada, Norway, Sweden, the Soviet Union, and South Africa. In recent years the mining of magnetite has become an important industry in the Adirondack Mountains of New York State.

Hematite, Fe_2O_3, comes in many varieties with different colors, hardness, lusters, and forms. *Specular hematite* is shiny, grayish black with a high metallic luster and a strong resemblance to mica. *Kidney ore* seems to consist of smoothly rounded lumps of mineral. *Red ocher* is dull, earthy, brownish red. Hematite may therefore be gray, reddish brown, or black. But all hematites have a reddish-brown streak. Fracture is

Hematite (Oölitic)

Hematite (Kidney Ore)

Limonite

uneven, lusters are metallic to earthy or dull, hardness ranges from 5 to 6.5, specific gravity from 4.9 to 5.3.

Limonite, a mixture of hydrous iron oxides, ranges in color from yellow through brown to black, but its streak is always yellowish brown. Its fracture is shell-like or earthy. Its hardness ranges from 1 to 5.5, its specific gravity from 3.4 to 4. Yellow and brown limonites cause the yellow color of many clays, soils, and weathered rocks. Limonite is also ground into paint pigments known as yellow ocher, sienna, and burnt umber. Common iron rust is limonite.

Taconite is not a mineral. It is the name given to the iron-bearing rock formation that covers a wide area in the Lake Superior region. Taconite contains magnetite and hematite in smaller percentages than the rich deposits mentioned above, but improved processing techniques now make the extraction of iron from this ore commercially practical.

4. Copper Ores

Copper is obtained as native copper or from the minerals chalcocite (*kal* ko sight), chalcopyrite (kal ko *pie* right) azurite, bornite, cuprite, and malachite. The prefix *chalco* means "copper."

Copper has a hardness of 2.5 and a specific gravity of about 9. The color of untarnished copper is "copper-red." When tarnished, copper may be black, blue, green, or red.

Chalcocite is a compound of copper and sulfur, Cu_2S. Its color is dark gray to black, its streak gray, and its luster metallic. Hardness varies from 2.5 to 3, specific gravity from 5.5 to 5.8. It has a conchoidal fracture.

Chalcopyrite is a compound of copper, iron, and sulfur, $CuFeS_2$. Like iron pyrite, it looks enough like gold to be called fool's gold. Its color is a brassy, iridescent yellow, its streak greenish black like pyrite's, its specific gravity about 4.2.

But whereas pyrite has a hardness of 6, chalcopyrite is considerably softer, its hardness ranging from 3.5 to 4. It is the most common mineral of copper.

Bornite, like chalcopyrite, is a compound of copper, iron, and sulfur. Its color is usually an iridescent purple, often described as "peacock color." Its streak is gray-black, its hardness 3, its specific gravity about 5.

Malachite is a carbonate of copper. Its color ranges from bright green to black, its streak is light green, hardness is 3.5 to 4, and specific gravity is about 4. It effervesces with hydrochloric acid. Malachite is used as an ornamental stone as well as a source of copper.

Azurite is also a carbonate of copper. Its color is light blue to deep blue, its streak light blue, its hardness 3.5, its specific gravity 3.8. It effervesces with hydrochloric acid.

Cuprite is copper oxide, Cu_2O. Its color is ruby-red, its hardness 3.5 to 4, and its specific gravity about 6.

5. Uranium Ores

Until the early 1940's uranium was a rare metal for which almost no use was known. Today it is of prime importance both for its explosive use in nuclear bombs and its use as a fuel in atomic power plants. The minerals described below are only two of the many varieties of uranium minerals.

Uraninite, the most important uranium mineral, is uranium oxide, UO_2. There are several varieties of uraninite, but the most common variety is **pitchblende,** a massive (noncrystalline) form. Pitchblende ranges in color from black to steel gray; the black may be grayish, brownish, or greenish in tint. Its powder is usually black or greenish black. Its luster is dull, glassy, or pitchlike—hence the name pitchblende. Its fracture is uneven or slightly shell-like. Pitchblende has a hardness that is between 5 and 6 and a specific gravity that ranges from 6 to 9.

Malachite

Chalcopyrite and Bornite

Carnotite

Bauxite

Bauxite may be white, yellow, brown, or reddish in color. Its streak varies. Its luster is dull or earthy, its hardness only 1 to 3, and its specific gravity about 2.5. Other aids to identification are its lumpy appearance and its earthy claylike odor.

✓ **Lead** is obtained from **galena,** a compound of lead and sulfur, with the formula PbS. Galena has a lead-gray color, a grayish-black streak, and a metallic luster. Its hardness is only 2.5 and its specific gravity is high—7.5. Its three excellent

Galena

Carnotite is a complex compound of uranium, vanadium, oxygen, and water. Its color is bright mustard or canary yellow. It has a yellow streak, waxy luster, and earthy fracture. Specific gravity is 5. It is very soft, with a hardness ranging from 1 to 2.

6. Other Metallic Ores

⌐ **Aluminum** is obtained from **bauxite** (*bawks ite*), a mixture of hydrous aluminum oxides.

Fig. 4-2. Cubic crystals of galena from the Tri-State Area.

Ward's Natural Science Establishment

Sphalerite

Sulfur

Graphite

cleavages result in the splitting off of perfect cubes from large specimens. Cubic crystals are also common. (See Fig. 4-2.)

Zinc is obtained from **sphalerite,** a compound of zinc and sulfur with the formula ZnS. Sphalerite is white when pure, but is generally colored yellow, green, red, or black, and is commonly known as *blackjack*. Its luster is resinous; its streak is white, light yellow, or brown. Hardness is 3.5 to 4, and specific gravity is about 4. It cleaves in six different directions.

Tin is obtained from **cassiterite,** a compound of tin and oxygen, SnO_2. Cassiterite is usually reddish brown, brown, or black in color. Its streak is white to pale brown, its luster diamond-like, its hardness 6 to 7, its specific gravity 7.

Mercury, or quicksilver, is obtained from **cinnabar,** which is HgS, mercury sulfide. Cinnabar is red to reddish brown. Its streak is bright red, luster adamantine to dull, hardness 2 to 2.5, specific gravity 8.1, fracture uneven.

Nickel is obtained chiefly from **pentlandite,** a compound of nickel, iron, and sulfur. Its color is a light bronze, hardness 3.5 to 4, and specific gravity 4.6 to 5.

Titanium is obtained from ilmenite and rutile (*ru* teel). **Ilmenite** is a compound of iron, titanium, and oxygen, $FeTiO_3$. It is black, brownish black, or deep red. Its streak may be black, brownish red, or yellow. Hardness is 5.6, specific gravity 4.5 to 5.5 **Rutile** is black, reddish brown, or red. Its streak is yellow or light brown. Hardness is 6 to 6.5, and specific gravity is 4.2 to 4.3. It occurs widely as a mineral in granites, gneiss, mica schist, and some limestones. Its formula is TiO_2, titanium oxide.

NONMETALLIC MINERALS

7. Important Nonmetallic Minerals

Sulfur occurs as a native mineral in limestone or gypsum rock, in volcanic areas, and in the vicinity of some hot springs. Sulfur is usually bright yellow, but may be darker. Its streak is white or yellow. It is soft and lightweight, with a hardness of about 2 and a specific gravity of about 2. Sulfur is used in making sulfuric acid and other vital chemicals.

Diamond, a native mineral, is the pure crystalline form of the element carbon. Though famous as the most precious of gems, diamonds are more important to the world today for their industrial uses in drilling, cutting, grinding, and polishing hard substances. Diamond is the hardest of all minerals, number 10 in the scale of hardness, Pure gem stones are perfectly transparent and colorless. Tiny amounts of other elements may produce yellow, blue, green, or red diamonds. *Bortz* is the name given to inferior diamonds that, because of poor color or crystallization, cannot be used as gems. *Carbonado* is a gray to black opaque variety of diamond. Both bortz and carbonado are used as industrial diamonds.

Graphite is another form of the mineral carbon. Graphite is gray or black, gives a black streak, and has a metallic luster. It has a greasy feel, a hardness of 1 to 2, and a specific gravity of about 2. The softness and greasiness of graphite make it useful as a lubricant and in "lead" pencils.

Asbestos, a mineral that can be separated into fibers, is used commercially to make materials that are fireproof or are insulators against heat. There are several asbestos minerals, but the most useful one is **chrysotile,** or short-fibered asbestos. Its color is white, yellowish, or green; its luster is silky; its streak is white; its hardness is 2.5 to 2.8.

Corundum is aluminum oxide, Al_2O_3. It is next in the hardness scale to the diamond and is similarly useful as an abrasive and a gem. Transparent red gems are called *ruby.* Transparent blue gems are *sapphires,* which may also be yellow, green, or purple. **Common corundum** is a dull mineral, which may be gray, blue, pink, or

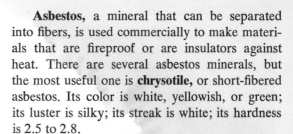

Corundum

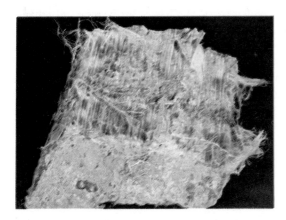

Chrysotile Asbestos

Beryl

Apatite

Halite (Salt)

Selenite (Gypsum)

brown in color. It gives a white streak. Its hardness is 9, and its specific gravity is 4. **Emery** is a natural mixture of corundum with magnetite and other minerals. It is dark gray to black, and its hardness is 7 to 9 depending upon the percentage of the softer minerals present.

Beryl, a beryllium aluminum silicate, is used commercially as a gem, in making glass that transmits ultraviolet light, in fluorescent lamps, and as a source of the newly important metal beryllium. *Common beryl* is grayish white, yellowish, or bluish green. Gem varieties of transparent beryl are known as *emerald* (green), *aquamarine* (blue to bluish), *morganite* (pink to red), and *golden beryl*. Beryl has a white streak, glassy luster, a hardness of 7.5 to 8, and a specific gravity of 2.6 to 2.8.

Apatite is a calcium phosphate mineral that is used principally in making fertilizer and phosphoric acid. Apatite may be white, gray, yellow, green, brown, blue, or red. It has a white streak, glassy luster, hardness of 5, and specific gravity of 3.1.

Borax is obtained principally from the mineral **kernite** (mined in Kern County, California) and by evaporation from the waters of Searles Lake and Owens Lake (both in southern California). Kernite is a compound of sodium, boron, oxygen, and water. It is colorless or white, with

a white streak and glassy luster. Its hardness is 2.5 to 3, and its specific gravity is 1.9. Borax is used in making glass, soap, water softeners, enamel, medicines, and in soldering. *Boron* is now used in making modern solid propellants for rockets.

Salt occurs in nature as rock salt or **halite.** It also occurs in solution in salt springs, salt lakes, and, of course, in the ocean. Halite is sodium chloride, NaCl. It is colorless or white when pure, but impurities may color it gray, green, blue, or even red. It has a white streak, glassy luster, hardness of 2 to 2.5, specific gravity of 2.2, and a salty taste. The principal uses of salt are as a

Fluorite

good cleavage, its hardness is 2, and its specific gravity is 2.2 to 2.4 Gypsum occurs in many varieties. Colorless, transparent crystals are *selenite*. A silky, fibrous variety is *satin spar*. A compact, grainy or massive variety is *rock gypsum*. A marblelike fine-grained variety is *alabaster,* which is used as an ornamental stone. The principal use of gypsum is as a source of *plaster of Paris,* which is made by heating gypsum to drive off most of its water.

Fluorite is calcium fluoride, CaF_2. Its principal use is as a "flux" which causes iron ore to melt more easily during the smelting process. It is also used in making hydrofluoric acid. Fluorite occurs frequently in limestones, dolomites, and some igneous rocks. Fluorite has many colors, especially light green, bluish green, yellow, and purple. It has a white streak, glassy luster, and good cleavage in four directions. Its specific gravity is 3.2, and it is number 4 in the scale of hardness. Some specimens of fluorite are weakly fluorescent.

source of sodium and its compounds, as a source of chlorine, and in the packing and preserving of meat, fish, and other foods.

Gypsum (*jip* sum) is a compound of calcium, sulfur, oxygen, and water. Its formula is $CaSO_4 \cdot 2H_2O$. It may be colorless, white, gray, yellow, or other colors. Its streak is white. It has one

TOPIC QUESTIONS

Each topic question refers to the topic of the same number within this chapter.

1. (*a*) What is a native mineral? Give examples. (*b*) What is an ore? the ore mineral? the gangue?

2. (*a*) Define magma, lava, and igneous rock. (*b*) Describe two of the first five ways discussed in this Topic for the origin of ores. Name specific examples. (*c*) Explain what a *placer* is and describe its origin. (*d*) What is a *mother lode?*

3. Give the formula or chemical composition and a brief description of the following ores: magnetite, hematite, limonite, taconite.

4. Give the name, formula or chemical composition, and a brief description of chalcocite, chalcopyrite, and malachite.

5. (*a*) Why is uranium important today? (*b*) Give the composition and a brief description of uraninite and carnotite.

6. Name and describe the ores from which aluminum, lead, zinc, and any two other metals (described in Topic 6) are extracted.

7. (*a*) What are diamond, bortz, carbonado, and graphite? (*b*) Briefly describe the composition and importance of chrysotile, corundum, emery, beryl, apatite, kernite, halite, gypsum, and fluorite.

GENERAL QUESTIONS

1. Make a list of metallic ores that are sulfides (compounds of the metal with sulfur).

2. Make a list of metallic ores that are oxides (compounds of the metal with oxygen).

3. Make a chart listing ten important metallic minerals with their composition, color, streak, hardness, specific gravity, luster, and cleavage or fracture.

4. Do the same (as in question 3) for five nonmetallic minerals.

STUDENT ACTIVITIES

1. Obtain specimens of magnetite, limonite (several varieties), and hematite (red and black varieties). Differentiate these specimens by use of magnetic tests and streak tests. (See Topic 3.) Use as strong a magnet as you can obtain. It may be necessary to break chips off your specimens to test their magnetism.

2. "Extract" mercury from cinnabar or from red oxide of mercury by heating strongly in a pyrex glass test tube over a Bunsen burner. Be careful not to inhale mercury vapor or to get mercury on your skin.

3. Extract lead from galena by heating a small amount of powdered galena and powdered charcoal on a charcoal block with a blowpipe. Use the same care as in Activity 2.

4. Demonstrate the radioactivity of uraninite, carnotite, and other uranium ores with a Geiger counter. See whether any of your other mineral specimens show radioactivity.

5. Obtain specimens of fluorescent minerals such as scheelite, willemite, fluorite, autunite, and wernerite. Note their colors in ordinary light. Then expose them to the ultraviolet radiations of a "black light" or argon bulb in a darkened room and observe the colors when the minerals "fluoresce."

6. Since limonite is $Fe_2O_3 \cdot nH_2O$, it should be possible to convert it into hematite, Fe_2O_3 by heating it strongly enough to drive off its water. Try it. Heat it in a metal dish or crucible with a Bunsen burner.

7. See if you can convert gypsum into plaster of Paris by heating it strongly to drive off part of its water. (See Topic 7.)

8. Strip some fibers from a specimen of asbestos. Test them in a flame to see if they burn.

9. Make talcum powder by crushing a small sample of talc.

CHAPTER 5

Origin of the Rocks

HOW DO YOU KNOW THAT . . . ?

The rocks of the earth's crust formed over long periods of time in three principal ways. You can "model" two of these ways.

1. Put two heaping tablespoons of sand into a clean paper cup or cut-down milk container. Add a few small pebbles and one tablespoon of cement. Mix thoroughly. Slowly add cold water and stir until a thick mixture is formed. Let it stand until it hardens. The "rock" you get is a sedimentary rock like those described in Topic 12.

2. Put one teaspoon of para (paradichlorobenzine) flakes into a test tube or small bottle. Stopper the test tube tightly. Stand it in a beaker of very hot water until the para melts. Remove the test tube and allow it to cool. The "rock" that forms is an igneous rock, comparable to those described in Topic 4.

1. Hutton's "Uniformity of Process"

Modern geology is said to have had its real beginnings in 1795. In that year the Scotch geologist James Hutton explained his *doctrine of uniformity of process,* sometimes called *uniformitarianism* by present-day scientists. Before Hutton, most geologists believed that the physical features of the earth had been formed by sudden spectacular events which they called *catastrophes.* Thus they explained the birth of mountains, the formation of canyons, the creation of waterfalls, and in general, the origin of almost all the landforms or "scenery" of the continents.

James Hutton's ideas were quite different. A geologist himself, Hutton had spent years in the study of geological processes in the field. His famous words that *"The present is the key to the past"* embodied his ideas that: (1) The geologic processes now operating on the earth were also active at about the same rate in past geologic ages; (2) The present physical features of the earth can be explained in terms of

these geologic processes, operating over long periods in the past.

According to Hutton, then, a canyon or great river valley was not the result of a sudden splitting open of the earth's crust. Instead, its formation could be explained by slow but ceaseless wearing away of the land by the river occupying the valley, aided by time and other natural processes of weathering and erosion still to be observed today.

2. Three Families of Rocks

Hutton's principles have been well applied by geologists in explaining the meaning and origin of the rocks. In Chapter 1 we spoke of the origin of the earth's crust, and said that the crust consists principally of *granite* and *basalt.* It would have been more accurate then to have said "granite, basalt, and rocks derived from or related to them." Actually, the number of different varieties of rock runs into the thousands.

There are white rocks, red rocks, green rocks, black rocks. There are rocks with enormous crystals, rocks that are coarse and granular, rocks that are smooth as glass. Some rocks are shiny; others lack luster. Some rocks are made of only one mineral, while others are bewildering in the number of different minerals to be found in them. Some rocks teem with fossils. Others show no signs of any relation to living things.

Despite the great variety of rocks and the complexity of the problems, geologists have found answers to many questions about how the rocks originated. They observe, for example, that erupting lava solidifies into rocks similar to rocks already found in many places on the earth. They see sands and clays, deposited on sea and lake bottoms, hardening into rocklike materials that resemble present-day sandstone and shale formations. They study the effects of hot lava on other rock materials, and apply their observations to an understanding of how rocks may be changed to other rocks. From these studies geologists conclude that all the rocks of the crust originated in one of three general ways, as follows:

Igneous rocks are those formed by the cooling and hardening of hot molten rock (magma) from within the earth's crust. **Sedimentary** rocks are those formed by the accumulation and hardening of sediments. The sediments may consist of rock fragments, plant and animal remains, or chemicals precipitated from solution. **Metamorphic** rocks are formed when rocks that already exist are transformed directly into new kinds of rock. The solidified lava of a volcano is igneous; sandstone, formed of sand, is sedimentary; and marble, derived from the transformation of limestone, is a metamorphic rock.

Does classification into these three groups solve all the problems of rock origin? Not all. As we study each group, we shall see that some problems still puzzle the geologists.

IGNEOUS ROCKS

3. Questions about Igneous Rocks

All rocks formed from magma, says the geologist, are to be called igneous. But how does he recognize that rocks are formed from magma? Why are there so many different varieties of igneous rocks? Why do they contain different minerals? Why do they have different textures? Most of these questions have been answered satisfactorily, but a number of questions have not. Here are just a few that are still being explored.

Where does magma come from? Why are most igneous rocks formed in volcanic eruptions in the basalt family, while most of those formed deep in the earth are in the granite family? Are all granites igneous rocks, or are some formed in other ways? Are there as many different kinds of magmas as there are different igneous rocks, or can a number of different rocks develop from a single magma?

4. Recognizing Igneous Rocks

When hot liquid magma pours out of the earth's crust in a volcanic eruption and then solidifies, it forms the kind of igneous rock called **extrusive** or **volcanic**. The geologist has no difficulty in recognizing such rocks as igneous. He can see some in the process of formation, and from them he can identify rocks formed in similar fashion in other times or places.

But igneous rocks also formed from magma that never reached the surface, and they solidified below a cover of rock that made direct observation of their origin impossible at any time. Such igneous rocks are called **intrusive** because they have intruded into other rock masses. They are also called **plutonic** because they originated within the earth. They become visible only after the rock that covers them is worn away. The geologist sees several evidences in these rocks that they were once liquid magma. They may

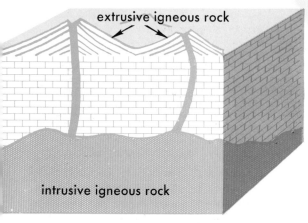

extrusive igneous rock

intrusive igneous rock

Fig. 5-1. When magma solidifies, it forms either intrusive or extrusive rock.

have striking resemblances in mineral composition to some of the volcanic rocks, though their mineral crystals are likely to be much larger. The crystal grains interlock as they would in forming from a hot liquid. These and other evidences make it possible to identify intrusive rocks as igneous, though not always with absolute certainty. For a long time all granites were believed to be igneous, but now most geologists think that some granites may have originated differently. (See Fig. 5-1.)

5. Two Types of Magma

What is a magma made of? Geologists are able to answer this question fairly well by actual observation and analysis of volcanic lavas and other materials.

Magma is called **lava** when it reaches the earth's surface. Magma can be simulated by melting rocks like granite and basalt in the laboratory. When the geologist analyzes volcanic lavas and laboratory-made magmas, he finds that they fall into two main types. They are all very hot solutions of silicates, with temperatures ranging from about 1100°F to 2200°F. But they differ in their chemical composition. One main

type has a high percentage of silica (SiO_2) and relatively little of the calcium, iron, and magnesium used in forming dark-colored minerals. This *high-silica* or *acid* type of magma is relatively thick and viscous. When it solidifies it forms mainly light-colored minerals like quartz and orthoclase feldspar, resulting in light-colored rocks such as granite. Most intrusive rocks are of this type.

The second main type of magma has a much lower percentage of silica and a correspondingly higher percentage of calcium, iron, and magnesium. This *low-silica* or *basic* type of magma is hotter and more fluid than the acid type. When it solidifies, dark ferromagnesian minerals like hornblende, augite, and black mica are common, and the resulting rocks are dark-colored rocks such as basalt. Most extrusive rocks are of this type.

6. Sources of Magma

Where does magma come from? The geologist has no definite answer for this, but he can offer a likely hypothesis from his study of available information. He estimates that at a depth of about 25 to 35 miles—probably in the upper part of the mantle—the rock is hot enough to melt at the earth's surface. In most parts of the mantle the great pressure of the overlying rock prevents melting. If the pressure is relieved, however, magma forms at that point and moves upward in the mantle and crust. The pressure may be relieved by cracking of the overlying rocks. It is also thought that in some places the mantle may become hot enough to melt despite the great pressure. In such places the extra heat may perhaps be produced by radioactive minerals. But we do not yet know the answer.

According to the hypothesis just given, all magma should be basaltic or low-silica, since it comes from the low-silica rock of the mantle. Where, then, does the high-silica type come from to form the great masses of intrusive granitic rocks that make up so much of the continents? One hypothesis says that granitic magmas may form by the melting of high-silica layers of the earth's crust, when movements of the crust drag them down into hot enough depths. Another hypothesis suggests that low-silica magmas may change into relatively high-silica magmas as they cool. This is because the first minerals to crystallize out of the magma are the dark-colored ones that use up the iron and magnesium. According to this hypothesis, if these settle out, they may leave a magma that can then form granitic rocks. This process is known as **magmatic differentiation.**

7. Texture of an Igneous Rock

Igneous rocks range in appearance from glassy-smooth rocks like obsidian to coarsely grained rocks like granite. This *texture* of the rock depends on the sizes, shapes, and arrangement of its mineral grains or crystals. How are these related to the origin of the rock?

The sizes of the mineral grains appear to depend largely on the rate at which the magma cools and solidifies. The longer the magma stays liquid the larger the mineral grains may become. This is because in the liquid the ions are free to move together to increase the size of the growing crystals.

Magmas that cool deep within the earth's crust cool very slowly and solidify slowly. Thus they form intrusive rocks with large, easily visible mineral grains of fairly uniform size. These rocks, of which granite is an example, are *granular* or *coarse grained* in texture. Magmas that cool close to or on the surface solidify more rapidly. They form intrusive or extrusive rocks with tiny crystals usually too small to be seen without a microscope. These rocks, of which basalt is an example, are *fine grained*. In some cases magmas flowing onto the earth's surface may solidify so rapidly that there is no time at all for crystals to develop, and the rocks that

form are as smooth as glass. Such rocks, of which obsidian is an example, have *glassy* texture.

Another factor that favors the growth of large crystals is the presence of a high percentage of dissolved gases in a magma. This is because the gases keep the magma liquid longer. Still another factor in texture is the order in which particular minerals crystallize from the magma. Those that are first to crystallize are likely to be larger and more regular in form than the minerals whose crystals have less time and less room to grow in.

8. Porphyritic Texture

Some igneous rocks consist of two distinctly different textures. Large crystals called **phenocrysts** (*fee* no krists) are surrounded by a **groundmass** that is fine grained or glassy. Such a texture is called **porphyritic** (por fi *rit* ik), and the rock is usually called a **porphyry** (*por* fi ree). Figure 5-2 shows a porphyry.

One explanation for the formation of a porphyry involves two stages of cooling. In the first stage the magma is at great depth, where it cools

Fig. 5-2. This trachyte porphyry consists of large light-colored phenocrysts of feldspar imbedded in a fine dark groundmass.

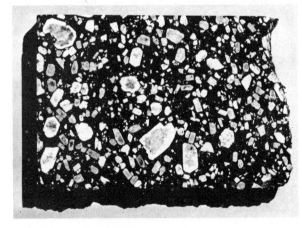

Dolerite Porphyry

Rhyolite Porphyry

slowly enough to permit the growth of large crystals of its earliest-forming mineral. The rest of the magma remains liquid. In the second stage the magma moves upward, possibly by breaking through overlying rock, until it comes close to the surface. Here it cools rapidly, and the remaining liquid solidifies into a groundmass of fine grains surrounding the first stage crystals.

9. Families of Igneous Rocks

Geologists classify the igneous rocks into families according to their mineral composition. Each family has its coarse-grained, fine-grained, and glassy member.

The **granite family** includes rocks derived from high-silica magmas. All of them consist mainly of orthoclase feldspar and quartz. Other minerals likely to be present are plagioclase feldspar, mica, and hornblende. Since orthoclase and quartz are light in color, the rocks in this family are usually light colored. In this family *granite* is coarse grained, *rhyolite* is fine grained, and *obsidian* and *pumice* are glassy. But all have similar mineral or chemical composition. (See Fig. 5-3.)

The **gabbro family** includes rocks derived from low-silica magmas. They consist mainly of *plagioclase feldspars* and *augite*. Other minerals likely to be present are olivine, hornblende, and biotite. Since the dark, heavy ferromagnesian minerals are very prominent in the gabbro family, these rocks are generally very dark in color and heavier than the granites. In this family *gabbro* is coarse grained, *basalt* is fine grained, and *basalt glass* is glassy. *Diabase* lies between gabbro and basalt in texture.

There is also a **diorite family** that is intermediate between the granite and gabbro families. Its members and composition are shown in the table on page 54. Also of interest are three coarse, dark, heavy rocks that may be like the rock of the earth's mantle. *Pyroxenite* is nearly all pyroxene; *dunite* is almost all olivine; *peridotite* is a mixture of pyroxene and olivine.

10. Descriptions of Igneous Rocks

Granite always contains quartz, orthoclase feldspar, and at least one other mineral such as mica or hornblende. The quartz grains look like little chips of cloudy or grayish glass; the feldspar crystals can be recognized by their smooth cleavage surfaces and by their color, such as white, gray, or pink. The mica flakes, usually black mica, can be chipped out with the fingernail or knife blade. Hornblende, also black or dark green, occurs in small chunks or sticks that cannot be removed so easily. Granites range in color from light grays to medium grays and pinks, with the color of the feldspar having the greatest influence on the over-all color of the rock.

Granite is the most abundant of all igneous rocks. It can be seen in the Rockies, the Adirondacks, the Black Hills of South Dakota, the White Mountains of New Hampshire, and many other mountain areas. Its presence at the surface indicates that erosion has removed thousands of feet of other rocks that once covered the now exposed granite. (**Syenite** is a rock that resembles granite, but contains almost no quartz.)

Rhyolite is white, gray, yellow, or pink in color. Formed in lava flows, it is often banded and flinty in appearance. Rhyolites can be seen in Yellowstone National Park and other volcanic or former volcanic regions. **Trachyte** resembles rhyolite, but it contains almost no quartz. Both rhyolite and trachyte are referred to as *felsites*—fine-grained, light-colored rocks.

Obsidian, formed by the rapid cooling of surface flows of lava, is usually dark brown to

Granite

Rhyolite

Fig. 5-3. Visible grains of quartz, feldspar, and mica or hornblende give granite its coarse texture.

Ward's Natural Science Establishment

black in color and glassy in texture. Obsidian is very hard but brittle. It breaks rather easily with a shell-like fracture. The dark color of obsidian is caused by the presence of particles of black minerals like magnetite scattered evenly throughout the "volcanic glass." Particles of hematite make a reddish obsidian. Because of its hardness, the ease with which it can be split, and the sharpness of its edges, obsidian was much used by primitive peoples for making knives, hatchets, arrowheads, and other implements.

Pumice is the name given to lava that solidified while steam and other gases were still bubbling out of it, forming a "fiberglass rock" that looks like a sponge with many fine holes in it.

Obsidian

Pumice is usually light gray, and its air holes may make it light enough to float.

,**Diorite** is a coarse-grained rock in which light-colored plagioclase feldspars and dark ferromagnesian minerals (such as hornblende, augite, and biotite) are fairly evenly divided, giving it a "salt and pepper" appearance.

Andesite is a fine-grained rock, usually gray or green, and often of banded appearance like rhyolite. It has the same composition as diorite.

Gabbro is the coarse-grained member of the basalt-diabase-gabbro family, all of which are dark green, dark gray, or black, and consist largely of plagioclase feldspars and augite, with some hornblende, olivine, and biotite.

ι **Basalt** is the most abundant of the rocks formed from flows of lava. In addition to its characteristic dark color and fine grain, basalt is distinguished by a heavy dense appearance and occasional small cavities sometimes containing crystals. It ranges in color from dark green to black. Large areas of basalt occur in the lava flows of Iceland, the Hawaiian Islands, and the Columbia Plateau of western United States.

ɔ **Diabase** is similar to basalt in color and minerals, but it is coarser in texture. It forms most of the Palisades of the Hudson River, the Watchung Mountains of New Jersey, and the volcanic hills of the Connecticut River Valley. Diabase is also known as *dolerite* and *trap rock*.

Granodiorite

Pumice

Olivine Gabbro

Scoria is similar in origin to pumice, but its holes are larger. It is usually much heavier and darker than pumice, and does not float in water.

Pegmatite is a very coarse rock, usually resembling granite in consisting largely of quartz, orthoclase feldspar, and micas. The crystals in pegmatite may range in length from less than an inch to many feet. Pegmatite usually occurs in thick flat or irregular masses cutting through the outer margins of masses of intrusive rocks like granite. The gigantic crystals are believed to have formed through slow cooling from very fluid (thin) magmas, or possibly from hot water solutions. Occasionally pegmatites contain enormous crystals of such minerals as beryl, topaz, apatite, and uraninite, which, like their micas and feldspar, may be of commercial importance.

Scoria

SUMMARY TABLE: COMMON IGNEOUS ROCKS

Texture and Origin	Light-colored Rocks		Medium-colored Rocks	Dark-colored Rocks	
	Colors: white, tan, gray, pink, red *Minerals:* Feldspar (mostly orthoclase), quartz; also some mica and hornblende		*Colors:* gray, green *Minerals:* Feldspar (mostly plagioclase) hornblende, augite, biotite	*Colors:* dark green, dark gray, black *Minerals:* Plagioclase feldspar, augite; also olivine, hornblende, biotite	
	With Quartz	*Almost No Quartz*	*Without Quartz*		
Glassy: cooled quickly at surface of earth	Obsidian Pumice		Obsidian	Basalt glass Scoria	
Fine grained: cooled more slowly at or near surface	Rhyolite (Felsite)	Trachyte	Andesite	Basalt Diabase	
Coarse grained: cooled very slowly, usually at great depths	Granite Pegmatite	Syenite Granodiorite	Diorite	Gabbro	*No feldspar* Peridotite Pyroxenite Dunite

Pegmatite

SEDIMENTARY ROCKS

If we believe that the earth originated as a hot liquid globe, then the entire crust of the earth must once have been igneous rock. Today, however, sedimentary rocks cover about three-fourths of the surface and make up more than one-tenth of the total volume of the crust's outer ten miles.

Sedimentary rocks have been defined as rocks formed by the accumulation and hardening of sediments. What are the different kinds of rock-forming sediments? How do they originate? How do they become changed into rock? In what ways are these "secondary" rocks different from the "primary" rocks from which they are derived?

11. Kinds of Sediments

There are three principal sources for the "sediments" that form sedimentary rock. **Clastic** sedimentary rocks are formed from such fragments of other rocks as clay, sand, and gravel. **Chemical** sedimentary rocks are formed from mineral grains that precipitate out of solution by evaporation or chemical action. **Organic** or **biogenic** sedimentary rocks are formed from the remains of plants and animals.

12. How Clastic Rocks Form

The fragments that may form clastic rocks are derived from the weathering of other rocks that are already in existence. These fragments range in size from coarse gravels to ultra-fine clays, and are simply classified in the following way:

Gravel   Larger than sand grains; pebbles
Sand   Diameters from 5/64 inch to 1/400 inch
Silt   Diameters from 1/400 inch to 1/6400 inch
Clay   Smaller than silt particles

These rock fragments form on mountains, on plateaus, on plains, along the sea coast, and wherever rock is exposed to the atmosphere. From their places of origin they are carried off by the agents of erosion—winds, waves, rivers, and glaciers—to places where they may accumulate in great deposits of sediment. The largest accumulations are those made by rivers on their flood plains or at their mouths in lakes and in the ocean. In lakes and oceans the sediments are usually spread out by waves and currents for great distances in the shallow-water areas bordering the land. (The shallow-water areas that border the continents are called the continental shelves.)

When the deposits of sediments become hundreds of feet thick, their lower layers may harden into rock. How? Geologists are not certain just how this takes place. It is believed, however, that in fine sediments like salt and clay the great pressure in the lower layers makes the particles stick together or "become compacted." In coarser sediments like sands and gravels the particles do not hold together unless they are cemented. But ocean and lake waters contain dissolved minerals such as silica (from quartz), lime (from calcite), and iron compounds (from limonite and hematite), all of which are natural cements. When chemically deposited between the fragments of sands and gravels, they cement them to rock.

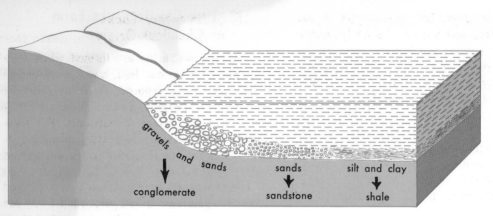

Fig. 5-4. How clastic sediments form sedimentary rock.

Silica and lime cements are usually gray or white; limonite is yellowish or rust colored; hematite is brown or reddish. They give the same colors to the rocks they cement.

13. Sorting the Sediments

When a river flows into a lake or ocean, it drops its sediment as it gradually loses its speed. The first sediments to be dropped are the heavy pebbles and gravels, which settle to the bottom in the shallow waters of the continental shelves nearest to shore. Next come the lighter sands, and finally the silts and clays. The process of **sorting** may not produce perfect separation; sand

may be found mixed with the pebbles and gravels in shallow water, as well as with silts and clays in deeper water. Nevertheless, the deposits are fairly definite. As the sediments become cemented together, the pebbles and gravels form a rock called **conglomerate,** the sands form **sandstone,** and the silts and clays form **shale,** or **mudstone.** The particles, both large and small, are generally rounded as a result of their having been carried by running water. (See Fig. 5-4.)

14. Conglomerate, Sandstone, and Shale

Conglomerate is the coarsest of the clastic rocks. It resembles a porphyry to some extent,

Red Sandstone

Conglomerate

but instead of crystalline phenocrysts it has rounded pebbles, and instead of a finely crystalline or glassy groundmass it has a mass of cemented sand grains. The pebbles in conglomerate may be any rock material, but quartz is most common because of its great durability. In some conglomerates the pebbles are barely larger than sand grains. In others they reach the size of boulders. Conglomerate is a natural concrete. *Breccia* (*bret* shee uh) is a rock similar to conglomerate, but its fragments are sharp and angular, not having been carried and rounded by running water.

Most **sandstones** are made largely of grains of quartz. Although the grains are cemented together, the cement never fills all the spaces between the grains, and sandstones may have up to 30 per cent of air space in them. For this reason they are *porous*, and since water can pass through them, they are also said to be *permeable*. Sandstones feel rough and gritty. They occur in a variety of colors: white, gray, red, and brown. The color and the durability of sandstones depend to a large extent on the mineral that cements the grains together. Silica cements usually form the most durable sandstones. *Shaly sandstones* contain a large proportion of clay. *Arkose* is a sandstone containing much feldspar.

The clays that make up **shale** or **mudstone** are usually composed of the mineral kaolin, although many other minerals may be mixed in. The pore spaces between the very fine particles in shale are so tiny that water is unable to pass through the rock. The rock is then said to be *impermeable*. In this respect shale is unlike sandstone. Because of their fine particles shales are smooth. They are comparatively soft and easily broken. Shales, like clays, occur in almost all colors. Black or dark gray shales appear to owe their color to carbon from decayed plant material. Mudstone is similar to shale except that it does not split easily into very thin layers as shale does.

15. Sedimentary Rocks of Chemical Origin

Chemical sediments are formed when minerals dissolved in sea, lake, swamp, or underground waters are deposited from the water by evaporation or chemical action. There are many rocks formed of chemical sediments. The most abundant are limestone, rock salt, and rock gypsum. Others will be described in the chapter on underground water.

Limestones of chemical origin are formed from tiny grains of calcite deposited from sea or lake waters. *Compact limestones* include a number of limestones, usually gray or tan, that are composed of grains nearly microscopic in size. These limestones are always dense in appearance and smooth to the touch, and may be confused with basalt or felsite. *Dolomitic limestone* or *dolomite* is a compact crystalline limestone containing magnesium carbonate as well as calcite, and it is therefore less subject to the chemical action of acids or the acid test. (Chapter 3, Topic 5.) Geologists believe that dolomite is not formed directly from sea water, but rather through the replacement of some of the calcium in limestone by magnesium.

Rock salt is the natural form in which our common table salt (sodium chloride) occurs as a sedimentary rock in thick layers or beds in

Rock Salt

many parts of the world. It consists almost entirely of the mineral *halite*.

Rock gypsum, like rock salt, occurs in sedimentary layers and veins of nearly pure mineral gypsum.

Both rock salt and rock gypsum are believed to have been formed by the continuous evaporation of the waters of salt lakes or ocean lagoons (shallow bays in back of sand bars). They are therefore known as *evaporites*.

16. Sedimentary Rocks of Organic Origin

Organic sediments are formed by the accumulation of the remains of once-living animals and plants. The most important rocks derived from organic sediments are **limestone** and **coal.**

The origin of organic limestone. Great numbers of lime-forming organisms live in the waters of the continental shelf. These organisms include clams, mussels, oysters, sea snails, corals, microscopic algae, and many others. When they die, their lime shells—sometimes whole, often broken into fragments by the grinding action of the waves—accumulate on the floor of the continental shelf and become cemented together into limestones. The limestones that form near the shore may contain a good deal of clay, whereas

Coquina

those that form in deeper water may be almost pure lime. The lime in these limestones represents the mineral *calcite* which was dissolved out of rocks on land, carried to the ocean (or lakes) by streams, and then extracted from the water by the lime-forming organisms named above. There are many different varieties of limestone because there are so many different kinds of shells or lime particles from which limestones have been formed.

Coquina (ko *kee* na), common in Florida, consists of shells and shell fragments of rather recent origin, loosely cemented together. *Fossiliferous* limestone is a much older rock than coquina, and its shells are highly compressed and thoroughly cemented. *Coral limestone* consists of coral fragments naturally cemented together. Coral limestone occupies areas of ancient or modern coral reefs. *Chalk* is made largely of the cemented shells of microscopic sea animals. It is soft, smooth, and very fine grained. Pure white chalk makes up the famous chalk cliffs of Dover, England. Chalk often contains lumps or *concretions* of flint or chert. (See Topic 21.)

Since most limestones are composed of the mineral calcite, they can readily be identified by the acid test. That is, cold dilute hydrochloric acid reacts with limestone, causing bubbles of carbon dioxide gas to form. Limestone has

Shell Limestone

Fig. 5-5. Miner testing for gas in a coal seam near Pittsburgh, Pennsylvania.

numerous uses: as a building stone; in making lime, cement, and concrete; as a chemical source of carbon dioxide gas; as a flux which helps to extract a metal from its ores. Two of the best-known limestone structures in the world are the Great Pyramid in Egypt and the Pentagon in Washington, D.C.

The story of coal. When ferns, mosses, twigs, and even tree trunks are buried in swamp waters and accumulate in great thicknesses, they undergo a slow decay by which they eventually lose almost all of their elements except carbon. At first they decay into *peat,* a brownish mass of mosses, leaves, and twigs. Peat burns well when

Bituminous Coal

dry. With further decay and with compression under other sediments, peat is converted into a harder and more compact material called *lignite,* or brown coal. Further change produces *bituminous coal,* commonly called soft coal. The entire transformation may take many thousands of years. One estimate is that a layer of peat 20 feet high is required to form a bed of bituminous coal 1 foot thick. Some sand or clay may mix with the accumulating plants to account for more or less ash or clinker when the coal is burned. Two factors may interrupt the accumulation of plants for a long period of time: (1) an increase in rainfall that turns a swamp into a lake, and (2) the submergence of coastal swamps through a rise in the sea level. During such intervals, large deposits of sand and clay may form on top of peat beds. Later these deposits are consolidated into beds of sandstones and shales with which coal beds are always found. On the other hand, if the swamp dries up, the wood decays normally and no peat is formed. (See Fig. 5-5.)

Not counting its ash content, an average soft coal contains about 85 per cent carbon. The remaining 15 per cent is largely hydrogen, oxygen, and nitrogen in the form of *volatile compounds.* These are gases or compounds that are easily changed into gases by heat. During mountain formation the folding of beds of soft coal

59

(bituminous) may allow the volatile compounds to escape through *joints* (cracks) in the crumpled rock layers, leaving behind a coal which may be from 90 to 95 per cent pure carbon. Even higher percentages are possible. Such a coal is called *hard coal* or *anthracite*. (See page 66.)

17. The Story of Petroleum

Petroleum is not usually regarded as a rock. However, it is found mainly in sedimentary rocks, and is believed to be of organic origin in most cases.

Many theories have been advanced for the origin of petroleum. It is now generally agreed that petroleum is derived from oil-forming plants or animals or both. Large accumulations of such organic remains are believed to have been deposited in shallow coastal waters. Just how the oil came from these deposits is not known, but three explanations have been suggested. According to one explanation, the plants or animals

Samuel N. Namowitz

Fig. 5-7. Stratified sedimentary rocks at the famous Red Rocks outdoor theater near Denver, Colorado.

Fig. 5-6. An oil well and a natural gas well in an anticlinal formation.

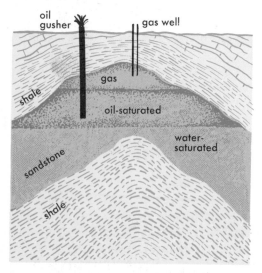

themselves contained oil, just as the castor bean and the codfish of today contain oil. A second says that oil was formed as the organic remains decayed but before they were buried by sediments. The third explanation is that the oil was formed by chemical action after the organic remains were buried in sediments.

In any case, the oil thus formed appears to have somehow accumulated in the pores of rocks like sandstone, or in the cracks and fissures of rocks like limestone, wherever shale was present as a cap rock to trap the oil and prevent its escape. (Shale is an *impermeable* rock—one through which liquids and gases cannot penetrate.) So-called *oil pools* or *reservoirs* are simply saturated areas of rock—usually sandstone or limestone. Where the rock formation is an upfold or anticline (Fig. 5-6), the oil is invariably found at the top, sealed in above by shale, and below by water (usually salt water).

Natural gas is often found together with oil, and it is probably derived from oil. When gas is present, it stands in the top of the anticline, above the oil. If its pressure is sufficient, it produces a gusher when a well is drilled into the formation. Otherwise the oil must be pumped out.

18. Sedimentary Features: Stratification

Sedimentary rocks are marked by a number of special features that help to identify them and tell their stories. The most important of these features is **stratification**—arrangement in visible beds or layers that separate fairly easily. How does stratification develop?

When any change occurs in the kind of sediments being deposited in one place, new rock layers are formed. For example, if a coarse clay is deposited on a fine one, or a yellow clay on a white one, different layers of shale will form, one on top of the other. On the other hand, if sand is deposited on clay, a layer of sandstone will form on a layer of shale. In this way sedimentary rocks become *stratified,* and their beds or layers are separated by bedding planes. Bedding planes are usually horizontal, but *cross bedding* may develop when beds are deposited in inclined positions on sand dunes and deltas. (See Fig. 5-7.)

Sediments change for many reasons. The river that brings the sediment to the ocean may be wearing away new kinds of rock; it may carry larger quantities and more varieties of pebbles, sand, and clay during flood times; it may carry its sediments farther out to sea than formerly or drop them closer to shore. These and many other events are responsible for changes in the nature of the sediments left at any one spot. The thousands of feet of sedimentary rocks exposed in the wall of the Grand Canyon of the Colorado River very well demonstrate layers of different color, hardness, texture, and thickness.

19. How Fossils Form in Sedimentary Rocks

As sediments pile up on continental shelves, lake bottoms, or swamp floors, animals that live in these waters may die, fall into the accumulating sands and clays, and be buried. The fleshy

Fig. 5-8. Formation of a fossil. When the mud hardens into shale, the remains or impression of the fish become part of the rock.

parts of the animals decay, but the hard parts may remain as **fossils** when the sediments turn to rock. The shells of clams, mussels, and snails are frequently found as actual remains inside layers of sandstone, limestone, and shale. Sometimes the shells themselves disappear but leave impressions that can be seen when the rock layers are split apart. Fish skeletons also form fossils, and plant remains or impressions are found in the rocks derived from swamp sediments. **Fossils are the remains, impressions, or any other evidence of the existence of plants or animals preserved in rock.** (See Figs. 5-8, 5-9, and 5-10.)

20. Ripple Marks; Mud Cracks

Sandstones often show ripples on the surface of a bedding plane. Apparently these **ripple marks,** formed by the action of winds, streams, waves, or currents on deposits of sand, were preserved when the sand became sandstone. (See Fig. 5-11.) **Mud cracks,** seen most often in shales, apparently developed when deposits of wet clay dried out and cracked before hardening into rock. The cracks were preserved by being filled with the different material (sand, lime, etc.) of a later layer of sediment. Ripple marks can be seen today on any sandy beach or stream bed. Mud cracks can be seen wherever muddy roads or beds of clay dry after a rain.

21. Concretions and Geodes

Limestone and dolomite often contain lumps of chert, flint, or other "foreign material." It is believed that these **concretions** may have been deposited from solution, bit by bit, around a

Fig. 5-11. Ripple marks in sandstone.

Mudcracks in Sandstone

nucleus of fossil material trapped in the rock. Concretions often consist of the same mineral as that which cements the rock together.

Limestones sometimes enclose small, fairly round cavities lined with crystals of quartz or calcite. These **geodes** (*jee* odes), like miniature caverns, are believed to have been formed by mineral-carrying waters which first formed the hollows and later filled them with deposits of crystals. (See Fig. 5-12.)

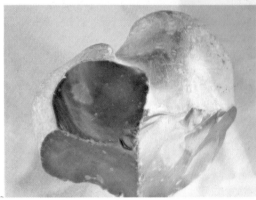

Flint Concretion in Chalk

Fig. 5-12. A geode lined with quartz.

METAMORPHIC ROCKS

22. What Metamorphic Rocks Are

Anthracite coal, marble, slate, gneiss, quartzite—these are fairly familiar names of rocks we have not yet described. These rocks fail to fit into either of our first two categories, for they are formed neither from magma nor from sediment. Yet in many respects they resemble members of our first two groups. Anthracite strongly resembles bituminous coal. Marble resembles some limestones, slate reminds us of shale, quartzite looks like crystallized sandstone, while gneiss contains minerals like those in granite. Geologists have determined that these resemblances are not mere coincidence. The rocks in these pairs are really related, with one actually being derived from the other as a result of changes produced by natural forces. These **metamorphic** (*meta,* change; *morph,* form) **rocks** are defined as **rocks formed from existing bedrock by the action of heat, pressure, and chemicals within the earth's crust.**

23. Agents of Metamorphism and Their Effects

The natural agents that change existing rocks into metamorphic rocks are *pressure, heat,* and *chemicals.* What is the source of these agents? What effects do they produce?

Examination of metamorphic rocks shows many evidences of great *pressures.* Quartzite is harder and denser than the sandstone from which it was formed, and unlike sandstone, it contains no pores. Slate no longer splits along bedding planes as shale did. Pebbles that are flattened and stretched out can be seen in metamorphosed conglomerates. Mineral grains in schist are lined up in parallel layers as though pressed into this new arrangement. Fossils still present are squeezed into distorted shapes. And in the field, rock layers that were once horizontal may be seen crumpled and deformed into great wavelike folds. The pressures that produced these effects are believed to come from two sources. First there is the downward pressure caused simply by the weight of overlying rocks. At a depth of 6 miles, this is about 20 tons to the square inch—enough to turn rock into a plastic substance. Secondly, there is the enormous horizontal pressure that results from movements of the earth's crust during periods of mountain formation.

Examination of metamorphic rocks also reveals evidences of changes produced by *heat* and *chemicals.* The crystals of calcite in marble are far larger than they are in the limestones from which marble is formed. Similarly, quartzite is more highly crystalline than sandstone. Anthracite coal is more nearly pure carbon than is bituminous coal. Slate and schist contain new minerals not present in the shales from which they originated. Geologists attribute these changes—larger crystals and greater degree of crystallization, changes in chemical composition, and the formation of new minerals—largely to the work of heat and chemically active liquids and gases. Hot magmas are sources of both heat and chemicals. Additional heat is believed to come from the friction between moving rock layers during movements of the earth's crust in mountain formation.

24. Classifying Metamorphism

Metamorphism may be classified as *dynamic* (from movement) or *thermal* (from heat). **Dynamic metamorphism** results chiefly from the crushing pressures exerted on the rocks during mountain formation. **Thermal metamorphism** results chiefly from contact with hot magmas.

Dynamic metamorphism usually produces great changes in the rocks. Many rocks develop *foliation* or *foliated* (leafy) *texture,* in which leaflike or flaky minerals like mica and chlorite, or needlelike minerals like hornblende, are arranged in parallel layers or bands along which

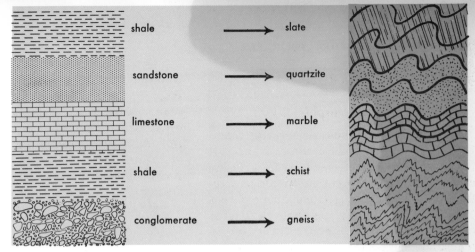

Fig. 5-13. This diagram represents the dynamic metamorphism of sedimentary rocks. (Standard geologic symbols are used.)

shale → slate
sandstone → quartzite
limestone → marble
shale → schist
conglomerate → gneiss

the rock splits easily. These layers are microscopically thin in *slate,* somewhat thicker in *phyllite,* plainly visible in *schist,* and cardboard-thick in *gneiss.* The sequence from slate to phyllite to schist, all derived from shale, represents increasing degrees of metamorphism. *Quartzite, marble,* and *anthracite* are also formed in dynamic metamorphism, but they have *unfoliated texture* because they contain little or no flaky minerals like mica. (See Fig. 5-13.)

In thermal metamorphism the rocks are usually "baked" by the heat from the intruding hot magmas. Because the baking effects are most intense in the zone of contact between the rocks and the magmas, such metamorphism is also known as **contact metamorphism.** The baking effects rarely extend more than a few hundred feet into the rock, but the area covered may be many square miles. Unlike dynamic metamorphism, thermal metamorphism does not produce foliation. *Hornfels* is an unfoliated rock commonly formed by the baking of shale.

25. Unfoliated Metamorphic Rocks

The following descriptions give the origin and chief characteristics of the unfoliated metamorphic rocks.

Quartzite is a metamorphosed quartz sandstone, in which all the pores of the sandstone have been filled with crystalline quartz. The original sandstone grains are so strongly cemented that when the rock breaks, it breaks across the grains rather than around them, as in sandstone. Quartzites have the same colors—white, gray, brown, or red—as the sandstones from which they are formed. Because they are almost immune to chemical attack, quartzites are among the most durable of rocks.

Marble is metamorphosed limestone or dolomite. It is harder, denser, and more crystalline than limestone, but reacts to the acid test as limestone or dolomite does. Pure marble is white, but may be colored red or brown by iron oxides, green by serpentine, and black by carbon.

Quartzite

Dolomite Marble

Hornfels

Hornfels is formed by contact metamorphism of shale. It is a hard, fine-grained rock which may be green, brown, or black in color.

Anthracite coal is metamorphosed soft or bituminous coal. It is much harder and more lustrous than soft coal, and splits with a conchoidal fracture. Anthracite is usually formed by metamorphism in folded mountain regions. Soft coal, on the other hand, is found in regions of unfolded rocks. Most of the anthracite in the United States occurs in the folded mountains of eastern Pennsylvania.

Anthracite Coal

26. Foliated Metamorphic Rocks

Slate is metamorphosed shale. Its microscopic mica flakes, formed from the clay minerals of shale, give it its foliated texture. Quartz is its second principal mineral, while small amounts of other minerals color it gray, black, purple, red, or green. Slate is much harder and smoother than shale, but it splits easily in a direction perpendicular to the direction of the pressure that formed it during metamorphism. This splitting, called *slaty cleavage,* makes large, thin slabs of slate available for chalk boards, roofing tiles, and similar uses.

Phyllite (*fill* ite) is a more highly metamorphosed shale than is slate. Its mica and chlorite

flakes are larger than those of slate, and it can easily be distinguished from slate by the silky luster of its cleavage surface. This luster is caused by flakes of muscovite mica.

Schist (shist) is very highly metamorphosed shale. It also may be formed from such rocks as rhyolite, basalt, impure sandstone, phyllite, and slate. Visible layers of flaky minerals like mica, chlorite, and talc, or needlelike minerals such as hornblende, give schist a highly foliated texture and a strong tendency to cleave. Schists differ in composition as they differ in origin, and are usually named for their most abundant mineral. Mica schist usually consists of muscovite mica, biotite mica, and quartz. Other varieties are talc schist, chlorite schist, and hornblende schist.

Gneiss (*nice*) is a highly metamorphosed rock. Like schist, it may originate from many different rocks. It may be formed from granite, gabbro, shale, sandstone, conglomerate, and other rocks. The minerals in gneiss are arranged in relatively coarse parallel bands in which light-colored minerals like quartz and feldspar often alternate with dark-colored ferromagnesian minerals like hornblende, biotite, or augite. Granite gneiss has the same minerals as granite but different texture. The composition of gneiss varies with its origin, but it commonly includes feldspar. Quartz, mica, hornblende, and garnet are also likely to be present.

Phyllite

Red Slate

Gray Slate

27. Can Granite Be Metamorphic?

Until recently geologists believed that all granites were formed from magmas, and were therefore igneous. Today, however, many geologists believe that some granites have been formed by metamorphism of sedimentary rocks or even of other metamorphic rocks. This particular kind of metamorphism is called **granitization,** and it is thought to occur when hot liquids and gases penetrate and react with overlying rocks. The evidence for this manner of origin is usually not conclusive, however, and geologists frequently disagree as to where and in which granites it has taken place.

Mica Schist

Hornblende Schist

Biotite Gneiss

RELATION OF PRINCIPAL SEDIMENTARY MATERIALS, SEDIMENTARY ROCKS, AND METAMORPHIC ROCKS

Sedimentary Material	Sedimentary Rock	Metamorphic Rock
Pebbles, gravel, and sand	Conglomerate	⎧ Quartzite conglomerate ⎨ Gneiss (also from granite and ⎩ rhyolite)
Sand grains (usually quartz)	Sandstone	Quartzite
Clay (usually kaolin); silt	Shale, mudstone	Slate, phyllite, hornfels, schist
Lime (shells, fragments, or grains)	Limestone	Marble
Peat	Bituminous coal	Anthracite coal

28. The Rock Cycle

In classifying the rocks of the crust according to their origin, we have seen how closely related they are. The igneous rocks, derived from magmas originating in the earth's interior, may be thought of as the *primary* or parent rocks of the crust. As these are attacked by forces of weathering and erosion, sediments are formed and deposited. The sediments harden to form *secondary* rocks which we name sedimentary rocks to describe their origin. If these rocks are buried beneath great weights of other sediments and then involved in mountain-making movements of the crust, they may be converted into metamorphic rocks. These, in turn, may be subjected in the crust to temperatures so high that they melt into magma, and then solidify into igneous rock to complete a "rock cycle."

The rock cycle also has short cuts and detours. Igneous rock may be metamorphosed directly. Sedimentary rock may be weathered without being metamorphosed. Metamorphic rocks weather or may be metamorphosed a second time. The story of the rock cycle is outlined in the accompanying diagram (Fig. 5-14). In brief form it is a large part of the story of geology.

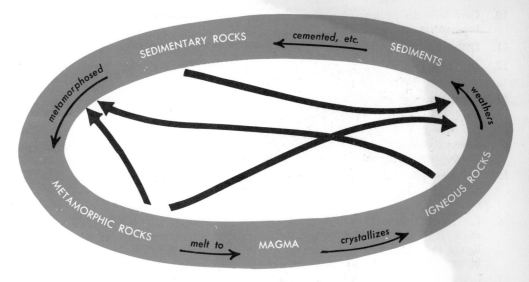

Fig. 5-14. The rock cycle is the never-ending story of rock formation.

TOPIC QUESTIONS

Each topic question refers to the topic of the same number within this chapter.

·1. (*a*) Before James Hutton how had geologists explained the origin of landforms? (*b*) What two principles are embodied in Hutton's "uniformitarianism"? (*c*) Compare Hutton's explanation of the origin of a canyon with that of a "catastrophist."

· 2. (*a*) Give illustrations of the ways in which geologists apply Hutton's principles to learning the origin of rocks. (*b*) Define the three families of rocks.

3. (*a*) List two questions about igneous rocks that the geologist can answer satisfactorily. (*b*) List two questions that are still being explored.

·4. What are extrusive rocks? Why are they easy to recognize as igneous?

5. (*a*) How can the geologist tell what magmas are made of? (*b*) Describe the acid type of magma. (*c*) Describe the basic type of magma.

6. (*a*) Explain how magma forms in the earth's mantle. (*b*) How does the geologist explain the formation of high-silica magmas?

·7. (*a*) What determines the size of the mineral grains in an igneous rock? (*b*) Explain when a magma will form a coarse-grained rock, a fine-grained rock, or a glassy rock. (*c*) What other factors favor the growth of large crystals?

8. What is porphyritic texture? How does it develop?

9. (*a*) Describe the granite family of igneous rocks. (*b*) Describe the gabbro family of igneous rocks. (*c*) What is the diorite family? (*d*) Why is dunite of special interest?

10. Give brief descriptions of granite, obsidian, pumice, ~~diorite, gabbro,~~ basalt, ~~diabase,~~ scoria, and ~~pegmatite.~~

11. Define the three groups of sedimentary rocks.

12. (*a*) Explain how gravel, sand, silt, and clay differ in size. (*b*) Explain how sediments form rocks.

13. Explain how rock sediments are sorted when deposited in water. Name the rocks formed from each sediment.

14. (*a*) How does breccia differ from conglomerate? (*b*) How does arkose differ from ordinary sandstone? (*c*) Explain why sandstone is permeable. (*d*) How does shale's composition explain its being impermeable?

15. (*a*) How are chemical sediments formed? (*b*) How do limestones of chemical origin form? Name two varieties. (*c*) Why are rock salt and gypsum called *evaporites?*

16. (*a*) Explain the origin of organic limestones. (*b*) Briefly describe coquina and chalk. (*c*) Describe a test for limestone. (*d*) How is peat formed? (*e*) How are lignite and bituminous coal formed? (*f*) Why are coal beds always found with layers of shale and sandstone? (*g*) How is anthracite coal formed from bituminous?

17. (*a*) Describe the probable origin of petroleum. (*b*) Describe the rock structures in which petroleum is usually found. (*c*) What makes an oil gusher?

18. What is stratification? How does it develop in sedimentary rocks?

19. What are fossils? How do they form in sedimentary rocks?

20. How did ripple marks and mud cracks form inside of sedimentary rocks?

21. (*a*) What is a concretion? How does it develop? (*b*) What is a geode? How is it formed?

22. Define metamorphic rocks. Name at least four examples.

23. (*a*) Name three agents of metamorphism. (*b*) Cite illustrations that show evidences of pressure in metamorphic rocks. What are the sources of the pressure? (*c*) What effects do heat and chemicals have in changing rocks? What are their sources?

24. (*a*) Distinguish between dynamic and thermal metamorphism. (*b*) Explain what foliated texture is and which minerals and rocks are involved. (*c*) What is contact metamorphism? How far can it extend?

25. (*a*) Describe quartzite, marble, and one other unfoliated metamorphic rock. (*b*) Why is anthracite found in folded mountain regions?

26. (*a*) Compare slate, phyllite, schist, and gneiss as to origin, principal minerals, and degree of metamorphism. (*b*) What is mica schist? (*c*) What is granite gneiss?

27. What is granitization?

28. Describe the rock cycle briefly either in words or by a simple diagram.

GENERAL QUESTIONS

1. Which minerals are likely to appear as phenocrysts in a porphyry? (See Topics 6 and 8.) Which are likely to be in the groundmass? Explain why.

2. (*a*) How can you "deduce" the hardness of pumice from the information given in Topic 7? (*b*) How would you determine its hardness experimentally?

3. (*a*) How may the "sharp fragments" in breccia have originated? (*b*) How may arkose have originated? (See Topic 14.)

4. Why are fossils more likely to be formed in shale and sandstone than in conglomerate?

5. Can fossils ever be formed in igneous rocks? Explain.

6. Why are fossils less likely to be found in metamorphic rocks than in the rocks from which the metamorphic rocks are derived?

7. Why does bituminous coal burn more readily than anthracite?

8. Explain several ways of distinguishing white marble from white quartzite.

STUDENT ACTIVITIES

1. Using the acid test, hardness tests, and any other means you have learned, differentiate the following rocks: (*a*) white limestone, white marble, and white quartzite; (*b*) dark gray limestone and basalt; (*c*) conglomerate and pegmatite; (*d*) gray sandstone and gray limestone; (*e*) red shale and red sandstone; (*f*) schist and gneiss.

2. Pair off the following metamorphic and sedimentary rocks, and then make a list of the similarities and differences you can observe in them: (Do these bear out the statement that metamorphic rocks are "pre-existing rocks that have been changed by heat, pressure, and chemicals?) (*a*) shale and slate, (*b*) bituminous and anthracite, (*c*) limestone and marble, (*d*) conglomerate and gneiss, (*e*) sandstone and quartzite.

3. Heat a small quantity of crushed soft coal in a pyrex test tube or metal dish. Do the same with hard coal. Which coal gives off more "volatile material"? Does this agree with what Topic 16 says? If you heat the coal until no more gases are given off, what will remain?

4. With the aid of a hand magnifier examine specimens of coarse granite, pegmatite, gabbro, marble, and conglomerate. Make a list of the minerals you can identify in each rock.

5. Make your own collection of igneous, sedimentary, and metamorphic rocks.

6. Take the following "field trips" to see how many different kinds of rock you can identify: (*a*) to your own school building (look at window sills, staircases, and ornamental stone in lobbies, auditorium, in front of the building, etc.); (*b*) to other public buildings in your town or vicinity; (*c*) to local parks and other outdoor areas; (*d*) to a monument works or graveyard.

CHAPTER 6

Topographic Maps

HOW DO YOU KNOW THAT . . . ?

Contour lines are used to represent land forms. Use modeling clay to make a cone-shaped "mountain" about 8 to 10 cm (4 in.) high with a base that will let it fit easily into a battery jar or transparent plastic box. Make the cone steeper on one side. With a glass-marking crayon, mark the outside of the box from the bottom up with short horizontal lines every half inch.

Put the mountain in the box. Pour in water until the first marker is reached. With the crayon draw a line all around the mountain showing the exact level of the water. Repeat this process at each level until the top of the mountain is reached. Each line drawn is a **contour line.**

Fasten a transparent cover (glass plate, plastic cover, or plastic sheet) to the top of the box so it does not move. Tape a sheet of paper to the cover. Looking straight down through the cover, draw each contour line as accurately as possible. The result is a contour map of your mountain.

How do the lines show the shape of the mountain? How do they show it is steeper on one side?

1. Mapmakers Have Their Problems

The making of a map is a complex problem. **A map is defined as the representation of all or part of the earth's surface on a plane** (a plane is a flat surface). Since the earth is a sphere, its surface is like the skin of an orange or the cover of a basketball, but vastly larger. Making a map of half the earth, for example, is like trying to make the skin of half an orange coincide with the flat surface of a table. It cannot be done unless the orange skin is torn or stretched out of shape. Making a single map of the whole earth is even more difficult and requires more tearing or stretching. On the other hand, if a small section of an orange skin is taken, it can be flattened with less tearing or stretching. *The smaller the area mapped, the less distortion required.*

Topographic, or contour, maps show the relief and physical features of a region by the use of symbols. Relief, the "ups and downs" of the earth's surface, is the difference in height between the highest and lowest points in a given region. The physical features include all the land forms and water forms.

2. How Map Projections Are Used

Mapmakers have suggested many schemes for showing the curved earth on a flat surface. Such schemes are called map projections. The ideal map would show *shapes, distances,* and *directions* correctly, but no map projection can do all of these things. Some projections show true shapes while distorting distances and directions. Some may show both shapes and distances correctly, but only by using a series of disconnected map sections, as one might do with an orange-skin peeled into quarters. However, maps of small areas can be made with very little distortion in any respect.

There are many useful map projections, but only four will be mentioned here. The **Mercator projection** is an old and still valuable scheme that shows the whole world (except the extreme polar regions) on one single continuous map. It is indispensable to the navigator because *it shows true directions by straight lines*. The captain who wishes to sail from New York to Cherbourg draws a straight line on his Mercator chart between the two cities. If he then sails in the direction indicated by this line, he will be heading directly for his destination. The chief fault of the Mercator projection is its tremendous exaggeration of distances in high latitudes (Fig. 6-1).

On the **gnomonic** (noh *mon* ik) **projection,** a straight line between two points shows the shortest route (great-circle route: see Chapter 31) between those points on the earth's curved surface. It is used in planning long voyages or flights, but since its directions and distances are distorted, other maps must be used to supplement it.

The **Lambert conformal conic projection** is used in making air navigation charts. For short flights, it shows true distances and great-circle routes by straight lines, but adjustments must be made for true directions.

For small areas, the **polyconic projection** is nearly correct in all respects. It is therefore ideally suited to the making of topographic maps. The topographic maps of the United States Geological Survey use this projection.

3. Which Way Is North?

On any map, directions are shown by parallels and meridians. **Parallels** are circles that run

Fig. 6-1. In the upper map, Greenland and South America are shown in approximately their true relative size. In the lower map, taken from a Mercator projection, Greenland appears larger than South America.

around the world in an east-west direction parallel to the Equator. **Meridians** are half-circles that run in a north-south direction from the North Pole to the South Pole. (See Chapter 31 for a fuller explanation.) North or south on a map is found simply by finding and following any meridian. East or west is found by following any parallel. Most of us are accustomed to maps in which north is at the top, south at the bottom, east to the right, and west to the left. But in many projections this arrangement does not hold true. In polar-view maps (Fig. 6-2), north is toward the center, while east and west are merely opposite directions around the parallel circles.

4. How Can Places Be Located on a Map?

The location of places on the surface of the earth is shown on maps by means of latitude and longitude.

Latitude is distance in degrees north or south of the Equator and is measured by parallels. The latitude of the Equator is zero degrees, written as 0°. The points farthest from the Equator are the two poles of the earth, the North Pole and the South Pole. Since the Poles are located one-quarter of the circular distance around the earth from the Equator, their latitudes are 90° N and 90° S respectively. (One-fourth of a circle is ¼ of 360°, or 90°.) Figure 6-2 shows the parallel circle which is one-third of the distance from the Equator to the North Pole, and therefore has a latitude of 30° N. It also shows the 60° N parallel. The center point in the map is the North Pole, with a latitude of 90° N.

One degree of latitude is 1/360 part of the whole earth's circumference of about 25,000 miles, and is therefore about 70 miles long. Degrees are divided into minutes, one degree (1°) being equal to 60 minutes. Since one minute (1') of latitude is 1/60 of a degree, its length is about 1⅙ miles (70 miles ÷ 60).

Longitude is distance in degrees east or west of the prime meridian, and is measured by

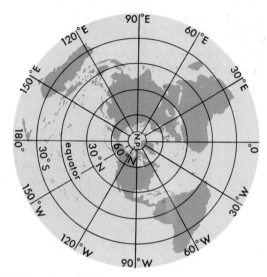

Fig. 6-2. *In this north polar projection, east and west are directions around the parallel circles, and northward is toward the North Pole at the center.*

meridians. Meridians are the semicircles that are drawn around the earth from the North Pole to the South Pole. The prime meridian (*prime,* first) is the meridian that passes through the borough of Greenwich (*gren* ich) outside London, England. Its longitude is 0° (see Figure 6-2). If we move equally in both directions away from the prime meridian, the farthest we can get from the prime meridian is 180°. The 180th meridian is half the distance around the earth. The half of the world that is west of the prime meridian has west longitude. The half that is east of the prime meridian has east longitude.

Longitude degrees are also divided into minutes, and 1° longitude = 60' longitude. But since meridians come closer together toward the Poles (see Fig. 6-2), there is no fixed number of miles in a degree of longitude. At the Equator 1° longitude is about as long as 1° latitude. But as the Poles are approached, the mileage of a longitude degree gets smaller and smaller. (A fuller explanation of latitude and longitude is given in Chapter 31.)

In locating a place, we give its latitude in degrees north or south of the Equator and its longitude in degrees east or west of the prime meridian. No matter what projection scheme is used or what distortions a map has, all maps must show the same latitude and longitude for any particular point on the earth's surface.

5. What the Scale Means

The scale of a map tells how the map compares in size with the piece of the earth's surface that it represents. With many world maps, as with the Mercator projection, the distortion of distance varies so much over the map that no single scale can be given. Small-area maps, such as topographic maps, present no such problem, however.

A map scale is usually defined as the ratio of distance on the map to distance on the earth. This ratio may be shown on the map in three different ways:

(1) **Verbally,** as a simple statement, such as "1 inch to 100 miles."

(2) **Graphically,** by a line divided into equal parts, and marked in miles or other units of length.

(3) *Numerically,* usually by writing a fraction to show what part of the *true* distances the *map* distances really are. The fraction is known as the R.F. or representative fraction. For example, the scale 1/1,000,000 (also written 1: 1,000,000) means that any distance on the map is one-millionth of its true length on the earth. This may also be expressed by saying that 1 *unit* of length on the map (1 inch, 1 foot, etc.) represents 1,000,000 of the *same units* on the earth.

Maps are always much smaller than the pieces of land they represent. The more closely the map approaches the land in size, the larger its scale is said to be. A map of the United States on an 8- by 10-inch sheet of paper would have to use a very small scale, such as 1 inch (of paper) to 300 miles (of earth). On the other hand, a large wall map of the same area would use a *larger scale,* such as 6 inches (of paper) to 300 miles (of earth), usually expressed as 1 inch to 50 miles. A still larger scale such as 1 inch to 1 mile would require a sheet of paper 300 feet long (the length of a football field) and almost as wide for all of the United States.

6. Showing Elevation

In order to show land forms, maps must show the relief or the changes in height of the earth's surface. This can be done in many ways, such as shading, coloring, or even miniature sketching of land forms. The simplest and most accurate method for large-scale maps, however, is by the use of contour lines. Contour lines give exact elevations (heights above sea level) and show the shape of the land at the same time. They can be explained best by an illustration. Figure 6-3a is a sketch of an island in the sea. This island is 6 miles long, 3 miles wide, oval-shaped, and 113 feet high at its highest point. In an ordinary map the island would look as shown in Figure 6-3b. Such a map gives little information about the island. The shoreline shows the shape of the island at *sea level* and the scale indicates the length and width of the island, but the map gives no information about the height of the island, the steepness of its surface, or its shape above sea level. So the mapmaker surveys the island and proceeds to turn this map into a contour map. On the map he locates a series of points shown by his survey to be 20 feet above sea level (Fig. 6-3c). He joins these points with a **contour line, a line drawn through points at the same height above sea level.** Every point on this line is 20 feet higher than the shoreline. The shoreline is also a contour line, since it joins points all of which are at sea level (zero feet above sea level).

The distance along the ground between any two points is still found by use of the map scale! Using the scale in Figure 6-3c, we see that between *A* and *B* the island reached the 20-foot elevation in one mile, whereas between *C* and *D* the same height is reached in only one-fourth of a mile. Obviously, then, the island is steeper between *C* and *D*. Instead of figuring this out each time, we use the rule that **where contour lines are close together, the slope of the ground is comparatively steep; where contour lines are far apart, the slope of the ground is comparatively gentle.**

Fig. 6-3. *Representing an island by a contour map: (a) sketch of Sea Island; (b) an "ordinary" map of Sea Island; (c) map b with a 20-foot contour added; (d) contour map of Sea Island.*

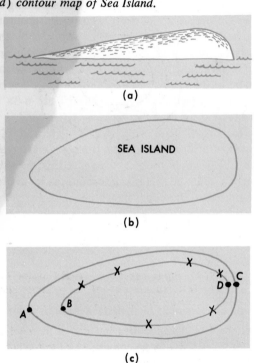

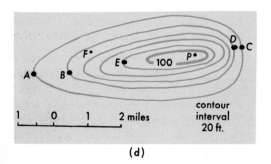

Now the mapmaker draws additional contour lines showing where the island reaches the 40-foot, 60-foot, 80-foot, and 100-foot elevations respectively (Fig. 6-3d). He is using a 20-foot **contour interval,** which is the **difference in elevation between two consecutive contour lines.** (Do not confuse the contour interval, which is difference in height, with distance along the ground. The horizontal distance between two points on consecutive contour lines is measured, as before, with the map scale.)

The contour interval differs according to the relief of the land. If the land to be mapped is high and steep, the mapmaker will use a large contour interval such as 50 feet or 100 feet; if it slopes gently or is nearly level, the mapmaker will use a small contour interval such as 10 feet, 5 feet, or even 1 foot. For moderately rough land, a 20-foot contour interval is used.

To make the reading of contour lines easier, every fifth line is made heavier and its elevation is marked on it. The other contour lines are not numbered, but the contour interval is stated at the bottom of the map (see Fig. 6-3d). Notice that the contour lines show three things: (1) elevation of the land; (2) steepness or gentleness of its slopes; (3) shape of the land at various heights.

7. Depression Contours

Up to now, we have been assuming that the farther you go on a hill, the higher it becomes. This is almost always true, but there are some exceptions. In climbing a volcano, for example, the highest point is reached when you come to the rim of the crater, the cup-shaped depression at the top of the volcano. If you go on from there, you go *down,* not up. To show this we use **depression contours,** which are drawn like contours but are hachured (shaded) on the inside.

Suppose we wish to draw a contour map of Dead Volcano Island, shown in Figure 6-4. The volcano rises from sea level to a height of 70 feet above sea level at the rim of the crater. The crater goes down to a height of 30 feet above sea level. At the center of the crater, a small cone rises from the floor to a height of 50 feet above sea level. If we use a 20-foot contour interval in our map, our fourth contour line takes us to a height of 60 feet (0, 20, 40, 60). The volcano continues to rise as far as the crater rim at 70 feet, but since our contour interval is 20 feet, we cannot draw a contour line at the 70-foot level. Passing the rim, we go down into the crater. When we reach the 60-foot level, we may again draw a contour line. However, if we draw it in the ordinary way, it will be interpreted as the 80-foot level of an ordinary hill rather than as the 60-foot level of one with a crater. So we hachure it (see Fig. 6-4), call it a depression contour, and read it *at the same height* as the surrounding regular contour. Remember this rule!

Continuing down into the crater, we reach the 40-foot level, which we show by another depression contour. The 30-foot low point cannot be shown by a contour line, since the next one would be at 20 feet. But now the floor of the crater *rises* again as we approach the central cone. To show its 40-foot level we draw a *regular* contour, and again we follow the rule of reading it at the *same* height as the depression contour that surrounds it. To simplify our illustration, each contour line has been numbered. Ordinarily this is not done.

Volcano craters are not the only kinds of depressions found on land. In desert areas there are often shallow depressions left by the evaporation of small lakes. In limestone areas there are depressions formed by cave-in of the bed rock. These and other depressions may appear on the contour maps of relatively level areas.

To summarize: In reading depression contours, the first one is read *at the same altitude as the ordinary contour* that encloses or precedes it. (Similarly, a regular contour has the same altitude as the depression contour that encloses it.) Thereafter, each depression contour is *lower*

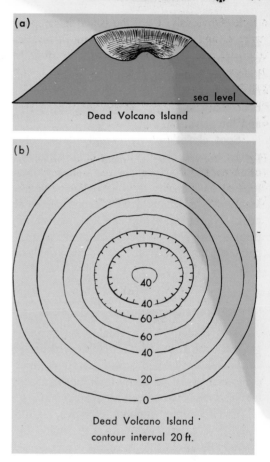

Fig. 6-4. At the top is a sketch of Dead Volcano Island. Below is a contour map of the volcano with depression contours showing its crater.

than the one that encloses it (and each regular contour is higher) by an amount equal to the contour interval of the map.

8. Bench Marks and Spot Elevations

During the course of a map-making survey the surveyors determine the *exact elevation* of many points in the map area. These may be shown on the map in a number of ways. **Bench mark** points are points whose exact elevation is inscribed on a brass or aluminum plate permanently set into the ground at the point of survey.

(See Figs. 6-5 and 6-8.) They are shown on the map by the letters BM, followed by a small cross or triangle to show the location, and then followed by numbers giving the elevation to the nearest foot. A survey point for which there is no benchmark is shown on the map by a triangle and the elevation.

Spot elevations are the elevations of such places as road forks, hilltops, lake surfaces, and other points of special interest. These points are located on the map by a small cross, unless the location is obvious, as at a crossroad or sharp peak. Numbers giving checked elevations are printed in *black*. Unchecked elevations are printed in *brown*. Water elevations are shown in *blue*.

9. U.S.G.S. Topographic Maps

The United States Geological Survey, engaged in the topographic mapping of the entire surface of the United States, has thus far made contour maps of far more than half of the country. The maps are issued in two principal series.

The 15-minute quadrangle series. Until the early 1940's, most contour maps made by the United States Geological Survey represented areas or quadrangles that covered one-fourth degree of latitude from north to south, and one-fourth degree of longitude from east to west. (Since one degree of latitude or longitude is equal to 60 minutes, one-fourth degree equals 15 minutes. Hence the name the *15-minute series.*) Each map or *sheet* was named for a prominent part of the quadrangle. Examples are the Brooklyn Sheet, the Shasta Sheet, and the Delaware Water Gap Sheet. The area covered by each sheet in the 15-minute series is approximately 18 miles (north to south) by 13 miles (east to west). The scale used on most of these sheets is 1:62,500. This means that one inch on the map represents 62,500 inches (nearly a mile) on the surface of the earth. (The exact number of inches in a mile is 63,360, but the round number 62,500

U.S. Geological Survey

Fig. 6-5. A United States Geological Survey bench mark.

is used to simplify calculations.) The contour interval found most often on these sheets is 20 feet, but fairly level areas may use a 5-foot or 10-foot interval, while very steep mountainous areas may use a 50-foot or 100-foot interval.

The 7½-minute quadrangle series. Since the early 1940's the Geological Survey has made most new quadrangle maps on a scale of 1:24,000 (one inch = 24,000 inches, or exactly 2,000 feet). This scale is more than twice as large as the 1:62,500 scale, making possible much greater detail. The map sheet is somewhat larger than those made on the 1:62,500 scale, but the area covered by each sheet is only half as much in each direction. Half of 15 minutes is 7½ minutes, so we have each map sheet showing an area 7½ minutes from north to south, and 7½ minutes from east to west. Many areas that were surveyed in the 15-minute series years ago are now being re-surveyed in the 7½-minute series. (See Fig. 6-6.)

Since maps in this series have a much larger scale than in the old series (more than 2½ inches to a mile), there is much more room for contour lines. So we find the 10-foot interval used much more than formerly. Other intervals commonly used in the 7½-minute series are 5, 20, 40, and 80 feet.

Other scales. Both the 15-minute and the 7½-minute series sometimes use mileage scales other than those mentioned above. The 15-minute sheets for Alaska have a scale of 1:63,360 (exactly 1 inch to 1 mile). Some 7½-minute sheets have a scale of 1:31,680 (exactly 1 inch to ½ mile, or 2 inches to 1 mile).

Other series. Where great detail is not needed, or large areas are to be shown on the usual size sheet, smaller scales are used. There is a 30-minute series that uses a scale of 1:125,000 (1 inch to about 2 miles). There is also a series that uses a scale of 1:250,000 (1 inch to about 4 miles) and takes in an area of 1 degree from north to south, and 2 degrees from east to west. In Antarctica, however, this series usually covers 1° latitude and 6° longitude. Why?

Fig. 6-6. The relation of 7½-minute quadrangles to the 15-minute quadrangle of Harrisburg, Pennsylvania.

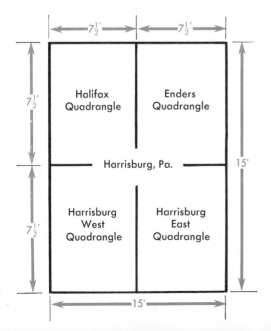

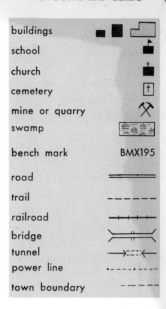

Fig. 6-7. Some common topographic map symbols.

Use of color. The various features of the contour map are shown in three colors. Contour lines are always printed in brown. Roads, railroads, and other works of man are printed in black, while water features—such as rivers, lakes, and swamps—are shown in blue. Many maps also show woodland areas in green and highways in red. A complete key to all symbols is obtainable from the United States Geological Survey. (See Fig. 6-7.)

10. Reading the Contour Map

Direction. As explained in Topic 3, directions are found by following meridians and parallels. If the map shows no meridians or parallels, it may have an arrow pointing to true north. Otherwise it can be assumed that north is at the top of the map. U.S.G.S. topographic maps also show the **magnetic declination** or **variation** of the compass from true north in each map region.

Distance. In measuring distances the scale of the map is first determined. If the scale is known in miles per inch, distances on the map

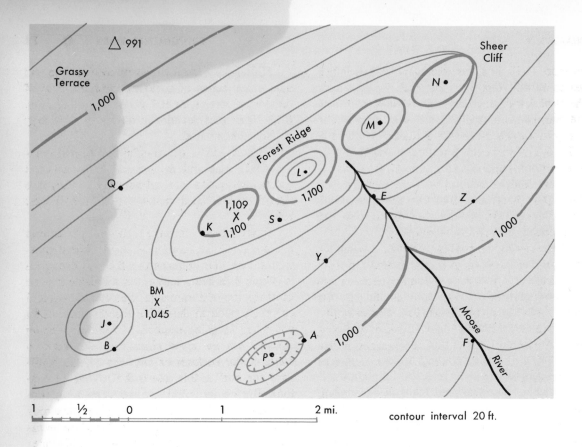

Fig. 6-8. *Simple landforms are easily identified on a contour map. Contour lines are far apart in level areas like Grassy Terrace, and closer together at steeper slopes. At a cliff they run together, as at Sheer Cliff. Oval contours show hills and ridges. Depression contours show basins, as at* P.

may be measured with a ruler and converted into miles. (On U.S.G.S. maps the common scale 1:62,500 may be regarded, for approximate work, as 1 mile to the inch.) When a graphic scale is printed on the map, the distance between two points can be marked off with any straight edge, such as the edge of a sheet of paper, or with a piece of string, and then held directly against the scale for reading. Zigzag distances along roads, rivers, etc., may be marked off in succession on the edge of a sheet of paper before measuring against the graphic scale.

Elevation. When a point is *on* a contour line, its *exact* elevation is known. For example in Figure 6-3d, point *B* is exactly 20 feet above sea level, and point *E* is exactly 80 feet above sea level. When a point is between two contour lines, its elevation is known to be *between* the elevation of the two lines. For example, point *F* is halfway between the 20-foot and 40-foot contour lines, so its elevation is approximately 30 feet. When the exact elevation of a hilltop is known, it is printed in the space at the top of the hill. Otherwise its elevation is estimated as more than that of the last contour line, but less than the elevation that the next contour line would have. For example, the elevation of point *P* is above 100 feet but under 120 feet. *P* may be anything from 101 feet to 119 feet.

It must be remembered that each elevation given on a contour map is *height above sea level*, not height above the lowest point on the particular map. Only those contour maps that include a sea coast will start from sea level. To determine the elevation of any point, one should start from the marked contour line that is nearest to it. For example, to determine the elevation of point Q (Fig. 6-8), we begin from the marked, 1,000-foot contour line and count *up* in 20-foot "rises," since the contour interval of the map is 20 feet. Point Q is therefore 1,040 feet above sea level. (We count *up* rather than *down* because we are approaching the top of the ridge.)

Determining the contour interval. When the contour interval is not given, it can be determined by noting the *difference in elevation* between any two marked contour lines, and dividing by the number of "rises" between them. For example, in Figure 6-8 the difference between two consecutive *marked* lines is 100 feet, reached in five "rises." Dividing 100 feet by 5 gives a 20-foot contour interval.

If only one marked contour line is shown, the contour interval can usually be figured out by reference to spot elevations. In Figure 6-8, for example, spot elevation X1,045 indicates that the contour line just south of it is 1,040, and the one north of it is 1,060, even without reference to the 1,100-foot line or the stated contour interval.

11. Landforms on Contour Maps

Level land. If a large part of a contour map shows no contour lines, it means that the rise or fall of the land in that area is less than the contour interval, and the land is therefore comparatively level. In Figure 6-8, for example, Grassy Terrace (in the northwest) has no contour lines on it and must be fairly level.

Cliffs. Where contour lines run very close together, the land is very steep. If contour lines coincide, it means that the higher ground is directly above the lower ground, and the contour lines therefore indicate a cliff. An example of this is shown at Sheer Cliff.

Hilltops. Closed circles or ovals at the end of a rising series of contours show the tops of hills or mountains, as at J, K, L, M, and N (Fig. 6-8). The exact elevation of the top of a hill may be indicated, as at K.

Ridges. Hills or mountains that are comparatively long and narrow and may include a number of peaks are called ridges. They are shown by long oval contour lines, as at Forest Ridge.

Depressions or basins are shown by hachured contour lines like those at A and P. The depression shown here differs from the one described in Topic 8 in being located on a hillside instead of at the top of a mountain. The rule of Topic 7 can be applied to determine the elevation of its contours: In going upslope, *the first depression contour has the same altitude as the ordinary contour that encloses or precedes it.* The "ordinary contour" in this case is the 1,000-foot contour. But on its uphill side the depression contour is 20 feet lower than the next ordinary contour, and this should be remembered to avoid error. For these cases we might use this rule: When going downslope into a depression, the first depression contour is one contour interval lower than the contour just crossed (see Fig. 6-8).

River valleys. Where a river has cut a valley through the land, contour lines plainly show the carved-out valley. As each contour line approaches the valley, it can stay at the elevation it represents *only by bending* in the direction of the high land from which the river is running down (see Fig. 6-9). On the map, then, *contour lines bend upstream where they cross river valleys.* This rule may be used to determine the direction in which a river flows. The direction of river flow can also be determined by noticing the elevations of marked contour lines. Common sense tells us, of course, that a river must flow from higher to lower elevations.

The *steepness of a river* is shown by the closeness of the contour lines that cross it. The

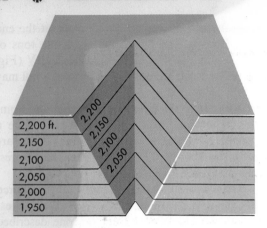

Fig. 6-9. *Contour lines must bend upstream where they cross a river valley in order to stay at the heights they represent.*

width of the valley is approximately shown by the width of the "V" made by a contour line where it crosses a river.

12. Determining the Average Slope or Gradient

The average slope or gradient between any two points of a hill, mountain, river, trail, or road is easily determined from a contour map. If we know how many feet our hill drops in a given distance, we have

$$\text{Average Slope} = \frac{\text{Drop in Altitude (ft.)}}{\text{Distance (mi.)}}$$

Both drop in altitude and mileage between two points can easily be read from a contour map. Let us calculate the average slope of a trail from *B* to *F* in Fig. 6-8. The altitude of *B* is 1,060 feet; the altitude of *F* is 960 feet. If the *distance* between them, *measured with the scale,* is 4 miles, then:

$$\text{Average Slope} = \frac{1060 - 960 \ (\text{ft.})}{4 \ (\text{mi.})}$$

$$= \frac{100 \ \text{ft.}}{4 \ \text{mi.}} = 25 \ \text{ft./mi.}$$

13. Profiles from Contour Maps

A **profile** which shows the ups and downs of a line across any part of a contour map, is easily made as shown in Figure 6-10. Wherever the line (or path to be followed on a hike, march, etc.) meets a contour, we know the exact height above sea level. If we plot this on some definite vertical scale, we get our profile. This is done most easily by placing the bottom edge of a sheet of paper on top of the line we wish to follow. Then we mark on the paper each point where our path crosses a contour. At each point we record the height of the point. When all points are marked, we use our vertical scale to raise each point to its proper height, keeping them as far apart as they were on the map, of course. Then we join the elevated points and have our profile. (Vertical scales may be ⅛ inch = 20 feet, ¼ inch = 20 feet, or whatever you wish. Plotting is easier if you use graph or cross-section paper.)

Fig. 6-10. *A profile—a line showing the "ups and downs" of a section across a contour map—can be made as shown in this sketch.*

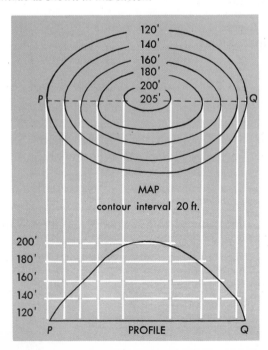

TOPIC QUESTIONS

Each topic question refers to the topic of the same number within this chapter.

Introduction. (*a*) What is a topographic map? (*b*) What is "relief"? (*c*) Of what value are topographic maps?

1. (*a*) What is a map? (*b*) Why is mapmaking a problem? (*c*) Why can a map of a small area be made with less distortion than a map of a large area?

2. What is a map projection? What three features do all maps show? Name four map projections and describe the feature that makes each one useful.

3. (*a*) What are parallels? (*b*) What are meridians? (*c*) How are north and south found on any map? east and west?

4. (*a*) What is latitude? How is it measured? What is the latitude of the Equator? the North Pole? the South Pole? How long is a degree of latitude? (*b*) What is longitude? How is it measured? Where is the 180th meridian?

5. (*a*) Define or explain what a map scale is? (*b*) Why is it impossible for a Mercator world map to have a single scale? (*c*) Describe three ways to express a map scale. Give examples. (*d*) Distinguish between a large-scale map and a small-scale map.

6. (*a*) What is a contour line? How are contour lines drawn on maps? (*b*) How does a contour map show whether a slope is gentle or steep? (*c*) Define contour interval. Give examples of large and small contour intervals and their uses. (*d*) Distinguish between the use of the contour interval and the scale. (*e*) How are contour lines drawn on maps to make it easier to read them?

7. Explain the meaning, use, and rules for drawing and reading depression contours.

8. (*a*) What is a bench mark? (*b*) How is a bench mark point shown on the map? (*c*) What are spot elevations? How are they shown?

9. (*a*) Describe the following features of a U.S.G.S. 15-minute topographic sheet: area, scale, contour interval. (*b*) Describe the use of color on U.S.G.S. topographic maps.

10. (*a*) How is direction found on a contour map? (*b*) How is distance measured on a contour map? (*c*) How is the elevation of a point determined on a contour map? Of a hilltop? When the map does not show sea level? (*d*) How can the contour interval be found when the map does not state it?

11. How does a contour map show: (*a*) level areas, (*b*) cliffs, (*c*) hilltops, (*d*) ridges, (*e*) river valleys, (*f*) the steepness of a river, (*g*) the width of a valley?

12. Explain the meaning of the gradient between 2 points and how it is determined.

13. Explain what a "profile" is and how one is made from a contour map.

GENERAL QUESTIONS

1. After plotting a great-circle route on a gnomonic projection, the navigator must transfer it to the Mercator projection. Why?

2. Globes are true representations of the earth's surface. Why aren't they used instead of maps?

3. Where are north, south, east, and west on a polar projection of the Southern Hemisphere?

4. Prove that the scale 1:62,500 is the same as "1 inch to nearly 1 mile." Prove that 1:24,000 is exactly "1 inch to 2,000 feet."

5. Draw graphic scales for: (a) 1:125,000; (b) 1:31,680; (c) 1:250,000; (d) 1:1,-000,000; (e) 1:62,500; (f) 1:24,000.

6. Express the above scales in words.

7. Answer the following questions about Figure 6-8. (a) What is the maximum elevation of each of the hilltops J, K, L, M, and N? How high is point S? Y? Z? A? B? (b) How high a cliff is Sheer Cliff? (c) From L in what direction is J? N? Q? Y? (d) In what direction does Moose River flow? (e) How far is it from Q to Y? from J to Sheer Cliff? (f) How wide is the Moose River Valley at the 980 contour? (g) How much higher than J is L? (h) At what elevation does Moose River start? (i) How many feet does Moose River drop in 1 mile on the average? (j) What is the feature at P called? What is the altitude of its lowest possible point?

8. Using a scale of 1 inch to 1 mile and a contour interval of 20 feet, draw a contour map of an ocean island 6 miles long, 5 miles wide (north to south), steepest on the north side, and rising to a single peak 167 feet above sea level. Show a stream whose source is at an altitude of 143 feet and which flows southwest to the sea.

STUDENT ACTIVITIES

1. Make a three-dimensional cardboard (or plywood) model of a region similar to the one represented by Figure 6-8. Use a separate sheet of cardboard for each contour level shown. Fasten the sheets together with glue or nail them to a baseboard with nails driven through high points J, K, L, M, and N.

2. Modeling clay may be used for making a model of Figure 6-8 or other topographic maps.

3. Using the method described in activity number 1, make a model of an area similar to that shown in Figure 6-9, illustrating why contour lines must bend upstream where they cross a river valley.

4. Parts of real topographic maps may be represented in models made by the method suggested in activity number 1. To reproduce the various contour levels accurately, use carbon paper under your map sheet to trace any given contour line onto a sheet of cardboard. Do this for each level you wish to reproduce. In general, only heavy (marked) contour lines need to be used. Thus, for a map with a 20-foot contour interval, each sheet of cardboard in your model will represent a height of 100 feet.

5. Using the method described in Topic 13, construct profiles across real topographic maps at regular distances. If these profiles are plotted on thin cardboard, they can be cut out and mounted vertically on the map. This is another way of showing the topography of a region represented by a topographic map.

TOPOGRAPHIC SHEETS

State index maps showing all quadrangle maps available for each state may be obtained from the U.S. Geological Survey, Washington, D.C. 20025, without charge. The index map also gives prices and detailed instructions for ordering.

For maps of areas east of the Mississippi River, order prepaid from the Geological Survey, Washington, D.C. 20025.

For maps of areas west of the Mississippi River, order prepaid from the Geological Survey, Federal Center, Denver, Colorado.

· The Boothbay, Maine, sheet (15-minute series) has long been a first choice for introductory exercises in the reading of topographic maps.

BIBLIOGRAPHY

ROCKS AND MINERALS

Desautels, P. E. *The Mineral Kingdom*. Grosset and Dunlap, N.Y., 1960.

Fenton, C. L. and M. A. *The Rock Book*. Doubleday, N.Y., 1970.

Fritzen, D. K. *The Rock Hunter's Field Manual*. Harper and Row, N.Y., 1959.

Holden and Singer. *Crystals and Crystal Growing*. Wesleyan University Press, Columbus, Ohio, 1960.

Hurlbut, C. S. *Manual of Mineralogy*. Wiley, N.Y., 1969.

Jensen, D. *My Hobby Is Collecting Rocks and Minerals*. Children's Press, Chicago, 1958.

LaFleur, R. G. *Field Identification of Rocks*. N.Y. State Education Dept., Albany, N.Y., 1964.

Lapham, D. M. and Geyer, A. R. *Mineral Collecting in Pennsylvania*. Department of Internal Affairs, Harrisburg, Pa., 1969.

Loomis, F. B. *Field Book of Common Rocks and Minerals*. Putnam, N.Y., 1957.

Luedke, Wrucke, and Graham. *Mineral Occurrences of New York State, with Selected References to Each Locality, 1959*. U.S. Government Printing Office, Washington, D.C. 20402.

Pearl, R. M. *Wonders of Gems*. Dodd, Mead, N.Y., 1963.

Pearl, R. M. *Rocks and Minerals*. Barnes and Noble, N.Y., 1969.

Pough, F. H. *Field Guide to Rocks and Minerals*. Houghton Mifflin, Boston, 1960.

Ransom, J. E. *Gems and Minerals of America*. Harper and Row, N.Y., 1973.

Sanborn, W. B. *Crystal and Mineral Collecting*. Lane Book Co., Menlo Park, Cal., 1960.

Sinkankas, J. *Prospecting for Gemstones and Minerals*. Van Nostrand Reinhold, N.Y., 1970.

Sinkankas, J. *Mineralogy; A First Course*. Van Nostrand Reinhold, N.Y., 1966.

Skinner, B. J. *Earth Resources*. Prentice-Hall, Englewood Cliffs, N.J., 1969.

Vanders, I. and Kerr, P. F. *Mineral Recognition*. Wiley, N.Y., 1969.

Zim, H. S. and Shaffer, P. R. *Rocks and Minerals*. Simon and Schuster, N.Y., 1957.

Also publications of state geological surveys, state museums, and the U.S. Geological Survey.

TOPOGRAPHIC MAPS

Hathaway, J. A. *The Story of Maps and Map-Making*. Golden Press, N.Y., 1960.

Lahee, F. H. *Field Geology*. McGraw-Hill, N.Y., 1961.

Lobeck, A. K. *Things Maps Don't Tell Us*. Macmillan, N.Y., 1956.

Marsh, S. *All About Maps and Mapmaking*. Random House, N.Y., 1963.

Raisz, E. *General Cartography*. McGraw-Hill, N.Y., 1948.

Raisz, E. *Mapping the World*. Abelard-Schuman, N.Y., 1956.

Strahler, A. N. *The Earth Sciences*. Harper and Row, N.Y., 1971.

Unit 2 The Crust Undergoes Attack

Have you ever seen a
snow-capped mountain in spring
or summer? The glacial cap of Mt. Rainier
is clearly shown in the photograph. What season
do you think is shown? How can you tell? Observe how far
the glacial snow on Mt. Rainier extends. What effect might
glaciers have on the crust of the earth? Do they build up the land or
wear it away? How? In the photograph look for evidences of other forces
that change the earth's crust. What are these forces? What might they do?

The national parks and national monuments of the United States include many
of the world's most fantastic landforms—the Grand Canyon, the towering cliffs
and waterfalls of Yosemite, the erosional forms of Bryce Canyon and Monument
Valley and the Badlands, the mountainous sand dunes of the Sangre de Cristo
Mountains, the famous geysers of Yellowstone, the spectacular basin of Crater Lake.

Each of these landforms, like all features on the earth's surface, represents some
stage in the continuing conflict between two sets of forces. On the one hand are
the forces of weather, winds, waves, rivers, and glaciers. Receiving their energy
from the sun, these forces constantly attack the rocks of the earth's crust. In
the billions of years of the earth's existence, they could have worn down the
continents to sea level many times.

But opposed to them is another set of forces starting in the
earth's interior. These forces build up the earth's crust. In
this unit we shall explore the forces that attack the earth's
crust. In Unit 3, we shall explore those that
counter the attack.

CHAPTER 7

Weathering, Mass Wasting, and Soils

HOW DO YOU KNOW THAT . . . ?

Rocks containing iron, in minerals like magnetite, are easily weathered under certain conditions. Try the following experiment to identify the conditions.

Take two dry pads of steel wool (soapless preferred, but not essential). Wet one thoroughly with water. Keep the other dry. Let them "weather" overnight in an open dish. Compare their appearance. If one weathered more than the other, explain why. Is the rusting of iron an example of chemical action or physical action? Why? In what way does rusting change the steel wool physically?

1. Weathering, Mass Wasting, and Erosion

The Palisades of the Hudson are the nearly vertical cliffs that form the west walls of the lower Hudson River Valley. (See Fig. 7-1.) The palisades consist of diabase, a hard tough crystalline rock. Like all rocks, diabase is affected by the weather. As time passes its smooth, dark-gray surface turns brown and crumbly. Cracks form on the face and top of the cliff, and spread inward and downward. Eventually material breaks away from the cliff in the form of brown claylike powder, rock chips the size of sand grains and pebbles, and occasional boulders. How and why do these changes in the rock come about? In a moment, we shall attempt to explain them. These changes are called **weathering,** which we define as **the physical and chemical breakup of rock at or near the earth's surface from exposure to atmosphere, weather, and plants and animals.**

Now what happens to the newly formed clay, sand, pebbles, and boulders? The heavy boulders and pebbles may fall all the way to the base of the cliff, where they continue to weather. The sands and clays may lodge temporarily part of the way down, and reach bottom some days or weeks later after being washed down by rain or melting snow. And finally, some day, some of this material will fall or be washed into the river. **All of the downslope movements of the loose rock material,** whether rapid or slow, sudden or steady, are called **mass wasting.**

What next? The sediment washed into the river is carried downstream to the sea. The river, which wears down or *erodes* its valley, and also carries off rock sediment, is an agent of erosion. **Erosion** may be defined as **the breakup and removal of rock by moving natural agents.** In addition to rivers, the other agents of erosion are glaciers (ice in motion); winds (air in motion); waves and currents (water in motion).

In summary, weathering attacks and breaks up the rock wherever it is exposed at the earth's surface. Mass wasting moves the weathered rock downslope. Erosion breaks up rock and carries it off as well.

New York Central System

Fig. 7-1. The Palisades of the Hudson River illustrate the effect of weathering. See Topic 1.

2. Types of Weathering

Sandstone crumbles into sand. Shale is shattered into thin fragments. Flakes of black mica in schist and gneiss turn golden brown and fall away. Dark basalts are stained reddish brown. Even granite is attacked until its quartz grains fall apart, no longer held together by feldspars and hornblendes which have decayed to clay. All these evidences of *weathering* can be seen in natural exposures of the bedrock, or they may be seen where man has used these rocks for buildings, monuments, and other purposes. Weathering includes a great variety of processes, but all of them are usually classed under two headings. **Mechanical weathering** or **disintegration** takes place when rock is cracked, split, or broken into smaller pieces of the same material without changing its composition or identity. The breaking of a *granite* cliff, for example into boulders and pebbles of *granite* is mechanical weathering. **Chemical weathering** or **decomposition** takes place through the alteration or decay of the minerals of a rock into different substances. The

crumbling of dark gray diabase rock into rusty brownish clay is an example of chemical weathering.

3. Why Mechanical Weathering Takes Place

A rock split in two by the blow of a hammer undergoes a mechanical change. In nature, rocks are weathered mechanically mainly as a result of weather changes, although the movements of plants and animals also cause some mechanical weathering.

Effects of temperature change. Rocks warm up in the daytime and cool off at night. The resulting temperature changes are very large in the bare rocks of mountain and desert areas. Since the different minerals in a rock expand and contract at different rates, changes in temperature might be expected to loosen the mineral grains until they fall apart. However, laboratory tests fail to produce such effects. Changing temperatures alone probably do little to weather rock, or at best work very slowly. There is one exception. In forest fires rocks are known to split and break if heated strongly enough.

Frost action. Water expands by about 10 per cent of its volume when it freezes into ice. This expansion exerts a tremendous force on the walls of any container in which the water may be held, whether that container is a water pipe or a crevice in a rock. In climates where the temperature goes below freezing, and especially in porous rocks or rocks that are already cracked, the freezing of water may be the most damaging of all weathering processes. The more often the ice melts and then refreezes, the more often will this *frost action, frost wedging,* or *wedgework of ice,* be able to split the rock. The exposed bedrock of mountain tops is particularly subject to frost action. As a result, the surface above the tree line may be entirely covered by large angular boulders in what are known as **block fields** or **boulder fields.** These are common in the Rocky Mountains, the White Mountains of New Hampshire, and many other mountain regions. The effects of frost action can also be seen in the many new pits and cracks that form in street pavements in northern United States every winter. (See Fig. 7-2.)

Exfoliation. In humid or moderately humid climates one may see exposures of rock that look as though successive layers have been stripped away from their surface. The rocks are always massive coarse-grained rocks like granite and gabbro, and they usually contain feldspars or other minerals that weather into clay. This *peeling* or *scaling off* of the outer layers of massive rocks is called **exfoliation.** Exfoliation's effects range from thin flakes of rock weathered from small boulders to enormous

Fig. 7-2. Boulder field formed by frost action high in the Big Horn Mountains of Wyoming.

Darton, U.S. Geological Survey

Fig. 7-3. Weathering by exfoliation has caused the rounded knoblike form of this boulder of gabbro.

sheets of rock splitting away from cliffs and mountain tops. At least two different processes are believed involved in exfoliation.

On a small scale, exfoliation results when rain water gets into tiny cracks in the rock. The water combines chemically with grains of feldspar just below the surface, causing the feldspar to swell and expand. The expansion splits off a thin flake or shell of the rock. As weathering continues, more and more layers split off. But the weathering is fastest at corners and edges—because of their greater exposure—and this results in rounding off the rock. If a rock mass contains many cracks or *joints* that run both vertically and horizontally, exfoliation may carve it into a large number of *rounded knoblike forms.* Those that break off become *rounded boulders.* (See Fig. 7-3.)

On a large scale, gigantic slabs of fresh rock may split away from the tops of exposed mountain peaks of granite or granodiorite. Granite is an intrusive rock formed far below the earth's surface. It is believed that when great weights of overlying rock are removed by erosion, the reduced pressure on the granite allows it to expand. The effect of this expansion is to cause extensive curved fractures or joints to appear in the rock *parallel to the surface* and at various depths. It is along these joints that exfoliation occurs. The rounded peaks formed by the process are called **exfoliation domes.** (See Fig. 7-4.) In the United States, many spectacular exfoliation domes occur in Yosemite National Park, California. Stone Mountain, Georgia, and Sugar Loaf Mountain, near Rio de Janeiro, are other

Fig. 7-4. Exfoliation has removed great sheets of rock from the surface of famous Half Dome in Yosemite National Park, California.

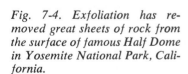

famous granite domes, but not all geologists agree that they were weathered by exfoliation.

Action of plants. Numerous tiny plants such as the grayish lichens (*lye* kens) and the green mosses are found growing on rocks. Small as they are, these plants help to split and decay the rock. They do this by the wedging growth of their hairlike roots in the tiny pores of the rock, and by the formation of rock-dissolving acids in the roots both as they grow and as they decay. Trees and shrubs may grow through cracks in boulders that lie on top of soil, or may send rootlets into crevices in the bedrock. (See Fig. 7-5.)

Action of animals. While animals do not attack rock directly, the burrowing animals contribute to weathering indirectly. Earthworms, ants, woodchucks, and other such animals dig holes in the mantle rock and bring rock particles to the surface. The holes permit air and water to penetrate to the bedrock and weather it below the surface.

4. Why Chemical Weathering Takes Place

Chemical weathering of rock results chiefly from the action of the *oxygen, rain water,* and *carbon dioxide* of the atmosphere. These three substances act as chemical agents. They get some help from tiny quantities of *nitric acid, ammonia,* and other active gases formed in the air by lightning. Chemical weathering is also aided by *acids formed in the soil* through the decay of plants and animals. Let us see how these chemical agents work.

The chemical union of *water* with other substances is called **hydration.** Common minerals that may undergo hydration include feldspar, hornblende, and augite. When these minerals are exposed to water, they unite with it slowly, swelling up and then crumbling into powdery clay. The clay formed by the hydration of feldspar is called kaolin. (See Chapter 3, Topic 12.)

American Museum of Natural History

Fig. 7-5. Lichens growing on rock cause the surface of the rock to crumble.

The chemical union of *oxygen* with other substances is called **oxidation.** The minerals most easily attacked by oxygen are compounds of iron such as magnetite, pyrite, and the dark-colored ferromagnesian minerals hornblende, augite, and biotite. Oxidation of these minerals forms iron rust, just as the oxidation of an iron nail does. If the oxidation involves only iron and oxygen, the rust is the red iron oxide called *hematite.* But when water is also present, hydration takes place at the same time, and the rust is the brown hydrous iron oxide called *limonite.* (See Chapter 4, Topic 3.) The hematite and limonite formed by weathering are usually responsible for the reddish or brownish colors of soils and weathered rocks. Red Bank, New Jersey, gets its name from its hematite-colored soil.

The chemical union of *carbon dioxide* with other substances to form carbonate compounds is called **carbonation.** Alone, carbon dioxide gas has almost no effect on rock minerals. However, carbon dioxide dissolves readily in rain water and ground water to form a weak acid called carbonic acid (the same acid as in soda water). This acid attacks many abundant rock-forming minerals, such as feldspar, hornblende, augite, and biotite mica. Its effect is to *leach* (dissolve out) such elements as potassium, sodium, magnesium, and calcium, with which the carbon dioxide unites to form soluble carbonates (such as calcium carbonate and potassium carbonate). When this happens, the original mineral crumbles into a residue of *clay*.

The process just described may be shown in two chemical equations as follows:

1) $$CO_2 + H_2O \rightarrow H_2CO_3$$
$$\underset{\text{dioxide}}{\text{carbon}} + \text{water} \rightarrow \underset{\text{acid}}{\text{carbonic}}$$

2) $$2KAlSi_3O_8 + H_2CO_3 + H_2O \rightarrow$$
$$\underset{\text{feldspar}}{\text{orthoclase}} + \underset{\text{acid}}{\text{carbonic}} + \text{water} \rightarrow$$

$$K_2CO_3 + Al_2Si_2O_5(OH)_4 + 4SiO_2$$
$$\underset{\substack{\text{carbonate} + \\ \text{(soluble)}}}{\text{potassium}} \quad \underset{\substack{\text{(insoluble)} \\ \text{clay}}}{\text{kaolinite}} + \underset{\substack{\text{(partly} \\ \text{soluble)}}}{\text{silica}}$$

Carbonic acid is even more effective with calcite than with the minerals mentioned above, for it dissolves calcite completely. Unless the calcite is impure, no residue of clay is left over. The same thing happens to gypsum and salt, both of which will dissolve slowly but surely, even in ordinary rain water. This dissolving action of carbonic acid hollows out the great underground caverns of the world from limestone bedrock, which is composed almost entirely of calcite.

Acids produced by lightning and by the decay or wastes of plants and animals are dissolved by rain water and carried down through the soil to the bedrock. Like carbonic acid, these acids dissolve some of the rock minerals and cause others to crumble. Their effects are considerable. Since water is so essential to chemical weathering, a humid, rainy climate favors this type of weathering. And since heat speeds up chemical action, chemical weathering is much more active in a warm climate than in a cold one.

5. Which Minerals and Rocks Are Most Resistant?

A very brief summary of the over-all effects of weathering on the principal rock-making minerals and their rocks is worth while at this point. Quartz, almost completely unaffected by water and acids, is practically immune to chemical weathering, and its hardness makes it extremely resistant to mechanical weathering as well. Crystals, grains, or masses of quartz weather very slowly into pebbles or sand grains. The pebbles or sand grains do not change chemically and are still pieces of quartz, usually white in color. Quartz is rarely worn down any finer than sand. Feldspar, hornblende, mica, augite, calcite, and gypsum are all subject to chemical weathering as well as to mechanical weathering. Mechanical weathering breaks them into pebbles and sands, but chemical weathering eventually decomposes these fragments into fine clays. Calcite and gypsum also disappear in solution, in which form they may be carried off to lakes or the sea by both surface and underground waters.

Most of the igneous rocks and many of the metamorphic rocks weather more rapidly in moist climates than in dry ones because they contain minerals that are attacked by oxygen and carbon dioxide aided by water. The first products of the weathering of these rocks are boulders, pebbles, sands, and clays, but in time even the boulders crumble to clay. Pebbles and sands will remain only if the rocks contain quartz or some other chemically resistant mineral.

Sandstones, quartzites, and quartz-pebble conglomerates are only as durable as the cements that hold them together. When they break up, however, their quartz fragments remain as boulders, pebbles, and sands. Quartzites and well-cemented sandstones and conglomerates (with silica cement) are among the most lasting of all rocks. Shales, weakest of the sedimentary rocks, split easily between layers and quickly weather into the clays from which they were formed. Marbles and limestones are fairly resistant to mechanical weathering, but their calcite undergoes slow attack by solution, making these rocks generally less durable in moist climates than quartzites or sandstones. In dry climates, however, limestone may be among the most durable of rocks. Even in moist climates limestones surpass shales in strength.

6. Weathering Is a Slow Process

When learning about weathering, one might get the impression that a building made of soluble limestone would wash away in the rain, or that a tombstone made of a quartz-feldspar-mica granite would crumble away to a mass of quartz pebbles and clay in a few years. Such is hardly the case. Under average conditions, weathering is a very slow process. It is estimated, for example, that even in moist climates the *rate of solution* of limestone exposed to the air is no more than one-fiftieth of an inch in a hundred years. At this rate it would take 60 million years to dissolve a thousand foot layer of limestone from the earth's surface. *At the same time, however, all the other weathering processes would account for the removal of far more rock.*

7. Cleopatra's Needle

The rate at which weathering takes place depends upon many factors, chief of which are the kind of rock, the climate, and the amount of protective cover on the bedrock. In general, weathering takes place most rapidly in weak rocks, in a moist climate with hot summers and cold winters, and where there is no soil cover to protect the bedrock from the atmosphere. Steep slopes and high altitude also favor rapid weathering.

An interesting illustration of the effect of climate on weathering is seen in the case of the granite obelisk called Cleopatra's Needle. In 1880 it was taken from the dry, hot, Egyptian

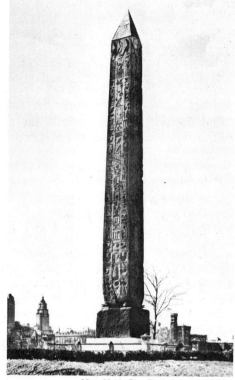

New York City Department of Parks

Fig. 7-6. The obelisk Cleopatra's Needle, in Central Park, New York City.

climate where it had stood almost unchanged for 3,000 years and was moved to the moist hot-and-cold climate of Central Park in New York City. Here chemical weathering and frost action attacked the obelisk. Frost wedging in the ready-made cracks provided by the hieroglyphics (inscriptions) on the obelisk caused more damage in a few years than in as many centuries in Egypt. A waterproof coating has been of little value in protecting the obelisk from the weather. (See Fig. 7-6.)

MASS WASTING OR MASS MOVEMENT

8. Mass Movements Caused by Gravity

Wherever the surface slopes, gravity may cause rock fragments to fall, slide, or move at invisibly slow speeds to lower levels. Geologists refer to such downslope movements of large masses of loose rock material as **mass movement** or **mass wasting.** Mass movement is usually divided into rapid movements and slow movements. Let us see what some of the more important types of mass movement are.

9. Rapid Movements

A **landslide** is the sudden movement of a mass of bedrock or loose rock or both down the slope of a hillside, mountain, or cliff. Some geologists now subdivide landslides into **rock slides** and **debris slides.** In the rock slide large masses of *bedrock* become separated from underlying layers and slide down steep mountainsides or valley walls. Such a slide took place in the valley of the Gros Ventre River southeast of Grand Teton (*tee* ton) National Park, in 1925, when a large mass broke off from the side of Sheep Mountain, crossed the valley, and dammed up the river to form a lake five miles in length. Another famous rock slide is the one that descended from the slopes of Turtle Mountain in Alberta, Canada, in 1903, to destroy the mining town of Frank located at the base of the mountain. In 1959, a landslide triggered by an earthquake caused extensive damage in the Madison

River Valley west of Yellowstone National Park. (See Figs. 7-7 and 7-8.)

A debris slide is a sudden movement of a mass of *loose rock material* down a slope or a cliff. When large debris slides are mixed with snow, they may be called **avalanches.** Both debris and rock slides are more likely to occur after heavy rains and on slopes made steeper by erosion or by the mining activities of man. Small debris slides are common on cliffs and steep hillsides bordering highways, particularly after heavy rains or during spring thaws.

A **mudflow** is a rapid movement of a large mass of "mud" formed from loose earth and water. Mudflows occur chiefly in the normally dry canyons of semiarid regions when heavy thunderstorms or rapid spring thaws suddenly flood the canyons. As the water washes down the loose rock of the canyon walls and floor, rock and water mix to form the mudflow, which moves down the canyon to its mouth.

Talus is an accumulation of rock fragments of all sizes at the base of a cliff. Boulders are most prominent in talus, but continued weathering of the boulders produces pebbles, sand, and clay as well. Talus hides the lower part of the cliff, resting against it at angles as high as 40°. *Talus slopes,* as they are called, are common wherever there are cliffs. (See Fig. 7-9.)

Fig. 7-7. Cross-sectional diagram representing the Gros Ventre rock slide of 1925.

After W. C. Alden

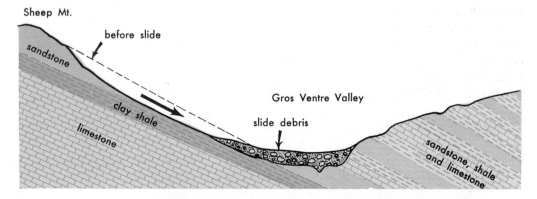

Cross, U.S. Geological Survey

Fig. 7-8. The scarred south face of Landslip Mountain, Colorado, is the result of a land-slide.

10. Slow Movements

Creep is a slow, invisible, downslope movement of the soil that takes place on even the gentlest of slopes. Creep can be detected by its effect in causing fence posts, poles, tree trunks and roots, and other objects fixed in the soil to lean downhill. Again, soil moisture is probably most helpful to gravity in causing this movement. (See Fig. 7-10.)

A **rock glacier** is a ridge or series of ridges of loose rock material that extends down mountain valleys in Alaska and elsewhere. The "glacier" apparently moves slowly downslope in the manner of glaciers of ice. Its origin is not known.

Fig. 7-9. A talus slope at the foot of a cliff bordering Crater Lake, Oregon

Diller, U.S. Geological Survey

11. Gravity Aids Weathering

Soil that lies on top of bedrock provides the bedrock with partial protection against the atmosphere, thereby slowing down the rate at which the bedrock weathers. On steep slopes, however, gravity tends to remove loose earth and thus keep the bedrock continually exposed. Gravity is therefore regarded as an aid to weathering and its action is largely responsible for the fact that steep slopes weather more rapidly than gentle ones.

12. Results of Weathering

The agents of weathering have maintained their attack on the earth's surface since the beginning of geological time. They have been instrumental in wearing down mountains and shaping countless land forms in this and past ages. They have provided tools for the agents of erosion and materials for the formation of sedimentary rocks and valuable mineral deposits. Perhaps of greatest importance, they have been chiefly responsible for the formation of the earth's most priceless resource—its life-supporting soil.

SOILS

13. What Is Soil?

The greatest value to mankind of weathering is its production of the soil, without which there could be no life on the lands. **Soil is the loose earth material in which plants with roots can grow.** A soil may be classified as residual or transported according to the **parent material** from which it is derived. A **residual soil** is a soil whose parent material is the underlying bedrock. A **transported soil** is one whose parent material is an underlying deposit of glacial, alluvial (from rivers), or "foreign" transported loose rock material *not* derived from the bedrock that it covers.

The soil of the famous Blue Grass Region of Kentucky is an example of residual soil formed from an impure limestone. The glacial soils of New England are transported soils.

14. What Determines Soil Makeup?

Soils differ widely in many ways. They differ in fertility, depth, texture, mineral composition, color, and amount of organic material. This is to be expected, for soils are derived from different kinds of parent material. But as soil scientists studied the origins and characteristics of soils, they discovered that different soils could be derived from the same bedrock or parent material if climatic conditions were different.

Today *climate* is regarded as being of even greater importance than *parent material* in determining the kind of soil that develops. Other factors of importance are the kind of *natural vegetation* whose roots and leaves are left in the soil, the hilliness of the *topography,* and the *length of time* in which the soil has developed. A fully developed soil is said to be *mature.* Such a soil is described on the next page.

Fig. 7-10. Some visible effects of creep on a hillside.

Soil Conservation Service

Fig. 7-11. A, B, and C horizons of a soil profile in Wayne County, Ohio.

15. Three Soil Horizons: The Soil Profile

Almost all of us have dug into the soil at one time or another and have observed a difference in color between the topsoil and the subsoil just beneath. Soil scientists have gone farther, reaching the parent material in thousands of samples of soils. In almost all of their samples they observe that the cross section exposed shows a "profile" of three distinct layers or zones. These zones differ in color, texture, mineral content, presence of organic material, and in other respects. Scientists name the top zone the **A-horizon,** the next the **B-horizon,** and the lowest zone the **C-horizon.** Regardless of the parent material, three horizons are to be seen in most mature soils. (See Fig. 7-11 and 7-12.)

The *A*-horizon is the top zone. Roughly it marks the top of the original bedrock when it first began to weather many years ago. The *A*-horizon has, therefore, been exposed to weathering longer than the other two horizons. Examination shows it to be darker in color than the *B*-horizon, and generally gray to black. This darkness is caused by organic material or **humus** (*hew* muss) from decayed plants and animals, and is most pronounced in the top few inches of the horizon. The *A*-horizon is sandy, for much of the fine clay formed by chemical weathering has been washed down by rain into the *B*-horizon. The *A*-horizon contains little soluble mineral matter, most of this having been leached out or washed into the *B*-horizon.

The *B*-horizon is the middle zone. Here we find more clay than in the *A*-horizon because clay formed here has not been washed out and

Fig. 7-12. General characteristics of the three horizons of a soil profile.

A-horizon : topsoil. Gray to black, sandy, contains humus.

B-horizon : subsoil. Reddish, brownish or yellowish; clayey; contains iron oxides and soluble carbonates.

C-horizon : weathered bedrock

unweathered bedrock

some has been added from above. The *B*-horizon is often reddish or brownish in color, being stained by iron oxides formed in the *A*-horizon and washed down. The *B*-horizon may also contain appreciable amounts of calcium and magnesium carbonates, and fragments of durable minerals from the original bedrock.

The *C*-horizon is the lowest zone, resting on the unweathered bedrock or other parent material. Here we find weathered bedrock in various stages of decomposition. The color of the *C*-horizon is determined largely by the color of the bedrock.

16. Soil Horizons and Climate

Now we come to the differences between soils that result from different climates. Continental United States is fairly typical of the temperate climate regions of the world. Soil scientists have found that, in general, two different types of soils have developed in continental United States *regardless of parent materials.* In the eastern half of the country, where *rainfall exceeds 25 inches a year,* the soils are largely of a type called **pedalfers** (ped *al* fers). In the western half, where *rainfall is less than 25 inches a year,* the soils are largely **pedocals.**

Pedalfers are defined as soils with an accumulation of iron oxides, clays, or both in the *B*-horizon. The name pedalfer is made up of *ped* for soil, *al* for aluminum, and *fer* for ferrum or iron. Aluminum is an important element in clay, iron in iron oxide. Why do pedalfers develop in *humid* temperate climates? Moisture accounts for the oxidation of iron minerals and the formation of iron oxides. Fairly heavy rainfall explains the carrying of the iron oxides and clays from the *A*-horizon into the *B*-horizon. It also accounts for the absence of soluble calcium and magnesium compounds from the *B*-horizon, since abundant rainfall would wash these out of the *B*-horizon and carry them off in ground water.

Pedocals are defined as soils in which there is an accumulation of calcium carbonate, particularly in the *B*-horizon. The name is made up of *pedo* for soil, *cal* for calcium. Why do pedocals develop in moderately *dry* temperate climates? We are told that in the hot summer of the western plains the small amounts of rainfall fail to leach soluble calcium and magnesium compounds (products of rock weathering) from the soil. Rain water carries soluble substances as far down as the *B*-horizon, but here it usually evaporates and leaves the minerals behind. This accumulation of soluble minerals in the *B*-horizon is added to in another way. Through capillary action, water from the ground may rise through the *C*-horizon into the *B*-horizon, where again it evaporates in the hot dry upper horizons. In these two ways a considerable quantity of calcium carbonate, with less magnesium carbonate, may be precipitated as a hard white material called caliche (cal *ee* che), meaning *lime.*

The development of pedocals seems to be favored by the natural vegetation of the western plains and desert states, because the thick roots of grasses and shrubs help to prevent the loss of soluble minerals from the upper soil horizons. The development of pedalfers, on the other hand, appears to have taken place largely in regions covered, now or formerly, by forests.

17. Podsols, Chernozems, and Laterites

Podsols (Russian for *ash-gray soils*) are pedalfer soils developed in areas of rich forests of pines and other conifers. They differ from other pedalfers in being extremely light in color —light gray or white—in the upper horizons. This lightness of color is the result of the removal of most of the iron oxides from the soil by strong acids formed from the decay of conifer needles.

Chernozem is the Russian word for *black earth.* The chernozems are fertile pedocal soils with a black or very dark brown *A*-horizon, rich in humus, from which they derive their name. Chernozems form the soil of the great Aralo-Caspian plain in Russia, and of the eastern edge of the Great Plains of North America from Saskatchewan south to Texas.

Laterites (*later* is Latin for *brick*) are hard red and yellow soils rich in hydrous iron and aluminum oxides. They are formed in parts of the tropics where rainfall is heavy but seasonal, and temperatures are continuously high. Laterites are unusual in having had their silica leached out along with ordinarily soluble elements like sodium, potassium, magnesium, and calcium. Some laterites in Cuba are so rich in iron that they are used as ores. Bauxite is a laterite consisting almost entirely of hydrous aluminum oxides and is the principal ore of aluminum.

SOIL EROSION

18. What Is Soil Erosion?

The removal of topsoil from land by rain or wind is **soil erosion.** Soil erosion is a serious problem in the United States, where over three billion tons of topsoil are washed or blown off our farms every year, causing 300,000,000 acres of farmland to be abandoned in recent years. Topsoil coincides roughly with the *A*-horizon of the soil profile. Particularly because of its humus content and other important qualities given it by organic material, topsoil is irreplaceable except through the slow and normal processes of many centuries of weathering. Its loss constitutes a national disaster.

19. Causes of Soil Erosion

Soil erosion has been caused largely by man's removal of protective natural vegetation—trees, shrubs, grasses—from the land. Figure 7-13 shows how little soil is lost from land covered by woods or grass. There are several reasons for this. First, the living trees, shrubs, and grasses stand in the way of the rain and prevent it from running downslope fast enough to wash soil away. Second, the humus of decaying leaves and other plant parts acts like a sponge to soak up and hold the rain. Third, the plant roots, especially of grasses, are highly effective in holding the soil together. Fourth, the leaves of trees and shrubs act like great umbrellas that keep much rain water from reaching the surface. When not protected by natural vegetation, topsoil is washed away by heavy rains, especially in humid regions, or blown away by winds in drier regions like the Great Plains during periods of drought.

Why does man remove natural vegetation? He may require the timber of the forests or he may need cleared land for farming. Natural vegetation may also be stripped away from ranch lands by overgrazing of sheep and cattle or it may be destroyed in forests by forest fires.

What are the remedies? Where trees have been cut or burnt down, the answer is reforestation, which also helps to prevent floods and to restore our timber. But where the land must be kept cleared for agriculture, natural vegetation—forest or prairie—cannot be restored.

Here, then, we have the problem of reducing soil erosion to a minimum while continuing to cultivate the soil.

20. Erosion by Rain: Sheet Wash

There are two types of soil erosion by rain. One is called *sheet wash;* the other, *gullying.* **Sheet wash** is the removal of thin sheets of soil from the entire area of even the most gently sloping farmland. It takes place whenever there is runoff from rain or melting snow. The removal of topsoil by sheet wash goes on so evenly that it can hardly be noticed. But sheet wash proceeds rapidly enough to strip a 6-inch layer of topsoil from moderately sloping cotton fields in 40 years (see Fig. 7-13).

Sheet wash can be greatly reduced by contour plowing, strip cropping, and rotation of

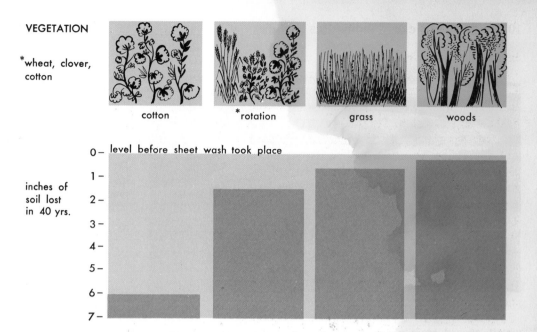

Fig. 7-13. *Soil Conservation Service data show that* natural vegetation, *such as grass or forest, gives almost perfect protection against soil erosion by sheet wash. When* cotton *is grown on sloping land, soil erosion is considerable. Rotation of wheat and clover with the cotton greatly reduces soil erosion.*

crops. **Contour plowing** is plowing along a contour line—a line that goes around a hill at a fixed level. This method of plowing forms *terraces* that hold the rain on the hillsides and give it time to soak in rather than run off. (See Fig. 7-14.) The old method of plowing up and down the hill created many miniature valleys through which much of the rain ran off. Contour plowing reduces sheet wash by reducing the runoff. In **strip cropping** strips of dense rainholding crops like alfalfa are made to alternate with the cotton, corn, or tobacco strips that are unable to absorb runoff because their plants must be so far apart (Fig. 7-14).

The effect of **rotation of crops** in reducing sheet wash is discussed in Topic 23.

21. Erosion by Rain: Gullying

Gullies are miniature river valleys that hold water only during rains. The formation of gullies on sloping farmlands is a more noticeable form of soil erosion than sheet wash and it is easily checked if promptly attended to. The usual procedure is to dam up the gully with boulders and brush (twigs, branches, leaves) or with boards. The dams not only check the flow of water, but also cause the deposition of any soil washed into the gully. Gullying is common in regions of steep slopes and heavy rainfall (Fig. 7-15). Gullies will not develop if moderately sloping land is properly cultivated. If the slope of the land is greater than 15 feet per hundred, gullying may be impossible to control on cultivated land. In such instances, the land should be restored to natural vegetation.

22. Preventing Soil Erosion by Wind

The dust storm of the western Plains States is the form in which soil erosion by wind takes place in times of drought. Here the farmers'

Fig. 7-14. Contour plowing and strip cropping in Vernon County, Wisconsin. From left to right, the fields are planted with corn, grain (light color), alfalfa, grain, alfalfa.

Caterpillar Tractor Co.

widely spaced grain plants provide little of the protection afforded by natural grasses, nor can they survive as well in periods of light rainfall. Dust storms cannot be prevented as long as droughts occur, but the effects of drought can be minimized. The best cure for abandoned farmland and grazing land is to give it time for restoration of its natural grass and brush cover. For farmland a number of measures are helpful. *Contour plowing* or *terracing* slows down the

Fig. 7-15. With each rainfall, this deep gully ate closer and closer to the peach orchard at the right, near Thomaston, Georgia.

Caterpillar Tractor Co.

runoff of rain water and helps get it into the soil. *Tree shelter belts* provide "windbreaks" to reduce the force of the wind.

23. Soil Depletion

When the same crop is grown year after year, the soil eventually loses the minerals needed for that crop. The soil is then said to be *depleted*. Soil depletion happens most rapidly with such crops as cotton and tobacco. There are two cures for soil depletion. One is the use of commercial *fertilizers* to restore the missing minerals. This expensive cure has been used in the depleted cotton and tobacco lands of the South.

Another cure is the rotation of crops on a particular plot each year. For example (see Fig. 7-13), wheat, sweet clover, and cotton may be rotated over a three-year period. Each one takes different combinations of minerals from the soil, so that no single mineral is removed too rapidly. Furthermore, the clover roots are rich in nitrates, formed by their nitrogen-fixing bacteria, so the clover may merely be plowed into the soil as fertilizer. Soil depletion is not merely a matter of fertility. It has been proven that runoff and sheet wash are much greater in depleted soils than in fertile ones. The prevention of depletion and the prevention of soil erosion and floods go hand in hand. (Flood prevention is discussed in Chapter 10.)

TOPIC QUESTIONS

Each topic question refers to the topic of the same number within this chapter.

1. Distinguish between weathering and erosion. Name the principal agents of each.

2. (*a*) Mention a few examples of weathering. (*b*) Define mechanical weathering and give an example. (*c*) Define chemical weathering and give an example.

3. (*a*) Explain how rocks are weathered by: (1) temperature change, (2) frost action, (3) exfoliation, (4) plants and animals. (*b*) What is a boulder field? an exfoliation dome?

4. (*a*) What substances cause chemical weathering? (*b*) In what type of climate is chemical weathering most active? least active? Why? (*c*) Explain the weathering action of (1) oxygen, (2) water, (3) carbon dioxide, (4) acids of plant and animal decay.

5. (*a*) Explain how weathering affects each of the principal rock minerals. (*b*) Explain how weathering affects the common rocks.

6. Discuss the length of time involved in weathering processes.

7. Under what conditions do rocks weather most rapidly?

8. What is mass wasting?

9. (*a*) What is a rock slide? Give one example. (*b*) What are debris slides? Where and when do they occur? (*c*) What is a mudflow? (*d*) What is talus?

10. (*a*) What is creep? (*b*) What is a rock glacier?

11. How does gravity aid weathering?

12. What are the over-all results of weathering?

13. Define soil. Distinguish between residual and transported soils. Give an example of each.

14. What factors cause different soils to develop from one parent material? Which factor is most important?

15. Briefly describe the three horizons of a mature soil.

16. (a) Define pedalfers. Explain why pedalfers are found in the humid eastern part of the United States. (b) Define pedocals. Explain why they develop in the dry western part of the United States. (c) How is vegetation related to the locations of pedalfers and pedocals?

17. Define and explain: (a) podsol, (b) chernozem, (c) laterite, (d) bauxite.

18. (a) What is topsoil? (b) What is soil erosion? (c) Why is soil erosion a "national disaster"?

19. (a) What is the chief cause of soil erosion? (b) Why do woods or grass prevent soil erosion? (c) Why does man remove natural vegetation?

20. (a) What is sheet wash? How can it be reduced? (b) What are contour plowing and strip cropping?

21. What are gullies? Where do they form? How are they checked?

22. (a) Why do dust storms take place more easily on cultivated land than on natural grasslands? (b) How do contour plowing and tree shelter belts help against dust storms?

23. (a) What is soil depletion? (b) How does rotation of crops cure or prevent depletion?

GENERAL QUESTIONS

1. Why is frost action likely to damage sandstone more than limestone?

2. In what respects does the weathering of a bare mountain peak differ from the weathering of the bedrock under the soil of a forest?

3. Sandstones cemented by lime usually weather much more rapidly than those cemented by silica. Why?

4. In parts of Bermuda where the limestone bedrock consists almost entirely of white calcite, with a small percentage of iron-containing minerals, the residual soil is a fine red material. How is this explained?

5. What should be the content of residual soil formed in a humid climate from a granite composed of quartz, feldspar, and black mica?

6. Why are the pavements of streets and highways damaged so much more in the winter months than in the summer months in most of the United States? (Compare the processes of weathering in the two seasons.)

STUDENT ACTIVITIES

1. Topic 3 states that "rocks are known to split and break if heated strongly enough." See if you can verify this by the following procedures: (a) strongly heat small samples of such rocks as obsidian, granite, sandstone, shale, slate, and schist in the flame of a Bunsen burner. Observe and note your results after comparison with unheated specimens of the same rocks. (b) Repeat the procedure of (a), but this time plunge your heated rock samples into cold water.

2. Use the acid test (1 or 2 drops of dilute hydrochloric acid on each) on samples of different varieties of sandstone to determine which of them contain lime or lime cements.

3. Place samples of limestone, shale, sandstone, granite, and other rocks in a beaker of dilute hydrochloric acid and let stand for at least 10 minutes. Remove the samples, wash carefully in cold water, and inspect for signs of "chemical weathering." Compare with fresh samples.

TOPOGRAPHIC SHEETS

1. *Landslides:* Red Rock, Washington; U.S.G.S., 15-minute series.

2. *Landslides:* Frank, Alberta (shows Turtle Mt. Landslide of 1903; obtain from Map Distribution Office, Ottawa, Canada).

3. *Exfoliation domes and cliffs:* Yosemite Valley, California; U.S.G.S., scale 1:24,-000.

CHAPTER 8

Ground Water

HOW DO YOU KNOW THAT . . . ?

This simple experiment serves as a model of the way underground water feeds springs, wells, rivers, lakes, and all growing plants. Fill a plastic or glass container to the top with coarse gravel or marble chips. Why isn't the container *really* full? Estimate what fraction of the space occupied by the gravel is air space. Now check your estimate. Fill a same-size container with water. Then pour the water from it into the gravel container until the gravel can hold no more water. Compare your estimate with your observation. Now carefully pour the water out of the gravel and back into the water container. A piece of wire gauze over the gravel will help to keep the gravel from spilling. Why doesn't all the water return from the gravel?

1. Water in the Earth

The water in the ground comes from three sources. A very small part of it is sea water that was trapped in the pores of sedimentary rocks as they formed long ago on the continental shelves. This salty water is called **connate water** (*nate* born; *con* with). Some of the water is newly born from the steam of magmas. Such **juvenile water** (*juvenile* means *young*) is most likely to be formed in volcanic regions. But the chief source of the water in the earth is the rain and snow that comes down on the earth from the atmosphere. This is called **meteoric water**. (*Meteoric* means *from the air.*) Meteoric water comes from the air and returns to the air in a process known as the **water cycle**.

2. The Water Cycle

The water cycle (Fig. 8-1) may begin at the surface of the oceans. The sun heats the water and makes it evaporate. Winds carry water vapor over the lands. Some of it condenses into clouds and falls as rain or snow (**precipitation**). As soon as it falls, rain journeys back to the sea by three different routes. In the most direct route, perhaps, some of the rain becomes the **runoff** that flows back to the oceans in the form of countless numbers of rivers and streams. Another part of the rain returns directly to the air by **evaporation** and may then be carried back to the oceans by winds. A third part of the rain seeps into the earth to become the **ground water** of springs and caverns and the soil water used by growing plants. Some of this ground water seeps slowly through the rocks until it reaches the sea, but most of it seeps into rivers to become part of the runoff, or returns to the air by evaporation from the ground or by **transpiration** from the leaves of plants that draw it up from the soil.

Rain also falls directly into ponds and lakes, while snow forms glaciers and snow fields. These, too, dispose of their excess water by runoff through outlet streams or by evaporation from their surfaces. And when the water that came from the oceans returns to the oceans, the water cycle is completed, only to begin again. Of course, as in the rock cycle, there are detours and short cuts. Water that evaporates from the

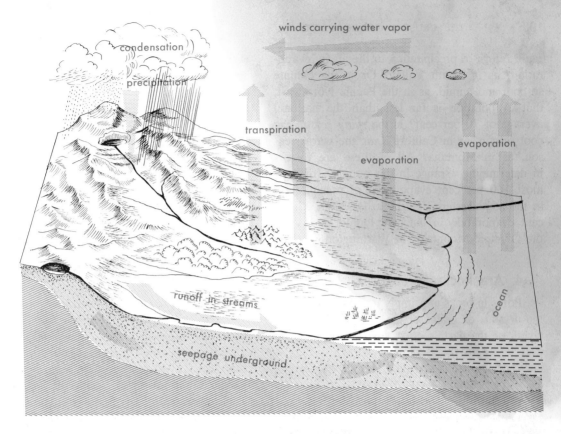

Fig. 8-1. The water cycle, also called the hydrologic cycle.

oceans may return directly to the oceans as rain. The same may happen with water from the land. Other variations are possible. But all are part of a ceaseless cycle that receives the energy for its "perpetual motion" from the sun.

3. The Water Cycle in the United States

It is interesting to take some actual figures related to the water cycle in the United States. The average yearly rainfall for the entire country is about 30 inches. Of this only 9 inches—30 per cent of the total rainfall—returns to the oceans as runoff. About 0.1 of an inch—a fraction of 1 per cent—returns as seepage. About 21 inches, or approximately 70 per cent, is returned to the air by evaporation and transpira-

tion. In transpiration, vast quantities of water are evaporated into the air from forests, grasslands, and fields.

But these figures are only averages. For any one locality the percentages and amounts of runoff, seepage, and evaporation depend on many factors. Does the region have 2 inches of *annual precipitation* as in parts of the Mojave (moh hah vee) Desert, or does it have 100 inches yearly, as in the Olympic Mountains of Washington? Is its *precipitation distributed* in steady rains that soak into the ground, or in heavy showers that run off in flooded streams? Does the *terrain* favor runoff by steep slopes and bare rock surfaces, or does it favor seepage into the ground by being level, porous, and covered with *vegetation?* Does the region have a climate with high *temperature* and low *humidity* that favor rapid return of precipitation to the air by evaporation, as in Death Valley? Or is the climate so cool and humid, as in the Pacific Northwest, that evaporation is far less than the national average of 70 per cent? Is the *rainy season* the cool season, as in California, or the warm season, as in Montana? All of these are factors in determining a range in this country from almost 100 per cent evaporation of precipitation in the southwestern deserts, to less than 25 per cent evaporation in the cool humid climate of the Olympic Mountains of Washington.

4. Are Rocks Porous?

Pores in rocks are simply the spaces between the crystals or grains of the rock. In the upper layers of the earth's crust all rocks have some pore space in them, ranging from less than 1 per cent in igneous rocks like granite to as much as 30 per cent in some sandstones. In igneous and metamorphic rocks the rare pores are unfilled spaces between the crystals. In sedimentary rocks the pores are the spaces between grains of sand, clay, etc. that have not been filled with cement. The amount of such space differs greatly, especially in sandstones. Unconsolidated deposits of gravel, sand, or clay, having little or no cement between grains, may be nearly half pore space. The percentage of pore space in sedimentary materials is greatest where the particles are round and all of the same size (well sorted). Where the material is poorly sorted, as in a mixture of sand and clay, small particles fill the spaces between large particles, and total pore space is greatly reduced. Angular or irregularly shaped particles also fit together more closely than do round particles, leaving less pore space. Pore spaces are usually filled with air unless the air has been forced out by water, or other fluids like petroleum, or natural gas. (See Fig. 8-2.)

The porosity of a rock tells us how much of its volume is open space. But no matter how porous a rock is, water will not pass through it easily if the pores are tiny, as they are in clays and shales. This is because water clings to the material. On the other hand, water passes readily through sediments or rocks with large pores, as in sands, gravels, and many sandstones. Thus to the geologist, the *permeability* of rock material is at least as important as its porosity. **Permeability** is the ability of the rock to transmit water or other liquids. In the origin of springs, wells, and other ground water features it is of great importance.

Materials—like sand, gravel, and sandstone—through which water passes easily are said to be **permeable.** Materials—like clay, shale, and most igneous and metamorphic rocks—through which water does not pass easily are **impermeable.** Notice that a material may be highly porous, like clay, and yet be impermeable. On the other hand, nonporous rocks, like limestone and some lavas, often become permeable because of the formation of cracks and fissures through which water can pass. This is sometimes true of crystalline igneous and metamorphic rocks as well.

Fig. 8-2. Pore space in sands, sandstone, and limestone.

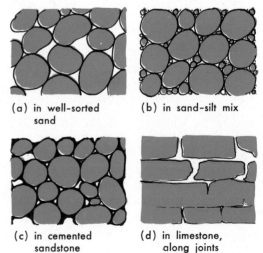

(a) in well-sorted sand

(b) in sand-silt mix

(c) in cemented sandstone

(d) in limestone, along joints

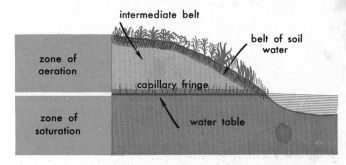

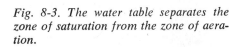

Fig. 8-3. The water table separates the zone of saturation from the zone of aeration.

5. Forming the Water Table

When rain falls on the ground, it passes into the pores and other openings in the soil or rock and adheres to the mineral particles. If the rain is light, this moisture may soon return to the air by evaporation. But if enough rain enters the soil to *fill* the pores of the upper layers, some of the water continues downward, stopping only when it reaches impermeable material such as clay or shale. Here, unable to penetrate deeper, the water fills the pores at the bottom of the permeable material, rising higher and higher as the rain continues, and forming what is known as the **zone of saturation.** The upper surface of the zone of saturation is called the **water table.** (The water table can also be defined as the surface below which the ground is saturated with water.)

Above the water table, the unsaturated earth is called the **zone of aeration,** because here the pores are largely filled with air. The zone of aeration consists of three parts. Just below the surface is the *belt of soil water,* where films of water adhere to the grains of topsoil but fail to fill the air spaces. Just above the water table is the *capillary fringe,* where water rises from the water table by the capillary attraction of the narrow tubes formed by the closely packed particles of subsoil. Between the belt of soil water and the capillary fringe there may be a drier *intermediate belt* which holds little water except during rains. (See Fig. 8-3.)

A **perched water table** is a water table in permeable material that lies above the local water table, but is separated from it by an impermeable layer. (See Fig. 8-4.)

6. Depth of the Water Table

How far below the surface is the water table? It may be a few feet or hundreds of feet down. This depends on many factors—the thickness of the porous rock, the slope, the amount of rainfall, the vegetation cover, and the amount of water already in the ground. In desert regions there may never be enough rainfall to form a water table. The position of the water table also varies from day to day with the weather, rising when the weather is rainy and falling when the weather is dry. Between rains, water slowly escapes from the ground in many ways. It evaporates into the air; it seeps into springs, swamps, and lakes; it rises into the soil and is absorbed by plants.

In hilly country the water table is nearer the surface in the valleys than in the higher land. Figure 8-5 shows the relation of the water table to the features of local topography in hilly country.

7. Ordinary Wells and Springs

Wherever the water table reaches the surface, the ground water seeps out. This rarely

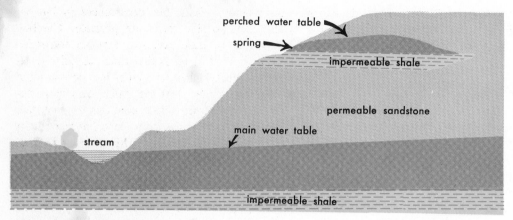

Fig. 8-4. A perched water table lies above the main water table.

happens in level ground unless heavy rains have saturated the entire zone of aeration, but it is quite likely to happen on hillsides. Here and there on hillsides where the water table cuts the surface, ground water may run into small natural basins called **hillside springs** (see Figs. 8-4 and 8-5). At camp sites, along hiking trails, and in farmland, it is common practice to drive a piece of narrow pipe horizontally into the hillside below the water table, in order to provide a path by which the ground water may come out in quantity. These, too, are called springs. Ground water is naturally filtered by the earth through which it seeps and is usually perfectly clear. Dissolved substances, however, may be present in it and its freedom from harmful materials depends on whether or not the ground

through which it passes has been contaminated by human or animal wastes or poisonous minerals.

In places where the water table does not reach the surface, the ground water may be reached by digging or driving wells into the ground (see Figs. 8-5 and 8-6). If these wells are to provide water in all seasons, they must go considerably deeper than the lowest level to which the water table is likely to fall in dry weather. If the well is lined, its lining must be perforated to allow the ground water to seep in at either the bottom or the sides, or at both places. A well of this type, known as an **ordinary well,** contains water from its bottom up to the level of the water table. As the water table rises and falls with weather changes, so does the level

Fig. 8-5. At hilltops the water table is usually far below the surface. In valleys the water table may rise above the surface to form lakes, swamps, and springs.

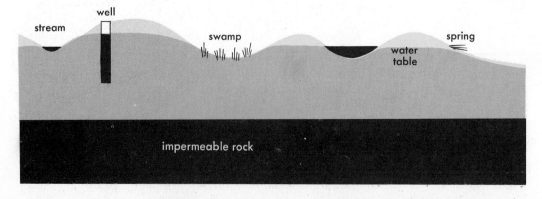

of the water in the well. Both the hillside spring and the ordinary well receive their water from the rains in their own vicinities.

8. Artesian Formations

In many parts of the world permeable beds outcrop on hillsides and mountainsides, then dip underground downslope between beds of impermeable rock. (See Fig. 8-6.) Rain that enters the permeable outcrop is confined to this layer of rock by the impermeable beds above and beneath. The upper impermeable layer, which is likely to be clay or shale, is known as the **cap rock.** The permeable layer, which is likely to be sand or sandstone, is known as the **aquifer** (water bearer). The water trapped in the aquifer follows its sloping course underground under the pull of gravity. As additional water from rains and melting snows enters the outcrop, the water level rises in the aquifer, and the water pressure at its lower end increases.

Artesian (ar *tee* zhun) **formations**—aquifers between impervious beds—usually are found in sedimentary rocks, but occurrences in igneous and metamorphic rocks are possible. The best known and most extensive artesian formation in the United States is that which supplies water to the Great Plains. Its aquifer is a porous sandstone more than 100 feet thick, known as the Dakota sandstone, which outcrops for hundreds of miles along the eastern slopes of the Rocky Mountains, the Big Horn Mountains of Wyoming, and the Black Hills of South Dakota. The formation dips eastward for hundreds of miles beneath the surface of the Great Plains. Thousands of wells are drilled into it in Montana, Wyoming, the Dakotas, Nebraska, and Kansas.

Other important artesian formations are found in the Atlantic Coastal Plain states; in Long Island, New York; in Florida; and in the Los Angeles area. The word *artesian* comes from Artois, France.

9. Artesian Wells and Springs

Rain and melting snows pour tremendous quantities of water into the aquifers of artesian

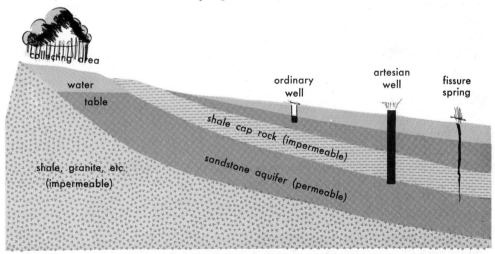

Fig. 8-6. The rain that enters the aquifer of an artesian formation is trapped under an impermeable cap. From here it may travel great distances underground before rising to the surface in an artesian well or spring.

formations where they outcrop in mountain regions. Like the water in a great sloping pipe, this water is under pressure. When wells are drilled into the aquifers at lower levels, even hundreds of miles away from the outcrops, water rises in the wells and may spout into the air if the water pressure is sufficient. **Artesian wells** are wells in which the water comes from aquifers below an impermeable layer. (See Fig. 8-6.) Unlike ordinary wells in the upper mantle rock, artesian wells do not obtain water from the local water table. Their water comes from distant outcrops, and they are therefore not dependent on local rainfall. This is particularly important for regions like the Great Plains whose rainfall is light and unreliable. Artesian wells can usually provide much larger quantities of water than ordinary wells, and their water is less likely to be contaminated.

Artesian wells differ greatly in depth. As a rule, the greater the distance from the outcrop, the deeper the aquifer. On the Great Plains, wells that are hundreds of miles from the outcrops may go down thousands of feet to reach the aquifer. In Long Island, most artesian wells are less than 200 feet deep, but the pressure in them is so low that the water must be pumped to the surface. (The water pressure in an artesian well depends upon the difference in level between the well and the top of the water in the aquifer.) Long Island's artesian formations consist of sands and clays, rather than of sandstones and shales. Florida's aquifer is a limestone full of fissures and cavities.

Artesian formations may be broken naturally by rock fissures through which **artesian springs** or **fissure springs** emerge without the need for drilling. Such a spring may form an oasis in the desert. Other large springs may also emerge from fractured igneous rocks and from limestone caverns.

10. Conserving Ground Water

Ground water supplies are far from inexhaustible. Unless the quantity of water returned to the ground in a given basin is at least equal to that removed from its wells and springs, the water table will drop and its wells and springs will shrink accordingly. In some artesian basins so many wells have been drilled and so much water has been pumped that the water table has dropped steadily. The Dakota sandstone formation of the Great Plains now has more than 15,000 wells drawing water from it. Excessive pumping has lowered water levels in Long Island, New York; Atlantic City, New Jersey; Miami, Florida; and Los Angeles, California. In coastal cities, another danger is that the lowered water table may allow salt water from the ocean to seep into the wells and contaminate them.

How is the ground water restored or "recharged"? Rains and melting snows must provide most of the replacement for the water drawn out of wells and springs. Where this is inadequate—and such is the case in many metropolitan areas today—artificial recharge methods are used. The principle is simple. After water has been used, as much as possible must be returned to the ground instead of being poured off into sewers that drain into rivers or the ocean. This can be done by running or pumping the water into **return wells,** into large shallow basins, or directly onto the ground. Many states now require such measures of large commercial users of water and of all commercial air-conditioning installations. In many cases the waste water must be purified before it is used to recharge the ground water.

11. Ground Water Is Usually Cool

Observations of temperatures within the earth show that at a depth of about 50 feet, protection from weather changes is so complete that the *ground stays at nearly the same temperature throughout the year.* The temperature near which it stays is the *average yearly temperature of its location,* which in most parts of the United States is somewhere between 40 and 60 degrees Fahrenheit. The water of an ordinary well or spring has practically the same temperature as the ground from which it comes. This explains why the water is comparatively cool in summer but never freezes in winter. Since spring or well water is close to the average temperature of its locality, such water is obviously colder in a cool climate like that of Maine than in a warm climate like that of Florida. In polar regions, where the average temperature is below freezing, there can be no wells or springs, for the water in the ground is always frozen.

12. Warm Springs, Hot Springs, Geysers, and Fumaroles

Below the 50-foot depth, heat from the earth's interior raises the earth temperatures at the rate of 1°F for about 50 to 75 feet, differing with the locality. Water from deep artesian wells or springs may therefore be considerably warmer than water from ordinary wells or springs. Fissure springs thousands of feet deep may be warm enough to be called **warm springs** or even **hot springs,** as at Warm Springs, Georgia, or Hot Springs, Arkansas. But ground waters may be hot without coming from great depths. In many regions of comparatively recent volcanic activity lava rock just a short distance below the surface is still hot enough to boil water. In such places the ground water may come to the surface as hot springs that are boiling or nearly so. Here and there in Yellowstone and other volcanic regions hot springs emerge through sticky colored clays formed by the weathering of the volcanic rocks. These sputtering hot springs are called **paint pots** or **mud volcanoes.** (See Fig. 8-7.)

Boiling hot springs that erupt from time to time as gushers of hot water and steam are called **geysers.** There are only a few parts of the world in which these scenic wonders occur, the most important being Yellowstone National Park in Wyoming, North Island in New Zealand, and Iceland. Old Faithful is not the largest geyser in Yellowstone, but it is famous for both its height and its regularity. (See Fig. 8-8.) Its average interval between eruptions is now about 66 minutes, though intervals may be as short as

Darton, U.S. Geological Survey

Fig. 8-7. Paint pots in Yellowstone National Park. Note the contrast between the light-colored mineral deposits of the paint pots and the dark hillsides of the background.

35 minutes or as long as 80 minutes. An eruption lasts several minutes, and usually reaches a height of 150 feet or more.

Geyser eruption is like the explosion of a hot water boiler or pressure cooker. The "boiler" is a fissure or "geyser tube" which extends many feet down into the hot rock. (See Fig. 8-9.) At the bottom of this tube, ground water, under pressure of the water above it, is "superheated" to a temperature far above water's normal boiling point. As the heated water expands, it causes the water above it to overflow onto the surface. This relieves the pressure. The superheated water explodes into steam, blowing out the water above it in the form of a geyser eruption.

Fumaroles (*few* meh roles) are holes or fissures in the ground from which steam and hot

Northern Pacific Railway Co.

Fig. 8-8. Old Faithful Geyser averages about 65 minutes between eruptions, but intervals range from 35 to 80 minutes.

gases escape. As might be expected, fumaroles are found in volcanic regions where relatively recent eruptions have occurred and where ground water comes in contact with very hot rock. The high pressure steam from fumaroles has been used commercially for heating and to generate electricity. (See Fig. 8-10.)

13. The Minerals in Ground Water

Rain water is water that has been "naturally distilled" by the heat of the sun. Therefore it

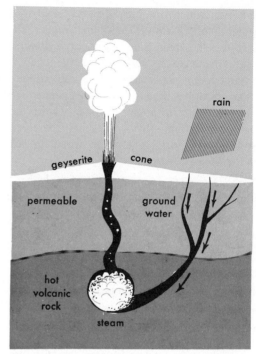

Fig. 8-9. The "plumbing system" of a geyser.

has no dissolved mineral matter in it. As ground water, however, its slow passage through the subsoil or bedrock gives it ample opportunity to dissolve minerals. The kind and quantity of mineral matter which it contains depend largely on the kind of rock through which it passes, the distance it travels underground, and its temperature.

Dissolved minerals that contain the elements calcium, magnesium, or iron make water *hard*. Of these, calcium (from calcite) is the commonest cause of hardness. The dissolved minerals in hard water interfere greatly with its use. In laundering they react with soap to form sticky curds instead of lather. In boiler tubes and hot water pipes they form deposits of *boiler scale* which eventually clog the pipes and make expensive cleaning or replacement necessary.

Artesian water is usually harder than ordinary ground water, since it travels farther and may be warmer (if it comes from great depth), enabling it to dissolve more mineral matter. Ordinary ground water is almost always harder than river water. In regions where the bedrock is limestone, practically all the water is hard, since limestone is largely calcite, $CaCO_3$, or dolomite, $CaMg(CO_3)_2$.

14. Mineral Springs

A spring whose water contains so much dissolved mineral that it cannot be used for ordinary drinking or washing purposes is called a **mineral spring.** The high mineral content of the water may be due to its passage through very soluble rock (such as the salt beds of Michigan) or to the fact that it contains large quantities of acid-forming gases such as carbon dioxide (example: Saratoga Springs, N.Y.) or hydrogen sulfide (example: White Sulphur Springs, W. Va.) or to the fact that it is very hot (example: Hot Springs, Arkansas). Many such mineral spring areas have become **spas** or health resorts.

Famous European spas include Vichy, France; Bath, England; Carlsbad, Czechoslovakia. But not all mineral springs are "good for the health." In desert regions *alkali mineral springs* may be poisonous.

15. Destructional Work of Ground Water

Although limestone is not a porous rock, limestone strata are frequently split by fissures or joints that run down from the surface and by cracks that run horizontally between the beds. (See Fig. 8-11.) Ground water always contains carbonic acid, formed by dissolved carbon dioxide. As ground water runs through these cracks and fissures in limestone, its carbonic acid slowly dissolves and removes more and more of the limestone and carries it away. After thousands of years, the fissures may grow into large, circular, surface openings, while the cracks between the

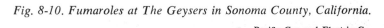
Fig. 8-10. Fumaroles at The Geysers in Sonoma County, California.

Pacific Gas and Electric Co.

Fig. 8-11. The fissures in this mass of limestone bedrock were formed by solution along the joints in the rock.

Wilson, Geological Survey of Canada

beds form networks of irregular underground tunnels many miles in length and hundreds of feet high in places. The surface openings are called **sink holes** or **sinks,** and the tunnels are called **caverns** or **caves.** Sink holes also form when parts of cave roofs collapse. Water often collects in sink holes which are below the water table, or are clogged at the bottom by broken rock, forming **sink-hole ponds** or **lakes.** There are many sink-hole lakes in central and northern Florida and in Kentucky. (See Figs. 8-12 and 8-13.)

When a large section of a cave roof collapses or is dissolved by sink hole growth and a middle section is left standing, a **natural bridge** may be formed. Natural bridges may also be formed when a surface river disappears into a fissure in the bedrock, runs underground a short distance, and then gushes out on the face of a cliff. As the

Fig. 8-12. This diagram shows the surface features and underground structure of a limestone region of caverns, sinks, and a natural bridge.

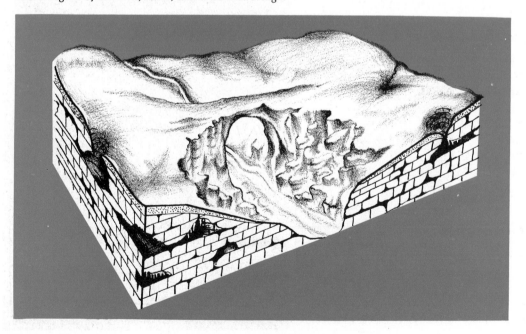

Fig. 8-13. A sink hole in limestone bedrock at Cambria, Wyoming.

Darton, U.S. Geological Survey

fissure is enlarged, the area between it and the cliff is left as a natural bridge. The famous Natural Bridge of Virginia is believed to have been formed in this manner. (See Fig. 8-14.)

Limestone is a common surface or near-surface bedrock, and limestone caverns are found in many parts of the world. Whether caverns were formed when the water table was above them (putting them in the zone of saturation) or when the water table was below them (putting them in the zone of aeration) is still one of geology's unsolved problems. Some of the best known caverns in the United States are Carlsbad Caverns (a National Park) in New Mexico; Mammoth Cave (a National Park) in Kentucky; Luray Caverns in Virginia; Howe Caverns in New York; Oregon Caves in Oregon; and Wind Cave (a National Park) in South Dakota.

16. Karst Topography

In regions of caverns almost all of the rain water enters the ground through sink holes and fissures, and there are very few surface rivers. **Lost rivers** are formed when surface streams disappear underground and emerge from caves miles

Fig. 8-14. The Natural Bridge of Virginia is a mass of limestone 90 feet long, 150 feet wide, and 215 feet high.

Virginia State Chamber of Commerce

Fig. 8-15. The great Dome Room of Carlsbad Caverns where thousands of slender stalactites hang from the ceiling. A few stalactites have joined stalagmites to form columns. As in most caverns, the rock is limestone, composed of the mineral calcite.

away. Regions characterized by sinks, sink-hole ponds, lost rivers, and underground drainage are said to have **karst topography.** This name comes from the typical Karst Plateau region of Yugoslavia. The Mammoth Cave region of Kentucky has karst topography. Other karst regions in the United States are found in Florida, Tennessee, and Indiana.

17. Mineral Deposits by Ground Water

The minerals dissolved in ground water are deposited by it in a variety of ways. In places

where ground water drips from the roof of a limestone cave, it very slowly deposits some of the calcite held in solution—partly because of evaporation and partly because of decreased pressure and the escape of acid-forming gases like carbon dioxide. Deposits shaped like icicles are formed, and they hang from the roof along the lines of the dripping water. These slender calcite formations are called **stalactites** (stuh *lak* tytes). At the same time, as each drop of water spatters and evaporates on the floor below the stalactite, it deposits additional calcite which grows upward in the form of a blunt, rounded mass called a **stalagmite** (stuh *lag* myte). When stalactites and stalagmites meet, **columns** or **pillars** are formed. All three are examples of **dripstone,** calcite deposits from dripping water in caverns. Dripstone can form only when a cave is *above* the water table, in the zone of aeration where water can evaporate. (See Fig. 8-15.)

Calcite deposits around mineral springs are called **travertine** (*trav* er tin). Among the most famous of such deposits are the delicately colored travertine terraces of the Mammoth Hot Springs in Yellowstone National Park (see Fig. 8-16). Here the hot water pours out of long hillside fissures in limestone bedrock, depositing some of its dissolved calcite as it cools. Tiny plants, called algae (*al* jee), grow on the moist terraces, producing a variety of beautiful colors. Thermopolis, Wyoming, is also famous for its active hot springs and terraces.

Around the openings of geysers, a white porous substance called **geyserite** is deposited, often accumulating in the shape of a cone. Geyserite consists of silica dissolved from the hot igneous rock through which the geyser waters pass on their way to the surface.

Hot ground water often deposits minerals in cracks and fissures in bedrock, forming *veins* which may contain such minerals as quartz, calcite, gold, and silver. **Petrified wood** is formed when minerals dissolved in ground water replace the decaying wood of buried trees. As each

Fig. 8-16. Travertine deposits on Cleopatra Terrace of the Mammoth Hot Springs. The hot spring waters have destroyed all vegetation on this part of the hillside.

Chicago, Milwaukee & St. Paul
Railway

microscopic particle of wood is replaced by a grain of mineral matter, many details of the wood structure are reproduced. The petrified trees of Arizona and Yellowstone National Park, originating in this way, consist of silica in the form of opal and chalcedony. (See Fig. 23-5.)

Perhaps the most important ground water deposit is the cement with which it binds together the sand grains and pebbles of sedimentary deposits to form sedimentary rocks. While calcite is the most common cementing mineral, silica and iron oxides are used in this way, too.

TOPIC QUESTIONS

Each topic question refers to the topic of the same number within this chapter.

1. Define meteoric, juvenile, and connate water. Compare their importance.

2. With the aid of a diagram briefly describe the water cycle.

3. (*a*) What are the "average yearly" figures for U.S. rainfall, runoff, seepage, and evaporation? (*b*) What factors affect the percentage of runoff, seepage, and evaporation for a particular place?

4. (*a*) Why do rocks have pores? (*b*) What determines the amount of pore space in sedimentary materials? (*c*) Distinguish between porosity and permeability.

5. (*a*) Explain what the water table is and how it forms. (*b*) Describe the zone of aeration. (*c*) What is a perched water table?

6. Explain why the depth of the water table varies.

7. (*a*) Explain what a hillside spring is. (*b*) Explain what an ordinary well is.

8. With the aid of a diagram explain what an artesian formation is. Define the aquifer and the cap rock.

9. (*a*) What is an artesian well? How does it originate? (*b*) In what ways may an artesian well be superior to an ordinary well? (*c*) Compare the artesian formations of Florida, Long Island, and the Great Plains (Topic 8). (*d*) What is a fissure spring?

10. (a) Why is the water table dropping steadily in some areas? (b) What special problems arise in connection with artesian wells in city areas and coastal regions? (c) What is a return well? (d) Describe one other method of recharging ground water.

11. (a) Why does spring water or well water seem so cold in summer? (b) Why doesn't well water freeze in winter? (c) Explain why well water is warmer in Florida than in Maine.

12. (a) Why is the water of deep artesian wells and fissure springs *warmer* than ordinary well and spring water? (b) Explain the source of the heat of boiling hot springs and geysers. (c) What is a geyser? (d) Where do geysers occur? (e) Explain the action of a geyser. (f) What is a fumarole?

13. (a) What factors determine the amount and kind of mineral matter dissolved in ground water? (b) What is hard water? (c) Compare the water of ordinary wells, artesian wells, and rivers in hardness. Explain. (d) Why is all the water hard in a limestone region?

14. Describe the different kinds of mineral springs.

15. (a) Explain how ground water forms sink holes, caverns, natural bridges, and sink-hole ponds. (b) Name several of the great limestone caves of the United States. (c) Why are limestone caves so common?

16. (a) What is a lost river? (b) What is karst topography? Give examples.

17. (a) Explain how stalactites and stalagmites are formed. (b) Explain the origin of travertine, geyserite, mineral veins, and petrified wood. (c) What is dripstone?

GENERAL QUESTIONS

1. In regions of cold climates less water enters the ground during winter than in any other season. Why?

2. What disadvantages may artesian water have as compared with ordinary well water?

3. Is a rainy climate necessary for the formation of limestone caves? Explain.

4. Which theory of limestone cavern origin do you favor? (See Topic 15, last paragraph.) Give your reasons.

5. Why cannot dripstone form when a cave is below the water table? (See Topic 17, paragraph 1.)

6. In some regions petrified wood is composed of silica, a form of quartz. In other regions it is composed of calcite. Why?

STUDENT ACTIVITIES

1. Fill 3 test tubes (or small beakers, cups, tumblers, etc.) with gravel, sand, and clay respectively. By pouring water from a graduated cylinder or small test tube, measure the quantity of water needed to "saturate" the material in each test tube.

2. Compare the permeability of gravel, sand, and clay by putting each material into a funnel (lined with filter paper) and then noting the time required to pour a given amount of water through the material.

3. Make a plasticene model of an artesian formation or of the water table.

4. Make a working model of an artesian well.

5. Compare the amount of dissolved mineral matter in samples of well water, lake water, river water, etc. by evaporating to dryness equal volumes of each.

6. Compare the hardness of different samples of water in the following way: (*a*) Adding liquid soap 1 drop at a time and shaking vigorously, measure the number of drops of soap needed to produce a lasting lather with distilled water. This is your standard of soft water. (*b*) Repeat this procedure with each sample of water. The more soap needed, the "harder" the water.

TOPOGRAPHIC SHEETS

(15-minute series, unless otherwise stated)

1. *Sink holes and karst topography:* Mammoth Cave, Kentucky (also in 7½-minute series); Garfield, Kentucky, 7½-minute series; Crystal Lake, Florida.

2. *Springs:* Thousand Spring, Idaho, 7½-minute series.

CHAPTER 9
Wind

HOW DO YOU KNOW THAT . . . ?

Figure 9-1 shows a dust storm arriving in Springfield, Colorado, on the Great Plains. The dust has been blown out of the soil of regions to the west of Springfield. It is being carried eastward by strong winds that blow steadily from west to east. Which soil materials are picked up by the wind as dust? What kind of weather in the region west of Springfield allows this to happen? Is this more likely to occur in cleared, cultivated land or in land with natural vegetation? Why? How does the photograph show that the winds are very strong? How are dust storms related to the origin of a surface like the one shown in Fig. 9-4? (See Topic 4.)

1. Where Does Wind Erosion Occur?

Is the wind an agent of erosion? To be one, it must attack and wear down some part of the earth's surface, carry off weathered and broken rock materials, and then deposit them. The wind does all of these things, although perhaps less conspicuously than they are done by rivers, waves, or even glaciers. Air is far lighter than water and ice, so wind is relatively ineffective in eroding areas of bedrock or even of soils held firmly together by trees or grasses. Wind is most effective where sands and silts and clays lie loose and dry and unprotected by natural vegetation. Such conditions are found in great deserts like the Sahara, the desert of Arabia, and the Mohave Desert of the United States. To a lesser extent they are found on the beaches of seas and lakes, even in humid areas, and they are also found in semiarid regions like the Great Plains at times when droughts dry out the topsoil and kill its protective vegetation.

Now let us see how the wind erodes these regions. What materials does it carry? How does it carry them? How does it attack the earth's surface? Can it erode solid rock? What deposits does it build? What landforms does it create?

Soil Conservation Service

Fig. 9-1. This dust storm, shown just arriving in Springfield, Colorado, one May afternoon, kept the city in total darkness for half an hour.

2. Transportation of Rock Material

The names *sandstorm* and *dust storm* tell us what materials the wind can carry. The sand carried by the wind is called its **bed load** because it is carried close to the ground. Dust can be carried high above the ground, in suspension for a time at least, and is therefore called the **suspended load.** (See Fig. 9-1.)

Geologists have measured the size of sand grains carried by winds in sand dune regions. The average size of these grains is close to $\frac{1}{100}$ inch in diameter. It has been shown by experiment that wind speeds of at least 11 miles an hour are needed to move grains of this size. Even then, the sand grains are not blown up into the air as dust is. At first the grains roll along the ground, but as they pick up speed and strike other particles, some of the grains become "airborne." Even then, however, they rise and fall in a pattern of short jumps and bounces called **saltation** (*saltare,* to jump) rather than move in a steady stream above the surface. Ordinarily, they rise only a few inches from the ground. As wind speeds increase, larger grains are rolled and lifted and the smaller grains fly higher. But even in very strong winds, almost all of the sand is carried within three feet of the surface. Pebbles and boulders are never carried by the wind, except possibly during hurricanes and tornadoes.

3. Abrasion by Wind-Blown Sand

Silt and clay particles are too soft and fine to scrape away or *abrade* most materials against which they blow. Sand grains, on the other hand, are decidedly abrasive, especially if they are quartz.

The sand grains driven by the wind act like a natural sand blast, grinding and scouring and polishing whatever materials they strike, but only at levels within about three feet of the ground. In desert and beach areas, the bases of utility poles and fence posts are protected from this undercutting action by the piling of stones about them. Rock outcrops may be undercut close to the ground too, though this is usually a minor

Campbell, U.S. Geological Survey

Fig. 9-2. The shiny surfaces of these ventifacts are bounded by sharp edges and marked by pits and grooves.

effect compared with the effects of weathering and streams on the entire rock mass.

One of the most interesting effects of the desert sand blast is the production of the curious wind-abraded pebbles and boulders called **ventifacts** (*venti,* wind; *fact,* made). In these rocks long continued abrasion has scoured the side facing the wind and has ground it down to a flat or gently curved shiny surface or *facet.* (See Fig. 9-2.) Ventifacts may have more than one facet, with fairly sharp edges between facets. Three-edged ventifacts called *dreikanter* (*dry kan ter*)—which means three edges—are rather common. Figure 9-3 shows the origin of one

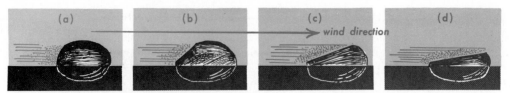

Fig. 9-3. The origin of a ventifact.

facet of a ventifact. How may a ventifact develop a second or third facet? One possibility is that the wind may have blown steadily from different directions at different times. Another possibility is that the rock was turned by frost or some other weathering action. What do you think?

4. Erosional Effects: Deflation

Deflation is the geological term for the removal of loose rock particles by the wind. (Derived from Latin roots, *inflate* means "to blow into," *deflate* means "to blow away.") Deflation is by far the most important erosional effect of the wind. In many desert areas the sands and clays formed by weathering are thoroughly removed by the wind until only pebbles and boulders are left at the surface. This pebble-and-boulder surface is a *desert pavement* which protects the materials beneath from further deflation. Stony deserts of this type are common in southwestern United States and in the Sahara. (See Fig. 9-4.)

Wherever sand and dust are being blown out of a region, deflation is occurring. In semiarid regions, like the Great Plains, deflation has probably produced thousands of depressions or *deflation basins*. Most of these are shallow and

Fig. 9-4. The stony surface of a desert pavement in Arizona.

U.S. Geological Survey

small, but some are miles long and hundreds of feet deep. If the bottom of the depression reaches the water table, the wet ground prevents further deflation just as effectively as when a desert pavement is formed. The growth of natural vegetation also prevents deflation. Some of the oases of great deserts like the Sahara are located in deep depressions probably formed by deflation.

5. Sand Dune Regions

Sand dunes are hills of sand formed by wind deposition. They originate when sand carried by the wind is piled up against any kind of obstruction, such as a rise in the ground, a boulder, a bush, a fence, or a house. Sand dunes form wherever there are strong winds and an adequate supply of loose sand. These conditions are met in three major types of places. The most extensive of these are the great sandy stretches of deserts like the Sahara, the Mohave Desert, and the desert of Peru. Then there are sandy river flood plains that are dry a large part of the year because they are in a semiarid climate. The flood plain of the Columbia River in Washington is such a flood plain. Finally there are the sandy beaches of sea coasts and lake shores.

6. Shape and Size of Dunes

If the wind blows steadily from a single direction, dunes develop a long gentle slope on the windy or *windward* side and a shorter steep slope on the sheltered or *leeward* side. To illustrate, winds blowing steadily from the west form dunes with gentle slopes on their west sides. Where winds are irregular in direction, sand dunes will not show any distinctly steep or gentle slope. Steady winds of medium strength often form beautiful crescent-shaped dunes called *barchans* (*bar* kans). The windward and leeward slopes of a sand dune are often duplicated in miniature by tiny *sand ripples* formed on the windward surface of the dune. (See Figs. 9-5 and 9-6.)

Dunes vary in size from tiny beach dunes a few feet high to mountainous dunes in the Sahara hundreds of feet high and miles long. Dunes always occur in groups which may cover extensive areas. In the Sahara they cover about 300,000 square miles. In Great Sand Dunes National Monument in Colorado, westerly winds have piled dunes nearly 1,000 feet high at the base of the Sangre de Cristo Mountains.

7. Migration of Dunes

Each time the wind blows against the windward side of a sand dune, some of the loose surface sand is carried over the top, where it falls down on the leeward side, also known as the **slip face.** The slip face of a dune makes an angle of about 34° with the horizontal. This **angle of repose** may be seen in Figure 9-7. As this process continues over a long period of time, the effect is the same as if the whole dune has been moved somewhat from windward to leeward. Such movement is known as **dune migration,** and may amount to as much as 100 feet a year.

Migrating dunes have buried towns, farms, and forests (see Fig. 9-7). On the southern shores of Lake Michigan prevailing westerly winds have

Fig. 9-5. These sand dunes in the New Mexico desert were formed by winds blowing from the right. Note the sharp crests that separate the gentle windward slopes from the steep leeward slopes. Also note the sand ripples on the windward slopes.

Soil Conservation Service

Fig. 9-6. Crescent-shaped dunes or barchans on the flood plain of the Columbia River in Oregon. Note the gentle windward (left) slopes and the steep leeward slopes.

Gilbert, U.S. Geological Survey

built up an extensive series of dunes which migrate inland, gradually burying the trees of a forested area known as Dune Park in Indiana.

Not all dunes migrate. Where grasses and shrubs grow in the dune sands, their roots may prevent further migration of the dune. Grasses and shrubs are planted on dunes to prevent their drifting over roads and buildings in beach developments on Cape Cod in Massachusetts, Jones Beach in Long Island, and many other places.

8. Sand Dune Materials

The term "sand" suggests a particular size of rock particle rather than a particular kind of material. Sand dunes may be made of any kind of sand. Most dunes are composed of well-sorted quartz grains. However, there are exceptions, and the beautiful white dunes of the White Sands National Monument near Alamogordo, New Mexico, where the world's first atomic bomb was exploded, are composed of gypsum sands.

Fig. 9-7. The steep leeward slope of a sand dune advancing on a pine forest.

U.S. Forest Service

Fig. 9-8. These cross-bedded layers of sandstone are believed to have originated in ancient sand dunes. This famous exposure of the Navajo sandstone is seen in Utah. (Note the many joints that cut through the rock layers.)

Gregory, U.S. Geological Survey

Bermuda's sand dunes are composed of calcite sands, eroded from its coral limestone bedrock. Dune sands show the effects of wind abrasion in their frosted appearance and rounded shapes. Dune sands may also contain flakes of mica and black grains of magnetite.

9. Ancient Sand Dunes

When the sand grains of a sand dune are cemented together, layers of sandstone are formed. This has happened many times in the geologic past. How does the geologist recognize these ancient sand dunes and distinguish their desert sandstones from those formed under water?

The individual grains of dune sands are more uniform in size and generally better rounded than water-worn grains, and they show a characteristic frosted or ground-glass surface. Furthermore, the layers of desert sandstones are tilted and *cross-bedded,* as shown in Figure 9-8. The strongly tilted beds are believed to have originated as tilted layers of sand on the slip face of a migrating dune. Layers tilting in different directions and at different angles were formed when the wind changed its direction and possibly its speed. The result was an intricate pattern of cross-bedding which was retained when the sands were cemented into sandstones. The Navajo sandstone in Figure 9-8 is a fine example of dune origin.

10. From Ancient Dust Storms

Large areas in China, northern Europe, north central United States, and many other parts of the world are covered by deposits of a fertile material called **loess** (lōs or lō ess). The loess ranges in thickness from a few feet to 300 feet. It consists of unstratified yellowish silt-sized particles of many different minerals and rocks. The particles are angular in shape and only slightly weathered.

Geologists believe that loess is a wind-transported sediment. The silt particles are the size carried by winds in dust storms. The lack of stratification and the upland locations at which the loess is found rule out deposition by rivers. But where did the materials come from? The principal deposits in the United States are found in the upper Mississippi and Missouri valleys, especially in Nebraska, Iowa, Kansas, Missouri, and Illinois. This distribution leads geologists to believe that the loess materials came from melting glaciers at the close of our recent Ice Age. Water and crushed rock from the glaciers drained into the Mississippi and Missouri rivers. These overflowed, depositing the sediments on their flood plains. When the ice disappeared, the rivers shrank and their flood plains dried out. Then the prevailing westerly winds blew the fine silts out of the flood plains in great dust storms, and the silts were carried south and east by the wind to their present locations. Loess

Fig. 9-9. Eroded loess deposits at Vicksburg, Mississippi, form nearly vertical cliffs.

Shaw, U.S. Geological Survey

deposits in northern Europe are believed to have a similar origin. The loess of north China, however, is believed to have been blown eastward into China from the great deserts of Mongolia.

Because of its excellent texture and its variety of unweathered minerals, loess forms a very rich soil. Despite the softness of its silts, loess holds together so well that when eroded, it splits off in columns to form almost vertical slopes. Many old cave dwellings are found in the loess cliffs of China and Europe, and in China ancient roads have been worn so deeply into the soft loess deposits that they now occupy the floors of small "canyons." (See Fig. 9-9.)

11. Wind as a Geological Agent

Erosion by wind produces many phenomena —dust storms and sand storms; rounded and frosted sand grains; flattened, shiny-faced pebbles and boulders; sand dunes in a variety of shapes and sizes; stony desert pavements. The landforms in desert areas are unmistakably different from those of humid regions. Nevertheless, most geologists believe that even in desert areas, the wind is not the most important geological agent. They believe that the combined effect of weathering, mass wasting, and stream erosion is far greater than that of the wind in eroding the desert surface and shaping its landforms. Although most desert streams run only briefly at times of infrequent rains, desert rains are likely to be of the cloudburst type, and the streams are likely to be raging torrents—short-lived but powerful.

The traveler who has experienced both the desert sandstorm and the desert cloudburst might offer an opinion as to the relative erosional power of wind and water in the desert. In the next chapter we shall see what running water can accomplish.

TOPIC QUESTIONS

Each topic question refers to the topic of the same number within this chapter.

1. In what kind of regions is the wind most active as an agent of erosion?

2. (*a*) What is saltation? How large are the sand grains? How high are they lifted? How strong is the wind?

3. (*a*) How does a ventifact form? (*b*) How does sand undercut rock outcrops?

4. (*a*) What is deflation? (*b*) How is a desert pavement formed? (*c*) How is a deflation basin formed?

5. Define sand dunes, explain their origin, and give examples of the three types of areas where they are found.

6. (*a*) Describe the shape of a sand dune formed by steady winds. (*b*) What effect does wind direction have on the shape of sand dunes? (*c*) What are sand ripples? (*d*) How large are dunes?

7. (*a*) Explain the migration of a sand dune. What is the slip face of a dune? The angle of repose? (*b*) How is dune migration prevented?

8. (*a*) What minerals are dune sands made of? (*b*) How do dune sands show the effects of wind abrasion?

9. What characteristics distinguish beds of sandstone which were formed from ancient sand dunes?

10. Describe the origin, characteristics, and occurrence of loess.

11. Discuss the importance of wind as a geological agent.

GENERAL QUESTIONS

1. Make sketches showing the windward and leeward sides of sand dunes for winds blowing steadily from (*a*) the north, (*b*) the south, (*c*) the east, (*d*) the west.

2. Topic 3 states that: (*a*) utility poles are easily protected from wind-blown sand by piling rocks at their bases; (*b*) that ventifacts may have been turned by frost or other weathering action. Explain these statements.

STUDENT ACTIVITIES

1. Obtain samples of dune sands from nearby beaches or other sources. Examine the sands with a hand magnifier or low power microscope. Which minerals can you identify (e.g., quartz, mica, feldspar, calcite, magnetite)? Do the grains appear frosted and rounded as described in Topic 8?

2. Examine sand grains rubbed from samples of sandstone. Analyze them as you did the sands in activity number 1.

3. If you live near an area of sand dunes, take a field trip to the dunes and observe: (*a*) the shapes of the dunes, (*b*) the relative steepness of their sides, (*c*) the materials of which they are made, (*d*) whether they are fixed or migrating, (*e*) their relation to the prevailing wind direction.

TOPOGRAPHIC SHEETS

(15-minute series, unless otherwise noted)

1. *Sand dunes:* Yuma, California-Arizona; Yuma, East and Yuma, West 7½-minute series; Barnegat, New Jersey; Cape Henry, Virginia.

2. *Barchan dunes:* Sieler, Washington, 7½-minute series; Moses Lake, Washington.

CHAPTER 10
Running Water

HOW DO YOU KNOW THAT . . . ?

Pour enough clay into a tall clear container to form a layer 2 cm deep. Cover this first with 2 cm of sand, then with 2 cm of coarse gravel or marble chips. Cover all of these with 15 cm of water. With a stirring rod, mix all the materials together until the sediment layers have completely disappeared. Stop stirring and observe the order and arrangement of the sediments as they settle out. Which materials settle first? Which settle last? Why? Why is there considerable mixing of the materials? Would a taller cylinder or jar improve their separation? Try it.

Stir the mixture again, but this time do not disturb the gravel. How can you manage this? Again change your stirring speed until only the clay remains in suspension. When you stop stirring, where is the clay? What does this experiment show about the relation between the speed of moving water and the size of material it can carry?

STREAM EROSION AND TRANSPORTATION

1. Running Water and Its Work

Running water is regarded as the most effective of all agents of erosion in wearing down the surface of the earth. Running water includes all the water that falls on the earth's surface as rain or snow and then moves downhill under the pull of gravity. The water trickling out of a hillside spring, the tiny brook flowing out of a pond, the overflow from a swamp, the runoff from melting snow, the rain washing down a hillside, the stream or creek or river running within its banks, or the same creek or river transformed into a torrent that floods its entire valley—all these are forms of running water.

2. River Terms

A **stream** is any appreciable flow of water. Streams are said to be *permanent* when their flow continues all year, and *intermittent* when they are dry for a part of the year. Many terms are used to indicate streams of different size, the most common being **river** for large streams, **creek** for smaller streams, and **brook** for still smaller ones.

All streams flow downhill, which may be in any direction on a map. On a map of the United States the Mississippi and Hudson rivers flow "down" to the south, the Red River in North Dakota flows "up" to the north, the Columbia River in Oregon flows "left" to the west, and the Platte River in Nebraska flows "right" to the east.

The **source** or **head** of a river is the place where it first makes its appearance on the earth as a surface stream. It is the highest point of a river. At its source the river may be no more than a trickle from a hillside spring or the overflow from a mountain pond. The source of the

Mississippi River is Lake Itasca high in the hills of Minnesota.

The mouth of a river is its lowest point or the point at which it ends, the mouth of the Mississippi River is in the Gulf of Mexico; the mouth of the Missouri River is in the Mississippi River.

A **tributary** is a river that flows into, and joins, another river which is usually larger and is called the **main stream.** The Ohio and the Missouri rivers are tributaries of the Mississippi. The **headwaters** of a river include those tributaries which are close to its head or source. A **river system** includes a main river and all of its tributaries. The **drainage basin** or **watershed** of a river includes all the land whose rainfall drains (runs) into the river, either directly or through its tributaries. The Mississippi's drainage basin, for example, includes almost all of the United States from the Rockies to the Appalachians. A

divide is the high land that separates one drainage basin from the next. We often speak of the Rocky Mountains as the Continental Divide, because its ranges split the continent into two drainage basins. In the United States rain falling east of this divide runs into the Mississippi system and then into the Gulf of Mexico. Rain falling west of the divide eventually runs into the Pacific Ocean.

A **river valley** is a lowland between the hills of a drainage basin, at the bottom of which a river runs. The valley is usually carved out by the river itself, though occasionally rivers flow in valleys formed by other natural agents. The **bed** or **channel** of a river is the part actually covered by its running water. (The word "channel" is also used for the deepest part of a river bed.) The **banks** of a river are the land alongside the river and just above it. Rock material carried by a river is called its **load.** (See Fig. 10-1.)

Fig. 10-1. Some of the features of river valleys.

3. Where Does River Water Come From?

It is easy to understand why a river should flow during and shortly after a rain. But where does the river's water come from in the period between rains? There are four sources of supply. Rivers like the Niagara River and the St. Lawrence River are permanently supplied with water by *lakes* at their sources. The Niagara River starts out as the overflow or outlet of Lake Erie. The St. Lawrence River starts out as the overflow of Lake Ontario. Lakes as large as these vary so little in level that their outlets have a very even flow of water throughout the year.

The small streams of mountains and forests are steadily supplied by *ground water* that trickles into their sources—springs, swamps, or small ponds high in the hills or mountains. If the water table drops too low or disappears completely during dry seasons, streams of this type run dry for part of the year and are intermittent. In desert regions there are intermittent streams which flow only when there are heavy rains, for there is no ground water to provide a flow at other times.

Large rivers like the Mississippi receive their water from thousands of *tributaries* scattered widely over tremendous drainage basins, and there is scarcely a time when it is not raining over some part of these basins. Such rivers vary enormously in volume, however, and may be subject to destructive floods at times when heavy rains fall over large parts of their vast watersheds.

Still another source of permanent water supply is the *melting of snow and ice* in high mountain areas. The Rhône River of Switzerland and France is constantly supplied by the melting of the Rhône Glacier from which it starts. In the United States the Colorado River receives its permanent supply from the snows of the Rocky Mountains.

4. How Water Wears the Land

Like the wind, running water wears down the surface of the earth by removing weathered rock and by wearing down bedrock. Rain running down a hillside carries loose rock to the bottom of the hill and into the nearest stream, while streams themselves wash material from their banks and beds.

Running water may break up the bedrock by both mechanical and chemical means. Its mechanical work is accomplished largely through the use of sand, pebbles, and even boulders as *cutting tools* with which it *abrades* or grinds away the rock of its bed and banks. Running water may also split off chunks of the bedrock by its *lifting effect* as it runs into cracks in the rock. As running water rolls, drags, and pushes rock fragments over its bed, it wears off their corners and edges, eventually producing the rounded boulders, pebbles, and sands characteristic of stream wear or *stream abrasion*.

The chemical action of running water is like that of ground water. Running water may break up bedrock chemically by dissolving its soluble minerals. Limestone, marble, and sandstones with soluble cements are the rocks most readily attacked by this process of *solution*. Rivers flowing over such bedrock form pits and holes in their beds.

5. Materials Carried by Streams

Like all agents of erosion, streams not only wear rock down but also carry it off. A stream carries its load of rock material in *solution*, in *suspension*, or as *bed load*. (See Fig. 10-2.)

Mineral matter in **solution** comes to the stream mainly from ground water. In limestone regions the dissolved mineral matter may be largely compounds of calcium and magnesium. Other dissolved minerals include silica and compounds of sodium and potassium derived from chemical weathering of the bedrock.

Material carried in **suspension** includes the clays, silts, and fine sands that give a muddy appearance to the water. Although these materials are heavier than water, they are stirred up and kept from sinking by the *turbulence* of stream flow. In much the same way, the turbulence of

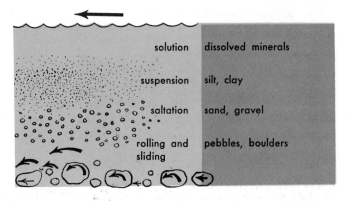

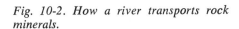

Fig. 10-2. How a river transports rock minerals.

air enables the wind to keep dust in the air. Similarly, turbulence in a stream of water means the existence of swirls and eddies that result from friction with the bed and banks of the stream. (Smooth flow, the opposite of turbulent flow, is *streamline flow,* in which water or air flows in smooth straight lines rather than in eddies and broken or curved lines.) The faster a stream flows and the rougher its bed is, the more turbulent it will be.

The **bed load** of a stream is the material the stream can move along its bed. This varies with the speed of the stream, but it may include heavy sands, gravel, pebbles, and even boulders. Here again, the turbulence of the water is important in lifting and moving the heavier-than-water sand grains. These grains move by *saltation,* being pushed along in jumps and bounces like grains of sand in a sandstorm. Pebbles and boulders move along by *sliding* or *rolling,* depending on their shape. As they abrade the river bed and move downstream, they become smaller and rounder.

It is estimated that the rivers of the United States carry a billion tons of rock into the oceans each year. About one-fourth of this load is in solution, about one-half in suspension, and the remaining fourth in the form of bed load. Large as this figure is, it represents a wearing down of the entire surface of the United States at the rate of only one foot in 8,000 years, emphasizing once again the extreme slowness characteristic of geologic change.

6. Carrying Power and Load

The carrying power of a stream depends simply on its **volume** (how large its cross section is) and its **velocity** (how fast it runs). If the cross section area in *square feet* is multiplied by the stream's velocity in *feet per second,* the flow of the stream in *cubic feet per second* can be calculated. The larger a stream is and the faster it runs, the more it can carry.

The size and weight of the largest rock particle a stream can carry depend on the stream's velocity. (Remember, too, that turbulence increases with velocity.) When a stream doubles its velocity, it far more than doubles the weight of particles it can carry. A slowly moving river, no matter how large it is, may be able to carry nothing larger than silt. A small swift stream may be able to move boulders.

The velocity of a stream depends chiefly upon the steepness or *gradient* of its bed. It also increases with increased volume and depth, as during heavy rains or flood seasons. In fact, the carrying power of a stream may be hundreds of times as large during floods as at other times. Consequently it does most of its work of erosion and transportation at such times. If it can remove all of the loose rock and sediment from its bed at such times, it is likely to cut into its bedrock floor and erode its bed deeper. (See Fig. 10-3.)

The load carried by a stream is brought in by tributaries, washed or pulled down from the valley sides by sheet wash and mass wasting, or scoured from the stream's bed and banks.

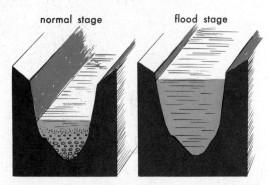

normal stage   flood stage

Fig. 10-3. At flood stage, a river swells in volume and increases greatly in velocity, enabling it to scour its bed clean of sediments and dig deeper into its rock floor.

7. Rate of Erosion

Every stream flows downhill under the pull of gravity until it reaches its mouth. As it flows, it wears down its bed. But it can never cut its bed any lower than the level to which it flows. This level is called **base level.** For rivers that flow into the ocean, base level is the same as sea level. Rivers that flow into lakes or into other rivers usually have higher base levels, though these may change in time as the level of the lake or main river changes.

The rate at which a river wears down its bed differs from river to river and from one part of the river bed to another. It depends upon many factors, chief of which are the velocity of the river, its volume, the kind of rock over which it runs, and its supply of cutting tools. A river that carries few cutting tools can perform little erosion. A river that receives more sediment from its tributaries than it can carry also does little to erode its bed, dropping sediment instead and forming sand bars. Such a river is said to be *overloaded.* Except at flood times, it winds in and out between so many sand bars that it is described as a *braided stream.* Streams flowing on wide flood plains in arid regions are likely to be braided.

SHAPING THE VALLEY

8. The Steep V-shaped Valley

As running water in any form moves over the surface of the earth, it wears out a depression or **valley** which is usually V-shaped in cross section, though the sides of the V may differ greatly in steepness (see Fig. 10-4). The cross section of a valley is a line drawn down one side of the valley, across the river, and up on the other side of the valley. The V-shape of a river valley is explained by the fact that **while the river deepens its valley by eroding its bed, it also widens its valley by eroding its banks.** In the widening process it is assisted by weathering, mass wasting, and the work of its tributaries. Since the upper valley walls are the first to be exposed as the river erodes its bed, they are attacked sooner than the lower valley walls, thus making the valley wider at the top than at the bottom.

The steepness of the cross section of a valley depends upon the *relative speed* of deepening by the river and widening by the other forces. If no widening at all took place, a vertical-walled valley or "box canyon" would be formed which would be no wider at the top than at the bottom. The nearest approach to this in nature is generally found in high arid plateau regions like those of southwestern United States. There steep, swift rivers cut rapidly through the rocks to great depths, while widening the valley by weathering

Fig. 10-4. How mass wasting aids a river in forming its valley.

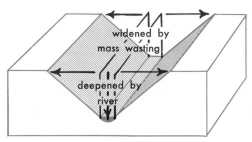

and mass wasting is slow because of the dry climate. But even in humid regions, the combination of rapid erosion of the bed and slow widening of the valley occurs. The deep, steep-sided valleys thus formed are known as **canyons** or **gorges.** *Ravine, chasm,* and *glen* are similar names.

The greatest of all canyons is the Grand Canyon of the Colorado River in Arizona, part of which is a national park. Ranging in depth from 4,000 to 6,000 feet, and in width from 7 to 15 miles, the canyon runs 200 miles through the Colorado Plateau in northern Arizona. Other superb examples of cliff-walled valleys are the canyon of Yellowstone River in Yellowstone Park, Wyoming; Zion Canyon in Zion Canyon National Park, Utah; and the Royal Gorge of the Arkansas River in Colorado. (See Fig. 10-5.)

9. Widening of the Valley

River valleys do not remain steep-sided forever. The deeper the river cuts into its valley, the closer it approaches its base level. (See Topic 7.) As its slope decreases, so does its speed. Thus it cuts down more and more slowly. But, while deepening of the valley is thus being checked, weathering and mass wasting go on as before with their work of widening the valley, and they "catch up." The result is a gradual but continuous change in the cross section of the valley. As the valley walls wear down, the valley becomes greatly enlarged, and its walls usually become increasingly gentle in slope (Fig. 10-6).

It is estimated that much less than one-tenth of a river's life history is spent in the canyon-shaped valley which it can produce only while flowing rapidly down steep slopes. The actual number of years differs with the river. A great river like the Colorado may take millions of years to form a canyon a mile deep in a plateau of resistant rock. A small, swift stream flowing over soft clays may complete its canyon stage in as little as a hundred years.

New York State Department of Commerce

Fig. 10-5. Ausable Chasm is the young valley of the Ausable River in the Adirondack Mountains.

LENGTHENING THE VALLEY

10. Gullies and Headward Erosion

A single heavy rain that runs down a soil-covered hillside may erode a miniature stream valley. Like larger river valleys, this valley will be V-shaped in cross section and may have a number of tributaries. When the rain ends, the "river" disappears, but its tiny valley remains and is known as a **gully.** Gullies may be seen on farmland, at roadsides, in deforested areas and, in fact, in any place where heavy rains may wash loose earth from some part of a sloping piece of land. Gullies may be only a few feet long and a few inches deep, or they may be hundreds of feet long and many feet deep.

Gullies grow in length, width, and depth with each new rainfall and even between rains. When

The Milwaukee Road

Fig. 10-6. A young river valley in which widening is overtaking deepening. The Grand Canyon of the Yellowstone River in Yellowstone National Park, Wyoming.

it rains, water runs into the head and sides of the gully from higher parts of the hillside. As this water runs into the gully, it washes in some of the surrounding earth. The result of this action is both a widening and a lengthening of the gully. Each rain moves the source or head of the gully farther up the hillside, making the gully longer than it was before the rain. (See Fig. 10-8.)

The term **headward erosion** refers to the wearing away of the land at the head of a gully or stream valley. While most of this is done by rains, some "erosion" is carried on by weathering and mass wasting even when it is not raining. The net effect of headward erosion is to lengthen a stream valley at its source, usually in steep hilly country. But remember, headward erosion does not mean that a stream is flowing toward its head or source. No stream does.

Gullies may be considered to be the valleys of intermittent streams. As a gully grows in length

and depth, it may cut below the water table and become a permanent stream. Tributary gullies may join it, and in time a complete river system may be born. Most of the world's rivers are believed to have originated in this simple way.

Fig. 10-7. These gullies form a miniature river system on easily eroded soil.

Caterpillar Tractor Co.

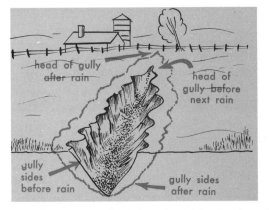

Fig. 10-8. *How a gully is lengthened by headward erosion.*

Desert cloudbursts cause large numbers of gullies to develop in regions of soft, impermeable clay deposits unprotected by vegetation. Such regions are so difficult to travel through that they are called *badlands*. Among the best known badlands in the United States are those of South Dakota, North Dakota, and Nebraska. (See Fig. 10-9.)

11. Stream Piracy

Stream piracy or **stream capture** results from the lengthening of a river by headward erosion. Figure 10-10 illustrates one way in which stream piracy occurs. As the source of river *A* moves farther and farther up the slope on which it originates, it cuts into the banks of river *B*. If, as headward erosion continues, *A*'s source wears down lower than *B*'s bed at point *P*, all of *B*'s water above point *P* will eventually flow into *A*. If the difference in level at *P* is large, there may be a waterfall at *P*. Stream *A* is known as the pirate stream and stream *B* as the beheaded stream. The headwaters lost by stream *B* are "captured headwaters." By such a process, one stream may grow larger at the expense of the neighboring ones and it is probable that

Fig. 10-9. *Scenery in Badlands National Park, South Dakota, is a result of gully formation.*

National Park Service

Fig. 10-10. Stream piracy is illustrated here as stream A (first seen in the left sketch) extends its source until it "beheads" stream B (in the right sketch). See Topic 11.

many of the great river systems of the world were aided in their development by stream piracy.

Stream piracy may be regarded as a result of differences in the rate of stream erosion, since the pirate stream must cut down its bed faster than the stream it captures. More rapid erosion by the pirate stream may be the result of steeper slope, softer rock, or greater volume. Many cases of stream piracy are known to have occurred in the Catskill Mountains and the Appalachian Mountains of eastern United States.

IRREGULAR DEEPENING

12. Potholes and Plunge Pools

No stream bed is perfectly smooth. As a swift stream moves over the irregular bedrock and boulders in its bed, it develops eddies and whirlpools at many places. If these whirlpools continue in the same places for any considerable length of time and are equipped with ample cutting tools such as pebbles and boulders, they grind out oval or circular basins called **potholes** in the bedrock of the stream. (See Fig. 10-11.)

Fig. 10-11. Potholes in the granite bed of the James River, Virginia. These potholes were ground out by whirlpools in the river during periods of flood.

Wentworth, U.S. Geological Survey

The grooves and scratches made by whirling pebbles and sands can be seen on the sides of the potholes.

Larger potholes called **plunge pools** may be ground out by giant whirlpools at the bases of waterfalls. Potholes may be seen in almost any rocky stream bed. They range in size from tiny ones measured in inches to great plunge pools that measure up to 40 or 50 feet in diameter and even more in depth. Jamesville Lake, south of Syracuse, New York, and similar lakes in the Grand Coulee in the state of Washington, occupy plunge pools made by great waterfalls in the beds of rivers that no longer exist.

13. Waterfalls and Rapids

River beds rarely maintain the same slope for any very great distance. The slope is likely to be steepest in the headwaters of a river and gentlest near its mouth. At some points the river bed may be so steep as to form **rapids** of fast-flowing, foamy, turbulent water. Where the river bed is vertical or nearly vertical, the water plunges over a cliff to form a **waterfall.**

The steep slopes and cliffs that are responsible for rapids and waterfalls may originate in many different ways: through earthquakes, volcanic action, unequal weathering, or unequal erosion. In some cases the steep slopes and cliffs were parts of the surface topography when the rivers first started to flow. Niagara Falls came into existence simply because the Niagara River had to pass over a cliff as it overflowed from Lake Erie to Lake Ontario. But in many cases the river itself, through unequal erosion, has worn steps or cliffs in a bed that was originally uniform in slope, thereby making its own rapids and waterfalls. The two great falls of the Yellowstone River in Yellowstone National Park are examples of this method of origin. (See Topic 16.)

Like canyons, rapids and waterfalls are regarded as only temporary features in the life of a river, lasting for perhaps no more than the first 5 per cent of the river's complete history. The greater speed and turbulence of the river at falls and rapids wears them down more rapidly than other parts of the bed, and they eventually disappear.

14. Undermining and Recession

Waterfalls often grind out potholes or plunge pools at their bases. In many types of waterfalls these holes *undermine* or weaken the waterfall cliff sufficiently to cause pieces of the cliff top to cave in. Each time this happens, the waterfall is left a little farther upstream than before and is said to recede (move back). Undermining and recession are fastest in waterfall cliffs made of horizontal layers of bedrock in which a hard "cap rock" rests on top of soft layers.

15. Niagara Falls Recedes Rapidly

Niagara Falls is the world's most famous example of the cap rock type of waterfall. At Niagara the cliff is about 160 feet high, the cap

Fig. 10-12. The rock structure of Niagara Falls.

is a hard dolomite layer about 60 feet thick, and the weaker layers consist largely of thin beds of shale. Great plunge pools, as deep as the falls are high, are formed in the weak shales at the foot of the falls. This undermines the hard dolomite cap until from time to time it breaks off because of its own weight, thus causing the falls to recede. (See Fig. 10-12.)

When the Ice Age ended in North America, Niagara Falls originated at a cliff 7 miles downstream from its present location. It has been estimated that it took Niagara about 10,000 years to recede from this original position, near which the city of Lewiston stands today. As Niagara Falls and its plunge pools wore back, they left a great gorge which is now 7 miles long, about

Fig. 10-13. Formation of a gorge by waterfall recession, as at Niagara.

300 feet deep, and from 200 to 400 yards wide. (See Fig. 10-13.)

At its present location, a small island (Goat Island) in the middle of the Niagara River splits Niagara into two falls known as the American Falls and the Canadian Falls. Goat Island extends diagonally upstream in such a way as to make most of the water go over the Canadian Falls. (See Fig. 10-14.) Erosion here is so rapid that the Canadian Falls is receding at the rate of almost 5 feet a year and is now worn back so much that it is also known as the Horseshoe Falls. Recession of the American Falls is much slower, averaging only a few inches a year, and its outline is fairly straight. When the Canadian Falls is eventually eroded beyond Goat Island, all of Niagara's water will flow into the Canadian Falls, leaving the American Falls dry.

16. Yellowstone's Falls Recede Very Slowly

The origin of the upper and lower falls of the Yellowstone River is a good illustration of the manner in which unequal erosion by a river creates its own waterfalls. At several places in the bed of the Yellowstone River vertical intrusions (dikes) of magma have formed rock that is much harder than the rest of the bed (see Fig. 10-15). The river wears down the softer rock *downstream* from the intrusion so much more rapidly than the dikes that it develops falls at this point. Since the dikes extend to great depths and are uniformly hard, little recession occurs, the falls simply wearing down slowly.

17. Other Waterfalls

The Shoshone Falls of the Snake River in Idaho is similar to Niagara Falls in having hard cap rock on top of soft rock, but its rocks are lavas rather than sedimentary rocks. The great Victoria Falls in Africa form where the Zambezi River flows from hard rock to soft rock. Rivers

Niagara Falls Chamber of Commerce

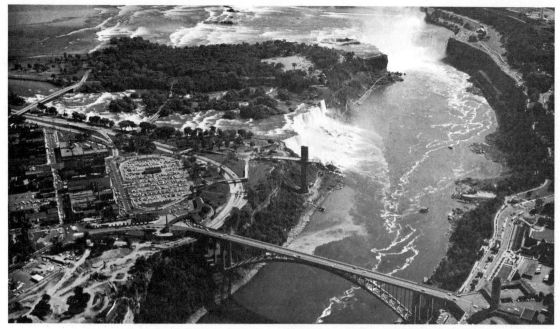

Fig. 10-14. The Niagara River, Niagara Falls, and Niagara Gorge. Goat Island separates the American Falls in the foreground from the Horseshoe or Canadian Falls in the background, splitting the river unevenly so that most of the water goes to the Canadian Falls.

in eastern United States form a Fall Zone of falls and rapids where they flow from the hard rocks of the Piedmont Upland onto soft coastal plain sediments. These falls and thousands of others are the result of unequal erosion in rocks of unequal hardness.

Many falls occur where tributary streams join main streams whose valleys are cut much lower than those of the tributaries. The tributary valleys are called **hanging valleys,** and the falls **hanging-valley waterfalls.** This type of fall occurs frequently in regions of glacial erosion. Its origin is explained in Chapter 11. Many of the great falls in Yosemite (yoh *sem* ih tee) National Park are of this type. (See Fig. 10-16.)

Fig. 10-15. At its Lower Falls the Yellowstone River drops 308 feet over a dike.

The Milwaukee Road

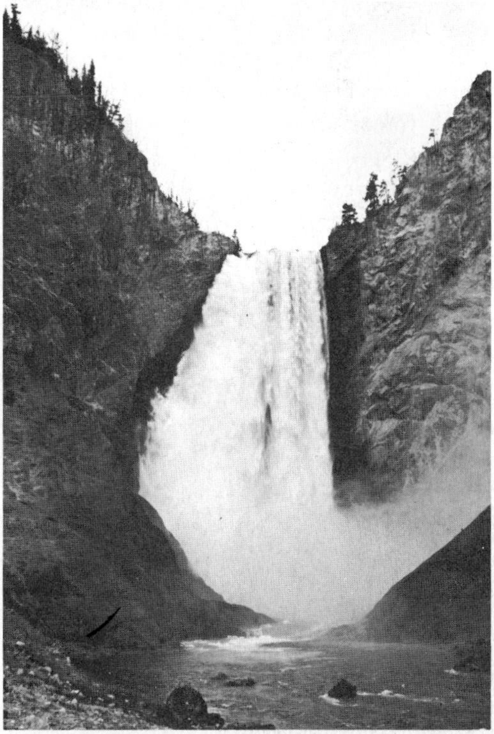

WIDENING OF THE VALLEY FLOOR

18. Flood Plain and Meanders

A fast-flowing river moves in a comparatively straight course which directs most of its cutting

Fig. 10-16. *From its hanging valley, Yosemite Falls drops 2200 feet in two great leaps as it joins the Merced River.*

power at its bed. The river deepens its bed, while other forces widen the valley walls above it, leaving the *floor* of the valley hardly any wider than the river bed itself. But as the slope and speed of the river decrease with the passing of

time, its ability to override large boulders, hard rock outcrops, and other obstructions is largely lost, and it is more easily deflected sideways against its banks (see Fig. 10-17). As the water is deflected against the bank on one side, it erodes that bank and begins the formation of a curve in the river's course. But from this bank it is now deflected diagonally downstream until it strikes the opposite bank, where both erosion of the bank and deflection downstream are repeated. In this way, rebounding from bank to bank, the river begins the development of a curving course which, in time, erodes the floor of the valley to form a wide flat area called a **flood plain.** (This name is given to it because the river overflows onto it during floods. At such times the flood plain is built up higher by sediments which the river deposits. See Topic 24.) The process by which the valley floor is widened by the swinging of the river is called **lateral erosion** or **side-cutting.**

Once begun, the curving course of the river becomes more and more pronounced. At each bend in the river the current swings against the bank at the *outside of the curve, undercutting it* and eroding it rapidly. At the *inside of each curve* there is so little water in motion that *sediment* is *deposited.* The net result is the shifting of the river bed in the direction of the outside of the bend. As the shifting of the bed occurs at each bend on alternate sides of the river, the course of the river eventually forms a series of broad

Fig. 10-17. *How a river side-cuts its valley, forms a flood plain, and develops meanders.*

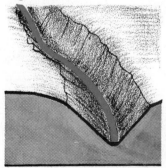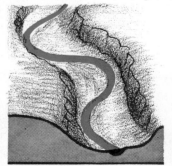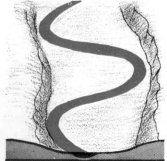

curves called **meanders** (mee *an* ders), which wind their way across an increasingly broad flood plain. (See Fig. 10-18.) Great rivers like the Mississippi, the Nile, the Ganges (*gan* jeez), and the Amazon may have flood plains dozens of miles wide and hundreds of miles long.

19. Cutoffs and Oxbow Lakes

As meanders swing wider and wider, their ends move closer together until they almost touch. The land separating the ends of a meander is called its **neck.** Since undercutting is taking

Fig. 10-18. A meandering river, and an oxbow lake formed from it, in northern Alaska.

U.S. Geological Survey

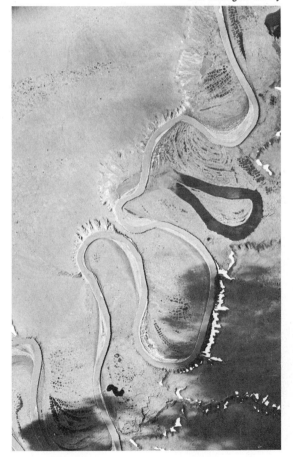

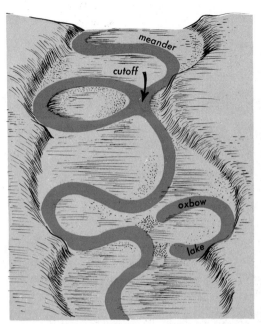

Fig. 10-19. A meandering river that has developed a cutoff and an oxbow lake.

place at the banks on both sides of the meander neck (Fig. 10-19), the river eventually breaks through the neck to form a **cutoff,** at the same time making an island of the land inside the meander curve. Most of the river goes through the steeper, shorter cutoff, and the meander becomes an abandoned channel full of sluggish water. Mud and silt are deposited by the river along the old entrances to the meander, which becomes completely separated from the river to form an **oxbow lake.**

Large numbers of oxbow lakes occur on the flood plain of the Mississippi. At flood times, silt is deposited in oxbow lakes, making them shallower. Vegetation grows in them, turning them into swamps or **bayous** (*bye* ews) and eventually filling them up completely.

20. Water Gaps and Wind Gaps

Where an extensive formation of resistant rock crosses the bed of a river, the river is unable

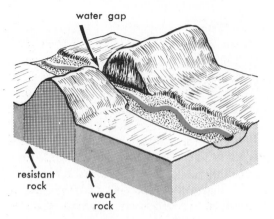

Fig. 10-20. The origin of a water gap.

to widen its valley as fast as in the softer rock above and below the formation. But the hard rock formation is also more resistant to weathering, so it usually stands above the rest of the countryside as a mountain or ridge (Fig. 10-20). Through this ridge the river runs in a narrow, canyonlike valley which is in marked contrast to its broad, open valley on both sides

of the ridge. The cut made by the river through the ridge is called a **water gap** or **narrows.** Most famous of such gaps in the East is the Delaware Water Gap, cut by the Delaware River through the hard conglomerate rock of the Kittatinny Mountains in New Jersey and Pennsylvania. Many other gaps occur in the Appalachian Mountains along the Susquehanna, the Potomac, and other rivers. The long, gorgelike "narrows" in the Hudson River Valley near West Point is a water gap. (See Figs. 10-21 and 22-13.)

Wind gaps are simply abandoned water gaps. Many wind gaps occur in the southern Appalachians, where stream piracy diverted a number of rivers after they made water gaps.

ALLUVIAL DEPOSITS

Like all agents of erosion, running water removes much of the rock debris it scours from the surface of the land and carries it off to lower levels to deposit it in a variety of forms and places. The end result is to bring the surface of

Fig. 10-21. Railways and highways follow the gap made through the Kittatinny Mountains by the Delaware River.

Pocono Mountains Vacation Bureau

the continents closer and closer to the level of the sea.

21. Why Deposition Occurs

Running water may deposit a part of its load of sediment with each decrease in either *velocity* or *volume.*

Rivers lose velocity where their *slopes decrease,* where their *beds widen,* or where they meet *obstructions* in the form of curving banks or rock outcrops. Rivers usually suffer their greatest losses in velocity when they *empty into the ocean or into lakes* where all their remaining sediment is finally taken from them.

In regions of humid climate, rivers usually grow larger and larger as they approach the sea and acquire new tributaries. In arid regions, however, the reverse is likely to be the rule, with *rivers shrinking in volume* as water is lost by *evaporation* in the dry air of the deserts through which they run. Losses in volume may also result from *diversion* of water by man for farmland irrigation or for city water supplies.

Whenever a river shrinks in volume, it also suffers a loss of velocity. The same river will flow much more swiftly in flood stage than during its normally shallower periods.

The deposits of sediment made by running water are called **alluvium** or alluvial deposits. They are likely to be stratified in layers of particles that are fairly well sorted by size and rounded by abrasion on the bed of the stream.

22. Deltas

When a river flows into a relatively *quiet* body of water such as a lake, inland sea, or ocean gulf, its loss of velocity is complete and all of its sediment is deposited at its mouth. The sediment, most often composed of sand, silt, and clay, usually forms a level, fan-shaped deposit called a **delta** (after its resemblance to the Greek letter delta, Δ). The shape of the delta varies considerably with such factors as the rate at which sediment is deposited and the rate at which it is removed by waves and currents. Deltas are unlikely to form along open ocean coasts because strong waves and currents carry the sediment off too rapidly.

The fan shape of a delta is due to the fact that as the river's deposits block its mouth, it swerves away from that point, often splitting into two or more branches. These branches spread additional deposits on both sides of the center. This blocking and shifting is repeated continually, spreading the sediment out until the fan shape is developed. The branches into which the river divides as it flows over its delta are called **distributaries** or **passes.** Unlike tributaries, they flow away from the main stream rather than into it. (See Figs. 10-22, 10-23, and 10-24.)

The delta of the Mississippi extends 200 miles into the Gulf of Mexico, covers an area far larger than Rhode Island, and is growing seaward at an average rate of about 350 feet a year. Other great deltas are those of the Nile in the Mediterranean Sea, the Danube in the Black

Fig. 10-22. Three stages in the growth of a delta are shown from left to right. Land is shown in white; water in black.

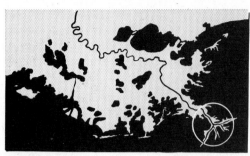

Fig. 10-23. Sketch map of the Mississippi River delta. The circled area shows the extreme southern end of the delta in the Gulf of Mexico. Figure 10-24 is a photo of this area.

Sea, the Rhine in the North Sea coast of Holland and Belgium, the Ganges and Brahmaputra in the Bay of Bengal, and the Volga in the Caspian Sea.

23. Alluvial Fans

Rivers sweeping down from steep mountain valleys onto comparatively level lands suffer great losses in velocity. As they come out of their mountain canyons, they drop a large part of their usually heavy loads of coarse sands and gravels at their mouths. These loads form deposits greatly resembling deltas both in shape and in the manner in which the streams divide into distributaries over their surfaces. The deposits are not flat-surfaced like deltas, however, and their sediments are much coarser. When their slopes are only moderately steep, these deposits are called **alluvial fans;** when very steep, they are called **alluvial cones.** (See Figs. 10-25, 10-26.)

The distributaries often disappear completely into the extremely porous materials of the fans, but emerge down the slope where the deposits thin out. Alluvial fans are best developed in the arid regions of western United States, at the bases of steep mountains like the Rockies and Sierra Nevadas. Some of these fans attain a diameter of 40 miles, spreading so far along the mountain base as to meet and merge with the fans of other rivers. Such a continuous series of fans is known as a **piedmont alluvial plain** (*piedmont,* foot of the mountain; the pronunciation is *peed* mont).

Fig. 10-24. Aerial view of the southern end of the Mississippi delta, circled in Fig. 10-23.

U.S. Army, Corps of Engineers

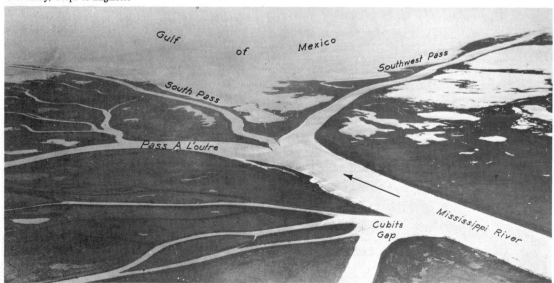

24. Flood Plain Deposits

The flood plain has already been explained as the flat portion of a valley floor formed by lateral erosion and subject to flooding by the river. A river is said to be in flood when it receives more water than it is able to contain within its banks. Because of its greatly increased volume and velocity at flood times, a river carries tremendous quantities of sediment. When it overflows its banks and spreads over its flood plain, sediment is deposited on the flood plain in large amounts, because the waters on the flood plains are shallower and slower than the waters in the river bed. Thus a layer of alluvium is spread over the valley floor with every flood, but some of the alluvium may be removed by lateral erosion before the next flooding of the valley occurs. (See Fig. 10-27.)

The deposit of alluvium is not uniform in either thickness or composition. Since the greatest loss of velocity takes place right at the banks, where the river waters are suddenly transferred from the deep bed to the shallow flood plain, more sediment is dropped here than farther back on the flood plain. Not only is the quantity greater, but the materials are coarser. In this way

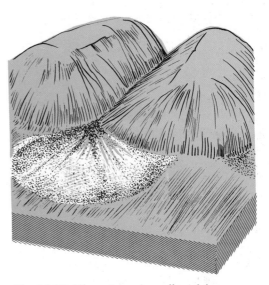

Fig. 10-25. The origin of an alluvial fan.

a thicker deposit is built up all along the banks, forming low ridges called **natural levees** (*lev* ees) on both sides of the river.

Beyond the levees the flood plains is lower and in some places the water table may stand above the surface to form areas called **back swamps.** Since the flood plain slopes *away from*

Fig. 10-26. An alluvial fan at the mouth of Aztec Gulch, Colorado.

Cross, U.S. Geological Survey

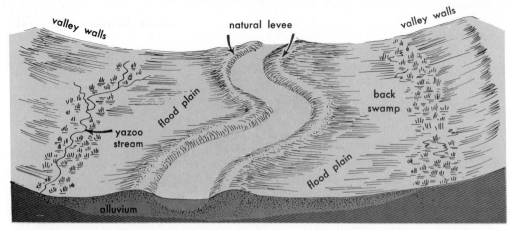

Fig. 10-27. *Sketch of a well-developed flood plain such as that of the lower Mississippi.*

the main river, tributary streams may flow great distances through the back swamps, more or less parallel to the main stream, before they can cut through the levees to join the main stream. Such tributaries are **yazoo streams**. They are named after the famous Yazoo River, which flows 175 miles through the back swamps of Mississippi before joining the Mississippi River.

Natural levees are never any higher than the height of water during the last flood that built

Fig. 10-28. *Sandbags being used to raise and reinforce a levee on the Mississippi River at Porter Lake, Arkansas.*

U.S. Army, Corps of Engineers

them. To provide further flood protection, natural levees are often built up into **artificial levees,** varying from elaborate concrete walls to simple heaps of sandbags. The "dikes" of Holland are artificial levees on the flood plain of the Rhine River. (See Fig. 10-28.)

FLOODS

25. Floods from Rain

The simplest and commonest cause of river floods is *heavy rainfall*. A single heavy downpour or cloudburst in the narrow valley of a young mountain stream may turn the stream into a violent torrent within a few hours. Floods of this type are known as **flash floods**. They are common in the dry gulches or arroyos (ah *roy* ohs) of the Southwest and in the steep valleys of the Rockies and the Sierra Nevadas. They may also

occur in the steep mountain valleys of eastern United States. Towns located at the bases of the mountains suffer severely from flash floods.

The lower courses of great rivers like the Missouri, the Ohio, and the Mississippi never have flash floods. Their floods are usually the result of many days of continuous rainfall over large portions of their great drainage basins. The larger the rainy areas, the higher the floods. As these floods move downstream, they may cover sections of flood plain far removed from the sources of the flood waters. (See Fig. 10-29.)

26. Floods from Snow

The *rapid melting of snow* is the second most important cause of floods. When heavy winter snowfalls are followed by periods of warm weather called thaws, there may be as much water

Fig. 10-29. Flooded railroad yards and industrial section in Paducah, Kentucky, at the junction of the Tennessee and Ohio rivers.

U.S. Air Force Photo

running into the rivers as during heavy rains. Thaws occur most frequently in the spring, but winter thaws are not unusual. If thaws are accompanied by even light rainfall, floods are very likely to occur.

27. How Much Runoff?

The occurrence of floods depends to a very great extent on the kind of ground on which the rains fall or the snows melt, as well as on the quantity of rain or melted snow. The percentage of runoff is much greater on bedrock and clay than on sandy soil; it is much greater on steep slopes than on level ones; it is greater on bare ground than on ground covered by vegetation. The greater the runoff, the greater is the likelihood of flood from a given quantity of rain. In winter and early spring there are many parts of the world in which the ground is frozen. **Frozen ground means ground in which all the pore spaces between rock particles are filled up by ice.** When rain falls or snow melts on such a surface, no water can seep in, and practically all the water runs off. In such cases even light rains or brief thaws may cause floods.

The percentage of runoff also varies with the heaviness of a rain. An inch of rain in a cloudburst or severe thundershower will cause far more runoff than an inch of slow, steady rain on the same surface. This is one reason why flash floods are likely to occur during short, heavy downpours.

28. Other Causes of River Floods

The **formation of a natural dam** that blocks a river and makes it overflow into its valley above the dam is an occasional cause of flooding. Small natural dams may be built by *beavers.* Larger ones may result from *lava flows* or *landslides.* A common type of natural dam is the *ice jam* that may result when a frozen river in northern United States breaks up in the spring. Great cakes of ice sometimes pile up at narrow places or at sharp bends in the river bed, damming up the river. When such a dam gives way suddenly, a flash flood downstream may also occur.

The **failure of a man-made dam** also causes floods. The famous Johnstown, Pennsylvania, flood of May 31, 1889, took place when an earth dam on the Conemaugh River, two miles above Johnstown, collapsed after days of heavy rain, and the entire reservoir burst down upon the sleeping city. More than 2,200 people were drowned. On December 14, 1963, the failure of a dam above the Baldwin Hills section of Los Angeles caused property damage estimated at $50,000,000. Great loss of life was prevented because warnings of the impending disaster, about four hours before the dam collapsed, allowed most residents to be evacuated.

Although the dam did not give way, the Vaiont Dam in the Alps of northeastern Italy, third highest dam in the world, was involved in a great flood disaster on October 9, 1963. That night a massive **landslide** from the bordering mountainside poured into the reservoir behind the dam, causing a mighty surge of water over the dam that wiped out the downstream town of Longarone and drowned nearly 3,000 people.

29. Flood Prevention

Flood prevention methods are of four different kinds. The first kind does nothing to reduce the quantity of water in a river, but simply tries to keep the water from overflowing onto the flood plain. This is done by *building up their levees* with sand bags, concrete, or other materials. One trouble with this method is that the levees may break. When they do, the river pours through the **crevasse** (break in the levee; the pronunciation is (krah *vass)* in a flood far worse than a mere overflow. A second fault is that levees may have to be built higher and higher each year, because sediments dropped in a riverbed between flood periods raise the bed. The higher the levees rise above the rest of the flood plain, the greater is the damage when the river does overflow. (See Fig. 10-28.)

A second method of flood prevention is used on the lower course of the Mississippi River. As the waters rise to flood stage, they are permitted to pass at certain points into *spillways* that carry the water into parallel channels running through the back swamps to the Gulf of Mexico or to Lake Pontchartrain.

The third kind of flood prevention attempts to reduce the quantity of water flowing in a river after heavy rains or thaws. It does this by building *dams across the headwaters and tributaries of the river,* thus storing up the excess runoff in great reservoirs. Hoover Dam helps to do this for the Colorado River. But in very rainy regions like the Tennessee Valley a single dam is not enough, for each part of the valley may collect enough rain to make its own flood. For this reason the TVA project includes 26 different dams along the Tennessee River and its tributaries.

The fourth kind of flood prevention attempts to reduce the runoff from a drainage basin of a river by restoring the natural vegetation that man has destroyed. In the humid lands of the United States where the threat of flood is greatest, the natural vegetation is chiefly forest growth. Restoring the natural vegetation here means *reforestation*—the planting of trees to take the place of those that were cut or burnt away. But such a program would be incomplete if it did not also provide for future conservation of the forests by limiting the amount of timber to be cut and by providing for its replacement with young trees. A young tree needs many years to become timber.

LIFE HISTORY OF A RIVER

30. The Three Stages

Many years ago the great physiographer William Morris Davis introduced the idea that land forms may be considered to pass through a *life history* (or cycle of erosion). The complete cycle of a land form includes its history from the time of its origin to the time of its complete removal by erosion. As with living things, the cycle is usually divided into the three principal stages of *youth, maturity,* and *old age.* These stages do not imply any fixed number of years, but rather a set of characteristics. Thus a land form that continues to show youthful characteristics is considered to be in youth, regardless of its age in years.

31. Youth

A river that is in the vigorous early stages of its development is a young river. Such a river flows rapidly over a generally steep, but irregularly sloping bed. Its fairly straight course is frequently interrupted by rapids and waterfalls, and occasionally by lakes through which it flows. It has few tributaries. An important part of its work is down-cutting. Thus its valley is steep-sided or canyonlike in form, and it has no flood plain. The interstream areas (areas between river valleys) are comparatively flat, and there are no well-marked highland divides to separate its drainage basin from the next.

The Niagara, the Colorado, the St. Lawrence, and the Yellowstone are excellent examples of young rivers. Since headward erosion is constantly adding to the length of a river at its source, the headwaters of almost every river are young.

32. Maturity

The end of youth and the beginning of maturity are marked by the elimination of almost all the irregularities of the bed of a river. Rapids and waterfalls have been worn away, and lakes have been filled in by the river's deposits. The mature river flows over a *graded bed*—just steep enough to enable the river to transport its load. With the bed cut closer to base level (see Topic 7), the slope is decreased, and down-cutting is now much slower than in youth. By late maturity the river has developed a broadly meandering course across its wide flood plain, and natural levees, oxbow lakes, and back swamps may be present. The valley cross section shows a flat floor. There are many tributaries, and the increased volume of the river makes up for its reduced velocity in enabling it to transport great quantities of sediment.

Except in their headwaters, rivers that have well-developed flood plains are mature. Thus the Mississippi is young in its hilly headwaters, early mature in its narrower northern valley, and mature to late mature or old in its southern portions.

33. Old Age

The characteristics of old age do not differ markedly from those of late maturity. The river bed is closer to base level. Down-cutting has practically stopped, and lateral erosion is less active than in maturity. The valley floor is very broad and flat, *with a flood plain far wider than the river's meander belt.* The valley sides are worn to very gentle slopes, and interstream areas are low. In a large region of old rivers the low rolling surface produced by erosion is so nearly flat that it is called a **peneplane** (*pee* neh plane). *Pene* means "almost"; *plane,* "flat surface."

There are very few examples of rivers in old age. Erosion is so slow in late maturity that tremendously long periods are required to bring

Fig. 10-30. Sketch of an entrenched meander.

about the characteristics of old age. In most cases the river's life cycle is interrupted long before old age is reached. The lower Mississippi River may be considered, however, as a close approach to the features of old age. Apparently rivers did reach old age in past geologic eras, for raised peneplanes exist in many parts of the world. They will be described in a later chapter.

34. Interruptions in the Cycle of Erosion

As suggested in the preceding paragraph, the life cycle of a river may be interrupted. If the region in which the river flows is *raised,* it has the effect of starting the river's life cycle all over again. The river becomes young again, and is said to be *rejuvenated.* The river flows fast once more, and begins to cut a new steep-sided valley that follows the course already made by the river on its mature flood plain. Thus, a meandering river which is rejuvenated may cut a strange new canyonlike valley with a meandering course. This is known as an **entrenched meander** (a meander that is dug in). The San Juan River in southeastern Utah and the Susquehanna River in southern New York and northern Pennsylvania show entrenched meanders. (See Figs. 10-30 and 10-31.)

Stream terraces frequently result when rejuvenation causes a mature river to cut down sharply into its flood plain. A stream terrace is therefore a remnant of the valley floor before rejuvenation. As its name suggests, the terrace is a "bench" running along the side of the valley. A steep slope separates it from the present valley floor.

When a region is *lowered,* the effect is to bring the river closer to old age, thus shortening the river's life cycle. The river slows down and erosion slackens. In the case of a river flowing into the sea, lowering of the land near its mouth may bring the valley below sea level. The river is then described as a **drowned river.** The part

La Rue, U.S. Geological Survey

Fig. 10-31. Entrenched meanders of the San Juan River in Utah.

that is flooded by the sea becomes a **bay** where it is wide at the mouth, and an **estuary** (*ess* tew air ee) where it is narrow farther inland. There are many drowned rivers along the Atlantic coast of North America. The Hudson River's drowned valley includes New York Bay; the Delaware's includes Delaware Bay; the Susquehanna's includes Chesapeake Bay.

TOPIC QUESTIONS

Each topic question refers to the topic of the same number within this chapter.

1. (*a*) Define running water and name some of its forms. (*b*) What geologic work is done by running water?

2. Explain or define each of the following or draw sketches to illustrate them: stream, river, creek, brook, intermittent stream, source, head, mouth, tributary, headwaters, river system, drainage basin, divide, valley, bed, banks, channel, load.

3. (*a*) Explain, with illustrations, what are the four sources of permanent water supply for rivers. (*b*) Compare these sources as to the likelihood that they will cause floods in their rivers.

4. Describe the mechanical and chemical action of running water in (*a*) removing loose rocks, (*b*) wearing away bedrock.

5. (*a*) Explain how a river carries rock material in (1) solution, (2) suspension, (3) as bed load. (*b*) Describe the movement of pebbles and boulders on a stream bed.

6. (*a*) What factors determine the carrying power of a stream? (*b*) What determines the size and weight of the largest object a stream can carry? (*c*) What factors determine the speed of stream flow? (*d*) What determines the total load carried by a stream?

7. (*a*) Explain what base level is. (*b*) What factors determine the rate of stream erosion?

8. (*a*) Explain why a young river valley is usually V-shaped. (*b*) Explain what canyons are, and how and where they are formed. Give examples

9. (*a*) Define base level. (*b*) Explain why the cross section of a river valley becomes less and less steep with time.

10. (*a*) Explain the formation of a gully. (*b*) Define headward erosion and explain how it lengthens a gully. (*c*) How are gullies related to the origin of river systems? (*d*) What are badlands?

11. (*a*) Explain how headward erosion may bring about stream capture. (*b*) Why is stream capture an effect of differences in the rate of erosion?

12. Describe the origin of potholes and plunge pools.

13. (*a*) What are rapids and waterfalls? (*b*) How do they originate? (*c*) Why do they eventually disappear?

14. (*a*) Explain why waterfalls often recede. (*b*) In which type of waterfall is recession fastest?

15. (*a*) Describe the structure of the Niagara type of waterfall. Explain why it recedes. (*b*) Explain how the Niagara gorge was formed. (*c*) Explain why the Canadian Falls recedes so much more rapidly than the American Falls.

16. Explain the origin of Yellowstone Falls. Why does little recession occur?

17. (*a*) Compare the structure of Shoshone Falls, Victoria Falls, or the Fall Zone with that of Niagara. (*b*) Describe the type of falls represented by Yosemite Falls.

18. (*a*) Explain what a flood plain is and how it is formed. (*b*) Explain what meanders are and how they develop.

19. With the aid of diagrams, explain how a meander forms a cutoff and an oxbow lake. What happens to oxbow lakes?

20. (*a*) Explain the origin of a water gap. (*b*) Define a wind gap and explain its origin.

21. (*a*) Explain how rivers may lose velocity. (*b*) Explain why rivers usually grow larger as they approach the sea, except in dry climates. (*c*) How does a river's volume affect its velocity? (*d*) What is alluvium? How is it identified?

22. (*a*) Describe the origin of a delta and the conditions that favor its formation. (*b*) What are distributaries? (*c*) Name and locate three great deltas.

23. (*a*) Describe the origin, shape, composition, and occurrence of alluvial fans. (*b*) How do fans differ from deltas? (*c*) What is a piedmont alluvial plain?

24. (*a*) Explain how deposition takes place on the flood plain. (*b*) Explain the origin of natural levees. (*c*) What are back swamps? (*d*) What is a yazoo stream? (*e*) Why are artificial levees built? How?

25. (*a*) What is the commonest cause of river flood? Explain what a flash flood is and how it occurs. (*b*) Explain how floods occur on great rivers like the Mississippi.

26. How does snow cause floods? When? What is a thaw?

27. (*a*) Give examples showing how the percentage of runoff varies with the kind of ground. (*b*) What is "frozen ground"? How does it help to cause floods? (*c*) How does the percentage of runoff vary with the kind of rain?

28. (*a*) Name several types of natural dams, and explain how they may cause floods. (*b*) How does the failure of a dam cause a flood? Give an example. (*c*) Explain the cause of the Vaiont Dam flood.

29. Names and describe briefly four different methods of flood prevention or control.

30. Briefly describe the idea that land forms have a life history.

31–33. (*a*) Make a table summarizing the characteristics of young, mature, and old rivers under these headings: (1) slope, (2) speed, (3) course, (4) tributaries, (5) principal work, (6) valley cross section, (7) flood plain, (8) divides, (9) special features, (10) examples. (*b*) What is a peneplane? Why are old rivers so hard to find? What evidence is there that rivers ever reach old age?

34. Explain what happens to a river and its valley when the region through which it flows is (*a*) raised, (*b*) lowered.

GENERAL QUESTIONS

1. Why should the Niagara River upstream from Niagara Falls have less eroding power than downstream, even where it flows at equal speeds?

2. The rock layers of Niagara are not perfectly horizontal, but dip into the earth toward Niagara's source. How will continued recession change the height of Niagara Falls? Explain.

3. Under what conditions may a river be able to build a delta along an open sea coast?

4. Can a tributary form a delta in its main stream? Explain.

5. Alluvial fans are made of more permeable sediments near the mountains than farther away. Why?

6. Why is a meandering river like the Rio Grande a very unsatisfactory boundary between the United States and Mexico?

7. What is the rate of discharge of a brook with a width of 10 feet, an average depth of 1 foot, and a rate of flow of 2 feet per second?

8. In flood time the brook (in Question 7) averages 5 feet in depth, 20 feet in width, and moves at a rate of 9 feet per second. How many times as much water does it discharge in a given time as in Question 7?

STUDENT ACTIVITIES

1. Make a plasticene model of a canyon, a water gap, a meandering river and its flood plain, an entrenched meander, a waterfall, a delta, an alluvial fan, or any other feature described in this chapter.

2. Make a series of models showing the development of (*a*) an oxbow lake, (*b*) a wind gap through stream piracy.

3. Take a field trip to observe the features of a stream valley in your vicinity and the activities of the stream.

4. Observe the formation of small gullies, alluvial fans, etc. in local parks, etc. after a heavy rainfall.

TOPOGRAPHIC SHEETS

(15-minute series)

1. *Canyon:* Bright Angel, Arizona.
2. *Waterfalls:* Niagara Gorge, New York.
3. *Alluvial fans:* Cucamonga, California.
4. *Meanders and flood plain:* St. Louis, Missouri.
5. *Natura levees and flood plain:* Donaldsonville, Louisiana.
6. *Delta and distributaries:* East Delta, Louisiana.
7. *Young valley:* Fargo, North Dakota.
8. *Mature valley:* Charleston, West Virginia.
9. *Water gaps:* Harrisburg, Pennsylvania.
10. *Stream piracy:* Kaaterskill, New York.
11. *Entrenched meander:* Rural Valley, Pennsylvania.

CHAPTER 11
Glaciers

HOW DO YOU KNOW THAT . . . ?

1. Glaciers form from snow that accumulates in mountain regions above the snow line. To see how ice can form from snow, take a handful of snow or crushed ice and squeeze it between your hands. Repeat the process. Is the "snow" still "snow"? Is it still a granular mass? Explain any changes that occurred.

2. Set up an inclined plane with a pan at one end. At the upper end, place an ice cube. Carefully adjust the slope of the plane until the ice cube just begins to slide slowly down the slope. Repeat the procedure. As the ice cube melts does it slide more easily? Why?

1. The Problem of the Strange Boulders

Geologists tell us that continental ice sheets, like those in Greenland and Antarctica, covered nearly all of Canada and much of northern United States until about 11,000 years ago. They tell us that this "Ice Age" probably lasted about a million years. We accept these statements because they are backed up by sound scientific evidence. But the concept of an Ice Age was not generally accepted by geologists until the middle of the last century.

In the early 1800's geologists noted that many rock outcrops in northern regions had polished and scratched surfaces unlike those of more southern regions. Giant boulders were different from the bedrock on which they rested and could sometimes be traced to outcrops many miles north and even from mountain tops. Pebbles and other mixed deposits of sediments were strange to the locality in many places. Geologists agreed that these features could not be explained by stream action. Many geologists, particularly the British, believed all this had happened in one great flood. The flood waters had carried the boulders, scoured the bedrock, and deposited the mixed sediments over a wide area. Because water had transported the "foreign" materials, the British called all such material **drift,** a name still in use.

Meanwhile, however, another explanation was coming into existence. Students of glaciers in the Alps saw how bedrock becomes marked by glacial erosion, and how boulders and transported soils are carried downslope. When they found these features miles down the valley from the glacier front or high above the glacier on the valley walls, they reasoned that the glacier had been longer and thicker not so long ago. A number of imaginative geologists then applied this reasoning to the "drift" that covered so much of northern Europe, and offered the radical idea of an Ice Age in which great ice sheets had covered the drift areas.

This new concept was not unopposed. The man who is given the major credit for its acceptance is the famous Swiss naturalist, Agassiz (*ag* ah see), who did extensive research to prove his theory and worked hard to publicize it.

ORIGIN, TYPES, AND OCCURRENCE

2. What Is a Glacier?

Imagine a steep young valley high in the Alps of Switzerland. But no narrow river runs in a thin stream at the bottom of this valley. Instead, the entire valley floor is covered with a thick mass of snow-clad ice. This mass of ice extends completely across the valley and hundreds of feet up the valley walls. It can be followed up the valley for miles to a source in vast fields of ice and snow just below the very highest peaks. Careful observation reveals that it is moving downhill at the rate of several feet a day. Followed down the valley, it thins out and suddenly ends. Milky water runs out from beneath the ice and flows down the now-open valley. This long, slow-moving, wedge-shaped stream of ice is a **valley glacier**. (See Figs. 11-1 and 11-8.)

Imagine a great land mass in the polar latitudes of the far north or south. The climate is so cold that only snow falls. For thousands of years snows have been falling, accumulating, and changing to ice. Almost the entire land mass, thousands upon thousands of square miles of lowland, hill, valley, and mountain, is covered by a thick mass of ice through which only the highest mountain peaks protrude. The ice is thousands of feet thick, and it moves outward from the center in all directions—north, south, east, and west—toward the sea coasts. In some places it reaches the sea through low valleys, and great chunks of ice break off to float away as icebergs. This moving mass of ice, far larger than a valley glacier, is called an **ice sheet.** (See Figs. 11-6 and 11-22.)

3. The Line of Perpetual Snow

Glaciers are born in regions of perpetual snow. These are regions where each year more snow falls than melts, and some is always left over to add to the accumulations of previous years. Climates cold enough to produce such conditions may occur in any part of the world, because air temperatures grow colder with increasing height above sea level, as well as with

Fig. 11-1. The Great Aletsch Glacier seen from Jungfraujoch in the Swiss Alps.

Southern Pacific Photo

Fig. 11-2. Snow line on Mount Shasta, California. Shasta is 14,162 feet high.

increased distance from the Equator. Even in equatorial regions, then, perpetual snows may occur on high mountains; farther from the Equator the mountains need not be as high; in the polar regions perpetual snows may exist even at sea level. The lowest level to which the perpetual snows reach in summer is called the **snow line.** A mountain that is completely covered with snow in winter, but from which the snows are all gone by summer, has no snow line. (See Figs. 11-2 and 11-3.)

The snow line is highest near the Equator and lowest near the poles. As climates become colder with increasing latitude (distance from the Equator), less altitude is needed to reach a snow line. The position of the snow line also varies with such factors as the total yearly snowfall and the amount of exposure to the sun. Thus no exact height can be given for each latitude. Going from the Equator through South America, Central America, and North America to the North Pole, the snow line drops with increasing latitude approximately as follows: Andes Mountains at the Equator, 18,000 feet or 3½ miles; Mexico,

15,000 feet; Sierra Nevada and Rocky Mountains in the United States, 13,000 to 9,000 feet; southern Greenland (60° N), 2,000 feet; North Pole, sea level (there is no land at the North Pole, but there is a great land mass at the South Pole).

4. Birth of a Glacier

Except for its bare rock cliffs, the entire mass of a mountain above the snow line is

Fig. 11-3. This diagram shows how the height of the snow line varies with latitude. The higher the latitude, the lower the snow line.

almost completely buried in its accumulated snows. Great basins and depressions below the highest peaks are filled with snows reaching hundreds of feet in thickness. In these vast *snow fields,* which in warmer climates might hold the waters of mountain lakes, the freshly fallen snows melt and freeze and become compressed until they are transformed into a rough granular icy material called **névé** (nay vay) or **firn.** (See Figs. 11-4, 11-5.)

The granules of firn are no larger than fine buckshot, and the firn is like the ice of old spring snow or a packed snowball. As the thickness of the firn increases, air is squeezed out from between the granules in the lower layers of the snow field, and solid ice is formed. When this ice begins to flow downward or outward because of the weight of the overlying firn and snow, it has become a glacier. A **glacier** may be defined as a mass of ice, formed on land from snow, that moves on land under the pull of gravity. It may move down a mountain valley, or outward in all directions over a continental land mass.

5. Where Valley Glaciers Occur

Although there are many types of glaciers, the two principal types are those described in Topic 2. **Valley glaciers** were first studied in the Alps and are also known as **alpine** or **mountain glaciers.** They occur in all parts of the world where mountains extend above the snow line. In other words, they occur wherever there is sufficient *altitude.* With the exception of Australia, every continent has mountains that reach above the snow line. The higher the mountain extends above the snow line, the larger its glaciers are likely to be.

Valley glaciers range in length from one to two miles up to 75 miles; in width from fractions of a mile to several miles; and in thickness to more than a thousand feet. Valley glaciers attain

Fig. 11-4. Sketch showing the origin and movement of a valley glacier.

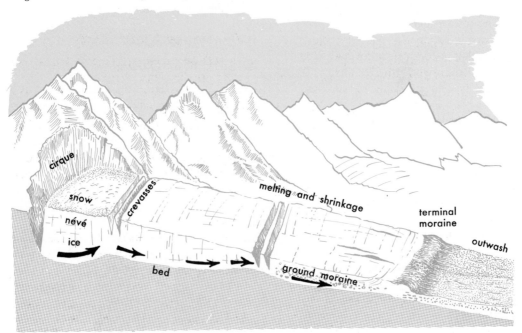

Fig. 11-5. Snow fields, firn, and glaciers high in the Swiss Alps above Zermatt. Here the glaciers reach almost to the tops of their valley walls. The sharp divides that separate adjacent glacial valleys are called arêtes. See Topic 10.

their greatest size in southern Alaska, where mountains with a snow line at 5,000 feet extend to heights above 20,000 feet. Western United States has many small glaciers in the Sierra Nevadas, the Rockies, and the Cascade Mountains, with glaciers being featured as scenic attractions in Glacier National Park in Montana and Mt. Rainier National Park in Washington. There are no glaciers in the United States east of the Rockies.

Notable systems of valley glaciers also occur in the Alps and the Caucasus Mountains of Europe, the Andes of South America, the Southern Alps of New Zealand, and the Himalayas of Asia. Where two or more valley glaciers merge at the base of a mountain—like merging alluvial fans—a **piedmont glacier,** like the Malaspina Glacier of Alaska is formed.

6. Where Ice Sheets Occur

Ice sheets owe their existence to *latitude* so high (close to the North Pole or South Pole) that the snow line is close to sea level and extensive areas are above the snow line. Whereas valley glaciers are long and narrow, ice sheets are roughly circular or oval in shape. Small ice sheets called **ice caps** exist in Iceland, Baffin Island, Spitzbergen, and other large islands of the Arctic Ocean. An ice cap may have a long dimension of about 100 miles and an area of several thousand square miles.

The vastly larger ice sheets of Greenland and Antarctica are **continental glaciers.** The Greenland glacier is about 650,000 square miles in area and thousands of feet in average thickness. It covers all of Greenland except a small coastal strip. The Antarctic glacier covers a far larger

United States Antarctic Service

Fig. 11-6. Surface of the Antarctic ice sheet seen from the air at an altitude of about 9,500 feet above sea level near Mount Sidley.

land mass with an area of about 5 million square miles. Here the ice reaches a maximum thickness of nearly 3 miles! Along the coast it may extend more than 5,000 feet below the level of the sea. In the interior great mountain peaks called **nunataks** project through the ice at heights of 17,000 feet above sea level. The earth's South Pole lies under the Antarctic glacier at a point where the ice is about 8,000 feet thick. (See Fig. 11-6.)

Slightly more than 10 per cent of the earth's land surface, nearly 6 million square miles, is covered by glaciers today. Of this total, continental glaciers cover all but about 5 per cent.

GLACIER MOVEMENT

7. How Glaciers Move

Geologists have studied the movement of glaciers by driving rows of stakes into the ice from one side of the valley to the other, marking their location and then observing their positions at regular intervals. From such observations they learn that small valley glaciers may move only a few inches a day, whereas parts of the Greenland glacier may move as rapidly as 100 feet a day. They learn that glaciers move more rapidly in the center than at the sides where friction with the valley walls holds them back. They see that glaciers move faster after winters of heavy snowfall, faster on steep slopes than on gentle ones, and faster in summer.

Gravity causes glaciers to move, but the exact manner of motion is not yet known. One explanation involves the melting of the bottom ice under pressure, its rolling forward a bit as water, then its refreezing. Another explanation is that the ice, at depths of more than about 100 feet, flows like wax under pressure. Still another suggestion is that layers of ice slide or are pushed over each other.

Observations show that the upper ice of a glacier, approximately 100 to 200 feet in thickness, is brittle. Beneath this brittle layer the pressure of the overlying ice makes the lower ice plastic. In the "brittle zone" the ice cracks wherever it moves faster in one part than in another. The cracks, called *crevasses*, may extend across the whole width of a glacier in gaps many feet wide and more than a hundred feet deep, closing up under pressure as they approach the bottom of the ice. (See Figs. 11-4 and 11-7.) Crevasses may form across the glacier because of irregular motion of the ice around a curve or on a steep slope. Lengthwise crevasses may form when a valley glacier spreads out like an alluvial fan at the open end of a steep mountain valley.

8. How Far Glaciers Move

Moving out of their feeding grounds in the upper snow fields, the glaciers flow slowly downhill. Here and there tributary glaciers, like tributary rivers, move in from side valleys to add bulk to the main ice stream. In general, however, the glacier shrinks steadily because of melting and evaporation as it moves into lower, warmer altitudes. *As long as the ice moves faster than it melts, the glacier continues to advance.* Most glaciers extend miles beyond the snow line to a level thousands of feet below it. Finally the glacier reaches its lowest limit at the level *where the ice melts as fast as it moves.* Here the glacier comes to an end (see Figs. 11-4 and 11-8). In Switzerland it is not at all unusual for this *snout* or *ice front* to reach almost into streets of the Alpine villages.

The glacier itself always moves forward, but as long as the rates of movement and melting are equal, the ice front will be *stationary*. After a winter of heavy snows the glacier may move faster than normal, advancing beyond its usual limit. In very warm summers, on the other hand, it may melt faster than normal, and the ice front will recede or move back.

In regions like Alaska and Greenland, where the snow line is close to sea level, many glaciers reach the sea. Even at sea level they do not melt as fast as they move, and as they extend into the water, great blocks break off to become icebergs. This is called **calving.** In Antarctica, where the snow line is at sea level, the ice sheet reaches the coast line everywhere. In a number of places it extends beyond the coast far into the sea in vast **ice shelves.** The largest of these, the Ross Ice Shelf, is hundreds of miles wide and nearly 1,000 feet thick at its margins. The icebergs that break off from an ice shelf are tremendous. At least one such iceberg was 40 miles long.

Fig. 11-7. A crevasse in Coleman Glacier on Mount Baker, Washington.

U.S. Forest Service

Fig. 11-8. The front of Norris Glacier, Alaska, extends far below the snow line.

9. Glaciers Transport Loose Rock

Like rivers, glaciers remove loose rock from the valleys through which they move. All rock material carried by a glacier is called **moraine** (moh *rayn*). There seems to be almost no limit to the size and amount of material carried by a glacier. Particles ranging in size from fine *rock flour* to giant boulders are picked up by the glacier from its valley floor, or fall into it from the valley walls. Additional material may be brought to it by tributary glaciers.

Rock flour is a mixture of fine sand and silt formed by the crushing of rock under the glacier. It is usually rich in angular fragments of feldspar. The meltwater pouring out of a glacier is likely to be filled with suspended rock flour. This gives it a milky gray color and the name of *glacial milk*. The similarity of rock flour to loess (Chapter 9, Topic 10) has led geologists to believe that the loess of northern United States and Europe originated as rock flour in the glaciers of

Fig. 11-9. The origin and position of ground, lateral, and medial moraines.

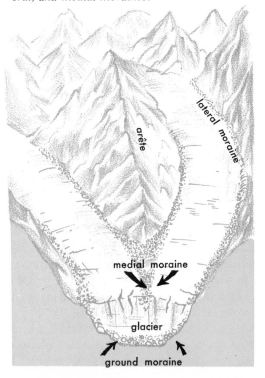

the Ice Age. Meltwater from these glaciers poured great quantities of rock flour into the Mississippi, the Missouri, and other rivers. When the rivers overflowed, the rock flour was deposited on the flood plains. In dry seasons, winds blew the rock flour away in dust storms that carried the material to its present locations.

Large accumulations of rock fragments frozen into the bottom of the glacier are known as the **ground moraine** (see Figs. 11-4 and 11-9). The two long lines of rock fragments that pile up along the valley margins of the glacier are called **lateral (side) moraines.** When two glaciers merge to form a single larger glacier, their inside lateral moraines move together in the middle of the new glacier to form a **medial (middle) moraine** (see Figs. 11-9 and 11-10). At the ice front, rock fragments brought forward by the glacier's motion accumulate as the ice melts, and pile up as a **terminal (end) moraine,** which may grow very large if the ice front is stationary for a long time. (See Figs. 11-4, 11-17, and 11-20.)

10. Glaciers Leave Their Mark

Glaciers, like winds and rivers, erode the bedrock largely through the use of rock fragments as cutting tools. These fragments, frozen into the bottom ice and subjected to enormous pressure, are dragged over the bedrock by the forward movement of the glacier. Particles of fine sand, acting like sandpaper, *smooth and polish* the bedrock. Coarse sand, pebbles, and sharp boulders leave long parallel scratches called **striations** which plainly show the general direction of ice movement. If the bedrock is especially soft, pebbles and small boulders may dig in so deeply as to leave long parallel *grooves*. The pebbles and boulders show signs of wear, too, becoming faceted (flattened) and scratched by the harder

Fig. 11-10. Medial moraines formed by the union of lateral moraines, Franklin Glacier, British Columbia.

Royal Canadian Air Force

Fig. 11-11. The striated, grooved, and polished rock wall of an ancient glacier's valley. Glacier Creek, Flathead National Forest, Montana.

U.S. Forest Service

minerals in the bedrock over which they are dragged. (See Figs. 11-11 and 11-12.)

Fig. 11-12. A glacial boulder flattened, polished, and striated from being dragged under the glacier.

U.S. Geological Survey

11. Shaping the Bedrock

Glacial erosion shapes the bedrock into many new forms. Outcrops of bedrock become smooth and polished on the side from which the glacier comes, but the opposite side may be left steep and rough where the glacier freezes onto and plucks away loose blocks of rock. Such outcrops are called **roches moutonnées** (rosh moo toe *nay*), meaning sheep rocks, because they suggest resting sheep. **Potholes,** like those formed in river beds, are ground out beneath glaciers in whirlpools formed by meltwater falling into crevasses.

Frost action and glacial erosion combine to wear back the rock walls of the mountain peak against which the head of the glacier rests and to transform them into towering cliffs. The enlarged, deepened semi-circular basin thus formed at the head of the glacial valley is called a **cirque** (serk). (See Figs. 11-4, 11-5, and 11-13.)

When two adjacent cirques are formed on a peak, the divide between them may become extremely narrow and sharp. It is then called an

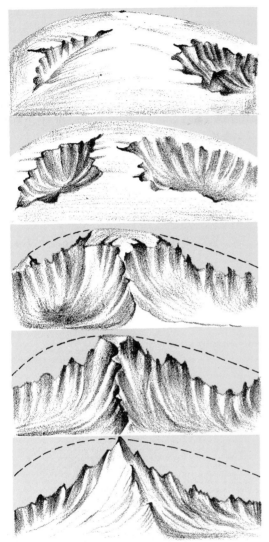

After W. M. Davis

Fig. 11-13. Starting at the top, this series of dia-grams shows how the growth of cirques in an alpine region leads to the formation of arêtes and a horn.

arête (ah *ret*) or knife-edge ridge (see Figs. 11-5, 11-9, and 11-13). Continued erosion of the arête may form a gap or pass in it called a **col.** When three or more cirques cut into the same mountain peak, it may be cut away so much that a spectacular pyramid-shaped peak is left. Such peaks are called **horns** or **matterhorns** after the famous Matterhorn in Switzerland (see Figs. 11-13 and 11-14).

12. Glacial Valleys Can Be Recognized

A river is in direct contact with only a small part of its valley floor. A valley glacier, on the other hand, is in contact with the entire valley floor and a large part of the valley walls as well. As it moves through its valley, the valley glacier scours away the rock until it flattens the entire valley floor and makes the valley walls nearly vertical. The result is a **glacial trough**—a glacial valley that is roughly U-shaped up to the point on the valley walls reached by the ice. Just as an arête may form between two cirques, so may an arête form if the divide between two glacial troughs is eroded until it forms a knife-edge ridge.

Main valley glaciers are usually much thicker than their tributary glaciers and erode their valleys much more powerfully. In regions from which warmer climates have caused glaciers to

Fig. 11-14. The famous Matterhorn of Switzerland, seen from Lake Riffel.

Swiss National Travel Office

disappear, the main valleys are found to be eroded to much greater depths than their tributary valleys, which end abruptly high on the cliff-like walls of the main glacial trough. The tributary U-shaped valleys are called **hanging troughs,** and the rivers which now run in them form **hanging-trough waterfalls** as they plunge over the cliffs into the main river below. Glacial troughs, hanging troughs, and hanging trough falls are common in all glaciated mountains. Two famous hanging trough falls are Yosemite Falls and Bridal Veil Falls in Yosemite National Park, California. (See Figs. 10-16, 11-15, and 11-16.)

13. Alpine Topography

The term **alpine topography** indicates the features resulting from erosion of a mountain region by valley glaciers. Such topography includes the many features described earlier and is quite different from the topography of mountains eroded only by rivers. The steep walls of glacial troughs and cirques produce knife-edge ridges and horns that cannot be seen in river-eroded regions. The entire alpine scene, even if its snows and glaciers have long since disappeared, is one of sharpness and angularity that is in marked contrast to the rounded slopes of water-worn regions. Alpine topography can be seen not only where alpine glaciers exist today but also in regions subjected to glacial erosion within recent geological time.

14. What Continental Glaciers Do

Like alpine glaciers, continental glaciers remove loose rock and soil, smooth and striate and groove bedrock, form roches moutonnées, and leave potholes. But their erosion of mountain

Fig. 11-15. Sketch showing a main glacial trough and hanging troughs after glaciers have disappeared.

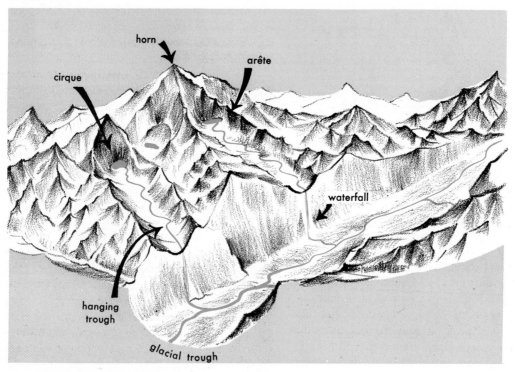

Yosemite Park Co.

Fig. 11-16. Bridal Veil Falls drops from its hanging trough into the Merced River in Yosemite National Park, California. Above it an exfoliation dome towers.

regions differs from that of alpine glaciers in several respects. A continental glacier deepens and widens only those valleys that run parallel to its direction of motion. Since it often covers even the mountain tops, it grinds down the peaks and leaves them polished and rounded, rather than sharpened as in alpine regions. In general, the topography of a region eroded by a continental glacier is considerably gentler than alpine topography.

DIRECT DEPOSITS BY GLACIERS

15. How Was It Deposited?

Much of the rock material carried by glaciers, like that carried by winds and rivers, is deposited on the land. Changes in velocity have practically no effect on the carrying power of a glacier, and its deposits are made almost entirely as a result

of its melting. All glacial deposits are known as **drift.**

Drift is divided into two classes. Deposits made directly by the glacier when it melts are called **till.** All till deposits are *unstratified,* because the morainal materials simply pile up on top of each other as the ice melts. Deposits made by streams of glacial meltwater underneath the ice or at the ice front are called **fluvio-glacial** (*flowing glacial*) deposits. Since these are made by running water, they are sorted and *stratified* like river deposits into gravels, sands, and silts.

16. Glaciers Leave Moraines

When a glacier melts, it leaves its moraines in nearly the same positions as they occupied in the glacier. The *ground moraine* forms a thin, fairly even deposit over the entire area occupied by the ice. *Lateral* and *medial* moraines form ridges running approximately in the direction of glacial movement. The *terminal moraine,* usually the thickest and most conspicuous of the moraines, forms a ridge all along the ice front, marking the farthest position reached by the advance of the glacier. The longer the ice front stays in one place, the larger the terminal moraine becomes. When a receding ice front stops in new positions for any length of time, new "terminal" moraines are formed behind the principal one. These moraines are called *recessional moraines.*

Since even a "stationary" ice front moves back and forth slightly with the seasons, terminal moraine deposits are spread over a fairly broad belt in front of a glacier. For this reason, as well as because no two parts of the ice front deposit exactly the same amount of material, terminal and recessional moraines are likely to consist of a series of irregular hills and hollows rather than a single straight ridge. Terminal moraines of continental glaciers may be hundreds of miles long, miles wide, and hundreds of feet high. The Harbor Hill and Ronkonkoma moraines are responsible for most of the hilly topography of northern

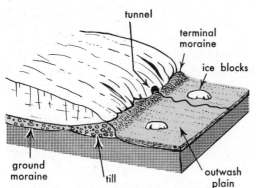

Fig. 11-17. Part of the front of a continental glacier, showing its moraine and outwash.

Long Island in New York. (See Figs. 11-17, 11-20, and 11-22.)

The materials of the moraines are boulders, pebbles, sands, rock flour, and clays, mixed in widely varying proportions, and always unstratified. Large glacial boulders are called **erratics,** indicating that they are different from the underlying bedrock. In regions of continental glaciation erratics weighing many tons may be found resting on mountain tops hundreds of miles from their place of origin. The melting of glaciers may let down giant erratics so gently that they remain delicately balanced in unstable positions, where they are known as **perched boulders** or **rocking stones.** (See Fig. 11-18.)

17. Drumlins

Drumlins are long, smooth, oval-shaped hills composed of till. They usually occur in swarms of hundreds of drumlins, all of which are more or less parallel to each other and pointing in the direction of glacier movement. A drumlin has the shape of an inverted canoe, with its steep end facing the direction from which the glacier came. Drumlins usually range in length from a quarter-mile to a half-mile, in height from 50 to 100 feet, and in width up to a few hundred feet. (See Figs. 11-19 and 11-20.)

The problem of drumlin origin is still unsolved. According to one theory they are formed when an advancing glacier overruns previous moraine deposits, sweeping the ground moraine into long strips or ridges. Another theory suggests that they were formed by deposition of sediment in lengthwise glacial crevasses. Drumlin swarms occur in southeastern Wisconsin, in New

Fig. 11-18. This "glacial table" forms because the boulder protects the ice beneath it from melting. When the boulder finally comes to rest on the bedrock at the ice front, it may be an erratic.

Swiss National Travel Office

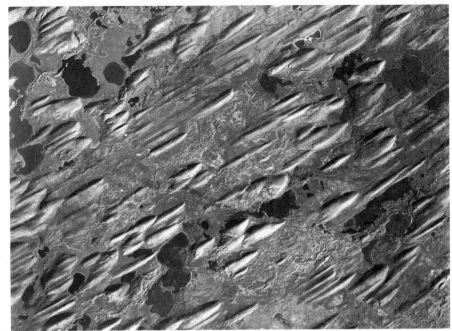

National Air Photo Library, Canada

Fig. 11-19. Drumlin swarm in northern Saskatchewan. Small discontinuous eskers wind among the drumlins.

York State south of Lake Ontario, and in the vicinity of Boston, Massachusetts. In other parts of glaciated United States, however, they are comparatively rare. Bunker Hill in Boston, near the site of the famous battle of the Revolution, is a drumlin. Drumlin swarms also are found in central Canada.

FLUVIO-GLACIAL OR INDIRECT DEPOSITS

18. Outwash Plains

The water from the melted ice of a glacier pours out at the ice front, over and through the terminal moraine, in streams filled with rock flour, sand, and gravel. Dropping the coarse gravels and sands first, while carrying the finer silts and clays much farther, these streams form gently sloping deposits that may extend for miles beyond the terminal moraine. The deposits resemble alluvial fans, and in front of large glaciers they merge to form broad, relatively flat areas called **outwash plains.** (See Figs. 11-17 and

11-20.) Like terminal moraines, outwash plains may parallel the ice front for hundreds of miles. A great outwash plain on Long Island runs southward from the terminal moraine to the sea, forming the level sandy southern half of Long Island for its entire length of almost 140 miles. Good examples of outwash plains are found in the prairies of Wisconsin. Where only a single stream emerges from a valley glacier, it may drop its deposits for miles along the valley floor down which it runs. Such a deposit of glacial sediment

Fig. 11-20. Depositional features left by a continental glacier that has melted away. See Fig. 11-17.

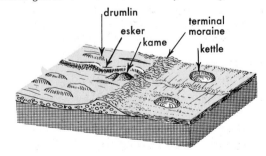

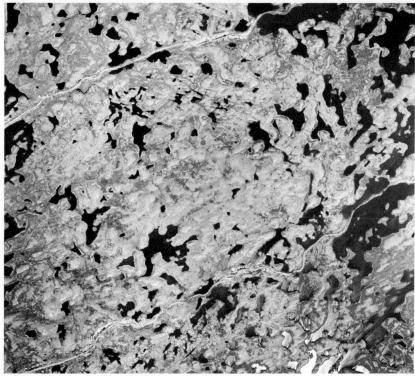

Fig. 11-21. Two nearly parallel eskers can be seen stretching across hummocky morainal topography in north central Canada.

is called a **valley train** (see Fig. 11-8). In both outwash plains and valley trains the sediments are stratified since they are deposited by running water.

19. Winding Hills Called Eskers

Much of the water of a melting glacier falls to the bottom of the ice through crevasses, forming *subglacial streams* which run in tunnels beneath the ice until they emerge at the ice front. The winding tunnels of these streams become partly filled with layer upon layer of roughly stratified sands and gravel. When the glacier disappears, the deposits slump down at the sides and are left as winding sand-and-gravel ridges called **eskers** (see Figs. 11-17, 11-20, and 11-21.)

Eskers resemble railroad embankments in appearance, with side slopes of about 30 degrees and with fairly level but narrow tops. The usual esker is about a mile long and anywhere from a few yards to a few hundred feet wide at its base. However, there are some unusual eskers over a hundred miles long. The height of an esker is in proportion to its width, rarely exceeding a hundred feet. In the United States, eskers are found especially in the glaciated states of the Mississippi Valley, the north central states, central New York, and Maine. Eskers often run in a direction roughly parallel to the direction of ice movement.

20. Kames, Kettles, and Deltas

Kames (kayms) are small cone-shaped hills of stratified sand and gravel. They are formed when streams from the surface of the glacier deposit their sediments in heaps at the ice-front margins of the glacier or at the bottom of circular "wells" (depressions) in the glacier itself. Kames may occur as parts of terminal moraines or in the areas between the moraines and the level outwash plains. (See Fig. 11-20.)

Where kames occur in groups, the depressions between them are called **kettles.** The term kettle or kettle hole is also applied to circular depressions found on terminal moraines and outwash plains. Kettles are formed when moraine or outwash deposits surround and bury large blocks of ice left by slight glacial recession. When the blocks melt, they leave the kettle holes (see Figs. 11-17 and 11-20).

Long, narrow kamelike deposits sometimes form terraces between the side of a glacier and the valley wall. These are called **kame terraces.**

When glacial streams empty into lakes at or beyond the ice front, **deltas** are formed. These consist largely of layers of gravel and coarse sands. Fine sands and clays may be spread evenly over the entire lake floor.

21. Lakes Made By Glaciers

Glaciation of a region usually results in the formation of many new basins or depressions in the land surface. If these basins are permanently filled with water, they form lakes, ponds, or swamps, depending on how large and deep they are. Three important types of lakes resulting from glaciation are *cirque lakes, kettle lakes,* and *moraine-dammed lakes.*

Cirque lakes are formed when water fills the rock-floored cirque basins left by alpine glaciers that have disappeared. Alpine glaciers may scoop out additional rock basins in soft rock areas below the cirques. Lakes in such basins are called **rock-basin lakes.** Cirque lakes and rock-basin lakes are also called **tarns.** Two famous examples are Lake Louise in the Canadian Rockies and Iceberg Lake in Glacier National Park.

Kettle lakes form in large numbers in the kettle holes of moraines and outwash plains. Small kettle holes may contain ponds or swamps.

Lakes, ponds, and swamps of this type are common in Minnesota, Wisconsin, New York, and New England. Lake Ronkonkoma, a kettle lake, is the largest lake on Long Island.

Moraine-dammed lakes are formed where river valleys are blocked by glacial moraines that prevent the flow of the river. In rising to the height of the moraine dam, the river floods its valley to form a long, usually narrow lake. Many of the larger lakes of northern United States originated in this way. Examples are Lake George in New York and Long Lake in Maine.

In many cases lakes were formed by a combination of glacial erosion and deposition which scoured out river valleys before damming them. The Finger Lakes of central New York State—Lakes Seneca, Cayuga, Canandaigua, and others—were formed by glacial deposits that dammed up the northern ends of glacier-scoured parallel north-south river valleys. Many of their former tributary valleys were left as hanging troughs high above the main troughs. One such hanging trough has since been eroded to form famous Watkins Glen. From another trough Taughannock Falls drops more than 200 feet. These lakes are called Finger Lakes because of their long narrow shape. The Great Lakes have a more complicated history, but they, too, occupy river valleys which were deepened and then dammed by glacial moraines.

THE ICE AGE

22. How It Happened

A million years ago it was as cold in much of northern North America and northern Europe as it is today in Greenland. Great ice sheets moved down from central and eastern Canada and northern Scandinavia. In North America the ice sheets extended about as far south as the present location of the Ohio and Missouri rivers and to central Long Island. Much of northcentral and northeastern United States was covered by ice.

In Europe the ice sheets covered most of Scandinavia, the British Isles, Denmark, Belgium, northern France, and the Baltic countries, and extended far into Germany and Russia.

In North America there were three areas in which the snow and ice were thickest, and from which the ice radiated out in all directions. The three **centers of accumulation** were the **Labrador center** east of Hudson Bay, the **Keewatin center** west of Hudson Bay, and the **Cordilleran center** in the Canadian Rockies. From the Labrador center came the ice that covered eastern Canada and northeastern United States; from Keewatin came the ice that covered central Canada and northcentral United States. Joining in northcentral United States, these two ice sheets somehow failed to cover part of the state of Wisconsin (Fig. 11-22). This area, about as large as New Jersey, is called the **Driftless Area.** The Cordilleran ice sheet covered the Canadian Rockies

Fig. 11-22. Areas shown in white were covered by ice sheets during the Ice Age. The uncovered Driftless Area of Wisconsin can be seen south of Lake Superior.

Fig. 11-23. At this stage the Great Lakes drained into the Atlantic Ocean through the Mohawk and Hudson rivers.

down to their foothills, but did not move south. Valley glaciers in the mountains of western United States were far larger than they are today.

The ice sheets advanced and receded four times during the past million years as the climate changed from cold to warm and back again. Geologists now believe that the last recession took place about 11,000 years ago, and many think we may now be in a warm or **interglacial period** which will be followed by a return of the ice sheets in perhaps 50,000 years. Others think that this warm period will last millions of years.

23. How The Great Lakes Were Formed

The Great Lakes were formed during the closing stages of the Ice Age. As the continental ice sheet receded from northern United States, it exposed a number of broad north-sloping river valleys. Since the ice front blocked the northward drainage of these valleys, they filled up with the waters from the melting glacier and became lakes. The farther north the glacier receded, the larger the lakes became. The lakes became so full that they overflowed southward, draining through the Illinois and Wabash rivers into the Mississippi, and through it into the Gulf of Mexico. As the recession of the ice sheet continued, many changes in the size and shape of the Great Lakes took place. With these changes came new points of overflow, and at one time the lakes drained eastward into the Mohawk River in New York State. The Mohawk flowed into the Hudson River, and thus glacial drainage went into the Atlantic Ocean. Then came the last stage. The ice sheet receded so far north that the St. Lawrence Valley was uncovered. This new outlet was lower than the Mohawk outlet. As the waters of the Great Lakes poured out through the St. Lawrence outlet, the old Mohawk outlet was left high and dry, while the Great Lakes shrank somewhat from their previous maximum size. With the final disappearance of the ice sheets, the north-flowing valleys into which the lakes had been poured were left permanently blocked by moraine deposits. And this is how they stand today—a chain of five great lakes, draining northeastward through the St. Lawrence River into the Gulf of St. Lawrence, just as they did at the close of the Ice Age.

Three stages of Great Lakes drainage have been described above: a southward drainage through the Mississippi River, an eastward-southward drainage through the Mohawk and Hudson rivers, and the present northeastward drainage through the St. Lawrence River. These are simply three of the most easily described highlights of the very complicated history of the Great Lakes.

24. Evidence of the Ice Age

Proof of the occurrence of an Ice Age is supplied by the many glacial features described in the preceding paragraphs. The southernmost extent of the ice sheets is marked by their terminal moraines. One of the most notable of these is the Long Island moraine that extends almost 140 miles from Brooklyn to Montauk Point, which it forms. Terminal moraines may also be seen running from New Jersey through Pennsylvania, Ohio, Indiana, Illinois, and westward to Puget Sound. South of the terminal moraine, outwash plains occur in many places.

U.S. Forest Service

Fig. 11-24. Glacial lakes in Superior National Forest, Minnesota, formed during the Ice Age. An old moraine, now fully forested, separates the two large lakes in the foreground.

Almost all of the United States and Canada north of the moraines is covered by a mantle of transported drift or glacial material. Glacial erratics are so numerous in the ground moraine soils of New England as to make cultivation exceedingly difficult. When removed by farmers, they were used to make the stone fences so typical of New England. Exposed bedrock is *striated, grooved,* and *polished,* even on mountain tops; north-south valleys are shaped into glacial troughs and east-west valleys are partly filled with drift. Kames, eskers, drumlins, and recessional moraines are found in many parts of the glaciated area. Numerous glacial lakes and swamps dot the landscape, greatly contrasting with the general absence of lakes in unglaciated areas south of the terminal moraine. Extinct glacial lakes have left dried-out lake bottoms, while lakes like the Great Lakes have left old shorelines and beaches from which we may read the history of their development. Rivers, blocked by glacial deposits and turned into new channels, have entered upon a new cycle of erosion and are young again. Some, like the Niagara, have dug out gorges in the short period since the close of the Ice Age.

In the Rockies and the Sierra Nevadas the proof of the existence of much larger glaciers during the Ice Age is shown by the glacial markings found high upon the valley walls. (See Fig. 11-11.)

25. Causes of Glacial Climates

The geologist who attempts to explain why the earth was cold enough to have the recent Ice Age must account for certain facts. He knows that widespread glaciation is a rare event in earth history, other ice ages having occurred only two or three times before in the past 600 million years, and not more recently than 225 million years ago. He knows that this Ice Age began about a million years ago and included four successive advances of the ice sheets. These are named Nebraskan, Kansan, Illinoian, and Wisconsin, in that order, after the states where their deposits were first studied. Each advance covered approximately 30,000 to 100,000 years. The warm interglacial periods were apparently longer, ranging from perhaps 100,000 to 200,000 years. We may now be in an interglacial period. The geologist also knows that during the last Ice Age, glaciers advanced and receded at the same time not only in North America and Europe but also in the Southern Hemisphere.

No satisfactory explanation of glacial climate has yet been offered, and this problem remains one of the great unsolved mysteries of geology. Geologists believe there is no simple explanation, and that the answer lies in a combination of the hypotheses that we now list with their shortcomings:

(1) *North America and Europe were higher, and therefore colder, during the Ice Age.* Increased altitude does make a colder climate. However, our continents would have had to rise and fall four times in the past million years to account for the four advances of the glaciers. Geologists find neither likelihood nor evidence for such occurrences.

(2) *Melting of the Arctic Ocean ice would cause more snow to be precipitated, and glaciers to form, in northern Europe and North America.* This hypothesis was proposed by Ewing and Donn of the Lamont Geophysical Laboratory. One objection is its failure to explain how the great Antarctic glacier was formed without any ocean at the South Pole to provide snow. Another objection is its failure to explain why glaciation would occur simultaneously in both hemispheres.

(3) *Changes in the inclination of the earth's axis and the shape of its orbit might cause colder climates in some parts of the earth.* Changes of this kind do take place over and over again at regular intervals in earth history. However, glaciation has not occurred at these regular intervals. Furthermore, such changes would probably not cause glacial climates in both hemispheres at the same time.

(4) *Volcanic dust, from great volcanic eruptions, reduced the amount of heat received from the sun.* But there is no geological evidence of unusual volcanic activity at times that coincide with glacial advances.

(5) *The amount of heat radiated by the sun varies. At times of minimum radiation, glacial climates may occur.* The sun's radiation does vary by small percentages, but we do not have enough information about the periods (length of time) of these variations to explain glaciation by them.

TOPIC QUESTIONS

Each topic question refers to the topic of the same number within this chapter.

1. (*a*) What were the strange phenomena that geologists of the early 1800's found difficult to explain? (*b*) What explanation was offered by British geologists? (*c*) What explanation was offered by Louis Agassiz?

2. In your own words describe (*a*) a valley glacier, (*b*) a continental glacier.

3. (*a*) Define the snow line and explain its meaning. (*b*) Explain how the snow line varies with latitude and give examples.

4. Describe the origin of a mountain glacier. What is névé or firn?

5. (*a*) Where are valley glaciers generally found? (*b*) How large are valley glaciers? (*c*) Describe the occurrence of valley glaciers in North America and elsewhere.

6. (*a*) Distinguish between ice caps and continental glaciers. Give examples. (*b*) What is a nunatak?

7. (*a*) What has been learned from studies of rows of stakes driven into a glacier? (*b*) How is glacier movement explained? (*c*) Why do crevasses form?

8. (*a*) Why do glaciers reach beyond the snow line? (*b*) What determines how far a glacier can go? (*c*) Explain when the ice front is stationary, advancing, or retreating. (*d*) When do glaciers reach the sea coast? (*e*) How are icebergs formed?

9. (*a*) Describe the kind, amount, and source of material carried by a glacier. (*b*) Explain what ground, lateral, medial, and terminal moraines are. (*c*) What is rock flour?

10. Explain the origin of polished, striated, and grooved bedrock and boulders.

11. Describe the origin of roches moutonnées, potholes, cirques, arêtes, and horns.

12. Describe the shape and origin of glacial troughs, hanging troughs, and hanging-trough waterfalls.

13. Explain what is meant by alpine topography.

14. How does erosion by a continental glacier differ from that done by alpine glaciers?

15. (*a*) Explain the words drift, till, and fluvio-glacial. (*b*) How do till deposits differ from fluvio-glacial deposits?

16. (*a*) Describe the appearance of the moraines of a glacier after they are deposited by the glacier. (*b*) What are recessional moraines? (*c*) Why are terminal moraines usually broad and irregularly hilly? Describe one example. (*d*) What are moraines made of? (*e*) Describe erratics and rocking stones.

17. Describe the shape, size, possible origin, and occurrence of drumlins.

18. (*a*) Describe the origin and structure of an outwash plain. Give an example. (*b*) How is a valley train formed?

19. Describe the origin, appearance, and occurrence of eskers.

20. (*a*) What are kames? How are they formed? (*b*) What are kettles or kettle holes? How are they formed? (*c*) How is a delta formed?

21. (*a*) Name and describe three important types of lakes resulting from glaciation. Give examples. (*b*) What part did glaciers play in the origin of the Finger Lakes? The Great Lakes?

22. (*a*) Describe the origin, centers of accumulation, and extent of the ice sheets in North America during the Ice Age. (*b*) How long did the Ice Age last? Was it continuous? Explain. (*c*) What is the Driftless Area?

23. Describe the origin of the Great Lakes.

24. Classify the evidences of glaciation given in Topic 24, using the two headings of erosion and deposition.

25. Describe any two theories of glacial climates.

GENERAL QUESTIONS

1. How should the total yearly snowfall and the direction in which a mountainside faces affect the position of the snow line?

2. Name five mountain regions in the United States which have no glaciers.

3. Why should glaciers move faster in warm weather than in cold weather?

4. Why should striations and grooves made thousands of years ago still be visible?

5. Many eskers go up and down hills. How is that possible?

6. Moraine-dammed lakes often have many irregular inlets and bays. Why?

7. How do scientists know where the centers of accumulation were during the Ice Age?

8. How did scientists identify the Driftless Area of Wisconsin?

9. After the ice sheet retreated from New England, valley glaciers existed for some time in the White Mountains of New Hampshire. What evidence would show this?

10. Manhattan is just north of Brooklyn in New York City. Why is the glacial soil of Manhattan so much thinner than that of Brooklyn? (Brooklyn is part of Long Island.)

STUDENT ACTIVITIES

1. Make plasticene models of any of the following: a region of alpine glaciers, a glaciated mountain region showing a main trough and hanging troughs, terminal moraine and outwash plain topography, eskers and drumlins.

2. If you live in a glaciated part of the United States, take a field trip to an area in which you can observe some of the features studied in this chapter. If you do not live in a glaciated region, you will have to do your "field tripping" by means of pictures and topographic maps for the time being.

TOPOGRAPHIC SHEETS

(15-minute series)

Alpine Glaciation

1. *Alpine glaciers:* Chief Mountain, Montana: Mt. Rainier, Washington.
2. *Matterhorns, cirques, hanging valleys:* Chief Mountain, Montana; Mt. Whitney, California.
3. *Terminal moraine* (*alpine*): Fremont Park, Wyoming.

Continental Glaciation

1. *Terminal moraine:* Whitewater, Wisconsin.
2. *Terminal moraine, outwash plain:* Brooklyn, New York; Hempstead, New York.
3. *Drumlins:* Palmyra, New York; Oswego, New York; Sun Prairie, Wisconsin.
4. *Eskers:* Passadumkeag, Maine; St. Francis, Minnesota.
5. *Finger Lakes:* New York (Skaneateles, Auburn, Genoa, Canandaigua).
6. *Driftless Area:* Lancaster, Wisconsin.

BIBLIOGRAPHY

Calder, N. *The Restless Earth.* Viking, N.Y., 1972.
Croneis and Krumbein. *Down to Earth.* University of Chicago Press, 1961.
Dyson, J. L. *The World of Ice.* Knopf, N.Y., 1962.
Fenton, C. L. *Giants of Geology.* Doubleday, N.Y., 1960.
Flint, R. F. *Glacial Geology.* Wiley, N.Y., 1971.
Folsom, F. *Exploring American Caves.* Crowell-Collier, N.Y., 1962.
Gamow, G. *Biography of the Earth.* Viking, N.Y., 1959.
Gilluly, et al. *Principles of Geology.* Freeman, San Francisco, 1968.
Leet, L. W. *The World of Geology.* McGraw-Hill, N.Y., 1961.
Leet and Judson. *Physical Geology.* Prentice-Hall, Englewood Cliffs, N.J., 1971.
Longwell and Flint. *Introduction to Physical Geology.* Wiley, N.Y., 1969.
Matthews, W. H. *Geology of Our National Parks.* Natural History Press, N.Y., 1967.
Matthews, W. H. *Introducing the Earth.* Dodd, Mead, N.Y., 1972.
Mather, K. F. *The Earth Beneath Us.* Random House, N.Y., 1964.
Mohr and Sloane. *Celebrated American Caves.* Rutgers University Press, New Brunswick, N.J., 1955.
Sharp, R. P. *Glaciers.* University of Oregon Press, Eugene, Oregon, 1960.
Shelton, J. S. *Geology Illustrated.* Freeman, San Francisco, 1966.
Shimer, J. A. *This Sculptured Earth.* Columbia University Press, N.Y., 1959.
Strahler, A. N. *Physical Geography.* Wiley, N.Y., 1970.
Strahler, A. N. *The Earth Sciences.* Harper and Row, N.Y., 1971.
U.S. Dept. of Agriculture. *Water, 1955 Yearbook; Soil, 1957 Yearbook.* Supt. of Documents, Washington, D.C. 20402.
Wycoff, J. *Story of Geology.* Golden Press, N.Y., 1960.

Unit 3   The Crust is Raised

An island is born! The
photograph shows one of the
volcanic eruptions that created a new island
in the North Atlantic. In the morning of November 14, 1963, a fisherman saw burning in the distance
off the coast of Iceland. Several miles away, an observer
photographed billowing clouds of steam. Great explosions went on
all day. On November 15, scientists discovered a new land mass about
25 feet high. By January 1965, after more than a year of eruptions, the
island named Surtsey was about 500 feet high with a diameter of almost a mile.

Suppose the attack made on the earth's crust from weathering and erosion described in Unit 2 were to go unchecked. Geologists estimate that only 25 million
years would be needed to wear all the continents down to sea level. Why has this
not happened in the billions of years since the earth was formed?

The answer is that the earth's crust is being rebuilt at the same time it is attacked.
A volcanic eruption may be the most dramatic activity building up the earth's
crust. There are others. Continental shelves emerge from the sea to become
coastal plains. Plains rise to become plateaus. Parts of the earth's crust are
crumpled up into new mountains.

Some of these activities, like the slow rise of a continental shelf, take
place quietly and almost unobserved over long periods of times.
Others, like volcanic eruptions and the building of a volcanic
island like Surtsey, are violent and rapid. Volcanoes,
often called "windows to the interior of the earth,"
give earth scientists great opportunities
to study forces that go on beneath the earth's crust.

CHAPTER 12
Diastrophism

HOW DO YOU KNOW THAT . . . ?

Rock layers of mountainous regions may be squeezed and crumpled into great wavelike folds (Topics 4, 5). A simple model may show how this is possible. Use several different colors of plasticene clay to make a "plateau" of four layers of "sedimentary rock." Each layer should be about 1 cm thick, 15 cm long, and 8 cm wide. Gently squeeze the two ends of the plateau toward each other to form an upfold of the rock layers called an *anticline*.

Level out the plasticene layers again. This time squeeze the ends of the plateau to form a downfold of the rock layers called a *syncline*. Repeat the procedure, this time seeing if you can produce both syncline and anticline together, as in Figure 12-5. Any cracks that form at the crest of the anticline or in the trough of the syncline are fractures or joints, like those described in Topic 8.

1. What Is Diastrophism?

Does the solid crust of the earth really move? There are many movements of the crust. All of them—the violent ones that cause earthquakes and the slow ones that go unfelt if not unnoticed—are recognized by the geologist as processes that help to rebuild the crust against the attacks of weathering, mass wasting, and erosion. The geologist calls all movements of the earth's bedrock crust **diastrophism** (dye *ass* troh fizm). These movements may be upward, downward, or sideward. They may be sudden or they may be slow. All of them are part of a process that opposes the leveling of the earth's crust.

2. Evidences of Ancient Diastrophism

The geologist can read evidences of ancient diastrophism in many parts of the earth's crust.

Fig. 12-1. A sea cave on the coast of California, raised high above the sea level at which it was formed many years ago.

U.S. Geological Survey

Throughout the world we find sedimentary beds of marine origin in mountains and plateaus high above sea level. In the Himalaya Mountains such beds reach altitudes over 20,000 feet. The fossils of marine animals, like the corals and the mollusks, tell us that the rocks were formed on the ocean floor. To reach their present elevations, they must have been raised by natural forces. Closer to the sea we find evidence of similar but more recent uplift. Along the California coast, along the coast of Labrador, and at many other locations throughout the world, we find marine shells on raised beaches and terraces, and barnacles on raised sea cliffs and in sea caves. Some of these are now hundreds of feet above the level of the waves that formed them. (See Fig. 12-1.)

Could lowering of sea level, instead of uplift of the land, account for these raised sea coast features? Yes, but then all coastal areas of the world would have been affected to the same height at the same time. Geological evidence shows that this did not happen.

Evidence from the past also tells us that the earth's crust may have moved downward in many parts of the world. Wells drilled hundreds of feet below sea level in coastal regions sometimes encounter soils and peat deposits that could have been formed only at the surface. Submerged river valleys form bays along the coast of Maine, and drowned channels of the Hudson River and the Sacramento River can be traced out to sea in New York Bay and San Francisco Bay, respectively. (See Fig. 12-2.) A drowned forest on the Dogger Banks, 60 feet below sea level in the North Sea, tells us that these Banks were once a part of the land.

These are but a few evidences that the land has risen or fallen in the past.

3. Evidences of Diastrophism in Historical Times

As geologists became aware of evidence pointing to crustal movements in the past, they began to seek evidence of movements taking

Fig. 12-2. *The submerged canyon of the Hudson River is evidence that sinking of the land may have occurred in recent geological time.*

place now or which took place within historical times.

Sudden *rapid crustal movements* were not difficult to find, for such movements often accompany great earthquakes. In the Yakutat Bay earthquake in Alaska in 1899, parts of the coast were found to have been raised 47 feet, while other parts were raised lesser amounts or even lowered. In the San Francisco earthquake of 1906, the rocks of the crust moved laterally (sidewise) along a break in the crust known as a **fault,** and fences and roads crossing the fault were offset as much as 21 feet on opposite sides of the fault. In the Mino-Owari earthquake of 1891 in Japan the rocks were displaced more than 10 feet both vertically and laterally in places along the fault. (See Figs. 12-3 and 12-11.)

Slow movements of the crust required careful measurement. Such measurements were begun more than 150 years ago on the Baltic shores of Sweden, where it has been found that the land is rising out of the sea at a rate up to 4 feet in

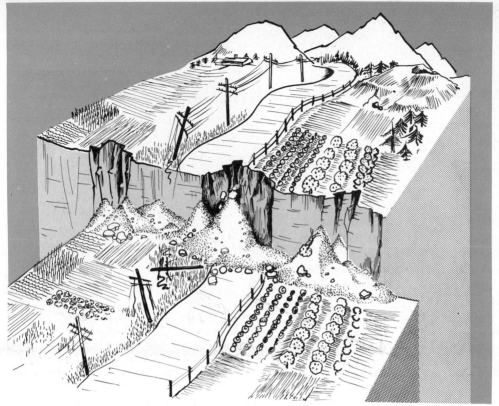

Fig. 12-3. Sketch showing how vertical and horizontal displacement of the crust may take place along a fault in an earthquake.

100 years. Further study by geologists of raised beaches in the northern Baltic shows that the land has risen about 900 feet since the melting of the Ice Age glaciers over 10,000 years ago. Why?

On the coast near Naples, Italy, the famous Temple of Jupiter Serapis gives evidence of both a sinking and a rising of the land since the days of ancient Rome. The three columns of the Temple, from the floor to a height of 18 feet, are marked with the borings of marine clams known as *lithodomi*. Above this height the columns are unmarked. Since the Temple was built on dry land, we infer from the evidence that first the land sank until the Temple was submerged to the depth shown by the borings and that some time later the land moved up to its present level.

4. Evidences of Diastrophism in the Rocks

The effects of movements of the earth's crust can be seen in the rocks themselves. As far back

as 1669 Nicolaus Steno, a Danish scientist, had pointed out that sediments deposited in water form strata that are almost perfectly horizontal. This generalization is known as the Law of Original Horizontality, and it means that unless something has changed their positions, sedimentary beds should be found in horizontal positions. Throughout the world, however, we find exceptions of all degrees. In the Mississippi Valley and the Great Plains, for example, the sedimentary strata slope gently but irregularly in a manner which indicates that diastrophism has *warped* (gently bent or tilted) the rocks of the entire region. A series of domes and basins may result from such warping. In mountain regions like the Appalachians, on the other hand, we find evidence of much more drastic changes produced by diastrophism. Here the sedimentary rocks are found crumpled into wavy **folds** of all sizes and angles. Nowhere are the rocks horizontal, and in places they even stand on end. (See Fig. 12-4.)

Diastrophism produces other kinds of *deformation* of the sedimentary rocks from their

Fig. 12-4. In the Green Mountains of Vermont, rock layers that were originally horizontal have been folded and crumpled by diastrophism.

"original horizontality." In many places the rocks have slipped along faults extending deep into the crust, and rock layers that were originally continuous are now offset at different levels on opposite sides of the fault. In some regions like the Colorado Plateau, the movement has been nearly vertical, so the rocks still retain almost their original horizontality. In the mountains of the Basin Ranges of Nevada and Oregon, on the other hand, the rocks are likely to be tilted as well as faulted.

Now let us look at folds and faults in greater detail.

5. Folds: Anticline, Syncline, Monocline

Folds in rocks may range in size from barely visible crinkles, like those seen in hand specimens of schist, all the way to folds many miles in extent running below the surface of great mountain ranges. Folds appear to have been formed in the

rocks when they were under sufficient lateral pressure to make them plastic.

Folds usually come in series. The arched or upfolded part of the fold is called an **anticline** (*anti,* opposite; *cline,* inclined), which may be remembered by the shape of its first letter, A. The downfolded part of the fold is called a **syncline** (*syn,* together; *cline,* inclined). The sides of a fold are called its **limbs.** In an anticline the limbs slope away from each other. In a syncline they slope toward each other. (See Fig. 12-5.) A **monocline** (*mono,* one) is a fold with only one limb. Above and below the monocline, the beds of rock are still horizontal. (See Fig. 12-6.)

The terms anticline and syncline refer only to the structure of the rocks and not to the surface topography. When first formed, large anticlines will be ridges, and large synclines will be valleys. Such relations are seen in young mountains. In older mountains like the Appalachians the anticlines may underlie valleys, and the synclines may underlie ridges. This more rapid erosion of an anticline may come about because the higher anticlines are more exposed to weathering than synclines, and the weak rocks at their cores are reached sooner.

6. Dip and Strike

The study of rock structures is known as structural geology. The structural geologist studying folds is interested in measuring and mapping the inclination and direction of the rock layers in the fold. He does this in specific terms.

The **dip** of a rock layer is simply its angle of inclination, or the angle it makes with the hori-

zontal. (The compass direction toward which the rock layers dip is the **dip direction.**) The **strike** of the rock layer is the compass direction of a line formed where the rock layer intersects an imaginary horizontal plane. Figure 12-7 shows dip and strike. Both may be illustrated simply by holding a closed book in a tilted position on a table, with the bound edge up at the left. The acute angle between the book and table is the "rock layer's" dip. The direction in which the top of the bound edge points is the strike. Notice that the *direction of the dip* is always at right angles to the strike direction. To illustrate, the bed in Figure 12-7 has a dip of 30° to the east. Its strike is due north.

Dip is easily measured in the field by an instrument called a *clinometer*. Direction is measured with a compass. The "Brunton compass" combines both instruments.

7. Fold Axis and Plunge

Folding of rock layers may be illustrated by holding several sheets of paper in both hands and pushing them together until they fold. The **axis** of your "anticline" is the line at the apex or top of the fold. Similarly, the axis of the syncline is the line that marks the bottom of the syncline. (See Fig. 12-9.)

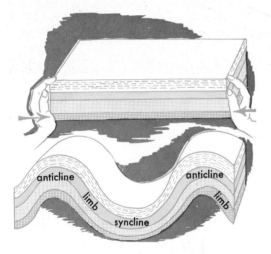

Fig. 12-5. Lateral pressure folds rock layers into anticlines (upfolds) and synclines (downfolds).

Fig. 12-7. Diagram illustrating the meaning of dip and strike.

Fig. 12-6. Rock structure of a monocline.

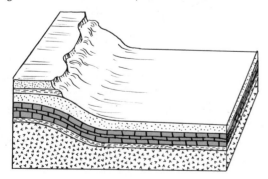

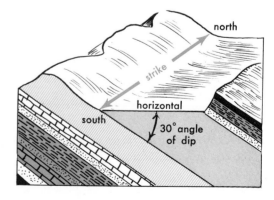

Fig. 12-8. The tilted rocks of the Dakota Hogback near Canyon City, Colorado. Compare with Fig. 12-7.

Darton, U.S. Geological Survey

Anticlines and synclines may have horizontal axes for great distances. In the earth's crust, however, folds must die out eventually—they cannot "float in air," but must come down to earth. At such places the axis of the fold is no longer horizontal, and the fold is said to be a **plunging anticline** or a **plunging syncline.** The angle the axis makes with the horizontal is the **plunge** of the fold. (See Fig. 12-9.)

A **dome** is an oval or circular elevation of rock layers dipping radially away from a central high point. Similarly, a **basin** is an oval or circular depression of rock layers dipping radially toward a central low point.

8. Fractures in Bedrock: Joints

Examination of the bedrock in any exposure shows it to be cut by cracks or **fractures** of all sizes and directions. Some fractures are only fractions of an inch in length. Others may be traced for miles or even hundreds of miles. Further study of the fractures shows that the rocks have slipped or been displaced along some frac-

Fig. 12-9. The features of a plunging anticline. See Topic 7.

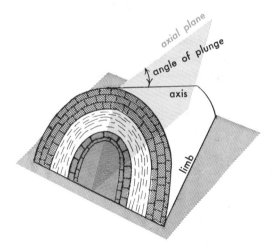

axial plane
angle of plunge
axis
limb

tures, but there has been no rock movement along most. Geologists clasify all fractures as either joints or faults on this basis: A **joint** is a fracture along which no movement of the rocks has taken place. A **fault** is a fracture along which movement of the rocks has taken place.

Russell, U.S. Geological Survey

Fig. 12-10. Highly jointed limestone in a quarry on Drummond Island, Michigan. The joints are nearly at right angles to the bedding planes.

Joints may run vertically, horizontally, diagonally, or along curved surfaces, and they always come in sets in which all the joints are parallel to each other. Vertical joints may develop when hot lava contracts as it cools. Most joints, however, are believed to have formed when the rocks were relieved of the pressure of overlying rocks

(as in Yosemite), or of pressures caused by diastrophism. As explained in Chapter 7, the exfoliation domes of Yosemite National Park are probably the result of "peeling" along curved joints. Such joints are common in granite. Geologically, joints hasten the weathering and erosion of rock, and provide openings for the entry

Fig. 12-11. A normal fault, also called a gravity fault because the hanging wall seems to have slipped downward.

Fig. 12-12. A reverse fault is one in which the hanging wall seems to have moved upward.

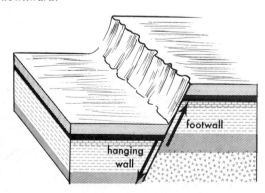

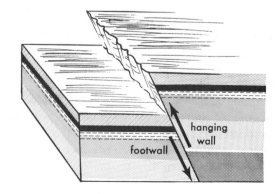

of ground water. Economically, they may be either help or hindrance. Blasting or quarrying is made easier by joints, but closely spaced joints make it difficult to obtain good sized blocks of stone like the blocks of granite and marble used for monuments or sculpture.

9. Fractures in Bedrock: Faults

Faults are believed to result when rocks break under the strain of folding or other pressures involved in diastrophism. Movement of rock masses along a fault is called **faulting.** Faulting is the leading cause of earthquakes. Faulting in a vertical direction can be recognized by offset rock layers at different levels. Lateral faulting —in a horizontal direction—can be recognized by the offset of surface features such as roads and streams.

Faults are classified according to the direction in which the two rock blocks on opposite sides of the fault moved. But first it is necessary to give names to these two masses, and this was done long ago by miners working mineral veins crossing faults. Faults are usually inclined, although close to the vertical. The face of the block that overhangs the fault surface is called the **hanging wall,** regardless of whether it has moved up or slipped down. Similarly, the face of the block below the fault surface is the **footwall.** (See Fig. 12-11.)

Now to return to our classification of faults. A **normal fault** or gravity fault is one in which the hanging wall appears to have slipped downward on the footwall (Figs. 12-11 and 12-13). Relative movement is all the geologist can determine in old faults, for the actual movement may have been up for the footwall, down for the hanging wall, or a combination of both. A **reverse fault** is one in which the hanging wall appears to have moved upward on the footwall (Figs. 12-12 and 12-14). Reverse faults may also be called **thrust faults,** but usually this name is

U. S. Geological Survey

Fig. 12-13. A normal fault in a sandstone formation.

Fig. 12-14. A reverse fault exposed in a road cut.

U.S. Geological Survey, W. H. Monroe

applied only if the dip of the fault (its inclination from the horizontal) is less than 45°.

The **strike of a fault** is simply the compass direction in which it runs. Since horizontal faulting means that the two blocks of rock have slipped or moved along the strike of the fault, such faults are called **strike-slip faults.**

10. Faulting and Land Forms

Faulting, like folding, is unquestionably related to the uplifting of the earth's crust. Though no known fault of recent times has caused elevation greater than 50 feet, there is no doubt that repeated vertical faulting over long periods of time helped to create great plateaus like the Colorado Plateau, or aided in the creation of great mountains like the Sierra Nevadas.

When vertical faulting has just occurred, cliffs called **fault scarps** are formed, rivers flowing over the new scarps form waterfalls, and landslides may occur. However, fault scarps are eventually leveled off by erosion, leaving evidence of the fault only in the offset rock layers. Active strike-slip faults may be marked by depressions resulting from rapid erosion of the broken rock along the fault line.

When hard rocks on opposite sides of a fault rub against each other, highly polished surfaces called **slickensides** are formed.

TOPIC QUESTIONS

Each topic question refers to the topic of the same number within this chapter.

1. Explain what diastrophism is.

2. (*a*) What are some evidences from the past that the earth's crust has been raised? (*b*) What are some evidences that the crust has moved downward?

3. (*a*) Cite evidence of rapid crustal movement in recent times. (*b*) Cite evidence of slow crustal movement in recent times.

4. (*a*) What is the Law of Original Horizontality? (*b*) What evidences in the rocks themselves show that diastrophism has taken place?

5. What is an anticline? a syncline? a monocline? How are anticlines and synclines related to ridges and valleys?

6. What is the dip of a rock layer? the strike? the dip direction? the clinometer?

7. (*a*) What is the axis of an anticline? of a syncline? (*b*) What is a plunging fold? What is "the plunge of the fold"? (*c*) What is a dome? a basin?

8. What are joints in rocks? How do they run? How were they formed?

9. (*a*) What is a fault? How do faults originate? (*b*) Distinguish between the hanging wall and the footwall of a fault. (*c*) Make a simple sketch of a normal fault. (*d*) Make a simple sketch of a reverse fault. (*e*) What is a strike-slip fault?

10. (*a*) What land forms may be produced by faulting? (*b*) What are slickensides?

GENERAL QUESTIONS

Examine the photographs of previous chapters to see which ones show: (*a*) joints, (*b*) "original horizontality," (*c*) tilted rock layers, (*d*) folded rocks. List the photos in each category, giving figure numbers and titles or locations.

STUDENT ACTIVITIES

1. Make plasticene, plaster of Paris, or wooden models of (*a*) a normal fault, (*b*) a reverse fault, (*c*) a strikeslip fault, (*d*) anticlines and synclines, (*e*) a monocline, (*f*) pitching folds, (*g*) a dome, (*h*) a basin.

2. Make a simple clinometer by mounting a protractor on a larger, rectangular piece of cardboard, with the straight edge of the protractor parallel to one of the edges of the rectangle. Fasten a string at the center of the protractor's straight edge, and tie a small weight to the end of the string. When the clinometer is held on a horizontal surface, the plumb line (made by the weighted string) will indicate a reading of 0°, or no dip. When held against a sloping surface, it will give the angle of dip.

3. Use your clinometer to measure the dip angles of any sloping surfaces. If your locality permits it, take a field trip to measure the dip of real rock formations. Observe other rock structures studied in this chapter.

4. Practice using a compass to determine the dip direction and strike of sloping surfaces in your classroom, home, or outdoor vicinity.

CHAPTER 13
Vulcanism

HOW DO YOU KNOW THAT . . . ?

Your teacher can simulate a volcanic eruption for observation. A small evaporating dish is the "crater" of a volcano. Mount it on a tripod or at the top of a plaster model of a volcano. Put two or three heaping teaspoons of granular ammonium bichromate in the dish. Insert a ribbon of magnesium metal into the bichromate as a "fuse." The fuse is ignited with a match or burner flame. The eruption is best observed in a darkened room at a safe distance of 2–3 meters. The bichromate burns to form gases (nitrogen, water vapor) and ashy material (green powdery chromic oxide).

1. Magma and Vulcanism

Molten lavas that erupt from volcanoes have temperatures ranging between 1100°F and 2200°F. What depths do they come from? What is the source of the liquid magma that erupts from volcanoes as lava? Geologists believe that the crust and mantle of the earth are solid. They think, however, that the huge pressures of the overlying rocks prevent the deep rocks from melting even though they are hot enough to melt *at the surface*. Then how do we explain volcanic regions? Geologists think that the hot deep rocks do melt in places where the pressure is relieved by breaks or faults in the crust. But magma may also form in the colder rocks close to the surface. Geologists believe that intense radioactivity or chemical action may produce enough heat in parts of the crust to melt the rock and form "pockets" of magma.

What happens to the magma? The hot molten rock is lighter than the solid rock around it, and it rises toward the surface. The movements of this magma, both inside and outside of the crust, are called **vulcanism** (vul kan ism). In its *extrusive activities,* magma reaches the surface

Fig. 13-1. The contrast between a quiet *volcanic eruption* (*on the left*) *and an* explosive *volcanic eruption* (*on the right*).

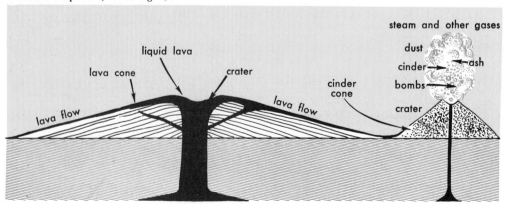

Fig. 13-2. Aerial view of the summit of Mauna Loa, the great Hawaiian volcano. The giant crater at the mountain top is 3 miles in diameter. Note the gentle slopes of this broad lava cone, only a fraction of which appears in the photo.

and erupts from it to form volcanic mountains and volcanic plateaus. In its *intrusive activities,* magma intrudes itself into the crust beneath the surface where it may cause faulting or slow rising of the overlying rock layers. In some cases the mass of intruded rock is so vast that it forms the core of a great mountain range.

EXTRUSIVE ACTIVITIES

2. Quiet Eruption

When hot liquid magma breaks through the earth's crust to emerge as lava, volcanic eruption is said to take place. The eruptions are classified as *quiet* or *effusive* when the liquid lava *flows out* of openings in the crust. When the lava is *blown out* of the crust in a violent explosion, eruptions are said to be *explosive.* (See Figs. 13-1 and 13-2.)

Quiet eruptions are typical of the Hawaiian Islands and Iceland. In the Hawaiian Islands, lava may overflow from circular openings at the tops of mountains, or pour out of small fissures in mountainsides. In Iceland, the lava may flow out along the entire length of narrow fissures miles in length, or it may overflow from a whole series of circular openings located along a single fissure. The liquid lava from these openings flows downhill until it solidifies into **lava rock,** such as basalt, andesite, rhyolite, obsidian, pumice, or scoria. Sometimes the hardened lava may have a rough, jagged surface, probably caused by the escape of large quantities of gases or by movement of liquid lava beneath the surface. Such lava is known in Hawaii as **aa** (pronounced *ah ah*). (See Fig. 13-3.) In other cases the surface of the lava is smooth and ropelike, and is called **pahoehoe** (*pah hoe* ay *hoe* ay). (See Fig. 13-4.) **Lava tunnels** may form temporarily when liquid lava

Fig. 13-3. The rough surface of aa *lava is seen here in the foreground of a lava flow from the volcano Parícutin in Mexico.*

continues to flow beneath a roof formed by the hardened outer lava crust. Such tunnels with lava stalactites hanging from them can be seen in Craters of the Moon National Monument at Arco, Idaho. When lava flows into lakes, swamps, or the ocean, it often solidifies in rounded forms resembling pillows, and is described as **pillow lava.**

3. Explosive Eruption

Explosive eruptions are typical of the East Indies and the Mediterranean region. In these eruptions lava and gases are blown out of the earth in violent explosions that may hurl the hot liquid miles into the air. The lava spray cools and hardens into solid fragments while still in the air. Since these fragments are formed from hot material, they have been named **pyroclastic** (*pyro,* fire; *clastic,* broken) materials. (See Figs. 13-1 and 13-5.)

The tiniest droplets of the lava spray form **volcanic dust** fine enough to be carried thousands of miles in the upper atmosphere before coming down to earth. Larger droplets of lava solidify into fragments comparable in size to silts, sands, and pebbles. These fragments are known as **volcanic cinders** (coarse) and **volcanic ash** (fine), because they are about the size and consistency of cinders and ashes. They do not, however, represent burnt-out materials. Volcanic cinders and ash are heavy enough to fall fairly close to the openings from which they are erupted. Occasional large blobs of lava solidify in the air as rounded or spindle-shaped **volcanic bombs** (so called because of their size and shape, not because of any explosive quality). (See Fig. 13-6.) Large angular lumps of solid lava are called **blocks.** Volcanic ash may become cemented to form a rock called **tuff.**

Explosive eruptions usually shatter great masses of the solid rock through which the eruption occurs. This shattered rock is mixed with

Fig. 13-4. The ropy surface of pahoehoe *lava inside the crater of Kilauea volcano in Hawaii.*

Fig. 13-5 Nuée ardente from Mt. Pelée descending on city of St. Pierre during violent eruption of May 1902.

the erupting lava and gases, adding to the total of dust and cinder produced by the eruption.

4. Gases from Volcanoes

Pumice and scoria form as a result of the hardening of lava while gas bubbles are still present. Lavas contain many different gases, including steam (water vapor), carbon monoxide, carbon dioxide, hydrogen sulfide, hydrogen chloride, and hydrogen fluoride, among others. Some of these gases are poisonous, and all of them are intensely hot as they escape from the lavas during eruption. Great quantities of condensing

Fig. 13-6. A volcanic bomb from the volcano Kilauea in Hawaii.

steam, mixing with fine volcanic dust and ash in an explosive eruption, often form a gigantic dark cloud reaching miles into the air over an erupting volcano.

5. Building a Volcano

Except in fissure eruptions, volcanic eruptions almost always form domes or cones of erupted material, built up around the opening in the earth from which the eruption occurred. The erupted material spreads fairly evenly in all directions from the central opening, with more material piling up near the opening than farther away. As eruption continues, the volcanoes grow until they become hills or mountains. The world's greatest volcano, Mauna Loa in Hawaii, has a circumference of about 400 miles at its base on the floor of the Pacific Ocean, above which it rises to a height of nearly six miles. This great pile represents the accumulations of more than a million years of eruption.

The term volcano refers both to the actual opening in the crust through which eruption takes place and to the pile of volcanic material. Most volcanoes have a cuplike depression at their tops, through which eruptions usually occur. These are called **craters.** Very large craters that are several miles in diameter are called **calderas** (kal *day* rahs).

6. Birth of a Volcano

The development of a new volcano in recent times is illustrated by the Parícutin (pah *ree* koo teen) volcano, which is 200 miles from Mexico City. Early in February, 1943, a series of slight earthquake shocks disturbed the residents in and near the village of Parícutin, a farming community. For weeks the shocks continued, until on February 20 a number of cracks appeared in a perfectly level corn field, hardly more than a mile from the village. Fiercely hot gases escaped into the air, and were soon followed by blasts that shattered the earth and opened outlets through which lava and cinders were ejected. Eruptions and earthquakes continued to rock the area, and in May the volcano became so violent that it was necessary to evacuate the residents for many miles around, lava flows even reaching into the village. By September, 1943, Parícutin's volcano had built a cone-shaped mountain 1,500 feet high and about a mile in diameter! In 1944 a great outpouring of lava flowed more than five miles from the volcano to bury all but the church steeple of the village of San Juan de Parangaricutiro. Parícutin became less active after this, but eight years later, in 1952, it was still pouring out lava at the rate of 200,000 tons a day. Today Parícutin is no longer active, but it will be many years before erosion destroys its cone. (See Fig. 13-4.)

7. Explosive or Quiet?

What determines whether a volcano erupts explosively or quietly? **Explosive eruptions** are believed to occur in volcanoes whose craters are plugged up by the solidification of old lava or in which the magma is so thick that gases cannot escape. Gases accumulate in these volcanoes until the terrific pressure blows out the rock plug with a mighty explosion. Shattered rock, liquid lava spray, great volumes of steam and other gases combine to form a fiercely hot and destructive cloud above the erupting cone. There is practically no flow of liquid lava in an explosive eruption. Volcanoes have been known to erupt so violently as to blast away a large part of their cones. This happened to the volcano Krakatoa in the East Indies in 1883 and to the volcano Katmai in Alaska in 1912.

In **quiet eruptions** very little solid rock is ejected from the volcano. The magma of the quiet volcano is fluid enough to allow the steady escape of dissolved gases, and its broad crater is but thinly covered by solidified lava. Even between eruptions, "lakes" and "fountains" of fiery liquid lava may be seen in some craters. Eruptions occur when internal pressure causes lava to rise in the crater and overflow, or to break through fissures in the sides of the cone. There is little explosion in these eruptions, but the blazing-hot lava destroys everything in its path.

8. Classes of Volcanoes

Volcanoes used to be classified as quiet or explosive according to their type of eruption. But many of the world's great volcanoes erupt in both ways, their eruptions often beginning explosively and being followed by flows of lava. So volcanoes are now classified largely by the materials of which they are made.

Shield volcanoes form domes composed almost entirely of lava, most of which is basalt or, less frequently, andesite. The eruptions of shield volcanoes are largely quiet ones, and their fluid lavas spread like thick syrup to form broad, gently sloping, shield-shaped domes with slopes usually much less than 10°.

Typical shield volcanoes occur in the Hawaiian Islands and in Iceland. Mauna Loa and Kilauea (kee lou *ay* ah), both on the island of Hawaii, are perhaps the most famous of all volcanoes of this type. Mauna Loa's slopes of approximately 6° are so gentle that it is difficult to believe that they are the flanks of a giant volcanic dome rising over 30,000 feet from the ocean floor and almost 14,000 feet above sea level. Its steep-walled, oval-shaped crater is a great caldera about three miles in diameter (Fig. 13-2).

Cinder cones are so called because they are cone shaped, and because they consist largely of cinders and other pyroclastic materials. Small cinder cones are often found growing out of the gently sloping sides of great shield volcanoes, where they are known as **parasitic cones.** Parícutin in Mexico, Sunset Crater in Arizona, and Mono and Amboy craters in California are cinder cones.

In contrast with a shield volcano, a cinder cone is made up largely of materials that do not flow away from the volcano opening, so it is comparatively steep sided and narrow at the base. Its slopes may reach 35°, its diameter about one mile, and its height about 1,500 feet. Cinder cones are usually eroded rapidly because of their loose materials and their steepness, and they never achieve the great size of shield volcanoes.

Composite volcanoes are composed of both lava and pyroclastic materials in alternating layers that correspond with periods of quiet and explosive eruption. The pyroclastic materials are usually erupted from the crater, while the lava is likely to have poured out of fissures in the sides of the volcano. Composite cones are steeper than shield volcanoes but gentler than cinder cones. Their average slope is between 20° and 30°. In general the more lava in the cone, the gentler its slopes and the broader its base. With the exception of the volcanoes of Iceland and Hawaii, most of the world's great volcanoes are composites. Among the best known are Fujiyama in Japan, Vesuvius in Italy, Mayon in the Philippine Islands, Popocatepetl (poh poh kah *tay* pet il) in Mexico, and Rainier in Washington. Mount Shasta, California, is a composite cone on whose flank a parasitic cone called Shastina can be seen. (See Fig. 13-7.)

9. Eruptions from Fissures

Hundreds of thousands of square miles in northwestern United States are covered by layer upon layer of basalts totaling thousands of feet in thickness and forming a high plateau. There are almost no volcanoes in this great Columbia lava plateau, and geologists believe that the layers of basalt were formed by vast **lava floods** that poured repeatedly out of long fissures in the earth's crust in the geologic past. The basalts formed by the lava floods are called **flood basalts** or **plateau basalts.** The rock of the lava beds is always basalt, apparently because only basalt-

Fig. 13-7. Mayon Volcano, a composite cone, is 7916 feet high and about 15 miles in diameter at its base.

American Museum of Natural History

forming magma is fluid enough to spread so widely on the earth's surface before solidifying.

A good example of fissure eruption took place in Iceland as recently as 1783. Numerous fissure eruptions of past ages are believed to have built up the great Deccan plateau of India, the Columbia plateau of northwestern United States, the plateaus of Iceland and northern Ireland, and such smaller lava plateaus as those in Yellowstone National Park. The total amount of material erupted in lava floods is far greater than that erupted by all the world's volcanoes. (See Fig. 14-14.)

10. Is the Volcano Alive?

To indicate the "liveness" of a volcano, the terms "active," "dormant," and "extinct" are used. An **active** volcano is one that erupts occasionally in our own times. A **dormant** (sleeping) volcano is one that has erupted in modern times, but not very recently. An **extinct** volcano is one that has not erupted within historic time. These terms are more or less relative. Now and then a supposedly extinct volcano such as Mount Vesuvius in Italy or Lassen Peak in the United States suddenly becomes active. There is no real security for the people who live in the immediate vicinity of a dormant volcano. Outstanding examples of densely settled volcanic regions are those near Vesuvius in Italy, Etna in Sicily, and Mount Pelée (peh *lay*) on the island of Martinique in the West Indies. All these regions have suffered many disastrous eruptions within historic times.

11. Famous Eruptions

Space does not permit full descriptions of some of the great eruptions of history, but a few interesting highlights can be presented.

Mount Pelée. Three miles from the crater of "dormant" Mount Pelée on the West Indian island of Martinique stood the capital city of St. Pierre. The inhabitants of that city expected no harm from a volcano that had been inactive since 1851. When the volcano showed signs of activity in April of 1902, few of the nearly 30,000 inhabitants paid any attention until it was too late. On May 8 a terrific explosion tore open the crater, and a great fiery cloud (in French, *nuée ardente*) of hot poisonous gases and volcanic fragments swept down upon the city to scorch and smother the entire population. The only survivor was a prisoner in the city jail who apparently owed his life to the poor ventilation of his deep dungeon. (See Fig. 13-5.)

Krakatoa. Krakatoa is a volcanic island in the East Indies between Java and Sumatra. On August 27, 1883, an explosive eruption took place that is usually described as "the most violent eruption of historic times." More than half of the island—over a cubic mile of rock—was destroyed and blown away in the explosion. The cloud over the volcano reached 17 miles into the air. The air wave broke windows 100 miles away, and the sound was heard 2,000 miles off in Australia. Great sea waves flooded nearby coasts, where 36,000 people were drowned, and the waves even reached the shores of South Africa, over 5,000 miles away. The fine volcanic dust from the eruption was carried completely around the world by the winds of the stratosphere. Taking months to drift down to the earth's surface, the dust produced strangely beautiful sunrise and sunset skies throughout a large part of the world for a long time after the eruption.

Mauna Loa. Mauna Loa has been consistently active in recent times, with eruptions occurring irregularly at intervals of about eight years. Between eruptions the great oval caldera, three miles long and two miles wide, is crusted over by basalt rock, underneath which lies hot molten lava. The coming of an eruption is usually foretold by the rise of lava in the crater. Breaking the crust at various points, the white-hot lava spurts up in "fountains" hundreds of feet high.

Before the lava can rise high enough to overflow the crater, it usually breaks through fissures on the volcano's sides. As these fissures split open, earthquakes may occur in the vicinity. The overflowing lava forms streams up to a mile in width and 40 miles in length, sometimes running into the ocean.

Kilauea. Kilauea is the second of Hawaii's active volcanoes. Like Mauna Loa, it is also located on the island of Hawaii. However, its crater is much larger than that of Mauna Loa. (See Figs. 13-4 and 13-6.)

12. Distribution of Volcanoes

Most of the active volcanoes of the world lie in two great belts. Outstanding in the **Circum-Pacific belt,** often called the "ring of fire," are the volcanoes of the Andes Mountains of South America, Central America, Mexico, Alaska, the Aleutian Islands, Japan, the Philippines, Indonesia, and New Zealand. In the **Mediterranean belt** are the volcanoes of the Mediterranean region itself, the Azores, the West Indies, the Hawaiian Islands, and Asia Minor. The volcanoes of Iceland and the Antarctic are in neither of the two great belts. (See Fig. 13-8.)

Fig. 13-8. This map shows the world's principal regions of active volcanoes.

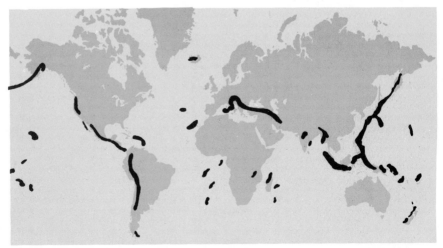

Both volcanoes and earthquakes occur along great fault lines in the earth's crust, in regions where the forces of the earth's interior are most active today in elevating the earth's surface by vulcanism and diastrophism.

13. Volcanoes of North America

Lassen Peak in Lassen Volcanic National Park, California, was thought to be extinct until

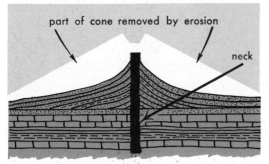

Fig. 13-9. *The origin of a volcanic neck.*

Fig. 13-10. *A volcanic neck in the Mount Taylor region of New Mexico.*

Dutton, U.S. Geological Survey

1914, when it suddenly became active. Alaska has two great active volcanoes, Katmai and Aniakchak. In 1912 Katmai had an explosive eruption rivaling that of Krakatoa in violence. Mexico has three great volcanoes which rank among the highest mountains in North America. The best known of these is Popocatepetl (17,887 feet); the other two are Orizaba (18,700 feet) and Ixtaccihuatl (17,343 feet).

There are many great cones of recently extinct volcanoes in the United States, including Mount Rainier (14,408 feet) in Washington, Mount Shasta (14,162 feet) in California, Mount Hood (11,225 feet) in Oregon, and San Francisco Mountain (12,794 feet) in Arizona.

14. Life History of a Volcanic Cone

The life history of a volcanic cone portrays in miniature the struggle that goes on all over the earth between the constructional forces of the earth's interior and the destructional forces of weathering and erosion. No sooner does a volcanic cone come into existence than it is attacked by weathering and erosion. Weathering and erosion work steadily and ceaselessly, while the building of the cone can occur only during eruptions. In *youth* the *active* volcano builds its cone faster than it is eroded, and the cone grows tall

Fig. 13-11. *The origin of a caldera like that occupied by Crater Lake. (See Fig. 13-12.)*

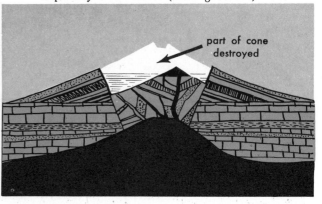

Fig. 13-12. Crater Lake occupies a caldera formed by the collapse of the crater floor of a prehistoric volcano that geologists call Mt. Mazama.

and symmetrical (evenly shaped). When the volcano becomes *extinct,* weathering and erosion soon wear gullies and valleys into its once-smooth slopes, and the volcanic cone is said to be *in maturity.* As erosion continues, it usually wears away the lava and ash layers more rapidly than the hard plug of intrusive rock below the crater. In time this plug may be left standing high above the remnants of the slopes of the volcano in *old age.* (See Fig. 13-9.) The plug is also known as a **volcanic neck.**

The necks of old volcanoes may be seen in western United States as spectacular, steep-walled masses of dark rock projecting from the landscape. (See Fig. 13-10.) The 1,300-feet high Shiprock in New Mexico is a famous example of a volcanic neck. Other necks occur in the Mount Taylor region of New Mexico, and at Mount Royal in Montreal, Canada. Volcanic necks also form the diamond-bearing rock of the great Kimberley mines of South Africa. Devil's Tower in Wyoming is thought by some geologists to be a volcanic neck. Others think it is a remnant of a lava flow or *laccolith.* (See Topic 18.)

15. Lakes in Craters

Rain and melting snows partly fill the craters of some extinct volcanoes to form **crater lakes.** In a few cases the craters have been tremendously enlarged into calderas, either by violent explosions that blew off the top of the volcano (as at Mount Katmai in Alaska) or by sinking of the top of the volcano into the lava below its crater floor (as in the Hawaiian volcanoes). (See Fig. 13-11.) Crater Lake in Crater Lake National Park, Oregon, lies in a caldera which was probably formed by one or the other of these processes. The caldera is nearly six miles in diameter. Its clifflike walls rise in places more than 2,000 feet above the surface of the lake, which reaches a maximum depth of 1,932 feet. Crater Lake is the second deepest lake in North America. A small cone, apparently formed after the destruction of the volcano top, rises from the crater floor as a small island in the lake. It is called Wizard Island. (See Fig. 13-12.) A hiking trail leads from its shoreline to the rim of its 300-foot-wide crater.

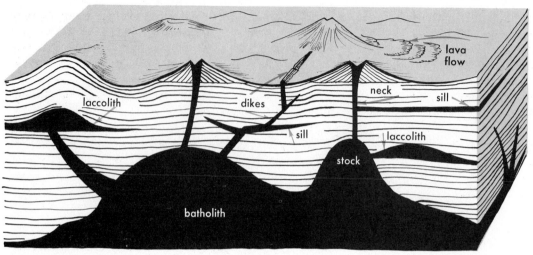

Fig. 13-13. Diagram showing the kinds of rock masses formed by vulcanism.

INTRUSIVE ACTIVITIES

Volcanoes and lava flows represent features produced by the extrusive activities of vulcanism, in which magmas penetrate the earth's crust and solidify on its exterior. But by far the greater part of the magma is engaged in intrusive activities, forcing its way into fractures or between rock layers, raising overlying rocks, and solidifying into masses of igneous rock in a variety of shapes and a wide range of sizes, all of them known as igneous intrusions. When erosion removes over-lying rock, igneous intrusions are revealed. (See Fig. 13-13.)

16. Dikes

Dikes are masses of igneous rock that cut *across* the structure of the rock into which they intrude. They appear to have been formed by the solidification of magma that was forced into existing fractures in the rocks. Dikes are *tabular* in shape. That is, they are actually *flat sheets of*

Fig. 13-14. This great dike radiates northward from West Spanish Peak, Colorado, where it has been exposed by more rapid erosion of the sedimentary rocks into which it intruded.

rock standing vertically within masses of other rock. Dikes range in thickness from inches to hundreds of feet, and in length up to many miles. Most dikes are made of basalt or diabase. Dikes may be stronger than the rocks they cut. If they are stronger, erosion will leave them projecting like walls from the surrounding rock. Excellent examples of such dikes radiate from the Spanish Peaks in Colorado. Dikes in the bed of the Yellowstone River are responsible for the formation of Yellowstone Falls, as explained in Chapter 10. (See Figs. 13-13 and 13-14.)

17. Sills

In contrast to dikes which cut *across* rock structures, **sills** are tabular igneous intrusions that are *parallel* to the layers of the stratified rocks they intrude. They were formed when magma was forced along bedding planes between rock layers. (Sills can be distinguished from buried lava flows by the fact that their heat has baked the rock both *above and below* them, whereas lava flows can only have baked the *underlying rock*.) Like dikes, sills usually consist of basalt or diabase, and they may be hundreds of feet thick and miles in length. (See Figs. 13-13 and 13-15.) When a river cuts through the rock

of a region in which a sill is buried, the sill may be exposed to view between the sedimentary layers into which it was intruded. In such a case the igneous rock of the sill may form the steepest part of the valley wall. It was in this manner that the cliffs known as the Palisades of the Hudson River in New York and New Jersey were exposed. The Palisades represent the face of a great diabase sill hundreds of feet thick and 30 miles long. Talus from the Palisades collects at its base and covers the sandstone layers that dip gently away from the Hudson beneath the diabase rock of the sill. (See Fig. 7-1.)

18. Laccoliths

Laccoliths (*lacco,* lake; *lith,* stone) are large mushroom-shaped igneous intrusions formed, like sills, between layers of stratified rock. The rocks of laccoliths are usually granite or diorite. Granite and diorite are formed from stiffer, less fluid magmas than basalt. This leads geologists to believe that laccoliths form when stiff magmas, unable to flow far between the rock layers into which they are intruded, push up the overlying rocks into oval domes. It used to be thought that all laccoliths were fed by magma coming from a "pipe" underneath the laccolith, as shown at the

Fig. 13-15. Sill of dark igneous rock intruded between ancient sedimentary rocks in Banks Island, northwestern Canada.

Darton, U.S. Geological Survey

Fig. 13-16. Bear Butte, South Dakota, is a laccolith exposed by erosion.

Fig. 13-17. Three great batholiths of western North America.

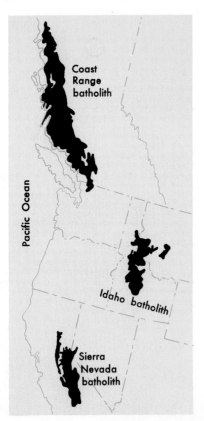

left in Figure 13-13. This would make laccoliths mushroom-shaped. However, recent studies in the Henry Mountains of Utah show that laccoliths there were fed by magma coming laterally from larger intrusions called *stocks*. (See Topic 19 and Fig. 13-13.) Such laccoliths would have no "stems." Groups of laccoliths, each up to several miles in diameter and thousands of feet thick, can be seen partly exposed by erosion in the Henry and La Sal Mountains of southeastern Utah. Laccoliths are also found in the Bearpaw and Little Rocky Mountains of Montana, and in the Black Hills of South Dakota. (See Fig. 13-16.)

19. Batholiths and Stocks

What is the source of the magmas that intrude rocks to form dikes, sills, and laccoliths? Geologists believe that these intrusive streams come from enormous reservoirs of magma located beneath the intrusions in the crust. Eventually the reservoirs also solidify to form the largest of all intrusive masses, the **batholiths** (*batho,* deep; *lith,* stone). Batholiths are usually composed of granite or granodiorite, and they form the cores of most of the world's great folded mountain ranges, where they may appear exposed by the erosion of overlying rock layers. Unlike laccoliths, batholiths seem to have no "bottom," broadening as they go deeper into the crust, insofar as direct observation is possible.

The dimensions of batholiths are usually long and narrow, like the mountains whose cores they form. The largest batholith in North America is the great *Coast Range batholith* of British Columbia. It is more than 1,000 miles long and from 20 to 150 miles in width. The *Sierra Ne-* *vada batholith* in California is about 400 miles long and up to 70 miles wide. The *Idaho batholith,* in the Rocky Mountains of Central Idaho, is even larger. (See Figs. 13-13 and 13-17.)

Stocks are formations similar to batholiths, but smaller. Geologists use the name "stock" if the exposed surface area of the intrusion is less than 40 square miles. Stocks are believed to be connected with underlying batholiths, and are also thought to have been reservoirs that fed magma to dikes, sills, and laccoliths. (See Fig. 13-13.) Like batholiths, stocks are usually granite or granodiorite.

TOPIC QUESTIONS

Each topic question refers to the topic of the same number within this chapter.

1. (*a*) Under what conditions does magma form in the earth's crust? (*b*) What does the liquid magma do in these places? (*c*) Define vulcanism. (*d*) Compare extrusive and intrusive vulcanism.

2. (*a*) Distinguish between quiet and explosive volcanic eruption. (*b*) What kinds of rock are formed by quiet eruption? (*c*) What is aa lava? pahoehoe lava? pillow lava? (*d*) Where do quiet eruptions occur?

3. (*a*) Where do explosive eruptions occur? (*b*) What are pyroclastic materials? (*c*) What is volcanic dust? ash? cinders? a volcanic bomb? tuff?

4. (*a*) What gases are erupted by volcanoes? (*b*) How are pumice and scoria formed? (*c*) What makes up the cloud above an erupting volcano?

5. (*a*) Explain how a volcano forms a mountain. (*b*) Make a simple labeled sketch showing the parts of a volcano? (*c*) What is a caldera?

6. Give a brief history of the volcano Parícutin.

7. (*a*) Why do explosive eruptions occur? (*b*) Why do quiet eruptions occur?

8. Describe the composition, shape, eruption, and locations of (*a*) shield volcanoes, (*b*) cinder cones, (*c*) composite volcanoes.

9. (*a*) How was the Columbia lava plateau formed? (*b*) Why is the rock of a lava bed always basalt? (*c*) Locate other plateaus.

10. What is meant by the terms "active," "dormant," and "extinct" as applied to volcanoes?

11. Describe some highlights of the famous eruptions of Mount Pelée and Krakatoa.

12. Locate the two great volcano belts.

13. (*a*) Name an active volcano in California, in Alaska, and in Mexico. (*b*) Locate three great extinct volcanoes in western United States.

14. (*a*) Give a brief description of the life history of a volcanic cone. (*b*) Give examples of volcanic necks.

15. (*a*) What is a crater lake? (*b*) How do craters become calderas? (Also see Topic 5.)

16. What is a dike? What is "tabular" shape? How large are dikes? Of what rock are they made?

17. (*a*) How do sills differ from dikes? (*b*) How do sills resemble dikes? (*c*) How were the Palisades of the Hudson River formed? (*d*) How can a sill be distinguished from a buried lava flow?

18. What are laccoliths? What rock are they made of? How are they formed?

19. (*a*) What is a batholith? Of what rocks are batholiths made? Locate some batholiths. (*b*) What is a stock?

GENERAL QUESTIONS

1. In the Hawaiian volcanoes lava breaks through fissures far more often than it overflows from the craters. How does this effect the shape of the volcanoes? Explain.

2. How is it possible for glaciers to exist on the slopes of an active volcano?

3. What evidence tells us that dikes and sills were not formed at the same time as the rocks in which they occur?

4. In what ways would the eruption of a volcano under water differ from an eruption on land?

5. Topic 17 mentions one way of distinguishing between a sill and a buried lava flow. Can you suggest any others?

6. How do laccoliths differ from sills?

STUDENT ACTIVITIES

1. Make plasticene or plaster of Paris models of (*a*) a shield volcano, (*b*) a cinder cone, (*c*) a composite cone, (*d*) a volcanic neck, (*e*) a crater lake, (*f*) dikes, sills, laccoliths, and other igneous intrusions.

2. If you live near enough to any features resulting from vulcanism, take a field trip to study these features.

3. Visit a museum or college geology department to study specimens of pyroclastic rocks such as volcanic dust, cinder, tuff, and bombs. Also look for specimens of aa, pahoehoe, and pillow lavas.

4. Construct profiles (as suggested in Chapter 6, Topic 14) from one of the topographic sheets listed below.

TOPOGRAPHIC SHEETS

(15-minute series, except as noted)

1. *Young volcano:* Lassen Volcanic National Park, California.

2. *Mature volcano:* Shasta, California.

3. *Mature volcano:* Dunsmuir, California (30-minute series).

4. *Volcanic neck and dikes:* Shiprock, New Mexico.

5. *Laccolith:* Fort Meade, South Dakota (Bear Butte; 7½-minute series).

CHAPTER 14

Mountains, Plateaus, and Plains

HOW DO YOU KNOW THAT . . . ?

One theory of how mountains are formed is the convection hypothesis (Topic 5). Set up this model of the convection process. Fill a large Pyrex beaker with cold water. Add some sawdust or grated blotting paper to the water and wait until it settles to the bottom. Heat the water over a small, narrow-tipped flame (Bunsen burner, alcohol lamp) that just touches the center of the beaker. Observe the convection currents produced by the heating. The sawdust particles will help you see the directions in which the currents move.

MOUNTAINS

1. Introduction: Mountains and Plateaus

Diastrophism and vulcanism create the elevated portions of the earth's crust called mountains and plateaus. Both mountains and plateaus stand high above at least part of their surroundings. Their relief—the vertical distance between the highest and lowest point—is measured in thousands of feet. But the geologist distinguishes between mountains and plateaus on the basis of their rock structure. **Plateaus** are regions of horizontal or nearly *horizontal rock structure*. **Mountains** are regions of disturbed or *distorted rock structure,* often underlain or penetrated by igneous intrusions. Mountains may also consist of individual volcanic peaks or of chains of volcanoes. In Chapter 12 we studied the structures that give evidence of the work of diastrophism in folding and faulting the rocks. In Chapter 13 we studied the activities of vulcanism in elevating the crust. How did the forces of diastrophism and vulcanism combine to build the mountains and plateaus of the earth's surface?

2. Problem of Mountain Origin

The origin of mountains is one of the great unsolved problems of geology. Attempting to "solve" this problem, geologists put together all the facts and observations at their disposal and from them try to reconstruct the past. What are some of these important facts about mountains?

First, every great mountain range in the world appears to include folded, faulted, and tilted beds of sedimentary rocks which are largely of shallow-water marine origin. On measuring the total thickness of these beds, geologists have estimated that in every case they represent an original thickness, before folding, of at least 30,000 feet. Second, many of the great mountain ranges border or lie parallel to the ocean margins of the continents. Third, every great mountain range appears to have a massive core of granite or other igneous rocks underlying its sedimentary layers.

From consideration of these facts and others, geologists today believe that all of the great mountain ranges were developed by much the same process. Let us describe this process.

3. Geosynclines and Mountain Origin

From the evidence described in the preceding topic, geologists concluded that at least 30,000 feet of sediments must accumulate before folding, faulting, and tilting take place to elevate the sedimentary rocks into mountains. But since almost all of the sediments are relatively shallow-water deposits (sandstone, shale, limestone) of marine origin, geologists reason that they must be deposited in great shallow ocean basins bordering the continents or in shallow inland seas. From the nature of the sediments and their fossils, it is reasoned that the basins cannot be more than about 1,000 feet deep. How, then, can sediments 30,000 to 50,000 feet in thickness accumulate in them? This can happen by having the floor of the basin slowly subside (sink) at a rate roughly equal to the rate at which sediments are deposited by rivers and other agents of erosion, so that the basin is never more than about 1,000 feet deep. Such a basin, in which slow subsidence permits sediments to accumulate in thicknesses of many thousands of feet, is a **geosyncline** (jee oh *sin* kline). It may be more than a thousand miles long and hundreds of miles wide. (See Fig. 14-1.)

When the thickness of sediment reaches at least 30,000 feet, something happens that causes the sediments to be crumpled and folded by horizontal compression, and mountain growth begins. Geologists do not know the cause of this compression, but they do have ideas about it, some of which will be described shortly.

The forces of horizontal compression have many effects. The whole geosyncline is squeezed together, shortened, and elevated. Great anticlines and synclines are produced. Faulting takes place, especially at the edges of the geosyncline, where great mountain blocks are forced upward but away from the center in gigantic thrust faults. Between the thrust faults the remainder of the elevated geosyncline forms a high plateau or smaller mountain masses of folded and faulted rocks. (See Figs. 14-3c and d.)

While compression is raising the geosyncline, hot magma enters the lower strata of the geosyncline to form the granite cores and other intrusions which may later be exposed by erosion. The magma helps the forces of horizontal compression to change many of the sedimentary rocks into metamorphic ones. Magma may also reach the surface and erupt in the form of volcanoes or lava flows. Fractures, including joints and all nor-

Fig. 14-1. A geosyncline is a great shallow basin which subsides slowly while sediments accumulate in it to thicknesses of thousands of feet.

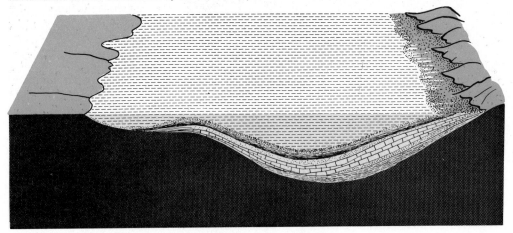

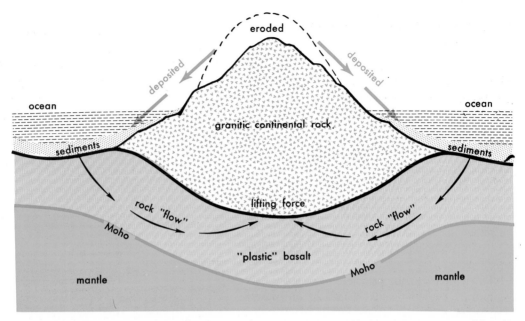

Fig. 14-2. According to the theory of isostasy, continental masses are supported by the underlying basalt. When erosion takes place, sediments from the continents are deposited on the floors of geosynclines. The added weight makes the geosynclines sink, whereas the continental masses rise because they have become lighter.

mal faults, may develop in the folded rocks when compression ends and the rocks are relieved of the squeezing pressures.

How long does the process described above take? Estimates differ, but certainly many millions of years are required.

4. Why Geosynclines Subside; Isostasy

To support the geosynclinal origin of mountains, geologists must explain what causes the floor of the geosyncline to subside. Without subsidence only 1,000 feet of sediments could be accommodated. Geologists believe that the *principle of isostasy* can explain a subsidence of several thousand feet. The rest of the subsidence must be accounted for by horizontal compression. First let us see what **isostasy** (eye *soss* tuh see) is. Incidentally, *iso* means *equal; stasy* means *standing.*

You will recall that in Chapter 1, Topic 6, the crust of the earth was described. The description told us that the granite rocks of the continents are underlain by somewhat heavier basalts. According to the theory of isostasy, the continents do not rest *on top* of the basalt. Instead, they *float* deep in the basalt like icebergs floating in water, with much of their mass submerged below the surface of the basalt. (The basalt acts like a plastic or fluid at great depths because of the tremendous weight of the continental blocks.) Where mountains are seen on the surface of the continents, there must be long thick "roots" of rock extending deep into the plastic basalt. Where the continents are lower in elevation, as in regions of plains and plateaus, the granite masses do not sink as deep into the plastic basalt. (See Fig. 14-2.)

Now how does isostasy explain the subsidence of the geosyncline? As erosion of a continent occurs, sediments are carried from the continent to the ocean, where they are deposited in the geosyncline. The net result is to make the continent lighter and the geosyncline heavier. The added weight on the floor of the geosyncline makes it subside and also increases its pressure on the underlying basalt. Since the basalt behaves like a plastic material, the increased pressure is transmitted through it. This produces a lifting force that raises the now-lighter continent, though not enough to compensate for the height lost by erosion. How long can this adjustment continue? Geologists calculate that a geosyncline originally 1,000 feet deep will sink about 1,500 feet while becoming filled with sediments up to sea level. But for further subsidence, we must find other explanations.

To summarize: the principle of isostasy tells us that 1) the continents "float" in the basalt layer of the crust; 2) mountain masses are thicker than lowland masses and have deeper roots into the basalt; 3) areas which lose weight by erosion will rise; areas which gain weight by deposition will subside. *Movements caused by isostasy are vertical, not horizontal.*

An interesting case of rising land that is attributed to isostasy is the case of the Baltic shores mentioned in Chapter 12, Topic 3. This area was covered by continental glaciers during the Ice Age, and the weight of the ice caused the land to sink deep into the underlying basalt. When the ice melted away, about 10,000 years ago, the land began a slow rise that will continue until it reaches its proper "floating" level. According to measurements this region has risen about 900 feet since the Ice Age ended. Similar rises have been determined in the Great Lakes region of the United States and Canada.

Now let us see what hypotheses have been advanced to account for further subsidence of geosynclines and for the horizontal compression that makes the crust fold and fault into mountains.

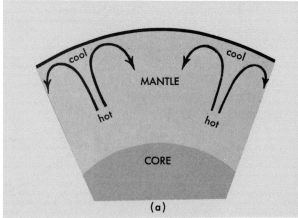

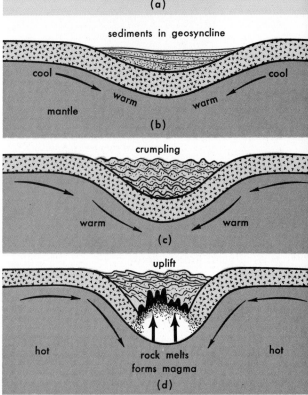

Fig. 14-3. Four stages in mountain building, according to the convection hypothesis.

5. Hypotheses of Mountain Building

The **convection hypothesis** supposes that pairs of great convection currents move slowly upward from the hot plastic mantle to the lower crust, then horizontally beneath the crust, and finally downward. The friction between the moving mantle and the crust creates a strong drag on the crust, causing geosynclines to form where the crust is dragged downward, and mountains to form on both sides of the geosyncline where crustal blocks are dragged horizontally and geosynclinal sediments are crumpled together. This hypothesis suggests that magma is formed by the melting of sediments that are forced deep into the hot mantle below the geosyncline. The magma then intrudes into the overlying sediments to form the granite cores of the mountains, as well as smaller intrusions. (See Fig. 14-3.)

There is as yet no proof for the convection hypothesis, and there are objections. One objection, again, is that it offers no explanation of the irregular distribution of the world's mountains. Another is that convection in the mantle seems unlikely. Nevertheless, this hypothesis has many supporters.

The **hypothesis of continental drift** starts out with the idea that the continents of the earth were once a single continent. In 1915 Alfred Wegener, a German physicist, proposed this hypothesis. Wegener was impressed by the striking similarity in outline between the east coast of South America and the west coast of Africa. To explain this "jig-saw puzzle" fit, as well as that of other continental outlines, Wegener suggested that all the present continents began from a single vast *protocontinent* which he called Pangea. Pangea, he said, split up many millions of years ago, and its continent-sized pieces slowly moved apart. North America and South America moved westward, the other continents moved eastward, and the Atlantic Ocean basin opened up between them. (See Fig. 14-4a.)

According to Wegener, the split between America and Europe took place at the Mid-Atlantic Ridge, the great undersea mountain chain that stretches from Iceland almost to Antarctica. (See Chapter 20.) The continents "drifted" apart on the plastic mantle under the earth's crust. As they did so, their leading edges were crumpled and folded into mountains like the Andes in South America and the Coast Ranges of Alaska.

Wegener's picture of drifting continents was an attractive one. First, it solved a global jig-saw puzzle. Then, it also explained why rocks and certain fossils from mountains in South Africa and Argentina—a whole ocean apart—were so much alike. But at the time of Wegener's death in 1930, very few scientists supported his hypothesis. Its critics argued that it failed to provide earth forces strong enough to make a protocontinent break up, drift, and crumple its rocks into mountains. It also failed to account for the origin of mountains in continental interiors, such as the Himalayas in Asia or the Rockies and Appalachians in North America. Wegener had no direct evidence of any continuous movement of the continents. So continental drift remained a curiosity, talked about but not accepted.

By 1969, however, the picture changed dramatically. Geologists discovered strong evidence that movement of the sea floor is taking

Fig. 14 -4a. According to Wegener's hypothesis of continental drift, the protocontinent looked like this about 50 million years ago.

place on both sides of undersea ridges like the Mid-Atlantic Ridge. How? The crest of the Mid-Atlantic Ridge—10,000 miles long—is split by a great depression, or *rift valley,* having many active volcanoes and rock fissures. From time to time hot magma rises from these openings and solidifies into new sea-floor rock on both sides of the ridge. This causes a slow but steady movement of the sea-floor crust away from the ridge. The movement is eastward toward Europe and Africa and westward toward the Americas. Scientists named this movement **sea-floor spreading** and calculated its rate at about one inch a year.

What is the evidence for sea-floor spreading? Measurements of the age of sea-floor rocks show very young rocks closest to the ridges and older rocks farther away. The age measurements also stress the relative newness of the sea-floor rocks. The oldest ones are only about one-tenth as old as the oldest land rocks. Other evidence is the fact that more heat flows out of the earth at the mid-ocean ridges than is normal for other parts of the crust.

Supporting evidence is the variation in magnetic field patterns of sea-floor rocks at varying distances from the ridges. These patterns are formed in the rocks when their magnetic minerals crystallize from the molten state. The rocks become magnetized in a direction parallel to the earth's magnetic field. So they provide evidence of the varying locations of the earth's magnetic poles at the times when the rocks were formed. Each new pattern is contained in two long bands of rock, one on each side of the mid-ocean ridge from which the rock poured out and parallel to it. (See Fig. 14-4b.)

If the sea floor is spreading from its center, what is happening at its continental edges? The answer is far from complete. However, records of deep earthquakes indicate that in many places the ocean crust is moving downward. Here it is being melted or destroyed in great deep ocean *trenches* like those which border the coasts of America and Japan. (See Chapter 20.)

What do these findings mean? Scientists became convinced that a moving earth's crust was a reality. So they revised their concepts of the earth's structure.

A new **hypothesis of plate tectonics** was proposed. This hypothesis explains how mountains grow and why and where earthquakes and volcanic eruptions take place. The word *tectonics* refers to the structure of the earth. The hypothesis of plate tectonics suggests that the entire surface of the earth is covered by a small number of vast blocks or *plates* of lithosphere (rock). The plates are irregular in shape and unequal in size. Six of them—the major plates—cover most of the surface. The irregular spaces between them are filled by smaller *subplates*. The plates are so named because they fit the curved surface of the earth, much as inverted dinner plates might fit the outside of a very large globe.

The six major plates are known as the American, African, Eurasian, Indian-Australian, Pacific, and Antarctic plates. (See Fig. 14-4b.) Unlike the moving masses in Wegener's hypothesis, plates include ocean floor as well as continents. They are much thicker than Wegener's floating continents, and they extend much deeper into the earth's mantle. The American plate, for example, includes a sector of earth "hide" from the Mid-Atlantic Ridge westward all the way to the Pacific Ocean. It is at least 50 miles thick. The eastern half is all sea floor, but the western half carries an "upper deck" of continental crust 15 to 30 miles thick. The Eurasian plate, similarly constructed, extends eastward from the Mid-Atlantic Ridge. But the great Pacific plate is almost all ocean floor.

Plates may move away from each other; they may move toward each other; or they may slide alongside each other. At their boundaries rock crusts may be formed or destroyed, mountains may be created, and earthquakes and volcanic eruptions may occur. The American and Eurasian plates move away from each other at the Mid-Atlantic Ridge. The Eurasian and Indian-

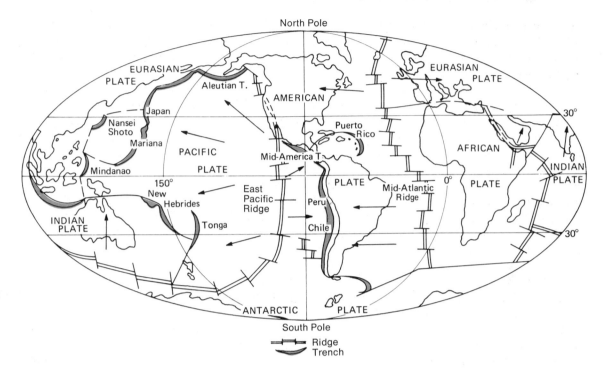

Fig. 14-4b. A view of the continents and ocean floor according to the hypothesis of plate tectonics. Symbols for mid-ocean ridges and deep trenches are shown in the legend.

Australian plates move toward each other and have collided to raise the Himalaya Mountains. The Pacific and American plates slide past each other at the earthquake-prone San Andreas Fault in California. A study of Fig. 14-4b will show many other examples of landforms produced along plate boundaries. There are great coastal ranges like the Andes of South America; mountainous island chains like the Philippines; and deep ocean trenches like those off the west coast of South America.

What makes the plates move? According to plate tectonics, the answer lies in convection cells in the earth's mantle. Plates spread and move apart where convection currents rise to the surface. Plates move together and clash where convection currents sink.

Plate tectonics has not yet provided all the answers to questions of earth movement. But it has represented a great step forward in the modern development of the earth sciences. Scientists hope that it will help us to forecast earthquakes and volcanic eruptions; that it will aid in the discovery of new mineral deposits; that it will give us a better explanation of past ice ages in regions that are now tropical and vice versa; and that it will lead to a better understanding of the earth's history.

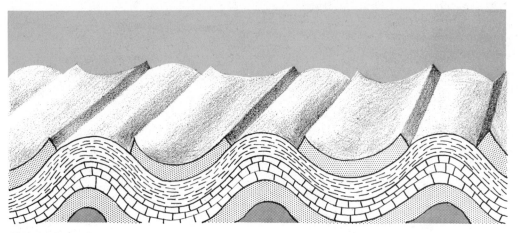

Fig. 14-5. Rock structure of young fold mountains like the Jura Mountains of Switzer-land.

6. Fold Mountains

The mountain-building processes just described are believed to account for the origin of most of the great mountain chains of the earth's surface. These include the Himalayas of Asia, the Andes of South America, the Rockies and Coast Ranges of western North America, the Urals and Caucasus of Russia, the Alps of Europe, and the Appalachians of eastern United States. The structures and rocks of these mountains are varied and complex. Both diastrophism and vulcanism appear to have played a large part in their formation. The rocks are folded and faulted in intricate patterns. Great stocks and batholiths lie at their roots, feeding a myriad of dikes and sills that slice across and between the beds of rock. But

Fig. 14-6. Parallel ridges in the Swiss Alps. The Alps are fold *mountains.*

Swiss National Travel Office

the outstanding features of these great mountain chains are the numerous long parallel folds, more than a thousand miles long in some mountains, that parallel the margins of the continents. These mountains are known as **fold** (or folded) **mountains.** (See Figs. 14-5 and 14-6.)

Fold mountains are the most important of the earth's mountains, but there are other types, too. These include *fault-block mountains, volcanic mountains,* and *dome mountains.*

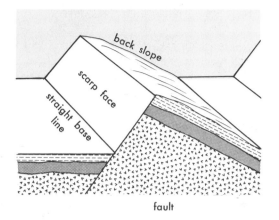

fault

7. Fault-Block Mountains

When diastrophism raises and tilts large blocks of the earth's crust by faulting, **fault-block mountains** are formed. Particularly in youth these mountains are characterized by long, straight base lines running along their fault scarps. The fault-scarp face of the mountain is also much steeper than the gentle back slope. (See Figs. 14-7 and 14-8.)

Fault-block mountains are usually rectangular in shape and several times as long as they are wide. They range greatly in size. Some blocks may be but a few miles in length and only a thousand feet high. Others may be hundreds of

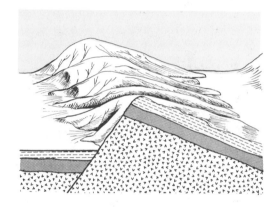

Fig. 14-7. Fault-block mountains before erosion (above) and after some erosion (below).

Fig. 14-8. A long, straight base line marks the steep eastern fault-scarp face of the Sierra Nevadas, at the foot of which is Owens Valley, California, part of the Great Basin.

Mendenhall, U.S. Geological Survey

miles in length and many thousands of feet high. Small block mountains abound in the Great Basin areas of Nevada, Utah, and Oregon. The Wasatch Range in Utah is over 100 miles long and almost a mile high. The Sierra Nevada Mountains, largest of all block mountains in the United States, are over 400 miles long. Facing eastward, the steep fault scarp of the Sierra Nevadas forms one side of the Great Basin.

Like fold mountains, fault-block mountains include a great variety of rocks and underlying structures. But in almost every case the faults that form the boundaries of the great blocks are normal or gravity faults.

8. Volcanic Mountains

Volcanic cones may stand up as individual mountain peaks like Mount Popocatepetl in Mexico and Mount Etna in Sicily. Others may form in chains, probably along great fault lines, to build up volcanic mountain ranges from the floor of the ocean, as in the Hawaiian and Aleutian Islands in the Pacific and the Azores in the Atlantic. Still others may make individual contributions to the mass of great folded or faulted mountain ranges, as in the Andes Mountains of South America.

The Cascade Range of California, Oregon, and Washington is a true volcanic range, with great peaks like Mt. Shasta in California, Mt. Hood in Oregon, and Mt. Rainier in Washington forming the crests of a 500-mile long mountain mass formed almost entirely of lava.

9. Dome Mountains

Some of our smaller mountain masses, like the Black Hills of South Dakota, the Adirondack Mountains of New York, the Henry Mountains of Utah, the Uinta (yoo *in* tah) Mountains of Utah, and the highlands of Labrador are classified as dome mountains. The over-all surface of these mountains forms a circular or oval dome in various stages of erosion. The rocks beneath the dome differ. In some mountains they are folded metamorphic rocks. In others they are groups of laccoliths or stocks. But in every case, the underlying rocks have apparently gently raised the sedimentary strata above them into a dome-shaped mountain mass. Dome mountains rarely exceed 150 miles in diameter. Some geologists prefer to call these mountains *upwarped mountains*. (See Fig. 14-9.)

10. Life History of Mountains: Youth

The life history of dome mountains is very different from the life history of fold mountains or block mountains or volcanoes. But as with other land forms, there are certain characteristics that are typical of each stage of mountain development, regardless of type.

During early *youth*, all mountains are growing and their growth may be indicated by earthquakes, by volcanic eruptions, by the slow rise of rock strata, or by all these events. Growth goes on for long periods of time, and as mountains grow they are immediately attacked by weathering and erosion. This causes young mountains to be both high and rugged, with sharp peaks, narrow valleys, and steep slopes on which landslides and avalanches frequently occur. Bare rock cliffs and ledges are common, and young

Fig. 14-9. A dome mountain whose igneous core has been exposed.

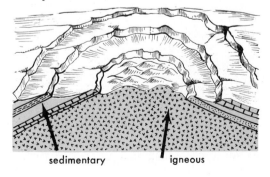

sedimentary   igneous

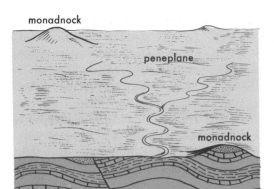

Fig. 14-10. *In old age a mountain region is worn down to a peneplane.*

mountains often reach high above snow line. (See Figs. 14-6 and 14-8.)

Because of the erosion that begins as soon as growth begins, even the youngest of mountains have their upper rock layers at least partly worn away. In dome mountains this may not yet expose the cores. In young fold mountains the tops of the anticlines are also the tops of hills and ridges and are likely to be the first rocks to be stripped away. Examples of young mountains are the Himalayas, the Andes, the Alps, the Coast and Cascade Ranges of western United States, the Sierra Nevadas, the Rocky Mountains, and the volcanoes of Hawaii. The world's young mountains are found on the great fault lines that mark the "zones of weakness" in the earth's crust, where diastrophism and vulcanism are most active today.

11. Mountains in Maturity

In *maturity* the mountains have stopped growing, but weathering and erosion continue to wear down their surfaces. Peaks are greatly lowered, slopes become gentler, valleys become wider, and interstream areas are narrowed. The locations of ridges and valleys no longer coincide with anticlines and synclines. Instead, ridges occur where

hard rock layers resist erosion, and valleys are found where softer layers are rapidly worn away. Examples of mature mountains are the Appalachian Mountains, the White Mountains, the Adirondacks, the Green Mountains of Vermont, the Black Hills, and the mountains of Scotland and Scandinavia. (See Fig. 14-9.)

12. Mountains in Old Age

When erosion continues for extremely long periods of time into *old age,* even mountains may be worn down almost to base level. The low-rolling surface of an old mountain region is called a **peneplane** (pee nuh *plane*). Peneplane means "almost flat." Here and there on the peneplane stand solitary rock masses known as **monadnocks.** These masses rise rather gently from the peneplane surface to modest heights that rarely exceed a thousand feet. Monadnocks have strongly resisted erosion because of their durable rocks or their location in interstream areas of which they are the last remnants. (See Fig. 14-10.)

Peneplanes may be seen in many parts of the earth, but almost all of them have been raised again by diastrophism and are no longer close to sea level. The development of a peneplane involves millions and millions of years, and it is not surprising that movements of the earth's crust occur during the late stages of peneplane formation or in the ages that follow. The rivers on raised peneplanes are said to be rejuvenated, or made young again. With newly increased slope, they begin a second cycle of life history, once more carving out young V-shaped valleys. But the level surface of the worn mountain rocks show unmistakably that the region had reached old age before being uplifted.

Southern New England is a raised peneplane on which Mount Monadnock in New Hampshire and Mount Greylock in Massachusetts stand as typical monadnocks. Manhattan, the Bronx, and Westchester County in New York are located at the southern end of this old mountain region of crystalline metamorphic rocks. Other raised peneplanes are the Piedmont Upland, the Laurentian Mountain region of eastern Canada, and the region north and south of Lake Superior. Stone Mountain, near Atlanta in Georgia, is a monadnock of the Piedmont region. (See Fig. 14-11.)

PLAINS

13. Plateau or Plain?

The major land forms of the earth's surface include not only the elevated regions we call mountains and plateaus but also the even more extensive lowlands we call plains. In North America these lowlands include the Atlantic and Gulf coastal plains, the interior lowlands of the Mississippi Valley, the Great Plains that stretch from Hudson Bay to the Gulf of Mexico, and many others. In Asia and Europe great plains reach across China, Siberia, and into the Ukraine. Other vast areas of plains are found in South America, Africa, and Australia.

Plains, like plateaus, are regions of nearly horizontal rock structure. How, then, do they differ? In the popular sense a plateau always stands above its surroundings—at least on one side—while a plain is always lower than adjoining land. The geologist may go further, however, distinguishing plateau from plain also on the basis of their relief. Thus he may define a **plain** as a *region of horizontal rock structure and low relief,* while a **plateau** is a *region of horizontal structure and high relief.* **Relief,** you will recall, is the difference in height between the highest and lowest points of a region.

No definite amount of relief is specified for either a plain or a plateau. As a rule, however, the relief of plateaus—like the Colorado Plateau, the Columbia Plateau, and the great plateau of Tibet—is thousands of feet. The relief of plains —like the Atlantic Coastal Plain—is more likely to be in the hundreds of feet. There are exceptions, however. The Great Plains of North America rise to a height of 5,000 feet above sea level at the base of the Rocky Mountains, and have a total relief of thousands of feet. But the rise is so gradual that "plain" still seems appropriate except where the normally flat surface has been

Fig. 14-11. Stone Mountain, Georgia, a granite monadnock of the Piedmont Upland.

U.S. Air Force Photo

deeply eroded, as in the "badlands" of the Dakotas and Nebraska. (See Fig. 14-12.)

14. Origin of Plains and Plateaus

Since plains and plateaus are regions of horizontal rock structure, they originate by any process that deposits rock materials in horizontal layers. Rivers may deposit sediments on continental shelves, on lake floors, at the base of mountains, or on their own flood plains. Glacial streams may deposit sediments beyond their terminal moraines. Volcanic eruptions through fissures may form horizontal layers of lava.

In some cases the regions covered by these horizontal layers of alluvial, glacial, or volcanic materials are already parts of the dry continental areas; in other cases they are under water and must "emerge" before they become plains or plateaus. Those regions that are high above sea level are likely to become deeply eroded and thus to have high relief. These will be known as plateaus. Regions that are not high above sea level will not be eroded deeply. They will have low relief and will be known as plains.

15. Classes of Plains: Marine Plains

Plains are usually classified according to the *origin* of their sediments or materials.

Marine (ocean) **plains** are plains formed by the emergence of shallow parts of ocean floors. (As explained in an earlier chapter, emergence may occur through either the rise of the ocean floor, the lowering of the ocean water, or a combination of both.) The largest plains in the world originated in this way. Marine plains may be either **coastal** or **interior** plains, depending on their locations. The Atlantic Coastal Plain, running along the Atlantic Coast from New Jersey to Florida, is a coastal plain. So is the Gulf Coastal Plain along the Gulf of Mexico. Both of these were formed by the emergence of continental shelves. The Great Plains region of the United States and Canada, though also originally

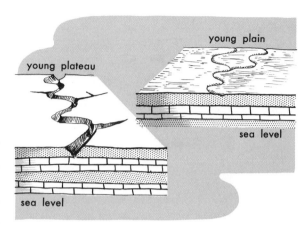

Fig. 14-12. Both plains and plateaus have horizontal rock structure, but plateaus have higher relief.

a marine plain, is an interior plain. It was formed by the emergence of the floor of a shallow inland sea that stretched from Hudson Bay to the Gulf of Mexico millions of years ago. Following its emergence, rivers flowing from the Rocky Mountains covered the plain with thick alluvial deposits.

Marine plains in Europe include the coastal plains of northern France, of southeastern England, and of western Scandinavia, as well as the great interior plains of central Europe and the Russian Ukraine.

16. Lake Plains

Lake plains are plains formed by the emergence (of all or part) of a lake floor. This may happen when the waters of a lake run out or evaporate, or when a lake floor rises. The greatest lake plain in North America extends over more than 100,000 square miles of North Dakota, Minnesota, and the Canadian province of Manitoba. This region was once the floor of a great Ice Age lake called Lake Agassiz. The natural drainage of this area is northward toward Hudson Bay. During the Ice Age the glacier itself blocked the drainage, damming up the water from the melting glacial ice into a tremendous lake larger

Fig. 14-13. How a glacier may stand in the way of its own drainage, thereby forming a temporary lake.

than all the Great Lakes combined. When the Ice Age ended, the lake drained away and disappeared, leaving its level floor and fine sediments as a great lake plain. Here and there a depression in the floor of Lake Agassiz retained its water and formed a smaller lake. The largest of these remnant lakes is Lake Winnipeg in Canada. Today the Red River of the North flows northward from Minnesota to Lake Winnipeg through nearly 600 miles of the lake plain. (See Fig. 14-13.)

Great Salt Lake in Utah is another remnant of a once-greater lake called Lake Bonneville, and the Great Salt Lake Desert is a lake plain that was once part of Lake Bonneville's floor. The broad belt of farmland south of Lake Ontario in New York State is also a lake plain. It represents the part of the floor of Lake Ontario that was uncovered by shrinkage of the lake at the close of the Ice Age.

17. Alluvial Plains, Glacial Plains, and Lava Plains

Alluvial plains (formed by rivers) include *flood plains, delta plains,* and *piedmont alluvial plains,* all of which were described in the chapter on streams. **Glacial plains** include *outwash plains*

like those of southern Long Island (described in the chapter on glaciers) and *till plains.* Till plains are regions in which glacial till, deposited in hilly country, has filled in hollows and created a fairly level surface. Till deposits are not stratified, so these regions are true plains only where the old rock structures that they cover are horizontal, as in northern Ohio and southern Illinois.

Lava plains, originating in fissure eruptions or in the far-spreading lava flows of quiet volcanoes, are found in parts of Iceland and the Hawaiian Islands.

18. The Life History of a Plain

In its *youth* a newly formed plain is a broad region of almost perfectly level topography. A few shallow river valleys occur at great distances from each other, and the very extensive interstream areas are so flat that drainage is poor and shallow lakes or swamps may be common. The swampy coastal plain of Florida, the muddy floor of Lake Agassiz, and the level plains of the Russian Ukraine are all examples of youth.

In *maturity* the plain is eroded by many new tributaries of the original streams. Frequent shallow valleys and narrow interstream areas create a rolling surface of low relief and good drainage. The Prairie Plains of Iowa and Illinois are mature plains.

In *old age* the plain is worn almost level again, but it is covered by a very thick layer of soil and weathered rock. There are few rivers, all of them in late maturity or old age. Parts of eastern Kansas are plains in old age.

PLATEAUS

19. Plateaus Formed by Diastrophism

Some plateaus are former plains that have been raised high above sea level by repeated vertical faulting through hundreds of thousands of years of recent earth history. Such plateaus are called **fault plateaus.** The Colorado Plateau of southwestern United States is an example of a great plateau region formed largely by upwarping and faulting. Its total relief is about 6,000 feet. The Appalachian Plateaus region of eastern United States (New York, Pennsylvania, West Virginia, Kentucky, Tennessee, and Alabama) was raised slowly with little faulting or tilting and is a **warped plateau** (warping means rising gently without folding or faulting). Both fault and warped plateaus are raised by the forces of diastrophism.

20. Plateaus Formed by Vulcanism

Vulcanism also forms plateaus. When successive horizontal lava flows build up a region to great heights, **lava plateaus** are formed—exactly like lava plains in origin, but having greater thicknesses and higher relief. The great Columbia lava plateau of Washington, Oregon, northeastern California, and southern Idaho covers an area of about 200,000 square miles and its *flood basalts* are thousands of feet thick. (See Fig. 14-14.)

The great Deccan lava plateau of India, roughly covering the triangle marked by the cities of Bombay, Madras, and Calcutta is even larger. (See Chapter 13, Topic 9.)

21. The Life History of a Plateau

The life history of a plateau is very similar to that of a plain, but high relief makes plateau scenery much more striking. *Young plateaus* are high and broad, and the few rivers that run through them carve out deep and often spectacular canyons or ravines. The Colorado Plateau and the Columbia Plateau are young. (See Fig. 14-15.)

As plateaus mature, increasing numbers of rivers cut many valleys and narrow their once-broad interstream areas, creating extremely rugged surfaces. (See Fig. 14-16.) The *mature plateaus,* also known as eroded or dissected plateaus, are still plateaus because of their *horizontal rock structure* and high relief. But in their own localities they are usually known as "mountains." The Appalachian Plateaus region of eastern United States—high, rugged, and densely

Fig. 14-14. Layer upon layer of basalt lava flows are exposed to view where the Columbia River cuts through the Columbia Plateau.

Carl B. Lewis

U.S. Geological Survey

Fig. 14-15. Marble Canyon, cut by a young river into a broad young plateau.

forested up to its even skyline—is a group of maturely dissected plateaus, known locally as the Catskill Mountains (in eastern New York), the Helderbergs (near Albany), the Allegheny Escarpment (in western New York), the Pocono Mountains and Allegheny Mountains (in Pennsylvania and West Virginia), and the Cumberland Mountains (in Kentucky, Tennessee, and Alabama).

In *old age* most of a plateau is worn down almost to base level. Here and there a few hard-capped hills, perhaps the last remnants of the old interstream areas, remain standing high enough to maintain the high relief of a plateau. In arid regions hills that are flat-topped and broad often remain. These are called **mesas** (*may suhs*). Smaller, narrow-topped hills are called **buttes** (bewts). Both mesas and buttes have steep, clifflike walls, sometimes hundreds of feet high, which isolate them from the rest of the plateau. Parts of Arizona, New Mexico, and Texas are old plateau regions. (See Figs. 14-17 and 14-18.)

Although young rivers are more likely to be found on young and mature plateaus than on old ones, there is no necessary correspondence be-

tween the river's age (youth, maturity, or old age) and the erosional stage of the plateau or plain into which the river cuts its valley.

22. Bedrock of Plains, Plateaus, and Mountains

The horizontal rock layers of plains consist of gravels, sands, clays, and lime in various stages of consolidation or hardening. In recently formed

Fig. 14-16. A mature plateau has a ruggedly dissected surface and is likely to be known locally as a mountain region.

plains, such as the outwash plain of Long Island, the floor of Lake Agassiz, the Atlantic Coastal Plain, or the flood plain of the Mississippi, the sediments are still likely to be loose rather than consolidated. In older plains, such as the interior Great Plains of the United States and Canada, the sediments are likely to be hardened into layers of conglomerate, sandstone, shale, and limestone. The rock layers of plains are rarely perfectly horizontal. Where porous layers outcrop between impervious layers, artesian formations like those of the Great Plains and the Atlantic Coastal Plain are created.

In plateau regions of sedimentary origin the horizontal rock layers are sandstones, shales, limestones, and occasional conglomerates, as found in the Colorado and Appalachian plateaus.

In lava plateaus like the Columbia the horizontal beds consist largely of basalts.

The rocks of mountain regions include largely folded, faulted, and tilted sedimentary rocks in such regions as the Appalachian Mountains and the block mountains of the Great Basin; igneous rocks such as granite in the Rockies, the Sierra Nevadas, the Black Hills, and the Adirondacks; metamorphic rocks such as gneiss, schist, and marble in the complex mountain regions of southern New York, southern New England, the Laurentians, the Piedmont, and the White Mountains of New Hampshire. (*Complex mountains* are so called because of their complicated origin. This may have included combinations of folding, faulting, doming, and igneous intrusion.)

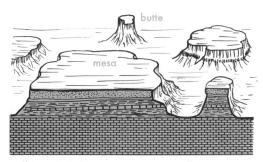

Fig. 14-17. Buttes and mesas are features of old plateaus in arid regions.

Darton, U.S. Geological Survey

Fig. 14-18. The cap rock of this butte near Cambria, Wyoming, is a layer of white gypsum thirty feet thick.

TOPIC QUESTIONS

Each topic question refers to the topic of the same number within this chapter.

1. (*a*) In what two respects are mountains and plateaus similar? (*b*) In what respect do they differ?

2. In trying to explain the origin of mountains, what facts must be taken into account?

3. (*a*) Why do geologists believe that mountain rocks were formed in great shallow basins? (*b*) What is a geosyncline? (*c*) Describe the process of mountain making that begins with horizontal compression.

4. Explain how the principle of isostasy accounts for some subsidence of a geosyncline.

5. Give a brief description of each of the following hypotheses of mountain origin: (*a*) convection, (*b*) continental drift and plate tectonics.

6. What is the principal feature of fold mountains? Name some examples of these mountains.

7. How do fault-block mountains form? Describe them and name examples.

8. How does a range of volcanic mountains originate? Give examples.

9. How do dome mountains originate? How large are they? Name some examples.

10. Describe the characteristics of young mountains. Give examples.

11. Describe mature mountains. Give examples.

12. (*a*) Describe an old mountain region, explaining what a peneplane and monadnocks are and how they are formed. (*b*) Why are peneplanes often found to be raised well above sea level? (*c*) Locate some raised peneplanes and monadnocks.

13. Define plain and plateau, explaining how they differ. Give examples.

14. (*a*) In general, how do "regions of horizontal rock structure" originate? Give examples. (*b*) When do these become plains? plateaus?

15. (*a*) How do marine plains originate? (*b*) Name two coastal marine plains in the United States. (*c*) How did the interior Great Plains originate? (*d*) Name regions of marine plains in Europe.

16. (*a*) What are lake plains? How did the great lake plain of North Dakota and Minnesota originate? (*b*) Describe two other lake plain areas in the United States.

17. (*a*) What are alluvial plains? Name three types of alluvial plains and give a specific example of each type. (See Chapter 10.) (*b*) Name and give examples of two types of glacial plains. (*c*) Where are lava plains formed?

18. Describe the three stages of the life history of a plain. Give examples.

19. (*a*) Why is the Colorado Plateau called a fault plateau? (*b*) Why is the Appalachian Plateaus region called a warped plateau?

20. How is a lava plateau formed? Give examples.

21. (*a*) Describe the three stages of a plateau's life history. Give examples. (*b*) Explain why the Catskill "Mountains" are a plateau. (*c*) Define butte and mesa.

22. (*a*) Discuss the kinds of bedrock found in plains, plateaus, and mountains. (*b*) What are "complex mountains"?

GENERAL QUESTIONS

1. Compare the following regions as to kinds of rock, rock structure, and topography: (*a*) the Appalachian Mountains and the Appalachian Plateau, (*b*) the Black Hills and the Columbia Plateau, (*c*) the Colorado Plateau and the block mountains of the Great Basin, (*d*) the Great Plains and the Atlantic Coastal Plain, (*e*) southern New England and New Mexico's old plateau region.

2. Mature folded mountains often have ridges with synclinal rock structure and valleys with anticlinal structure. (*a*) Draw a cross-section diagram to show this. (*b*) Explain how these anticlinal valleys and synclinal ridges may have developed. (See Chapter 12, Topic 5.)

3. Why are alluvial fans likely to develop on the steep side of a block mountain?

4. Make a contour map of an oval-shaped domed mountain 40 miles long, 20 miles wide, rising from a base at 3,000 feet above sea level to a summit at 6,000 feet above sea level. Select your own scale and contour interval.

5. Make a contour map of an old plateau with a butte and a mesa.

STUDENT ACTIVITIES

1. Make plasticene or plaster of Paris models of (*a*) a geosyncline, (*b*) fold mountains, (*c*) fault-block mountains, (*d*) dome mountains, (*e*) a young plateau, (*f*) a mature plateau, (*g*) buttes and mesas.

2. Make a series of models to represent (*a*) the hypothesis of continental drift, (*b*) the convection hypothesis.

3. Make a set of weighted blocks of different sizes, shapes, and weights that will illustrate isostasy when they are floated in water.

4. Determine the sources of rock specimens available in your school. Classify them according to source region as plain, plateau, mountain, and type of each.

TOPOGRAPHIC SHEETS

(15-minute series, except as noted)

1. *Young coastal plain:* Trent River, North Carolina.
2. *Young lake plain:* Fargo, North Dakota.
3. *Young plateau:* Soda Canyon, Colorado.
4. *Mature plateau:* Kaaterskill, New York.
5. *Mesas and Buttes:* Natural Bridges, Utah.
6. *Block mountain:* Furnace Creek, California.
7. *Folded mountain:* Harrisburg, Pennsylvania.
8. *Dome mountain:* Hot Springs, South Dakota (7½-minute series).
9. *Monadnock:* Mt. Monadnock, New Hampshire.

CHAPTER 15
Earthquakes

HOW DO YOU KNOW THAT . . . ?

The damage done in an earthquake results from shaking of the earth's crust (Topic 3). Take a long thin stick; a piece of lath about the size of a meterstick or yardstick will work. Hold one end down firmly at the side of your desk. Allow most of the stick to project beyond the desk. With your free hand, push down gently on the free end of the stick. Why does the stick bend rather than break? Remove your free hand suddenly. What happens to the stick? Why would a similar motion in the earth's crust be destructive? How is pressure on the crust "suddenly released"? Try this with your stick.

1. What Is an Earthquake?

Earthquakes are defined as any shaking or trembling of the earth's solid crust. Here is a description of one great earthquake, striking without warning during the night of December 16, 1811, in a region where earthquakes had previously been almost unknown. "Early in the morn-ing another shock, preceded by a low rumbling . . . , was experienced. The ground rose and fell as earth waves, like the long, low swell of the sea, passed across its surface, tilting the trees . . . and opening the soil in deep cracks. . . . Landslides swept down the steeper bluffs and hillsides; considerable areas were uplifted;

Fig. 15-1. One scene from the Alaskan earthquake of 1964. Note the deep crack in the ground. What other effects of the quake do you see? Scientists estimate that every year more than 150,000 earthquakes shake the earth strongly enough to be felt by us. But perhaps only 100 a year cause great property damage or loss of life.

NOAA

and still larger areas sank and became covered with water emerging from below through fissures or little craterlets. On the Mississippi, great waves were created which overwhelmed many 'boats and washed others high upon the shore . . . High banks caved and were precipitated into the river; sand bars and points of islands gave way; whole islands disappeared."

W. H. Norton described the Charleston, South Carolina, earthquake of 1886 as follows: "A slight tremor which rattled the windows was followed a few seconds later by a roar, as of subterranean thunder, as the main shock passed beneath the city. Houses swayed to and fro, and their heaving floors overturned furniture and threw persons off their feet as, dizzy and nauseated, they rushed to the doors for safety. In 60 seconds a number of houses were completely wrecked, 14,000 chimneys were toppled over, and in all the city scarcely a building was left without serious injury. In the vicinity of Charleston, railways were twisted and derailed."

2. Causes of Earthquakes

Faulting is the principal cause of earthquakes, and nearly all the destructive earthquakes of history originated through faulting. But earthquakes do result from other causes. A violent explosion of any kind, whether it be of gas, TNT, or a nuclear bomb, will rock the vicinity and shake the earth for varying distances. Violent explosions occur naturally in the eruptions of many volcanoes, and in some cases these have resulted in destructive earthquakes. In general, however, such earthquakes are far less extensive and less damaging than those caused by faulting. Minor earthquakes of very limited extent may be caused by landslides and cave-ins of various kinds.

3. Faulting and Earthquakes: Elastic Rebound

Faulting, the sudden slipping of great blocks of rock along faults, is usually explained by the

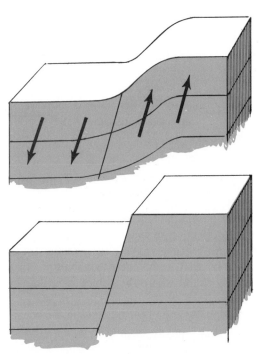

Fig. 15-2. Faulting results when rocks yield suddenly to bending pressures.

elastic rebound theory. According to this theory the rocks in two adjacent sections of the earth's crust are subjected to tremendous pressures in *opposite directions* for long periods of time. The pressures may be either up and down or sideways. In the immediate vicinity of the pressures the rocks may bend slowly and increasingly for many years, without any changes being noticed on the earth's surface. Eventually, however, the strain becomes so great that the rocks suddenly rip apart along a *fault* that may be hundreds of miles long. Vertical pressures may lift one block many feet higher than the other; horizontal pressures may slide the two blocks in opposite directions along the fault. (See Fig. 15-2.)

The trembling and vibration of the solid rock immediately after faulting produce earthquake shocks which may be strong enough to shake an entire continent, or they may be so slight that only the most sensitive instruments detect them. The shocks are strongest along the fault, decreasing in intensity with distance from the fault.

Severe shocks may last for several minutes, slight shocks but a few seconds.

Once developed, the fault torn in the rocks remains a zone of weakness for ages to come, for it is here that strains in the earth's crust are most easily relieved. Erosion, too, is more rapid along faults than elsewhere, and valleys often develop in them.

4. Faulting in the Ocean; Tsunami

Faulting may also take place in the rocks of the ocean basins, and deep-sea soundings show clearly the location of many fault scarps on the ocean floor. When breaks develop in the trans-ocean cables that lie on the ocean bottom, they are usually found where the cables cross known fault scarps.

Occasionally strong earthquakes in the ocean, for reasons still unknown, may produce gigantic sea waves called **tsunami** (tsoo *nah* mee) by the Japanese. Geologists think that tsunami occur in conjunction with vertical faulting or with massive landslides on the sea bottom. Tsunami may travel thousands of miles across the oceans at speeds of 450 miles per hour, and break over low coastal areas in destructive waves rising as high as 60 feet. One of the most disastrous tsunami occurred when the volcano Krakatoa erupted in 1883. It caused the drowning of 36,000 people living on islands in the Pacific Ocean near the East Indies. In 1964 tsunami from the great Anchorage, Alaska, earthquake rolled to almost every part of the North Pacific Ocean, dealing death and destruction throughout the Gulf of Alaska and as far south as Crescent City, California. Tsunami are erroneously called tidal waves.

5. Destruction by Earthquakes

From the geologic point of view, faulting is an upbuilding process. But to man, the earthquakes that follow faulting are the most destructive of all natural occurrences. The violent shaking of the earth's crust causes flimsily constructed buildings to collapse, crushing and trapping their inhabitants within the shattered walls. An earthquake in Shensi Province, China, in 1556, is estimated to have killed nearly a million people; one in Calcutta, India, in 1737, killed 300,000 people. Two great earthquakes in Italy in 1908 and 1915 took 105,000 lives. In 1920, 120,000 lives were lost in a quake in Kansu Province, China. Other regions suffering disastrous quakes in this century were Peru, Chile, Turkey, Tibet, Burma, India, Algeria, Greece, Morocco, Iran, Philippine Islands, Central America, and Mexico. All in all, in this century alone, over 600,000 people have been killed in earthquakes.

Fires (from overturned stoves, lamps, and electrical short circuits) add greatly to the loss of life and property in earthquakes, while broken water pipes and disrupted communications hinder fire fighting and rescue work. Property damage of $350,000,000 in the San Francisco earthquake of 1906 was largely the result of fire. In the great earthquake of 1923 in Japan, nearly 150,000 lives were lost and half a million buildings destroyed. Here, too, fire played a major part in the disaster.

Tsunami may make fearful contributions to the destructiveness of earthquakes in coastal areas. In the terrifying earthquake of 1755 in Lisbon, Portugal, a 60-foot sea wave smashed into the city immediately after the first violent shocks, and many of the 60,000 deaths in this disaster were caused by drowning. In an even greater disaster involving tsunami, nearly 200,-000 people lost their lives in the great earthquake of 1900 in Sicily.

6. Earthquakes and Buildings

The ability of earthquakes to destroy buildings varies tremendously with the foundation and construction of a building. Earthquake shocks are generally more destructive in loose earth than in bedrock. This difference may be illustrated by taking a large bowl of gelatin dessert and striking it a sharp blow. The gelatin, like the loose earth, quivers from the blow. The bowl, like the bedrock, hardly moves after being struck.

In the San Francisco earthquake of 1906 damage was far greater in the loose ground of the dock area than in the rocky hills of the city, even though the hills were nearer the point of most intense shock.

7. How Deep Do Earthquakes Originate?

Earthquakes may take place along faults hundreds of miles long. Nevertheless, each quake seems to begin in a particular part of the fault, perhaps only a few miles in extent, and almost always below the earth's surface. The point at which an earthquake appears to originate is called its **focus.** The point on the surface vertically above the focus is called the **epicenter** (*epi =* above). (See Fig. 15-3.)

Seismologists (size *mol* oh jists), scientists who specialize in the study of earthquakes, classify earthquakes according to depth of focus as follows: shallow-focus earthquakes originate at depths up to 40 miles; intermediate-focus earthquakes originate at from 40 to 200 miles; deep-focus earthquakes originate below 200 miles. The deepest focus yet recorded is 435 miles. Only about 3 per cent of all recorded earthquakes are deep focus. The large majority, about 85 per cent, are shallow-focus earthquakes. Most destructive earthquakes are in this group.

8. Earthquake Waves

When earthquakes occur, energy is released at the focus of the earthquake and all along the fault on which movement of the crust takes place. Seismologists estimate that a great earthquake may release the energy equivalent of over a million atomic bombs. How does this energy travel from the focus to be felt hundreds or even thousands of miles away?

When the rocks at the focus of the quake

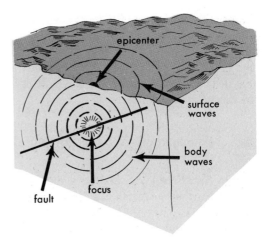

Fig. 15-3. Where earthquake waves come from.

vibrate, earthquake waves carry energy away from the focus in all directions. These waves travel *through the body* of the earth, so they are called *body waves.* They are of two types. The **primary waves,** also known as P waves and push-pull waves, travel through the earth by alternately pushing together and pulling apart the particles of rock through which they pass. Like sound waves, the P waves travel in the same direction as the particles they push and pull. P waves travel through the earth at speeds of more than three miles per second near the surface, and higher speeds at greater depths. P waves can pass through solids, liquids, or gases.

The **secondary waves,** also known as S waves and shake waves, travel through the earth by causing rock particles to shake or vibrate "sideways." S waves are like waves in a rope, with the particles vibrating at right angles to the forward direction in which the wave travels. S waves travel at speeds of about two miles a second near the surface, their speed increasing with depth. But unlike P waves, *S waves cannot pass through liquids or gases.*

When both P and S waves reach the surface (this would occur first at the epicenter, directly above the focus), they set up new waves that travel *along the surface* of the earth like ripples on the surface of a pond. These **long waves** or L waves travel at a uniform speed of about two miles per second. Since they stay at the surface, there is no change in speed for depth, so L waves are slower than both P and S waves. L waves pass through all materials.

9. Seismographs Record Earthquake Waves

How can a seismologist know, within a matter of minutes, that an earthquake is occurring a thousand miles away? How can seismologists locate the epicenter of an earthquake that occurs in the ocean or in uninhabited areas of the Antarctic or Alaska? How do seismologists determine the depth of an earthquake focus? The answer to these questions lies in the **seismograph** (*size* mo graf), the instrument that records earthquake waves on a sheet called a seismogram. (See Figs. 15-4, 15-5.)

The principle of the seismograph is a simple one. A heavy weight is attached to a base that is anchored in the bedrock. The weight is flexibly mounted in such a way that it remains almost stationary (because of its inertia) even when the bedrock and base are vibrating rapidly during an earthquake. The seismogram sheet is mounted on a drum turned by accurate clockwork and attached to the base. A pen attached to the heavy weight rests on the rotating drum. As long as the bedrock is unshaken, the pen makes a straight, unbroken line on the turning seismogram. But when the bedrock vibrates, the drum

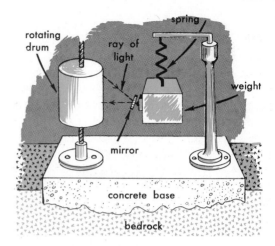

Fig. 15-4. This form of the seismograph will record vertical shaking of the earth.

shakes under the nearly motionless pen. The result is a zigzag line that shows an earthquake is taking place. Different forms of seismographs are used to record either horizontal or vertical shaking.

As one would expect, the seismogram of an earthquake shows three distinct groups of "zigzags" to mark the arrival of the P, S, and L waves. Traveling fastest, the P waves arrive first, hence their name of "primary." The S waves arrive second and the L waves arrive last.

Instead of a pen, seismographs now use a ray of light reflected from a mirror attached to the heavy weight. Instead of ordinary paper the seismogram sheet is photographic film.

Fig. 15-5. A seismogram shows the differences both in time of arrival and in intensity of the P, S, and L waves.

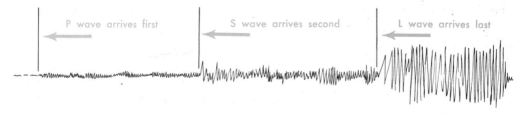

10. Where and When Did It Happen?

It is possible to determine the *distance* of an earthquake's epicenter from a single seismogram's record of the *difference in arrival time of the P and S waves*. Again the principle is a simple one. Let us assume that P waves traveling through the earth average 6 miles a second, and S waves average 4 miles a second. Then for every second of travel from the source, the S waves will fall 2 miles behind the P waves, and take ½ second longer to arrive at a given seismograph. Suppose the seismogram shows that the S waves arrived 60 seconds (120 half-seconds) later. This means that the P waves traveled 120 seconds to reach the seismograph. At 6 miles a second, this gives the epicenter's distance as 720 miles. (S waves at 4 miles a second take 180 seconds for the same distance.)

Fig. 15-6. Graph showing the different speeds of P, S, and L waves.

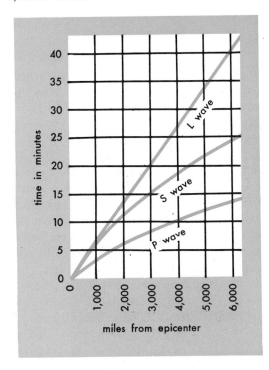

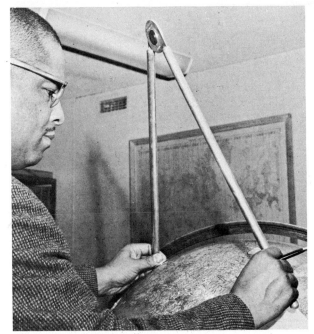

ESSA

Fig. 15-7. Geophysicist Waverly Person of National Earthquake Information Center locating earthquake epicenter of globe.

Obviously, the more distant the earthquake, the greater the difference in arrival time between P and S waves. In actual practice seismologists use graphs (Fig. 15-6) that show the distances traveled by P, S, and L waves in a given time, or tables that give the distance of an earthquake when the lag in arrival of the S wave is known.

The *time* at which a quake occurs is determined merely by subtracting the time the waves take to arrive, from the time at which they did arrive. For example, suppose the P waves (in paragraph one) arrived at 9:10 P.M. on the seismogram. Since they left their source 120 seconds earlier, the quake must have occurred at 9:08 P.M.

11. Finding the Epicenter and Focus

To find the location of an earthquake epicenter, its distance from at least three places must be known. Suppose a seismologist in St. Louis determines from his own seismogram that a quake has occurred 1,125 miles away. Seismologists in

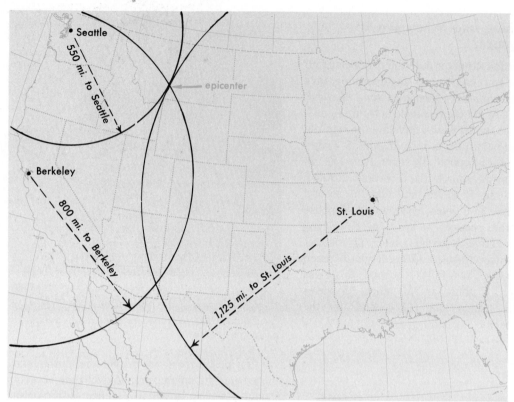

Fig. 15-8. Finding the epicenter of an earthquake. See Topic 11.

Seattle give its distance as 550 miles, while Berkeley, California, finds it to be 800 miles distant. The St. Louis seismologist knows that if he draws a circle on the globe, with St. Louis as center and 1,125 miles as radius, the epicenter must be somewhere on the circle. An 800-mile circle centered at Berkeley will intersect the first in two points, one of which must be the epicenter. Finally a third circle, 550 miles in radius and centered at Seattle will meet the others in a single point. *This must be the epicenter,* since it is at the proper distance from all three stations. (See Figs. 15-7 and 15-8.)

How is the *depth of focus* determined? The method used is similar to that used for finding the distance of the epicenter. Remember that L waves begin at the surface. Obviously, the deeper the focus, the longer the L waves will lag behind P and S waves in arriving at a given station. From a study of arrival times, depth of focus can be calculated.

12. Intensity and Magnitude

The **intensity** of an earthquake is generally determined by seismologists in terms of its effects on people and property. For example, in the popular Modified Mercalli Scale there are twelve degrees of intensity, I to XII. An earthquake intensity of II is "felt only on upper floors," and causes "swinging of some suspended objects." Intensity VII causes considerable damage to poorly built structures, breaks some chimneys, makes almost everyone run outdoors, and is noticed by some auto drivers. Intensity XI destroys bridges, buildings, pipes; forms cracks in the ground; and causes landslides. Earthquakes are most intense near the epicenter. Lines drawn on a map to show areas of equal earthquake intensity are called **isoseismals** (eye so *size* mals).

Even a small earthquake may be very destructive in a limited area close to the epicenter. Great earthquakes, on the other hand, may spread intense destruction over much larger areas. To compare earthquakes more accurately as to their *total energy,* seismologists use the Richter scale of earthquake **magnitude,** with steps from 1 to 10. In this scale, the energy or magnitude of the quake is judged by its calculated effect on a standard seismograph located at a standard distance from the epicenter. Each step in the scale represents 60 times the energy of the preceding step. On the Richter scale magnitude 7 is a destructive earthquake. The strongest earthquakes recorded in modern times had magnitudes of 8.6.

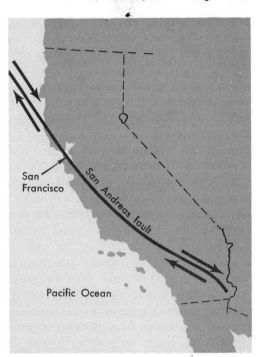

Fig. 15-9. The location of the San Andreas fault.

13. Earthquake Regions

Although earthquakes may occur in any part of the earth, most of the world's quakes occur in two "regions," coinciding to a large extent with the regions of active volcanoes and growing mountains. (See Fig. 13-8.) Foremost is the **Circum-Pacific belt** which rings the Pacific Ocean with the great mountain chains of western North America, Central America, South America, the islands of Japan, the Philippines, New Zealand, and islands in the South Seas. Next comes the **Mediterranean and trans-Asiatic region,** including Italy, Greece, Turkey, North Africa, Burma, China, India, and Iran. About 80 per cent of all earthquakes occur in the Circum-Pacific belt; about 15 per cent occur in the Mediterranean belt. Of the remaining 5 per cent, a large number occur along the Mid-Atlantic Ocean Ridge and the Mid-Indian Ocean Ridge.

14. Earthquakes in the United States

The only part of the United States that lies in a major earthquake belt is the Pacific Coast region, particularly California and Alaska. Most earthquakes in California occur near San Francisco, to the west of which runs the 600-mile-long San Andreas fault or rift. It was along this fault that the earth's crust slipped in the earthquake of 1906. (See Fig. 15-9.) In Alaska, most earthquake activity occurs along the Alaska Peninsula and the Gulf of Alaska. On March 27, 1964, the most powerful earthquake ever recorded in North America devastated the city of Anchorage and caused property damage of $250 million in the Alaska Bay region alone. Its magnitude was 8.4, its depth of focus about 18 miles. (See Fig. 15-1.)

Earthquakes also occur in other parts of the United States, though they are much less frequent and generally less intense. Other western states in which severe shocks have occurred in recent years are Utah, Idaho, Nevada, Wyoming, and Montana. In the East there were violent earthquakes in 1811 in the lower Mississippi Valley (the New Madrid, Missouri, quake) and another in 1886 over an area of 2,000,000 square miles in the southeast (the Charleston, South Carolina, quake). Minor shocks are also felt in New England and New York from time to time.

All earthquakes in the United States are caused by faulting. In the West the faulting appears to be associated with the growth of young mountains. In New England minor slipping along old fault lines is also explained as an "elastic rebound" of the rock strata. In this region of old mountains, however, the rebound is not connected with mountain growth. Instead, it is believed that the rocks are still readjusting themselves after being relieved of the weight of the great glaciers of the recent Ice Age.

15. Seismic Prospecting for Oil

Earthquake waves travel at slightly different speeds in different kinds of rock. This principle is used in modern methods of prospecting for oil. The oil geologist sets off his own private "earthquake" by exploding a charge of dynamite in the earth above the formation he is testing for oil. By analyzing the waves that are reflected back to the surface from the strata underneath, it is possible to determine whether the rock structure is the type in which oil may be found.

16. Earthquake Waves, the Crust, and the Moho

The study of earthquake waves has been our greatest source of information about the structure and composition of the earth's interior described in Chapter 1. In 1909 the Yugoslav seismologist Mohorovicic was able to prove from a study of seismograms that P and S waves traveled at sharply increased speeds when they reached depths of about 20 to 40 miles. His in-

Fig. 15-10. How the core of the earth affects P and S waves.

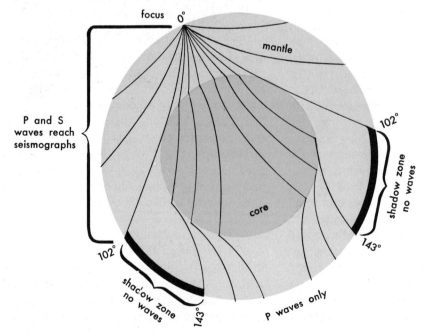

terpretation of this fact, widely accepted by other seismologists, is that here the P and S waves were entering a distinctly different rock of much higher specific gravity than the rocks of the crust. In other words, the crust merely forms an outer layer that ends rather abruptly where it meets the main body of the earth's interior. The base of the crust became known as the **Mohorovicic discontinuity** or **Moho,** and the denser rock beneath it was called the mantle.

As explained in Chapter 1, the crust itself is not uniform, being largely granite in the upper continental crust and basaltic at greater depths and under the oceans. These facts, too, were learned through study of the higher speeds of earthquake waves in the deeper crust and under the oceans.

17. Earthquake Waves and the Core

P and S waves are body waves. This means that P and S waves penetrate deeper and deeper into the earth to reach more and more distant stations. Studying wave records of strong quakes, seismologists discovered that both P and S waves reached all stations up to about 102° (about 7,000 miles) away from any given epicenter. But beyond this distance the *S waves disappeared completely.* (See Fig. 15-10.) Since S waves cannot pass through liquids, seismologists reasoned that the interior of the earth must become liquid-like at the depths reached by waves going beyond the 102° limit. This depth, approximately 1,800 miles, marks the beginning of the earth's **outer core.**

P waves pass through the outer core, but they too are strongly affected by this new liquid-like material. First, they undergo a marked drop in speed when they enter the core. Second, they are strongly bent, as if the core acts like a lens, toward the earth's center. The result is a "shadow zone" between 102° and 143° from the epicenter, in which the P waves are also missing from seismograms. Beyond 143°, however, the P waves reappear. The S waves never reappear.

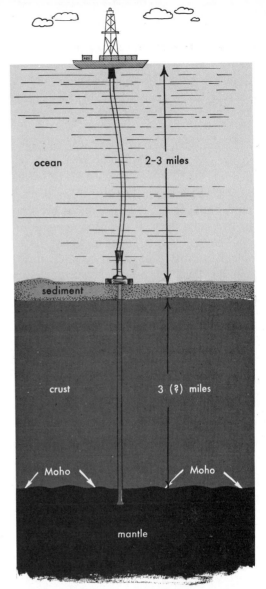

Fig. 15-11. How Project Mohole had hoped to reach the mantle.

P waves speed up markedly at about 1,350 miles into the core. Seismologists believe this means that the outer liquidlike core ends at this depth, and that the remainder of the core—the inner core—is solid right to the earth's center.

18. Project Mohole

In 1959 the National Academy of Sciences began a project to drill through the Moho and into the mantle. The project was known popularly as Project Mohole. In 1967, however, the project was still far from completion, and Congress refused to appropriate the funds needed to continue it. Perhaps it will be revived some day in the near future.

The project's key problem was to find the best place to drill the Mohole. If it were to be drilled on land, it would have to penetrate a crust believed to be at least 20 miles thick. Up to now, our deepest land drilling has been in oil wells five miles deep. If the Mohole were to be drilled on the ocean floor, it would have to penetrate a crust believed to be only three to five miles thick in places. Unfortunately the places where the ocean crust is thought to be thin are also the places where the ocean waters are several miles deep. Drilling would have to be done from a gigantic floating platform in very deep water. Man's only experience in drilling under water had been in the shallow waters of tidewater oil fields like those in the Gulf of Mexico.

Project Mohole chose the undersea route to Moho. In experimental drilling in deep water in 1962, it penetrated 601 feet into the floor of the Pacific Ocean near Guadalupe Island, west of lower California. Here the sea is 11,700 feet deep.

Project Mohole had hoped to learn much about the crust, the Moho, the history of the earth and the oceans, and the kind of rock in the mantle. From the properties of the mantle now known, many geologists believe that it may be composed of a dense rock very rich in the mineral olivine, such as *dunite* or *peridotite*. Stony meteorites consist of such rocks.

TOPIC QUESTIONS

Each topic question refers to the topic of the same number within this chapter.

1. (*a*) What is an earthquake? (*b*) What happens in an earthquake?

2. (*a*) What is the chief cause of earthquakes? (*b*) What are some minor causes?

3. (*a*) How is faulting explained by the elastic rebound theory? (*b*) How are earthquake shocks related to faulting and the fault? (*c*) Why do earthquakes occur repeatedly in the same places?

4. What is a tsunami? How does one originate? Describe it.

5. Describe the variety of ways by which an earthquake may cause destruction. Give examples.

6. Discuss the effect of foundation and construction on a building's resistance to earthquake shock.

7. (*a*) What is the focus of an earthquake? the epicenter? (*b*) Classify earthquakes according to depth of focus.

8. (*a*) Describe P waves and their travel. (*b*) Describe S waves and their travel. (*c*) What are L waves?

9. What is the seismograph? Explain how it works.

10. Explain the principle by which we can determine how far off an earthquake occurs.

11. (*a*) Explain how the epicenter of a quake can be found. (*b*) Explain how depth of focus is found.

12. (*a*) How is the intensity of an earthquake measured? What are isoseismals? (*b*) How is the magnitude of an earthquake measured?

13. Describe the regions or belts in which earthquakes occur.

14. (*a*) What is the San Andreas rift? (*b*) Name states other than California in which earthquakes occur. (*c*) What is the cause of earthquakes in western United States? eastern United States?

15. How are earthquake waves used in prospecting for oil?

16. What is the Moho? How was it discovered?

17. (*a*) How do the S waves reveal the presence of a liquid outer core for the earth? (*b*) Explain the shadow zone that exists between 102° and 143° from an epicenter. (*c*) How do P waves show that the earth's inner core is solid?

18. (*a*) What was Project Mohole? (*b*) What problems were involved in the choice of a location for the "Mohole"? (*c*) What did the Project hope to learn?

GENERAL QUESTIONS

1. Slight earthquakes occur in the vicinity of Niagara Falls every few years. What is the probable cause?

2. Why are accurate maps of the sea floor important for cable companies?

3. Where would the "zone of greatest damage" be located in (*a*) earthquakes caused by faulting, (*b*) earthquakes caused by volcanic eruption?

4. Prove that 102° from an epicenter is a distance of about 7,000 miles. (See Topic 17.)

5. How much later than the P wave does the S wave arrive when the epicenter is (*a*) 2,000 miles off, (*b*) 3,000 miles off, (*c*) 5,000 miles off, (*d*) 6,000 miles off? (Use Figure 15-6.)

STUDENT ACTIVITIES

1. Use Figure 15-6 to determine the distance of an earthquake epicenter when the interval between arrival of P and S waves is (*a*) 5 minutes, (*b*) 10 minutes.

2. On a map of the United States locate the epicenter of an earthquake whose distance from three seismic stations is as follows: Seattle, 750 miles; Salt Lake City, 625 miles; Denver, 975 miles.

3. Locate the epicenter of a quake whose distance from seismic stations is Washington, D.C., 800 miles; New Orleans, 500 miles; Chicago, 400 miles.

4. Visit a seismic station or museum where you can see a seismograph.

TOPOGRAPHIC SHEETS

(15-minute series)

Fault line scarp: Meriden, Connecticut; Glacier National Park, Montana; Redlands, California.

CHAPTER 16

Lakes

HOW DO YOU KNOW THAT . . . ?

1. One of the main ways in which lake basins form is the damming up of a river valley. People make use of this process when they create artificial lakes. Use plasticene or modeling clay to make a model of a river valley. Place the lower end of the "valley" over a sink or large container. Pour water into the upper part of the valley. A stream will form that runs into the sink. Now build a plasticene dam across the lower part of the valley. Again pour water into the head of the valley. What happens? How can you make your lake larger?

2. Lakes moderate the climate of the nearby area. Try this experiment to identify the reason. Place two identical containers (pans or small aquarium tanks) equal distances from a light bulb. Fill one container with water. Fill the other with soil, rock, plant materials, or a mixture of these. Put a thermometer in each container, with one bulb just covered. Keep each thermometer in, at this depth, until no further change in temperature is noted. Record each of these starting temperatures. Record air temperature by setting up a thermometer at equal distances above each container. Now turn on the light. After 20 minutes, record all temperatures again. What changes and variations are there? How would you explain them? Vary the experiment by putting both containers in a cold place. Repeat your measurements and observations. What do you find?

LAKE BASINS

1. The Depth of Lakes

Despite occasional claims to the contrary there are no "bottomless" lakes. The world's deepest lake, Lake Baikal in eastern Siberia, is more than a mile deep. The deepest lake in North America, Great Slave Lake in Canada, is 2,010 feet deep. Most lakes, however—even very large ones—are much shallower. Lake Erie, with an area of nearly 10,000 square miles, is only 210 feet deep. Lake Chad in Africa, though larger than Lake Erie, is only 20 feet deep during its wet season, and only 6 feet deep in its dry season!

2. Sources of Lake Water

Lakes receive their water in a number of ways. *Rain* falls directly into a lake or runs into the lake from surrounding high land. *Rivers* may empty into lakes. In humid climates *ground water* seeps into lakes. Since lakes found in regions of humid climate usually receive a fairly steady supply of water from these sources all year round, they usually stay at rather uniform levels.

3. Lake Basins

Lakes are usually defined as bodies of water that occupy closed depressions in the surface of the land. These "closed depressions," called **ba-**

Fig. 16-1. Convict Lake in the Sierra Nevada Mountains occupies a basin formed by the damming of a glacial valley by the moraines marked T, R_1, R_2, and R_3.

sins, represent the areas that are completely surrounded by higher land—as a wash basin or bathtub is completely surrounded by its walls. Lake basins may be of almost any shape and any depth. A teacup set into a heap of sand might be comparable to the deep round basin of Crater Lake in Oregon. A saucer set into a level sandy beach might be compared to the large shallow basin of Lake Okeechobee on the coastal plain of Florida. Lake Chelan in Washington has a deep, narrow trenchlike basin, while the Finger Lakes of New York State have deep narrow basins of very irregular form.

4. The Outlet

If water is poured into a wash basin or saucer, no water can run out until the basin is filled. In the same way, when rain or rivers or ground water pour into a lake basin, no water runs out until the basin is filled. Basins in dry regions may never fill up and may often be without any water at all. In humid regions, however, lake basins usually fill up until they overflow. The overflow takes place at the lowest point in the surrounding land, and the stream that runs out of the lake at this point is called its **outlet.**

The Niagara River is the outlet of Lake Erie, the St. Lawrence River of Lake Ontario, and the Yellowstone River of Lake Yellowstone.

5. Origin of Lake Basins

Lake basins may originate in a great variety of ways, many of which have already been described. Basins are formed by diastrophism, by vulcanism, by rivers, glaciers, winds, waves, currents, ground water, gravity, and even by plants and animals.

The preceding chapters have described many methods of lake origin. Ground water forms **sink-hole lakes** in limestone regions. Rivers form **plunge-pool lakes** at the base of large waterfalls, **delta lakes** on the uneven deposits of deltas, and **oxbow lakes** on mature or old flood plains. Glaciers form **cirque lakes** and **rock basin lakes** in alpine regions. Continental glaciers form **kettle lakes** in moraines and outwash plains, and **drift-basin lakes** in unevenly deposited ground moraine. Both alpine and continental glaciers may form **moraine-dammed lakes** in valleys (see Fig. 16-1), and temporary **marginal lakes** like Lake Agassiz when the glacier prevents its own meltwater from flowing downhill. Vulcanism is re-

Fig. 16-2. Lake basins may result from faulting.

sponsible for the formation of **crater lake** basins. Waves and shore current form bars which cut off bays from the ocean and turn them into closed **lagoons** or coastal lakes.

6. Basins by Crustal Movement

As smooth as the continental shelf is, it nevertheless contains many broad shallow basins on its surface. When the shelf is *uplifted* to form a coastal plain, the deeper basins form lakes and the shallower basins form swamps. There are many examples of these coastal plain lakes and swamps on the young coastal plain of southern Florida. The largest of the lakes is Lake Okee-

chobee; the largest of the swamps is the great Everglades covering an area of about 4,000 square miles of dense semitropical wilderness.

A second method by which diastrophism forms lake basins is faulting. Great blocks of the crust have sunk in many parts of the world to form the basins of lakes such as Lake Baikal in Siberia, the Dead Sea in Palestine, and the Great Lakes of Africa—including Lake Nyassa, Lake Tanganyika, and Lake Albert. In other cases large blocks of the crust have been faulted and tilted, as in the formation of block mountains, to create basins of such lakes as Lake Warner and Lake Albert in Oregon. (See Fig. 16-2.)

7. How Dams Create Lakes

Any mass of material that stretches across a river valley may block the flow of the river until the river rises to the lowest point in the mass. Such a mass of material is called a **dam,** and it changes a river valley into a lake basin. In order to get over the dam, the river must rise, overflowing its banks and flooding its valley. The lake formed by this overflow is as deep (at the dam) as the dam is high but becomes more and more

Fig. 16-3. A landslide dam blocks a river and creates a lake.

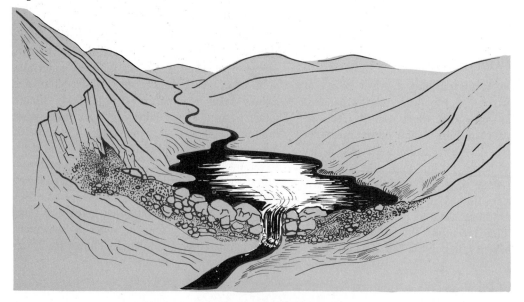

Fig. 16-4. Hoover Dam dams up the Colorado River at Black Canyon, forming 115-mile-long Lake Mead.

shallow upstream. The lake extends upstream to the point in its bed that is *as high as the top of the dam*. The river is said to "back up" to this point. The greater the height of the dam and the gentler the slope of the river bed, the longer the lake will be.

8. Dams Made by Nature

Dams across river valleys are made by a great number of natural agents. Glaciers may leave *moraine* dams. Volcanic action may leave *lava* dams, as at Lake Tahoe on the California-Nevada border. Tributary streams may dam their own master streams with the *alluvial fans* deposited at the mouths of the tributaries, as at Lake Tulare in California. Gravity causes *landslide* dams to form across steep-walled river valleys in many parts of the world. (See Fig. 16-3.) Winds may cause migrating *sand dunes* to dam up streams in sandy coastal areas. Beavers

may make dams of small *trees* across streams, thereby forming ponds in which they can build their homes. Streams running through swamps have been dammed by the rapid growth of *swamp vegetation,* as at Lake Drummond in the Dismal Swamp of Virginia. In a few cases large accumulations of tangled fallen trees have formed so-called *rafts* or *log jams* in large rivers, damming up the mouths of tributaries and turning them into lakes. The best known occurrence of this kind took place in the Red River of Louisiana and Arkansas during the last century.

9. Why Man Builds Dams

Man makes artificial lakes or **reservoirs** by building dams across river valleys. The great quantities of water stored in them may be used for irrigating dry farmlands, for providing a city's water supply, or for running hydroelectric generators. (See Fig. 16-4.) In regions where heavy rains cause floods in the river valleys, the great artificial lake basins provide storage space for the rain water, helping to prevent floods downstream from the dam and providing deep water for navigation upstream from the dam. Then this stored water may be released slowly between rains, supplying the river below the dam with an even flow of water in dry weather as well as in rainy weather. Lakes are also made in order to provide recreational facilities such as bathing, boating, fishing, and skating.

Whether artificial or natural, lakes may serve some or all of the same valuable purposes mentioned above. These may be summarized as irrigation, community water supply, water power, flood control, navigation, regulating stream flow, and recreation. Large lakes also have a moderating effect on the climate of their surroundings. Because of the relative slowness with which water warms up and cools off, lakes keep their surroundings cooler in summer and warmer in winter than they would be otherwise. They also cause increased precipitation and more fogs.

THE DESTRUCTION OF LAKES

10. Lakes Have Short Histories

As geological time is measured, lakes do not last very long. Shallow lakes may disappear almost within the lifetime of a human being. Deep lakes exist longer, but they too disappear in times much shorter than those in which the life histories of mountains or rivers are measured.

Lakes disappear because their basins are destroyed or because they lose their water. Basins are destroyed either by being filled in or by having parts of their surrounding high land worn down. Water may be lost by increased evaporation resulting from a change in climate.

11. Destruction by Filling

Many natural agents may take part in the destruction of a lake basin by filling. Foremost among these agents are the rivers that flow into a lake, leaving all of their *rock sediments* deposited in the quiet waters of the lake, often in the shapes of deltas. Other lesser contributors of rock sediment are winds, waves, and gravity. Winds blow in dust and sand, especially in dry regions. Waves wash in materials from the shores. Gravity may cause landslides from the steep walls of mountain lakes.

Plants and animals may contribute *organic sediments* to the filling of a lake basin. Swamp grasses, ferns, mosses, and pond lilies grow and die in the shallow marginal waters of a lake, accumulating on the bottom and decreasing the size of its basin. Entire lakes are turned into swamps in time, and the large accumulations of *swamp plants* may be converted into beds of peat, and perhaps some day into coal. Freshwater clams and other *lime-forming animals* also add to the organic sediments that help to fill the basin of a lake.

12. Destruction by Erosion

As the outlet river runs out of the lake, it steadily erodes the low point in the rim of the lake basin at which it starts. *Erosion of the outlet,* as this process is called, is extremely slow, however, because the clear overflow waters of the lake contain no cutting tools for erosion. Almost invariably lakes are filled with sediment long before their outlets are worn down low enough to destroy them.

13. Destruction by Evaporation

Lakes may *receive* water from inflowing streams, from ground water, from direct rain or snow, and as runoff from surrounding land. Lakes may *lose* water by overflow through an outlet stream, by seepage through their beds, and by evaporation. In humid climates lakes rarely lose as much water by seepage and evaporation as they receive. Thus they overflow and always have outlets. In dry climates, on the other hand, lakes usually lose at least as much water by seepage and evaporation as they receive. Evaporation accounts for the greater amount of water loss. Lakes in dry climates therefore do not overflow and have no outlets. In fact, losses by evaporation may be so great that the shallow lakes formed after a rare rain dry out completely in only a few days. Such temporary lakes are called *playas,* a Spanish word meaning "beaches."

Many lakes of long ago are known to have been destroyed by evaporation when their humid climates were changed to dry ones. The plains left by these lakes are covered with salt and other mineral deposits instead of with the fine soils of sediment-filled lake plains. In this manner Lake Bonneville in Utah and Lake Lahontan in Nevada disappeared many thousands of years ago, leaving Great Salt Lake and Pyramid Lake behind in deep parts of their dried-up basins.

FRESH AND SALT LAKES

To most people the story of lakes is incomplete until one puzzling question is answered.

How do salt lakes, such as the Great Salt Lake of Utah or the Dead Sea of Asia, originate? Let us see what the explanation is.

14. Fresh-Water Lakes

Fresh lake water is a mixture of rain, river water, and ground water. This "fresh" water contains a very small percentage of dissolved mineral matter carried into it by its river and ground water. *Because lakes in humid climates overflow,* as much dissolved mineral matter is constantly being carried out of them as comes into them, so their percentage of mineral matter does not increase. Thus such lakes stay fresh. (See Fig. 16-5.)

15. Fresh to Salt-Water Lakes

In dry climates lakes lose water so fast by evaporation that *they have no outlets.* During evaporation, the water escapes, but the dissolved minerals are left behind in the lake. Through the ages, rivers and ground water have been carrying

Fig. 16-5. Where a lake's water comes from, and where it goes to.

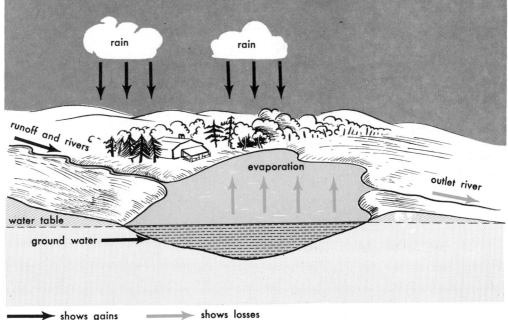

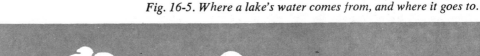

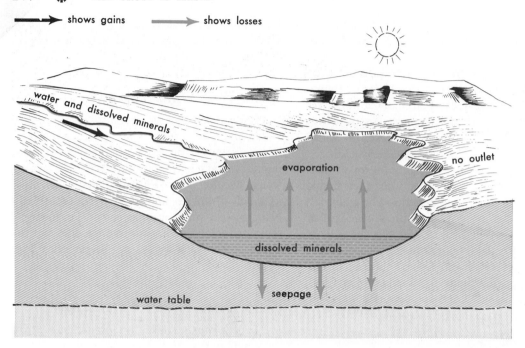

shows gains → shows losses →

Fig. 16-6. Origin of a salt lake. Lakes in dry climates lose water mainly by evaporation. Dissolved minerals are left behind, become concentrated, and make the water "salty."

water and dissolved minerals into these dry-climate lakes. Evaporation has removed as much water as has been brought in, but the dissolved minerals have been concentrated in the remaining water to make it "salty." The longer the lake exists under these conditions, the saltier it becomes. (See Fig. 16-6.)

The actual composition of the mineral matter in a lake depends on the rocks of its region. Great Salt Lake, a small remnant of the destruction of Lake Bonneville by evaporation, contains water with over 20 per cent mineral matter by weight. Most of this mineral matter is common salt. The waters of the Dead Sea of Israel and Jordan contain 24 per cent dissolved mineral matter, but only one-third of this is common salt, the rest being largely magnesium chloride. Lake Van in Turkey has waters that contain 33 per cent dissolved mineral matter! These waters are far denser than ocean waters, which have 3½ per cent of mineral matter. Their composition is

quite different, too, making it obvious that the salt lake waters are not derived from the ocean. Since their waters are denser than the human body, people can float in them without any exertion whatever.

The production of minerals from the waters and deposits of salt lakes is a big industry today. Large quantities of common salt are extracted from Great Salt Lake. Borax and sodium carbonate are extracted from Searles Lake. Owens Lake and Mono Lake are also rich in valuable minerals, while Death Valley is laden in many places with the mineral deposits of lakes destroyed by evaporation. With the exception of Great Salt Lake, these locations are all in the desert region of California.

16. Why the Sea Is Salt

When the ocean was formed by the first rains that fell upon the earth, the ocean was probably

Fig. 16-7. Without any effort, a person floats much higher in Great Salt Lake than in fresh or sea water, because of the much greater density of its water.

Salt Lake Chamber of Commerce

all fresh water. Since then, however, rivers from the lands have been carrying dissolved minerals into the ocean for millions and millions of years. Like a lake in a dry climate, the ocean loses water only by evaporation and has no outlets. As the river waters pour in and evaporate and return over and over again through the ages, more and more dissolved minerals are concentrated in the ocean waters. Lime and silica are removed by shell-forming animals, but salt and other soluble minerals remain to make the ocean salty. The older the ocean, the saltier it is.

TOPIC QUESTIONS

Each topic question refers to the topic of the same number within this chapter.

1. Discuss the depth of lakes.

2. Compare the sources of lake water in humid and dry regions. How is the size of a lake affected by its climate?

3. (*a*) What is a lake basin? (*b*) How are lake basins shaped?

4. Explain what the outlet of a lake is. Give examples.

5. Make a list of types of lakes formed by ground water, rivers, glaciers, and waves.

6. Explain how lake basins are formed by (*a*) uplift, (*b*) faulting.

7. What is a dam? How does it make a lake? What determines the depth and length of the lake formed by a dam?

8. Name five or six ways in which natural agents may dam up rivers to form lakes.

9. (*a*) Name and discuss six or seven reasons why man makes lakes. (*b*) How does a large lake affect the climate of its surroundings?

10. What makes lakes disappear?

11. (*a*) Explain how a lake basin may be filled with rock sediment. (*b*) Explain how organic sediments may help to fill a lake basin.

12. (*a*) Explain how a lake basin may be destroyed by the erosion of its outlet. (*b*) Why is this process usually so slow?

13. (*a*) List the ways in which a lake may receive and lose water. (*b*) Why do lakes in humid climates almost always have outlets? (*c*) Why do lakes in dry climates

have no outlets? (*d*) What is a playa? (*e*) Name two ancient lakes that no longer exist and explain why they disappeared.

14. Describe the composition of "fresh" lake water and explain why lakes with outlets stay fresh.

15. (*a*) Explain how lakes in dry climates become salt lakes. (*b*) What determines the mineral composition of the water of a salt lake? Give some examples. (*c*) Why can people float more easily in salt-lake waters than in the ocean? (*d*) What minerals are commercially produced from salt lakes?

16. How did the sea become salty? Explain.

GENERAL QUESTIONS

1. Why must earth dams be thicker than concrete dams? What natural dams are made of materials comparable to earth and concrete?

2. (*a*) Why are man-made dams thicker at the bottom than at the top? (*b*) How do natural dams usually achieve the same effect?

3. Crater Lake has no outlet, yet it stays fresh. How can this be explained?

4. How can a salt lake become fresh?

STUDENT ACTIVITIES

1. Make relief models to illustrate the different ways in which lake basins originate. (See Topics 5, 6, and 7.)

2. Set up an experiment to demonstrate the process by which a salt lake is formed from "fresh" water containing a small percentage of dissolved mineral matter.

3. Show how a constant flow of fresh water into a "salt lake" will make the lake fresh. (See General Question 4.)

TOPOGRAPHIC SHEETS

(15-minute series)

1. *Crater lake:* Crater Lake, Oregon.

2. *Coastal plain lakes and swamps:* Norfolk (Special), Virginia.

3. *Finger lake:* Skaneateles, New York.

4. *Glacial lakes and swamps:* Madison, Wisconsin.

CHAPTER 17

Physiographic Provinces of the United States

HOW DO YOU KNOW THAT . . . ?

Your locality may be named for its geology. Look at Fig. 17-1. In which "physiographic province" of the United States do you live? Now look at the cross sections shown in Figs. 17-2, 17-3, and 17-6 to see if your province is shown there, too.

The number and letter shown on each province in Fig. 17-1 tells you in which paragraphs the province is described. Read the description. Now make a list of the features described for your province that you yourself have observed. Make a list of those you have not seen, but know about. As far as your locality is concerned, is the name of the province justified? Why? Be sure your list includes the rock structure, surface topography, and principal economic minerals in your region.

1. The Laurentian Upland Division

This great physiographic division, hundreds of thousands of square miles in area, includes the Laurentian Upland of Canada, the Superior Highlands of north central United States, and the Adirondack Mountains of New York State. These three areas are all complex mountain regions of granite, gneiss, or other crystalline rocks.

(a) The Laurentian Upland of Canada. The Laurentian Upland, reaching from the Great Lakes to the Arctic Ocean, is a low rolling peneplane covered by forest in the south and tundra in the north. Glacial action during the last Ice Age has left numerous young streams, thousands of lakes, and only a thin cover of soil. The principal industries of this region are mining, lumbering, and trapping. The province of Ontario includes the world's richest nickel deposit at Sudbury and rich uranium ores near Blind River. Iron is mined in the Quebec-Labrador region.

(b) The Superior Highlands. The Superior Highlands, including the northwestern peninsula region of Michigan, northern Wisconsin, and northeastern Minnesota, are similar in topography to the Laurentian Upland but somewhat hillier. The Mesabi Range of hills extends 100 miles along the northern shores of Lake Superior in Minnesota; the Keeweenaw Range projects into Lake Superior from its southern shores in Michigan. Mesabi is famous for its rich iron mines; Keeweenaw is famous for its native copper mines, now almost completely exhausted.

(c) The Adirondack Mountains. The Adirondack Mountains are higher and more rugged than the Laurentian and Superior Uplands. Mining, especially of garnet, and of iron and titanium

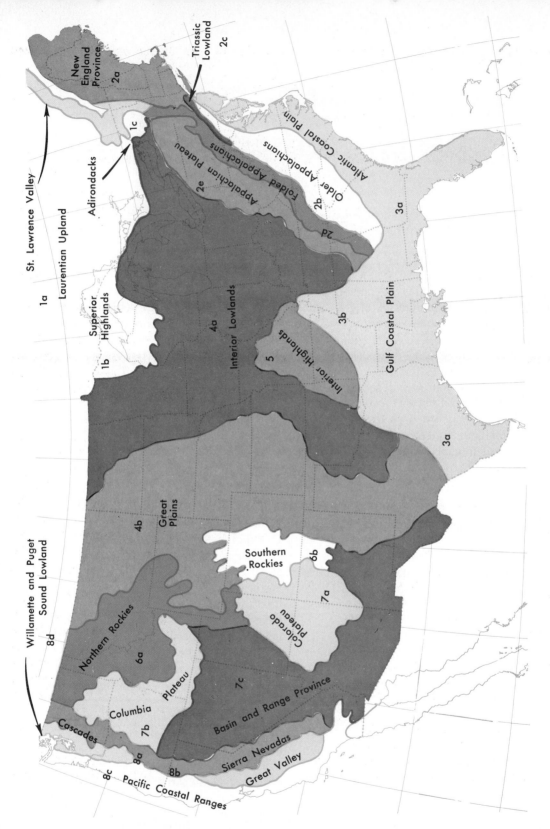

Fig. 17-1. The principal physiographic provinces of the United States. The number next to each name is the number of the text paragraph in which the province is described.

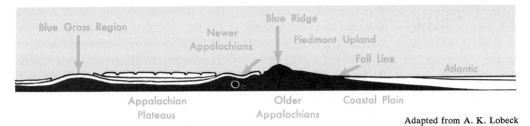

Fig. 17-2. Cross section of the United States at about the 39th parallel (Washington, D.C. to San Francisco). Part 1: from the Atlantic Ocean to the Central Lowlands.

ores, has become of increasing importance in recent years. The famous Thousand Islands located at the outlet of the St. Lawrence River represent the low, narrow rock "bridge" joining the Adirondacks to the rest of the Laurentian Division.

2. The Appalachian Highland Division

This major division includes all the mountain and plateau areas of eastern United States.

(a) The New England Province. The New England Province includes Canada's New Brunswick and Nova Scotia, all of New England, and parts of New York, New Jersey, and Pennsylvania. Like the Laurentians, this is an area of old or mature complex mountains of crystalline rocks, such as granite, gneiss, schist, and occasional slate and marble. Here, too, glaciation has left young rivers with numerous lakes and waterfalls, and the glacial mantle is generally thin and full of boulders.

Southern New England is a moderately rugged raised peneplane, above whose surface rise many monadnocks, including Mount Monadnock in New Hampshire. Northern New England, much higher and more rugged, includes the Green Mountains of Vermont, the White Mountains of northern New Hampshire, and such peaks as Mt. Katahdin in Maine. Mount Washington in the White Mountains is the highest

peak in northeastern United States. It is 6,288 feet high.

West of the Green Mountains and the southern New England peneplane lie the Taconic Mountains, a raised peneplane. Mount Greylock, Massachusetts, a monadnock, is the best-known peak in the Taconic Range. A southward continuation of the Taconics in Massachusetts is called the Berkshire Hills.

From Connecticut two slender projections or "prongs" of the New England Province's crystalline rocks extend southwestward. The smaller southern one, known as the Manhattan Prong, forms the bedrock of part of Westchester County, the Bronx, and Manhattan, where it ends. The larger Reading Prong, through which the narrows" of the Hudson River (a water gap) passes from Newburgh south to Stony Point, forms the Ramapo Mountains and Hudson Highlands of New York and New Jersey.

(b) The Older Appalachians. The Older Appalachians, extending from Pennsylvania southward to Georgia and Alabama, include the *Piedmont* and the *Blue Ridge*. Like the Laurentian and New England Provinces, the Older Appalachians are an area of complex mountains and crystalline rocks. However, they were not subjected to glaciation during the Ice Age, and are covered by fairly thick residual soils. There are very few lakes.

The Piedmont, lower eastern portion of this province, has the low rolling surface of an old mountain region. Like southern New England, it has its monadnocks, of which the best known is Stone Mountain near Atlanta, Georgia. East of the Piedmont lies the Atlantic Coastal Plain. The junction between the two is known as the Fall Zone, so named because of the falls or rapids that occur in the many rivers flowing from the harder rocks of the Piedmont onto the Plain. Atlanta, Georgia, is the only large city within the Piedmont, but many cities are located along its Fall Zone. Trenton, Philadelphia, Baltimore, Washington, Richmond, Raleigh, and Augusta, Georgia, are some of the largest.

From the Fall Zone the Piedmont slopes gently upward toward the west until it reaches the thickly forested Blue Ridge. The Blue Ridge, much higher and more rugged than the Piedmont, rises steeply above it to form the Great Smoky Mountains in western North Carolina and Tennessee; the "Skyline Drive" in Shenandoah National Park, Virginia; the Unaka Mountains in Georgia; and other mountain groups. Mount Mitchell, in the Black Mountains of North Carolina, is the highest mountain peak east of the Mississippi. It is 6,684 feet high.

(c) The Triassic Lowland. The Triassic Lowland lies between the New England Province and the Older Appalachians. It extends from New York southwestward through New Jersey, Pennsylvania, Maryland, and Virginia as a belt of sandstones and shales. Since these rocks are weaker than the crystalline rocks which lie on either side, they are weathered more rapidly to form a "lowland," marked by red soil and a very gentle surface.

Resistant igneous beds occur between the sedimentary layers, standing out in such formations as the Palisades of the Hudson River and the Watchung Ridges of New Jersey.

(d) The Folded Appalachians or Newer Appalachians. The Folded Appalachians or Newer Appalachians Province (also called the Valley and Ridge Province) extends from Lake Champlain in New York State to Alabama, running as a long narrow area west of the New England Province and the Older Appalachians. The Folded Appalachians are mountains formed by the folding of sedimentary layers of sandstone, limestone, conglomerate, and shale. Just west of the crystalline rocks of the New England and Older Appalachians provinces, outcropping weak limestone has been worn down into the *Great Valley,* stretching 1,000 miles from Vermont to Tennessee. West of the Great Valley, the Folded Appalachians form a series of long parallel ridges and valleys, the ridges usually being formed by resistant sandstone or conglomerate outcrops. Rivers like the Delaware, the Susquehanna, and the Potomac have cut water gaps through the ridges.

The slate beds and anthracite coal beds of eastern Pennsylvania lie in the rocks of this province. They were formed when sedimentary shale and soft coal were metamorphosed by the intense folding that created the mountains. At the southern end of the province in Alabama valuable deposits of iron ore are found not far from deposits of soft coal and limestone needed in the smelting of iron ore.

(e) The Appalachian Plateaus. This province lies west of the Folded Appalachians. Though generally higher and more rugged than the Folded Appalachians, the province's horizontal rock structures make it a plateau. It includes the following regions: the Catskill "Mountains" of eastern New York; the Helderberg Escarpment near Albany; the Allegheny Escarpment in western New York and the Finger Lake district; the Pocono "Mountains" in eastern Pennsylvania; the Allegheny "Mountains" in western Pennsylvania and West Virginia; the Cumberland Plateau of Kentucky, Tennessee, and Alabama.

Vast deposits of soft coal outcrop from horizontal layers on open valley walls from western Pennsylvania to Alabama. These exposed coal beds are easily dug into in "open-pit" mines in contrast to the deep drilling required in the hard coal mines. Oil and natural gas are also important resources.

3. The Atlantic Plains Division

This major division includes the Atlantic and Gulf Coastal Plains and the Mississippi Valley Plain.

(a) The Coastal Plains. This province includes the Atlantic Coastal Plain and the Gulf Coastal Plain. The "rocks" consist for the most part of layers of sand and clay which are not yet hardened into sandstone and shale. The surface is generally flat.

The Atlantic Coastal Plain extends from Long Island to Florida and from the Atlantic Ocean to the Piedmont. Large cities are located either along the Fall Zone or at the heads of bays formed by the recent partial submergence of river valleys. Offshore bars are common along most of the coast.

The Gulf Coastal Plain extends from western Florida to southern Texas. It is similar to the Atlantic Coastal Plain in structure, topography, and natural vegetation, but its shoreline has almost no harbors. Oil, natural gas, and sulfur form valuable mineral deposits in Texas and Louisiana.

(b) Mississippi Valley Plain. The flood plain of the Mississippi River extends from the mouth of the Ohio in southern Illinois to the mouth of the Mississippi in the Gulf of Mexico, 600 miles to the south. It has an average width of nearly 75 miles, and is from 100 to 200 feet below the cliffs or "bluffs" that enclose it. The principal city of the flood plain is New Orleans, built on the levees nearly 100 miles from the mouth of the river.

4. Interior Plains Division

This division includes the Interior or Central Lowlands and the Great Plains.

(a) The Central Lowlands. The Central Lowlands province extends westward from the Appalachian Plateaus to the Great Plains (at about the 100th meridian), and southward from the Laurentian Uplands to the Gulf Coastal Plain. This province was once the floor of a sea that reached from Hudson Bay to the Gulf of Mexico. Horizontal layers of sediments make up its bedrock. With the exception of Lake Superior, which is in the Laurentian province, all of the Great Lakes lie in the Interior Lowland. From near Rochester, New York, to eastern Wisconsin, a long low cliff known as the Niagara Escarpment extends across the Great Lakes region. Niagara Falls originated at the Niagara Escarpment, from which it has since receded a distance of seven miles.

Except in the Driftless Area of southwestern Wisconsin, the sediments are covered by glacial deposits about as far south as the Ohio and Missouri rivers, which mark the approximate limit of the great glaciers of the Ice Age. *Glacial lake deposits* form the very level plain of the bed of Lake Agassiz in North Dakota and Minnesota, while *till deposits* form the level till plain of northern Ohio. Elsewhere the surface varies from gently rolling prairies, as in Iowa, Illinois, Ohio, and Indiana, to somewhat greater relief, as in Kentucky and Tennessee. Thousands of lakes occur in the morainal deposits of Minnesota, Wisconsin, northern Iowa, and the Dakotas.

Fig. 17-3. Cross section of the United States at about the 39th Parallel. Part 2: from the Central Lowlands to the Rocky Mountains.

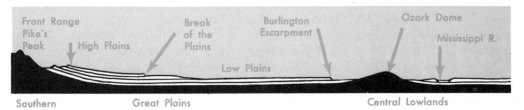

Caterpillar Tractor Company

Fig. 17-4. The Great Plains near Roswell, New Mexico. Preparing to plant cotton.

(b) The Great Plains. The Great Plains may be divided into the High Plains, the Low Plains, and the Missouri Plateau. The High Plains cover the western part of the province from the Rocky Mountains in Colorado and New Mexico eastward for about 200 miles, reaching into western Kansas, western Oklahoma, and the Texas panhandle. This level region of horizontal sediments, over 5,000 feet high at the base of the Rocky Mountains, has sufficient relief to be called a plateau.

The High Plains end abruptly to the east in a very rough escarpment known as the "Break of the Plains," from which the Low Plains extend eastward to the Central Lowlands at about the 100th meridian. The Low Plains include central Kansas, Oklahoma, and Texas. North of the High Plains, the Great Plains extend through Wyoming, Montana, and the Dakotas to the Canadian border as a rugged plateau region drained by the Missouri River and its tributaries. This region is the Missouri Plateau. Beyond the Missouri Plateau the Great Plains continue through Canada all the way to the Arctic Ocean.

Within the boundaries of the Great Plains are found a number of other physiographic features. The domed Black Hills rise high above the plain in western South Dakota. Their lower

sandstone layers form the outcropping aquifer of the Dakota artesian formation, while their igneous cores contain valuable gold and silver deposits. Western Nebraska has a great area of "sandhills" or dunes. In some parts of the Great Plains, *badlands* of deeply gullied clay deposits form fantastic scenery. Buttes and mesas are numerous throughout the Missouri Plateau, as well as in parts of Colorado, New Mexico, and Texas. Near Roswell, New Mexico, are located the great Carlsbad Caverns.

Mineral resources of the Great Plains include vast deposits of brown coal and the great oil and natural gas deposits of Texas, Oklahoma, Kansas, and Wyoming.

5. The Interior Highlands Division

The Interior Highlands include the Ozark Plateaus of southern Missouri and northern Arkansas and the Ouachita (*wash* ih tuh) Mountains of westcentral Arkansas and eastern Oklahoma.

(a) The Ozark Plateaus. The Ozark region is a maturely dissected plateau. Lumbering and the mining of lead and zinc are its chief industries.

(b) Ouachita Mountains. The Ouachita Mountains are mature folded mountains similar

Fig. 17-5. This mesa in Scotts-bluff National Monument, Nebraska, was a landmark on the Overland Trail.

to the Folded Appalachians. The ridges and valleys run in an east-west direction. The valley of the Arkansas River forms a broad east-west lowland between the Ouachitas and the Ozarks.

6. The Rocky Mountain Division.

This division consists of two major parts: the Northern and Southern Rocky Mountains.

(a) The Northern Rocky Mountains. The Northern Rockies are complex mountains whose various ranges show a great variety of structures. Rising steeply from the Great Plains on the east, they extend through western Montana, northern Idaho, western Wyoming, and northeastern Utah and include the Lewis Range in northern Mon-

tana, the Grand Tetons and the Bighorn Mountains of Wyoming, and the Wasatch and Uinta Mountains of Utah. Alpine topography is best developed in the area of Glacier National Park, where fairly large valley glaciers occur. Copper, gold, silver, iron, and coal are important mineral products.

(b) The Southern Rocky Mountains. The Northern Rockies are separated from the Southern Rockies by an extension of the Great Plains known as the Wyoming Basin, running almost diagonally across Wyoming from northeast to southwest. The Southern Rockies consist principally of two long granite domes that rise high above the Great Plains to the east and the Colorado Plateau to the west. The eastern dome is

Fig. 17-6. Cross section of the United States at about the 39th parallel. Part 3: from the Rocky Mountains to the Pacific Ocean.

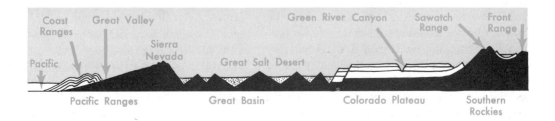

Fig. 17-7. Rainbow Natural Bridge in Utah is 309 feet high and 278 feet long.

Gregory, U.S. Geological Survey

known as the Front Range. It extends from southern Wyoming almost to the southern border of Colorado. Among its highest peaks are Longs Peak north of Denver, and Pikes Peak in the south near Colorado Springs. Both peaks are over 14,000 feet high. The Arkansas River has cut its famous Royal Gorge through the Front Range south of Pikes Peak.

The western dome is known as the Sawatch Range. It parallels the Front Range through Colorado and extends far beyond it into New Mexico. Between the two ranges in Colorado lies a series of basins or *parks*.

The Southern Rockies are higher than the Northern Rockies, but because of their lower latitude, they have not been eroded as extensively by glaciers. Rocky Mountain National Park in the Front Range in Colorado is a popular area for hikers and mountain climbers. Silver, gold, lead, zinc, molybdenum, and coal are mined in Colorado.

7. Intermontane Plateaus Division

This division of "between-the-mountain plateaus" includes the Colorado Plateau, the Columbia Plateau, and the mountains and valleys of the Basin and Range Province.

(a) Colorado Plateau. Starting at the base of the Southern Rockies, the lofty Colorado Plateau stretches westward to include western Colorado and New Mexico, more than half of Utah, and the northern half of Arizona. On its northern side it is partly enclosed by the Uinta Mountains of Utah. On its western and southern rims it looks down upon the Basin and Range Province. The Colorado is a young plateau formed largely by faulting. Its extraordinarily level surface is slashed here and there by the great canyons of the Colorado River and its tributaries. Occasional small mountain groups project above its surface.

In Arizona the Grand Canyon of the Colorado River pierces the entire 4,000-foot thickness of the sedimentary strata and continues through

2,000 feet more of underlying granite. The Green River, the Grand River, the San Juan, and other tributaries have carved smaller but still spectacular canyons. The principal mountain groups owe their origin to vulcanism. Mount Taylor in New Mexico and the San Francisco Mountains in Arizona are extinct volcanoes. The Henry Mountains in Utah and the Zuni Mountains in New Mexico are dome mountains.

The uranium ores of this region are the richest in the United States and among the richest in the world. The region also includes many national parks and "monuments." The best known are Mesa Verde in Colorado; Bryce Canyon, Zion Canyon, Cedar Breaks, Arches, and Rainbow Natural Bridge in Utah; and Grand Canyon, Petrified Forest, Canyon de Chelly, and Meteor Crater in Arizona.

The Colorado River, master stream of the region, carries almost all of its drainage southwest and through the adjoining Basin and Range Province into the Pacific Ocean.

(b) Columbia Plateau. The Columbia Plateau extends from the Northern Rockies west to the Cascade Mountains and south to the Great Basin. It includes southern Idaho, eastern Washington, and nearly all of Oregon. Its rocks are flood basalts up to 5,000 feet in total thickness. Through this vast sheet of lava the Snake and Columbia Rivers have cut spectacular gorges, that of the Snake River being more than 100 miles long and having a maximum depth of 6,000 feet. Except for these gorges, most of the plateau surface is fairly flat.

(c) Basin and Range Province or Great Basin. The Basin and Range Province is bounded on the north by the Columbia Plateau, on the east by the Wasatch Range and the Colorado Plateau, and on the west by the Sierra Nevada and Coast Ranges of California. Reaching south to the Mexican border, it includes western Utah, all of Nevada, southeastern California, southern New Mexico, and Texas.

This province consists of numerous fault-block mountains and the basins between them.

Most of the blocks are long and narrow, running in a north-south direction, and are half-buried in the sediment of the alluvial fans formed along their straight bases. Two of the great basins have no outlets. One of these, once the floor of great Lake Bonneville, is now occupied in part by Great Salt Lake in northern Utah. The other, once the floor of Lake Lahontan, is now occupied in part by Carson Sink and Pyramid Lake, both of which are alkali lakes located in northwestern Nevada.

With the moisture of the Pacific Ocean locked out by the lofty Sierra Nevada Mountains on the west, this province is the "Great American Desert." In California it includes the vast Mohave Desert and, between the ranges to the north, the famous Death Valley desert, which is 280 feet below sea level. Despite the extreme dryness of the climate, three great rivers cross the southern part of this province, bringing waters largely from the Southern Rockies. These rivers are the Colorado and Gila in the southwest and the Rio Grande in the southeast.

8. Pacific Mountain System

Parts of the System. From the Pacific Ocean on the west to the Columbia Plateau and Basin and Range Province on the east, the surface of the United States resembles a long, narrow, curved letter "H." Each of the three lines in this "H" represents a mountain chain, while the openings between the lines represent two great lowlands.

The eastern mountain chain in the "H" runs from the Canadian border to central California and includes the Cascade and Sierra Nevada Mountains. The western mountain chain runs the entire length of the Pacific Coast from Washington through Southern California and includes the Coast Ranges. These two great parallel mountain chains are joined for over 200 miles in southern Oregon and northern California by the Klamath Mountains. The lowland north of the

Klamath Mountains contains the Puget Sound Lowland in Washington and the Willamette Valley in Oregon. The lowland south of the Klamath Mountains is the Great Valley of California.

(a) The Cascade Mountains. The Cascade Mountains of Washington and Oregon are complex mountains with a fairly level surface except where volcanic peaks rise to great heights. These volcanic peaks include Mount Rainier, Mount Baker, and Mount St. Helens, all in Washington, and Mount Jefferson, Mount Hood, and Crater Lake in Oregon.

(b) The Sierra Nevadas. The Sierra Nevada Mountains of northern and central California are formed from a great fault block whose steep scarpside faces east. The southern portion of the range, known as the High Sierras, includes Mount Whitney, our highest mountain peak outside Alaska. It is 14,501 feet high.

On the long western back slope of the Sierras, numerous rivers have carved out magnificent canyons, including the Yosemite Valley of the Merced River in Yosemite National Park, Kings Canyon, and the canyon of the Tuolumne River. Glacial erosion has added to the beauty of these canyons. Large alluvial fans are formed where the rivers leave the mountains.

The northern end of the Sierras contains Mount Lassen, our only active volcano outside Alaska and Hawaii. Farther north, between the Sierras and the Klamath Mountains but still in California, stands beautiful Mount Shasta, a volcanic mountain but one which is extinct. The gold rush of 1849 in California began an important industry which is still carried on in California's Sierras.

(c) The Coast Ranges. The Coast Ranges are young folded mountains that rise steeply from the ocean floor along most of the Pacific Coast. Faulting occurs frequently in these mountains, which are still growing; consequently there are many earthquakes in this region, especially in California. The Coast Ranges reach their greatest heights in Washington's Olympic Mountains, more than 8,000 feet high.

At San Francisco partial submergence of the Sacramento River's break in the Coast Range has formed one of the best harbors in the country. The Coast Ranges in Southern California are commercially important for their great oil fields.

(d) The Willamette and Puget Sound Lowland. This region, surrounded by the Coast, Klamath, and Cascade Mountains, has a fairly flat surface covered largely by alluvial soils deposited by the mountain streams. In northern Washington there are morainal deposits of the Ice Age. Seattle and other fine harbors border Puget Sound.

(e) The Great Valley of California. The Great Valley of California lies between the Coast, Klamath, and Sierra Nevada Mountains. The underlying bedrock of the Coast Range and the Sierras is covered by as much as two thousand feet of alluvial deposits carried down from the mountain slopes by the many rivers of the Sierras. The northern half of the Valley is drained by the Sacramento River, the southern half by the San Joaquin (wah *keen*) River. The surface of the Valley is generally flat and rarely more than 400 feet above sea level. Oil and natural gas are important mineral resources.

TOPIC QUESTIONS

This chapter is largely descriptive, and the student is *not* expected to "memorize" it. He may, however, become familiar with the location, rock structure, general topography, and principal minerals of each of the important physiographic provinces or sections that have been described.

Each topic question refers to the topic of the same number within the chapter.

1–8. For each major division make a chart showing (*a*) subdivisions (provinces or sections), (*b*) location of each subdivision, (*c*) rock structure and bedrock, (*d*) general topography, (*e*) scenic features, (*f*) minerals.

STUDENT ACTIVITIES

1. Study and label a copy of Lobeck's Physiographic Diagram of the United States, Small-Scale Edition with text. (Obtain from The Geographic Press, C. S. Hammond, Maplewood, New Jersey.)

2. Use plasticene or plaster of Paris to make a simple physical map of the United States.

3. On an outline map, make a "mineral map" of the United States by gluing to each state samples of the principal minerals it produces, as listed in this chapter.

BIBLIOGRAPHY

Bascom, W. *A Hole in the Bottom of the Sea—the Mohole Project.* Doubleday, N.Y., 1961.

Bullard, F. M. *Volcanoes.* University of Texas Press, Austin, 1962.

Calder, N. *The Restless Earth.* Viking, N.Y., 1972.

Cloos, H. *Conversation With the Earth.* Knopf, N.Y., 1953.

Croneis and Krumbein. *Down to Earth.* University of Chicago Press, 1961.

Eiby, G. A. *About Earthquakes.* Harper and Row, N.Y., 1957.

Emmons, et al. *Geology.* McGraw-Hill, N.Y., 1961.

Fenton, C. L. *Giants of Geology.* Doubleday, N.Y., 1960.

Gamow, G. *Biography of the Earth.* Viking, N.Y., 1959.

Gilluly, et al. *Principles of Geology.* Freeman, San Francisco, 1968.

Hunt, C. B. *Physiography of the U.S.* Freeman, San Francisco, 1967.

Leet, L. W. *The World of Geology.* McGraw-Hill, N.Y., 1961.

Leet and Judson. *Physical Geology.* Prentice-Hall, Englewood Cliffs, N.J., 1971.

Lobeck, A. K. *Physiographic Diagram of the United States.* Geographical Press, Maplewood, N.J.

Lobeck, A. K. *Panorama of Physiographic Types.* Geographical Press, Maplewood, N.J.

Longwell and Flint. *Introduction to Physical Geology.* Wiley, N.Y., 1969.

MacDonald G. A. *Volcanoes.* Prentice-Hall, Englewood Cliffs, N.J., 1972.

MacKenzie, D. P. *Plate Tectonics and Sea Floor Spreading. American Scientist,* Vol. 60, 1972.

Matthews, W. H. *Geology of Our National Parks.* Natural History Press, N.Y., 1967.

Matthews, W. H. *Introducing the Earth.* Dodd, Mead, N.Y., 1972.

Mather, K. F. *The Earth Beneath Us.* Random House, N.Y., 1964.

Pough, F. H. *All About Volcanoes and Earthquakes.* Random House, N.Y., 1955.

Shelton, J. S. *Geology Illustrated.* Freeman, San Francisco, 1966.

Shimer, J. A. *This Sculptured Earth.* Columbia University Press, N.Y., 1959.

Strahler, A. N. *Physical Geography.* Wiley, N.Y., 1970.

Strahler, A. N. *The Earth Sciences.* Harper and Row, N.Y., 1971.

U.S. Dept. of Agriculture. *Water, 1975 Yearbook; Soil, 1975 Yearbook,* Supt. of Documents, Washington, D.C. 20402.

Wilson, J. T. (ed.) *Continents Adrift.* Freeman, San Francisco, 1972.

Wycoff, J. *Story of Geology.* Golden Press, N.Y., 1960.

Unit 4 The Oceans of the Earth

What does the photograph on the opposite page show? Where do you think a scene like this takes place? How does the photograph show the struggle between the forces that build up the earth's crust and the forces that wear it away? How might waves affect a sandy shore? A rocky coast?

The shorelines are the boundaries between the earth's continents and its oceans. The oceans cover more than 70% of the surface of the earth, and there are thousands of miles of shorelines each with a life history of its own.

The study of the oceans is called oceanography. Oceanography uses many basic sciences. It uses chemistry to analyze the waters of the sea and the minerals of the sea floor; it uses physics to measure the depths of the oceans and the temperatures of their waters; it uses geology to study the topography and sediments of the ocean floor; it uses biology to study the plant and animal life of the ocean waters. Tides are studied with the aid of astronomy; waves and currents are studied with the aid of meteorology and climatology.

Oceanographers may go to sea in specially equipped ships on long expeditions that may last for years. They may make a base on an ice floe or an ice island that will drift into areas ships cannot reach. They may descend to the depths of the sea in a submersible that can cruise along the sea bottom for short distances. They may live and work for weeks in sea labs several hundred feet below the water surface. Today oceanography is deeply involved in what has become known as the exploration of "inner space."

CHAPTER 18
Exploration of the Sea

HOW DO YOU KNOW THAT . . . ?

The "drift bottle" is a simple device used to study the movement of ocean currents. Its principle is very simple. It floats just below the surface of the water where it is moved by currents but not by winds. To make a drift bottle, fill a small bottle or test tube with water. Cover or stopper it tightly. Place it in a large aquarium, battery jar, or beaker of water. What happens to it? Why?

Remove the bottle. Now pour off water, a little at a time, and test the bottle each time until it just floats fully submerged. Using a medicine dropper to remove or add water will help you make your final adjustment.

Drift bottles are usually weighted with sand rather than water. Why? If you have time, try making one that way. What information must be enclosed in a drift bottle if it is to be of any use?

1. The Oceans of the Earth

Even though the sea is continuous, the continental masses divide it up in a manner that has led geographers to give names to these divisions, calling each an ocean. The Pacific Ocean, larger than all the land areas together, stretches from the west coast of the Americas as far as Asia and Australia. Next largest is the Atlantic Ocean, reaching eastward from the Americas to Europe and Africa. The Indian Ocean, third in size, lies south of Asia. The Arctic Ocean covers the north polar region of the earth. Some geographers speak of the Antarctic Ocean as a fifth division of the sea, but many others regard these waters of the south polar region merely as parts of the Atlantic, Pacific, and Indian oceans from which they extend.

2. The Extent of the Oceans

The surface area of the earth is approximately 197 million square miles. About 57 million square miles—only 29 per cent of the total—represents the great continental masses of the earth, standing like enormous islands above the level of the sea that surrounds them. The sea, really a single continuous body of water, covers the remaining 140 million square miles that make up 71 per cent of the earth's surface.

The oceans greatly exceed the land in volume as well as in area. The oceans have an average depth of about two and a half miles, as compared with an average height of only a half mile for the land surface. The deepest point in the ocean is nearly seven miles deep, while the earth's highest peak, Mount Everest, is less than six miles high. As you can see, if the continents were completely eroded to sea level, the oceans would have no trouble in accommodating them. (See Fig. 18-1.)

3. Famous Names in Oceanography

Not until the 1800's did oceanography begin to become a science. Its first big step in this direction resulted from long and systematic

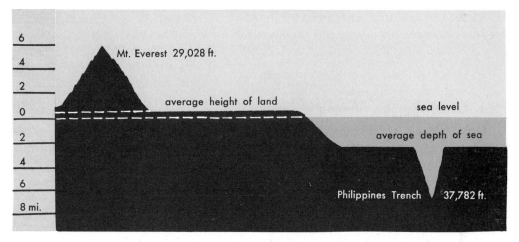

6
4
2
0

2
4
6
8 mi.

Mt. Everest 29,028 ft.

average height of land

sea level

average depth of sea

Philippines Trench   37,782 ft.

Fig. 18-1. Comparison of the height of the land with the depth of the sea.

studies of ocean winds, storm tracks, and surface currents by Lieutenant Matthew Fontaine Maury of the U.S. Navy. In 1855 Maury published his *Physical Geography of the Sea,* and his observations formed the basis for valuable Pilot Charts of the oceans issued by the Navy Hydrographic Office.

In England during the early 1800's a famous naturalist named Edward Forbes helped to introduce the use of the *naturalist's dredge* in collecting samples of the life of the sea floor. Forbes spent many years of his life in studying the waters off England and in the Mediterranean. He is generally regarded as the founder of marine biology. Forbes believed that below 300 fathoms (1,800 feet) the ocean was an Azoic Zone (*a,* without; *zoic,* life) in which neither plants nor animals could exist. This theory was later proved to be incorrect.

In the late 1860's the British government became interested in oceanographic research, and in 1872 it made possible the first great study of the world's oceans. A British Navy corvette, HMS *Challenger,* was fitted up as an oceanographic laboratory, staffed with scientists, and stocked with provisions for a long journey. The *Challenger* set sail from England on December 7, 1872, and did not return until three and a half

years later, on May 24, 1876, having covered nearly 70,000 nautical miles in the Atlantic, Pacific, Indian and Antarctic oceans. The *Challenger* "stopped" at a total of 362 "stations." Each station's latitude and longitude were determined so that the location of the station might be plotted on the ocean charts. Then *samples of the deep sea water and sediments of the sea floor* were taken, the *depth of water* was determined, and the *deep water temperature* was measured. Dredges and nets were used to capture marine animals and plants at various depths, and ocean currents were studied. When the *Challenger* returned to England in 1876, it had collected enough material to form the basis of a 50-volume report so exhaustive that it was not completed until almost 20 years later. The scientific leaders of the *Challenger* expedition were Sir Wyville Thomson, Professor of Natural History at Edinburgh University, and Sir John Murray, famous naturalist at the same university.

Further contributions to oceanographic research following the *Challenger* expedition were made by Alexander Agassiz, wealthy American mining engineer (and son of the famous naturalist Louis Agassiz) and Prince Albert of Monaco. Agassiz improved many of the instruments used by oceanographers, using these in his studies of tropical ocean waters. Prince Albert, too, improved old instruments and invented new ones, including floats used to track ocean currents.

4. Oceanographic Research Today

Oceanographic research is enormously expensive, since it requires the use of specially fitted vessels and professionally trained personnel. The years following the *Challenger* expedition saw considerable growth in the number of both private and government-supported expeditions in the United States and Europe. But very few individuals combine a deep love for oceanography with the means to pursue their interest—as did Alexander Agassiz and Prince Albert. Today almost all oceanographic research is carried on by government agencies and privately endowed institutions.

Fig. 18-2. How the echo sounder measures ocean depths.

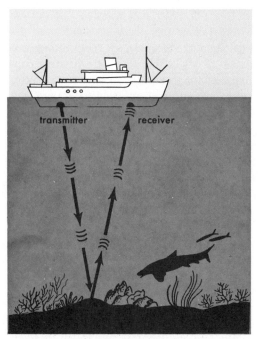

Oceanographic research is growing at a great pace. The First International Oceanographic Congress was held in the United States in 1959. It was attended by more than a thousand scientists representing 30 countries. When the Second Congress was held in the Soviet Union in 1966, the number of countries had increased to 57, and the total attendance was nearly 2,000. The United States delegation numbered almost 200 scientists.

The leaders of oceanographic research in the United States today include both government and private agencies. Among government agencies are the Naval Oceanographic Office and the Coast and Geodetic Survey. Private agencies include the Scripps Institution of Oceanography of the University of California, the Lamont Geological Observatory of Columbia University, the Wood's Hole Oceanographic Institution in Massachusetts, and the Institute of Marine Science of the University of Miami. In addition to those already mentioned, colleges offering programs leading to degrees in oceanography include the University of Washington, Texas A and M University, Johns Hopkins University, and the University of Rhode Island.

5. Oceanographic Methods and Instruments

The oceanographer uses many special instruments and methods to make his measurements and obtain his specimens.

(a) Measuring depth of water. The depth of any part of the ocean is found by **sounding.** In the days of the *Challenger* sounding meant reeling out a lead-weighted line of rope or wire until it reached bottom. In very deep water a single sounding would take hours. But in the early 1920's the **echo sounder** came into use. The echo sounder sends a high-pitched sound wave from the ship's hull through the sea water at the rate of about 4,800 feet per second. If the sound sent to the sea bottom is "echoed" back to the ship's receiver in two seconds, it means that the sound took one second to go to the bottom and one more second to return; the water is therefore 4,800 feet deep—in this example.

$$\text{Depth} = \frac{\text{number of seconds}}{2} \times 4,800 \text{ feet}$$

Echo sounders can measure the ocean's greatest depths in seconds instead of hours, and they are accurate to within about one part in 200. In the early days of echo sounders each depth shown on the instrument had to be recorded and plotted by hand. Today there are instruments that automatically plot a continuous record of depth as the ship cruises along, thus giving a profile of the sea floor. (See Figs. 18-2, 18-3 and 18-4.)

(b) Measuring thickness of sediments on the sea floor. This can be measured by the Sonoprobe, an instrument which uses a small underwater explosion to create low-pitched sound waves. These waves penetrate the soft sediments on the sea floor, but are echoed back from the underlying bedrock. By subtracting the

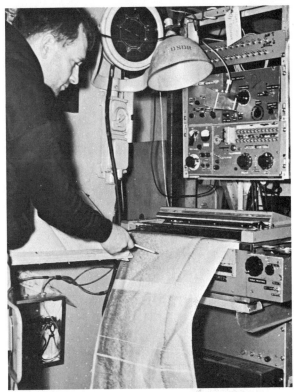

Woods Hole Oceanographic Institution

Fig. 18-3. An echo sounder automatically records the results of its soundings.

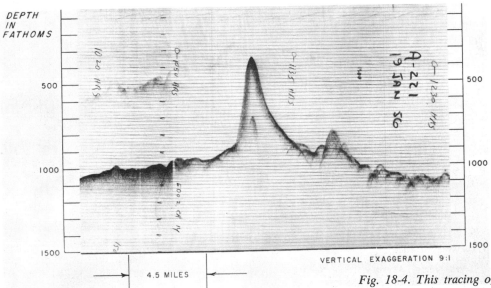

VERTICAL EXAGGERATION 9:1

4.5 MILES

DEPTH IN FATHOMS

Woods Hole Oceanographic Institution

Fig. 18-4. This tracing of echo soundings covers a distance of about 22 miles on the sea floor, and was made in about two hours.

Woods Hole Oceanographic Institution

Fig. 18-5. The Ekman current meter measures the speed and direction of deep ocean currents.

depth of the water from the depth of the bedrock, the thickness of sediments is determined. Sonoprobe records are plotted automatically.

(c) Measuring speed and direction of currents. The speed and direction of surface currents used to be measured by releasing dated **drift bottles** or floats, weighted so they would float just below the surface. In this position they were not affected by winds. The bottles carried instructions for the finders to return them to the research institution. From the date and location where they were picked up, the direction and speed of the current could be calculated.

Nowadays **current meters** of various types can be used to measure the speed and direction of currents below the surface as well as at the surface. (See Fig. 18-5.) An electronic instrument called the **Swallow float** or **Swallow pinger** may be floated beneath the surface at any chosen depth, and its movements tracked by the sound

signals or *pings* its transmitter sends out. The Swallow float was invented by Dr. John B. Swallow of the National Institute of Oceanography of Great Britain.

(d) Getting samples of deep-sea water. In the *Challenger* days *water-sampling bottles* closed automatically when they were pulled upwards, after reaching the desired sampling depth. Modern sampling bottles, known as **Nansen bottles,** are closed by a "messenger weight" that slides down the wire by which the bottle is attached. When the weight strikes the bottle, it releases a catch, permitting the bottle to turn upside down, close its valves automatically, and trap the water inside it. The sample is analyzed for both mineral content and the presence of living things. (See Fig. 18-6.)

(e) Measuring underwater temperature. Special *thermometers* attached to the Nansen bottles automatically record the temperature at

Fig. 18-6. Rack of Nansen bottles on board oceanographic research ship.

Woods Hole Oceanographic Institution

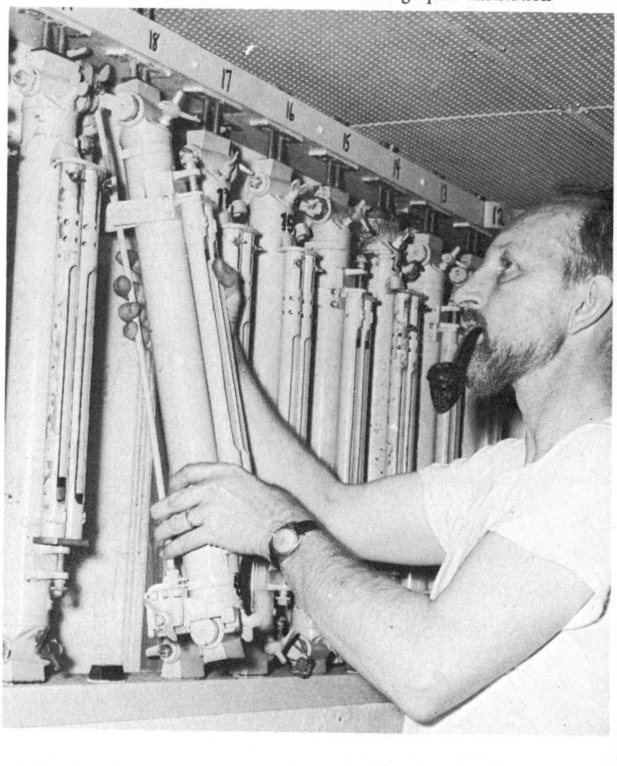

Woods Hole Oceanographic Institution

Fig. 18-7. Bathythermograph being lowered to measure the water temperature down to 900 feet.

the depth sampled. For a continuous record of temperatures in the water through which a thermometer is lowered, a **bathythermograph** (*bathy*, deep) has been developed. (See Fig. 18-7.) Its range of depth is only about 900 feet, however.

(f) Measuring surface temperature. The temperature of the water at the ocean surface is measured most simply on shipboard by dipping up a sizeable sample and promptly using a thermometer on it. The bathythermograph may also be used close to the surface to give a continuous record of the temperature. A most recent development is to measure the temperature of the surface by the infrared radiation it emits. This can be done from airplanes flying over the ocean. (The same method is used by satellites and space probes investigating the surface temperatures of the moon and the planets.)

(g) Getting samples of sea-floor sediments.

In the earlier days of oceanography tiny samples of sea-floor sediments were picked up by having them adhere to tallow placed in a hollow on the bottom of the sounding line's weight. The development of *grabbing devices* like the "clam-shell buckets" (similar to a small steam-shovel) has made somewhat larger samples possible. Metal **dredges** are now used to scrape up loose rock samples that may lie on the sea floor. (See Fig. 18-8.)

(h) Getting cores of sediments. The coring tube or corer is a device used by the oceanographer to obtain slender cylinder-shaped samples of "undisturbed" ocean floor sediments in their naturally layered arrangement. There are many kinds of corers, and the cores they can take range in length from a few feet up to about 100 feet.

Fig. 18-8. This device for obtaining samples of seafloor sediments is called an orange peel grab.

Woods Hole Oceanographic Institution

Fig. 18-9. The Phleger corer shown here is driven into the ocean floor by the heavy weight at its top. It uses a plastic liner which can be removed with the sediment core inside it.

The simplest type of corer is merely a steel tube with a heavy weight at the top to drive it into the sediments. The cores it brings up are somewhat compressed.

Cores that are longer and less disturbed can be obtained with the **piston corer** or **Kullenberg corer,** which was invented by Dr. Börje Kullenberg, Swedish oceanographer, in the early 1940's. This corer consists of a long, slender, steel coring tube with a piston inside it. The tube is lowered slowly by weight and cable. When almost at the sea floor, the tube is released suddenly, the piston still being held in place. The tube bores deep into the ocean floor. A partial vacuum is created inside the tube under the piston, and a core of sea-floor sediments is drawn into the tube. The cores, up to 100 feet in length, are brought to shore and studied in the labora-

tories of the oceanographic institutions. (See Fig. 18-9.)

The National Science Foundation is presently sponsoring a Deep Sea Drilling Project to study the bottom materials in ocean waters. Using the ship *Glomar Challenger* as a floating drill platform, the Project has already brought up thousands of sediment and rock cores from hundreds of places in the Atlantic, Pacific, and Indian oceans. The drilling has penetrated as much as 2,000 feet of ocean sediments and even cut into the underlying bedrock. Cores are studied to find the age of sediments, their relation to ocean currents, changes of climate they indicate, and origin of ocean basins.

(i) Getting samples of sea life. Samples of microscopic and small marine plants and animals are obtained in water-sampling bottles or in fine-meshed *silk or cotton tow nets.* (See Fig. 18-10.) *Coarser rope nets,* like fishing nets, may be trawled (dragged) through the water to trap larger specimens, or they may be used in conjunction with steel dredges to trap specimens dug up from the sea floor by the teeth of the dredge.

To make certain that the specimens in a net are all from a single known depth of water, nets are now made that can be closed automatically by "messenger weights" like those used with the Nansen water-sampling bottles.

(j) Underwater photography. Photographs of the sea floor and the deep sea are taken by special cameras equipped with synchronized electronic flash units and automatic film advance. The camera is lowered to the bottom by cable. When the camera touches the sea floor, the shutter is released, the light flashes, and the picture is taken. Each time the camera is lifted and dropped at a new location, the process is repeated.

Deep water television cameras can be used for continuous observation of objects in the deep sea and on the sea floor. They have been used to guide the operators of offshore oil drills. A similar use is in connection with the operation of mechanical arms under water. Marine biologists may use deep-water television to observe and make videotapes of marine life.

6. Direct Observation: SCUBA

Professional divers have been able to explore the sea directly to a maximum depth of about 300 feet, using waterproof suits with hoses connected to a surface supply of oxygen. In 1943 the invention of the Aqua-lung marked the beginning of an era of skin-diving. Now oceanographers as well as amateur sports enthusiasts may descend to depths of up to 180 feet with relatively inexpensive SCUBA (Self-Contained

Underwater Breathing Apparatus) equipment in which each diver carries his own oxygen supply.

7. Direct Observation: The Bathyscaphe

In 1934 William Beebe, famous explorer, set a record by descending in his **bathysphere** to a depth of 3,028 feet in the ocean floor near Bermuda. In 1949 this record was broken by Otis Barton, whose **benthoscope** touched bottom at a depth of 4,500 feet off the coast of California. Both devices were thick-walled hollow steel spheres attached to heavy steel cables that

Fig. 18-10. Woman scientist-aquanaut explores coral reef and gathers samples of sea life in a collection net. She is wearing a rebreather system that is bubbleless and lighter than SCUBA gear.

General Electric Company

Fig. 18-11. Artists's drawing of the U.S. Navy bathyscaphe Trieste II, *now used to train deep submergence rescue personnel.*

lowered and raised them from a supporting ship. Through thick glass portholes, Beebe and Barton were able to make direct observations and take photographs of deep-sea life. But neither sphere seemed capable of safely approaching the much greater depths of the deepest parts of the sea.

In the late 1940's the famous Swiss inventor and balloonist, Professor Auguste Piccard, developed the **bathyscaphe,** often referred to as the "underwater balloon." Piccard eliminated the need for a supporting cable in a most ingenious way. His spherical steel cabin, with walls about four inches thick and a plexiglas porthole six inches thick, was attached to the bottom of a much larger submarine-shaped "float." The float was basically a thin-walled steel tank, divided into compartments and filled with gasoline. Why gasoline? Any liquid would keep the tank from being crushed by the pressure of the deep sea. But gasoline, much lighter than sea water, also made the tank a "float" that was buoyant enough to support the heavy cabin of the bathyscaphe. (See Fig. 18-11.)

Unlike the bathysphere, then, the bathyscaphe supported itself afloat. To sink it, tons of *steel shot* were used as ballast (held inside the float by electromagnets) and the bathyscaphe allowed to descend to the desired depth. When ballast was released, the ship automatically floated to the surface—like a balloon rising in the air.

Under Piccard's direction, two bathyscaphes were built, and a number of successful dives made, easily breaking Barton's record. On January 23, 1960, Piccard's son, Jacques, and Lieutenant Don Walsh of the U.S. Navy set a world record of 35,800 feet on the floor of the Mariana Trench in the Pacific Ocean 250 miles southwest of Guam. Their U.S. Navy bathyscaphe, the *Trieste,* took nearly 5 hours to go down and a little over 3 hours to come up again. The *Trieste* was later used in attempts to locate the lost atomic submarine *Thresher* when it sank off the coast of Maine in 1963. (See Fig. 18-11.)

8. Submersibles for Research

In recent years there has been tremendous interest in the development of research "submersibles" that can explore the waters and floor

Fig. 18-12. Deepstar 4,000 *is designed to operate at a depth of 4,000 feet. Its manipulator arm is shown extended.*

of the deep ocean. Conventional navy submarines do not operate much below 400 feet, although their maximum depth is a military secret. The bathyscaphe can reach any depth, but its underwater horizontal range is only about .four miles. It moves underwater very slowly, and it has to be towed to the place where it is to make its dive. The new submersibles are generally designed to go to greater depths than conventional submarines, to have more maneuverability and greater range than the bathyscaphe, and to be able to do a number of different jobs underwater.

The *Diving Saucer* was designed by the famous French oceanographer Jacques-Yves Cousteau (koo *stow*) and launched by him in 1960. The crew of two must lie prone in this tiny saucer-shaped craft, which though only 6½ feet long, weighs four tons. The Diving Saucer goes to a maximum depth of about 1000 feet, which includes all of the continental shelves. It is easy to maneuver underwater. Cousteau has made many dives in his Saucers, and his underwater movies have been seen by millions of people.

More recently, submersibles that can stand the tremendous pressures of greater depths—thousands of tons per square inch—have been built. These vessels may be equipped with manipulator arms, sea-bottom corers, external lights, TV cameras, and sonar navigation instruments. Their power is provided by electric batteries or from surface "mother ships" connected by cables. *Deepstar* is like the Diving Saucers, but it is larger and descends more than 4,000 feet. (See Fig. 18-12.) The new *Sea Cliff Turtle*, and *DOWB* are designed to cruise at depths of 6,500 feet. The *Deep Quest,* designed especially for submarine rescue and salvage operation, holds the deep-diving record for submersibles other than bathyscaphes. In 1968 it went 8,310 feet down on the floor of the Pacific Ocean southwest of San Diego, California.

The *Alvin* is the tiny research submarine tha became famous when it located the hydroge bomb that fell into the Mediterranean Sea fi miles off the coast of Spain on January 17, 196 The *Alvin* is 22 feet long, weighs about 13 tor carries a two-man crew, and is designed f depths of at least 6,000 feet. (The bomb w located at a depth of 2,500 feet.) The *Al* can cruise underwater at a top speed of th miles an hour. Its range is about 30 miles.

The *Aluminaut,* which worked with *Alvin* in the search for the hydrogen boml larger and more like a conventional subma in shape than the other research submersi

It is about 50 feet long, weighs about 75 tons, and has comfortable facilities for a crew of three. Its horizontal range is 80 miles, and its top speed is nearly four knots. It is designed for a maximum depth of 15,000 feet. As its name implies, aluminum plays a large part in its construction, for its pressure hull is made of aluminum 6½ inches in thickness. In June 1969 *Aluminaut* "rescued" *Alvin* from a depth of 5,052 feet on the floor of the Atlantic Ocean 120 miles southeast of Cape Cod. *Alvin* had sunk October 1968 when her mother ship's cable broke as she was lowering *Alvin* for launching.

A 7-man nuclear-powered research submarine of "virtually unlimited endurance and range" was launched in 1969 by the U.S. Navy.

The **FLIP** ship derived its name from the words floating instrument platform. But as its name suggests, it actually flipped from the horizontal to the vertical when it took up its observation post. The FLIP ship was 355 feet long, and looked like a long narrow tube to which half a ship was attached. The FLIP ship was actually a manned buoy. It was used to study water waves both above and below the surface, sound waves, marine life, and other features of the sea.

Sealab was a research program developed by the U.S. Navy. Sealabs were stationary submerged shelters in which men could live for weeks at a time hundreds of feet down on the floor of the sea. The Sealabs were used as a base of operations from which undersea research could be conducted with scuba diving equipment. Some activities engaged in by Sealab were the collection of mineral, plant, and animal specimens; experimentation with "mining" techniques; working with tools to make underwater repairs on ships; "salvaging" sunken vessels; using a pet porpoise as a messenger.

TOPIC QUESTIONS

Each topic question refers to the topic of the same number within this chapter.

1. Name the oceans of the earth.

2. (*a*) Compare the area of land and sea on the earth's surface. (*b*) Compare the height of the land with the depth of the sea.

3. (*a*) What were the contributions to oceanography of Maury and Forbes? (*b*) Describe the oceanographic work of the *Challenger*. Who were its scientific leaders? (*c*) What were the contributions of Alexander Agassiz and Prince Albert of Monaco?

4. (*a*) Why is oceanographic research today carried on largely by institutions rather than individuals? (*b*) Name some of the leaders in present-day research.

5. Explain how oceanographers (*a*) measure depth of water, (*b*) measure thickness of sediments, (*c*) measure speed and direction of currents, (*d*) obtain samples of deep sea water, (*e*) measure underwater temperature, (*f*) measure surface water temperature, (*g*) get samples of sediments, (*h*) get cores of sediments, (*i*) get samples of sea life, (*j*) get underwater photographs.

6. What is SCUBA? How is it used in oceanography?

7. (*a*) What kind of vessels were the bathysphere and benthoscope? (*b*) How is a bathyscaphe built? How does it work? Describe its record dive.

8. (*a*) What are the new submersibles designed to do? (*b*) Give brief descriptions of the *Alvin* and the *Aluminaut*.

9. (*a*) How did the FLIP ship get its name? (*b*) What were some of the uses of the FLIP ship? (*c*) Briefly describe some of the activities that the Sealab personnel engaged in.

GENERAL QUESTIONS

1. Make an approximate calculation of how the volume of ocean water compares with that of the continents. (*Hint:* area × depth or height = volume)

2. Make an approximate calculation of the average daily distance covered by the *Challenger* in its expedition.

3. Approximately how long would it take a sound wave to go to the sea floor and return at the depth reached by the bathyscaphe *Trieste*? (See Topics 5 and 7.)

4. Suppose the batteries that give power to a bathyscaphe's electromagnets were to fail. Would this endanger the bathyscaphe? Explain.

5. How would a drift bottle (Topic 5c) differ if made for (*a*) the ocean, (*b*) the Great Lakes?

STUDENT ACTIVITIES

1. Make a model to represent the relative depth and volume of the oceans and the continents.

2. Make a drift bottle (see Topic 5c) that will just float beneath the surface of water.

3. Experiment with materials such as tallow, putty, wax, soap, etc. to see which is most effective in picking up sea-floor sediments such as sand, mud, and small pebbles. (See Topic 5g.)

4. Make a model of a bathysphere.

5. Make a model of a bathyscaphe.

CHAPTER 19

The Composition and Temperature of Ocean Waters

HOW DO YOU KNOW THAT . . . ?

Oceanographers use chemical tests to find out which minerals are dissolved in sea water. For example, they know that when a solution of silver nitrate is added to water containing chlorine ions (from salt or other chlorides), a milky white powder forms in the water. So they can use this procedure as a "test for chlorides."

Try this test yourself. Make salt water by dissolving a few grams of salt (sodium chloride) in about 25 milliliters of water. Using a medicine dropper or dropping bottle, add a few drops of silver nitrate solution. (Get this chemical from your teacher.) Be careful not to get silver nitrate on your skin or clothes. It may stain them.

What happens to the salt water? Would this happen with another chloride such as potassium chloride? With tap water? Try it. What conclusions do you draw?

1. How Minerals Enter Sea Water

For millions of years the earth's rivers have probably been carrying rock fragments and dissolved minerals down to the sea just as they are doing today. The rock fragments settle largely on the continental shelves, where they eventually form sedimentary rocks. But the dissolved minerals remain in the water, to accumulate through the ages and make the sea more and more "salty." They accumulate because evaporation from the surface of the sea removes only water, not the minerals dissolved in the water.

Attempts have been made to calculate the age of the earth's oceans from the rate at which their dissolved minerals are accumulating today. (See Chapter 23, The Rock Record.) Of course we cannot be certain that the rate was the same in the past as it is today. It is estimated that each year the earth's rivers add more than three billion tons of dissolved minerals to the ocean waters. This sounds like a vast quantity, but the oceans presently contain more than 500 million times that much mineral matter in solution.

2. Dissolved Minerals Form Ions

When a mineral dissolves in water it becomes invisible. Why? The water has caused the billions of ions that form the mineral's crystals to separate into individual ions that cannot be seen. (See Chapter 2, Topics 11 and 15.) Ions, you may recall, are atoms or groups of atoms that have an electric charge. Thus, when sodium chloride (common salt) is dissolved in water, its molecules split up into positively charged sodium ions and negatively charged chlorine ions. This can be shown by placing the electrodes of a storage battery in the solution. The positively charged sodium ions are attracted to the negative electrode, while the negatively charged chlorine ions go to the positive electrode.

Here are a few other examples of ionization of minerals found in sea water: calcium carbonate (lime) forms positively charged calcium ions and negatively charged carbonate ions; magnesium sulfate (Epsom salt) forms magnesium ions and sulfate ions; sodium silicate forms sodium ions and silicate ions. When sea water evaporates, the process is reversed. The ions recombine to form the solid minerals that went into the water, and the minerals reappear as a mixture of white crystals.

When chemists analyze the mineral composition of water, they usually do it in terms of percentages of ions in the solution, rather than in terms of the compounds that went into it. When they do it in this way, they group together all of one kind of ion, regardless of its source. For example, chlorine atoms coming from both sodium chloride and potassium chloride cannot be distinguished from each other, and would be counted together. This "counting" —actually the determination of the weight of

chlorine ions in the solution—is done by chemical tests.

3. River Water Versus Sea Water

It might be expected that ocean waters would have much the same mineral composition as the rivers that feed them, but such is far from the case. A comparison of river water with sea water in terms of percentage of particular ions shows the following striking differences:

PERCENTAGE OF TOTAL DISSOLVED MINERALS (BY WEIGHT)

Ion	In River Water	In Sea Water
carbonate	35.15	0.40
calcium	20.39	1.15
silicate	11.67	0.0004
chloride	5.68	55.04
sodium	5.79	30.62
magnesium	3.41	3.69
potassium	2.12	1.10
sulfate	12.14	7.68

Notice that the first three ions listed above —the carbonate, calcium, and silicate ions—together comprise more than 67 per cent of the dissolved minerals in river water, but only about 1.5 per cent in sea water. In sharp contrast, the chloride and sodium ions rise from about 11.5 per cent in river water to nearly 86 per cent in sea water. What is the explanation? One reason is that the carbonate, calcium, and silicate ions are constantly being extracted from sea water by living plants and animals to make their shells or skeletons. Corals and shellfish of many kinds, including abundant microscopic animals, make shells of calcium carbonate (lime). Other microscopic animals and plants make skeletons of silica. But while the concentration of calcium, carbonate, and silica ions in the water is kept more or less constant through the ages, sodium and chlorine ions are accumulating steadily and increasing in concentration. They are not extracted by marine organisms to any appreciable extent.

Some oceanographers believe that appreciable quantities of the dissolved minerals in the ocean —chlorine in particular—may have originated in undersea volcanic eruptions. Still others think at least part of the minerals entered the ocean when it first formed from hot gases early in earth history.

4. Salinity of Sea Water

When 1,000 pounds of sea water are evaporated to dryness, approximately 35 pounds of white solids remain. About three-fourths of this mineral matter is common salt (sodium chloride). The remainder includes many other minerals, but only a few of them in relatively sizable amounts. To express the ratio of the weight of dissolved mineral matter to the total weight of sea water, the oceanographer uses the term **salinity** (saltiness). Thus, *the average salinity of sea water is said to be 35 parts per 1000.* (We could also say 3.5 parts per 100, or 3.5 per cent, but by using parts per thousand we avoid one decimal place. The symbol for 35 parts per thousand is 35‰.

The seven most abundant minerals in sea water, expressed in parts per thousand, are:

sodium chloride	$NaCl$	27.2‰
magnesium chloride	$MgCl_2$	3.8‰
magnesium sulfate	$MgSO_4$	1.7‰
calcium sulfate	$CaSO_4$	1.3‰
potassium sulfate	K_2SO_4	0.9‰
calcium carbonate	$CaCO_3$	0.1‰
magnesium bromide	$MgBr_2$	0.1‰

5. Variations in Salinity

The salinity of ocean waters averages just under 35‰, and in most of the world ocean it is very close to that figure. This is particularly true in the deeper waters of the ocean. In the surface waters, however, there are places where the salinity may be distinctly more or less than the average. (See Fig. 19-1.)

Where unusually large amounts of fresh water enter the sea, salinity is lower than average. This is true in equatorial regions and in other regions of heavy rainfall. It is also true at the mouths of rivers and in polar regions at places where glaciers enter the sea. In the Baltic Sea, for example, melting glacier ice and river water combine to freshen the water to a salinity of only 30‰.

Salinity is higher than average in places where the climate is hot and dry, and the ocean loses fresh water rapidly by evaporation. This is generally true in latitudes of about 20 to 30 degrees north and south of the Equator. (On land these are the regions of the great tropical deserts.) In the Mediterranean Sea and the Red Sea, these conditions help raise the salinity to about 40‰. Salinity may also be higher than average in polar waters where the ocean freezes over. Why? When salt water freezes, only fresh water ice forms, and the remaining water is left saltier than before.

Fig. 19-1. How and why the salinity of sea water may vary from its average salinity of 3.5 per cent.

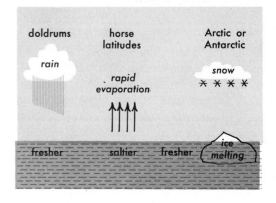

Fig. 19-2. "Harvesting" salt extracted from sea water by solar evaporation in shallow ponds near San Francisco, California.

Leslie Salt Company

6. Uniformity of Composition

One of the most remarkable characteristics of sea water discovered by the oceanographer is its uniformity of composition. No matter where a sample is taken from—whether it be Northern Hemisphere or Southern Hemisphere, Equator or polar regions, surface or bottom water—the *relative amounts of the dissolved substances in the water are the same.* This holds true regardless of the salinity of the water. It means that the oceanographer can calculate the complete analysis of a sample of ocean water after testing for just one element. Chlorine is usually tested for, because the amount of chlorine in solution is easily determined. From this the amounts of all other substances can be calculated on the basis of the uniform composition tables.

7. Commercial Extraction of Minerals

At least 55 elements are found in solution in sea water. Among these are uranium, radium,

gold, silver, copper, magnesium and many other elements of economic importance. The total quantities of these substances in the ocean are tremendous. There are 15 billion tons of copper, 500 million tons of silver, 2,000 billion tons of magnesium, and so forth. But most of them are present in such small percentages—about four parts of gold per 1,000 billion parts of sea water, as an example—that economical methods of extraction have not yet been devised. A cubic mile of sea water may contain about 40 pounds of gold, but the water from which it must be extracted weighs about five billion tons.

Some minerals can be extracted profitably, either because the quantities available are large or the process of extraction is comparatively inexpensive, or for both reasons. Ordinary *salt* is easily obtained by solar evaporation of sea water in hot sunny climates. A cubic mile of sea water contains about 120 million tons of salt. *Magnesium,* the lightweight metal much used in airplanes, is extracted more cheaply from sea water than from its ores. About six pounds of magnesium are obtained from every ton of sea water. *Bromine* from sea water is used for photographic chemicals and for making ethylene dibromide, the "ethyl" in high test gasoline. These three—salt, magnesium, and bromine— are presently the only dissolved substances being extracted in commercial quantities from sea water. (See Fig. 19-2.)

8. Gases in Sea Water

All of the gases in the atmosphere are found dissolved in sea water but in different percentages than in the atmosphere, because some are more soluble in water than are others. Thus carbon dioxide, quite soluble in water, is plentiful in sea water, even though it forms only 0.03 per cent of the air. The most important gases dissolved in the sea are carbon dioxide and oxygen. Carbon dioxide is needed by green plants in photosynthesis. Oxygen is needed by both animals and plants for respiration.

Oxygen and carbon dioxide are both plentiful in the surface waters. A short distance down, however, the carbon dioxide decreases in amount because it is used up by the many plants in the sunlit upper few hundred feet of the sea. This same layer of water becomes richer in oxygen given off by the plants in photosynthesis. But below about 300 feet little light penetrates, and there are few plants to consume carbon dioxide and produce oxygen. Deep-sea currents originating at the surface of the Arctic and Antarctic Oceans continue to bring a small supply of oxygen from the surface to deep waters, but this oxygen is quickly consumed by the animals of the sea and converted to carbon dioxide. *Thus the deep waters are rich in carbon dioxide and poor in oxygen.*

9. How Ocean Waters Are Heated

Unlike the water in a teakettle on a stove, the ocean is heated mainly from above—by the sun. The sun's rays do not penetrate very far. Most of the long wave radiations—invisible infrared, and visible red, orange, and yellow—are quickly absorbed and converted to heat in the top layer of water. The shorter radiations— green, blue violet, and ultra-violet—penetrate to greater depths, but no farther than about 300 feet. Many of these rays are reflected back to the surface, accounting for the dark green or blue color of deep waters. If the ocean waters were perfectly motionless, very little heat would pass below the top few feet of the ocean, because water is a poor conductor of heat. But winds, waves, and currents mix the heated upper water with the water below it down to varying depths, to form what is called the **mixed layer.** The mixed layer is nearly uniform in temperature. At the Equator it is about 300 feet deep. In middle latitudes it may extend down to 1000 feet.

How warm is the mixed layer? Its exact temperature varies chiefly with the latitude and the season. In equatorial regions it may reach a high of 85°F. In polar regions where floe ice or icebergs are present, it may never go above 28°F. (The freezing point of salt water is lower than that of fresh water, which is 32°F. The exact temperature at which sea water freezes depends on its salinity. The higher the salinity, the lower the freezing point. The usual range in sea water is from 28°F to 31°F.)

10. Daily and Annual Temperature Change

The mixed layer changes in temperature through the year, but again the amount of change differs with the latitude. Furthermore, the change is much less than on land because of water's slowness to warm up and cool off. The greatest change takes place in middle latitudes (about 40°N) where seasons change most. Here the waters are about 15°F colder in winter than in summer. In equatorial regions the range may be as little as 2°F. In polar regions there may be no change at all throughout the year.

At the surface the temperature of the mixed layer also changes between day and night, but the change is rarely more than 2°F in the open ocean. In shallow-water areas near shore both the daily temperature change and the seasonal temperature change may be much larger than in the open ocean.

11. Temperatures Under the Mixed Layer

In contrast with the rather *uniformly warm* surface layer, the waters from about 2,000 to 3,000 feet all the way to the bottom are generally almost *uniformly cold*. Between the warm mixed layers and the cold main mass of the ocean there is a boundary layer called the **thermocline** (*thermo,* heat; *cline,* slope). In the thermocline the temperature falls rather sharply with increasing depth for about 2,500 to 3,000 feet until the cold-water mass is reached. From this point temperatures drop very slowly indeed until the bottom is reached. Even in tropical waters with a surface temperature of 85°F the temperature at 3,000 feet has usually dropped to about 40°F. But from 3,000 feet to the floor of even the deepest parts of the ocean temperatures fall only a few degrees more to a low of about 35°F. All in all, except for the thermocline, ocean temperatures change very slowly with depth. (See Fig. 19-3.)

In polar waters the ocean is generally cold from top to bottom. In temperate latitudes the surface waters are colder in winter than in summer, but they are still much warmer than the deep waters. The low temperatures of the deep waters are maintained by currents moving slowly from the polar regions toward the Equator at great depths. The cold deep currents, sometimes collectively called **polar creep,** are described in Chapter 21. Where the ocean floor is high enough to keep out polar creep, as at the Straits

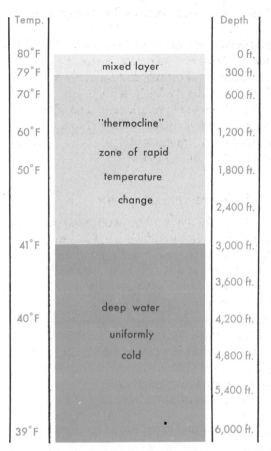

Fig. 19-3. *This diagram shows how ocean waters in equatorial regions change in temperature from the surface downward. Only in the thermocline is temperature change relatively rapid.*

of Gibraltar, an inland sea like the Mediterranean may have bottom temperatures as high as 55°F, even at a depth of 14,000 feet.

12. Ice in the Sea

The two main types of ice found in the sea are *pack ice* and *icebergs.* **Pack ice** (also called floe ice) forms during the winter, when the surface of the Arctic Ocean freezes to a depth of 7 or 8 feet. There may be cracks or *leads* in this ice and occasional patches of open water, but it is usually easy to travel by dog team over it. During the short summer the pack ice breaks up

U.S. Coast Guard Photo

Fig. 19-4. The U.S. Coast Guard icebreaker North Wind *driving through pack ice in McClure Strait, Arctic Ocean.*

and melts around the shores of the Arctic Ocean. (See Fig. 19-4.) On the Atlantic side ocean currents carry the ice south along the coasts of eastern Canada and Greenland. North of the Canadian Arctic Islands the pack ice never melts completely and no ship has ever penetrated into this part where the ice is very rough (hummocky) and may be 10 or 15 feet thick. In this area there are also a few **ice islands.** These may cover more than a hundred square miles and be over 150 feet thick. They drift slowly through the pack ice. Oceanographers have used some of these for months as floating bases of operations.

Icebergs are gigantic blocks of ice broken from glaciers that terminate in the sea. Almost all the icebergs in the Northern Hemisphere come from the Greenland glaciers and are carried by ocean currents into the North Atlantic Ocean off Labrador and Newfoundland. During

the summer they are a serious danger to shipping, forcing it to travel southerly routes. Ever since 1912, when the steamship *Titanic* was wrecked on an iceberg off Newfoundland, the U.S. Coast Guard has maintained an International Ice Patrol which charts icebergs, broadcasts their position and direction of drift, and blows up the smaller ones. Despite all precautions icebergs still take their toll. In 1959 the "unsinkable" Danish ship *Hedtoft,* built especially for service between Denmark and Greenland, collided with an iceberg on her first return voyage from Greenland. The ship sank with all 95 hands aboard. Stormy seas thwarted all rescue efforts, and not a trace of the ship was found in the week-long search that followed the disaster.

The largest icebergs in the north are one-half to one mile in length and may show 300 feet of ice above the water. Since only about one-ninth of the total iceberg is visible above water, such icebergs actually may attain heights of up to 2,700 feet. The greatest of all icebergs are those that are broken off the Antarctic glaciers. Some of these icebergs are over 40 miles long and a thousand feet thick. They are usually flat both top and bottom, and are described as tabular.

13. Fresh Water from Sea Ice

Both icebergs and pack ice can be used as sources of fresh water. Icebergs consist almost entirely of fresh-water ice, since they are derived from the snows of glaciers.

Pack ice, on the other hand, is formed by the freezing of sea water. When sea water freezes, however, it does not form a uniformly salty mass of ice. Instead, fresh-water ice crystals form and leave behind a more concentrated solution of salt water or brine. The resulting mixture is salty, of course, because the brine is trapped between growing ice crystals. But as time passes, the surface of the pack ice may melt by day and refreeze at night many times. At each melting, some of the trapped brine runs off and eventually only fresh ice may be left. The older the ice, the less salty it becomes. Snows that accumulate on its surface also add to its fresh-water content.

Fig. 19-5. A great North Atlantic iceberg broken off from the Greenland ice sheet. Nearly 90% of the mass of the iceberg is beneath the surface.

U.S. Navy

TOPIC QUESTIONS

Each topic question refers to the topic of the same number within this chapter.

1. (*a*) What is believed to be the origin of the minerals dissolved in sea water? (*b*) Why is the ocean getting saltier?

2. (*a*) What are ions? Explain what happens to a mineral like common salt or lime when it dissolves in water? (*b*) In what terms does the chemist usually describe the mineral composition of water?

3. (*a*) Describe the principal differences in the mineral composition of river water and sea water, and explain how they developed. (*b*) Besides river water, from what other sources may the sea have received its dissolved minerals?

4. Explain what is meant when we say that the salinity of sea water is 35 parts per thousand.

5. Explain where and why the salinity of the ocean waters is (*a*) below average, (*b*) above average.

6. What is meant by the uniformity of composition of sea water? How does this simplify the chemical analysis of a sample of sea water?

7. Why is magnesium extracted commercially from sea water, whereas gold is not?

8. (*a*) Why is carbon dioxide relatively more plentiful in sea water than in air? (*b*) Why is there less carbon dioxide a few hundred feet down than in the surface waters? (*c*) Why are the very deep waters poor in oxygen and rich in carbon dioxide?

9. (*a*) Explain how the sun heats the ocean waters. (*b*) Why do deep waters look dark green or dark blue? (*c*) Explain the origin of the mixed layer. How deep does it go? What is its temperature? (*d*) Why doesn't all sea water freeze at the same temperature?

10. Describe the variations in temperature of the surface waters of the ocean (*a*) from summer to winter, (*b*) from day to night.

11. (*a*) What is the thermocline? How far does it extend? (*b*) Describe the temperature in the deep waters beneath the thermocline. (*c*) Explain what keeps the deep waters of the ocean cold.

12. (*a*) What is pack ice? How does it form? (*b*) What are icebergs? Where do they originate? Where are they found?

13. Explain how sea ice forms, and why it gets less salty as it gets older.

GENERAL QUESTIONS

1. Is the ocean becoming more salty or less salty? Explain.

2. From the figures given in Topic 7, calculate the weight of gold in one cubic mile of sea water.

3. The temperature of ocean waters is found to rise very slightly at the bottom of the very deepest parts of the oceans. What source of heat may account for this rise?

STUDENT ACTIVITIES

1. If samples of sea water are available, evaporate to dryness 100 grams of sea water. Weigh the residue of mineral matter to determine its percentage by weight.

2. Float an ice cube in water and measure the relative volume of the part that is submerged and the part above water.

CHAPTER 20

The Sea Floor and Its Sediments

HOW DO YOU KNOW THAT . . . ?

1. Figure 20-2 shows the floor of part of the North Atlantic Ocean. For a rough idea of the area covered, look at the upper left-hand corner showing parts of Canada and the United States. Compare it with Fig. 20-3. Find one canyon that is definitely traceable to a river on the land. Find two mid-ocean canyons and two great plains. Locate a deep trench and a mountain range.

2. Microscopic shells form a large part of oozes (fine muds) found on the deep ocean floor. Many shells are the remains of one-celled marine plants called *diatoms* (dye-uh-toms). Pick up a bit of diatomaceous earth on the end of a toothpick. Spread it out in a drop of water on a microscope slide. Place a cover glass over it. Examine it under the microscope. Make sketches.

1. The Shape of the Sea Floor

The ocean floor is a vast basin that covers 71 per cent of the earth's surface. Its edges are rimmed by *continental shelves* that slope gently seaward from the continents. The continental shelves give way to much steeper *continental slopes* which lead downward to the main floor of the ocean basin. The continental slopes are scarred by many small valleys and occasional *submarine canyons* that may begin on the continental shelves. At the foot of the slopes the gradient becomes much gentler (this area is called the *continental rise*) until the basin floor is finally reached. But the floor of the ocean basin is not level. It is marked by many features. Approximately one-third of its total area is covered by great undersea mountain ranges or *mid-ocean ridges*. Thousands of additional isolated peaks called *seamounts* dot its surface. Vast areas of level sedimentary deposits form *abyssal plains*. Thousand-mile long depressions called *trenches* plunge to depths two and three times as great as those at which the continental slopes

end. Let us examine all of these features of the ocean basin in greater detail. (See Figs. 20-1, 20-2.)

2. Continental Shelves: Rims of the Ocean Basin

The **continental shelves** slope outward gently from the shores of the continents until they reach the steeper continental slopes. The depth of water at this end of the shelves generally ranges from 300 to 600 feet (50 to 100 fathoms; 1 fathom = 6 feet) with an average of about 400 feet. The average width of the shelves is about 40 miles. Dividing 400 feet by 40 miles, we get an average slope of 10 feet per mile—a rise of less than one foot in 500. Obviously, then, the shelves are very nearly level surfaces, although their smoothness is interrupted by low hills and ridges, by shallow depressions, and by occasional valleys. On some continental shores the shelves are hundreds of miles wide, as between Alaska and Siberia, or off the coast of Brazil. In other

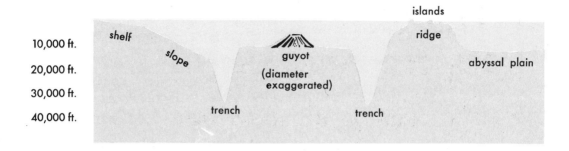

Fig. 20-1. *A generalized cross section of a part of the ocean floor to show its principal features. The vertical scale is greatly exaggerated.*

places the shelves may be very narrow or almost non-existent, as along the west coast of South America.

3. Continental Slopes: Walls of the Ocean Basin

The **continental slopes** begin at the outer edges of the continental shelves. Here the sea floor becomes abruptly steeper, with slopes ranging from about 150 feet per mile up to 900 feet per mile. The width of the slopes is usually between 10 and 20 miles. The slopes drop to an average depth of about 12,000 feet. They may go miles deeper, however, where they merge with the sides of deep sea trenches, as they do off the west coast of South America. The continental slopes are cut by many gullies and small valleys. These are believed to be scars left when great masses of mud slide off the steep slopes into the deep sea.

4. Submarine Canyons: Scars on the Slopes

Spectacular **submarine canyons** also cut into the continental slopes. These canyons usually begin on the continental shelf, sometimes as the apparent extension of a river on the coastal plain, and continue down the continental slope as far as the deep ocean. There are many such canyons on the continental slope off eastern United States. The best known of these is the Hudson River Canyon, which has been traced nearly 200 miles on the floor of the continental shelf and slope before it disappears at a depth of nearly three miles. Another great submarine canyon is the Monterey Canyon off the California coast, which rivals the Grand Canyon of the Colorado River in size.

How did submarine canyons originate? No simple answer can be given. It is probable that different canyons have originated in different ways. Furthermore, the part of a canyon on the continental shelf may have a different origin from the part on the continental slope. Canyons on the continental shelves may have been cut by rivers at a time when the continental shelves were coastal plains above sea level. Such canyons would now appear to be extensions of drowned river valleys.

Can canyons be formed right on the sea floor? Many geologists believe that canyons on the continental slope are actually carved out of the sea floor by swift currents running like rivers down the steep slopes. These currents are created when great masses of mud and sand break off from the upper part of the continental slope, perhaps because they are shaken loose by earthquakes, or because the accumulations become too steep. The avalanche of sediment sweeps water ahead of it, until the two merge to form

Fig. 20-2. This sketch shows the principal feature of the floor of the western side of the North Atlantic Ocean.

Newfoundland

Grand Banks

Mid-ocean Canyon

Sohm Abyssal Plain

Mid-Atlantic Ridge

Canada

Continental Shelf

Hudson River Canyon

Mid-ocean Canyon

Bermuda

United States

Hatteras Submarine Canyon

Hatteras Abyssal Plain

Bahama Is.

Cuba

Puerto Rico Trench

a dense and powerful stream filled with cutting tools of sand and possibly coarser materials. Such streams are called **turbidity currents** because they are turbid (muddy). Can such currents carve canyons out of granite bedrock, as Monterey Canyon seems to have been carved? We do not know. We do know that turbidity currents exist, that they move at high speeds, and that they are capable of strong erosional effects. Many breaks in submarine telephone and telegraph cables have been traced to the movements of turbidity currents, and great fan-shaped deposits of sediment are found at the mouths of submarine canyons.

5. Ocean Basins and Mid-Ocean Ridges

The main floor of the ocean basin begins at the foot of the continental slopes, and includes all the area between the slopes except for the mid-ocean ridges. The **mid-ocean ridges** are great undersea mountain ranges characterized by frequent earthquakes and volcanic eruptions. They form a more or less continuous chain of mountains 40,000 miles in length, with a total area equal to that of all the continents. They rise steeply from the ocean basin floor to heights of at least a mile. In some places their highest peaks protrude above the sea surface as oceanic islands. Their effect is to split every ocean basin into two or more smaller basins.

The best known of the mid-ocean ridges is the 1,000-mile-wide Mid-Atlantic Ridge, which zigzags 10,000 miles from Iceland almost to Antarctica, roughly paralleling the shorelines of the surrounding continents. (See Fig. 20-3.) Among its volcanic peaks that have grown above sea level are the Azores Islands in the North Atlantic Ocean, and Ascension Island, St. Helena, and Tristan da Cunha in the South Atlantic. On the average, the Mid-Atlantic Ridge rises from one to two miles above the floor of the ocean basin. Even so, its summits are usually about 9,000 feet below the level of the sea. A

Fig. 20-3. The Mid-Atlantic Ridge splits the Atlantic Ocean into two great basins.

striking feature of the ridge is a great "rift valley" or depression that runs along the length of the ridge near its center. The rift is as much as two miles deep and up to 30 miles wide. Rifts have also been discovered in other ocean ridges.

The origin of the mid-ocean ridges is a problem that greatly intrigues the geologist. One explanation of their origin is like that given in the hypothesis of continental drift and the hypothesis of plate tectonics. (See Chapter 14, Topic 5.) Some geologists believe that the rifts on the ridges show that *sea-floor spreading* is taking place. If so, it would lend support to the hypothesis of an expanding crust.

6. Abyssal Plains

Most of the basin floor lies at a depth of two and a half miles or more. In general, the floor has a rolling surface of low hills, but vast areas of the floor have been buried in sediments

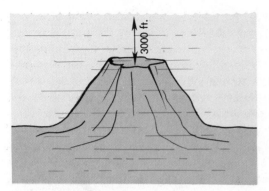

Fig. 20-4. A guyot is believed to be a volcanic cone whose top was planed off by wave action before it was submerged to its present depth.

to form great **abyssal plains.** The abyssal plains are said to be flatter than any of the plains on the continents. The sands and clays that form their surface are believed to have been deposited by turbidity currents.

Abyssal plains are relatively rare in the Pacific Ocean. It is believed that the sediments carried by turbidity currents in the Pacific are "trapped" in the deep *trenches* that parallel much of the Pacific coast. (See Topic 8.) In the Atlantic, on the other hand, no such coastal trenches are present to keep the sediments from being deposited on the main ocean basin floor.

7. Seamounts and Guyots

Oceanographers define **seamounts** as isolated elevations that rise more than 3,000 feet from the sea floor. Thousands of seamounts have been discovered, and they are particularly abundant in the Pacific Ocean. Most seamounts are shaped like volcanic cones, and in many cases evidence of their volcanic origin has been obtained in the form of volcanic rock and actual volcanic eruptions. The largest seamounts may rise two and a half miles above the sea floor, and their bases may reach 35 miles in diameter.

Some seamounts look as though they have had their tops sliced off. These flat-topped sea-

mounts are called **guyots** (*ghee* ohs). Like other seamounts, they are most abundant in the Pacific Ocean. Their tops are usually at least 3,000 feet below the sea surface. It is believed that they were volcanic cones that grew above sea level, were planed off to sea level by wave action, and were then deeply submerged by sinking of the ocean floor. (See Fig. 20-4.)

8. Trenches and Island Arcs

The basin floor has an average depth of about 12,000 feet, but this is far short of the greatest depths of the ocean, which reach a maximum of over 36,000 feet. The ocean's greatest depths are found in long narrow **trenches** that ring the Pacific Ocean, and in similar trenches in the Atlantic and other oceans. The trenches may exceed a thousand miles in length and a hundred miles in width, and they plunge as much as four miles below the general level of the floor of the ocean basin. In the Pacific Ocean, in particular, the greatest trenches are found on the seaward side of great chains of volcanic islands called **island arcs.** These island arcs include the Aleutian Islands, the Kuril Islands, the islands of Japan, the Philippine Islands, and the islands of Indonesia. In the Atlantic Ocean the West Indies form a similar island arc. The island arcs are usually crescent-shaped, with the convex side of the crescent facing the sea and the adjacent trenches. There are no island arcs in the Pacific Ocean off South America, but here the 2,000-mile Peru-Chile Trench runs parallel to the great coastal range of the Andes Mountains.

Soundings of more than 34,000 feet have been made in the Mariana and Mindanao (or Philippine) trenches of the North Pacific, and in the Tonga Trench of the South Pacific. The U.S. Navy bathyscaphe *Trieste* touched bottom at 35,800 feet in the Mariana Trench in 1960. In 1962 the British survey ship HMS *Cook* sounded the record depth of 37,782 feet in the same Mindanao Trench. The record depth for the South Pacific is 34,884 feet, sounded by the *Horizon* in 1952 in the Tonga Trench. The record depth for the Atlantic Ocean is 30,246 feet in the Puerto Rico Trench.

Both the trenches and the island arcs with which they are often associated are regions of great volcanic and earthquake activity. Some geologists believe that the trenches are in a part of the earth's crust that is being dragged down by convection currents in the mantle, as explained in the convection hypothesis of mountain building. (See Chapter 14, Topic 5.)

SEDIMENTS OF THE SEA FLOOR

9. Sea-Floor Sediments from the Land

The sediment that covers the sea floor from its continental shelves to its deepest trenches is highly varied in kind and in origin. Much of it comes directly from erosion of the land. Such sediments are called **terrigenous sediments.** From the land, rivers bring gravel, sand, silt, clay, and minerals in solution. In higher latitudes, glaciers perform a similar function. Along the sea coasts, waves and winds add to the mass of sediment. Most terrigenous materials are deposited on the continental shelf and the upper part of the continental slope, on which they are spread out by waves and currents, although thicker accumulations are found where rivers and glaciers enter the sea.

In shallow tropical waters where corals thrive, fragments of coral are eroded by waves from coral reefs to form **shallow-water calcareous sediments,** so named because coral is calcium carbonate (lime). Similar sediments may form anywhere on the continental shelf where lime is deposited by chemical action, or in the form of shell fragments and shells of shellfish.

Most of the terrigenous sediment is deposited on the continental shelf and upper slope and stays there. But there are some exceptions.

Dust, particularly from volcanic eruptions, may be carried far out to sea by the wind. Icebergs, breaking off glaciers entering the sea in high latitudes, may carry boulders and coarse gravel hundreds of miles from the coast before melting. Turbidity currents may sweep relatively coarse materials—sands and silts as well as clays—from the continental shelf and slopes to deeper waters. Such deposits are called **turbidites,** and they may be found on the floors of submarine canyons, in fanshaped deposits at the mouths of canyons, or even farther out at sea on the floors of abyssal plains.

Thick ocean-floor deposits of volcanic ash and pumice may result from the eruptions of volcanoes on oceanic islands.

10. Sediments on the Deep-Sea Floor: Oozes

Most of the sea floor beyond the continental slopes is covered by a thick deposit of fine-grained sediments. With the help of the microscope, these sediments are seen to include two main kinds of material. One kind is of organic origin. It consists of shells or skeletons of the tiny floating one-celled animals and plants of the sea known as **plankton.** The other kind is of inorganic origin, and consists chiefly of tiny particles of clay, quartz, mica, and other rock minerals. The sediments are slimy and soft to the touch. Those that contain more than 30 per cent of the organic shell material are called **oozes.** Those with less than 30 per cent organic material are called **red clays.** But all oozes and red clays are mixtures of both materials.

The shells and skeletons of the plankton are made of either lime (calcium carbonate) or silica (silicon dioxide), but lime-forming organisms are much more abundant. An ooze consisting mainly of lime shells is a *calcareous ooze.* The most abundant calcareous ooze is that formed from the sand-grain-sized shells of a protozoan called **Globigerina.** (See Fig. 20-5.) Globigerina ooze covers nearly half of the ocean

Fig. 20-5. Calcareous oozes consist largely of the shells of microscopic animals called Globigerina.

basin. The **pteropods** (*ter* oh pods) are other important limemaking protozoans.

Oozes consisting mainly of silica shells are *siliceous oozes.* They are formed largely from the remains of tiny one-celled animals called **Radiolaria** (see Fig. 20-6) or even smaller one-celled plants called **diatoms.** Although calcareous oozes are much more abundant than siliceous oozes, siliceous oozes are more likely to be found in cold waters. The reason is that cold waters contain more carbon dioxide, in which lime dissolves more readily than silica. Therefore siliceous oozes are more likely to be found in the cold waters of the ocean floor at depths greater than about 15,000 feet. They are also more likely to be found in high latitudes, and diatom oozes are abundant near Antarctica. Siliceous oozes are also abundant in the equatorial Pacific Ocean where Radiolaria thrive.

Plankton shells show a great range in size, from microscopic diatoms to sand-sized globigerina and pteropods. The larger shells may settle to the deep ocean floor in just a few days. The smallest shells may take years to sink the same distance. The rate at which the oozes *accumulate* is also exceedingly slow. It is esti-

mated that it takes 3,000 years or more to form a deposit of ooze one inch in thickness. This is a rate of one foot in about 36,000 years.

11. Sediments of the Deepest Sea: Red Clay

The deep waters of the ocean trenches are very rich in carbon dioxide, so both lime and silica shells are likely to be dissolved before they reach the bottom. As a result, inorganic materials predominate on the floors and walls of the trenches, and red clay deposits are formed. The particles of clay and other minerals in these deposits are believed to come from the rocks of the continents, but they are so tiny that ocean currents have been able to carry them to all parts of the ocean. Some of the clay particles are so fine that they take hundreds or even thousands of years to sink to the lowest depths of the sea. The red clays accumulate at an even slower rate than the oozes—about one inch in from 5,000 to 50,000 years.

Red clay is not always red in color. More often it is likely to be brown, yellowish, or almost any other color. A red or brown color is probably due to oxidized iron. Red clay may also contain bits of meteorites, the teeth of

Fig. 20-6. Siliceous oozes may consist of the shells of the microscopic animals called Radiolaria.

sharks, the earbones of whales, and lumps of manganese dioxide. The relatively large amount of these materials present in small thicknesses of red clay emphasizes the slowness with which the red clay accumulates.

12. Thickness of Deep-Sea Deposits

The thickness of ooze and red-clay deposits on the sea floor is measured by seismic sounding devices like the Sonoprobe, described in Chapter 18. As might be expected, the deposits vary greatly in thickness, from little or none to as much as 10,000 feet. Sediments are generally thicker in depressions and thinner on elevations of the sea floor, particularly on the mid-ocean ridges.

On the basis of seismic soundings, the thickness of sediment is estimated to average about 1,000 feet in the Pacific Ocean and about 2,000 feet in the Atlantic Ocean. Why is there so much less in the Pacific? Perhaps because fewer large rivers carry sediments into the Pacific, and because its many great coastal trenches trap much of the sediment before it can be carried out to the main ocean basin floor.

On the basis of the age of the earth as obtained from other measurements, oceanographers had expected to find much greater thicknesses of sediment on the sea floor. Many scientists believe that the sediments measured by soundings rest on another layer of consolidated sediments at least 1,000 feet thick. This would bring the total thickness much closer to expectations. But other scientists think this "second layer" is volcanic rock, not sediment.

13. Reading Sediment Cores

When the oceanographer brings up from the deep-sea floor a core of ooze or red clay 15 feet long, he is bringing up materials that may have been accumulating for half a million years or longer. But if part of the core is a one-foot layer

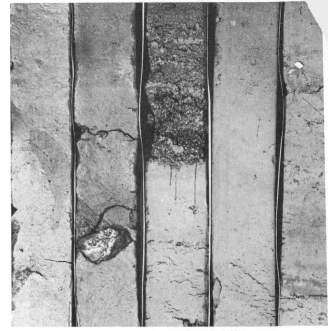

Lamont Geological Observatory

Fig. 20-7. Sediment core taken at a depth of nearly half a mile in the Arctic Ocean.

of volcanic ash, which might have been deposited in just a few days, it would reduce the time represented by the core accordingly. It would also indicate that vulcanism had occurred not too far away at a time that could be estimated from the position of the volcanic ash in the core. Layers of sand or silt in the core would indicate that turbidity currents originating in distant continental slopes had probably reached here in the past.

Changes of climate might be deduced from cores in which a layer of ooze rich in warm-water plankton shells rests on top of a layer of cold-water plankton remains, or vice versa. Many cores showing a change to a warmer climate in the past 11,000 years have been taken from the North Atlantic Ocean. The dating of the thin layer of "warm" sediments at the top of the core is done by measuring its radiocarbon (carbon 14) content, as explained in Chapter 23. Thus we have another method of determining when the Ice Age ended. This measurement also tells us how fast the top layer of sediment accumulated.

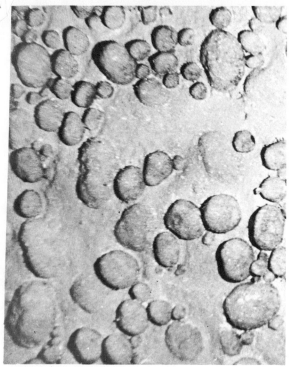

Fig. 20-8. Manganese nodules on the ocean floor at a depth of 18,000 feet.

Then the sediments beneath it can be dated by assuming the same rate of accumulation for them. (See Fig. 20-7.)

14. Mining the Sea Floor: Manganese Nodules

In 1875 the *Challenger* expedition discovered metallic lumps or **nodules** on many parts of the deep-sea floor in the Pacific. These potato-shaped nodules consist chiefly of oxides of manganese and iron, with smaller amounts of cobalt, copper, and nickel oxides. They range in size from less than an inch to nearly a foot in diameter. Exceptionally large nodules may weigh several hundred pounds. They appear to have formed by deposition of the oxides around such nuclei as bits of bone, shark's teeth, or volcanic glass.

The rate of deposition is estimated to be one inch in 25,000 years. (See Fig. 20-8.)

Recent oceanographic exploration by dredge and deep-sea camera has shown that manganese nodules are relatively abundant in parts of the Atlantic and Indian oceans as well as in the Pacific. Millions of square miles of the eastern Pacific Ocean floor have been estimated to average about 10,000 tons of nodules per square mile, giving each square mile a value of at least $500,000 worth of manganese. Manganese is very important in the manufacture of steel, and research is presently under way to develop economical methods of mining it on the sea floor. Engineers are considering such possibilities as sucking the deposits up with a great "vacuum cleaner" type of machine or dredging them up with buckets. (See Fig. 20-9.)

15. Other Sea-Floor Minerals

Another substance that is found on the sea floor in the form of nodules is *phosphorite* (calcium phosphate). Phosphorite can be used as a fertilizer or as a source of phosphorus for use in chemical industries. Phosphorite nodules are abundant off the coast of southern California, where they may soon be mined commercially. Other possibilities for future development include oozes rich in lime for cement and red clays rich in aluminum.

Diamonds are presently being mined by dredging gravels from the Atlantic sea floor off the coast of Southwest Africa. Gold may be mined in similar fashion in an area off the coast of Alaska, and "prospectors" are now looking for gold on the continental shelf of eastern United States. The most valuable sea-floor material actually being extracted today is petroleum. Many off-shore wells have been drilled off the Gulf and Pacific coasts of the United States, and they have yielded billions of dollars worth of oil.

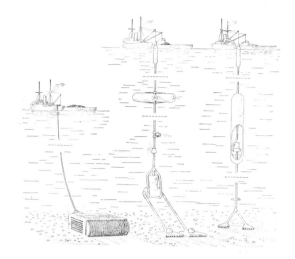

Fig. 20-9. Types of devices that may some day be used to bring up minerals such as manganese nodules from the sea floor.

Scientific American

TOPIC QUESTIONS

Each topic question refers to the topic of the same number within this chapter.

1. (*a*) How does the oceanographer study the topography of the ocean floor? (*b*) Give a simple description of the ocean basin.

2. Describe the location, appearance, width, and depth of the continental shelves.

3. Describe the continental slopes. How did their gullies originate?

4. (*a*) Explain what submarine canyons are. (*b*) Briefly describe two hypotheses of their origin. (*c*) What is a turbidity current?

5. (*a*) What are mid-ocean ridges? Where are they found? (*b*) Describe the outstanding features of the Mid-Atlantic Ridge.

6. (*a*) What is an abyssal plain? How is it formed? (*b*) Why are abyssal plains rare in the Pacific Ocean?

7. (*a*) What is a seamount? How did seamounts form? (*b*) Explain what guyots are, and how they formed.

8. (*a*) Explain what trenches and island arcs are, and how they are related. (*b*) Give the greatest depths of the North Pacific, South Pacific, and Atlantic Ocean.

9. (*a*) What are terrigenous sediments? Where are they found? (*b*) What are shallow-water calcareous sediments? Where are they found? (*c*) Give some examples of terrigenous sediments found farther out at sea than the continental shelf and slope.

10. (*a*) Describe the organic and inorganic materials found in deep sea floor sediments. (*b*) Define *ooze* and *red clay*. (*c*) Distinguish between calcareous and siliceous oozes. (*d*) Why are siliceous oozes more likely to be found in cold ocean waters? (*e*) How fast do ooze deposits accumulate?

11. (*a*) Why does red clay, rather than ooze, form on the deepest ocean floors? How fast does it accumulate? (*b*) Is red clay always red? Explain. (*c*) What may red clay contain besides minerals of continental origin?

12. Compare the average thickness of sea-floor deposits in the Atlantic and Pacific oceans.

13. (*a*) How many years of accumulation are represented in a 15-foot core of ooze or red clay? (*b*) How would you interpret the presence of a layer of volcanic ash, or of sand and silt, in a core consisting mainly of ooze? (*c*) How may a core show that changes of climate had occurred?

14. What are manganese nodules? Where are they found?

15. (*a*) What is phosphorite? Where is it found? (*b*) What other minerals are being mined from the sea floor? Where?

GENERAL QUESTIONS

1. Draw a sketch to illustrate the continental shelves and slopes as they are described in Topics 2 and 3.

2. Calculate the number of years represented by a deposit of red clay, 1,000 feet thick, using the slowest rate of accumulation given in Topic 11.

3. Verify the figure given in Topic 13 for the age of the 15-foot core. Calculate its possible ages both as ooze and as red clay.

STUDENT ACTIVITIES

1. Examine diatomaceous earth under the microscope. Make sketches of individual diatom shells.
   (A slide may be prepared by taking a tiny bit of diatomaceous earth on the end of a toothpick and spreading it out in a drop of water or oil on a microscope slide. Cover with a cover glass before examining.)

2. Make a plasticene or plaster of Paris model of part of the sea floor.

CHAPTER 21
Ocean Currents

HOW DO YOU KNOW THAT . . . ?

A density current is formed when dense water sinks below lighter water next to it. Set up a density current. Fill an old-fashioned soup plate—one with a flat rim—with water. Imagine the plate to be a model of the ocean: the rim is the continental shelf, the wall of the bowl is the continental slope, the bottom of the bowl is the ocean basin. Squirt a few drops of ink into the water at the very edge of the plate. Watch how the denser ink forms a "current" that slowly moves down the "continental shelf," then streams swiftly down the "slope" until it reaches the "basin."

1. Movements of Sea Waters

The waters of the sea take part in many different movements. Some, like the tides, the tsunami, and the swells familiar to bathers at ocean beaches, cause the surface of the sea to rise and fall in rhythmic patterns. Such movements are **waves.** Others, like the great Gulf Stream in the Atlantic Ocean or the longshore currents and undertows of coastal waters, are masses of water flowing through the main body of relatively stationary surrounding water. These are known as **currents.**

2. Forces That Create Currents

An ocean current may be defined as a streamlike mass of water moving through the surrounding ocean water. What forces can make water move through water?

Major ocean currents that move along the surface are called surface **currents.** The Gulf Stream, the Kuroshio or Japan Current, the Labrador Current, and the California Current are all famous examples of surface currents. The chief force responsible for surface currents appears to be the wind. Surface currents are dis-

cussed further in Topics 7 through 10.

Currents that move beneath the surface are called **subsurface currents** or **density currents.** Density currents usually consist of water that starts to flow downward because it is heavier (denser) than the water adjacent to it. This flow continues until the dense water sinks completely underneath the lighter water, or at least until it reaches a level where it is no heavier than the water next to it.

How does the water in one part of the ocean become denser than neighboring water? One way is through the rapid evaporation that occurs in a warm, dry climate. This makes the water saltier and therefore denser. A second way is through excessive cooling, as in the polar regions. This makes water contract and become denser. A third way is through the mixing of mud or silt with the sea water on parts of the continental slope. The muddy water is denser than the surrounding clear water. This muddiness is called **turbidity.** In all of these cases, when the dense water sinks beneath the lighter water next to it, a density current is formed.

In his book *Realms of Water* the Dutch oceanographer Kuenen describes a simple demonstration of a turbidity type of density current.

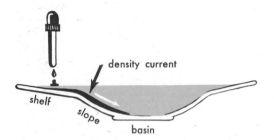

Fig. 21-1. Ink forming a "density current" in water.

An old-fashioned soup plate with a flat rim is filled with water. Then a few drops of ink are squirted into the water at the very edge of the plate. The denser ink forms a "turbidity current" that moves slowly down the "continental shelf" (the rim) and then streams swiftly down the "continental slope" (the steep wall of the bowl) until it reaches the floor of the "ocean basin" (bottom of the bowl). (See Fig. 21-1.)

Now a few examples of density currents in the ocean will be described.

3. Density Currents through Evaporation

The most famous illustration of a density current produced through evaporation is provided by the Mediterranean Sea. Here the hot, dry climate evaporates far more water than the Mediterranean receives in rain and river inflow.

The Mediterranean would shrink, except for the fact that it is connected with the Atlantic Ocean by the Strait of Gibraltar, the floor of which is about 900 feet below sea level, with deeper water on both sides. On the Atlantic side the water has a salinity of about 35‰. On the Mediterranean side its salinity is much higher—about 39‰. So a two-way flow results, with light Atlantic water pouring in at the surface and denser Mediterranean water running out to the Atlantic beneath the inflowing surface current. (During World War II, submarines made use of these currents to slip in and out of the Mediterranean without running their engines.) The Mediterranean water sinks to a depth of more than 3,000 feet in the Atlantic, where its flow has been traced as far north as Greenland and as far west as Bermuda. The total flow of Mediterranean water in this density current is many times that of the Mississippi. (See Fig. 21-2.)

4. Density Currents from Polar Waters

Oceanographers have traced three great density currents of cold water at different depths in the Atlantic Ocean. Two of these currents originate in the Antarctic. The third originates in the Arctic Ocean near Greenland. (See Fig. 21-3.)

Fig. 21-2. Dense Mediterranean water flows outward into the Atlantic Ocean as a subsurface density current. See Topic 3.

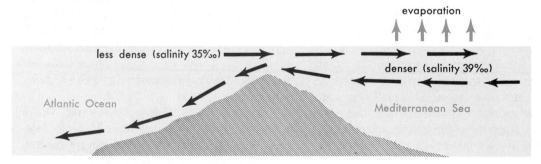

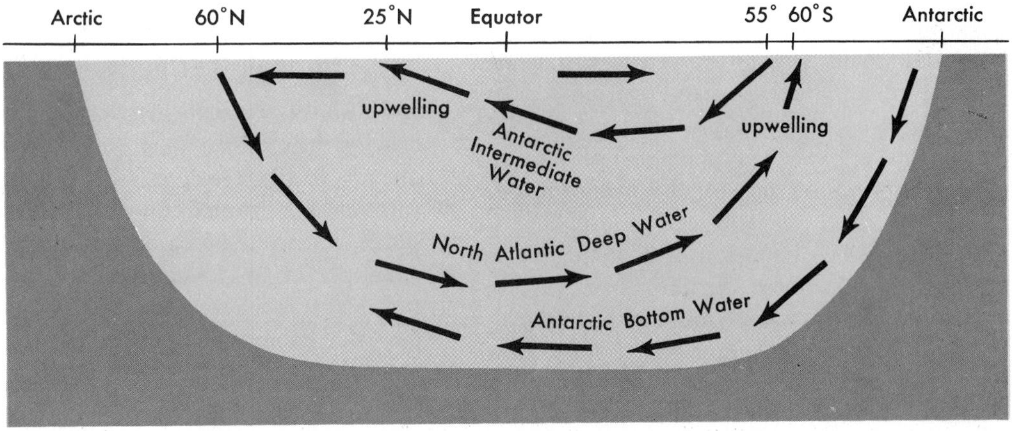

Fig. 21-3. Subsurface cold currents in the Atlantic Ocean. See Topic 4.

The first current—nearest to the surface—originates in the northern part of the Antarctic Ocean, nearest to the Equator. Here the water is cold and fairly dense, even though its salinity is somewhat less than average because of melting snows and heavy rains. Starting northward as a surface current, this water meets the warmer and lighter waters of the South Atlantic Ocean at about latitude 55°S to 50°S. Here it sinks below the warm water to a depth of about 2,000 to 3,000 feet and continues northward across the Equator all the way to between 20° and 30° north latitude before it returns to the surface. This current is sometimes called the **Antarctic Intermediate Water.**

The current next in depth originates in the North Atlantic Ocean near the southeast coast of Greenland. Here cold, dense polar waters meet the warm, lighter waters of a branch of the Gulf Stream. The polar waters sink deep beneath the warmer waters, reaching depths of 7,000 to 13,000 feet as they creep south. Known as the **North Atlantic Deep Water,** this current can be traced into the Antarctic as far as 60°S, where heavier Antarctic water forces it to the surface.

The coldest and deepest of the Atlantic's currents is the **Antarctic Bottom Water.** This water originates near the margins of the Antarctic Continent, and its density is high for two reasons.

First, its temperature is close to freezing. Second, when the surface waters freeze over in winter, only water freezes, and salt is left behind, increasing the salinity of the rest of the water. This densest of all ocean waters sinks to the very bottom of the sea and creeps northward along the floor of the ocean deeps into both the Atlantic and Pacific Oceans beyond the Equator. In the Atlantic it underlies the North Atlantic Deep Water described in the preceding paragraph, and is believed to merge with it after crossing the Equator.

5. Importance of Polar Creep: Upwelling

The cold heavy waters of the density currents described in Topic 4 are known collectively as **polar creep**—*polar* because of their place of origin and *creep* because of the slowness with which they move. Even now, oceanographers do not have enough data to determine accurately the speed of polar creep. However, estimates range from one-half mile to one mile a day. At this rate it takes between 20 and 40 years for polar water to cross the Equator.

Oceanographers regard polar creep as of great importance to the animal life of the sea. First, the sinking polar waters carry dissolved oxygen from the surface to the deep waters which otherwise would have no oxygen to sustain life. Even more important, perhaps, is what happens when the deep waters rise to the surface. Such movements are called **upwelling.** The tiny animals and plants of the sea, the **plankton,** need minerals such as nitrates and phosphates for their growth. The bottom waters of the sea are especially rich in these "fertilizer minerals" because the bottom waters are the resting place for the dead plants and animals that "rain" down from the surface. In upper waters where the plankton lives, the fertilizer minerals are soon used up. Upwelling replaces these minerals and permits the plankton to flourish. The plankton, in turn, provide food for the many larger animals of the sea, including even the great whales. As an example, the upwelling of North Atlantic Deep Water in the Antarctic is believed responsible for the abundance of fish and whales in these waters.

Another example of the value of upwelling is seen in the Peru Current on the west coast of South America. Here again, marine life thrives and the waters abound in fish. In this region upwelling results when steady winds blow surface water away from the coast, and cold water rises from the depths to take its place. Upwelling occurs for the same reason along the west coasts of Africa and California. Where deep water does not rise to the surface, as in much of the tropics, the seas are relatively barren "deserts."

As a result of the downward movement of density currents, and their return to the surface through upwelling, the oceans literally undergo an "overturning" over long periods of time. By measuring the amount of radiocarbon (carbon 14) in samples of polar creep, oceanographers can determine how long ago this water sank from the surface. With such observations they expect some day to make reliable estimates of the speed of overturning.

6. Density Currents through Turbidity

Turbidity currents are density currents made heavier than surrounding water by the addition of mud or silt. Geologists believe that turbidity currents are formed on the steep continental slopes when landslides or earthquakes stir large quantities of mud into the bottom water. The currents are believed by some geologists to be powerful enough to have eroded the submarine canyons found on the continental slopes. Other geologists doubt this, but agree that turbidity currents may be strong enough to scour these canyons and keep them from being filled by sediments. Most geologists agree that turbidity currents may account for deposits of sand and shallow-water shells found far out on the continental slope or even beyond the slope on the deep ocean floor.

Turbidity currents have been seen where muddy rivers empty into fresh water lakes, and they have also been created in laboratory tanks, but they have never actually been observed in the ocean. Nevertheless, many geologists are convinced that they do exist, and that they are responsible for breaking transoceanic cables from time to time.

7. Major Surface Currents and Their Origin

If the Equator is regarded as dividing the Atlantic and Pacific oceans into northern and southern halves, we find that each of these "oceans" has a circulation of surface waters moving around its margins. In the Northern Hemisphere this movement around the "ocean" is in a clockwise direction; in the Southern Hemisphere it is counterclockwise.

How do we know that this surface circulation owes its existence to the driving force of the wind? A strong clue is provided by the currents

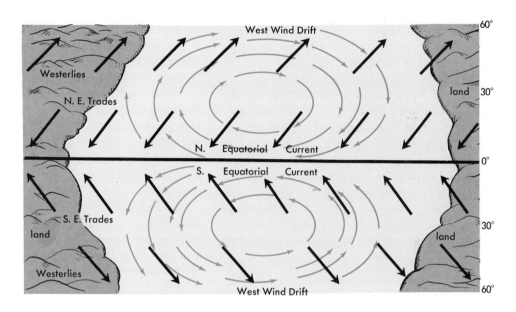

Fig. 21-4. The origin of the surface currents of an ocean.

of the northern Indian Ocean. In this region there is a semiannual reversal of wind direction known as the summer and winter monsoons. And as the winds change, so do the currents reverse their direction of circulation with the seasons.

All the surface ocean circulations appear to originate through the steady blowing of two great sets of world-wide winds in each hemisphere—the **trade winds** of the tropics and the **prevailing westerlies** of middle latitudes. (The origin of these winds is taken up in Chapter 35.) (See Fig. 21-4.)

Blowing strongly and constantly *from the east* in tropical latitudes on both sides of the Equator, *the trade winds drive the surface waters of the oceans westward* in two great streams. The stream north of the Equator is called the North Equatorial Current. The stream south of the Equator is called the South Equatorial Current. If there were no land masses to interrupt

their flow, these currents would probably girdle the globe. But in both hemispheres there is land in these latitudes, and when the currents reach the land masses, *they swing mainly away from the Equator*—northward in the Northern Hemisphere, southward in the Southern Hemisphere, Why away? First and foremost because *the outlines of the land masses* are usually such as to turn them away from the Equator. Secondly, because *the effect of the earth's rotation* is to deflect moving streams to their right in the Northern Hemisphere and to their left in the Southern Hemisphere. This effect, which is known as the **Coriolis force,** is quite small near the Equator, but it increases as distance from the Equator increases.

The currents continue away from the Equator until they reach the latitudes of the prevailing westerly winds at about 35° to 40° north and south of the Equator. Here the currents turn eastward in all oceans, through the combined effect of the earth's rotation and the driving force of the prevailing westerlies. (The westerlies, like all winds, are named for the direction *from which they blow*. Thus, they come from the west and blow toward the east.) Where the currents move with the west winds, they are usually named West Wind Drifts. The "Drift" indicates that the current is no longer as concentrated a stream or as fast moving as it had been. When the Drifts arrive at the eastern ends of the oceans, they turn toward the Equator and complete the circulations—clockwise in the Northern Hemisphere ocean; counterclockwise in the Southern Hemisphere. (See Fig. 21-4.) The speed of most surface ocean currents ranges between one-half and two miles per hour.

8. The South Atlantic Circulation

Now let us take a detailed look at the surface currents of the Atlantic Ocean, beginning south of the Equator. Here the **South Equatorial Current** flows west until it meets the projecting coast of Brazil, which splits it into two branches. The southern branch follows Brazil's east coast southward to about 35°S as the Brazil Current, swings eastward across the ocean to Africa as a West-Wind Drift, and then turns northward along Africa's west coast as the Benguela Current. The northern branch, however, is forced in a northerly direction by the north coast of Brazil, which it follows until it *crosses the Equator. Here it joins and strengthens the North Equatorial Current.* (See Fig. 21-5.)

9. The North Atlantic Circulation; Gulf Stream

The **North Equatorial Current** and its southern ally flow westward until they reach the West Indies, which split the current into two branches. One branch flows northwestward past the Bahama Islands as the **Bahamas Current.** The

other branch continues westward into the Caribbean Sea, through which it moves to the mouth of the Gulf of Mexico at the Straits of Yucatan between Yucatan and Cuba. But the Gulf of Mexico is a "dead end" blocking the path of the current, which therefore swings sharply to the east and into the Straits of Florida between Florida and Cuba. Here it is called the **Florida Current.** Finally, the Florida Current pours into the Atlantic Ocean as the **Gulf Stream**—a mighty "river" 100 miles wide and 2,000 feet deep, flowing at a speed of four to five miles an hour.

It should be pointed out that neither the Gulf Stream nor any other current flows as a single straight body of water. Observations show that the Gulf Stream, like a braided stream on the land, usually consists of interconnecting branches; that it may wind like a meandering river; and that it may shift course in unpredictable fashion, although occupying the same general area of the ocean.

Now the Gulf Stream follows the east coast of Florida. Off northern Florida it is rejoined by its "other half," the Bahamas Current. Thus enlarged, the Gulf Stream continues along the coast of the United States as far as Cape Hatteras, where it leaves the coast and heads northeast toward Newfoundland. By the time it reaches the Grand Banks of Newfoundland, the Coriolis force has turned it to the right so much that it is heading nearly due east. Moving towards Europe, it spreads out and slows down to become the **North Atlantic Drift,** with a speed of only a few miles a day.

The North Atlantic Drift sends out finger-like branches to the shores of Iceland, the British Isles, and the Scandinavian peninsula, giving these regions climates far warmer than normal for their latitudes. Another branch turns southward past the Canary Islands as the **Canary Current,** thereby completing the circulation begun by the North Equatorial Current. The complete circulation of any ocean is called an **eddy.**

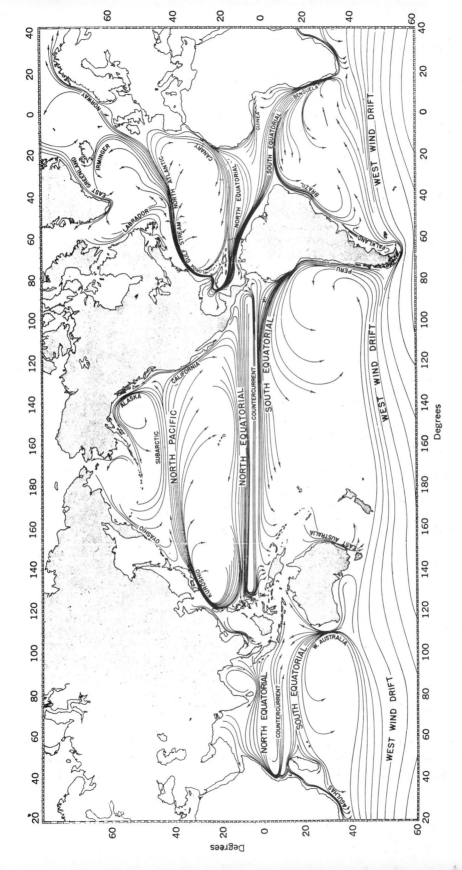

Fig. 21-5. Detailed map of the ocean currents of the world.

10. The Sargasso Sea

Inside the **North Atlantic Eddy,** away from currents and in the calm air between the trade winds and the westerlies, great masses of floating **sargassum** seaweed accumulate to form the Sargasso Sea with its remarkably clear blue waters. The Sargasso Sea supports relatively sparse sea life because no upwelling occurs to bring essential minerals to its surface waters. It is a "sea desert." Other sargasso seas are found in similar locations in the other oceans. The Sargasso Sea was once believed to be capable of trapping sailing vessels in its tangle of seaweed, but this is now known not to be true. Sailing vessels have, however, undoubtedly been becalmed many times in its quiet waters.

11. The Labrador Current

The **Labrador Current** is a cold current that flows out of the Arctic Ocean into the North Atlantic. Following the east coasts of Baffin Island and Labrador, it brings with it icebergs, pack ice, and icy waters. At the Grand Banks of Newfoundland the Labrador Current meets the Gulf Stream. Some of their waters mix, but the larger part of the Labrador Current continues south along the Atlantic coast, at and beneath the surface, as far south as Cape Hatteras.

The famous fogs of Newfoundland are caused by the cooling effect of the Labrador Current on warm moist air blown over it from the Gulf Stream or from Newfoundland in summer.

12. The Pacific Circulation

In the Pacific Ocean the *North Equatorial Current* flows west until it meets the Philippine Islands, the East Indies, and the mainland of southeast Asia. From here a warm current emerges between the Philippines and Taiwan. Swinging northeast as the **Kuroshio** or **Japan Current,** it crosses the ocean as a West Wind Drift. This divides into a north-flowing **Alaska Current** which warms the southern coast of Alaska and a south-flowing **California Current** which follows the coast of Washington, Oregon, and northern California to complete the **North Pacific Eddy.** Upwelling along the California coast makes the coastal waters cooler than the adjacent land, at least in summer.

In the South Pacific the *South Equatorial Current* is uninterrupted as it flows westward to Australia and the southwestern ocean. Turning south, it joins the West Wind Drift, with which it returns across the Pacific to the west coast of South America. Here some of the water, deflected northward by the coast of South America, forms the **Peru** or **Humboldt Current.**

In the southern oceans the West Wind Drift circulates completely around the globe, for in these latitudes there is no land to bar its flow.

13. Countercurrents at the Surface

In both the Atlantic and Pacific surface circulations **Equatorial Countercurrents** flow eastward just north of the Equator between the North and South Equatorial Currents and *opposite in direction* to them. These countercurrents lie in a belt of calm air, the **doldrums,** which separates the northern and southern trade-wind belts. The water of the countercurrents is believed to be water returning from the inner margins of the westward-flowing Equatorial Currents. (See Fig. 21-5.)

14. Countercurrents Beneath the Surface

Countercurrents also exist beneath the surface, but until recently they were not detected. Perhaps the best known is the **Cromwell Current,** first discovered in 1952 and carefully studied by an oceanographic expedition during the International Geophysical Year. The Cromwell Current was discovered flowing *eastward* at a depth of a few hundred feet below the *westward-flow-ing* South Equatorial Current of the Pacific Ocean. The Cromwell Current appears to be about 700 feet deep and about 250 miles wide. Its speed is more than three miles per hour, and its has been traced through the Pacific more than 3,000 miles. Its flow equals that of the Gulf Stream.

During the International Geophysical Year another great subsurface countercurrent was discovered, this time deep in the Atlantic beneath the Gulf Stream. Incidentally, the Swallow float was invented specifically to explore this **Gulf Stream Countercurrent,** the existence of which had been suspected by scientists. This countercurrent is 9,000 feet below the Gulf Stream surface, flowing south (the Gulf Stream flows north) at about eight miles a day. Continued oceanographic exploration will undoubtedly reveal more deep currents and countercurrents, and perhaps with them will come a better understanding of the overall circulation of the world ocean. (See Fig. 21-6.)

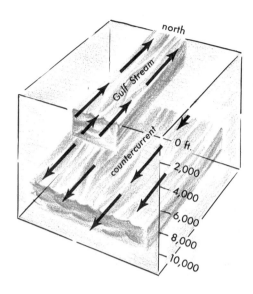

Fig. 21-6. The relation of the Gulf Stream to its countercurrent.

TOPIC QUESTIONS

Each topic question refers to the topic of the same number within this chapter.

1. Using examples of each, distinguish between ocean waves and currents.

2. (*a*) Distinguish between surface currents and subsurface currents. (*b*) Give three ways in which density currents may originate.

3. Describe the origin of the density current that flows from the Mediterranean into the Atlantic Ocean.

4. Briefly describe the three cold-water density currents of the Atlantic Ocean.

5. (*a*) What is polar creep? (*b*) What is upwelling? What is plankton? Why is upwelling so important to plankton? Where does upwelling take place? (*c*) Why is polar creep important to deep sea animals?

6. What are turbidity currents? How do they originate? What do they do?

7. Describe the origin of the clockwise ocean currents of the Northern Hemisphere and the counterclockwise currents of the Southern Hemisphere. Use a simple diagram.

8. Describe the surface currents of the South Atlantic Ocean.

9. Describe the surface currents of the North Atlantic Ocean. Mention the North Equatorial Current, the Bahamas Current, the Florida Current, the Gulf Stream, the North Atlantic Drift, and the Canary Current.

10. Where is the Sargasso Sea? How does it gets its name? Why is it a sea desert?

11. (*a*) Describe the course of the Labrador Current. (*b*) How does it cause fog?

12. (*a*) Describe the North Pacific's surface currents. (*b*) Describe the South Pacific's surface currents. (*c*) Why does the West Wind Drift circle the globe in the southern oceans?

13. What are the Equatorial Countercurrents?

14. (*a*) What is the Cromwell Current? Describe it. (*b*) Describe the Gulf Stream Countercurrent.

GENERAL QUESTIONS

1. Topic 3 describes the two-way flow of water through the Straits of Gibraltar. Is the volume of inflowing Atlantic Ocean water equal to the volume of outflowing Mediterranean water? Explain your answer.

2. On an outline map of the world trace the approximate course of the density currents described in Topic 4.

3. On the same outline map as in 2, mark the places where upwelling occurs in coastal areas, as indicated in Topic 5.

STUDENT ACTIVITIES

1. Make a "turbidity current" as described in Topic 2.

2. To demonstrate a density current due to "saltier water," do the following: (*a*) Make a strong solution of salt water. Add a few drops of dye or ink to color it. (*b*) Slowly pour this denser salt water into the side of an aquarium or large jar of ordinary tap water and observe its flow.

3. (*a*) Make a map or model of the surface currents of the North Atlantic Ocean. (*b*) Do the same for the North Pacific Ocean.

CHAPTER 22
Waves and Shorelines

HOW DO YOU KNOW THAT . . . ?

1. At shorelines, diastrophism and vulcanism struggle with waves and currents in an endless contest that constantly changes the shape of the boundaries separating land and water. Look at some physical maps of the world, for example, those on pages 284 and 299. Compare the photographs in this chapter. What kinds of shorelines are shown? Which ones are straight? Crooked? Where do mountains border on the shores? Where are coastal plains? Which shores are lined with sand bars? With coral reefs? Make a chart listing the different kinds of shorelines you can identify. For each one, find out (using the index in this book and other references) whether that area is a site of earthquake or volcanic activity. What relationships do you find?

2. The kinds of sand found on beaches are described in Topic 12. If a sample is available, spread it on paper and examine it with a magnifying glass. Can you identify any minerals from their colors (white, glassy chips of quartz; black grains of magnetite, of mica)? How would you differentiate the magnetite from the mica? What other materials can you identify? Now feel the sand minerals. Do they seem rounded and smooth? What does this tell you?

WAVES IN THE SEA

1. How Winds Make Waves

Except for tides and the occasional "long waves" due to earthquakes and other causes, almost all ocean waves are made by the wind. An ocean wave is a rhythmic rise and fall of the water surface. The energy for this motion comes from the wind. How does the wind impart its energy to the water?

When the wind blows over the water surface, friction between the moving air and the water creates a *drag* that starts the water in motion. The turbulence of the wind (the movement of the air in spinning eddies and whirlpools) adds a *lifting effect* that ripples the surface of the water. As the wind strikes the ripples, it rocks the water surface until the ripples grow into waves. The size of the waves is determined by the *speed* of the wind, the length of *time* it blows, and the *fetch* or length of open water over which it blows steadily. Ocean waves more than 100 feet high have been created by storm winds blowing for hours with a fetch of 1,000 miles. Because of shorter fetch, lake waves can never be as high as ocean waves. The smaller the body of water, the smaller its maximum waves.

Fig. 22-1. *Waves created by winter storm along the coast at La Jolla, California.*

2. Features of Water Waves

As a wave passes through water, the surface of the water rises and falls. The highest point to which the water rises is called the **crest** of the wave; the lowest point to which it falls is called the **trough** (see Fig. 22-2). The **height** of the wave is the difference in level between its crest and its trough. The **wavelength** is the *distance* from one crest (or trough) to the next. Strong winds make waves longer as well as higher. Storm waves often exceed 500 feet in length, and waves 2,000 feet long have been encountered in the great storms of the Pacific Ocean. On the average, the length of sea waves is between 20 and 30 times their height. For example, a wave 5 feet high is generally between 100 and 150 feet in length.

The **period** of a wave is the *time* it takes for a wavelength (two successive crests or troughs) to pass a given point. For most ocean waves the period ranges from two or three seconds up to about 10 seconds. The speed at which a wave travels can be calculated by dividing the wavelength by the period. For example, if a wave 80 feet long has a period of four seconds, its speed is 20 feet per second—about 14 miles per hour.

Expressing this as a formula,

$$\text{velocity} = \frac{\text{wavelength}}{\text{period}}.$$

3. How the Wave Travels

The passage of the wave through the water is like the passage of a wave through a rope. When a rope is snapped, each bit of the rope rises in its turn to a crest and then falls into a trough, and a wave is said to pass through the rope. But every bit of rope is still in the same place in the rope, having done nothing but rise and fall in a circular path (see Fig. 22-3), while passing on its energy to the next bit of rope. The same thing happens in a water wave. Each particle of water at the ocean surface stays in its place except for a circular motion (in which the diameter of the circle is equal to the wave height), but the wave form is passed on through

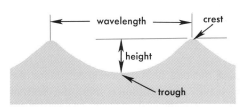

Fig. 22-2. Features of water waves.

the ocean for great distances. Such waves are called **waves of oscillation.**

Wave motion takes place below the surface, too, but the water particles move in smaller and smaller orbits as depth increases, and motion finally dies out. Usually the motion is hardly perceptible *at a depth equal to half the wavelength,* and only great storm waves are likely to scour the bottom of a deep channel or harbor.

4. Whitecaps and Swells

An observer at the beach on a stormy day may look in vain for neat crests and troughs like those shown in Figure 22-2. Instead, he is likely to find a choppy sea with waves of different heights, lengths, and even directions, all capped by a foamy surface of wind-torn crests known as **whitecaps.** This complex pattern is normal for areas of strong winds, and it occurs because the wind usually blows in gusts of differing speed and direction.

On calm days an observer is likely to see a procession of smooth waves that are smaller than the waves of stormy weather. These smooth waves have longer periods, perhaps up to 10 seconds. How, the observer may ask, can there be waves without wind? These waves are **swells** that originated as wind waves in stormy areas far out at sea. The distant storms, like storms close to shore, produce a jumble of waves of many heights and lengths. But the higher, shorter waves die out more rapidly than the lower and

longer waves because of greater internal friction in their steep crests. The long, low waves, with less internal friction to consume their energy, are more likely to maintain themselves and reach distant shores. Arriving in regions of calm weather, they are said to have "outrun the storm."

Swells become longer and lower with increasing distance from their source, and their period increases. Swells with periods of more than 10 seconds are common on the beaches of California in summer, and they are believed to originate in Pacific storms thousands of miles to the west. Swells with shorter periods, such as those common to the Atlantic and Gulf coasts of the United States, originate in storms closer to shore. When swells from two different storm areas arrive together, unusually large waves may result. The next time you go to the ocean beach, time the swell and see how regular a period it has.

5. The Origin of a Breaker

An advancing wave usually approaches the shoreline smoothly until it reaches water so shallow that the wave "feels the bottom." (This takes

Fig. 22-3. The movement of water particles in a wave of oscillation. Note how the movement decreases with depth.

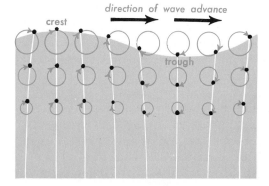

place near the lower depth of wave motion mentioned in Topic 3, where the water is about half as deep as the wavelength. For example, a wave 50 feet long will scrape bottom at 25 feet.) As the wave trough scrapes bottom, the lower part of the wave is slowed down. Meantime, the upper part of the wave moves ahead, the crest steepens, the wave becomes higher and less stable, and finally the crest topples over and breaks into a pounding mass of *surf* that washes up onto the beach. The line along which the successive crests break is called the *line of breakers*. The depth of water at the breakers is usually between one and two times the original height of the breaking wave. The higher the waves, the farther out they break. In the deep water beyond the breakers a swimmer may float like a cork, bobbing up and down with little forward motion. In the breakers he will be pounded and driven toward the beach by the forward-moving water or *swash*. On gently sloping sea floors like that at Waikiki Beach, Hawaii, breakers form at great distances from the shore, making it possible for surfers to enjoy a long "ride". (See Figs. 22-4 and 22-5.)

When waves break, the surf that is formed becomes a powerful agent of erosion. On beaches the surf scours the bottom and moves sediment along the shoreline. On rocky or hilly shorelines the surf pounds and wears down rocks and cliffs.

6. Undertows and Rip Currents

When waves break on a beach, large masses of water are thrown above sea level, and they return immediately under the pull of gravity as the *backwash*. Most of the water usually runs back down the beach in a thin sheet under the incoming wave, and continues along the bottom as a gentle **undertow** that sucks sand away from the feet of bathers and carries some of the sand to deeper water. Undertows were once thought to be dangerous currents capable of carrying swimmers out to sea, but it is now believed that they die out harmlessly even before they reach the line of breakers.

Rip currents are different. They are strong surface currents that flow directly away from the beach in occasional narrow channels through the incoming breakers. Rip currents form when there are large breakers, for it is then that great quantities of water are thrown onto the beach, and must return to the sea. When rip currents pass through gaps in offshore sand bars, their speed increases dangerously to perhaps three or four miles an hour. Swimmers who attempt to swim against the rip currents are likely to exhaust themselves and be swept out to sea. The most effective technique is to go with the rip current until able to escape laterally across the narrow current before attempting to swim back

Fig. 22-4. The formation of breakers and surf.

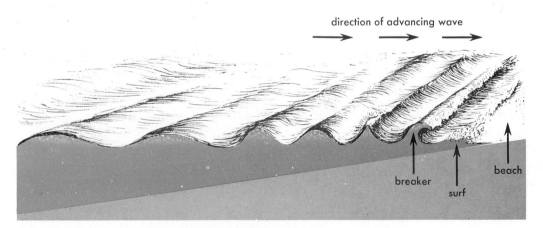

direction of advancing wave

breaker

surf

beach

Fig. 22-5. Surfing on the breakers at Waikiki Beach, Hawaiian Islands.

to shore. Rip currents are intermittent, appearing and reappearing at short but irregular intervals of time.

7. Oblique Waves: Beach Drifting; Longshore Currents

Waves, like the winds that form them, may come from any direction. By the law of averages most waves strike shorelines at oblique angles. As the wave breaks onto the beach, it pushes sand, shells, and gravel *diagonally up* the beach. Then as the water runs back, it drags the sediment almost *straight down* the beach back to sea. Each breaking wave repeats this process, and the net result is a zigzag movement of rock particles along the beach in the general direction of the oblique waves. This movement is called **beach drifting.** (See Fig. 22-6.)

Another product of oblique waves is the **longshore current.** Some of the returning backwash from oblique waves apparently forms a current running more or less parallel to the shoreline and in the general direction of the waves. Such a current is an "along-the-shore current"; hence the name *longshore* or *shore current.* Shore currents may also be made by winds blowing steadily parallel to the shoreline. They are important agents of transportation of sand, and play a large part in the formation of sand bars.

8. Refraction of Waves

Most waves approach a shoreline obliquely. Yet when they reach the shallow water of a smoothly sloping bottom, they swing around and tend to become parallel to the shoreline and to approach the shoreline "head on." This bending of waves is called **refraction.** It is explained by the fact that when a wave first scrapes bottom (in water about half as deep as the wavelength), it slows down. In a wave that approaches obliquely, the end of the wave closest to shore feels the bottom first. As it slows down, the end still in deep water keeps going at its normal speed

Fig. 22-6. How oblique waves cause beach drifting and form longshore currents.

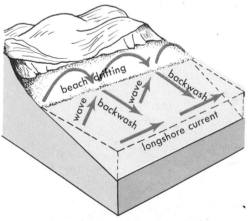

307

and tends to catch up. The net result is a wave front more nearly parallel to the shore, regardless of the original direction of the wave.

Refraction of ocean waves helps to explain why the projecting headlands or peninsulas of an irregular shoreline are worn away rapidly. The approaching waves reach shallow water sooner and slow up sooner in front of the headland than they do in the adjacent bays. So the wave is bent more nearly parallel to the headland until it strikes it from all three sides, concentrating both its water and its energy here. (See Figs. 22-7 and 22-8.)

Waves may strike a shore without refraction if the water remains deeper than half a wavelength right up to the shoreline.

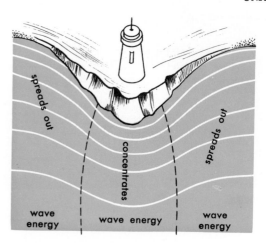

Fig. 22-7. The refraction of waves tends to make them parallel to the shoreline, and thus concentrates their energy against projecting land.

9. Long Waves

Long waves are defined as waves with longer periods than swells, but shorter periods than the tides. The periods of long waves range from 5 minutes to 60 minutes. The best known of the long waves is the *tsunami* produced by some submarine earthquakes. The tsunami was described in Chapter 15. A typical Pacific tsunami in 1946 had a wavelength of about 90 miles and a period of 12 minutes, giving it a speed of about 7.5 miles a minute, or 450 miles an hour. Typhoons far out at sea are also believed to generate long waves, but the origins of many other long waves are still unsolved mysteries of oceanography. Among the mysteries are the long waves known as *surf beats* that roll in to ocean shores at approximate 5-minute periods. Long waves are studied at mid-ocean stations in many parts of the world. Tsunami warnings are broadcast by our Seismic Sea Wave Warning System.

Fig. 22-8. Waves attack the headlands of an irregular shoreline and drive much of the eroded rock material into the coves. Midway Point, Monterey Peninsula, California.

Southern Pacific Photo

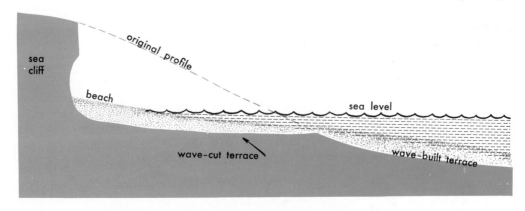

Fig. 22-9. The origin of a sea cliff, a beach, and terraces.

SHORE FEATURES FORMED BY WAVES AND CURRENTS

Regardless of the origin of a shoreline—whether it be through river action, glacial action, vulcanism, or diastrophism—all shorelines will develop features due to waves and currents. These features are classified as *erosional* if they are largely the result of the removal of rock material by wave action. Features that result largely from deposition of rock material are classified as *depositional*.

10. How Waves Erode Rock Materials

The pounding breakers of great waves are among the most powerful of all agents of erosion, especially along deep-water coasts where all the energy of the breakers is concentrated against the points of first impact. The force of a storm wave may reach thousands of pounds per square foot.

The smashing impact of the breakers easily removes large masses of loose materials such as sands and clays. Bedrock is split and "quarried" into blocks by water driven hard into joints and fissures. It is scoured away by the grinding action of sands and pebbles. Boulders that fall from rock cliffs are pounded into pebbles and sands that become rounder and smaller with time. Soluble minerals are dissolved in such rocks as limestone, causing them to crumble.

The breaking waves may also trap and compress the air that is in cracks and hollows of the cliffs. The air thus compressed becomes a powerful force in splitting the bedrock.

11. Erosion of Irregular Shorelines

On irregular, zigzag shorelines the areas that project into the water are called **headlands** or **promontories,** and the indentations of the shoreline are called **coves** or **bays.** Wave erosion against the headlands of a deep-water shore causes sea cliffs or **wave-cut cliffs** to form when the waves *notch* or cut away the rock at water level and the overhanging rock caves in. As the waves drive deeper into the headland, level **wave-cut terraces** slightly below sea level are worn at the base of the cliffs. (See Fig. 22-9.)

The rock fragments eroded from cliffs are used repeatedly by the waves as cutting tools until they are ground into small pebbles and sands. Some of these fragments are carried by the waves onto the shores of the quieter coves. As the fragments accumulate, they form **shingle**

Fig. 22-10. *Sketch of an irregular shoreline with the erosional features described in Topic 11.*

beaches of pebbles or **sand beaches.** Other fragments may settle in the deep water beyond the wave-cut terrace to form a fairly level deposit called a **wave-built terrace** (see Fig. 22-9). The rocks of a headland may differ somewhat in hardness. Where the rocks are less resistant, waves may dig in deeper to form short **sea caves** that are exposed at low tide. Waves may also cut through vertical joints in the sides of narrow headlands or through the walls of sea caves to form **sea arches** or small **natural bridges.** When the roof of a sea arch collapses, one side of the arch is left in the water as a high, narrow rock island called a **stack.** Good examples of these features can be seen on the coasts of California, Oregon, Washington, Maine, and the Gaspé peninsula of Canada. (See Figs. 22-10 and 22-11.)

Fig. 22-11. *Sea stacks carved by waves from stratified rocks at Bay of Islands, Australia.*

12. Depositional Features: Beaches

To the geologist **beach** means the area that lies between the lines of high tide and low tide. This area is usually covered with sands or gravels ground down by the waves from materials eroded from the shore. On an irregular shoreline beaches are more likely to be deposited in the quiet waters of the bays and coves than at the heads of promontories.

Beach materials may range in size from sand to boulders, and in composition from common minerals to precious ones. The size of the materials depends largely on the nature of the coastal rocks and the steepness of the sea bottom. The steeper the sea floor, the more easily are the finer sediments washed out to sea, leaving the larger fragments to form pebble or even boulder beaches. As for mineral composition, most sand beaches are composed principally of quartz sand. The beaches of Bermuda and other coral islands may consist largely of shell fragments. Grains of black magnetite are also found in small amounts in many beach sands. In rare cases enough gold has been found in beach sands to make a placer deposit worth mining. More than two million dollars in gold has been mined from the beach at Nome, Alaska.

13. Depositional Features: Sand Bars

A large percentage of the sand carried by waves and currents is deposited offshore in the form of long, narrow deposits known as sand bars. Some of these bars are *attached at one end* to projections of the mainland, and are known as *spits*. Others stretch completely across the mouths of bays, and are called *baymouth bars*. Still others are completely *unattached* to the mainland, and are called *offshore bars*. All three types of bar run more or less parallel to the mainland, and all or parts of the bars may be under water, especially at high tide. How do these different types of sand bar originate? What are their characteristics? (See Fig. 22-12.)

14. Origin of Attached Bars

On irregular shorelines, longshore currents carry sand and pebbles away from the wave-eroded cliffs of the headlands into deeper and quieter waters. Such waters occur in coves and bays and behind islands. On the shores of the coves the sediments may be deposited to form beaches; in open water they may form sand bars of many kinds. Some of the sand bars appear to

Fig. 22-12 Features formed by deposition along an irregular shoreline.

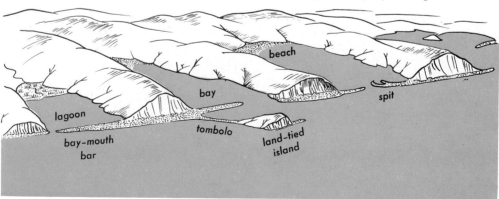

grow out from the ends of the very headlands from which their sediments are derived. Bars with one end attached to the headland and the other end in the open water across the bay or cove are called **spits.** Other bars grow from one side of a bay to the other to form **baymouth bars.** Still others grow from islands to the mainland to form bars called **tombolos.** The islands become **land-tied islands.** Nantasket Beach near Boston is a tombolo. Waves or crosscurrents may drive the ends of spits shoreward, forming spits with curved ends called **hooks.** The protected waters of the bays behind the bars become **lagoons.**

Sandy Hook in New Jersey, Rockaway Beach in New York, and Cape Cod in Massachusetts are famous examples of hooks which have grown many miles long and thousands of feet wide. Winds and waves have combined to pile their sands many feet above sea level.

15. Origin of Unattached Bars

An **offshore bar** or **barrier beach** is a sand bar that runs parallel to a straight shoreline and is nowhere attached to it. Offshore bars are common wherever straight shorelines with gently sloping sea floors are found.

The origin of offshore bars is not certain. Geologists think that at least some offshore bars may have been formed when large spits were separated from the mainland by storms or by a rise of sea level after the Ice Age. Until recently another theory was most in favor. This theory holds that offshore bars are long piles of sand scooped up in the zone of breakers by the scraping action of the breaking waves on smooth, sandy sea bottoms. Shore currents may also bring sand to help build the bar. When a bar grows to sea level, its surface may be raised still higher by wind and waves. (See Fig. 22-13.)

An offshore bar protects the shallow water on its landward side from winds and waves. This area of quiet water between the bar and the mainland is a lagoon. Lagoons may become salt marshes through filling with sediment and growth of vegetation.

16. Examples of Offshore Bars

There are many examples of offshore bars along the coast of the United States from southern Long Island all the way to Texas. Many of the larger bars in populated areas have become popular bathing resorts, as at Fire Island and Jones Beach in Long Island and Atlantic City in

Fig. 22-13. This diagram of an offshore bar suggests its formation by the scraping action of breaking waves. See Topic 15.

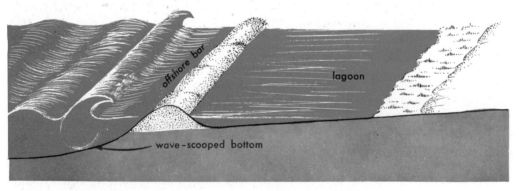

Fig. 22-14. Fire Island, an offshore bar parallel to the southern shore of Long Island, New York. Note its hooked end.

New Jersey. To reach an offshore bar, a lagoon must be crossed, usually by bridges or roads called *causeways*. (See Fig. 22-14.)

All offshore bars are low and very narrow in comparison with their length. Fire Island is about 30 miles long but nowhere more than a mile in width. Its greatest heights are those reached by the tops of its sand dunes—about 30 feet above sea level. One offshore bar, Padre Island, runs a hundred miles along the coast of Texas. Galveston, Palm Beach, Daytona Beach, and Miami Beach are also located on offshore bars.

The lagoon between an offshore bar and the mainland is rarely so named. Examples are Biscayne *Bay* between Miami Beach and Miami, *Lake* Worth between Palm Beach and West Palm Beach, Indian *River* and Banana *River* between Cape Kennedy and the Florida mainland, and Great South *Bay* between Fire Island and Long Island, New York. Despite their names these are all lagoons.

SHORELINES

17. Classifying Shorelines: Johnson's Classification

Many classifications of shorelines have been suggested by geologists, but no classification yet devised has been entirely satisfactory.

Shorelines are classified into four groups in the classification suggested by Professor D. W. Johnson of Columbia University. **Shorelines of emergence** are formed when parts of the continental shelf rise out of the sea or are uncovered by a drop in the level of the sea. Such shorelines can be identified by their *regularity* or straightness and by the *offshore bars* and *lagoons* that form in front of them.

Shorelines of submergence are formed when coastal land masses are flooded by the sea, either through their own sinking or by a rise of sea level. Such shorelines are identified by their *irregularity*, which results from the flooding of their valleys

Fig. 22-15. The estuary or drowned valley of the Hudson River at West Point, New York. In the background the Hudson flows through the water gap it carved into the Hudson Highlands.

Fairchild Aerial Surveys

and lowlands. The flooded valleys are *bays.* The unflooded highlands between valleys are *headlands* or *promontories.* Low hills may be covered to become dangerous underwater *shoals,* and higher hilltops may stand above sea level as *continental islands.* These shorelines may also be characterized by *sea cliffs, sea caves, sea arches, stacks, spits, tombolos,* and *baymouth bars,* as shown in Topics 11 and 14.

Neutral shorelines are formed without either emergence or submergence. For example, the shorelines of a volcanic island, a coral reef, an outwash plain, and a large river delta are considered "neutral."

Professor Johnson knew that many shorelines seemed to show features of at least two of his first three classes, so he included a fourth class of **compound shorelines** to cover these difficult cases. Johnson's classification also embodies the idea of a life history for all his four classes of shorelines, in which each one passes from youth to maturity, and finally to old age. In old age all shorelines are straight and are fronted by wide, sloping wave-cut terraces which protect them from further attack by the waves.

18. Shorelines of Submergence

The general features of a shoreline of submergence were described briefly in Topic 17. The specific features of such a shoreline depend, however, on the kind of land eroded and the chief agent of erosion.

The coast of Maine was formed by partial drowning of mountainous land eroded by rivers and glaciers. Its bays are rather short, narrow, and many-branched. Its waters are fairly deep near shore. Its islands and shoals are rocky and numerous. The coast of Scotland and the northwest coast of Spain are other examples of this *ria coast* or *partly submerged mountain coast.*

When a coastal plain is partly submerged, its bays are longer and wider than those of a ria coast. The water close to shore is not as deep, nor are islands as numerous or rocky. The Chesapeake Bay and Delaware Bay regions are examples of *partly submerged coastal plains.* Delaware Bay is the drowned valley of the lower Delaware River. Chesapeake Bay is the drowned valley of the lower Susquehanna River and its tributaries, including the Potomac River. New York Bay is the drowned valley of the lower

Hudson River. San Francisco Bay is the drowned valley of the lower Sacramento River. These drowned valleys usually extend inland many miles before reaching the part of the river that is still above sea level. With their floors far below sea level, and the ocean filling their valleys from wall to wall, drowned rivers are much wider and deeper than true rivers, and are known as **estuaries.** The Hudson River below Troy, New York, is an example of an estuary. (See Fig. 22-15.)

19. Shorelines of Submergence: Life History

Johnson theorized that shorelines of submergence were always irregular in their youth,

were straightened by continuous baymouth bars in early maturity, and eventually were eroded back into a *straight shoreline* without bays and headlands. (See Figs. 22-16 through 22-19.)

20. Fiord Shorelines

In many of the colder regions of the world, as in Greenland today, glaciers of past ages came down to the sea through valleys which they scoured out below sea level near the coast. When climates grew warmer and the glaciers melted away, the sea entered into and submerged the parts of the glacial troughs that were below sea level. In some cases sinking of the land helped to drown the valleys. These partly sub-

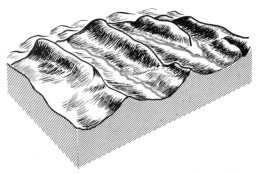

Fig. 22-16. A mountainous region dissected by river valleys. Submergence of this region will produce an irregular shoreline. See Fig. 20-17.

Fig. 22-17. Here the region of Fig. 20-16 has been partly submerged to form a youthful shoreline. Its valleys have become bays, its ridges are headlands, and some hills have formed islands.

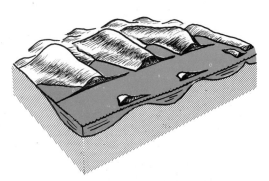

Fig. 22-18. The shoreline of Fig. 20-17 has reached maturity here, with its bays nearly closed by the growth of sand bars.

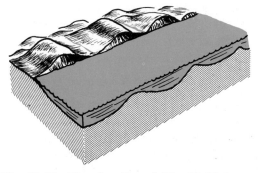

Fig. 22-19. The shoreline of Fig. 20-18 has now been worn back to the heads of its bays by wave erosion, and is fully mature.

Norwegian National Travel Office

Fig. 22-20. Geirangerfiord, West Norway. A fiord is a partly drowned glacial trough.

merged glacial troughs along sea coasts are **fiords.** Down their clifflike sides tumble the waterfalls of many hanging tributary troughs, making fiord coasts the most spectacular of all sea coasts. Fiords occur along the coast of Norway, Alaska, Greenland, New Zealand, Chile, and Labrador. (See Fig. 22-20.)

21. Shorelines of Emergence

Almost the entire west coast of North, Central, and South America from Oregon to central Chile has a comparatively straight shoreline produced by the emergence of young folded coastal mountain ranges. Narrow strips of coastal plain occur in places, but for the most part the ocean floor slopes steeply down to great depths not far

from shore, and the coast is bordered by rocky sea cliffs and stacks carved out by the direct attack of the waves. Above sea level at short distances inland, numerous raised sea cliffs and terraces show that emergence of the land has been taking place steadily in recent periods of time. (See Fig. 22-21.)

The Atlantic Coast of the United States from North Carolina to Florida, and the Gulf Coast from Florida to Mexico, may be classified as coastal plain shorelines of emergence. These regular coasts are marked by numerous sand bars, most of them unattached to the mainland, from which they are separated by lagoons. Erosion on the seaward side of the bars tends to shift them toward the mainland. At the same time the lagoon may be filling with sediment and swamp vegetation. Eventually, then, the bars and the filled lagoon may merge with the mainland to make a relatively straight continuous shoreline.

22. Neutral Shorelines

Specific examples of neutral shorelines include the delta shorelines of great rivers like the Mississippi and the Nile, outwash plain shorelines like that of southern Long Island, volcanic island shorelines like those of Hawaii, and coral island shorelines like those of Bermuda, east Australia, and the many coral islands of the South Pacific.

CORALS

23. Growth of Corals

Corals are tiny sea animals that live in colonies. Except in youth the coral animals do not move about but remain fastened to rocky sea floors in regions of warm, clear, fairly shallow water. Corals must have a water temperature of from 65°F to 70°F, and they do not grow at depths below about 150 feet. Since corals do

Fig. 22-21. Raised sea cliffs and terraces along the coast of California near Point Harford are evidence of recent emergence of the sea floor.

Stose, U.S. Geological Survey

not move, they depend upon waves and currents to bring food to them. From the sea water corals also extract dissolved lime to make the shells in which they live. The many different varieties of corals—the brain coral, the fan coral, the staghorn coral, and others—form an equally great variety of beautifully shaped colonies. (See Fig. 22-22.) When the corals die, the shells of their colonies remain, and other generations of corals grow up above them. These large accumulations of coral are called **coral reefs.** Shellfish and calcareous algae (simple plants) also grow on the reef and help to build it.

Although corals can grow only to the surface of the sea, waves may break the coral shells and pile them up above sea level. Fragments of coral form coral sands, and coral sands may become cemented together with other sediments to form coral limestone.

24. Coral Reefs

Coral colonies growing close to shore form coral reefs or **fringing reefs.** Such reefs occur along the coasts of Florida and Bermuda. The growth of a reef is most rapid on its ocean side, to which food is brought by waves and currents.

As reefs grow oceanward, they may become **barrier reefs,** which are separated from the mainland by broad lagoons of quiet water. The Great Barrier Reef of Australia is over 1,200 miles long and up to 90 miles wide. Between it and the mainland is a broad lagoon known as the Inland Water Way.

25. Coral Atolls

An atoll is a narrow ring-shaped island or chain of islands around a central lagoon. Most

Fig. 22-22. Top row, left to right: rose coral; many-pored coral; branching coral. Bottom row: brain coral; pink branching coral; organ-pipe coral; mushroom coral.

Ward's Natural Science Establishment

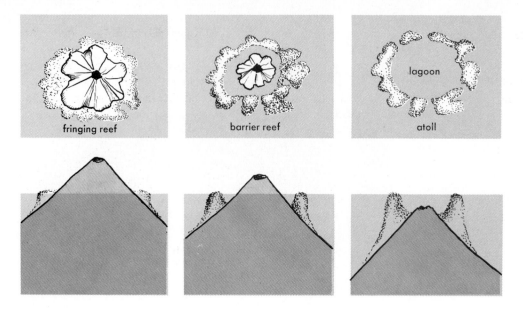

Fig. 22-23. The origin of an atoll is shown in three stages from left to right. Top views are shown in the upper half; cross-sections are shown below.

atolls are made of coral limestone, and drill borings and soundings show that they rest on the slopes of deeply submerged volcanic cones. These atolls appear to have originated in a manner first explained by Charles Darwin more than 100 years ago. The atoll started as a fringing reef or chain of reefs growing around a volcanic island. Then the island began to sink, but its subsidence was slow enough for the upward growth of the reef to keep pace with it. (Corals do not grow at depths greater than about 150 feet.) The reef grew outward as well as upward and became a barrier reef enclosing a lagoon and an island. With continued subsidence, the top of the island sank below sea level, and the barrier reef became an atoll around a central lagoon. (See Figs. 22-23 and 22-24.)

Atolls are found mainly in the open waters in the middle of the Pacific Ocean. There is usually at least one break in the coral ring of an atoll

Fig. 22-24. Aerial view of an atoll in the South Pacific Ocean.

through which boats may enter. The lagoon inside the atoll offers protection from wind and waves, and large atolls like Wake Island and Midway Island are important refueling bases for trans-Pacific airplanes. Bikini and Eniwetok atolls are well known as sites of nuclear bomb tests. Drill borings on Eniwetok showed about 4,600 feet of coral limestone resting on volcanic rock, apparently supporting Darwin's theory of atoll formation.

TOPIC QUESTIONS

Each topic question refers to the topic of the same number within this chapter.

1. (*a*) Explain how the wind makes water waves. (*b*) Name the factors that determine the size of the waves.

2. (*a*) With respect to waves, explain the meaning of wavelength, crest, trough, and period. (*b*) What is the usual ratio of length to height of ocean waves? (*c*) How can the velocity of a wave be calculated?

3. (*a*) Explain the motion of the particles of water in a "wave of oscillation." (*b*) At what depth does wave motion practically die out?

4. (*a*) What are whitecaps? (*b*) What are swells? How do they originate?

5. (*a*) How do breakers and surf originate? (*b*) Why is the surf important geologically? (*c*) What is "swash"?

6. (*a*) What is "backwash"? undertow? (*b*) What are rip currents? When and why do they form?

7. (*a*) Explain the origin of the zigzag motion of beach drifting. (*b*) What is a longshore current?

8. What is refraction of waves? How does it happen? What is one of its effects?

9. What are "long waves"? Name three kinds of long waves.

10. How do breakers erode rock?

11. Describe the features produced by wave erosion on irregular shorelines.

12. (*a*) Define beach. (*b*) Where do beaches form on irregular shorelines? (*c*) What materials are beaches made of? Why? (*d*) Why is the beach at Nome, Alaska, famous?

13. Explain how spits, baymouth bars, and offshore bars differ.

14. How does a spit originate? a baymouth bar? a tombolo? a land-tied island? a hook? a lagoon?

15. What is an offshore bar? How does it originate? What is the lagoon?

16. (*a*) Name and describe a few well-known offshore bars. (*b*) Name examples of lagoons that are not called lagoons.

17. Define the four classes of shorelines in Johnson's classification.

18. Define, describe, and give examples of (*a*) the ria type of shoreline, (*b*) the partly submerged coastal plain type.

19. Outline the life history of a shoreline of submergence.

20. What is a fiord shoreline? Describe it and give examples.

21. (*a*) Define and give examples of folded-mountain shorelines formed by emergence. (*b*) Define, describe, and give examples of coastal plain shorelines. (*c*) Briefly describe their life history.

22. Give examples of neutral shorelines.

23. (*a*) What are corals? Under what conditions do they grow? (*b*) How do coral sands form? coral limestone?

24. How does a fringing reef form? a barrier reef?

25. What is a coral atoll? How does it form?

GENERAL QUESTIONS

1. According to Topic 2, how high is a wave 500 feet long likely to be?

2. What is the velocity of a wave 1,000 feet long with a period of 25 seconds?

3. According to Topic 3, at what depth will a wave 1,000 feet long first be felt on the sea floor? a wave 30 feet long?

4. Make the necessary calculation to verify the figures given in Topic 9 for the velocity of the tsunami.

5. Magnetite grains are frequently found concentrated in parts of a beach. Why?

STUDENT ACTIVITIES

1. Make models representing (*a*) the features of an irregular shoreline of submergence, (*b*) the features of a coastal plain shoreline of emergence, (*c*) the origin of an atoll.

2. Examine beach sands with a magnifying glass. Use a magnet to separate any magnetite grains from the other minerals. List the minerals you identify. Compare beach sands with sands from other sources.

3. Make a series of models to represent the life history of a shoreline.

4. If you live near a lake or the ocean, take a field trip to study features described in this chapter. At the seashore see if you can estimate the length, the height, and period of the incoming waves and swell.

TOPOGRAPHIC SHEETS

(15-minute series)

1. *Shoreline of emergence and offshore bar:* Atlantic City, New Jersey; Fire Island, New York; Lake Como, Texas.

2. *Shoreline of submergence in hilly region:* Boothbay, Maine; Bar Harbor, Maine.

3. *Shoreline of submergence on a coastal plain:* Kilmarnock, Virginia; Barnegat, New Jersey.

4. *Spits and hooks:* Sandy Hook, New Jersey; Brooklyn, New York; Provincetown, Massachusetts.

5. *Sea cliff:* Wellfleet, Massachusetts.

6. *Shoreline of emergence, elevated beaches, wavecut cliffs:* Oceanside, California.

7. *Bay-mouth bars, hooks, cliffed headlands, estuaries:* Point Reyes, California.

BIBLIOGRAPHY

Barton, R. *Oceanology Today*. Doubleday, N.Y., 1971.

Bascom, W. (ed.) *The Oceans*. Freeman, San Francisco, 1969.

Behrman, O. *New World of the Oceans*. Little, Brown, Boston, 1969.

Brindze, R. *All About Undersea Exploration*. Random House, N.Y., 1960.

Burton, M. *Under the Sea*. Franklin Watts, N.Y., 1960.

Carrington, R. *A Biography of the Sea*. Basic Books, N.Y., 1960.

Carson, R. L. *The Sea Around Us*. Oxford University Press, N.Y., 1951.

Clarke, A. C. *Challenge of the Sea*. Holt, Rinehart and Winston, N.Y., 1960.

Clemens, E. *Waves, Tides, and Currents*. Knopf, N.Y., 1967.

Colman, J. S. *Sea and Its Mysteries*. Norton, N.Y., 1950.

Coker, R. E. *This Great and Wide Sea*. Harper and Row, N.Y., 1961.

Cousteau, J. Y. *The Silent World*. Harper and Row, N.Y., 1953.

Cowen, R. C. *Frontiers of the Sea*. Doubleday, N.Y., 1969.

Cromie, W. J. *Living World of the Sea*. Prentice-Hall, N.Y., 1966.

Daugherty, C. M. *Searchers of the Sea*. Viking, N.Y., 1961.

Dubach & Taber. *Questions About the Oceans*. Govt. Printing Office, Washington, D.C., 1967.

Engel, L. *The Sea*. Time, Inc., N.Y., 1961.

Gaskell, T. F. *World Beneath the Oceans*. Natural History Press, N.Y., 1964.

Groen, P. *The Waters of the Sea*. Van Nostrand-Reinhold, N.Y., 1967.

Gross, M. G. *Oceanography*. Merrill Publishing Co., Columbus, Ohio, 1971.

King, C. A. M. *Introduction to Oceanography*. McGraw-Hill, N.Y., 1963.

Kuenen, P. H. *Realms of Water*. Wiley, N.Y., 1963.

Leip, H. *River in the Sea*. Putnam, N.Y., 1957.

Mero, J. L. *Mineral Resources of the Sea*. Elsevier, N.Y., 1965.

Miller, R. C. *The Sea*. Random House, N.Y., 1966.

Naval Oceanographic Office. *Science and the Sea*. Govt. Printing Office, Washington, D.C., 1967.

Piccard, A. *Earth, Sky, and Sea*. Oxford University Press, N.Y., 1956.

Piccard, J. and Dietz, R. S. *Seven Miles Down*. Putnam, N.Y., 1961.

Pincus, H. J. *Secrets of the Sea*. American Education Publications, 1966.

Raitt, H. *Exploring the Deep Pacific*. Norton, N.Y., 1961.

Ross, D. A. *Introduction to Oceanography*. Appleton, N.Y., 1970.

Shepard, F. P. *The Earth Beneath the Sea*. Johns Hopkins Press, Baltimore, 1959.

Skinner, B. J. and Turekian, R. K. *Man and the Ocean*. Prentice-Hall, Englewood Cliffs, N.J., 1973.

Soule, G. *The Ocean Adventure*. Appleton-Century-Crofts, N.Y., 1967.

Stewart, H. B., Jr. *The Ocean Adventure*. Van Nostrand, Princeton, N.J., 1966.

Sullivan, W. *Assault on the Unknown*. McGraw-Hill, N.Y., 1961.

Vogel and Caruso. *Ocean Harvest*. Knopf, N.Y., 1961.

Yasso, W. E. *Oceanography*. Holt, N.Y., 1965.

Unit 5 Earth History

What kind of animals
do you see in the painting on the
opposite page? Make some observations as
though you were studying the painting for clues.
How big are these dinosaurs compared to the objects
around them? What is the land like where they lived? What is
the climate like? What do these dinosaurs eat? In what ways is this
scene different from one you might see today?

The picture is not a photograph, because these dinosaurs were believed to
live millions of years ago, long before people were on the earth. How do you
suppose the artist knew what they looked like? What their environment was
like? The painting is based on scientists' findings about past life on the earth.

Finding out about the earth and the life on it long ago is like a mystery story. Scientists have discovered clues that suggest what may have been and what may have happened. From these clues, scientists try to reconstruct the past. In that story, scientists describe the history of the earth from when it was believed to start—
over 4 billion years ago.

As part of the story, scientists tell us roughly when the first forms of life developed and what kinds of plants and animals lived at different times.
Scientists tell us when and where there were hot climates, cold climates,
wet climates, or dry climates. They tell us about ancient ice ages and
draw maps showing ancient continents with strange outlines.

In this unit you will explore some of the methods
used to reconstruct the past. And you will
read some chapters in the story
of the earth's history.

CHAPTER 23

The Rock Record

HOW DO YOU KNOW THAT . . . ?

Most fossils found in rocks are not the original remains of prehistoric plants and animals. In most cases, the fossils are *imprints*—molds or casts left in rock after the original remains have disappeared. Make a "fossil" mold. Flatten a small block of plasticene or clay to represent a layer of sediment. Use any object to represent your prehistoric organism. To keep the object from sticking in the clay, rub a little petroleum jelly on it. Press the outside of the object firmly into the clay until a clear impression is made. Remove the object and examine your "fossil" mold.

Now make a thick mixture of plaster of Paris and water. Rub a thin layer of petroleum jelly into all parts of the mold. Pour the plaster into the mold. When the plaster hardens, remove it. You now have a "fossil" cast.

1. The Geologic Timetable

The main events in the earth's history have been summarized into a **geologic timetable.** (See outline on p. 325.) Geologists have classified the earth's history into five great **eras** and smaller time divisions called **periods.**

2. A Sample of Earth History

As in our own times, weathering and erosion attack the surface of the continents everywhere. The bedrock of the continents is broken and shattered, and the resulting rock fragments are carried down from mountain and highlands by all the agents of erosion, even as they are today. Rivers deposit their sediments in horizontal layers of gravels, sands, and clays. These are deposited on flood plains, on lake floors, and on the shelves of the continents. In time these and other sediments, like the lime deposits of the continental shelf, are consolidated into sedimentary rocks. Plants and animals live and die on land and in the waters of lakes and oceans. As they die, these plants and animals are buried in the accumulating sediments into which they fall. When the sediments form layers of rock, many plants and animals are preserved in them as fossils.

Erosion and deposition continue for millions of years. More sediments are deposited, and more layers of rock are formed. The oldest layers are at the bottom, the most recent ones at the top. In geosynclines the sediments are many thousands of feet in thickness. The mountains and highlands of the continent are being worn down; the shallow areas of the ocean are being filled in.

And then one day great changes begin. Vulcanism and crustal movements raise extensive sections of the surface high above their former levels. Great mountain ranges are created. Horizontal rock layers are folded, tilted, faulted, and intruded by lava. Sedimentary rocks may be metamorphosed. With changing topography and climate many forms of life die out, while others are evolved. From within the earth has come a **revolution,** itself lasting millions of years, to end an era of earth history.

GEOLOGIC TIMETABLE

Era	Period	Epoch	(Millions of Years Ago) Began	(Millions of Years) Duration	Characteristic Life	Physical Events
CENOZOIC "Age of Mammals"	Quaternary	Recent	—	(11,000 yrs.)	Man dominant. Domestic animals develop.	West Coast uplift continues. Great Lakes form.
		Pleistocene	1	1	Primitive man appears, develops. Elephants flourish in N. America, then die out.	Ice Age. Raising of mountains and plateaus in western U.S.
	Tertiary	Pliocene	11	10	Modern horse, camel, elephant develop. Sequoias decline; tropical trees driven south.	N. America joined to S. America. Sierras and Appalachians re-elevated.
		Miocene	25	14	Horse migrates to Asia, elephant to America. Grasses, grazing animals thrive.	N. America joined to Asia. Vulcanism in northwest United States, Columbia Plateau.
		Oligocene	40	15	Mammals progress. Elephants in Africa. Monkeys die out in N. America.	Alps and Himalayas forming. Vulcanism in western United States.
		Eocene	60	20	Pygmy ancestors of modern horse, other mammals. Diatoms, flowering plants thrive.	Coal forming in West.
		Paleocene	70	10	Many new mammals appear.	Uplift in West continues.
MESOZOIC "Age of Reptiles"	Cretaceous		135	65	Dinosaurs, ammonites die out. Mammals, birds advance. Flowering plants, hardwoods rise.	Uplift of Rockies begins. Colorado Plateau raised. Coal swamps in West.
	Jurassic		180	45	Age of *Dinosaurs*. First birds, more mammals. Conifers and cycads abundant.	Rise of Sierra Nevadas, West Coast mountains, Basin and Range mountains.
	Triassic		225	45	Reptiles thrive. First mammals. Forests of conifers and cycads.	Vulcanism in New England, New Jersey. Palisades of Hudson formed.
PALEOZOIC "Age of Amphibians"	Permian		270	45	Trilobites, seed ferns, scale trees die out. Corals abundant.	"Ancestral Appalachians" formed. Ice Age in South America. Salt-forming deserts in western U.S.
	Pennsylvanian		330	60	First reptiles. Many giant insects. Spore-bearing plants, amphibians flourish.	Great coal-forming swamps in North America and Europe.
	Mississippian		350	20	Amphibians and crinoids flourish. Ferns, conifers abundant.	Extensive submergence of continents.
"Age of Fishes"	Devonian		400	50	First amphibians; fishes abound. First land plants, forests.	Mountain building in New England and Canada. White Mountains raised.
"Age of Invertebrates"	Silurian		440	40	First land animals (spiders, scorpions). Fish develop; marine invertebrates thrive.	Salt-and-gypsum-forming deserts in eastern U.S.
	Ordovician		500	60	First vertebrates (fish). Marine invertebrates thrive: mollusks, trilobites, graptolites.	Taconic and Green Mts. form. Half of N. America submerged.
	Cambrian		600	100	Many marine invertebrates (trilobites, brachiopods, snails, sponges). Many seaweeds.	Extensive deposition of sediments in inland seas.
PROTEROZOIC ARCHEOZOIC			(Estimated) 4,600	(Estimated) 4,000	No life on land. Simple marine plants (algae, fungi) and marine worms. Others probably existed, but fossil evidence is lacking.	Great volcanic activity, lava flows, metamorphism of rocks. Formation of iron, copper, and nickel ores.

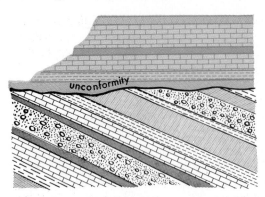

Fig. 23-1. An unconformity is an erosion surface that separates the rocks of two different ages of earth history.

No sooner do the new highlands and mountains rise than they too begin to be attacked by weathering and erosion, and a new era begins. Again long intervals of time pass. Eroded areas in coastal regions may be submerged by the sea. Sediments may be deposited on the eroded surfaces of folded or tilted rocks.

The new sediments are in horizontal layers. It can easily be seen that they do not belong to the same era in earth history as the rocks on which they rest. The rocks beneath are folded or

Fig. 23-2. An unconformity in which horizontal Paleozoic strata rest on the eroded surface of gneiss of Precambrian age.

tilted; they may be metamorphosed and intruded by lava; they contain different fossils; they do not "conform" or fit in with the younger rocks resting on them; their surface is weathered and eroded. Such an erosion surface, which separates the rocks of two different ages of earth history, is called an **unconformity** (Figs. 23-1 and 23-2).

3. Which Rocks Are Oldest?

The relative age of the sedimentary rocks in any one area is easily determined. The oldest layer of undisturbed sedimentary rocks is always at the bottom. The youngest or most recently formed layer of undisturbed sedimentary rocks is always at the top. Any igneous intrusions found in these rocks—dikes, sills, or laccoliths—must have come after the rocks they intrude were formed. Igneous intrusions are therefore obviously younger than any rocks into which they have intruded—sedimentary, metamorphic, or other igneous rocks. (See Fig. 23-3.)

In volcanic regions lava flows and volcanic cones may lie on top of other rocks. Here, too, the lavas are obviously younger than the rocks on which they rest, and the youngest layers of lava are the top ones.

The relative age of sedimentary rocks in different areas can usually be determined by the fossils they contain. Metamorphic rocks—such as those of the Piedmont and New England mountain areas—are generally older than sedimentary rocks. In fact, the metamorphic rocks include some of the oldest of all the surface rocks of the earth.

In a sequence of *undisturbed* sedimentary rocks, the younger rocks must always be on top of the older rocks. This rule is known as the **law of superposition.** But older rocks are sometimes found lying on younger rocks. This happens in mountain regions where diastrophism has overturned the rock layers. In such cases fossils are particularly useful in deciding the relative ages of the rocks.

4. How Do We Know There Were Five Eras?

In Topic 2 it was explained that eras are ended by geological revolutions. In these, extensive volcanic activity and uplift may produce changes in the physical appearance of the earth, and great changes may occur in the forms of plants and animal life. The historical geologist recognizes revolutions through unconformities, through different rock formations, and especially through marked differences in the fossils of these different rocks. From his studies of these features he has come to the conclusion that there were five great eras of earth history.

The five eras are given names that indicate the kind of life that existed in them. The oldest era is the **Archeozoic** (beginning or primitive life) era. It ended with peneplanation of its rocks after prolonged erosion. Then came the **Proterozoic** (earlier life) era, which also ended with peneplanation. The **Paleozoic** (ancient life) era which followed ended with the Appalachian revolution, which appears to have been the culmination of repeated folding during this era.

Then came the **Mesozoic** (middle life) era, also known as the Age of Reptiles. This was the era in which the dinosaurs lived. The Laramide revolution brought this era to a close, creating the Rocky Mountains and re-elevating the nearly peneplaned Appalachian Mountains.

The **Cenozoic** (recent life) era, also known as the Age of Mammals, is the latest of the five great eras of earth history. Most geologists regard the Cenozoic era as still with us. Others prefer to see our present time as the start of the Psychozoic (mind-life) era. The latter part of the Cenozoic era has been marked by a continuing Cascadian revolution. Though creating no new mountains in North America, the Cascadian revolution has added considerable height to the mountains of western United States.

5. How Are Eras Divided Into Periods?

The Paleozoic and Mesozoic eras have been separated by geologists into a number of divisions called periods. Like eras, periods differ from each other in such characteristics as the relative position of land and sea, the kinds of climates, and, most important, the forms of plant and animal life that developed and existed. However, the differences between two successive periods are not as great as those between two successive eras.

While eras are separated by revolutions, periods are sometimes separated by **disturbances.** These are similar to revolutions, but the changes they produce in topography, climate, and forms of life are not as widespread or as drastic. Where disturbances have occurred, they can be identified by unconformities similar to those of revolutions.

Fig. 23-3. The relative ages of the rocks in this diagram are given by the numbers. (See Topic 3 for explanation.) The surface that separates layers 1 and 3 is an unconformity.

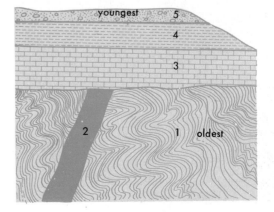

Both revolutions and disturbances are described briefly in the physical events column of our geological timetable. Disturbances, like revolutions, are usually named for some prominent feature they produce. For example, the Palisade disturbance at the close of the Triassic period faulted and tilted the rocks from which later came the famous Palisades of the Hudson River.

It should be made clear that mountain-making and other movements of the earth's crust, like those which created ocean basins and inland seas, were by no means confined to the ends of eras or periods. Where they did reach a climax at the end of an era or period, the historical geologist has named such events revolutions or disturbances. His chief bases for ending one period and beginning another in his geological timetable are, however, marked changes in living things, as disclosed by fossil evidence.

6. What Are Epochs?

The rock record of the Cenozoic era shows a number of divisions that are shorter and less distinct than the periods of the Paleozoic and Mesozoic eras. The geologist prefers to call these **epochs** rather than periods. We are now living in the Recent epoch, which began when the Great Ice Age ended about 11,000 years ago. The Ice Age itself occurred during the Pleistocene epoch.

7. How the Life of the Past Was Recorded

The paleontologist, a geologist who specializes in the study of prehistoric life, is able to tell us what living things existed in past ages because he has found their record in the rocks. This record consists of **fossils,** which are **any evidence of the existence of life preserved in the rocks.** With this record the geologist is able to trace the evolution of life on the earth from the simple beginnings of Archeozoic or Proterozoic time to the highly developed forms of today. But fossils do more than tell us about the evolution of life. They give us clues to the climates of the past (see Topic 16). Fossils also give us information about the conditions under which the rocks they are found in were formed.

The formation of a fossil has been described briefly in Topic 2 of this chapter and in Topic 19 of Chapter 5. There are four principal ways in which fossils are formed:

Fig. 23-4. Limb bones of a carnivorous dinosaur before removal from famous Bone Cabin Quarry, Wyoming.

American Museum of Natural History

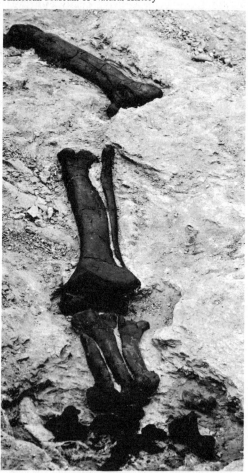

(a) Original remains. In rare cases fossils represent the actual remains of plants or animals. The entire bodies of woolly mammoths, great elephantlike creatures of Pleistocene time, have been found almost perfectly preserved in the perpetually frozen earth of Siberia. Here they were trapped in glacial moraines at the close of the Ice Age.

Other examples of original materials are the shells of shellfish, which became consolidated to form fossil varieties of limestone, and the teeth of sharks.

(b) Replaced remains. Many fossils no longer contain the original materials of which they were made, although they may look unchanged. Ground water may have replaced the lime of shells and bones with silica. The petrified trees of Arizona, of Yellowstone, and of other localities were formed when ground water replaced the decaying wood of these buried trees with silica (see Fig. 23-5).

(c) Molds and casts. Sometimes a fossil shell or bone is completely dissolved out of the rock in which it was preserved. This leaves a hollow **mold** which shows only what the shape of the fossil had been. The filling of such a mold with new mineral material may produce a **cast** of the original fossil. Molds and casts of shellfish are common fossils. (See Fig. 23-6.) The molds of ferns, leaves, and fish are also found in many rocks.

On the shores of the Baltic Sea in Europe molds of insects of millions of years ago have been found perfectly preserved in the hardened resin of pine trees on which the insects had crawled. This hardened resin is what we call **amber.** (See Fig. 23-7.)

(d) Impressions. Even the impressions left in the muds and sands of flood plains and deltas by moving animals may be preserved when the sediments become rock. In such shales and sandstones geologists have found the footprints of dinosaurs, the trails of ancient worms, and many

Iddings, U.S. Geological Survey

Fig. 23-5. Petrified tree trunks in Fossil Forest, Yellowstone National Park.

Fig. 23-6. Molds and casts of trilobites in Lockport dolomite.

American Museum of Natural History

Fig. 23-7. Baltic amber containing molds of insects trapped about 35 million years ago.

Fig. 23-8. Dinosaur tracks in Cretaceous rocks near Glen Rose, Texas. The large footprints are those of a four-legged "vegetarian" dinosaur. The three-toed prints belonged to a two-legged flesheater.

Roland T. Bird, American Museum of Natural History

other impressions of living things of the past. (See Fig. 23-8.)

8. What Are Index Fossils?

Fossils that are typical of a particular period or epoch of earth history are very useful to the historical geologist. When he finds one of these fossils in a layer of rock, no matter in what part of the world, it immediately tells him the relative geological age of the rock. These **index** or **guide fossils** help to correlate the geological histories of different parts of the United States or of different continents.

Index fossils are a great aid to the oil geologist. Suppose he knows that many oil deposits have been found in the rocks of a particular period. In seeking new oil deposits he uses his knowledge of the index fossils of this period in helping him to identify other rock formations of the same geological period.

What makes a good index or guide fossil? There are three important qualifications. The ideal index fossil represents a plant or animal that existed for a very short time in earth history. When such a fossil is found, there is no doubt about the relative age of the rocks in which it occurs. (This existence-for-a-short-time is known technically as **narrow vertical range.** Why?) A second requirement is that the fossil be plentifully distributed over a large area—continental or even world-wide distribution—otherwise its value would be negligible. (This is called **wide geographic** or **horizontal range.**) A third requirement is that it be easy to recognize. This is called **distinctiveness.**

An animal called the trilobite is often used as an index fossil. Trilobites were scorpionlike animals that lived in the oceans during the Paleozoic era, at the end of which they became extinct. Fossil trilobites are plentiful and world-wide. Any trilobite immediately identifies its rocks as of the Paleozoic era. A particular trilobite species that lived during only a part of the era makes an even better index fossil. (See Fig. 23-6.)

9. Measuring Geological Time: The Old Ways

How does the historical geologist calculate the figures given in our geological timetable? In some cases the figures are in billions of years. In other cases they are in millions of years. At the very top of the table where the Recent period begins, we are given a figure of but a few thousand years. How are such measurements made?

Modern methods of measuring geologic time are based largely on radioactivity. They are regarded as highly accurate. These are discussed in Topic 12. But first, let us see how geologic time was estimated before methods based on radioactivity came into use.

(a) Rate of deposition. Geologists have made careful studies to determine the rates at which sediments are deposited on the continental shelves. Rates of deposition vary widely. On the average, however, it seems to take between 4,000 years and 10,000 years for a layer of sedimentary rock one foot thick to be formed.

Suppose it is found that the total thickness of rock deposited during a single geological period was 6,000 feet. At the rate of one foot in 5,000 years, this would mean that deposition had been going on for 6,000 × 5,000 years, or 30,000,000 years for this period.

(b) Rate of erosion. The rate of erosion probably varies even more than the rate of deposition. Suppose that careful studies of the Colorado River lead the geologist to estimate a rate of erosion of one foot in 1,000 years. Using this figure, the geologist may calculate the time taken by the Colorado River to erode its canyon 6,000 feet deep. Multiplying 6,000 by 1,000 years, he gets a total of 6,000,000 years. Of course such calculations are not exact, but they have a basis in studies of facts.

(c) Salt in the ocean. Attempts have been made to determine the age of the ocean. To do this, geologists first calculate how much salt there is in the entire ocean. Then they estimate how much salt is being carried into the ocean by all the rivers of the world each year. From these two figures it is possible to calculate how long it took for the ocean to acquire its salt. This method can give us no exact answer, however, since the rate of salt accumulation must have varied widely through the ages, being greater during humid periods than during dry ones. Using a rate close to that of today, we obtain an answer of about 500,000,000 years.

Because all of the above methods depend so much upon estimates, average rates, and other assumptions, the figures arrived at are not very reliable. Now let us see how methods that use radioactivity operate.

10. Radioactive Elements and Radioactivity

What is a radioactive element? It is an element whose atoms emit radiations from their nuclei. What kinds of radiations? There are three kinds, and they are known as alpha, beta, and gamma rays, respectively. **Gamma rays** are highly penetrating rays similar to X rays. **Beta rays** are actually particles—electrons traveling at high speed. **Alpha rays** are also particles. In fact, each alpha ray is a bundle of two protons and two neutrons—the equivalent of a helium nucleus. Each time an alpha ray is shot out of an atomic nucleus, the atom changes to a new lighter element. The alpha ray (also called an alpha particle) becomes helium gas. If the new element is also radioactive, radiation will again take place and will continue until an element is formed that is not radioactive. (See Fig. 23-9.)

Let us take an illustration. The most common nuclide of uranium has an atomic weight of 238. It is radioactive. When an atom of this nuclide emits an alpha particle, it becomes an atom of thorium, also radioactive. The reaction is written as follows:

$$U^{238} \rightarrow He^4 + Th^{234}$$

Radiation continues with alpha, beta, and gamma rays being emitted, until finally an element is formed that is not radioactive. This is the nuclide of lead (symbol Pb), whose atomic weight is 206. In the process, eight alpha rays in all are emitted. This can be written as follows:

$$U^{238} \rightarrow 8 \ He^4 + Pb^{206}$$

The uranium atom has become transformed into eight atoms of helium and one atom of lead 206.

11. What Is Half-Life?

How can radioactivity be used to measure time? The answer lies in the remarkable fact that **radioactive disintegration takes place at an absolutely constant rate.** It is completely unaffected by conditions, such as temperature and pressure, that alter the speed of ordinary chemical reactions. Unlike the rates of deposition, erosion, and salt accumulation discussed in Topic 9, radioactive disintegration can be assumed to have proceeded at an unvarying rate throughout earth history.

Radioactivity—the emission of alpha, beta, and gamma rays—can be detected by instruments like the well-known Geiger counter. With the aid of such instruments, scientists are able to calculate the rate at which a radioactive element decays into its non-radioactive end product. The time it takes for half of the atoms in a sample of a radioactive element to change into a non-radioactive element is called its **half-life.** At the end of this time, the sample will emit only half as many rays in a given time as it had originally.

Each radioactive nuclide has its own rate of decay and its own half-life. Half-lives range from fractions of seconds to billions of years. The element protactinium formed from Th^{234} has a half-life of about one minute, whereas the half-life of U^{238} is 4.5 billion years.

To clarify the idea of half-life, let us take a specific example. Thorium 234 has a half-life of about 24 days. (See Fig. 23-10.) This means that *every 24 days* a sample of this element will lose half of the thorium atoms with which it be-

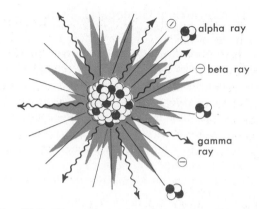

Fig. 23-9. The radioactivity of an atom of uranium 238.

gan that period. An original sample of one pound of thorium 234 will decay as follows:

After 24 days, 1/2 pound of Th^{234} is left (1/2 × 1)

After 48 days, 1/4 pound of Th^{234} is left (1/2 × 1/2)

After 72 days, 1/8 pound of Th^{234} is left (1/2 × 1/4)

After 96 days, 1/16 pound of Th^{234} is left (1/2 × 1/8)

If all the helium gas, lead, and other elements formed are kept together, the sample will always weigh one pound, but its thorium 234 content will decrease as shown above.

12. Measuring the Age of Rocks by Radioactivity

In the early 1900's the geological timetable could show only the relative age of geologic eras, not their absolute ages or actual age in years. Now the geologic timetable on page 325 gives the absolute age of each era and period. All of these figures come from measurements based on the decay of radioactive minerals in the rocks, by methods developed in relatively recent years. Let us see what these methods are.

(a) The uranium-lead method. Uranium 238 is the element used most often in measuring long periods of geologic time. If its half-life were a matter of days or even years, it would be of little value in measuring geologic time. But the rate at which uranium decays into lead is almost unbelievably slow. The half-life of uranium 238 is about 4½ billion years! Research has shown that *in one year,* one gram of uranium 238 yields only $\dfrac{1}{7,600,000,000}$ gram of an uncommon nuclide of lead with atomic weight 206.

How does the scientist use this knowledge? First, he must find rocks which contain uranium minerals that were "born" in the rock when the rock itself originated. Igneous rocks are such rocks. Then he measures both the amount of uranium in the rock and the amount of lead derived from the uranium. (Lead derived from uranium differs slightly from ordinary lead, and can be distinguished from it.) The greater the percentage of lead present, the older the rock. To determine the actual age, the geologist uses a formula based on the rate of decay given in the preceding paragraph:

$$\text{Age} = \frac{\text{Wt. of lead}}{\text{Wt. of uranium}} \times 7{,}600{,}000{,}000$$

or

$$\text{Age} = \text{lead-uranium ratio} \times 7{,}600{,}000{,}000$$

Let us take a specific example. Suppose the lead-uranium ratio in a uraninite crystal from pegmatite rock is 0.10. Then:

$$\text{Age} = 0.10 \times 7{,}600{,}000{,}000$$
$$= 760{,}000{,}000 \text{ years}$$

Using the uranium-lead measures, scientists have learned that some rocks in South Africa are almost 3½ billion years old; rocks in southeast Manitoba, Canada, are more than 2½ billion years old; rocks in the Black Hills of South Dakota are more than 1½ billion years old; some rocks in Connecticut are about one-quarter billion years old; and so forth. Unfortunately, the wonderful uranium-lead clock has its limitations. Uranium minerals suitable for this method of dating are rarely found in sedimentary or metamorphic rocks. Neither are they found in all igneous rocks. Furthermore, because the rate of uranium-lead decay is so slow, the method does not give reliable results unless the uranium-bearing rocks are at least 10 million years old! Therefore scientists have sought and developed different radioactive clocks for determining the age of other minerals.

(b) The rubidium-strontium method. Another radioactive element used in measuring the age of rocks is the relatively rare rubidium 87. Its half-life is about 49 billion years! It decays into the element strontium. Rubidium occurs in the feldspars and micas of igneous rocks. Where both rubidium 87 and uranium 238 occur in the same rock, one age measurement can be checked against the other.

(c) The potassium-argon method. An important and newer method of dating uses the

Fig. 23-10. This graph illustrates the decay of 16 ounces of radioactive Thorium 234, which has a halflife of about 24 days.

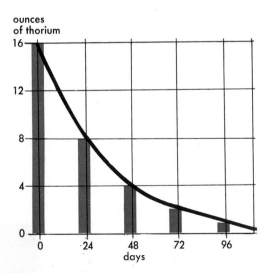

ounces
of thorium

decay of radioactive potassium 40 into the gas element argon. The half-life of potassium 40 is about 1.3 billion years. One great advantage of this method is that potassium, unlike uranium and rubidium, is a very common element, being part of potash feldspar and biotite mica. Minerals suitable for dating by this method are found in metamorphic rocks as well as in igneous rocks. This makes possible the dating of many rocks that cannot be dated by the uranium or rubidium methods. Another advantage of this method is that it can date rocks as "young" as about 1½ million years.

13. Measuring Ages of Thousands of Years

The methods described in Topic 12 measure rock ages millions or even billions of years old, but they are unable to measure periods of time under about 1½ million years. In 1947 Dr. Willard F. Libby developed a method of measuring absolute ages from about 1,000 to 40,000 years. (However, we are still in need of methods to fill the gap between ages of 40,000 and 1,500,000.) Let us examine Dr. Libby's discovery.

All living plant and animal cells have been found to contain a tiny, but constant, proportion of a radioactive form of carbon. (**Radiocarbon,** as it is called, has an atomic weight of 14, whereas ordinary carbon has an atomic weight of 12. Radiocarbon is formed from ordinary nitrogen in the atmosphere through the action of cosmic rays.) The half-life of this radiocarbon is about 5,700 years. As long as the plant or animal is alive, the ratio of radiocarbon to ordinary carbon in its cells remains fixed. But **as soon as the plant or animal dies, its radiocarbon begins to decrease** at an absolutely definite rate. By measuring the amount of radiocarbon left in a sample of wood, for example, it is possible to tell how old the wood is or how long ago the tree from which it came died. When geologists find wood or other organic materials buried in "recent" deposits such as those formed at the close of the Ice Age, they can determine the age of these materials through radiocarbon dating.

Radiocarbon dating is now regarded as accurate for periods ranging from about 1,000 years to as much as 40,000 years, after which too little radiocarbon is left for accurate measurement. Since carbon is found in the implements used by ancient peoples, archeologists use radiocarbon dating to determine accurately the time when certain peoples or cultures thrived. From radiocarbon dating, we now believe the last of the Ice Age glaciers to have vanished from the United States about 11,000 years ago. Radiocarbon dating has also been used to measure the "age" of deep Atlantic Ocean water. Using radiocarbon techniques, scientists have found that it takes 1,600 years for water from the Arctic Ocean surface to move down to depths of several miles in the Atlantic.

14. Ice Age Dating by Varves

A botanist can determine the age of a tree by actually counting the annual rings in its trunk. Before the discovery of radioactive dating, geologists used similar methods to find out the rate of recession of glaciers during the last part of the Ice Age. Instead of counting annual rings, they counted the layers of sediment deposited each year by the retreating glacier. How are these layers recognized?

Wherever lakes occurred at the ice front, streams from the melting ice carried sediment into the lakes. In summer, when the glacier melted rapidly, the streams carried a mixture of sands, silts, and clays into the lakes. The sands and silts, coarser than the clays, soon settled to the bottom in a light-colored layer. But the fine clays remained in suspension, being kept from settling by the motion of currents created by the wind. When winter came, the lakes froze over. With winds unable to reach and stir the water, the clays settled slowly to the bottom to form a layer of very fine, dark sediment. Thus each year two distinct layers of sediment were deposited—a light-colored sandy layer in summer and a dark-colored clay layer in winter. (See Fig. 23-11.)

The layers of sediment are called varved (banded) clays or simply **varves.** Each pair of layers is one varve and represents the deposits of a single year. By careful and painstaking research, specialists in glacial geology have traced glacial lake deposits from the extreme southern positions of the ice sheets in Europe and North America all the way north to their centers of accumulation in much higher latitudes.

15. Age of Niagara Falls

Attempts have been made to estimate the age of Niagara Falls in the following way. Niagara is known to have originated at Lewiston, New York, from which it has receded seven miles to its present position. Knowing the rate at which Niagara is receding today, the geologist *assumes* an average rate of recession since its origin. From this he can calculate how long it may have taken to recede seven miles. Niagara Falls is known to have originated during the close of the Ice Age, so such a calculation can also be used to estimate when the Ice Age was ending. If an average rate of recession of four feet a year is assumed, we have:

$$\text{Age} = \frac{7 \text{ (mi.)} \times 5{,}280 \text{ (ft. per mi.)}}{4 \text{ (ft. per year)}}$$

$$= \frac{36{,}000 \text{ (approx.)}}{4}$$

$$= 9{,}000 \text{ years (approx.)}$$

16. Clues to Climates of the Past

The geologist can often read the climates of past ages from the rocks. Deposits of coral limestone tell us of warm climates, for corals grow

American Museum of Natural History

Fig. 23-11. Seasonally banded glacial clays are called varves. Those on the left are from an Ice Age lake named Lake Passaic. Those on the right are from former Lake Hackensack. Both lakes were in New Jersey.

only in waters whose temperature is between 65°F and 70°F. Deposits of consolidated glacial tills (called tillites) in equatorial Africa tell us of the existence there of ice ages and glacial climates hundreds of millions of years ago.

Thick deposits of salt and gypsum, which could have been formed only by long-continued evaporation, tell us of ancient ages of hot, dry climates. Coal beds in Antarctica are a sure sign that temperate or tropical climates existed there in some extended period of long ago. These are but a few of the more obvious indications of the climates of the past.

17. Paleogeography

At the beginning of this chapter we asked how the historical geologist could determine what the outlines of the continents, ocean basins, and inland seas had been at various periods millions of years ago in earth history. This study is called **paleogeography** (*paleo,* ancient; *geography,* drawing of the earth). Let us see whether

Fig. 23-12. Thick deposits of rock salt were formed by continuous evaporation of sea water during long ages of hot dry climates. Avery Island Mine, Louisiana.

International Salt Co.

we can explain a few of the principles used by the paleogeographer in drawing his maps of the earth as it was during the various periods of prehistoric time.

Suppose the paleogeographer wishes to draw a map showing North America at the close of the Paleozoic era. (1) He reasons that stratified sedimentary rocks with marine fossils of late Paleozoic age should have been formed wherever continental shelves or shallow inland seas existed at that time. Next he proceeds to locate outcrops of such rocks. Upon locating these outcrops, he must try to determine how far the rocks extend below the surface and how much rock formerly at the surface has been removed by erosion. With this information, he can draw a reasonably good estimate of the location of land and sea in late Paleozoic time. (2) He can determine the location of inland fresh-water lakes in similar fashion. In this case the paleogeographer looks for lake deposits containing fresh-water fossils. (3) From the texture of the rocks the paleogeographer may be able to learn a good deal about the topography of the land from which the sediments had been eroded. Conglomerates or coarse sandstones suggest swift young streams running down the steep slopes of hills or mountains not far from the waters into which they emptied. Fine sandstones or shales suggest streams flowing slowly over gently sloping beds through broad lowlands. Pure limestones—without sand or clay—suggest an origin at relatively great distances from the shorelines.

These are but a few of the basic principles that help the paleogeographer to reconstruct the outlines of ancient continents.

TOPIC QUESTIONS

Each topic question refers to the topic of the same number within this chapter.

1. What information about the earth's past does the historical geologist give us? What is the geologic timetable?

2. Summarize the principal events in the geological history of an era. What is a revolution? What is an unconformity?

3. (*a*) How do we determine the relative age of sedimentary and igneous rocks in a particular area? (*b*) How do we determine the relative age of rocks in different areas? (*c*) What is the law of superposition? How do exceptions to this law occur?

4. (*a*) How do we know there were five eras of earth history? (*b*) What does the name of each era mean?

5. Explain how eras are divided into periods. (*b*) What is a disturbance? (*c*) Did mountain-building take place only at the ends of geological periods? Explain.

6. (*a*) What is an epoch? (*b*) Why is the Cenozoic era divided into epochs rather than periods?

7. (*a*) What is a fossil? (*b*) How is a fossil formed? (*c*) Give a brief explanation of the four principal kinds of fossils.

8. (*a*) What is an index fossil? (*b*) What use do geologists make of index fossils? (*c*) What three qualities make an ideal index fossil?

9. Describe three different methods formerly used to determine the duration of geological time.

10. (*a*) Describe the radiations given off by radioactive elements. (*b*) Describe the radioactive decay of uranium 238.

11. (*a*) Why is radioactivity more reliable for measuring time than rates of erosion and deposition? (*b*) What is meant by the half-life of an element? Use thorium 234 to illustrate your answer.

12. (*a*) Explain the uranium-lead method for measuring geological time. What are its limitations? (*b*) Give brief descriptions of the rubidium-strontium and potassium-argon methods.

13. Explain the way in which radiocarbon is used in measuring short periods of time.

14. Explain what varves are and how they were used in determining the rate of glacier recession.

15. Describe a method by which attempts have been made to calculate the age of Niagara Falls.

16. Describe the evidences that provide clues to the climates of the past.

17. Explain some of the principles used by the paleogeographer in drawing maps of the earth in past ages.

GENERAL QUESTIONS

1. Why are metamorphic rocks likely to be older than sedimentary rocks?

2. What factors would cause variations in the rates of deposition during a geological era? of erosion?

3. Why are the methods of radioactivity less useful for determining the ages of sedimentary or metamorphic rocks than for igneous rocks?

4. What factors may have caused the rate of salt accumulation in the ocean to vary through the ages?

5. Summer varves are usually reddish or brownish in color because of greater weathering by oxygen. Explain this.

6. Fall-winter varves are usually blackish because they contain more organic matter than spring-summer varves. Why?

7. What evidences of glaciation would be found in tillites?

8. The geologic timetable says that there were four glacial periods during the Pleistocene epoch. What evidences might indicate this?

9. In what way are the flakes of graphite found in Archeozoic schists and gneisses (see the geologic timetable) possible indicators that life existed in that era?

STUDENT ACTIVITIES

1. Visit the nearest museum or college geology department where you can study an exhibit of fossils of different types and different geological ages.

2. Refer to a textbook on historical geology for more information on types of unconformities. Then make models to represent these types.

3. Make "fossil" impressions, molds, and casts of leaves, shells, etc., using plasticene or modeling clay and plaster of Paris.

4. Make a diorama to represent the life of any selected prehistoric period.

CHAPTER 24

Precambrian Through Paleozoic

HOW DO YOU KNOW THAT . . . ?

1. Many scientists believe that simple forms of life developed first and more complex forms arose later. This idea is sometimes used to date rocks. The relative age of fossils helps scientists tell when the rocks were formed. Suppose you found a fossil print of a scorpion in one rock and a fossil print of a deer's foot in another rock. Which rock would you judge to be older? Why? (Clue: See the timetable, p. 325.)

2. Study a sample of fossiliferous limestone. Test for lime (calcite) by the acid test. A drop of dilute hydrochloric acid on the rock will fizz. What forms of shellfish can you identify in the rock? Are the fossils molds, casts, or both? Use a magnifying glass to study the details of the shells. Find out, with the help of your teacher, the era and period in which this rock was formed.

1. The Origin of the Earth

Many hypotheses about the origin of the earth have been suggested. We shall describe three of the more likely hypotheses.

Stars colliding. A number of hypotheses have suggested that the solar system originated as the result of a near-collision of two or three stars, one of which was the sun. One version of this hypothesis was proposed by the astronomer F. R. Moulton and the geologist T. C. Chamberlain in 1895, and is commonly known as the **planetesimal hypothesis.** Another version called the **tidal** or **gaseous hypothesis** was proposed by the astronomer Sir James Jeans and the geophysicist Harold Jeffries in 1917.

Our sun is one star in an enormous galaxy that includes billions of stars. Within this galaxy each star moves at high speed, each with its own direction. Some stars move away from each other; some move toward each other. But the distances between stars are so great that the chances of collision or near-collision are almost nonexistent. Yet, according to the tidal or gaseous hypothesis our sun did have a near-collision with another star about 5 billion years ago.

As the story goes, these two stars had gradually been approaching each other through countless eons of time. Finally they came close together. Closeness is a relative thing. In this case scientists believe that the distance must still have been many millions of miles. But whatever the distance, the stars were close enough to exert irresistibly great gravitational forces on the hot gaseous masses that each contained. (See Fig. 24-1.)

As the larger star moved away, it tore great fiery streamers from the very heart of the smaller one and drew them many millions of miles out into space. Then as the larger star moved on, the streamers were released. Many fell back into the body of the smaller star. Not all, though. Some of the streamers had acquired so much forward velocity that they did not fall back. Instead they moved around the smaller star in

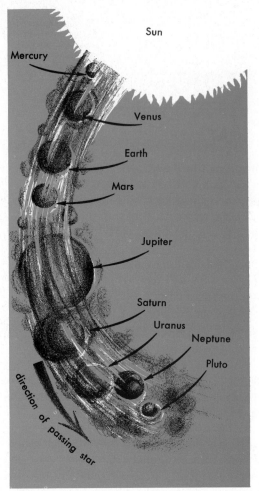

Sun

Mercury

Venus

Earth

Mars

Jupiter

Saturn

Uranus

Neptune

Pluto

direction of passing star

Fig. 24-1. Artist's conception of a stage in the tidal or gaseous hypothesis of the origin of the solar system.

elliptical orbits, gradually condensing into spheres. Thus the planets were born. Smaller masses of material became satellites around the planets. Still other masses are believed to have become the planetoids, comets, and meteor swarms of the newly born solar system, all revolving about the star we now call our sun.

The fiery birth of the earth must have been followed by a long period of cooling. During this cooling process the solid crust of the earth formed. Further cooling must have brought rain down in torrents to fill the ocean basins. Some

gases did not cool enough to condense, and they remain as our atmosphere.

The nova explosion hypothesis. This hypothesis was proposed by the astronomer Hoyle in 1944. A nova (*nova,* new) is an inconspicuous star that suddenly flares into extreme brightness, stays bright for a short time, and then fades to its former faintness. According to Hoyle's hypothesis a star may have flared or exploded as a nova just as it passed near the sun. The event caused it to throw off large shells of gaseous material. Parts of these shells may have been captured by the gravitational pull of the sun to form the planets. As the nova moved away, it faded beyond the possibility of identification.

The protoplanet hypothesis. This hypothesis was proposed by astronomer Gerard P. Kuiper about 1950. It states that the solar system began some five billion years ago as a vast rotating spherical cloud or globule of cosmic dust and gas. The cloud reached far beyond the present orbit of Pluto, our most distant planet. As time passed, the cloud contracted under the pull of its own gravitational force. Most of the cloud's mass concentrated around its center, continuing to contract and becoming so hot by compression that it eventually became the glowing fiery star we call the sun. About 10% of the total mass formed a disk that rotated rapidly around the center. Friction within the disk caused most of its material to collect in great swirling eddies. Then these contracted into more compact masses called protoplanets, and eventually into the bodies we call the planets and their satellites. Some "uncollected" materials still remain as meteors, planetoids, and comets (See Fig. 24-2.)

2. The Oldest Rocks on Earth

Using the radioactive clocks described in the preceding chapter, geologists have measured the age of rock samples in many parts of the earth. The oldest "rocks" yet discovered are meteorites more than 4½ billion years old!

Within the earth's crust itself, the oldest rocks dated so far are the uranium ores found in pegmatite dikes in southern Rhodesia, Africa. These are nearly 3½ billion years old. In the United States the oldest rocks thus far dated are pegmatites found in the Black Hills of South Dakota. They are about 1½ billion years old.

In many cases of dating, the igneous rocks whose age is being measured have intruded into more ancient rocks which must have been there first. In other words, the intruded rocks are even older, but just how old cannot so far be determined, since they do not contain "radioactive clock" minerals like uranium or rubidium. Nor do we find anywhere the igneous rock that must have been the earth's original crust 4 or 5 billion years ago. Either this original crust has been completely eroded away, or it has been buried deep beneath later deposits of sediments and lava flows.

PRECAMBRIAN TIME: THE ARCHEOZOIC AND PROTEROZOIC ERAS

3. What Does Precambrian Mean?

Look back for a moment to the geologic timetable. You will see that the Cambrian period is the first "chapter" in the Paleozoic era. (Remember, you must read the timetable from the bottom up, just as if these periods were layers of rock. Oldest is at the bottom, youngest at the top.) Beginning with Cambrian rocks more than one-half billion years ago and continuing to modern times, we find that the rocks of the earth's crust abound with fossils. We experience little difficulty in reading from these fossils most of the story of the development of life on the earth.

Just the opposite is true of the earlier Archeozoic and Proterozoic rocks. Except for a remarkable recent discovery in South Australia there are almost no distinct fossils to tell us about the living things that preceded the Cambrian period. So marked is the difference that historical

Fig. 24-2. Four stages in the origin of the solar system according to the protoplanet hypothesis.

Fig. 24-3. Artist's conception of widespread volcanic activity in the Archeozoic era. The earth has cooled enough to allow the oceans to form, but no life has yet developed in them.

geologists often speak of the 3 to 4 billion years of the Archeozoic and Proterozoic eras together as **Precambrian** (before Cambrian) time. Similarly, they speak of both Archeozoic and Proterozoic rocks as Precambrian rocks.

4. What Living Things Existed in Precambrian Times?

Precambrian rocks include igneous, sedimentary, and metamorphic rocks. Signs of past life are most likely to be found in the sedimentary rocks. But even in these rocks very few distinct fossils have thus far been found anywhere on the earth. Consequently, most of our knowledge of Precambrian life is deduced from indirect evidence. The only plant fossils found in Precambrian rocks are the lime-containing deposits of blue-green algae—one of the very simplest forms of plant life—and some simple fungi. Animal fossils in the South Australia rocks include jellyfish, soft corals, and segmented worms. Elsewhere, only the trails and burrows of wormlike creatures have so far been found. Both plants and animals of Precambrian time were marine (ocean) forms. Apparently no life existed on land.

Since remains of very simple marine life do occur in Precambrian rocks, we assume that a good deal of such life probably existed in the Precambrian oceans. The scarcity of fossils is explained by the fact that most forms were very tiny and lacked hard parts (shell, bone, etc.) that could be preserved as fossils through the ages.

Vast amounts of carbon occur in Precambrian graphite deposits, black shales, and black slates. Geologists believe that the carbon may be derived from the tissues of simple plants and animals buried in the accumulating sediments many hundreds of millions of years ago.

5. Geological Events of Precambrian Time

The geological events that took place in Precambrian time were complicated and difficult to read from the rock record. Let us see what the historical geologist believes took place.

The **Archeozoic** (*archeo,* ancient; *zoic,* life) **era** lasted from about 4½ billion years ago to about 2½ billion years ago—altogether nearly 2 billion years. It was a time of great igneous activity, during which vast quantities of lava came from the depths of the earth. The lava forced its way into already existing ancient sedimentary rocks whose origin is unknown. In many places the lava broke through the crust and poured out onto the ancient sedimentary rocks. But the Archeozoic era was also a time of repeated cracking and crumpling of the earth's crust, often followed by periods of erosion and deposition. The climax of its great continuing upheaval of the crust was called the **Laurentian-Algoman revolution.** Before the era closed, prolonged erosion peneplaned the mountains created by the Laurentian-Algoman revolution.

The **Proterozoic** (*protero,* earlier; *zoic,* life) **era** lasted from about 2½ billion years ago to about 600 million years ago. Again there was intensive vulcanism and diastrophism interrupted by periods of erosion and deposition. But there was also another kind of event. The first recorded ice age of earth history took place in eastern Canada. It left striated boulders and other glacial deposits as evidence. Before the Proterozoic era came to a close, its **Killarney-Grand Canyon revolution** had created the Killarney Mountains found in the Lake Superior region, block mountains found in the present Grand Canyon region, and the Adirondack Mountains found in New York.

Mountain-building "revolutions" like the Laurentian-Algoman and Killarney-Grand Canyon were not sudden brief upheavals, but are known to have continued through many millions of years. Where revolutions reached their climax near the close of an era, it is tempting to say that "the era was closed by the revolution." It must be remembered, however, that the historical geologist bases his divisions of geological time on *great changes of life,* not on the occurrence of mountain-building, which may or may not reach a peak at the same time.

6. Where Are Precambrian Rocks Found Today?

Precambrian rock is the surface rock of about one-fifth of the area of all the continents. Over the rest of the land surface rocks of more recent geological ages appear, but geologists believe that Precambrian rock lies beneath these younger rocks. At least one extensive area of exposed Precambrian rock is found in each of the continents. These areas, called **shields,** have apparently remained well above sea level since their formation. The shields have been neither completely worn down by erosion nor extensively covered over by sediments of later eras. The largest of these shields is the African Shield. Second largest is the Canadian Shield, which covers nearly 2 million square miles in eastern and central Canada. Its principal rock is a tough,

Fig. 24-4. This map shows the location of the Canadian Shield and other surface exposures of Precambrian rocks in North America.

Minnesota Division of Publicity

Fig. 24-5. The sedimentary strata in this open-pit iron mine are of Proterozoic age.

durable, pinkish-colored granite or granite-gneiss, but many smaller areas of ancient sedimentary rocks and lava flows lie within the main mass of the gneiss.

Outcrops of Precambrian rock also appear in places where younger overlying rock has been removed by erosion. Some outstanding examples of such outcrops are found in the United States. The best known is the exposure of Precambrian rocks that form the walls of the inner gorge of the Grand Canyon of the Colorado River. There ancient schist rocks rise more than 2,000 feet from the very bottom of the gorge and then are covered by additional thousands of feet of ancient sedimentary beds. Other exposures of Precambrian rocks can be seen in the Northern Rocky Mountains of the United States and Canada, the Adirondacks and Hudson Highlands of New York, and the Piedmont Upland. In the New York City vicinity the bedrocks known as Manhattan schist, Fordham gneiss, and Inwood marble may be Precambrian. (See Fig. 24-4.)

7. What Great Mineral Deposits Are Precambrian?

Some of the world's most important metallic mineral deposits were formed in the Precambrian rocks. In North America these include the great nickel deposits of Sudbury, Ontario; the great iron deposits of the Lake Superior region of Minnesota and Canada; the iron ores of the Adirondacks; the rich copper ores of the Keeweenaw Peninsula of Michigan; and the rich deposit of uranium ore at Great Bear Lake in northwestern Canada. In South Africa they include the world-famous gold ores of the Transvaal.

THE PALEOZOIC ERA

8. Highlights of the Paleozoic Era

We can characterize the Paleozoic era by considering various aspects of life during that time.

Paleozoic "firsts." The **Paleozoic** (ancient life) **era** began about 600 million years ago and ended about 230 million years ago. Great changes in life took place during this era. It progressed from the Age of Invertebrates to the Age of Fishes and the Age of Amphibians. Among the "firsts" of this era were the first vertebrates (animals with backbones), the first land animals, the first insects, the first land plants, the first forests, and the first seed plants.

Paleozoic climates. The Paleozoic era was also marked by the variety of its climates. These included long periods of warm, dry climate in which great salt deposits were formed; periods of warm, humid climate in which coal-forming swamp plants flourished; and periods of very cold climate in which extensive glaciation took place during great ice ages.

Paleozoic periods. Seven periods of the Paleozoic era are generally recognized. They were named after places where rocks of the period were first studied, and are accordingly known as the Cambrian, Ordovician, Silurian, Devonian, Mississippian, Pennsylvanian, and Permian periods. These periods are listed in chronological order, with Cambrian the oldest and Permian the youngest. (Some European writers refer to the Mississippian and Pennsylvanian periods together as the Carboniferous, or coal-forming, period.) The **Appalachian revolution** that took place during the Paleozoic era culminated in the folding of the Paleozoic rocks near the close of the era.

Paleozoic geography. At various times during the Paleozoic era large inland seas were formed when rising ocean waters flooded interior areas of North America. At other times uplifts occurred, the seas receded, and mountains may have formed. The inland seas of the seven periods of the era varied considerably in location and extent. Their origin and disappearance followed no regular pattern or sequence. Some lasted for very long periods of time, others for shorter periods. Some formed at the beginnings of periods, others in the middle or at the close of periods. The three largest inland seas of the era occupied broad, but shallow, depressions known respectively as the Appalachian Trough, the Cordilleran Trough, and Ouachita Trough. The Appalachian Trough was located roughly where the Appalachian Mountains are today. The Cordilleran Trough occupied the Rocky Mountains area. The Ouachita Trough stretched across Oklahoma, Texas, and New Mexico.

Now let us see what the highlights of each of the seven periods were.

9. Cambrian Period: Trilobites and Brachiopods

The **Cambrian period** is the first period in earth history in which the rocks contain abundant fossils. But they are fossils of marine life only. Not a single trace of land animals is found in Cambrian rocks. The plant kingdom was

Fig. 24-6. North America in Late Cambrian time. Dark areas are land; light areas are sea.

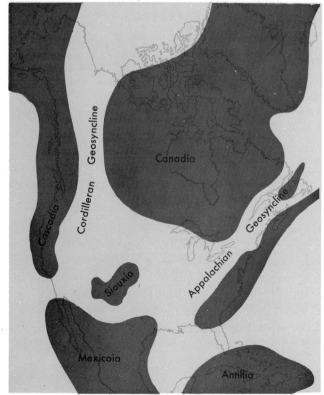

represented by a variety of seaweeds and other algae. The animal kingdom was represented by almost all of the divisions of invertebrate (without backbone) sea animals known today. Many of these bore shells or other hard parts that were readily fossilized when they died.

The most common animals of Cambrian seas were the now extinct *trilobites* (*tri,* three; *lobite,* parts; the pronunciation is *try* lo bites), of which there were probably thousands of different kinds. Most species of these crablike animals were less than 4 inches long, but the largest Cambrian trilobite reached a length of 18 inches. (See Fig. 24-8.)

The second most abundant animal of Cambrian time was the *brachiopod* (*bray* kee oh pod), a tiny "shellfish" with some outward resemblance to the clam. Relatively few species of brachiopods exist today. Sponges and small snails also lived in the Cambrian seas, but they were greatly outnumbered by the trilobites and brachiopods. (See Fig. 24-9.)

10. Ordovician Period: First Vertebrates Appear

North America was so extensively flooded by marine waters during this period that it became

New York State Museum

Fig. 24-7. The concentric rings of calcium carbonate in this limestone reef near Saratoga Springs, New York, were formed in Late Cambrian time by algae called Cryptozoöns.

Fig. 24-8. This trilobite from Jince, Bohemia, lived during Middle Cambrian time.

Ward's Natural Science Establishment

Fig. 24-9. An Early Devonian brachiopod from the New Scotland limestone, Albany County, New York. Brachiopods lived throughout Paleozoic time.

New York State Museum

Ward's Natural Science Establishment

Fig. 24-10. A cephalopod that lived in Indiana during the Mississippian period. These cephalopods resemble our chambered nautilus.

a group of islands rather than a continent. When submergence was greatest, about one-half of the entire continent was covered by inland seas! Tremendous quantities of sediment were deposited in these seas. Later these sediments hardened into vast areas of sedimentary rocks containing millions of fossils. The seas teemed with trilobites and brachiopods. *Gastropods* (snails), *cephalopods* (like the nautilus of today), and *graptolites* were also abundant. Graptolites (*graptos,* written; *lith,* stone) are extinct marine animals. Their carbonized remains look like thick pencil lines on the dark shales in which they are found. Pelecypods (clams) and corals appeared for the first time. But the big "news" in this period was the arrival of the earth's first vertebrates (animals with backbones). These were primitive fishes called *ostracoderms* (oss *track* oh derms). Fossil remains of ostracoderms are rare, but some have been found in Colorado and Wyoming.

The **Taconian disturbance,** which reached its climax at the close of the period, created a range of mountains that extended from Nova Scotia and New England all the way through Virginia and North Carolina. In this period the Green Mountains of Vermont and the Taconics of western New England were first raised.

11. Silurian Period: Corals, Salt and Gypsum Beds, First Land Animals

Much less submergence of North America took place during the Silurian period than in the Ordovician. During much of this period North America looked more like a continent. In Middle Silurian time many volcanoes in eastern Maine and Quebec erupted lava and ash at frequent intervals. The climate was warm and dry, and corals flourished and built reefs in the ocean waters as far north as northern Greenland. (See Fig. 24-11.) The seas still swarmed with trilobites, brachiopods, cephalopods, graptolites, sponges, snails, and clams. Primitive fishes were increasing in number. In Late Silurian time ancient sea scorpions which are called *eurypterids*

Fig. 24-11. Chain corals from the Lockport dolomite of Middle Silurian time.

New York State Museum

Fig. 24-12. The eurypterids, prehistoric sea scorpions, were common in Late Silurian seas.

New York State Museum

(you *rip* tuh rids) attained lengths up to nine feet. (See Fig. 24-12.)

Land animals appeared for the first time. Although the fossil record of these animals is rather scanty, it reveals the existence of such invertebrates as spiders, millipedes, and scorpions. Simple land plants such as mosses and lichens probably grew on bare rock surfaces, but there are no fossils to prove this.

In Late Silurian time the climate of northern United States became very dry. Shallow seas that existed in eastern North America evaporated continuously. As a result of evaporation, thick beds of rock salt and gypsum were left from central New York to Lake Michigan—including parts of West Virginia, Michigan, Pennsylvania, Ohio, and New York. The commercially impor-

tant salt deposits in the vicinity of Detroit, Michigan, and Syracuse, New York, are in this belt. The famous Lockport dolomite, cap rock of Niagara Falls, also originated during this period.

12. Devonian Period: Age of Fishes; First Amphibians, Land Plants, Forests

Again during Devonian time North America strongly resembled a continent. When submergence did occur, inland seas formed principally in the Appalachian, Cordilleran, and Ouachita troughs described in Topic 8. Invertebrates of all kinds, especially brachiopods, still filled the seas, and corals flourished as they had in the preceding period. Vertebrates now included more freshwater fishes, many new species of marine fishes, and sharks. The *armored fishes* were the giants of these Devonian seas, reaching lengths of 30 feet. Because fishes were so varied and plentiful, this period is called the **Age of Fishes.** (See Figs. 24-9, 24-13.)

Among the newcomers was the *lungfish,* a species of fish which could actually breathe air outside the water. (Lungfishes still exist today.) Before the Devonian period ended, a most important development took place. One group of fishes similar to the lungfish possessed strong fins which enabled them to crawl out of the water and then live for short periods on land. The "lobe-finned" fishes, as they are called, gave rise in the Devonian period to the first *amphibians*

Fig. 24-13. Osteolepis, *a fish common in Devonian seas, resembles our gar pike and sturgeon. Unlike most modern fish, its scales do not overlap.*

American Museum of Natural History

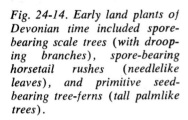

Fig. 24-14. Early land plants of Devonian time included spore-bearing scale trees (with drooping branches), spore-bearing horsetail rushes (needlelike leaves), and primitive seed-bearing tree-ferns (tall palmlike trees).

Chicago Natural History Museum

(land-and-water animals, represented by the frogs and salamanders of today). These first amphibians were large-headed crawling animals that bore some resemblance to giant salamanders.

In the plant world important things were also happening. For the first time in earth history plants unmistakably invaded the land. Woody plants grew profusely in both swamp and forest. There were true (spore-bearing) ferns, seed-bearing ferns, giant rushes (horsetails), scale trees with scaly bark that resembled snakeskin, and *Cordaites* (primitive conifers resembling our cone-bearing pines and fir trees). (See Fig. 24-14.)

The **Acadian disturbance** reached its climax in the middle of the Devonian period with an uplift of the continent that was most pronounced in the Northeast. Mountains were raised from Newfoundland through New England and south into the Appalachian region. In New England intensive igneous intrusions helped to form the White Mountains of New Hampshire.

13. Mississippian Period: Foraminifera; Sea Lilies

Advances in the evolution of life were not as striking in this period as in earlier periods. Fresh-water lakes, great inland seas, and ocean waters

were still teeming with invertebrates and fishes, while amphibians developed and became more numerous. Tiny shell-forming protozoans called *Foraminifera* thrived in the ocean waters. Among the larger invertebrates the *crinoids* (*cry* noyds) became very prominent. Crinoids are related to the starfish. Unlike the starfish, however, crinoids spend most of their lives attached to the sea

Fig. 24-15. A crinoid or sea lily of Mississippian age from Le Grand, Iowa.

Ward's Natural Science Establishment

Fig. 24-16. Coal-forming swamp forests of Pennsylvanian time included true ferns, seed-bearing tree-ferns, horsetail rushes, Cordaites, and scale trees. In the right foreground can be seen two kinds of amphibians and a giant dragonfly.

floor. Because of their petal-like arms, they are referred to as sea lilies. But they are animals, not plants. (See Fig. 24-15.)

Trilobites continued a slow decline that had begun in Ordovician time and was to continue until their complete extinction at the close of the Paleozoic era.

In the swamps and forests of this period plants flourished as in Devonian time. The plant life did not undergo any great changes, although many new species developed.

14. Pennsylvanian Period: Coal from Swamps, Giant Insects, First Reptile

During most of this period the great interior basins of eastern United States were covered alternately by shallow inland seas (when the sea rose or the land sank) and then by freshwater swamps (at times when the sea fell or the land rose slightly above sea level). The climate seems to have been warm and humid most of the time. Conditions were therefore favorable for the rapid growth of great true ferns, seed ferns, giant rushes, scale trees, *Cordaites,* and newly developed true conifers. All of these plants abounded in the widespread swamps and forests. As these Pennsylvanian plants died and fell into

the swamp waters, they underwent only partial decay, turning into peat, then much later into coal. Today these deposits form the rich "Pennsylvanian" coal fields of Pennsylvania, Ohio, West Virginia, Illinois, and Indiana. (See Fig. 24-16.)

During the intermediate times when inland seas covered the swamp regions, marine deposits of lime, mud, and sand were laid down. These deposits formed the limestones, shales, and sandstones that are found today with the Pennsylvanian coal beds.

Some important changes in the animal world took place in this period. Amphibians thrived in and out of the waters; many new species developed in lengths up to a maximum of 10 feet. But the most important development was the evolution of the first reptile. A lizardlike creature, this reptile can be regarded as the first true all-land vertebrate. In contrast to amphibians which lay their eggs in water, reptiles lay their eggs on land. Thus the reptiles may live their entire life cycles without going into the water. Not being bound to the water, reptiles were able to spread into land areas impossible for amphibians to reach.

The invertebrate animals, particularly the insects, also made important advances. Although insects had already appeared during Devonian time, their fossil record was scanty. In the Pennsylvanian period, however, insects underwent a remarkable development. Many different kinds of insects in a wide range of sizes flourished. The largest insects were giant dragonflies with a wingspread of about two and a half feet! Cockroaches reached lengths of four inches, and were so abundant that this period has been called the Age of Cockroaches.

15. Permian Period:
Salt Beds, Ice Age

Much less of the continent was covered by ocean waters in Permian time than in any preceding Paleozoic period. The submerged areas were principally in Mexico, western Texas, the western part of the Great Plains, and western United States through Canada and into Alaska.

The Permian period is noted for a long siege of desert climate. During this time the world's largest deposits of sea minerals were formed as the sea water that filled shallow inland seas evaporated continuously. In the United States great Permian deposits of rock salt and gypsum extend through Nebraska, Kansas, Oklahoma,

Adams, U.S. Geological Survey

Fig. 24-17. A gypsum bed of Permian time caps this butte called Glass Mountain in Woods County, Oklahoma.

and Texas, and give Oklahoma its nickname of the "Gypsum State." (See Fig. 24-17). Extensive coral reefs of Permian age occur in the Guadalupe Mountains of west Texas. The world-famous potash deposits of Stassfurt, Germany, were formed at this time.

The Permian period is also notable for the occurrence of a great ice age in South Africa,

Fig. 24-18. Reptiles and amphibians of the Permian period. The fin-backed flesh-eating Dimetrodon (to the right) *has long, spearlike teeth. The equally fin-backed but plant-eating* Edaphosaurus *is at the left. At the extreme left are the small lizard-shaped amphibians* Casea.

Chicago Natural History Museum

Australia, and South America (all in the Southern Hemisphere), and in India. The evidence for this time of glaciation is found in the form of glacial boulders, cemented glacial tills called *tillites,* and glacially polished and striated bedrock. These are all identified with deposits of Permian age.

16. The Paleozoic Era Closes

The ending of the Paleozoic era is marked by the following significant developments:

The Appalachian revolution. As the Permian period and the Paleozoic era drew to a close, the great Appalachian revolution, which had begun in Mississippian time, reached its climax. Large parts of the continent were elevated, especially in the East. Paleozoic rocks were formed all the way from Nova Scotia in Canada through New England and New York to Alabama. Where coal beds were strongly folded, as in eastern Pennsylvania, they were metamorphosed into anthracite. In Arkansas the Ouachita Mountains were formed, and in parts of western United States and Mexico mountain-building on a small scale included much volcanic activity.

Some forms of life disappear. The Paleozoic era represents nearly 400 million years of earth history. Thus it is not at all surprising to find that while many forms of life evolved, others became extinct at various times during the era. Graptolites, declining through Silurian and Devonian time, died out in the Mississippian period. Eurypterids, most abundant in Silurian time, gradually decreased in number until their complete disappearance in the Permian period. Trilobites, too, declined from a dominant position in Ordovician seas, until they became extinct during the Permian period. Although some experts attribute the rather high "mortality" of the marine invertebrates in Permian time to cold climates and shrinking seas, the evidence indicates that decline had already begun in earlier periods. In the world of land plants, the seed ferns, scale trees, and *Cordaites* declined slowly after their Pennsylvanian peak. By the close of the Permian period they had almost become extinct.

Most forms of life survive. While many individual *species* of plants and animals became extinct during the Paleozoic era, most groups of living things continued their existence into the Mesozoic era. The reptiles made the greatest advances of all groups of living things during the Permian period. They developed from the first primitive forms into species resembling modern lizards and alligators. Insects made progress, too, as beetles, wasps, May flies, and other new orders developed.

TOPIC QUESTIONS

Each topic question refers to the topic of the same number within this chapter.

1. In your own words briefly describe three hypotheses of the origin of the solar system.

2. Describe the oldest rocks which have been dated thus far. Explain why they are probably not the "oldest rocks on the earth."

3. Why does the geologist often speak of both the Archeozoic and Proterozoic eras as Precambrian?

4. (*a*) Describe the life of Precambrian time. (*b*) Why are the Precambrian fossils so scarce? (*c*) What do Precambrian carbon deposits tell us about Precambrian life?

5. (*a*) Describe the principal geologic activities of the Archeozoic era. (*b*) Do the same for the Proterozoic era. (*c*) Do revolutions always close geologic eras? Explain.

6. Describe the principal locations of Precambrian outcrops in North America.

7. Name and locate some important mineral deposits of Precambrian time.

8. (*a*) What are some Paleozoic "firsts"? (*b*) Describe the variety of Paleozoic climates. (*c*) List the seven periods of the Paleozoic era. What is the Carboniferous period? (*d*) Name and locate the three great Paleozoic seas in North America. What changes in geography took place during this era?

9. Describe the chief plants and animals of Cambrian time.

10. (*a*) Describe the flooding of North America in Ordovician time. (*b*) What animals lived in this period? (*c*) Describe the Taconian disturbance.

11. Describe (*a*) the marine life of Silurian time, (*b*) the land animals of Silurian time, (*c*) the origin of Silurian salt and gypsum deposits.

12. (*a*) What were the highlights in the Devonian animal world? Why were the lobe-finned fishes so important? (*b*) What were the highlights in the Devonian plant world? (*c*) What was the Acadian disturbance?

13. What were the highlights of the Mississippian period? What were the crinoids?

14. (*a*) Explain how Pennsylvanian coal was formed and what plants were involved. (*b*) How do reptiles differ from amphibians? (*c*) Describe Pennsylvanian insects.

15. (*a*) Describe the Permian deposits of salt, etc. (*b*) Describe the Permian ice age.

16. (*a*) Describe the Appalachian revolution and its mountain-building results. (*b*) What forms of life died out by the close of the Paleozoic era? (*c*) What forms of life survived?

GENERAL QUESTIONS

1. State one argument for and one against the assumption that the age of the meteorites mentioned in Topic 2 is the same as the age of the earth.

2. Compare the locations of the salt and gypsum deposits of Silurian and Permian time. How can Silurian salt beds be distinguished from Permian beds?

3. Summarize the mountain-building results of the various disturbances and revolutions of the eras taken up in this chapter.

4. Trace the changes in animal life as it developed through the entire Paleozoic era.

5. Trace the changes in plant life from the beginning to the end of the Paleozoic era.

STUDENT ACTIVITIES

See list at end of Chapter 23.

CHAPTER 25

Mesozoic Through Cenozoic

HOW DO YOU KNOW THAT . . . ?

Coquina, a common bedrock in Florida, is a variety of limestone that formed in relatively recent times. Examine a sample. Use the acid test—a drop of dilute hydrochloric acid. What does the reaction tell you about the coquina? What kind of shellfish formed its shells? Are they original remains or molds and casts? How can you tell? Compare coquina with the more ancient fossiliferous limestone of Chapter 24. In what ways does coquina seem more recent?

THE MESOZOIC ERA: AGE OF REPTILES

1. Highlights of the Mesozoic Era

The **Mesozoic** (*meso*, middle; *zoic*, life) **era** lasted about 165 million years. It began at the close of the Appalachian revolution and it closed with the Laramide revolution that created the Rocky Mountains. It was an era that saw the development and extinction of dinosaurs, giant flying reptiles; and strange toothed birds. In this era flowering plants developed, and hardwood trees rose to challenge the dominance of evergreens in the primitive forests. It was a time of mild climates that persisted for remarkably long ages. But perhaps the most significant event of this era was the first appearance on earth of the mammals, highest class in the animal kingdom.

The Mesozoic era consisted of three periods: **Triassic, Jurassic,** and **Cretaceous.** During the entire Mesozoic era in North America most of the submergence, most of the marine deposition, and most of the mountain-building took place in the western part of the continent. The eastern half of the continent was above sea level for the most part, and underwent steady erosion. In both the East and the West, nonmarine sediments formed red sandstones. Many newly discovered deposits of uranium occur in red sandstones of Mesozoic age in the Colorado Plateau.

2. Triassic Period: Evergreen Forest, Reptiles, Ammonites

Physical events. In the Far West during Triassic time a number of large inland seas were accumulating marine sediments. At the same time nonmarine deposits, including uranium-bearing red sandstones (the redness is due to the presence of red hematite), were being formed by winds and rivers in Wyoming, Utah, Colorado, Arizona, and New Mexico. In the East there were no inland seas, and the Appalachian Mountains were gradually being eroded. Then faulting in the Appalachians created block mountains with great north-south basins between them. One of these basins ran through Massachusetts and Connecticut; another extended from southeastern New York across New Jersey and Pennsylvania into Virginia. Streams running from the mountains carried coarse sediments into the basins to form Triassic red sandstones. Those in the Connecticut Valley are world-famous for the many dinosaur

Fig. 25-1. Petrified tree trunks weathered out of strata in which they were buried in Triassic time. Petrified Forest, Arizona.

National Park Service Photo

footprints found in them. Red conglomerates and red shales were also formed.

Great lava flows occurred at different times to interrupt the deposition of sediment. These lava beds were then covered over by more sediments. Igneous intrusions also formed dikes and sills in the Triassic beds. By the close of the Triassic period the **Palisade disturbance** had uplifted and faulted the region again, and a new series of block mountains was formed all the way from Nova Scotia to South Carolina. Some of the buried flows and sills were later exposed by erosion, forming the Watchung Ridges (flows) and the Palisades of the Hudson River (a sill) in New Jersey. In the western part of the continent there was no mountain uplift at the close of the period.

Plant life. The record of Triassic life begins with the survivors of the Paleozoic era. Among the plant survivors were spore-bearing ferns and tree ferns, rushes, and conifers. New plants included great conifers (similar to modern pine, yew, and cypress trees), ginkgo trees (like today's ginkgo or maidenhair trees), and cycad palm trees (related to today's sago palms). *Conifers* and *cycads* were the dominant members of the forest community. The famous Petrified Forest of Arizona was formed at this time. This "forest" came into being as follows. Conifers that had fallen into streams were carried into a shallow lake. Here they were buried in sediments

consisting of mud, sand, and volcanic ash. The sediments consolidated into beds of shale and sandstone. At the same time the buried wood was replaced by silica deposited from solution in ground water. Thus the trees were petrified. (See Fig. 25-1.)

Marine animals. The marine invertebrate life of the Triassic period included very few of the species of Paleozoic time. In their place new species of corals, snails, clams, and lobsters developed. The most abundant forms were cephalopods called *ammonites* (shelled animals resembling today's pearly nautilus, Fig. 25-2) and

Fig. 25-2. An ammonite. Ammonites abounded throughout the Mesozoic era, but became extinct at the close of the Cretaceous period.

Ward's Natural Science Establishment

National Park Service Photo

Fig. 25-3. The famous "Great White Throne" in Zion National Park, Utah, consists largely of sandstone of Jurassic age.

Fig. 25-4. Brachiopods such as these abounded in Jurassic seas.

Ward's Natural Science Establishment

belemnites (related to today's squids). Marine vertebrates were represented by numerous species of fishes and amphibians.

Land animals. On land there were some significant events. Insects capable of metamorphosis (change in body structure in developing from a wormlike larva to an adult insect; example, caterpillar to moth) made their debut. Even more important was the arrival of the first mammals of all time. They were tiny, primitive creatures, of which only a few fossil remains have been found. But the dominant vertebrate of the Triassic period was the reptile, represented by the earliest ichthyosaurs (who resembled swordfish and spent most of their time in the sea), turtles, and the many early dinosaurs who left their footprints in the Triassic sands of the continent.

3. Jurassic Period: Age of Dinosaurs; Toothed Birds; Flying Reptiles

Physical events. In eastern North America the newly raised northern Appalachians were continually attacked by the forces of erosion. In the West, inland seas covered more of the continent than in Triassic time. Both marine and nonmarine sediments were deposited. From the latter came many uranium-bearing sandstones in the Colorado Plateau, as well as the famous Morrison formation of Wyoming, one of the world's richest sources of dinosaur fossils. The period included the **Nevadian disturbance** in which folding and volcanic activity combined to form a great chain of mountains reaching from California to British Columbia. Igneous intrusions produced the rich gold-in-quartz veins that have made California one of the leading gold-producing states in the United States. In Europe the Rock of Gibraltar is Jurassic limestone.

Marine life. Plant and animal life flourished. Jurassic marine invertebrates now included the dominant clams and brachiopods (Fig.

Fig. 25-5. Giant reptiles thrived in Jurassic seas. The long-necked plesiosaurs were fish-eaters that pushed themselves through the water with their flippers. The fish-shaped ichthyosaurs fed mainly on squids, and propelled themselves with their powerful tails.

Fig. 25-6. Archeopteryx. These photos show the fossil as it was found in rock, and its "restoration" by paleontologists.

25-4), abundant ammonites and belemnites, newly developed shrimps, and others. Sea-going reptiles grew larger. Twenty-five-foot ichthyosaurs and 50-foot plesiosaurs (snakelike sea reptiles) preyed upon the fish, squids, and brachiopods of the sea water. (See Fig. 25-5.)

Land plants and animals. Jurassic forests looked very much like those of Triassic time. Cycads and conifers were the dominant forms. But animal life on the land had undergone great changes. New insects such as grasshoppers, termites, flies, and moths arrived on the scene. New primitive mammals were better developed than those of the Triassic period. And then there was *Archeopteryx,* the first bird of history (*archeo,* ancient; *pteron,* wing; the pronunciation is are key *op* tuh rix). Like most reptiles, *Archeopteryx* had teeth and laid eggs. He looked very much like the reptiles from which he was descended. But unlike a reptile, he had wings and a tail with feathers. A queer-looking bird (his wings ended in claws!), but a bird nevertheless (see Fig. 25-6). Reptiles on land now included the *pterosaurs* (flying reptiles) and large numbers of various kinds of dinosaurs. Because of the teeming dinosaur population, the Jurassic period is often called the **Age of Dinosaurs,** even though dinosaurs existed throughout the Mesozoic era, becoming extinct at its close.

Fig. 25-7. Tyrannosaurus rex, *"king of the dinosaurs," attacking the horned dinosaur* Triceratops. *These dinosaurs lived only in Cretaceous time.*

4. Dinosaurs: "Terrible Lizards"

Dinosaurs are probably the most famous of prehistoric animals. They originated in the Triassic period. However, they were comparatively small then, the largest being about 15 feet long. In the Jurassic and Cretaceous periods great creatures such as the *Tyrannosaur, Brontosaur, Triceratops,* and others came into being. Let us see what these "terrible lizards" were like and when they flourished.

Flesh eaters or carnivores. Dinosaurs may be divided into *carnivores* (flesh eaters) and *herbivores* (plant eaters). The most famous of all carnivorous dinosaurs is *Tyrannosaurus rex,* "king" of the dinosaurs and probably the most terrifying creature of all time. *Tyrannosaurus* at full growth was about 50 feet long, stood about 20 feet high on his hind legs, and weighed many tons. His enormous jaws enclosed razor-edged teeth which protruded as much as six inches beyond his gums. (See Fig. 25-7.)

Carnivorous dinosaurs lived throughout the Mesozoic era, but *Tyrannosaurus* did not appear until the Cretaceous period. *Allosaurus,* another powerful carnivorous dinosaur, lived during the Jurassic period.

Plant eaters or herbivores. The plant-eating dinosaurs are usually classified into four types: the armored dinosaurs, sauropods, horned dinosaurs, and duck-billed dinosaurs. The *armored dinosaurs* were represented by the 30-foot-long *Stegosaurus,* whose armor consisted of two long rows of great bony plates that stretched down his back from his tiny head to his spiked tail (see Fig. 25-8). The *sauropods* (lizard foot) included the gigantic *Apatosaurus,* a member of the family of Brontosaurs or "thunder lizards" (see photo p. 323). This creature was 70 feet long, 18 feet high (on all legs, for he could not stand up on his hind legs as *Tyrannosaurus* did), and 35 tons in weight. Another sauropod was *Diplodocus,* lighter in weight than

Fig. 25-8. Stegosaurus, *a plant-eating armored dinosaur of Jurassic time.*

Fig. 25-9. Trachodon, *one of the duck-billed dinosaurs, walked on its hind legs.*

Apatosaurus, but with a neck so long that his total length reached 87 feet! But the largest dinosaur of all was *Brachiosaurus,* whose weight is estimated at 50 tons. *Stegosaurus, Apatosaurus, Diplodocus,* and *Brachiosaurus* all lived during the Jurassic period and into at least a part of the Cretaceous period.

The *horned dinosaurs* included *Triceratops,* a ferocious-appearing, but probably mild, creature about 25 feet long and many times the weight of an elephant. Two long, menacing horns projected forward from either side of an immense bony plate that protected his neck. A third smaller horn protruded above his nose (see Fig. 25-7). The *duck-billed dinosaurs* included the strange *Trachodon* (see Fig. 25-9), who walked on hind legs as *Tyrannosaurus* did. *Triceratops* and *Trachodon* lived during Cretaceous time.

Not all of the dinosaurs were giants. In fact, the smallest adult dinosaurs were only a few inches long. But large or small, dinosaurs are noted for their tiny brains. *Triceratops,* for example, is said to have had a brain no larger than a walnut. In some of the dinosaurs enlarged portions of the spinal cord as far down as the tail may have helped to relay messages from the brain.

5. Cretaceous Period: Dinosaurs Die Out; Flowering Plants Enter

Physical events. Midway during this period one of the greatest inland seas of earth history stretched from the Arctic Ocean to the Gulf of Mexico. It covered approximately the area now covered by the Rocky Mountains, and it split North America into two unequal "halves." Altogether, including coastal areas that were then submerged, about half of the present North American continent was covered by sea waters. The land had not been submerged so since the Ordovician period early in the Paleozoic era.

During the Cretaceous period the important Dakota sandstone, part of an artesian formation of the Great Plains, was deposited, and more uranium-bearing sandstones were formed in Wyoming, South Dakota, Utah, and New Mexico. Also during this period the famous chalk cliffs of England and France were made from the microscopic shells of tiny marine animals. In western United States great swamps formed peat bogs that were later transformed into the great Cretaceous coal beds of California, Montana, Wyoming, Utah, and New Mexico. In Arkansas and Louisiana, warm dry climates during early

Fig. 25-10. Giant sea lizards, turtles, and flying reptiles of Late Cretaceous time. The 30-foot mosasaur is called Tylosaurus. *The sea-turtle* Protostega *had a shell up to six feet long. The pterosaur called* Pteranodon *had a wing spread reaching 25 feet.*

Cretaceous time were responsible for the formation of large salt deposits.

The Laramide revolution. The climax of the Laramide revolution brought this period and, with it, the Mesozoic era to a spectacular close. Intense folding, faulting, and volcanic activity took place along the entire length of the continent from Alaska to Central America and on to the tip of South America as well. In Canada and the United States the Rocky Mountains were created. The Laramide revolution takes its name from the Laramie Range of the Rockies in Wyoming.

Fig. 25-11. Closeup photo of a famous find of 12 fossilized dinosaur eggs in the Gobi Desert of Mongolia. Most dinosaurs were egg-layers.

Marine life. Plant and animal life of the seas continued to multiply. The invertebrates included abundant microscopic protozoans with chalk-forming shells (*Foraminifera*), sponges, corals, starfish, mollusks (clams, snails, cephalopods), and crabs. Among the vertebrates there were many kinds of sharks and bony fishes. The great swimming reptiles of earlier periods—*ichthyosaurs* and *plesiosaurs*—abounded, as did also the greatest "sea serpents" of all time, the *mosasaurs*. These ferocious creatures made their first appearance in Cretaceous time. (See Fig. 25-10.)

By the close of the Cretaceous period, a number of forms of marine life had become extinct. These included all of the great swimming reptiles —ichthyosaurs, plesiosaurs, and mosasaurs— and the invertebrate ammonites and belemnites.

Plant life on land. Plant life made its greatest progress during the Cretaceous period with the coming of the *flowering plants*. Chief among these were the deciduous trees. (Deciduous trees are broad-leaved trees that shed their leaves in the fall. They are generally hardwood trees. Their "opposites" are the evergreen trees, which are softwoods.) The deciduous trees appeared early and developed rapidly until they crowded the forests. First came magnolia, sassafras, fig, willow, laurel, and the tulip tree. Later came oak, maple, beech, birch, walnut, chestnut, and other familiar trees of the present day. Evergreen conifers continued in existence, while the *sequoia,* the ancestor of California's giant redwoods, made its first appearance.

Animal life on land. Insects continued to thrive and develop throughout the Cretaceous period. There were relatively few amphibians, but reptiles were abundant. Dinosaurs dominated the animal life of the period, but giant pterosaurs with 25-foot wingspreads, turtles, crocodiles, and the first snakes were also present. Although birds and mammals were not prominent, both made important advances in their development. The most highly developed mammal of Late Cretaceous time was the *insectivore* or *anteater.*

When the Cretaceous period came to its close, the dinosaurs and pterosaurs had become extinct.

Dinosaurs vanish. We do not know why dinosaurs became extinct, but many reasons have been offered to explain their disappearance. A possible explanation is that the rise of the land eliminated swamps as a habitat for dinosaurs. Another explanation is that the great size and clumsiness of the dinosaurs caused their own downfall. The dinosaurs may also have died for

lack of food when flowering plants displaced the vegetation to which they had become adapted.

THE CENOZOIC ERA: AGE OF MAMMALS

6. Divisions of the Cenozoic Era

Early in the nineteenth century geologists divided the **Cenozoic** (modern life) **era** into two periods. The first, covering the time before the Ice Age, had already been called the *Tertiary.* The second, including the time from the Ice Age to the present, was named the *Quaternary.* These names extended a classification in which the oldest known rocks were called *Primary* and the next oldest called *Secondary.*

Geologists now recognize six or seven divisions of the Cenozoic era, but these divisions are not regarded as distinct enough for true periods, so they are called *epochs.* The first five—Paleocene, Eocene, Oligocene, Miocene, and Pliocene —are all included in the Tertiary period. The last two epochs, the Pleistocene and the Recent, are included in the Quaternary period. Although

Fig. 25-12. Natural bridge in strata of Eocene age in Bryce Canyon, Utah.

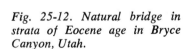
Union Pacific Photo

present-day geologists no longer regard the Tertiary and Quaternary as separate periods, the names still persist in the geologic timetable, and are often used in references to pre-glacial and glacial deposits.

Most European geologists, and some American geologists, prefer to divide the Cenozoic era into a *Paleogene* period (Paleocene, Eocene, and Oligocene epochs) and a *Neogene* period (Miocene, Pliocene, Pleistocene, and Holocene or Recent epochs).

7. Crustal Activity in the Cenozoic Era

When the Cenozoic era opened, the shape and size of North America were very much as today. Throughout the era there was little submergence of the continent, except for the Atlantic and Gulf Coastal Plains and a large part of California. These areas were covered and then uncovered by sea water several times. In the East the Appalachian Mountains were first peneplaned and then later uplifted to their present position.

In the West during this era the newly formed Rocky Mountains were peneplaned and then raised again. The Colorado Plateau was elevated a number of times, and then the Colorado River dug into the plateau during its last uplift to carve out the famous Grand Canyon. Faulting on a giant scale created the block mountains of the Basin and Range Province. The Cenozoic era saw the Sierra Nevadas, first raised in Late Jurassic time, now tilted into a vast single mountain block. Its steep eastern slope plunged over two miles into the Great Basin.

Vulcanism was also active during this era. Extensive outpourings of lava were building the Columbia Plateau to a thickness of up to 5,000 feet over a vast area of more than 200,000 square miles in Washington, Oregon, Idaho, and California. Lesser outbursts of lava and ash were burying trees and forming "petrified forests" in the Yellowstone National Park area, while erupting volcanoes studded the landscape from the Cascade Mountains into the Southwest.

Much of the mountain-building described above took place in the early epochs of this era, but the climax reached in the past million years has been called the **Cascadian revolution.** This revolution has re-elevated all of the major mountain ranges of western United States—the Rockies, the Sierra Nevadas, the Cascades, and the Coast Ranges. The earthquakes that every so often shake the Far West, particularly the Pacific Coast Ranges, demonstrate vividly that the Cascadian revolution is not over yet. Two of the world's great mountain ranges, the Alps and the Himalayas, were created on other continents during this era. The Andes of South America had already been in existence, but they, too, were raised a good deal higher in late Cenozoic time.

8. Cenozoic Climates: The Great Pleistocene Ice Age

Warm, humid climates prevailed over North America in the early part of the Cenozoic era. Then the temperature began to drop slowly. It continued to drop throughout the latter half of the Cenozoic era. Finally the climate became so cold that glaciers formed in northern Canada and then extended south through Canada into the United States. Elsewhere—in northern Europe, in Greenland, in Siberia, in Antarctica, and on nearly all of the world's high mountain tops—glaciers also formed. All in all, more than one-fourth of the land was covered by ice sheets and alpine glaciers.

No one yet knows why the earth cooled. But during the next million years—the Pleistocene epoch—ice sheets formed four times and melted away four times. There were four cold glacial ages interrupted by warm interglacial ages. The glacial ages lasted from about 30,000 to 100,000 years each. Interglacial periods were longer. The most recent glacial age ended not more than 11,000 years ago and we may be living even now

Fig. 25-13. An outcrop of white diatomaceous earth of Middle Miocene time, Santa Barbara County, California.

Arnold, U.S. Geological Survey

in another interglacial interval. Some scientists believe that the persistence of the great ice sheets in Antarctica and Greenland means that our last Ice Age is not yet ended.

9. Plant Life of the Cenozoic Era: Modern Trees, Grasses, and Other Flowering Plants

The modern trees that had developed during the Cretaceous period were present at the beginning of the Cenozoic era. Most of them continued into the present. However, the location and distribution of many of these trees changed because of climatic variations. As long as warm climates persisted, palm trees, ferns, fig trees, camphor trees, and other tropical vegetation grew in northern United States. Cypresses, laurels, and sequoias grew as far north as Greenland. The sequoias were especially abundant; many species spread through vast forest areas in both North America and Europe by middle Cenozoic time. But as climates cooled off late in the era, all tropical vegetation was driven southward. By the end of the era, camphor, fig, palm, cypress, and other tropical trees had disappeared from western North America, and the sequoias had been reduced to only two species. These two are the "Big Trees" (*Sequoia gigantea*) of the California Sierras and the redwoods (*Sequoia sempervirens*) of coastal California and Oregon.

As for the lowly grasses that cover the savannas and prairies of the earth today, no fossil evidence is available to prove their existence until about the middle of the era—during the Miocene epoch. The arrival of grasses provided the richest source of food for grazing animals, including today's domestic animals like the cow, the sheep, the goat, and the horse. As the grasses evolved into wheat, corn, rice, oats, barley, rye, and other grains, a source of food vital to modern life came into existence.

A single-celled water plant called the *diatom* (*die* uh tom) was abundant in seas and lakes of this era, especially from Eocene to Miocene time. Diatoms make microscopic shells of snow-white silica. As the diatoms died in Cenozoic seas, their shells accumulated in many places to form thick deposits of a lightweight and porous white rock called *diatomite* or *diatomaceous* earth. Today diatomite is quarried for use in abrasives, paints, and other industrial materials. (See Figs. 25-13 and 25-14.)

Fig. 25-14. Diatoms as seen under the microscope.

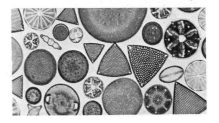

Fig. 25-15. These ostrich-like giant moas (Dinornis) *were great flightless birds that developed early in Cenozoic time.* Dinornis *lived in New Zealand until 5000 years ago, but is now extinct.*

10. Invertebrates of the Cenozoic Era

Cenozoic seas and lakes contained much the same invertebrate animals as we have today. Among the single-celled protozoans, lime-forming *Foraminifera* were particularly abundant in the early and middle parts of the era. Sponges, corals, starfish, sea urchins, and sand dollars were, and still are, fairly common, but brachiopods and cephalopods were rare. The *mollusks*—clams, oysters, mussels, and snails—thrived throughout the era. They increased both in numbers and types until today they are more abundant than ever in their history. Crabs and barnacles were also quite common throughout the era.

On land the spiders, centipedes, scorpions, and insects of Cretaceous times continued their development. Insects were especially abundant and varied. Moths, butterflies, wasps, bees, ants, beetles, and hosts of other insects thrived on the lush vegetation of field and forest, just as they do today. During the Oligocene epoch, the famous fossil "insects in amber" were formed in the Baltic Sea region of Europe. *Resin,* oozing from pine trees, trapped crawling insects and then hardened into *amber* to preserve molds of the insects as fossils.

11. Cenozoic Fishes, Amphibians, Reptiles, Birds

Throughout the era, Cenozoic fishes were much like those of late Mesozoic time. Sharks and rays were unusually abundant in early and middle Cenozoic time. Some sharks were 70 feet long and had jaws six feet wide! Amphibians— frogs, toads, and salamanders—were no more conspicuous than today. Reptiles included turtles, snakes, lizards, and crocodiles much like those we have today. Birds became more numerous and continued their development into the modern forms of today. Early in the Cenozoic era there was an abundance of ostrich-like types that could not fly. Some of these were 10 feet tall (Fig. 25-15).

12. The Rise of the Mammals

The Cenozoic era is the era in which the mammals rose from obscurity to the dominant position in the animal kingdom. **Mammals are warmblooded animals who suckle their young and whose skin is covered with fur or hair.** Primitive mammals had first appeared in the Triassic period. In the 150 million years or so of the Mesozoic era that followed their origin, they had made slow progress. When the Cenozoic era opened, most of the existing mammals were small animals somewhat resembling our modern woodchucks. There were also small monkey-like mammals called *lemuroids,* from which we believe monkeys to be descended. Unimpressive as the mammals were then, they were destined to make greater strides forward in the next 70 million years than any group of animals before them. Let us follow their rise epoch by epoch.

13. Paleocene epoch: Many New Mammals

Mammals increased greatly both in number and in variety during this epoch, becoming the dominant members of the animal kingdom for the first time in earth history. Survivors from Cretaceous time included anteaters, opossumlike animals, and small animals resembling woodchucks. These were now joined by tiny *rodents* resembling modern mice and squirrels, tiny monkeylike *lemuroids,* small catlike and doglike flesh eaters called *creodonts,* plant eaters called *amblypods,* and many other new mammals. The largest of these were about the size of a small bear, but most Paleocene mammals were much smaller.

14. Eocene Epoch: Preview of Modern Mammals

Many of our well-known mammals made their appearance in Eocene time in the form of pygmy ancestors. One of these was *Eohippus,* a primitive horse about as large as a small fox. Others included the first-known rhinoceroses, rodents, lemurs, and monkeys. Camels originated at this time in North America. *Creodonts* were abundant. Before the epoch ended, mammals that could live in the sea had developed. Other mammals took to the air. Thus the ancestors of our modern whales and bats appeared.

15. Oligocene Epoch: More and Larger Mammals; Brontotherium

In Oligocene time the pygmy forms of Eocene times changed in size. Camels, horses, and rhinoceroses developed larger species. The monkeys gave rise to a gibbonlike form of great ape in Europe but mysteriously became extinct in North America at the close of the epoch. New arrivals included wild pigs, small carnivorous dogs and cats, gnawing mice, beavers, rabbits, and squirrels. Small elephants originated in Africa, but there were none in North America.

Many strange mammals that no longer exist also lived in this epoch. Perhaps the strangest were the abundant *titanotheres* ("giant beasts"),

Fig. 25-16. Brontotherium, *largest of the* titanotheres, *was eight feet tall at the shoulders. His skeletons have been found in the Badlands of South Dakota. At the lower right are flesh-eating* hyaenodons, *probably descended from* creodonts. *At the lower left are Oligocene tortoises.*

Chicago Natural History Museum

who were distant relatives of the rhinoceros. The largest of the titanotheres was *Brontotherium,* a slender-legged creature with a rhinoceroslike horned head and an elephantlike body. The titanotheres originated in Eocene time and became extinct early in the Oligocene epoch. (See Fig. 25-16.)

Creodonts, too, became extinct by the close of the epoch. But the abundant *oreodons,* about the size of sheep and bearing resemblances to both deer and hogs, flourished in this epoch and lived into Miocene time. The oreodons were grazing animals.

16. Miocene Epoch: Grazing Animals Thrive; Land Bridge from Alaska to Siberia; Baluchitherium

During this epoch grasses began to cover the plains and the prairies. As a result, the grazing animals thrived in North America. Horses, camels, and rhinoceroses grew larger and roamed the grasslands. Horses were now as large as ponies; camels reached the height of giraffes.

North America and Asia were joined during this epoch by a "land bridge" that resulted from the emergence of part of the floor of the Bering Straits between Alaska and Siberia. Two-way traffic developed. Horses, hitherto only in North America, migrated into Asia. In the other direction, mastodons spread from Africa into Europe and Asia, and then migrated into North America. Monkeys continued their development in Europe and Asia, where great apes were now numerous.

The carnivorous dogs and cats also gave rise to larger forms and new species. The dog family was evolving such animals as wolves, foxes, raccoons, and (in Europe only) bears. The cats were evolving into modern lynxes and leopards, as well as into saber-toothed forms which are now extinct.

Among the strange mammals that no longer exist was the largest land mammal of all time, *Baluchitherium.* A slender-necked hornless member of the rhinoceros family, it is named after

Fig. 25-17. Baluchitherium, a hornless rhinoceros, was the largest land mammal of all time. He lived in Asia during the Miocene epoch.

American Museum of Natural History

Fig. 25-18. Early Pliocene mammals in North America. At the right is Gomphotherium, *a mastodon. At the left is* Teleoceras, *a rhinoceros.*

Baluchistan in Asia, where it lived. This giant grew to a length of 25 feet and was 18 feet tall at the shoulders—nearly twice the size of our largest elephants of today! (See Fig. 25-17.)

17. Pliocene Epoch: A One-Toed Horse

Mammals of the Miocene epoch continued their development. The first one-toed horse, *Pliohippus,* made its appearance. (Earlier horses had feet with 4, 3, or 2 toes. Modern horses have only one toe, which means that the foot is not divided.) Near the close of the epoch, the formation of the Isthmus of Panama created a land bridge between North America and South America. Migration of animals began between the two continents, much as it had occurred in Miocene time between North America and Asia. To North America came the giant armadillo *Glyptodont* and the great sloth *Megatherium.* To South America went camels, horses, mastodons, and wild pigs. This intermigration continued into the next epoch, the Pleistocene, until more than twenty different animal families had representatives in both continents.

Before the epoch closed, *mammoths,* or true elephants, had arisen, and *Equus,* our modern horse, had developed from earlier one-toed horses.

18. Pleistocene Epoch: Great Elephants Become Extinct in North America

The Pleistocene epoch was the time of the great Ice Age. In North America it was especially noteworthy for its great elephants that became extinct at the close of the epoch. These "elephants" included the mastodons, the imperial mammoths of the Southwest (14 feet tall at the shoulders), and the famous woolly mammoths of the North. (See Fig. 25-19.) The woolly mammoths are the animals whose fleshy carcasses were found perfectly preserved in the frozen soil of eastern Siberia in the year 1900, thousands of years after they had died. Other prehistoric animals that became extinct during Pleistocene time were the dire wolf, the giant ground sloth, the giant armadillo, and the great saber-toothed cat. Remains of these animals have been found well preserved in the famous natural tar pits of

Fig. 25-19. The woolly mammoth inhabited Europe, Asia, and North America in Pleistocene time, often wandering close to the Pleistocene ice sheets.

Rancho La Brea in Los Angeles. (See Fig. 25-20.)

During Pleistocene time great herds of horses, camels, and bison grazed the plains of North America, but only the bison survived into the Recent epoch, which followed the last retreat of the ice. Horses and camels disappeared from this continent as completely as did the great elephants and the saber-toothed cats. Not until the early Spanish explorers brought horses from Europe in their ships did horses return to North America.

19. Recent epoch: The last 11,000 Years

The Recent epoch is the name given to the years following the last retreat and disappearance of the Pleistocene ice sheets of the great Ice Age. The story of this epoch is still being written for us by the geologic agents studied earlier.

Fig. 25-20. Animals coming to drink from Pleistocene water holes were sometimes trapped in underlying asphalt pits like those at Rancho La Brea in Los Angeles. In the right foreground is the great saber-toothed cat. The large birds are vultures. At the far left is the dire wolf. In the right background are horses.

TOPIC QUESTIONS

Each topic question refers to the topic of the same number within this chapter.

1. Briefly state the highlights of the Mesozoic era with respect to its mountain formation, animals, plants, and minerals. Name its three periods.

2. (*a*) Describe the important physical events of the Triassic period. (*b*) Describe Triassic plant life. (*c*) Describe the marine life of the Triassic period. (*d*) Describe the land life of the Triassic period.

3. (*a*) Describe the physical events of the Jurassic period and some of its important mineral occurrences. (*b*) Describe Jurassic marine life. (*c*) Describe Jurassic land animals and plants.

4. Classify and describe some of the great dinosaurs of the Mesozoic era.

5. (*a*) Describe the principal physical events of the Cretaceous period and some of its important mineral occurrences. (*b*) What was the Laramide revolution? (*c*) Describe Cretaceous marine life. (*d*) Describe Cretaceous plant life on land. (*e*) Describe Cretaceous animal life on land. (*f*) What reasons have been given for the extinction of the dinosaurs?

6. Explain how the Cenozoic era is divided.

7. Describe the principal crustal activities of the Cenozoic era. What mountains were formed during this era?

8. (*a*) Describe Cenozoic climates. (*b*) How long were the glacial and interglacial intervals?

9. Describe Cenozoic trees, grasses, and diatoms.

10. Describe the invertebrates of the Cenozoic era (*a*) in the sea, (*b*) on land. (*c*) Explain the origin of "insects in amber."

11. Describe the Cenozoic fishes, amphibians, reptiles, and birds.

12. (*a*) What are mammals? (*b*) When did mammals first appear? (*c*) What were the first Cenozoic mammals like?

13. (*a*) What advances did mammals make in Paleocene time? (*b*) Which new ones appeared?

14. (*a*) Which modern mammals appeared in Eocene time? (*b*) What were creodonts?

15. (*a*) Which modern mammals appeared in Oligocene time? (*b*) What kind of animal was *Brontotherium?* (*c*) What were the oreodons (*d*) Which mammals became extinct in Oligocene time?

16. (*a*) Why did grazing animals thrive in North America during the Miocene epoch? (*b*) What new modern mammals developed? (*c*) What were the effects of the land bridge between Asia and North America? (*d*) Describe *Baluchitherium.*

17. (*a*) In what way did horses develop in Pliocene time? (*b*) What were the effects of the land bridge between North and South America?

18. (*a*) Name the principal mammals that lived in North America during the Pleistocene epoch. (*b*) Which mammals became extinct at the close of the epoch?

19. What is the Recent epoch?

GENERAL QUESTIONS

1. Red sandstones of Triassic and Jurassic age in eastern and western United States are of great interest for a variety of reasons. Locate three such sandstones (see Topics 1, 2, and 3) and explain what makes each interesting.

2. Do you believe the Recent epoch to be an interglacial age or still part of the glacial age? Give your reasons.

3. Summarize the changes in plant life that took place through the Mesozoic era.

4. Continue the summary of the development of plant life through the Cenozoic era.

5. Trace the development of animal life through the Mesozoic era.

6. Trace the development of animal life through the Cenozoic era.

STUDENT ACTIVITIES

See list at end of Chapter 23.

BIBLIOGRAPHY

Andrews, H. N. *Ancient Plants*. Cornell University Press, Ithaca, 1964.

Andrews, R. C. *All About Dinosaurs*. Random House, N.Y., 1953.

Berry, W. B. N. *Growth of a Prehistoric Time Scale*. Freeman, San Francisco, 1968.

Carrington, R. *A Guide to Earth History*. New American Library, N.Y., 1961.

Cloud, P. E. Jr. (ed.) *Adventures in Earth History*. Freeman, San Francisco, 1970.

Colbert, E. H. *Dinosaurs, Their Discovery and Their World*. Dutton, N.Y., 1961.

Colbert, E. H. *Evolution of the Vertebrates*. Wiley, N.Y., 1969.

Darling, L. L. *Before and After Dinosaurs*. Morrow, N.Y., 1959.

Dott, R. H. Jr. and Batten, R. L. *Evolution of the Earth*. McGraw-Hill, N.Y., 1971.

Fenton, C. L. and M. A. *The Fossil Book*. Doubleday, N.Y., 1958.

Fenton, C. L. and M. A. *Tales Told by Fossils*. Doubleday, N.Y., 1966.

Goldring, W. *Handbook of Paleontology: Fossils*. Paleontological Research Institution, Ithaca, N.Y.

Hotton, N. *Dinosaurs*. Pyramid Books, N.Y., 1963.

Howell, F. C. *Early Man*. Time-Life Books, N.Y., 1965.

Matthews, W. H. *Fossils*. Barnes and Noble, N. Y., 1963.

Matthews, W. H. *Wonders of Fossils*. Dodd, Mead, N.Y., 1968.

McCarthy, A. *Giant Animals of Long Ago*. Prentice-Hall, Englewood Cliffs, N.J., 1963.

Moore, R. *The Earth We Live On*. Knopf, N.Y., 1956.

Reed, W. M. *The Earth for Sam*. Harcourt, Brace and World, N.Y., 1960.

Rhodes, F. H. T. *Fossils: Guide to Prehistoric Life*. Golden Press, N.Y., 1962.

Rhodes, F. H. T. *The Evolution of Life*. Penguin, Baltimore, 1962.

Silverberg, R. *Clocks for the Ages*. Macmillan, N.Y., 1971.

Simpson, G. G. *Life of the Past*. Yale University Press, New Haven, 1961.

Swinton, W. E. *Wonderful World of Prehistoric Animals*. Garden City Books, Garden City, N.Y., 1961.

Verrill, A. H. *Strange Story of Our Earth*. L. C. Page, Boston, 1952.

Unit 6 Astronomy and Space Science

Have you ever seen the
star patterns called constellations?
In the winter you can see the constellation
Orion in the nighttime sky. Orion was a legendary
hunter. The three bright stars that make up his belt will
help you find this constellation. The photograph of *Orion* on
the opposite page was taken with a large telescope. It shows many
more stars than you can see with unaided eyes or even with binoculars
or a small telescope.

Astronomy is the study of objects in the universe. Until Galileo invented
the telescope, the only ones that could be studied were those visible to the
unaided eye—the sun; the moon; the planets Mercury, Venus, Earth, Mars,
Jupiter, and Saturn; meteors and occasional comets; and about 5,000 stars.

Galileo's simple telescopes revealed thousands of stars inivisible to the unaided
eye in the region early astronomers named the Milky Way. Now our largest telescopes show that the Milky Way is made up of billions of stars, and that there
are billions of other galaxies, each one with millions or even billions of stars.

Our sun is only one of billions of stars in the universe. With so many other
stars, surely there must be other solar systems! In 1963, astronomers observed a strange motion of Barnard's star, a near neighbor of our sun.
Astronomers concluded that this motion was caused by a planet-
sized object—invisible to the telescopes—that must be
revolving around Barnard's star and must be about as
large as Jupiter. This discovery represents the
first indirect evidence that other planets
may exist outside our own
solar system.

CHAPTER 26

Stars and Galaxies

HOW DO YOU KNOW THAT . . . ?

Fewer than 3000 stars are visible to the unaided eye in the Northern Hemisphere sky. See for yourself. Start with a clear moonless night. Choose any part of the sky convenient to you. Count the number of stars you can see. Estimate what part of the sky's total area you observed. Multiply your count by the proper number. If your observation covered $1/20$ of the sky, multiply by 20, and so on. Compare your answer with the figure given above. What factors will influence the "accuracy" of your count? How can you increase its accuracy?

Look at "your" stars again. How many degrees of brightness can you detect? (See Topic 16.) How many different colors can you recognize? (See Topic 14.)

1. Optical Telescopes

On a clear moonless night the sky seems to be studded with an infinite number of stars. A careful count, however, reveals that only about 5,000 stars are visible to the unaided eye in the heavens of both the Northern and Southern Hemispheres. With the aid of powerful telescopes, however, millions of stars can be seen, and more millions of fainter stars can be photographed.

The optical telescope is an instrument whose lens or mirror, much larger than the lens of the human eye, can gather together a much greater quantity of light from a star and focus it in one spot. If the eye is placed near that spot, it sees hundreds or thousands of times as much light from the star as it can see alone. Stars already visible look much brighter, and millions of stars invisible to the unaided eye become visible. Sensitive photographic plates, placed at the focus of the telescope and exposed for many minutes, show large numbers of stars that the eye is un-

able to perceive. Furthermore, the photographs make permanent records that can be studied at the astronomer's convenience.

The light-gathering power of a telescope depends on the *area* of its lens or mirror. Since the area of a circle varies with the *square* of its radius ($A = \pi r^2$), doubling the radius of a circular lens or mirror gives it four times the light-gathering power.

2. The Refracting Telescope

A telescope that uses a large glass lens to gather and focus starlight is called a **refracting telescope** or **refractor,** because the lens *refracts* or bends the rays of light to bring them to a focus and form the image of the star. (See Fig. 26-1.) The action of the lens is just like the action of a magnifying lens that is used to focus the rays of the sun on a piece of paper. The bright spot of sunlight on the paper is actually an image of the sun.

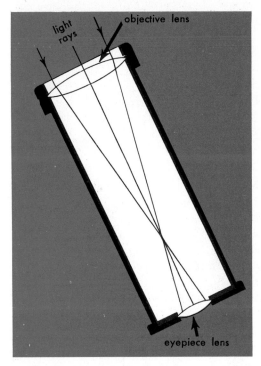

Fig. 26-1. The optical system of a refracting telescope.

The refractor lens is placed at the top of a telescope tube. A smaller lens is placed at the bottom or viewing end of the tube, where it magnifies the image formed by the large lens. The larger lens is known as the *objective*. The smaller one is the *eyepiece*.

The world's largest refractors are those of the Yerkes (*yerk* eez) Observatory at Williams Bay in Wisconsin and of the Lick Observatory at Mount Hamilton in California. The Yerkes objective lens is 40 inches in diameter; the Lick lens is 36 inches in diameter. Telescope observatories are usually located on isolated mountain tops in dry climates where "seeing" is better because the air is steady and clear and the disturbing lights of cities are far away. (See Figs. 26-2 and 26-3.)

3. The Reflecting Telescope

The **reflecting telescope** or **reflector** uses a concave mirror to gather and focus starlight. The mirror is made by grinding one face of a large circular glass disk into the proper curved surface, and then coating it with a thin film of aluminum. This mirror is called the *objective*.

The objective mirror is mounted at the bottom of a telescope tube. When the objective reflects a star's rays, it forms a small bright image of the star near the top of the tube, from whence it must be reflected to the observer. This may be done by a small flat mirror placed so that it reflects the image of the star out to the side of the telescope. (See Fig. 26-4.) The light rays may also be reflected straight down the tube and through a small opening in the objective. As in the refractor, the observer views the image through an eyepiece.

Fig. 26-2. The 36-inch refracting telescope of the Lick Observatory at Mount Hamilton, California.

Lick Observatory

Mount Wilson and Palomar Observatories

Fig. 26-3. Aerial view of the site of the Mount Wilson Observatory in California.

The world's largest reflectors are the 200-inch Hale telescope at Mount Palomar, California; the 120-inch reflector of the Lick Observatory; the 104-inch telescope of the Crimean Astrophysical Observatory in Russia; the 100-inch Hooker telescope at Mount Wilson, California; the 84-inch telescope of the Kitt Peak National Observatory in Arizona; and the 82-inch telescope of the McDonald Observatory on Mount Locke, Texas. The first two are so large that the observer can sit in a special cage located inside the tube where the light rays come to a focus.

4. Advantages of the Reflector

You may have noticed in the preceding paragraphs that the largest reflector mirrors are far larger than the largest refractor lenses. Why? There are several reasons. First, since light rays do not pass through a mirror, its block of glass need not be as perfect as the glass used for a refractor lens. Second, only one face of a mirror must be ground to the perfect curved surface needed. Third, the whole back of a mirror can

Fig. 26-4. The optical system of a reflecting telescope.

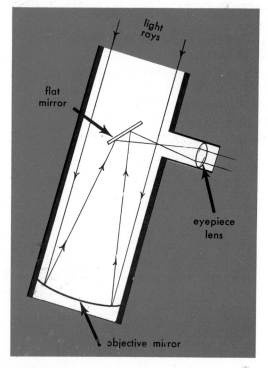

be supported, whereas a lens can be supported at its edges alone. Fourth, a refractor needs a longer tube than a reflector. Why? (See Figs. 26-1 and 26-4.)

5. The Telescope as a Camera

To use the telescope as a sky camera, the astronomer removes the eyepiece and puts a photographic film in its place. This may be done with both the refractor and the reflector. However, the field of view for such "cameras" is rather small.

The *Schmidt telescope* is a special form of reflecting telescope built solely for the purpose of photographing the sky. Like a wide-angle camera, it has a large field of view. The largest Schmidt telescope yet built is the 48-inch telescope of the Palomar Observatory.

6. The Electromagnetic Spectrum

Energy is radiated through space by means of electromagnetic radiations or electromagnetic waves. Examples of these radiations are the gamma rays emitted in the radioactive decomposition of uranium; X rays emitted by metals bombarded by high-speed electrons; invisible ultraviolet light and invisible heat or infrared rays given off by hot bodies like the sun; and radio waves emitted by rapidly oscillating electrons.

Mount Wilson and Palomar Observatories

Fig. 26-5. The Hale reflector at Mount Palomar is the world's largest optical telescope. Its mirror is 200 inches in diameter.

All of these radiations travel at the same speed, but they differ greatly in wavelength. Their speed is the familiar speed of light—about 186,000 miles a second. Their wavelengths range from less than one hundred-millionth of an inch for

Fig. 26-6. The electromagnetic spectrum includes all forms of energy from the longest radio waves to the shortest cosmic rays. Visible light forms only a small part of the spectrum.

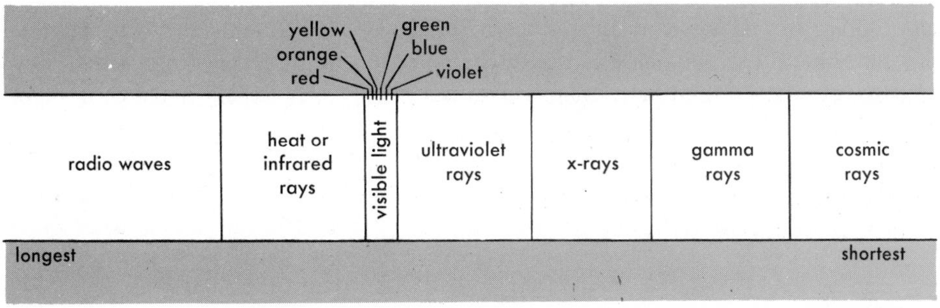

radio waves	heat or infrared rays	visible light	ultraviolet rays	x-rays	gamma rays	cosmic rays

yellow, orange, red — green, blue, violet

longest   shortest

Fig. 26-7. The great steerable radio telescope at Jodrell Bank, England is 250 feet in diameter.

gamma rays to as much as hundreds of feet for radio waves. All of these radiations are included in what physicists call the **electromagnetic spectrum.** Visible light occupies only a small part of this spectrum, as shown in Figure 26-6. All other radiations are invisible to the human eye.

How can the invisible radiations of the electromagnetic spectrum be detected? Gamma rays can be detected by a Geiger counter. X rays, ultraviolet rays, and infrared rays can be detected by photographic plates. Radio waves can be detected by receivers that transform the energy into sound. When energy is radiated from the heavenly bodies to the earth in any of these forms, the earthbound astronomer has the opportunity of detecting these radiations and trying to interpret them. He uses the optical telescope and the photographic plate to see and photograph objects that radiate visible light. Using special film, he can also photograph objects radiating in-

visible ultraviolet and infrared light. And with the radio telescope, he can map areas of the sky that emit invisible radio waves.

7. Radio Astronomy and Radio Telescopes

Radio waves are invisible, but with proper equipment they can be heard. In 1931 Karl Jansky of the Bell Telephone Laboratories, trying to trace the source of staticlike noises on his radio receivers, finally concluded that they were caused by radio waves coming from outer space. Astronomers now know that these radio waves are *thermal radiations* produced by the ions in clouds of hot gases or *nonthermal radiations* of high-speed atomic particles like those in the cyclotron.

Radio waves come from the sun, from our Milky Way, from distant galaxies, and even from galaxies in collision! Because these radio waves can pass through the great clouds of fine dust that lie between stars in space, they bring us information about parts of the heavens from which we can receive little or no light. Radio waves from space can also penetrate the clouds in our atmosphere, and they can be received by day as well as by night.

Radio astronomy is the study of radio waves from outer space to determine the nature of their sources. To collect and concentrate the radio waves, the radio astronomer uses a **radio telescope.** Instead of the glass lenses or mirrors that collect light waves in the optical telescope, radio telescopes use enormous saucer-shaped or radar-type antennas that collect radio waves and feed them into special radio receivers. These record the strength and wavelengths of the signals and the direction from which they come.

A "dish" 250 feet in diameter is the antenna for the great radio telescope of the University of Manchester at Jodrell Bank in England. (See Fig. 26-7.) This dish can be rotated to face in different directions, so it is said to be steerable.

Fig. 26-8. The world's largest radio telescope in Arecibo, Puerto Rico covers an area of 18.5 acres.

Commonwealth of Puerto Rico

The great non-steerable radio telescope at Arecibo, Puerto Rico, has an antenna 1,000 feet in diameter. (See Fig. 26-8.)

8. The Spectroscope

The optical telescope enables the astronomer to see the heavenly bodies. The spectroscope makes it possible to determine their composition, their speed of motion, and their temperatures. How does the spectroscope work?

Everyone is familiar with the visible **spectrum** or rainbow of colors formed when sunlight passes through a triangular glass prism. Sunlight or "white" light is a mixture of many colors of light. Each color has a different wavelength, with red having the longest wavelength and violet the shortest. As the light waves pass from air into the glass prism and out again, they are bent or *refracted*. But because long waves are refracted less than short waves, the different colors are separated or *dispersed* from one another, forming the wide colored band called the spectrum. (See Fig. 26-9.)

The **spectroscope** is basically a combination of a glass prism and a tiny viewing telescope.

Fig. 26-9. A triangular prism disperses sunlight into its colored components to form the visible spectrum.

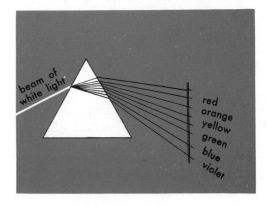

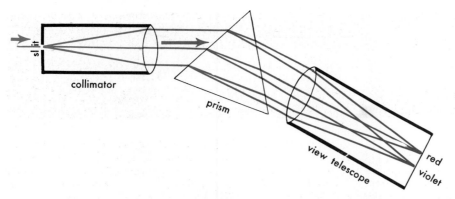

Fig. 26-10. The optical system of a spectroscope includes a slit, a collimator for forming parallel rays of light, a triangular prism to disperse the light into its component colors, and a small telescope for viewing the spectrum.

The prism disperses the light it receives into a spectrum of different wavelengths. This is focused and viewed through the view telescope. If the spectrum is to be photographed, a photographic plate is put in the place of the eyepiece of the view telescope. (See Figs. 26-10 and 26-11.) The spectroscope then becomes a *spectrograph*.

Fig. 26-11. In this spectroscope the slit and collimator are at the left, and the view telescope is at the right.

Welch Scientific Company

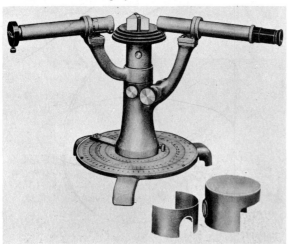

To study the spectrum of a star, the eyepiece of an astronomical telescope is removed, and the spectroscope is put in its place.

9. Reading the Spectrum

A spectroscope may form three different types of spectra, each one telling a story about the source of its light. A **continuous spectrum** or unbroken band of colors shows that its source is sending out light of *all* visible wavelengths. Such a spectrum is produced by a glowing solid like the incandescent filament of an electric light, or by a glowing liquid, or by the compressed gases in the interiors of stars.

A **bright-line spectrum** is an unevenly spaced series of lines of different colors and brightness, showing that its source is sending out light in specific wavelengths only. Such a spectrum is made by a glowing gaseous element such as neon or sodium. **Each gas has its own set of lines by which it can be identified.** (See Fig. 26-12.)

A **dark-line spectrum** is a continuous spectrum interrupted by dark lines **in exactly the same locations as the bright-line spectra of glowing gases.** The dark lines are found to be formed when the light from a glowing solid (or other source of a continuous spectrum) passes through

Lick Observatory

Fig. 26-12. This photograph shows part of the spectrum of the sun (the middle horizontal band) being matched above and below with the comparison spectrum *of glowing iron vapor. The spectrum of the iron vapor is a* bright-line spectrum. *The matching of the bright lines of iron with dark lines in the solar spectrum shows that iron vapor is present in the sun's atmosphere. Other elements would be identified in similar fashion.*

cooler gas. The gas then absorbs the very same wavelengths it is capable of emitting, and thereby identifies itself just as surely as if it were emitting those wavelengths in a private bright-line spectrum. Because the dark lines are caused by absorption, a dark-line spectrum is also called an **absorption spectrum.** Such a spectrum is formed when light from the sun passes through its own cooler atmosphere and that of the earth. The thousands of dark lines in the solar spectrum, first distinguished by Joseph Fraunhofer in 1814, may tell us what elements the sun contains. To do so, they must be matched with the bright-line spectra of the elements. (See Fig. 26-12.)

Absorption spectra can also give us clues to the composition of the atmospheres of other planets. The planets shine by reflected sunlight. If the spectrum of a planet includes dark lines that the sun's direct spectrum does not contain, they must be the result of absorption by elements or compounds in the planet's atmosphere.

10. The Doppler Effect in the Spectrum

By matching the spectrum of a star with the spectrum that a particular element produces in the laboratory (called a *comparison spectrum*), the astronomer can tell whether the star contains that element. (See Fig. 26-13.) But astronomers may find that the matching lines in the star's spectrum are displaced slightly either

Fig. 26-13. The Doppler effect as shown in the spectrum of the brighter member of the double star Castor in the constellation Gemini. (See Topic 22.) The top and bottom bands in this photograph are part of a bright-line spectrum being used as a comparison spectrum. The other two bands are absorption spectra of the star. In the upper of the two spectra the matching dark lines are displaced to the right—the red end of the spectrum—because the orbital motion of the star is away from the earth. In the lower spectrum the matching dark lines are displaced to the left—the violet end of the spectrum—because the orbital motion of the star is now toward the earth.

Lick Observatory

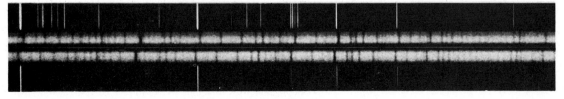

to the left or right of the lines in the comparison spectrum. If displaced toward the red end of the spectrum, it means that these lines represent slightly longer wavelengths than the comparison element's light. If displaced toward the violet end, it means shorter wavelengths.

Astronomers explain these displacements or **shifts** as caused by the motion of the star "in the line of sight" away from or toward the earth. A shift of spectral lines toward the red end of the spectrum is called a *red-shift,* and it means that *the star is receding* from the earth (or the earth is moving away from the star), thereby apparently lengthening somewhat the wavelengths it radiates. The faster it recedes, the greater the red-shift. Conversely, a shift toward the violet means that the star is moving toward the earth (or the earth toward the star), thereby apparently shortening somewhat the wavelengths it radiates. If a star is moving at right angles to the line of sight, no shift occurs in its spectral lines.

This principle was first explained by the physicist Doppler in 1842. It also applies to sound waves. All of us have noticed the Doppler effect in the rising pitch of a train siren or automobile horn as the train or automobile approaches us. Similarly, we notice the falling pitch of the same sound as its source recedes from us.

CHARACTERISTICS OF THE STARS

Using the tools described in the preceding paragraphs, and applying physics, chemistry, and mathematics to his observations, the astronomer is able to learn many things about the distant and mysterious stars in the heavens. We shall set down some of his findings in the following paragraphs, and wherever possible we shall give simple explanations of how his findings are made. In those cases where the astronomer's methods are too advanced for your present understanding, perhaps your scientific curiosity will lead you to further study.

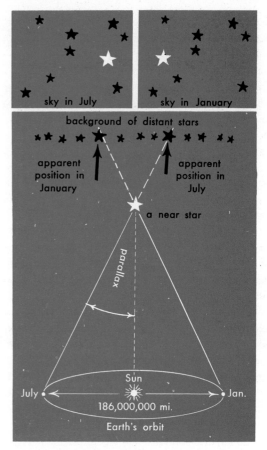

Fig. 26-14. *As seen against a background of very distant stars, the position of a relatively near star shows a distinct change from opposite ends of the earth's orbit.*

11. How the Astronomer Finds Out: A Summary

The astronomer is able to determine the distance, diameter, surface temperature, mass (total amount of matter), density, and chemical composition of many of the stars. The methods he uses are varied, but a simple idea of his basic methods can be given here.

The *distance* between the earth and about 6,000 "near" stars can be measured by trigonometry, just as a surveyor may measure the distance from one point to another. (For more distant stars, other methods must be used.) The astronomer uses the diameter of the earth's orbit as the base line of a triangle from which he sights the star at two different dates six months apart. The two "lines of sight" to the star form the other two sides of the triangle. Knowing the length of the base and the size of the two angles, the astronomer can calculate the distance to the star. (See Fig. 26-14.)

The *surface temperature* of the star may be determined from a study of its spectrum. In general, the bluer the star's light, the higher its temperature.

The *diameter* or *size* of a star (whose distance and temperature are known) may be obtained by observing its brightness or *magnitude* and calculating how large its surface must be to radiate the light that we get from it.

The *mass* of a star may be determined in a number of ways too advanced to explain here. When the mass and diameter of a star are known, its *density* can be calculated from the simple formula:

Density = Mass ÷ Volume

The *chemical composition* of a star is determined from its spectrum, as explained in Topic 9, with each element identifying itself largely by its dark lines.

Now for some details of the astronomer's findings about the stars.

12. Size, Mass, and Density of Stars

Our sun is regarded by astronomers as an "average star" in many respects. Its shape is spherical; its diameter is about 864,000 miles; its average density is about 1.4 times that of water; its mass is more than 300,000 times that of the earth. The sun is our star. How do the other stars in the universe compare with the sun?

Stars cover an enormous range in **size.** The smallest stars may be smaller than the earth, which is about 8,000 miles in diameter. The largest star known, Epsilon Aurigae (awe *rye* jee), is about 2 billion miles in diameter—about 2,300 times the diameter of the sun. Were it located at the center of our solar system, it would reach out to the orbit of Saturn! (See Fig. 26-15.)

Fig. 26-15. How our sun compares in size with the giant and supergiant stars.

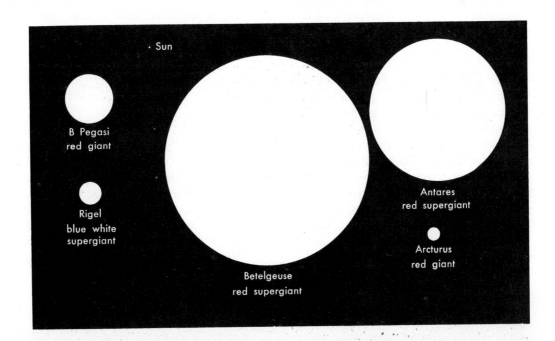

The range of **density** in stars is even greater than their range in size. The "red supergiant" star Betelgeuse (*bet* el juz) has a density about one ten-millionth that of the sun, which makes it more rarefied than most of our highest vacuums. At the other extreme, the "white dwarf" companion of Sirius (*sir* ee us) is believed to be so dense that one teaspoonful of it weighs about a ton! Most stars, however, lie well within the two extremes represented by Betelgeuse and Sirius' companion.

The range of **mass** in stars is much smaller than the range of either diameter or density. Stars range from about ten times the sun's mass to about one-fifth of its mass. Most stars are fairly close to the sun in mass.

13. Distances of Stars

The average distance between the earth and its star, the sun, is about 92,900,000 miles, which astronomers call the **astronomical unit** (A.U.). Imagine for a moment that the earth is a dot with the sun one inch away from it. The next nearest stars, both about 270,000 times as far from the earth as the sun, would be more than four miles away! The names of these stars are Alpha Centauri and Proxima Centauri (*proxima,* near; *Centauri,* of the constellation Centaur), and their real distance from the earth is about 25,000,000,000,000 (25 trillion) miles. Alpha Centauri is the second brightest star in the Southern Hemisphere sky, but Proxima is invisible to the unaided eye.

Because star distances are so large, special units are used to express them. One unit is the **light-year—the distance a ray of light travels in one year.** Since light moves at a speed of about 186,000 miles a second, the number of miles in a light year is approximately equal to 186,000 × 60 (seconds) × 60 (minutes) × 24 (hours) × 365 (days). This comes to nearly 6 trillion miles. In terms of light-years, then, Alpha and Proxima Centauri are about 4.3 light-years from the earth.

Other "near" stars are Sirius, brightest star in the sky, about 9 light-years distant; Vega, our brightest summer star, about 27 light-years distant; and Procyon, about 11 light-years away. Polaris, the North Star, is 680 light-years away from us. Our sun is about 8 *light-minutes* from the earth—in other words, light takes about 8 minutes to go from the sun to the earth.

Another unit of distance used by the astronomer is the **parsec.** When astronomers measure star distances as explained in Topic 11, they determine the star's shift of position as seen from the earth in terms of an angle called the **parallax** of the star. (See Fig. 26-14.) The nearer the star, the larger its parallax. **The parsec is the distance at which a star would have a parallax of one second of arc.** (A *second* is a sixtieth of a *minute;* a minute is a sixtieth of a *degree.* A second is therefore a 3,600th of a degree.) As small as this parallax is, no star is close enough to have a parallax of one second. Proxima Centauri's parallax is about three-fourths of a second of arc. The smallest parallax that can be measured accurately is about one hundredth of a second, and only about 6,000 stars are near enough to have measurable parallaxes. The distances of stars farther off must be determined by different methods.

A parsec is equal to 3.26 light-years. (The word *parsec* comes from *par*allax of one *sec*ond.) It is about 20 trillion miles, or about 200,000 times the distance from the earth to the sun.

14. Star Colors and Temperatures

Even to the unaided eye stars differ in color. Antares and Betelgeuse are red, Capella and our sun are yellow, Sirius and Vega and Rigel are blue. Spectrum analysis of the stars shows that the hotter the star, the bluer is its color. The cooler the star, the redder is its color. All stars emit all colors of light, but the hotter stars emit more light at the blue end of the spectrum, while the cooler stars emit less blue and more red. Much the same thing is seen when an iron bar is heated. As its temperature rises it changes in color from red to orange, to yellow, and finally to white or blue.

Astronomers classify stars into these seven main classes on the basis of their spectral lines:

Class	Color	Surface Temperature	Example
O	blue	above 30,000°C	Zeta Puppis
B	blue-white	15,000°C–30,000°C	Rigel, Spica
A	white	8,000°C–11,000°C	Sirius, Vega
F	white-yellow	about 7,500°C	Canopus, Procyon
G	yellow	about 6,000°C	Sun, Capella
K	orange	about 4,000°C	Arcturus, Aldebaran
M	red	about 3,000°C	Antares, Betelgeuse

Except for Zeta Puppis, all the stars listed here are familiar bright stars easily seen by the unaided eye.

15. What Stars Are Made Of

Spectrum analysis indicates that stars are composed of the same elements as those found on the earth, but in vastly different proportions. Most stars consist chiefly of hydrogen and helium, with such heavier elements as iron, titanium, calcium, sodium, and all others making up only about one per cent of their entire mass. Our sun is estimated to be about 70 per cent hydrogen and about 28 per cent helium. This leaves only two per cent for all the other elements, of which more than 60 have been identified from their spectral lines, as explained in Topic 9.

The differences in the spectra of the stars are apparently caused more by differences in temperature than by differences in composition.

16. Star Brightness

If the sun is only a medium-sized star of medium temperature, why does it look so much larger and brighter than all other stars? We all know the answer. It looks larger and brighter because it is so much closer. The **true brightness** of a star depends on its size and surface temperature, but its **apparent brightness** depends on its distance too. The stars that look brightest to us in the nighttime sky may not be truly brighter than the other stars. They may look brighter only because they are nearer. How, then, does the astronomer classify stars as to brightness?

Astronomers use the word **magnitude** in defining the brightness of a star. The **apparent magnitude** of a star is its brightness as observed either by the eye, by the photoelectric cell, or by photography. Long before the telescope was invented, astronomers had classified the stars they could see into six classes of "magnitude." *First magnitude* stars were the brightest stars, such as Sirius, Capella, and Betelgeuse. *Sixth magnitude* stars were those barely visible to the eye. Today, with the great 200-inch Hale telescope of Mount Palomar able to photograph twenty-fourth magnitude stars with less than a billionth the apparent brightness of Betelgeuse, astronomers have found it important to give an exact mathematical value to apparent magnitudes. The system they use is easily understood.

Roughly, the ratio of brightness of any two consecutive magnitudes is 2.5. For example, a star of fifth magnitude is 2.5 times as bright as a star of sixth magnitude. A star of first magnitude is 2.5 times as bright as a star of second magnitude. First magnitude stars are 100 times as bright as sixth magnitude stars ($2.5 \times 2.5 \times 2.5 \times 2.5 \times 2.5$). To provide for small differences in brightness of stars, magnitude numbers include decimals. The apparent magnitudes of some "first-magnitude" stars are, for example, Fomalhaut 1.16; Spica 1.0; Altair 0.80; Pollux 1.16.

Stars that are brighter than first magnitude may have magnitudes between 1 and 0, as for example: Altair 0.80; Rigel 0.15; Capella 0.09; Vega 0.04. A few stars are even brighter, so their magnitudes have to be expressed as negative numbers: Alpha Centauri −0.27; Canopus −0.73; Sirius −1.43. (Alpha Centauri and Canopus are Southern Hemisphere stars.)

The use of magnitudes for brightness is also applied to the sun, moon, and planets. At their brightest, Venus, Mars, and Jupiter surpass all stars in brightness, with magnitudes of −4.4, −2.5, and −2.8 respectively. The full moon's magnitude is −12.6. The sun's magnitude is −26.8. Remember, the lower the magnitude number, the brighter the star or planet.

17. Absolute Magnitude

The apparent magnitude of a star is simply a measure of how bright it looks to us on the earth, not of its true brightness or **luminosity.** To compare stars as to their luminosity, we should have to place them all at the same distance from us. Of course we cannot actually do this, but if we know their apparent magnitudes and distances from us, it is easy to calculate how bright each star would look at any given distance. To standardize this calculation, the astronomer defines a star's **absolute magnitude.** The absolute magnitude of a star is the apparent magnitude it would have at a distance of 10 parsecs (32.6 light-years). Rigel and Betelgeuse have very high absolute magnitudes of −6.4 and −5.8 respectively, whereas our sun's absolute magnitude is only 4.8, making it barely visible to the eye at 10 parsecs. Yet most of the stars in the heavens are not even as luminous as the sun.

18. Giants, Supergiants, Dwarfs

In general, the bluer the star, the higher its luminosity and absolute magnitude. This should mean that the most luminous stars are the blue or blue-white stars, and the faintest are the red stars. Such is the case for most stars, but there are many exceptions—red stars that are highly luminous and white stars that are very faint. Let us take some examples of both the rule and the exceptions.

Sirius and Vega are two examples of many hot blue-white stars, and they are highly luminous, as we expect. But Capella, Arcturus, and Aldebaran have absolute magnitudes near −1 and are even more luminous, yet they are cooler red stars. Their luminosity is explained by their enormous size, which enables them to radiate more light than hotter but smaller stars. Capella, Arcturus, and Aldebaran are exceptions to the rule, and they are known as **red giants.**

Other stars have even higher absolute magnitudes, and are hundreds of times as luminous as the giants. These **supergiants** include blue-white Rigel, white-yellow Canopus, and the **red supergiants** Antares and Betelgeuse. Again, the red supergiants must be much larger than the blue ones in order to be as luminous. They are the largest of all stars.

The less luminous stars (absolute magnitude, +1 or less) are known as **dwarfs.** We would expect the dwarfs to be the red and orange and yellow stars, and most of them are—our sun among them. But again there are exceptions—usually stars that are white to yellow, yet are very faint because they are really very small. These **white dwarfs** are also very dense, for the nuclei of their atoms are packed so closely that

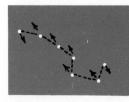 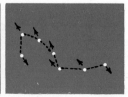

Fig. 26-16. *The present shape of the Big Dipper is shown at the left. The arrows show the proper motion (see Topic 19) of its stars. Because of this proper motion, the Dipper will look as shown at the right in about 50,000 years.*

one cubic inch of material may weigh many tons, as in the white dwarf companions of Sirius and Procyon. (See Topic 12.)

19. Motions of the Stars

All of the stars in our galaxy (Topic 23) rotate with the galaxy at high speeds that differ with each star's distance from the galaxy's center. (Our sun's speed is about 135 miles a second.) The astronomer may detect a star's motion in two different ways. **Proper motion** is the rate at which the star changes its position among the other stars in the sky. Proper motion is detected simply by comparing two photographs— one taken long after the other—showing the star against its background of more distant stars. Because of their enormous distances from us, very few stars show appreciable proper motion over short periods of time such as a few years.

In 50,000 years, however, proper motion will cause distinct changes, readily observable with the unaided eye, in the shapes of many of our constellations. (See Fig. 26-16.)

Radial velocity is the rate at which the star is moving toward us or away from us. As explained in Topic 10, radial velocity is detected by a shift of the star's spectral lines. A shift to the red means that the star is receding. Most stars have radial velocities of from 20 to 30 miles a second, but some exceed 60 miles a second. Our sun is moving through the stars in the direction of the constellation Hercules at a rate of 12 miles a second.

20. Variable Stars: Red Variables and Cepheids

Many stars in the sky can be seen to vary in brightness. Such stars are known as **variable stars.** They include *red variable stars, pulsating stars,* and *explosive stars.*

The **red variable stars** are red giants and supergiants whose brightness may change by several magnitudes in a cycle of months or even years. Betelgeuse, a red variable, changes in diameter as it changes in brightness.

Pulsating stars change in brightness as they expand and contract in regular cycles. Expansion causes them to become cooler. Contraction makes them hotter and brighter.

Examples of pulsating stars are the *cepheid* variables (named for the constellation Cepheus; the pronunciation is *see* fee us), yellow supergiants whose bright-dim-bright periods range from about one day to 50 days, with most around five days.

Astronomers have found that the true brightness (absolute magnitude) of a cepheid star is related to its period of pulsation. The longer the period, the greater the absolute magnitude. Furthermore, they have worked out tables giving the absolute magnitude for any period. With this information available, they can easily calculate how far away any cepheid or galaxy containing a cepheid is (comparing its apparent and absolute magnitudes). Thus the cepheid provides the astronomer with a remarkable new measure of distance in the universe—especially useful because of the brightness and wide distribution of the cepheids.

21. Explosive Variable Stars: Novae and Supernovae

Explosive stars are faint stars that flare up suddenly into a brightness thousands or even hundreds of thousands of times as great as before. Before the invention of the telescope, such a star might appear where no star had been seen before, and it was therefore called a *nova stella* (new star.) Astronomers believe that the flaring of a **nova** is the result of an explosion that blows away the outer atmosphere of the star and temporarily allows the radiation of tremendous amounts of energy from the star's interior. The star loses material, but the loss appears to be a very small fraction of its total mass. The brightening may take from a few days to a few weeks, and it may reach an absolute magnitude equal to that of a supergiant star. Eventually the star returns to its former luminosity. This may take months or even years. The stars that become novae are always small dense stars that resemble

Mount Wilson and Palomar Observatories

Fig. 26-17. The Crab Nebula is the vast cloud of gas left from the explosive flareup of a supernova in 1054 A.D.

white dwarfs. The cause of their explosion is not known.

On a few rare occasions recorded by astronomers, stars have flared into such brilliance that they have been called **supernovae**. A supernova may represent an increase in brightness of a million times, and its absolute magnitude may equal that of an entire galaxy. In its explosion a large part of its mass is blown away and lost, and the star itself may be destroyed. Such an explosion was observed in the year 1054 A.D., when it was recorded as a supernova by Chinese astronomers. After a year it faded, but left behind a great and still-expanding cloud of gas known today as the Crab Nebula in the constellation Taurus. (See Figure 26-17.) Other supernovae in our galaxy (see Topic 23) were recorded by the Danish astronomer Tycho Brahe in 1572 and by the German astronomer Johannes Kepler in 1604. All three of these now emit radio waves. No supernova has been observed in our own galaxy since 1604, so it is obvious that they are rare phenomena.

22. Binary Stars

Astronomers have thus far discovered, through the use of the telescope and the spectroscope, that about 40,000 of the stars in the sky are double or **binary stars.** A binary star is defined as a pair of stars that are "physically connected." The connection consists in their revolving around each other.

A **visual binary** is a pair of stars that can be seen as two stars in the telescope. The first visual binary discovered was the star Mizar in the handle of the Big Dipper. Sirius and its famous white dwarf companion form another visual binary.

A **spectroscopic binary** is a double star which cannot be separated by the telescope, but which is identified by alternating red shifts and blue shifts of its spectral lines, or by the alternate appearance of double and single lines in its spectrum, as its two stars separate and come together. The bright stars Capella, Spica, and Castor are spectroscopic binaries. (See Fig. 26-13.)

An **eclipsing binary** is a spectroscopic pair of stars whose orbit is edgewise to the earth. As they revolve, they eclipse each other. Periodically, therefore, their light grows weaker and then stronger. An eclipsing binary is also a variable star. The most famous of these stars is Algol, the "Demon Star" of ancient astronomers. Every 69 hours, approximately, Algol fades to about one-third its normal brightness as the brighter star is eclipsed by its fainter companion.

GALAXIES

23. Galaxies: Island Universes

Even before Galileo's use of the telescope, sky watchers noticed that in addition to the several thousand sharp points of light they called stars, there were a few hazy, blurred patches in the nighttime sky to which they gave the name of *nebulae* (clouds). Early telescopes revealed thousands more of these, and modern telescopes have shown that many of these nebulae are really systems or families containing millions or even billions of stars. Today we call these systems **galaxies.** Although galaxies are millions of light-years apart, our giant telescopes indicate that space contains at least a billion galaxies, each including millions or even billions of stars! The eighteenth century astronomer Sir William Herschel gave these galaxies the picturesque name of "island universes" to emphasize the vast emptiness of space between them. (See Fig. 26-18.)

The galaxy to which we belong is called the **Milky Way** or **the galaxy.** In it our sun is one star among 100 billion, and its nearest neighbor is Proxima Centauri. *Every star that we can see with the naked eye is part of our Milky Way.* Astronomers think that our galaxy is shaped like

a large, thin convex lens with a pronounced central bulge; that its diameter is about 80,000 light-years and its greatest thickness about 10,000 light-years; and that the sun is about two-thirds of the way from the galaxy's center to its edge. (See Fig. 26-19.) When we look along the plane of the galaxy, we see so many stars that the sky appears "milky." When we look at right angles to the plane of the galaxy, we see fewer stars. The entire galaxy rotates in one direction, but its stars may move at different speeds and in different directions within the galaxy.

Our galaxy belongs to a small cluster of 17 galaxies that astronomers have named the Local Group. Figure 26-18 shows the relative positions of part of the group. Our nearest neighbor galaxies are the Large Magellanic Cloud and the Small Magellanic Cloud, which were so named before telescopes showed them to be galaxies. They are visible to the unaided eye in the sky

Fig. 26-18. The position of our galaxy in space, with respect to a few "neighbor" galaxies.

American Museum of Natural History

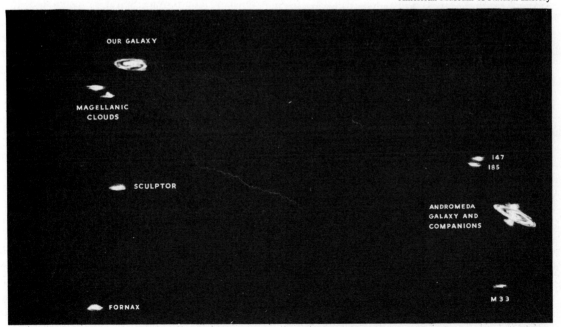

Fig. 26-19. A cross-section through our galaxy, the Milky Way. The surrounding dot-like objects are nearby globular clusters.

Fig. 26-20. M 31, the Great Spiral in Andromeda, is a spiral galaxy *even larger than our own. Two* elliptical galaxies *also appear as small bright oval spots, one above the Great Spiral's bright center, the other below it at the left.*

Lick Observatory

of the Southern Hemisphere, and are about 160,000 light-years from the earth. (See Fig. 26-22.) Another galaxy in the Local Group that is faintly visible to the unaided eye is the famous Great Spiral in the constellation Andromeda. (See Fig. 26-20.) The Great Spiral is estimated to be about 2 million light-years from the earth. It is believed to be even larger than our galaxy. All the other galaxies in the Local Group are considerably smaller. Powerful telescopes reveal individual stars in nearby galaxies.

24. Types of Galaxies

Galaxies appear to be of three main types. **Spiral galaxies** have a central lens-shaped bright nucleus made up of millions of stars. The nucleus may be surrounded by a fainter flat disk of stars. Spiral arms, usually two and often branched, extend from opposite sides of the nucleus. The arms curl around the galaxy in the same direction, trailing behind it as it rotates. Like the nucleus, the arms consist of millions of stars, but they also include great clouds of dust and gas not found in the nucleus of the galaxy. The region between the arms appears to contain few stars and almost no dust or gas. Photographs of spiral galaxies show a great variety of shapes, depending on the shape and relative size of the nucleus and the arms. The appearance of a galaxy also depends on whether it is turned fully toward us (see Fig. 26-21) or whether we see it obliquely or on edge (see Fig. 26-20). About three-fourths of all galaxies are believed to be spirals. Our own galaxy and the Andromeda Galaxy are spirals.

Elliptical galaxies have shapes ranging from nearly spherical to lens-shaped. Their distribution of stars, as shown by their brightness, is densest near the center and thins out gradually toward the edges. They have no arms, and they contain almost no dust or gas. Two elliptical galaxies can be seen near the Andromeda Galaxy in Figure 26-20.

Irregular galaxies are generally smaller, fainter, and less common than the others. Their shapes and distribution of stars are irregular. The two Magellanic clouds are irregular galaxies. (See Fig. 26-22.)

25. Cosmic Dust, Gas, and Star Populations

In 1904 astronomers first obtained proof that great clouds of gas and dust exist in interstellar (between the stars) space. The clouds are not found everywhere, and they differ in density, but the densities are always so low that even the highest vacuums produced on earth are dense in comparison. Nevertheless, the total quantities of material they contain in their enormous volumes are as large as those found in the stars. About 99 per cent of the mass of the cloud is gas, believed to be mainly hydrogen. The remaining one per cent is dust in the form of tiny grains, each only about four-millionths of an inch long. The composition of the "dust grains" is not known but they are thought to consist mainly of ice-like crystals of hydrogen compounds such as

Mount Wilson and Palomar Observatories

Fig. 26-21. Famous spiral galaxy *M 51 in the constellation Canes Venatici, the Hunting Dogs. The plane of M 51 is nearly perpendicular to our line of sight from the earth, giving us a "top view" of the galaxy. Notice especially its two spiral arms above and below, and the satellite irregular galaxy at the right. (M 51 means "Messier's Catalog, Object No. 51.")*

Fig. 26-22. The Large Magellanic Cloud is an irregular galaxy and a satellite of our own Milky Way galaxy.

Yerkes Observatory

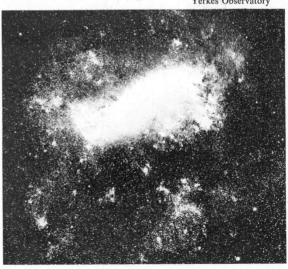

water, ammonia, and methane formed from the gases in the clouds. Tiny metallic particles may also be present. The dust grains are so far apart, on the average, that only one would be found in a space 100 feet long, 100 feet wide, and 40 feet high. Where do these clouds of gas and dust come from? Some may be left over from the "original" material from which the universe and its stars were first formed. But astronomers believe that most of the material in the clouds has been ejected from already existing stars during eruptions like those that form novae and supernovae, or during less spectacular flareups of other stars.

Now astronomers have found that there is a relation between the type of star found in a galaxy and the presence or absence of interstellar clouds. Where no gas and dust are present—in the nuclei of spiral galaxies, in elliptical galaxies, in globular star clusters (Topic 32), and in the regions between the arms of spiral galaxies —the stars are poor in heavy elements such as metals, and there are no stars brighter than red supergiants. The astronomer Walter Baade called these *Population II* stars. But where great clouds of gas and dust are present—in the arms of the spiral galaxies—the stars are somewhat richer in heavy elements, and the brightest stars are the much hotter blue-white giants. These stars Baade called *Population I* stars.

Astronomers believe that the hot Population I stars are young stars born relatively recently from the same kind of gas and dust as now surrounds them in the arms of the spiral galaxies where stars are created. The cooler Population II stars are relatively old stars, for the regions in which they are found are completely devoid of star-making gas and dust, and no new star has been born there for billions of years. They are poor in heavy metallic elements because they were formed at a time when the universe was mainly hydrogen, from which heavy elements are built up very slowly in the hot interiors of stars. But Population I stars were formed from

"second-hand" materials like those ejected from the interiors of already existing stars in supernova explosions. Therefore Population I stars start out with appreciable amounts of heavy elements to which they add during their own development. Our sun is a Population I star, so its atoms and those of its planets may once have existed in another star in a remote part of the universe.

26. Life History of a Star

According to modern theory stars are forming continually in different parts of the universe wherever great clouds of interstellar dust and gas are present. These clouds are believed to be at least a light-year in diameter and as massive as a thousand suns. The mutual gravitational attraction of the atoms of gas and grains of dust in the denser parts of the cloud causes these parts to contract and become heated. As contraction continues, the temperature of the shrinking but still enormous globular cloud rises, the denser parts begin to glow, and stars are born. Many stars may thus be born in a single vast cosmic cloud.

As contraction continues, the stars become hotter and brighter. The more massive ones, having shrunk more and faster, have higher temperatures and become blue and white stars. The less massive ones are cooler, and they become yellow and orange stars. The hotter stars are more easily seen not only because they are brighter but also because they have blown away the excess dust that surrounded them.

Contraction continues until the star's center becomes so hot that its hydrogen begins to be converted into helium. Once begun, this **fusion reaction** (which is the same as the reaction in a hydrogen bomb) continues to supply the star with all the energy it radiates. (See Chapter 27, Topic 6.) The star stops contracting, because the outward pressure of the hot gaseous interior just balances the weight of the overlying gases at any level. The massive blue stars may reach this stage in a few hundred thousand years. Yellow and orange stars may take millions of years to arrive at this stage.

Millions or even billions of years may pass in this stable state of star size and radiation. But eventually the time comes when so much of the hydrogen in its core has been converted to helium that the star loses its stability. The core contracts until it becomes so hot—perhaps 100,000,000°C —that its gas pressure makes the star's outer layers expand. This increases the star's surface area, so it radiates more light and appears brighter. Meantime the hydrogen of the core is largely consumed, and fusion begins to occur in the outer layers. The star expands still further, and even though its surface cools somewhat, its enormous surface area now radiates enough light to make it a red giant or supergiant.

If the temperature in the star's core goes high enough during this stage, helium may "burn" in a reaction that forms heavier carbon atoms. When temperatures exceed 3 billion degrees C, iron and other heavy metallic elements may be formed.

Finally, the time comes when nearly all the star's available nuclear fuel is used up, and its core can no longer support the weight of its outer layers. When this happens, it is conjectured, the red giant collapses. The nuclei of all its atoms are squeezed together into a tiny fraction of their original volume, and the star becomes a hot white dwarf no larger perhaps than the earth, but so dense that every teaspoonful of its mass weighs many tons. Since its nuclear fuel is exhausted, it can generate no more heat. Nevertheless, its residual heat is sufficient to keep it glowing faintly for perhaps a billion years, because it loses heat very slowly from its small surface area. Eventually it will become cold and dark.

Astronomers think that stars may pass through two intermediate stages before changing from red giants to white dwarfs. The red giant may become a red variable star before it begins its collapse. Then in the early stages of its collapse, it may go through a period in which it blows off outer layers to become a nova or even a supernova.

Our sun is believed to be at least 5 billion years old now, and still in the stable stage. This means we can expect it to sustain itself at its present size and temperature for another 5 billion years before it swells to a red giant. When it does, it will consume the entire solar system.

27. Origin of the Universe: Expanding Universe

How did the universe of galaxies originate? In the hypothesis of the **expanding universe**— also known as the **big-bang** hypothesis—it is suggested that all matter in the universe was once concentrated in a single dense globular mass of hydrogen not much larger than our sun. About 10 billion years ago this "primitive atom" exploded into a gigantic expanding cloud in which some parts moved faster than others. As the great cloud masses moved outward they condensed into galaxies. Billions of galaxies were formed, while continuing to move away from the center and from one another in all directions. In this expanding universe, the galaxies with the highest speeds are found farthest out in space.

What is the evidence for this hypothesis? In 1929 astronomer Edwin Hubble discovered that red-shifts occur in the spectra of all galaxies, indicating recession relative to the earth. (See Topic 10: The Doppler Effect.) The more distant the galaxy, the faster it recedes. The most distant galaxies observed appear to be receding at speeds as high as 85,000 miles a second, or nearly half the speed of light. This speed is so great that some astronomers are now questioning it. They believe that the red-shifts in the spectra of the galaxies may not be a Doppler effect, but may be due to some cause as yet unknown. (See Fig. 26-23.)

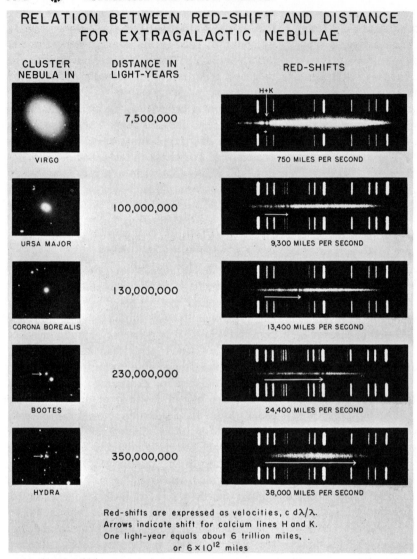

RELATION BETWEEN RED-SHIFT AND DISTANCE FOR EXTRAGALACTIC NEBULAE

CLUSTER NEBULA IN	DISTANCE IN LIGHT-YEARS	RED-SHIFTS
VIRGO	7,500,000	750 MILES PER SECOND
URSA MAJOR	100,000,000	9,300 MILES PER SECOND
CORONA BOREALIS	130,000,000	13,400 MILES PER SECOND
BOOTES	230,000,000	24,400 MILES PER SECOND
HYDRA	350,000,000	38,000 MILES PER SECOND

Red-shifts are expressed as velocities, c dλ/λ.
Arrows indicate shift for calcium lines H and K.
One light-year equals about 6 trillion miles,
or 6×10^{12} miles

Mount Wilson and Palomar Observatories

Fig. 26-23. These spectra show that the more distant the nebula, the greater the red-shift in its light waves. This, in turn, means that the more distant the nebula, the higher its speed of recession from the earth. ("Extra-galactic nebulae" are nebulae outside our own galaxy.)

In the theory of the expanding universe, the universe must in some distant day come to a cold end, because no new matter is being created to replace that which is being consumed to create energy in the interior of the stars.

28. Origin of the Universe: Steady-State Hypothesis

Astronomers Hoyle and Gold believe that matter, probably hydrogen, is formed continuously in space at a rate that exactly compensates for the loss of hydrogen converted into energy or into heavier elements. The **steady-state universe** has no beginning and no end. It has always had galaxies spread throughout space, and as its present galaxies are destroyed, they will constantly be replaced by others.

GROUPINGS OF STARS; NEBULAE

29. Constellations: Star Patterns in our Galaxy

The stars that the ancients saw close together in the sky are in most cases not near each other

at all. They are located in the same direction in space, but may in reality be vast distances apart, just as an airplane and a bird may appear to be near each other though actually far apart. All of these stars, however, are in our galaxy. To these groups, or "constellations" of stars, the Greeks, Romans, Egyptians, Chinese, Arabs, American Indians, and in fact star watchers over all the world, gave names often taken from their mythologies. Most of the names in use today are of Greek or Latin origin.

The best-known of the constellations is probably Ursa Major, the Great Bear, in which the Big Dipper forms the tail and part of the back. A line through the "pointer" stars in the bowl of

Fig. 26-24. Constellations of summer in the Northern Hemisphere sky.

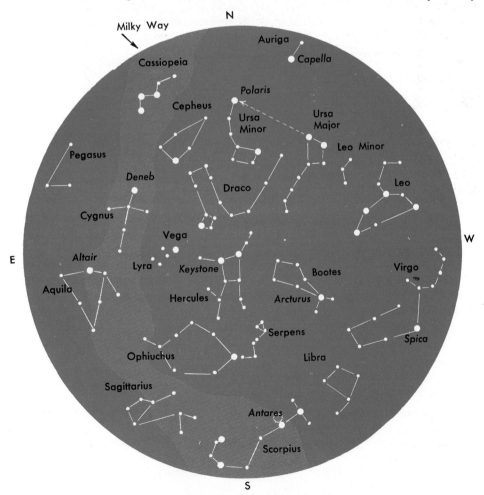

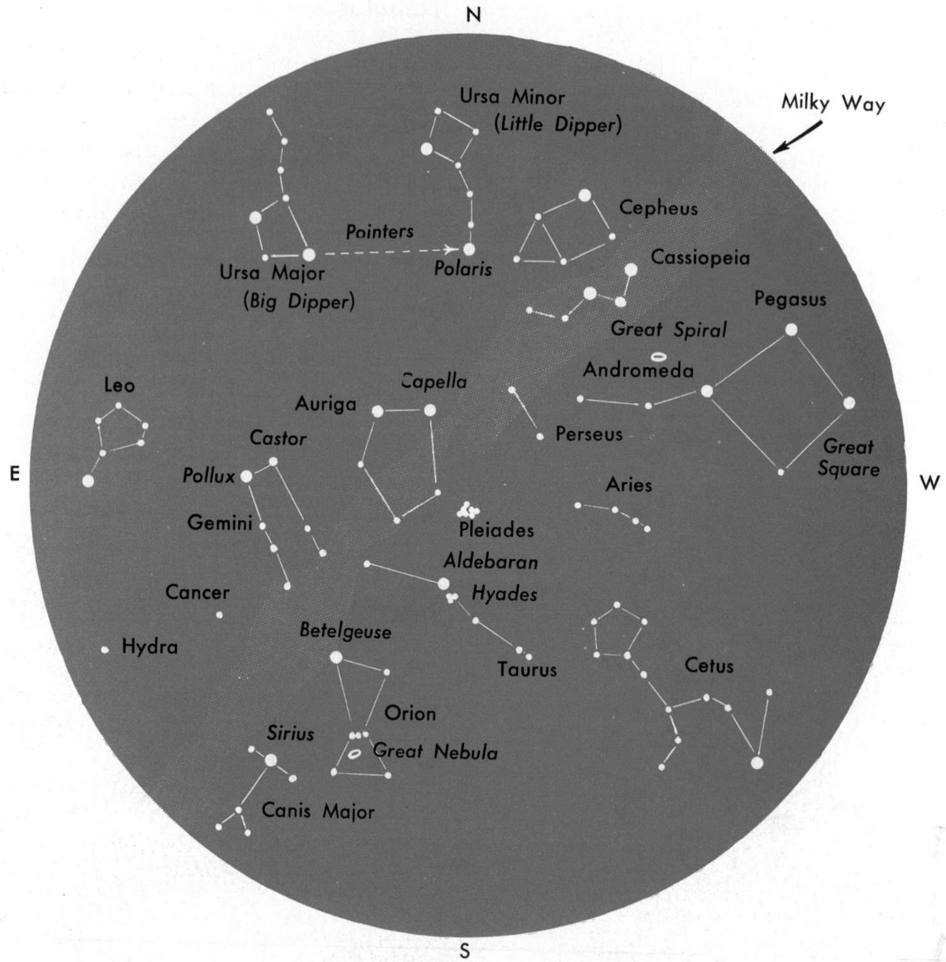

Fig. 26-25. Constellations of winter in the Northern Hemisphere sky.

the Big Dipper points to Polaris, the North Star. When you look at Polaris, you are looking north. Polaris itself is the last star in the handle of the Little Dipper. Opposite the Big Dipper can be seen Queen Cassiopeia's Chair. These three "circumpolar" constellations (the ones around the North Star) can be seen all year. Conspicuous in summer are the constellations Lyra, the Lyre, with the brilliant star Vega; Cygnus, the Swan, in which lies the Northern Cross; Scorpius, with Antares; and Aquila, the Eagle, with the bright star Altair. In winter we see Orion, the Mighty

Hunter, with its brilliant red supergiant star Betelgeuse and its hot-blue supergiant star Rigel; Canis Major, the Big Dog, with Sirius, brightest of all our stars; and Taurus, the Bull, with the Pleiades (the Seven Sisters) not far away. (See Figs. 26-24 and 26-25.)

30. Turning of the Heavens

The whole sky dome appears to turn from east to west. This appearance of turning is a result of the turning of the earth from west to east on its axis. Since the axis is pointed almost exactly at Polaris, the North Star, this star seems to remain almost stationary in the sky, while the stars near it appear to go around it in circles from east to west and can be seen all night. The farther the stars are from Polaris, the larger their circles become. The farthest stars simply appear to rise in the east and set in the west, and may be seen for only a part of the night. The tracks made by the stars as they pass through the sky each night can be photographed with an ordinary camera by time exposure. The circumpolar stars (those near Polaris) make circular "trails," while those far from Polaris produce straight trails. (See Fig. 26-26.)

31. Nebulae

In Topic 23 we learned that many of the "nebulae" or hazy patches of brightness in the night-time sky are distant galaxies or island universes. There are, however, other nebulae which are not galaxies. These **diffuse nebulae** are actually great clouds of interstellar gas and dust. The brightest and best known of the diffuse nebulae is the Great Nebula in Orion. Just barely visible to the naked eye, it is near the middle star in the sword of the constellation Orion, the Mighty Hunter. In the telescope this nebula is a brilliant sight. (See Fig. 26-27.)

Diffuse nebulae have no light of their own, and therefore their brightness depends upon how

Lick Observatory

Fig. 26-26. Circumpolar star trails are all-night photos of the North Star and the adjacent stars. The bright trail almost at the center is the North Star's.

Lick Observatory

Fig. 26-27. The Great Nebula in Orion.

Mount Wilson and Palomar Observatories

Fig. 26-28. Horsehead Nebula in Orion.

Fig. 26-29. The Great Cluster in Hercules.

Lick Observatory

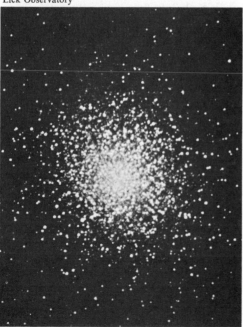

close they are to stars that can illuminate them. If no bright star is near enough, a diffuse nebula appears as a **dark nebula.** Thus it causes an area in the sky where few or no stars can be seen through the cloud. Two such dark areas in the Milky Way—one in Cygnus, the other near the Southern Cross—are called **coal sacks.** One of the best known of the dark nebulae is the famous Horsehead Nebula, also in the constellation Orion. (See Fig. 26-28.)

32. Star Clusters

In some parts of our sky groups of stars can be seen in which the stars are much closer together than is usual. Three of these groups are easily visible to the naked eye. They include the famous Pleiades or Seven Sisters in the constellation Taurus, the Hyades in the same constellation, and the constellation Coma Berenices. When the telescope is used, many more stars become visible in these groups, and many more star groups appear in the sky. Astronomers call these groups **star clusters,** because they have found that the stars are actually clustered closer together than other stars, and they move through space together. It is believed that all the stars in a cluster developed together from a single cloud of gas and dust.

About 600 star clusters have been discovered so far, and they fall into two quite different classes. The Pleiades, the Hyades, and Coma Berenices are all examples of **open clusters** or **galactic clusters.** (See Fig. 26-25.) These clusters are called *open* because their irregularly arranged stars are fairly widely spaced. They are called *galactic* because they are found mainly along the Milky Way in the spiral *arms* of our galaxy. About 500 open clusters have been counted. Their stars are relatively young and belong to Population I. The smallest open clusters include only a few dozen stars. The largest include more than a thousand.

Globular clusters are so called because each one is seen in the telescope as a dense circular mass of stars apparently occupying a globular section of space. About 100 globular clusters have been identified. All of them are located in the region of space centered around the *nucleus* of our galaxy, and even the nearest of them is thousands of light-years from the earth. (See Fig. 26-19.) They are larger than open clusters and contain many more stars, ranging as high as 100,000 or more in a cluster. The stars are strongly concentrated toward the centers of the clusters. Most globular clusters are invisible to the naked eye. Those that are visible look like single hazy stars. The brightest globular cluster in the sky of the Northern Hemisphere is the Great Cluster in the constellation Hercules. (See Fig. 26-29.) Globular clusters contain no clouds of gas and dust. Their stars are relatively old and belong to Population II.

33. Quasars

In the last decade astronomers have discovered a remarkable new type of celestial object that resembles a star, but in many respects is spectacularly different from any known star. Because these objects emit radio waves, they have been named **quasi-stellar radio sources** (radio sources that resemble stars) or **quasars** for short. Individual quasars are referred to by their numbers in Cambridge University's Third Catalogue of Radio Sources. For example, a quasar in the constellation Virgo is called 3C-273.

How do quasars resemble stars, yet differ from them? Let us examine 3C-273. In a telescope it looks like a faint star of about 13th magnitude. But when its distance is calculated from its red-shift, we find it to be about 2 billion light-years away. At this vast distance, no *star* we know could be visible, and even galaxies of billions of stars are visible only in the most powerful telescopes. But a study of 3C-273 shows it to be much smaller than any galaxy, though many times larger than any known star. So in order for it to be visible to us as a 13th magnitude star, 3C-273 must be billions of times as bright as our sun—brighter than our entire galaxy. Its mass is equal to hundreds of millions of suns.

Quasars appear to be by far the most luminous objects yet found in the universe. They are vastly larger and more massive than any stars. They radiate energy in the form of light and radio waves at a rate so high that thus far it defies explanation. They may include the most distant objects observed in the heavens up to the present time.

TOPIC QUESTIONS

Each topic question refers to the topic of the same number within this chapter.

1. (a) Compare the number of stars visible without and with the telescope. (b) How does the telescope make faint stars visible? (c) Why does a 2-inch lens have four times the light-gathering power of a 1-inch lens?

2. (a) What is a refractor? What does the name mean? (b) How is a refractor constructed? (c) Describe and locate our largest refractors.

3. (a) What is a reflector? (b) How is a reflector constructed? (c) Describe and locate our largest reflectors.

4. Why can large reflectors be built more easily than large refractors?

5. (a) How is the telescope used as a camera? (b) What is a Schmidt telescope?

6. (*a*) Name the different forms of electromagnetic radiation. (*b*) How are these different radiations detected? (*c*) Which radiations does the astronomer make use of?

7. (*a*) What are the sources of radio waves that come from outer space? (*b*) Why can these waves bring us information unobtainable from light waves? (*c*) What is a radio telescope? How does it work? (*d*) Name and locate some famous radio telescopes.

8. (*a*) What use is made of the spectroscope by astronomers? (*b*) What is the spectrum? How is it formed? (*c*) What does the spectroscope consist of? (*d*) How is a spectroscope used to take a photograph? (*e*) How is the spectroscope used to study the spectrum of a star?

9. (*a*) Describe the appearance and source of: 1. a continuous spectrum, 2. a bright-line spectrum, 3. a dark-line spectrum. (*b*) How are elements identified from: 1. bright-line spectra, 2. dark-line spectra? (*c*) How can absorption spectra tell us about a planet's atmosphere?

10. (*a*) What is a *red-shift?* What does it mean? (*b*) Why is the shifting of spectral lines called the Doppler effect? How is this effect noticed in connection with sound?

11. In simple terms explain how an astronomer determines a star's (*a*) distance, (*b*) surface temperature, (*c*) diameter, (*d*) density, (*e*) chemical composition.

12. (*a*) What are the sun's "dimensions"? (*b*) Describe how stars range in size, density, and mass.

13. (*a*) What is an astronomical unit? (*b*) Name the two nearest stars to the sun. How far distant are they? (*c*) What is a light-year? How many miles is it? Express the distance of a few stars in terms of light-years. (*d*) What is a parsec? What is the origin of the word? How many light-years in a parsec?

14. (*a*) How is the color of a star related to its temperature? (*b*) Name examples of stars of various colors.

15. (*a*) Of what elements are stars made? (*b*) Why do star spectra differ?

16. (*a*) What is the apparent magnitude of a star? (*b*) In the early days of astronomy how were star magnitudes defined? (*c*) How is magnitude compared today? Give some examples. (*d*) How is magnitude designated for stars brighter than first magnitude? Give examples. (*e*) How bright are the planets? the full moon? the sun?

17. (*a*) What is absolute magnitude? (*b*) Compare the absolute magnitude of Rigel, the sun, and most of the stars.

18. (*a*) What is a *red giant?* Give examples. (*b*) Why must a *red supergiant* be larger than a *blue-white supergiant?* Name examples of each. (*c*) How is a *dwarf* star defined? Give examples. (*d*) What is a *white dwarf?* How dense are they? Why?

19. (*a*) What is proper motion? How is it detected? (*b*) What is radial velocity? How is it detected?

20. (*a*) What are variable stars? (*b*) What is a red variable? (*c*) What is a pulsating star? (*d*) What is a cepheid? (*e*) What is the great importance of cepheids?

21. (*a*) What is an explosive star? (*b*) Describe the formation and decline of a nova. (*c*) What is a supernova? How does it form? What is the Crab Nebula?

22. (*a*) What is a binary star? (*b*) What is a visual binary? Give examples. (*c*) What is a spectroscopic binary? (*d*) What is an eclipsing binary? Describe a famous example.

23. (*a*) What are galaxies? (*b*) What is the Milky Way? Describe its shape and size. (*c*) Describe the Great Spiral galaxy in Andromeda.

24. Name and describe the three main types of galaxies.

25. (*a*) Describe the density and composition of the great gas and dust clouds of interstellar space. (*b*) What are Population II stars? Where are they found? (*c*) What are Population I stars? Where are they found?

26. (*a*) How are stars born? (*b*) How are blue or white stars formed? yellow or red stars? (*c*) Explain how fusion begins and contraction stops. How long does this take? (*d*) How does a star become a red giant? (*e*) Why does the star become a white dwarf? (*f*) In what stage is our sun now?

27. Describe the *big-bang* theory and the evidence for it.

28. Describe the *steady-state* theory.

29. Name some of the familiar constellations of summer, winter, and circumpolar skies.

30. What are star trails? What do they show?

31. (*a*) What are diffuse nebulae? Name one. Where do they get their light? (*b*) What is a dark nebula? Name one. What are the *coal sacks?*

32. (*a*) Describe open star clusters. (*b*) Describe globular clusters.

33. Explain how quasars differ from stars and galaxies.

GENERAL QUESTIONS

1. Why is it possible to photograph stars that are invisible to the eye?

2. If the diameter of Betelgeuse is 400 times as great as the sun's diameter, how does the volume of Betelgeuse compare with the volume of the sun? (Volume of a sphere $= \frac{4}{3}\pi r^3$.)

3. The moon is about 240,000 miles from the earth. How long does it take moonlight to reach us?

4. Why should the interior of a star be hotter than its surface?

5. How can planets be brighter than stars?

6. If an observer stays up late on an autumn night, he sees winter constellations. Why?

7. Star trails in the United States can never be complete circles. Why?

8. Where would one have to go in order to photograph star trails that were complete circles? Why?

9. Why is the Mount Palomar telescope four times as powerful a light-gatherer as the Mount Wilson telescope?

10. Compare the masses of Betelgeuse and the sun. (See Topics 11 and 12, and General Question 2.)

11. Approximately how many times as bright as Mars is the full moon? (Use figures given in Topic 16.)

STUDENT ACTIVITIES

1. "Measure" the distance from the sun to you in the following way: (*a*) Form a sharp image of the sun with a magnifying glass on a sheet of paper or screen. (See Topic 2.) (*b*) Measure the diameter of the image as accurately as possible. (*c*) Measure the distance from lens to screen. (Be careful not to look *at* the sun.) Now from geometry we know that

$$\frac{\text{Diameter of the sun}}{\text{Diameter of image}} = \frac{\text{Distance of sun}}{\text{Distance of image}}$$

Assume the sun's diameter to be 1 million miles for very approximate calculations, or 864,000 miles if you wish to try for more accuracy. Use the above equation to calculate the sun's distance.

2. Make a simple astronomical telescope with two convex lenses as follows:
(*a*) Determine the focal length of both lenses by doing the experiment described in Activity 1 or by forming an image of any distant object on a wall or screen. The image distance is the focal length. If the lenses have different focal lengths, use the longer focal length lens as your telescope objective lens and the shorter one as your eyepiece. (*b*) Hold the eyepiece lens close to your eye. Now place the objective lens in front of your eye, at a distance slightly less than the sum of the two focal lengths, and aim at any distant object. (*But not at the sun, or you will injure your eye.*) "Focus" by moving the objective back and forth slightly until a clear image is seen. The image is inverted. Why? (See Fig. 26-1.)

   To make a permanent telescope, mount the objective lens in one tube, and the eyepiece lens in a smaller tube which slides inside the first tube.

3. Make a simple spectroscope as follows:
(*a*) Obtain a cardboard tube about 8 inches long and 1½ inches in diameter. (*b*) Glue a replica diffraction grating* across one end of the tube. (*c*) Glue or fasten a sheet of heavy aluminum foil across the other end. Cut a straight narrow slit in the foil. (Other materials may be used for the slit end.)

   Observe the spectra of daylight, an incandescent light, or glowing gas tubes, etc.

4. Photograph the trails of circumpolar stars by exposing your film for at least 3 hours with an open shutter and your camera, mounted on a stand or tripod, pointed at the North Star. Your location must be shielded from all other lights. Choose a night with no moon.

5. Learn to identify the major constellations of summer and winter skies. Locate the first magnitude stars listed in this chapter, and see if their colors and relative brightness appear to you as they are described in the text.

6. Visit a planetarium or observatory.

* Obtainable from Edmund Scientific Co., Barrington, N.J.

CHAPTER 27
The Solar System

HOW DO YOU KNOW THAT . . . ?

A magnifying glass concentrates the rays of the sun on a piece of paper. If you have tried this perhaps you did not realize you were forming a bright image of the sun on the paper screen. Get as large a magnifying glass as possible. Set up a white paper or cardboard screen at right angles to the direction from sun to screen. Now, holding the magnifier parallel to the screen, move it to the position near the screen at which it forms the smallest and sharpest bright spot possible. This is your "image" of the sun. In effect, the magnifying glass has taken all the sunlight that strikes its large area and focused it into a much smaller area. That is why the "image" is so much brighter and hotter than direct sunlight.

Can you see any sunspots in your "image"? How is the size of a lens related to the size of the image of the sun it forms? How is the curvature of a lens related to the size of the image of the sun it forms? Use lenses of different diameters and different curvatures to find out.

THE SUN

1. Instruments for Solar Observation

We already know a good deal about the sun from our study of the stars in Chapter 26. With the sun so close at hand, however, it is possible for us to learn far more about it than about the other stars. Special instruments for observing the sun are devised by the astronomer. Long-focus **tower telescopes** can photograph images of the sun up to almost three feet in diameter. Other photographs of the sun have been taken by special telescopes carried by unmanned balloons high above the clouds and dust of the earth's atmosphere. **Spectroheliographs** make photographs of the sun from the light of a single element such as hydrogen or calcium. **Coronagraphs** make it possible to study the sun's corona even when the sun is not eclipsed. The **pyroheliometer** measures the rate at which we on the earth receive solar radiation. (See Fig. 27-1.)

Fig. 27-1. The solar telescope at Kitt Peak National Observatory near Tucson, Arizona, is the largest in the world. It is 110 feet tall, but the slanting shaft into which the sun's rays are reflected extends below the surface for a total length of 480 feet. The telescope forms an image of the sun 34 inches in diameter.

NSF Photo

The sun must not be viewed directly with the unaided eye or through the telescope, for its strong rays will injure the eye, especially when the rays are focused by the telescope.

2. Dimensions and Temperature

The sun is only an average-sized star, but compared to the earth its size is tremendous. Its diameter is about 110 times that of the earth, and its volume is so great that more than a million earths could fit into it. The sun is composed entirely of gases, but these are packed so tightly in its interior that its average specific gravity is more than one-fourth that of the solid earth. If we multiply the sun's volume by its specific gravity, we find that its mass is more than 300,-000 times that of the earth. In fact, the mass of the sun is about 700 times as great as the mass of all the rest of the solar system put together.

Among the stars, the sun is average in temperature as well as in size. By our standards, however, it is intensely hot. Its temperature ranges from an average of about 6,000°C at the surface to an estimated 15,000,000°C at its center. Most of the interior is believed to have a temperature over 1,000,000°C.

3. The Sun's Surface Features

The bright visible surface of the sun is its **photosphere,** a layer of relatively dense gas extending 250 miles into the sun's interior. Through the telescope the smooth yellow surface of the photosphere appears as a mottled or granulated surface of bright spots crowded together on a darker background. The bright spots or **granules,** hundreds of miles in diameter, appear to be great "bubbles" of hot gases that boil up from the sun's interior and disappear within minutes. (See Fig. 27-2.)

Above the photosphere lies the sun's atmosphere. First comes the **chromosphere** (chromo, color), colored red by glowing hydrogen and extending to about 5,000 miles above the photosphere. The lower part of the chromosphere is the cause of the dark lines in the solar spectrum. It creates these by absorbing some of the radiation passing through it from the hotter photosphere.

Solar prominences are great flamelike clouds of gas that may extend as high as a million miles above the sun's surface. Most of them seem to originate high above the chromosphere, floating above it or sending streamers down into it at high speed. Prominences glow bright red against the sky during a solar eclipse. (See Fig. 27-3.)

The **corona** or outer atmosphere of the sun surrounds the sun to a height of a million miles. The corona changes in size and shape, and streamers may extend millions of miles out into space from its outer surface. The corona glows with a faint pearly light that is invisible except during a solar eclipse. The invention of the coronagraph has made it possible to photograph the brighter inner corona without an eclipse. The gases of the corona are highly ionized. Their temperature is estimated to be about 1,000,-000°C.

4. Sunspots and the Sun's Rotation

Sunspots are dark spots on the surface of the sun. They range in size from spots barely visible through large telescopes to great spots 90,000 miles in diameter that reach more than one-tenth of the way across the surface of the sun. The spots are comparatively cool parts of the photosphere, and they appear dark by contrast with the brighter background of the photosphere. However, measurements show the spots to have

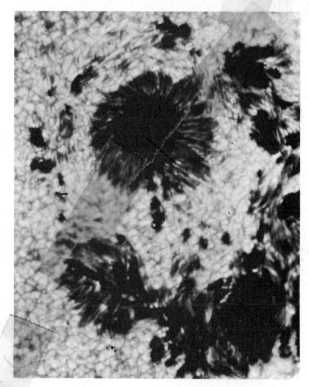

Perkin-Elmer Corporation

Fig. 27-2. This remarkably detailed photograph of the mottled appearance of the sun's photosphere was taken with a special 12-inch telescope from an unmanned balloon at a height of over 80,000 feet.

Fig. 27-3. This solar prominence, extending 205,000 miles above the surface of the sun, was photographed on July 2, 1957.

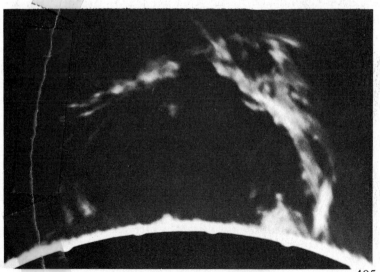

Mount Wilson and Palomar Observatories

405

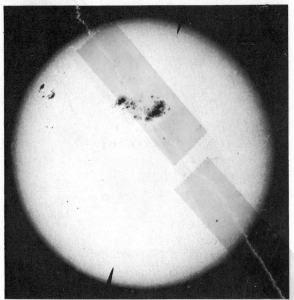

Mount Wilson and Palomar Observatories

Fig. 27-4. The large sunspot group of the upper photo is shown greatly enlarged in the lower photo. In estimating the true size of these spots, remember that the sun's diameter is 864,000 miles.

a temperature of about 4,000°C. This is cooler than the photosphere's 5,500°C, but it is very hot nevertheless. (See Fig. 27-4.)

Astronomers think that sunspots may be storms in the lower atmosphere of the sun. Like storms on the earth, sunspots are temporary features that form from a previously clear solar "sky," and then either disappear shortly or grow

larger. Those that grow larger usually form in groups that last for weeks or even months. The spots always move regularly across the disk of the sun from its eastern edge to its western edge. It was this movement that first revealed the rotation of the sun on its axis. Unlike the solid earth, the gaseous sun rotates more rapidly near its equator than near its poles. At its equator the period of rotation is about 25 days. Near its poles its period is 33 days or more.

Most sunspots are found in latitudes 5° to 30° north or south of the solar equator. They are never found close to the sun's poles. The *number* of spots is continually changing, reaching a maximum approximately every 11 years. The cause of this cycle is unknown. Sunspots have strong magnetic fields that may be related to their origin.

5. Solar Flares, Magnetic Storms, and Auroras

Large sunspot groups that are still growing are likely to be accompanied by occasional spectacular **solar flares.** These flares seem to be great masses of glowing gas erupting violently into the photosphere in the areas close to sunspots. Despite their intense brightness, the flares are hardly noticeable on the solar surface directly, but they are conspicuously bright in the hydrogen-light photographs taken by the spectroheliograph. Small flares may last only a few minutes. Large flares may exist for more than an hour and rise to a height of 30,000 miles. A solar flare produces remarkable effects on the earth. Its intense visible light and ultraviolet radiations travel at the speed of light to arrive at the earth's atmosphere simultaneously about 8 minutes after eruption of the flare. The visible light enables the flare to be seen. The ultraviolet radiations so disturb the ionized layers of our upper atmosphere that radio communications are badly disrupted. The flares also project high-speed atomic particles into the sun's corona, and their effect is to generate radio waves which produce continuous static in radio sets on the earth for from 10 to 20 minutes.

Many of the particles projected into the corona continue to the earth. Some travel at about one-sixth the speed of light and reach our ionosphere in less than an hour, continuing the disruption of radio communications begun by the ultraviolet waves. Slower particles travel at about 1,000 miles a second and take about 26 hours to reach the earth. Their effects are to produce **magnetic storms** and **auroras.** The magnetic storms are disturbances of the earth's magnetic field which deflect the magnetic compass from its normal readings, and may interfere with telegraph and long-distance telephone communication. The **aurora borealis** and **aurora australis** (the auroras near the northern and southern polar regions respectively) are the spectacular shimmering displays of "lights" seen in the nighttime sky, especially in high latitudes. They are believed to be caused by radiations resulting from the union of the solar protons and electrons with the ions of oxygen, ions of nitrogen, and the electrons of our upper atmosphere.

We now know from observations by space probes that the sun is continuously emitting a thin stream of protons (positively charged hydrogen nuclei) that move into space in all directions, passing the earth at a speed of nearly a million miles an hour and distorting its distant magnetic field. Scientists have named this stream of particles the **solar wind.** It is harmless to humans, but may help to explain some of the phenomena we observe in our atmosphere. It may also help to explain why the tail of a comet always points away from the sun.

6. Source of the Sun's Energy: Fusion

In describing the life story of a star in the preceding chapter, the fusion of hydrogen into helium was given as the source of a star's energy.

How does this fusion reaction take place? Why does it provide energy?

Astronomers have long wondered about the source of the energy of our sun and the other stars. Early astronomers may have thought, as some people do today, that the sun's energy came from the combustion of gases. Others thought that the impact of meteors might provide its energy. And in 1854 the physicist Helmholtz suggested that the sun's energy might come from continual contraction. All of these theories, however, failed to account for either the tremendous rate at which the sun radiates energy, or for its continuous production in the 5 or 6 billions of years we now believe to be the age of the sun.

Albert Einstein provided the key to the answer in 1905 with his famous $E = mc^2$ equation, which stated that **matter could be converted into energy.**

Calculations showed that the amounts of energy that would be obtained by the **nuclear reactions** predicted by Einstein's equation were vastly greater than the energy released by ordinary chemical reactions such as those which take place in the explosion of TNT. Then in the early 1940's scientists learned how to split the nuclei of uranium atoms and release nuclear energy, demonstrating the truth of Einstein's equation in the awesome light of the first atomic bombs. Not long afterward, scientists showed that far greater release of energy could be brought about in the thermonuclear or hydrogen bomb, where matter is converted into energy through the fusion of hydrogen nuclei into helium nuclei at temperatures in the millions of degrees.

Four hydrogen nuclei weigh about 4.030 units of atomic weight. One helium nucleus weighs about 4.003 units. Thus when a helium nucleus is formed from four hydrogen nuclei, the difference in mass is converted into energy. How much energy? Calculations show that the total conversion of one pound of matter would release enough energy to raise a weight of more than 3 billion tons a mile above the earth's surface. Astronomers believe that about 4 million tons of matter are being converted into energy in the sun every second, as 564 million tons of hydrogen fuse into 560 million tons of helium. How long can the sun keep this up? The mass of the sun is so great that it can continue to provide energy at this rate for another 5 billion years.

In 1938 physicist Hans A. Bethe of Cornell University suggested two possible processes for the hydrogen-to-helium reaction. In the **carbon cycle** carbon atoms "help" the hydrogen nuclei to fuse and form helium nuclei. In the **proton-proton reaction** hydrogen nuclei unite to form *heavy hydrogen* nuclei, which fuse to form helium nuclei. The proton-proton reaction probably takes place at the centers of "cooler" stars like our sun. The carbon cycle is believed to occur mainly in the interiors of the much hotter blue-white stars.

THE PLANETS

7. The Solar System

The sun's family is known as the **solar system.** It includes a multitude of objects ranging in size from tiny sandlike grains to gigantic spheres many thousands of miles in diameter. In the sun's family there are nine planets, 32 satellites, thousands of asteroids, millions of meteors, and numerous comets. These bodies travel around the sun at high speeds in paths which are known as **orbits,** located at distances that range from millions of miles to billions of miles. (See Fig. 27-5.)

8. Recognizing a Planet

How do we recognize members of the solar family? Our sun is unmistakable. So is our moon. Meteors are familiar to us as "shooting stars." Comets are seen rather rarely, but almost all of us have seen pictures that would help us identify a comet if we saw one. Five planets can easily be seen with the naked eye, but the asteroids and the most distant planets can be seen only through telescopes.

To the naked eye planets look very much like stars, but several visible differences enable us to tell them apart. First, since planets are so very much closer to the earth than the stars are, their motion around the sun is plainly noticeable as a shifting of their positions in the sky. As the ancient astronomers observed, the planets "wander" among the constellations, while true stars

Fig. 27-5. A diagram of our solar system.

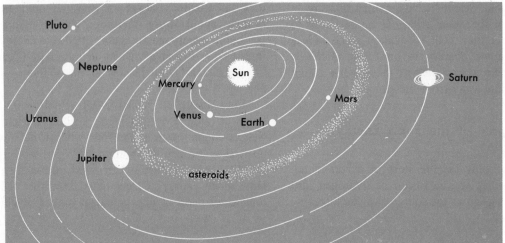

always keep the same formations. Again, because stars are so very far away, the telescope can only make them look brighter but not larger. Most planets, on the other hand, are near enough to the earth to be magnified by the telescope into bright circles rather than mere bright pinpoints of light. On these circles, which the astronomer calls visible disks, details of the surfaces of the planets may be seen. A third difference between stars and planets is that stars always twinkle, while planets shine steadily except when they are close to the horizon. (Twinkling is explained in Chapter 40, Topic 4.)

9. Classifying the Planets

In order of increasing distance from the sun, the planets are Mercury, Venus, Earth, Mars, Jupiter, Saturn, Uranus, Neptune, and Pluto. Between Mars and Jupiter are the **asteroids** or **minor planets.**

Scientists classify the planets in a number of different ways. *Inferior planets* are those nearer to the sun than the earth, and *superior planets* are those farther from the sun than the earth. If the asteroids are used as a "dividing line," then Mercury, Venus, Earth, and Mars are the *inner planets,* and the other five are the *outer planets.* If size is to be used as a basis for grouping, then Mercury, Venus, Earth, Mars, and Pluto are called *terrestrial planets,* whereas Jupiter, Saturn, Uranus, and Neptune are *major planets.*

10. What Is an Ellipse?

A circle is a line on which every point is at the same distance from another point called its center. An **ellipse** is a line drawn with respect to two points called its *foci* (singular: *focus*). For any point on the ellipse, the *sum of its distances from the two foci* is the same as such sum for any other point on the ellipse. An ellipse can be drawn in the following way. Suppose we want to construct an ellipse whose

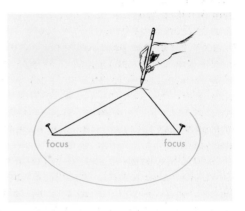

Fig. 27-6. This diagram illustrates the construction of an ellipse as described in Topic 10.

long diameter is 6 inches. Tie together two ends of a string to make a loop 8 inches long. Mark the two foci by placing thumb tacks 2 inches apart on a piece of cardboard. Loop the string around the tacks, and then pull the string tight with a pencil held vertically inside the loop. Continuing to hold the string *tight* and the pencil point against the paper, move the pencil completely around the two foci until a closed curve is completed. For every point on this curve, the sum of the distances from the two foci is equal to the length of the string minus the distance between the foci. (See Fig. 27-6.)

If the foci are placed farther apart, a "flatter" or more *eccentric* (off center) ellipse will be formed. If the foci are closer together, the ellipse will be more nearly circular. In fact, when the two foci meet, the ellipse becomes a circle.

11. How the Planets Move: Kepler's Laws

Copernicus published his theory of the motions of the planets around the sun in 1543. He believed that the planets revolved around the sun in circular orbits or in combinations of circles. In the latter part of the same century

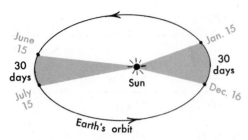

Fig. 27-7. The Law of Equal Areas. The area swept over by the earth's radius vector in a given time is the same in any part of the orbit. This means that the earth revolves faster near the sun and slower farther away.

the Danish astronomer Tycho Brahe made many observations of the planets which did not quite fit Copernicus' theory, but Brahe was unable to explain why. In 1609, eight years after Brahe's death, Brahe's former assistant Johannes Kepler published his first and second **laws of planetary motion,** based on Brahe's observations. These laws correctly described the movements of the planets as follows: **(1) The orbit of each planet is an ellipse in which the sun is at one of the two foci. (2) Each planet revolves so that a line from the planet to the sun** (called the "radius vector") **sweeps over equal areas in equal times.** This is known as the Law of Equal Areas. (See Fig. 27-7.)

Kepler's first law means that the distance between a planet and the sun is continually changing, increasing during half of each orbit and decreasing in the other half. Kepler's second law means that each planet's speed of revolution around the sun is also changing continually, for in order for the *radius vector* to cover equal areas in equal time, the planet must move faster when it is nearer the sun, and more slowly when it is farther away.

After publishing his first two laws of planetary motion, Kepler still puzzled over the possible relationships among the rates at which the different planets revolved around the sun. In 1618 he published the answer to this problem in his *third* law of planetary motion. This

law is also known as the Harmonic Law. It states that the **squares of the periods of revolution of any two planets are in the same ratio as the cubes of their average distances from the sun.**

This can be stated in the formula

$$\frac{P_1{}^2}{P_2{}^2} = \frac{D_1{}^3}{D_2{}^3}$$

where P_1 and P_2 are the periods of revolution of any two planets, and D_1 and D_2 are the average distances of the same planets from the sun. To illustrate this law, let us find the period of the planet Jupiter, if we know its distance from the sun. We shall use approximate numbers.

Let $P_2 =$ the earth's period of revolution $= 1$ year

Then $D_2 =$ the earth's distance from the sun $= 1$ A.U. (92,900,000 miles $= 1$ astronomical unit $= 1$ A.U.)

Let $P_1 =$ Jupiter's period of revolution

Then $D_1 =$ Jupiter's distance from sun $=$ about 5.2 A.U.

Then $\dfrac{P_1{}^2}{1^2} = \dfrac{(5.2)^3}{1^3}$

$P_1{}^2 = 140$ (approx.) $P = 12$ years (approx.)

Using Kepler's third law, we find that Jupiter's period of revolution is about 12 earth years. The farther a planet is from the sun, the longer is its period of revolution. This is not only because its orbit is larger, but also because it moves more slowly than do nearer planets. The average speed of the earth in its orbit is about 18.5 miles a second. Mercury, nearest to the sun, has an average speed of about 30 miles a second. Jupiter's average speed is about 8 miles a second. Pluto, farthest from the sun, moves at only 3 miles a second.

12. Orbits of the Planets

As Kepler stated, the orbit of each planet is an ellipse in which the sun is at one focus. At one end of each orbit, then, there will be

STATISTICS OF THE PLANETS

Name	Average Distance in Miles from Sun	Average Diameter in Miles	Period of Revolution	Period of Rotation	Number of Natural Satellites
Mercury	36 million	2,950	88 days	55 days	0
Venus	67 million	7,600	225 days	243 days	0
Earth	93 million	7,913	365¼ days	23h. 56 m.	1
Mars	142 million	4,212	687 days	24h. 37m.	2
Jupiter	486 million	89,000	12 years	9h. 50m.	12 16
Saturn	892 million	75,100	29½ years	10h. 14m.	10 23
Uranus	1,790 million	29,400	84 years	10h. 45m.	5
Neptune	2,810 million	28,000	165 years	15h. 48m.	2
Pluto	3,780 million	3,700	248 years	6.4 days	?

a point at which the planet is nearest to the sun. This point is called its **perihelion** (peri = near, helion = sun). At the opposite end of the orbit, the planet is farthest from the sun. This point is called its **aphelion.** Although the orbits of the planets are ellipses, all but those of Mercury and Pluto are nearly circular. Pluto's orbit is so eccentric that at aphelion it is almost twice as far away as at perihelion. Mercury, the planet nearest the sun, has an average distance of about 36 million miles; Pluto, farthest planet, is at an average distance of 3,670 million miles—just about one hundred times as far as Mercury. From Pluto the sun would look no larger than does a star in our sky. (See Fig. 27-8.)

All the planets revolve in their orbits *from west to east.* Except for Mercury and Pluto,

the orbits lie in almost the same plane as the *plane of the ecliptic* (the plane in which the earth travels around the sun). Mercury's orbit is inclined about 7° to this plane; Pluto's orbit is inclined 17°.

The time a planet takes to travel once around its orbit is its **period of revolution.** Pluto's period is 248 of our years. Mercury's period is only 88 days, which means that it circles the sun about a thousand times while Pluto goes around just once. (See the table on this page.)

13. Shape, Size, Density, Rotation

All of the planets are roughly spherical in shape, and all but Venus and Uranus rotate

Fig. 27-8. This diagram gives a rough approximation of the relative distances of the planets from the sun.

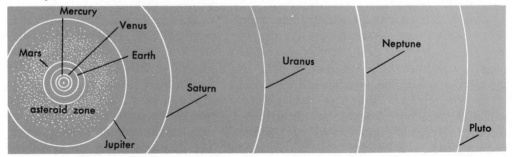

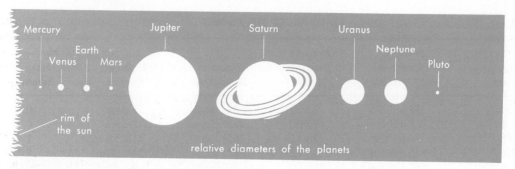

Fig. 27-9. How the planets compare in size with one another and the sun.

on their axes (plural for axis) from west to east. The rotation tends to make a planet bulge at its equator and flatten at its poles, forming a shape called an **oblate spheroid.** The amount of "oblateness" depends on the planet's speed of rotation, its size, and its density. The more oblate a planet, the larger is the difference between a diameter through the equator and the diameter through the poles. Our table of planetary statistics gives the approximate *average diameters* of the planets, ranging from little Mercury's 3,000 miles to giant Jupiter's 87,000 miles. (See Fig. 27-9.)

The planets present a great range in density. The minor planets apparently consist largely of rock, and have relatively high densities. The four major planets are apparently much more gaseous, and their densities are much lower. Mercury and Earth lead the planets in density, being about 5.5 times as heavy as water. The approximate densities of the others are Venus, 5; Mars, 4; Neptune, 2.3; Uranus, 1.6; Jupiter, 1.3; Saturn, 0.7.

Now to return to the oblateness of the planets. Which ones bulge most? Jupiter and Saturn are not only the two largest planets, but they are also the least dense. If they also rotate rapidly, they should bulge the most. A glance at the table shows us that Jupiter and Saturn also rotate most rapidly on their axes. Actual observation of these two planets shows them to be indeed highly oblate, with Saturn more oblate because of its lower density.

Note in the table that Mars and Earth have nearly the same rotation period: that all four major planets rotate more rapidly than the other planets; and that Mercury and Venus rotate very slowly. Mercury rotates only once in 59 days. Venus takes 243 days for one rotation.

14. Studying a Planet from Afar

Life, as we know it on the earth, depends on the presence in our atmosphere of water vapor, oxygen, and carbon dioxide. It also depends on favorable temperatures. Can life exist on other planets? The answer to this question must rest to a large extent on the nature of their atmospheres and their weather. Astronomers study the atmosphere and weather of a distant planet in a variety of ways. Optical telescopes may show clouds and possible evidence of winds and storms. Radio telescopes, radiometers, and photometers measure the intensity of a planet's reflected radiations, giving information about its temperature and its surface. The spectroscope analyzes its reflected light to give us clues as to the composition and pressure of its atmosphere. Observations with both optical and radio telescopes help us to determine a planet's period of rotation, from which we get the length of its day and night. From its period of revolution we can calculate the length of its seasons. From its distance from the sun we can calculate the amount of solar energy it receives. The astronomer puts all available information together to form a picture of the atmosphere and weather of a distant planet.

In recent years scientists have learned a good deal about the planets from instruments carried high above the earth's atmosphere by balloons, and especially from the planetary probes sent to Venus and Mars. Venus and Mars are our nearest planetary neighbors, and the ones we think most likely to contain some form of life.

15. The Atmospheres of the Planets

The following paragraphs will describe our present knowledge of the atmospheres and weather of the distant planets.

Mercury is difficult to observe through a telescope because it is small, relatively far off, and so close in the sky to the sun that it can be seen only briefly at sunrise or sunset. Scientists think its surface may resemble the moon's, but evidence is lacking. Until recently Mercury was believed to have no atmosphere, because its gravity was too weak to hold gas molecules to its surface. But new observations indicate a very thin atmosphere that may be composed entirely of carbon dioxide.

Until recently it was also believed that Mercury's periods of rotation and revolution were equal. This meant that one side always faced the sun and might be hot enough to melt lead, while the other side was always in darkness and as cold as −400°F. We know now that Mercury does turn both sides to the sun, but so slowly that its day and night are still very long. Measurements indicate the expected maximum temperature of about 800°F at its sunny surface. The dark side, however, is not nearly as cold as expected, with an astonishing maximum of about 60°F. To explain this, there must be some way in which heat is carried from the daytime side to the nighttime side.

Venus comes closer to the earth than any other planet. At its nearest, it is only 26 million miles away. Even so, its cloud cover is so complete that nothing can be seen of its surface even with our best telescopes. Through the use of radar waves, however, astronomers have learned that much of the surface of Venus is pitted by huge shallow craters.

Most of our current information about the atmosphere of Venus has come to us from radar studies and space probes. In 1962 the American space probe Mariner II flew within 22,000 miles of Venus, and in 1967 Marine V flew within 2,500 miles of Venus. Also in 1967 and 1969, Russian scientists parachuted instrumented capsules onto the surface of Venus. All of these devices radioed signals to the earth giving the results of their observations of the Venusian atmosphere.

We presently believe that the atmosphere of Venus may be as much as 100 times as dense as ours! Its "air" seems to be about 93% carbon dioxide, less than 7% nitrogen, and about 1% water vapor. Its clouds are probably frozen carbon dioxide (dry ice).

Venus' slow rotation gives it a day as long as 100 days on earth, and a night equally long. The average temperature of its entire surface is estimated to be about 800°F—hot enough to melt lead. During its long exposure to the sun, temperatures on the daytime side may go as high as 1100°F. Strangely, though, the temperatures go no lower than 400°F even through the long night on the dark side of Venus. One explanation offered by scientists is that large amounts of heat are carried regularly from the sunny side to the dark side by strong winds. Recent evidence seems to indicate that the upper atmosphere of Venus rotates around the planet once every four days.

Mars, unlike Venus, showed distinct surface features in photos taken by great telescopes. Among these were the famous white polar caps that appear in Mars' winter and disappear in its summer. Another was the set of apparent markings called "canals" that were thought to be made by "intelligent creatures." Other features included extensive bright reddish-orange areas and gray areas. Again, seasonal lightening and darkening of these areas was thought by some astronomers to mean that vegetation grew on Mars.

But beginning in 1965, our knowledge of the Martian surface increased dramatically. On July 14, 1965, the "fly-by" planetary probe *Mariner 4* came within 6,000 miles of Mars after a journey of 7½ months and 325 million miles. *Mariner 4* took 22 "closeup" photos of Mars. Two more space probes, *Mariner 6* and *Mariner 7,* came even closer to Mars in 1969 and transmitted nearly 200 more photos back to Earth. Then on November 13, 1971, the space probe

Fig. 27-10. The change of seasons on Mars is seen in the three photos of spring on the left, and the three photos of summer on the right. The dates given are "Mars dates."
Lowell Observatory

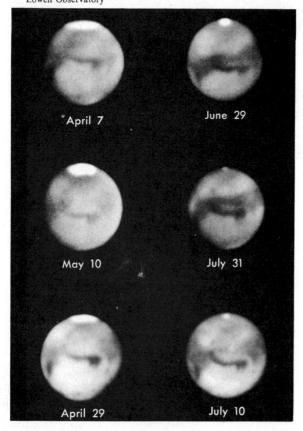

Mariner 9 reached Mars, *went into orbit around it,* and began a series of observations that continued for nearly a year. These observations included more than 7,000 photos covering all of the Martian surface: its two tiny moons; the structure, pressure, and composition of its atmosphere; the temperature and composition of its surface.

When the observations of the *Mariner* space probes are studied, we get a picture of Mars very different from that conceived by early astronomers. We know that the surface of Mars, like that of our moon, is marked by many craters and extensive lava flows. These are signs that its interior is still "alive" enough to produce volcanic activity. No "canals" are found, but many features resembling meandering river beds appear on the photographs, suggesting that water once existed on Mars. But the most spectacular features revealed by the photographs are a Grand Canyon and volcanic mountains that dwarf anything found on Earth. The Grand Canyon runs along Mars' equator. It is about 2,300 miles long, up to 150 miles wide, and nearly 4 miles deep. But unlike our own river-eroded Grand Canyon, it is believed to have formed mainly by crustal movement. The largest volcanic mountain, named Nix Olympica, is 355 miles in diameter and 15 miles high. At its summit is a caldera 40 miles across.

A thick layer of rock dust, probably formed by billions of years of meteorite bombardment, covers the Martian surface. Strong winds cause violent dust storms that shift large quantities of the rock dust from place to place on the surface. This shifting dust may cause the changes in color once thought to indicate the presence of vegetation.

The atmosphere of Mars is only one-hundredth as dense as ours. More than half of it seems to be carbon dioxide. The remainder is believed to be nitrogen or argon, with little or no oxygen. Water vapor is present, but only about one-thousandth as much as in our atmosphere. Mars has no magnetic field.

The day on Mars is only slightly longer than ours. Its seasons are similar to ours but about twice as long. Recent observations indicate an *average* surface temperature for the whole planet of about −58°F, with summers much warmer and winters much colder than this average. In summer at Mars' equator, it may be as warm as 68°F, so a "growing season" is a possibility. In the northern hemisphere's winter, a white polar cap covers almost the entire hemisphere from the north pole to the equator. In spring and summer this disappears almost completely, and as it disappears the surface exposed beneath it appears to darken in color. Scientists believe that the polar caps consist of a thin layer of ice that disappears in summer by evaporation without melting. The ice is either frozen carbon dioxide, frozen water, or both. When summer comes to the northern hemisphere, it is winter in the south, and a polar cap forms at the south pole. (See Fig. 27-10.)

Jupiter, like Venus, is surrounded by thick cloud layers that hide its surface. Above the clouds the atmosphere consists chiefly of hydrogen and helium, plus some poisonous methane and ammonia. The temperature of the clouds seems to be about −210°F or lower. This temperature is cold enough to freeze ammonia, so the clouds are believed to consist of ammonia crystals. Seen through a telescope, Jupiter's disk is covered by a series of alternating light and dark bands running parallel to its equator. A mysterious oval-shaped area 30,000 miles long and reddish in color seems to float in Jupiter's atmosphere. It is known as the Great Red Spot.

Jupiter, largest of the planets, has a mass more than twice as great as all the other planets together. Beneath its atmosphere, Jupiter is thought to be nearly all solid and metallic hydrogen.

On December 3, 1973, the space probe *Pioneer 10* marked another milestone in space history when it flew by Jupiter only 81,000 miles from its surface at a speed of 83,000 miles an hour. It had covered 620 million miles from the

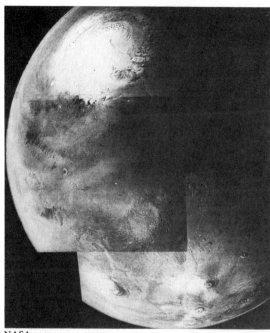

NASA

Fig. 27-11. Three photos by Mariner 9 *8,500 miles above Mars: polar cap area (top left); huge volcanic mountains (bottom); long canyon (bottom right).*

time of its launching 21 months earlier. Continuing "outward," *Pioneer 10* will escape from the solar system in 1987 and head toward the constellation Taurus. It carries a plaque intended to describe the earth's location and its inhabi-

Fig. 27-12. Pioneer *photo of Jupiter shows its belts, its Great Red Spot, and shadow of its moon (center).*

NASA

tants—should it ever reach another inhabited planet! Observations of *Pioneer 10's* television cameras and other instruments are still being studied. Among *Pioneer*'s findings are that Jupiter has a strange disk-shaped magnetic field eight times as strong at its surface as the earth's; that at least two of its larger satellites, Io and Callisto, have atmospheres, but the atmospheres are millions of times as thin as the earth's; that Jupiter radiates 2½ times as much heat as it receives from the sun; that it is surrounded by an intense radiation field.

Saturn's atmosphere strongly resembles that of Jupiter, but it contains less ammonia. This is believed to be due to Saturn's lower temperature of about −270°F, which freezes most of the ammonia out of the atmosphere. Like Jupiter, Saturn has a banded cloudy surface, is extremely oblate, and is believed to have a small dense center surrounded by a thick atmosphere in which some of the gases are frozen solid.

Uranus and **Neptune** are so distant from the sun that they are even colder than Saturn. The spectrum shows that their atmospheres contain hydrogen and methane, and they probably resemble Saturn and Jupiter in having small solid cores of frozen gases. **Pluto** is so far off and so tiny that almost nothing can be learned of its surface.

16. Asteroids: Minor Planets

The **asteroids** were unknown until 1801. For a long time, however, astronomers had felt that the space between Mars and Jupiter was too large not to be occupied by a planet. Then on January 1, 1801, the Italian astronomer Piazzi discovered the "planet" Ceres, which soon turned out to be merely the largest of many asteroids, or minor planets. Since Piazzi's discovery, astronomers have seen or photographed in telescopes more than 30,000 asteroids, and have calculated the orbits of about 1,600. The asteroids look like faint stars, hence the name

asteroid, which means *starlike*. They are also called *planetoids* (planetlike). They appear to be solid rocklike masses, only two of which are spherical in shape. These two, the largest of the asteroids, are Ceres, with a diameter of 480 miles, and Pallas, with a diameter of 300 miles. All the rest have irregular shapes, as is indicated by the great variation in the amount of sunlight they reflect as they rotate on their axes. The smallest known asteroids are about a mile long. There are probably many smaller ones.

All of the asteroids revolve around the sun in a counterclockwise direction, as the planets do. Most of their orbits are nearly circular, but a few are very eccentric and greatly inclined to the plane of the ecliptic. Most of the orbits lie between Mars and Jupiter, but there are exceptions.

How did the asteroids originate? According to one hypothesis this region of space originally held perhaps four or more spherical asteroids about as large as Ceres and Pallas. At least two of these are supposed to have collided and shattered into thousands of irregular fragments

17. Natural Satellites of the Planets

Until 1957, when Russia sent the first artificial satellite into orbit, it was unnecessary to say "natural" when referring to satellites like our moon. Satellites revolve around their parent planets, and in our solar system there are 32 natural satellites. The table on page 411 shows that except for Mercury, Venus, and probably Pluto, each of the planets has at least one satellite. Our earth's only satellite, the moon, is 2,160 miles in diameter, is about 240,000 miles from the earth, and revolves around it in 27⅓ days. How do other satellites compare with our moon?

Mars has two tiny satellites, Phobos and Delmos. Phobos, the larger and nearer one, is 17 miles long, 12 miles wide, and shaped like a lumpy, cratered potato. It is less than 4,000 miles from the surface of Mars, around which it races in about 8 hours— three times a day! Jupiter has 12 satellites, one of which was discovered as recently as 1951. Two of its satellites are nearly as large as our moon, and two are larger. Saturn has 10 satellites, one of which was discovered by French astronomers at the beginning of 1967. It is believed to be only 150 miles in diameter, and located just beyond the famous rings of Saturn. Saturn's largest satellite, Titan, is about as large as the planet Mercury. Like Io and Callisto, two of Jupiter's larger satellites, Titan has a very thin atmosphere probably containing methane gas. Three of Uranus' five satellites are nearly as large as our moon, and Neptune's Triton is larger than the moon.

Most of the natural satellites revolve from west to east, as the planets and asteroids do. The exceptions include Jupiter's four outermost satellites, Saturn's outermost satellite, and Neptune's Triton.

Saturn is unique in the possession of the rings which make it one of the most beautiful of all telescopic sights. There are four rings, one inside the other, all in the plane of its equator. (See Fig. 27-13.) The very faint innermost ring was discovered in 1969. The next ring, which is nearly as dark, is called the *crape ring*. It comes within about 8,000 miles of Saturn's surface. Then comes the *bright ring*. The *outer ring* is narrower and not as bright as the *bright ring,* from which it is separated by a 3,000-mile gap named the *Cassini division* after the Italian astronomer who discovered it in 1675. The outer ring reaches to nearly 50,000 miles from the surface of Saturn.

For many years astronomers thought that the rings consisted of tiny particles—"snowballs" of ice, frozen gases, and bits of rock. But recent radar studies suggest that at least some of the particles are rocks 3 feet or more in diameter. These particles may be the fragments of a satel-

Mount Wilson and Palomar
Observatories

Fig. 27-13. Saturn and its rings.

lite that was torn to bits when it came too close to the planet. Another hypothesis, however, suggests that the particles are simply remnants of the original nebula from which Saturn consolidated. Like the planets, the rings shine by reflecting sunlight. The thickness of the rings is estimated to be no more than 10 miles, and American astronomer Kuiper thinks that it is only about *5 inches.*

18. Comets

Comets are generally regarded as among the most spectacular of heavenly objects, yet most people have never seen a comet except in photographs. Most comets can be seen only through telescopes. A comet visible to the naked eye is not too common; a spectacular comet is rare.

The photograph of a comet shows a glowing *head* and a long luminous *tail*. (See Fig. 27-14.) The head appears to have a bright small *nucleus* surrounded by a hazy *coma*. According to astronomer F. L. Whipple, the nucleus of a comet is a loose spongy mass of icy material only about

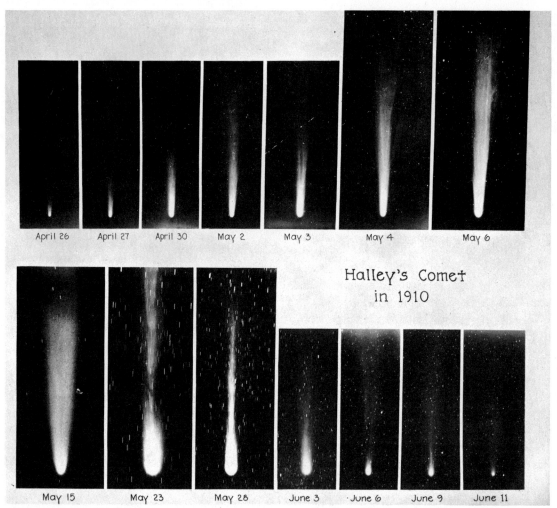

April 26 April 27 April 30 May 2 May 3 May 4 May 6

Halley's Comet
in 1910

May 15 May 23 May 28 June 3 June 6 June 9 June 11

Mount Wilson and Palomar Observatories

Fig. 27-14. Halley's comet in its most recent visit to the earth in 1910. Notice how the tail changed in length as it approached the sun and then receded from it.

a mile in diameter. Billions of tiny particles of rock are frozen into the "ice," which is largely frozen water, ammonia, and methane. Ordinarily a comet has no tail, and its head shines by reflected sunlight. However, when a comet comes close to the sun, some of the ice evaporates with explosive violence to form a broadening tail of gas and meteoric rock particles that may stretch millions of miles into space. The tail always points away from the sun because the pressure of the solar wind repels the gases. The gases of the tail glow—like the gases in a neon tube—as a result of the energy absorbed from the sun's radiations. (See Fig. 27-15.)

Most comets have steeply inclined and highly eccentric orbits in which they come very close to the sun at *perihelion* and then go very far away at *aphelion*. Many comets have been seen

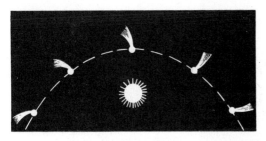

Fig. 27-15. The tail of a comet always points away from the sun.

only once, and appear to have *nearly parabolic* orbits that may not return them to the sun for thousands of years. Others have definite *elliptical* orbits with periods ranging from 3.3 years (Encke's comet) to hundreds of years. These comets may go from the vicinity of the sun to beyond Pluto, but they are certain to return to the sun. The first of these **periodic comets** to be identified was the famous Halley's comet, named after Edmund Halley, Astronomer Royal of England from 1721 to 1742. Halley correctly predicted its appearance in the skies in 1758, after a study of astronomical records convinced him that three bright comets observed in 1531, 1607, and 1682 were really the same comet returning to the sun about every 76 years. Halley's comet appeared again in 1835 and 1910, and should reappear in 1986. Halley's comet revolves from east to west, as do many of the very distant comets, but most periodic

comets revolve from west to east. (See Fig. 27-16.)

Nowadays a comet is named by the year of its discovery and also after its discoverer. Hundreds of comets have been named, catalogued, and their orbits calculated. Bright comets easily visible to the unaided eye are not too common a sight, but in 1957 there were two. The first was Comet Arend-Roland, brightest since Halley's comet in 1910. The second was Comet Mrkos. In 1973 Comet Kohoutek was visible.

19. Meteors and Meteoroids

Meteors or **meteoroids** are solid objects, considerably smaller than asteroids, moving in interplanetary space. They are pieces of stony or metallic rock, most of which are about the size of sand grains, though some are as large as gigantic boulders. The meteors are widely scattered throughout the solar system, some traveling alone and others revolving around the sun in great **meteor swarms** that include billions of particles.

Meteors travel at speeds up to 26 miles a second. The earth revolves around the sun at a speed of 18½ miles per second. Thus, meteors that collide head-on with the earth may plunge to the earth's surface at speeds up to 44½ miles a second (26 + 18½). Even those that overtake the earth from behind may strike the surface at

Fig. 27-16. The eccentric orbit of Halley's comet extends from a point near the sun to far beyond the orbit of Neptune. It will return to our sky in 1986.

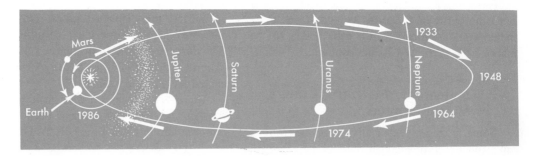

Fig. 27-17. Ahnigito, the nickel-iron meteorite found at Cape York, Greenland, by Admiral Peary in 1895, is 11 feet long, 5 feet wide, 7 feet high, and weighs about 34 tons.

more than 7 miles a second (26 — 18½). In its rapid plunge through the atmosphere a meteor is intensely heated by friction with air molecules. Usually at about 60 miles above the surface of the earth the meteor becomes white hot, and for about a second it leaves a brilliant *trail* of light in its wake as it burns up or vaporizes in the upper atmosphere. **Fireballs** are meteors whose light is unusually large and bright. These may form *dust trains* that remain visible for many minutes after the fireball has vanished. (Space scientists use the term *meteoroid* for rock fragments traveling in space and the term *meteor* for the light that is produced when a meteoroid streaks through our atmosphere.)

It is estimated that nearly 100 million meteors enter the earth's atmosphere every day. Most of these are tiny, and they burn up or vaporize in the atmosphere. The steady "rain" onto the earth of the dust and gas from these meteors adds at least a few tons a day to the mass of the earth and its atmosphere.

20. Meteorites; Meteorite Craters; Meteor Showers

Some meteors, especially large ones, may not vaporize completely in their plunge through the atmosphere. The part that "survives" to reach the earth's surface is called a **meteorite.** Very small meteorites less than one twenty-fifth of an inch in diameter are called **micrometeorites.** (Particles of this same size in space are called *micrometeors* or *micrometeoroids.*)

Meteorites are of two main types. The **stony meteorites** or **stones** strongly resemble our gray-black crystalline igneous rocks. The largest known stone weighs more than a ton. It landed in Furnas County, Nebraska, in 1948, and is now on display at the Institute of Meteoritics of the University of New Mexico. **Iron meteorites** or **irons** are usually black on the outside and silvery beneath. They consist largely of iron alloyed with nickel, and they are much heavier than the stones. One of the largest in the world is the 34-ton meteorite found in Greenland by Admiral Peary in 1895. This and many other meteorites are displayed in the Hayden Planetarium in New York City. (See Fig. 27-17.) The largest known iron still lies buried in the ground where it fell in South Africa. Its estimated weight is 60 tons.

At a few places on the earth gigantic meteorites are believed to have blasted out deep meteorite craters when they crashed onto the surface. The Barringer Meteorite Crater (better known as Meteor Crater) in Arizona is almost a mile in diameter and nearly 600 feet deep. Most scientists believe it was made long ago by a meteorite weighing more than a million tons. When this meteorite smashed into the earth, its friction-heated surface exploded in a mighty burst of gases that blasted out a crater and sprayed the landscape for miles around with fragments of the shattered meteorite. (See Fig. 27-18.)

Where do meteors originate? Many "individual" meteors—especially the "giants"—are believed to form from collisions of asteroids. Meteor swarms, on the other hand, seem to be the streams of tiny rock particles formed in the tails of comets. The astronomer Whipple estimates that the nucleus of a comet loses 1/200th of its mass of ice and rock every time it passes near the sun.

Meteor showers occur when the earth crosses the orbit of a meteor swarm. Large numbers of meteors are seen on such nights, the "showers" usually being named after the constellation in the sky from whose direction they seem to come. Four of the best-known meteor showers are the *Perseids* (*per* seh ids), which occur every year about August 12; the *Orionids* (oh *ry* un ids), which occur about October 20; the *Taurids,* about November 10; and the *Geminids* (*jem* uh nids), about December 10.

Do meteoroids constitute a serious menace to spaceships? Apparently not. Spaceships have been struck by numerous micrometeoroids without being damaged, undoubtedly because of the tiny size of the particles. Larger meteoroids seem to be so rare as to make the probability of a damaging collision almost zero.

Have large meteorites struck the earth within relatively recent times? Apparently yes. In 1908 a spectacular meteor fall in the Tunguska River region of Central Siberia was followed by an explosion that destroyed a large area of forest and left the ground pitted by a series of craters, the largest about 150 feet across. Strangely enough, no meteorite fragments seem to have been found here. In 1947 a great meteor fall occurred in southeastern Siberia. Many small craters were formed, and many iron meteorites were recovered.

21. Evening and Morning Stars

Venus is nearer the sun than the earth is, so it can appear in our sky when we face in the general direction of the sun. During most of the daytime the sun is too bright to allow us to see Venus, especially if it is nearly in line with the sun. When Venus is to the left (east) of the sun, however, the sun sets before it, and Venus becomes clearly visible in the evening twilight of the western sky, where it is called the "evening star." Being brighter than any of the stars, it makes a beautiful sight, and is frequently

Fig. 27-18. Air view of the Barringer Meteorite Crater, better known as Meteor Crater, Arizona.

U.S. Air Force Photo

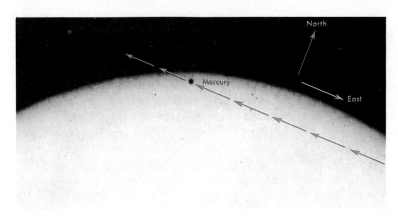

Fig. 27-19. A transit of Mercury. Mercury is seen as a small black dot as it passes across the face of the sun.

U.S. Navy Photo

thought by imaginative viewers to be a strange visitor from outer space or some other kind of "unidentified flying object." The orbit of Venus carries it far enough out from the sun to allow us to see it in the sky for as long as three hours after sunset, before it finally sets in the west. When Venus is to the right (west) of the sun, it rises in the eastern sky before the sun does, and is then a "morning star." Since Venus can never be on the night-time side of the earth, we can never see it in our sky in the hours close to midnight.

Mercury lies even closer to the sun than Venus, so it too is seen only as a morning or evening star. Mercury is smaller than Venus and not as bright; it moves much more rapidly in its smaller orbit and is much nearer the sun. As a result, Mercury is very difficult to see. Venus, on the other hand, is visible most of the year as either a morning or an evening star. On rare occasions either Mercury or Venus may pass directly between the earth and the face of the sun, looking like a dark spot on the solar disk. These crossings are called **transits.** (See Fig. 27-19.)

When Mars, Jupiter, and Saturn are close to the sun in the sky, they also are seen as morning or evening stars. But since these planets have orbits beyond the earth's, they appear in our nighttime sky during a large part of the year.

22. Planets in the Sky

The planets are easily identified. Venus is the brightest "star" in the heavens. It is seen only in the western sky in the evening or in the eastern sky in the early morning. Through a telescope it shows phases like those of the moon, a result of its position between us and the sun. It is brightest at its crescent phase, since it is then nearest to the earth.

Mercury, like Venus, can be seen only as a morning or an evening star, very close to the sun, and about as bright as a first-magnitude star. Venus has a silvery glow; Mercury is somewhat reddish in color. Mercury, like Venus, also shows phases.

Jupiter is next in brightness to Venus; it can often be seen in the nighttime sky long after Venus may have set. Its steady light is silvery in color. Through the telescope Jupiter's belts are seen. The telescope (or even good binoculars) also easily reveals the four largest of Jupiter's moons.

When Mars is close to the earth, it may be brighter than Jupiter. Ordinarily, it is about first-magnitude brightness and is distinctly red in color. The telescope shows many details of Mars' surface, such as its red "deserts" and its white polar caps.

Saturn, almost as large as Jupiter but much farther from both the sun and the earth, is about as bright as a first-magnitude star and is yellow in color. A telescope shows its remarkable rings.

23. Life on Other Planets?

Because of their extreme temperatures and their poisonous or nonexistent atmospheres, all of the planets except Venus and Mars are believed to be almost certainly devoid of life. What possibility is there that life exists on either Venus or Mars?

Most astronomers believe Venus to be a barren, lifeless desert. Its temperatures are fearfully hot, even on its nighttime side. Some scientists think its atmosphere may be filled with dust blown up from its deserts in wind storms. Even

so, we still know too little about Venus to be able to say that no form of life can exist there.

Do the conditions observed by space probes rule out any chance of life on Mars? Some scientists believe that primitive forms of life are still possibilities. Its polar caps may contain essential water. But its lack of oxygen, its thin atmosphere, and its generally low temperatures do not favor the existence of earthlike life. Scientists believe that the vegetation most likely to exist under these conditions is something related to the gray-green lichens that grow on rocks everywhere, and flourish especially in our arctic tundras. (See Chapter 7, Topic 3, and Chapter 42, Topic 19.) Perhaps the answer will be provided by the Russian and American space probes scheduled to land on Mars in 1974 and 1976.

TOPIC QUESTIONS

Each topic question refers to the topic of the same number within this chapter.

1. What does each of the following instruments do? (*a*) tower telescope, (*b*) spectroheliograph, (*c*) coronagraph, (*d*) pyroheliometer.

2. (*a*) Compare the sun's dimensions with those of the earth. (*b*) How hot is the sun?

3. Explain what each of the following is: photosphere, chromosphere, prominence, corona.

4. (*a*) Describe the appearance, size, and temperature of sunspots. (*b*) What do sunspots tell us about the sun's rotation? (*c*) Where are most sunspots located? What is their "cycle" of 11 years?___

5. (*a*) What is a solar flare? (*b*) How do solar flares disturb radio communications and cause static? (*c*) How do solar flares cause magnetic storms and auroras? (*d*) What is a magnetic storm? (*e*) How are auroras produced? (*f*) What is solar wind?

6. (*a*) How did Helmholtz try to explain the sun's production of energy? (*b*) How does Einstein's equation explain the sun's energy? (*c*) Explain simply why the fusion of hydrogen into helium provides energy. (*d*) What processes were suggested for the fusion reaction by Bethe?

7. What does the solar system include?

8. How can planets be distinguished from stars?

9. Explain how the planets are classified as (*a*) inferior and superior, (*b*) inner and outer, (*c*) terrestrial and major.

10. What is an ellipse? What determines how eccentric it is?

11. (*a*) What part was played by Copernicus, Brahe, and Kepler in explaining planetary motion? (*b*) State and explain Kepler's laws.

12. (a) How eccentric is Pluto's orbit? Explain. Define perihelion and aphelion. (b) Compare the distances of Mercury and Pluto from the sun. (c) In what direction do the planets revolve? In what plane? (d) What is the period of revolution? (e) Name the planets in order of distance from the sun.

13. (a) Which way do the planets rotate? (b) What is an oblate spheroid? (c) What is the range of planetary diameters? (d) How do the planets differ in density? (e) Why are Jupiter and Saturn most oblate?

14. Describe some of the ways in which scientists study the atmosphere and weather of a distant planet.

15. Describe the surface, weather, and atmosphere of (a) Mercury, (b) Venus, (c) Mars, (d) Jupiter.

16. (a) Describe the size, shape, and orbits of the asteroids. (b) How may they have originated?

17. (a) What is a satellite? (b) Which planets have no satellites? (c) Describe some of the interesting satellites of Mars, Jupiter, Saturn, and Neptune. (d) Describe Saturn's rings. How did they originate?

18. (a) Describe the appearance of a comet. (b) What is the head made of? (c) How is the tail formed? Why does it glow? (d) What kind of orbits do comets have? (e) What are periodic comets? (f) How are comets named?

19. (a) What are meteors? meteor swarms? (b) What is the speed of a meteor? What makes a meteor glow? (c) What is a fireball? a dust train? (d) Distinguish between meteor and meteoroid.

20. (a) What is a meteorite? a micrometeorite? a micrometeor? (b) Distinguish between stones and irons. (c) How is a meteorite crater formed? (d) Where do meteors originate? (e) What are meteor showers? Name some.

21. (a) Why can Mercury and Venus never be seen near midnight? (b) Why is Venus seen only as a morning or evening star? (c) What is a *transit?*

22. Explain how we can recognize Venus, Mercury, Jupiter, Saturn, and Mars.

23. (a) Discuss the possibility of life on Venus. (b) Discuss the possibility of life on Mars.

GENERAL QUESTIONS

1. Even planets twinkle when they are close to the horizon. Why?

2. Why are seasons on Mars almost twice as long as those on the earth?

3. Compare Mars' Phobos with our own moon in relative size, distance from its planet, and time of revolution.

4. Phobos revolves from west to east around Mars faster than Mars rotates on its axis from west to east. In what direction does Phobos rise and set?

5. As an evening star, Venus can be seen only in the west; as a morning star, it can be seen only in the east. Why?

6. Using the equation given in Chapter 26, Student Activities 1, determine the approximate focal length of the tower telescope mentioned in Topic 1 of this chapter.

7. Which is better for "focusing the sun's rays to a point," a long focus lens or a short focus lens? Explain your answer.

8. Perform the calculations necessary to arrive at the figures given in Topic 5, beginning of paragraph 2.

9. Vesta is the only asteroid ever visible with the unaided eye, yet Ceres is larger than Vesta. How is this explained?

10. Calculate the period of a planet that is four times as far from the sun as the earth is.

STUDENT ACTIVITIES

1. To illustrate Kepler's second law that a planet moves faster when it is nearer the sun: (a) Tie a small weight to a string. Swing it in a circle around your head with just enough velocity to keep it moving "in orbit" by itself for several circuits. (b) Shorten the string and repeat the experiment.

2. Vary the above experiment as follows:
   (a) Tie the string to a stick. Again, swing it around your head until the weight "orbits" by itself. (b) Now let the string wind up on the stick. Notice how the "orbiting" speed of the weight increases as its string shortens.

3. With the aid of weekly or monthly sky maps in such publications as *Science News Letter, Sky and Telescope,* or local newspapers, locate the planets currently visible. Observe their changes of position on successive nights. Notice their differences in appearance to the unaided eye and, if possible, observe them through a small telescope or good binoculars.

CHAPTER 28
Exploring Space

HOW DO YOU KNOW THAT . . . ?

The principle of jet propulsion is expressed in Sir Isaac Newton's Third Law of Motion: To every action, there is an equal and opposite reaction. A very simple illustration of jet propulsion can be shown with a balloon. Blow up a toy rubber balloon—the larger, the better. Pinch the neck. Now release the balloon and observe its behavior. What does it do? Explain what makes it behave this way.

To control the "flight" of the balloon, try this variation. Inflate a long narrow balloon and close the mouth. Suspend it from a stretched "clothesline" or wire by means of two paper clips, one at each end of the balloon. Each clip will have to be attached to a paper "collar" running around the balloon. Now open the mouth of the balloon. What happens? Why?

1. Birth of the Idea: Rockets to Explore Space

In 1903 a Russian mathematics teacher named Konstantin Ziolkovsky published an article in which he suggested that rockets be used for powering space ships. In 1919 Dr. Robert H. Goddard wrote of *A Method of Reaching Extreme Altitudes* by the use of rockets which might even reach the moon. In 1926 he launched the world's first liquid fuel rocket to a height of 184 feet.

In Germany the situation was somewhat different. In 1923 Professor Hermann Oberth published a book entitled *The Rocket into Interplanetary Space*. Oberth's followers organized the German Society for Space Travel and developed the V-2 rockets with which the Germans bombed England in World War II.

When World War II ended, intensive rocket research was continued in both the Soviet Union and the United States. In their plans for the International Geophysical Year of 1957–1958 both countries listed the launching of instrument-carrying artificial earth satellites. The Soviet Un-

ion opened the Space Age by launching *Sputnik I* into orbit around the earth on October 4, 1957. The United States followed suit with *Explorer I* on January 31, 1958. Since then many other launchings have taken place. Men have orbited the earth in "Skylabs" for as long as 84 days, and have worked in space outside their ships. Space vehicles have met and docked while circling the earth. Space "probes" have traveled to other planets. Moon probes have sent thousands of lunar photographs back to the earth, and robot exploration devices have made soft landings on the moon and have dug into its soil. The information provided by these lunar explorations was used to select landing spots for manned expeditions to the moon.

2. The Law of Gravitation

What principles are involved in man's newly found ability to "defy" the law of gravitation that had always forced objects thrown from the earth's surface to return to it? Let us see first exactly what the law of gravitation—discovered by Isaac Newton—says: **All objects in the universe attract each other with a gravitational force. The larger their masses are and the closer they are together, the stronger is the force between them.**

The physicist and the mathematician state the law of gravitation by saying that "the force of gravitation is directly proportional to the product of the masses and inversely proportional to the square of the distance between them." To illustrate this law, let us consider the attraction between the earth and the moon. If the moon's *mass* were doubled, the force between earth and moon would be doubled. If the *distance* between earth and moon were doubled, the force between them would decrease to one-fourth of what it is now.

The force with which objects are attracted to the center of the earth is known as the force of gravity. Your *weight* is a measure of the pull of gravity on your body. Because the surface gravity of Mars and of the moon are much less than the earth's, you would weigh much less there than you do here. On massive Jupiter, where the great increase in mass more than makes up for the greater distance from its center, you would weigh about two and a half times what you weigh on the earth.

The force of gravity can also be measured by the *acceleration* it gives to a freely falling body. Acceleration is the rate at which velocity changes. Near the earth's surface it is about 32 feet per second for every second of fall. In other words, a freely falling body will have a speed of 32 feet per second after one second of fall, 64 feet per second after two seconds, and so on. This acceleration is called "one gravity," or "1 *g*." A rate of change of velocity of 64 feet per second is an acceleration of 2 *g*'s, and so forth. At takeoff and re-entry into the atmosphere, a rocket may be subjected to an acceleration of as much as 10 *g*'s.

As the law of gravitation tells us, gravity decreases as distance from the earth's center

Fig. 28-1. Astronaut Ed White in space outside his orbiting Gemini IV spacecraft on June 3, 1965.

increases. At 4,000 miles above the earth's surface, your distance from the center of the earth is just doubled, and gravity is therefore only one-fourth as great as at the surface. At 4,000 miles, therefore, your weight would be one-fourth of your weight at the earth's surface, and you would fall with an acceleration of only about 8 feet per second for every second of fall.

3. "Escaping" from Gravity

Since gravity becomes weaker with increasing distance from the earth's center it would seem possible for an object—a rocket, for example—to escape from the pull of gravity if it could be shot high enough above the earth's surface. Strictly speaking, however, this is not so, because the earth's gravitational effect extends throughout space, and it would pull the rocket back to earth from wherever it stopped rising—if the earth were the only celestial body. But our solar system space is populated by other celestial bodies—the moon, the sun, the other planets. If the rocket comes to a region in space where the gravitational "sphere of influence" of one of these is stronger than that of the earth, the rocket escapes from the earth. Its "escape" comes about, however, because it is "captured" by another body on which it may land, or around which it may orbit. A rocket to the moon must have enough speed to reach the moon's sphere of influence, or it will fall back to earth.

4. Escape Velocity

How does a rocket or spacecraft escape from the earth's gravity? Escape from gravity has been compared to rolling a ball over the top of an incline that becomes more and more gentle as the top is approached. The top of the incline is like the edge of the "sphere of influence" which a rocket must reach to escape the earth's gravity. If the ball is rolled up from the bottom, it goes slower and slower as it approaches the top. No matter how close it comes, if it fails to reach the top, it will roll back to the bottom, arriving with a speed equal to its starting speed. If pushed fast enough, it will go "over the top."

The minimum speed needed to escape from a celestial body is called the **velocity of escape** or **escape velocity.** For the earth's surface, escape velocity is about 7 miles a second, or 25,000 miles an hour. At 500 miles altitude, escape velocity is only 23,600 miles an hour. At a height of 5,000 miles, it is 16,630 miles an hour. Escape velocity varies with the pull of gravity. On the moon, with its weak gravity, escape velocity is only 1.5 miles a second; on Mars it is about 2 miles a second; on Jupiter it is about 38 miles a second.

There are three different ways for a body to escape from the earth. One way is *to propel it hard enough to give it escape velocity at the earth's surface.* The second way is *to propel it after lifting it* to a height where it will not need as high an escape velocity as at the surface. The third way is *to keep propelling it* steadily as slowly as you like—until it reaches the point where its velocity equals escape velocity.

The first method requires single-stage rockets more powerful than have yet been developed. The second method requires multistage rockets, which are what we actually use now. The third method requires a long slow-burning fuel supply which has not yet been developed. In the multistage rocket, two, three, four, or even more rockets are joined in series. The largest is at the rear with progressively smaller ones ahead, and the payload (space vehicle, instruments, passengers) at the nose. Each rocket is fired in turn and then discarded, thereby reducing the weight to be driven by the next stage, until only the payload is left to be accelerated by the final stage.

5. Why the Moon and the Planets Stay in Orbit

How is a rocket or space vehicle put into orbit around the earth? To answer this question, let us first see why the moon revolves around the earth, or the earth and planets around the sun.

In his first law of motion Isaac Newton described a property of all matter which we call its **inertia.** The law states that **every body continues in a state of rest, or of motion at constant speed in a straight line, unless acted on by an outside force.** The moon moves at a speed of about 0.6 mile a second. Newton's first law tells us that the moon will continue to move at this speed *in a straight line,* unless an outside force acts on it. Although there is no outside force that alters the moon's speed, there is a force that acts to change its direction. That force is the earth's gravity, which acts to pull the moon toward the earth's center, in a direction at right angles to the moon's inertial (straight line) motion. (See Fig. 28-2.) Gravity thus makes the moon move in a curved path in which it orbits the earth. In similar fashion the earth and the planets travel in curved paths around the sun.

A weight swung around the hand on a string illustrates orbital motion very simply. When the weight is swung fast enough, its inertial motion keeps it full length away from the center around which it revolves. The pull of the string, representing gravity, keeps the weight from flying off into "space" and makes it move in a curved orbit.

How can the nine planets, the asteroids, and the comets all revolve around the sun at different distances? The answer is that for each distance, the pull of the sun's gravity is different, and so the orbital speed needed is different for each body. The nearer planets must move faster because the sun's pull on them is stronger. The more distant planets move more slowly. Again, an experiment with a weight and string will illustrate this point. (See Chap. 27, Student Activities 2.)

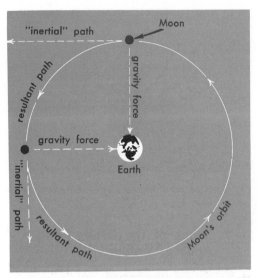

Fig. 28-2. The moon's curved path results from the effect of gravity on what would otherwise be inertial motion in a straight line.

6. Going Into Orbit: Artificial Satellites

Putting a satellite into orbit is different in several respects from making a rocket escape from the earth's surface. First the satellite must be lifted to the desired orbiting level. At this level it must be turned into a horizontal path (parallel to the earth's surface) and given just the right speed to *inject* it into orbit around the earth.

"Just the right speed" means a speed high enough to keep the satellite from falling back to earth, despite the downward pull of gravity. The higher the level at which *injection into orbit* occurs, the less the speed needed, because the earth's gravity weakens with distance from its center. Thus, at 200 miles altitude the speed needed is about 5 miles a second, or 18,000 miles an hour. At 1,000 miles altitude, orbital speed is about 4.5 miles a second. At 240,000 miles, the distance of our moon, it is about 0.6 mile a second, or about 2,200 miles an hour.

The farther off the satellite is, the slower it goes, and the longer it takes to complete its revolution. In a 200-mile orbit a satellite takes about 90 minutes to circle the earth; at 1,000 miles, 2 hours; at the moon's distance of about 240,000 miles, more than 27 days. At 22,235 miles a satellite will take exactly one day to circle the earth. If such a satellite is placed into a circular orbit above the earth's Equator, moving from west to east as the earth does on its axis, the satellite will always stay above the same spot on the earth. It is then said to be a *synchronous* satellite, and its orbit is a *synchronous* orbit, because it is in time with the earth.

The orbiting of a satellite may also be thought of in this way. The curvature of the earth's surface is 8 inches to the mile. Suppose we launch a satellite near the earth's surface, and *make it go a mile horizontally in the time that gravity makes it fall 8 inches.* At the end of the mile, our satellite will be just as far from the surface as when it started. This is precisely what happens to a satellite traveling at about 5 miles a second in an orbit a few hundred miles above the earth. It falls around the earth. (See Fig. 28-3.)

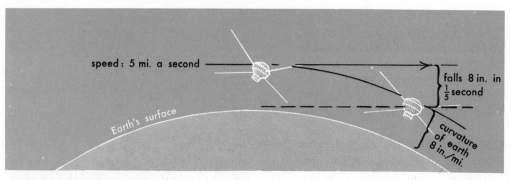

speed: 5 mi. a second

falls 8 in. in $\frac{1}{5}$ second

Earth's surface

curvature of earth 8 in./mi.

Fig. 28-3. A satellite is always falling toward the earth, but never reaching it.

7. Shape of the Orbit; Perigee, Apogee, Visibility

According to Kepler's first law all planets revolve around the sun in elliptical orbits. Satellites also revolve around the earth in elliptical orbits, in all of which the center of the earth is at one focus of the ellipse. The point in the orbit where the satellite comes nearest to the earth is called its **perigee** (*peri,* near; *gee,* earth). The point farthest from the earth is called **apogee** (*apo,* from). (See Fig. 28-4.)

Theoretically a circular orbit is possible for any satellite. To get into a circular orbit, however, an exact injection speed has to be given to the satellite, and it must be launched perfectly parallel to the earth's surface. (Astronomers can easily calculate the correct injection speed for each level. See Fig. 28-5.) If either of these conditions is not met exactly—and they probably never will be—the satellite follows an elliptical orbit. The greater the variation from ideal conditions, the more eccentric the orbit becomes. Let us see how.

If the injection speed is slightly less than needed for a circular orbit, the satellite will swing in towards the earth to begin an elliptical orbit in which its launching point is its farthest point or apogee. If the speed is too great—but less than escape velocity—the satellite will swing out to begin an elliptical orbit in which its launching

point becomes its perigee. If the injection angle is not perfectly horizontal, the orbit will be an ellipse whose perigee is lower than the point of launching. A perigee that is too low may bring the satellite into relatively dense air. This may slow it down enough at each orbit to shorten its life appreciably. On the other hand, a satellite orbiting thousands of miles above the earth is unretarded by atmosphere, and may orbit for hundreds of years. (See Fig. 28-6.)

When are artificial satellites visible? Like Mercury and Venus, they can be seen only as

Fig. 28-4. The meaning of perigee and apogee.

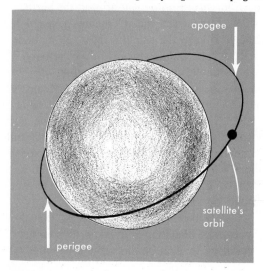

apogee

satellite's orbit

perigee

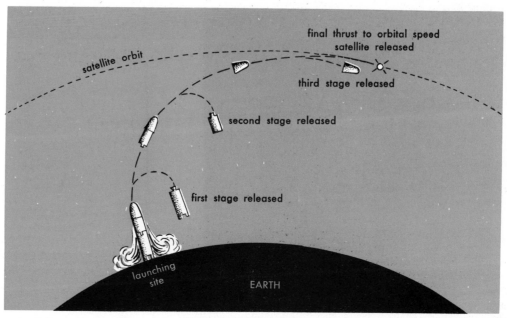

Fig. 28-5. Three stages in launching a satellite from the earth.

"morning stars" or "evening stars"—before sunrise or after sunset. The reason is that on the daytime side of the earth the glare of sunlight makes a satellite invisible. On the nighttime side the satellite is eclipsed by the earth's shadow. So the satellite is visible only during the period of time when the sun is below the observer's horizon, but the satellite is still high enough in the twilight sky to catch the rays of the sun. (See Fig. 28-7.)

8. Artificial Planets

What happens to a rocket that escapes from the earth? To answer this question fully, we must remember that everything on the earth is traveling around the sun with the earth at the earth's orbital speed of 18½ miles per second. Any velocity given to an object on the earth is *in addition* to the 18½ mile-a-second velocity it already has. Therefore, if an escaping rocket is launched eastward—in the same direction as the

Fig. 28-6. How injection speed is related to shape of orbit. See Topic 7.

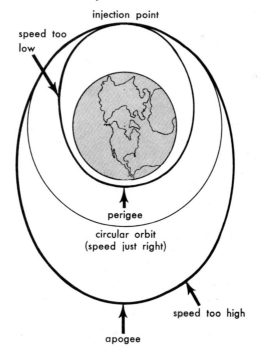

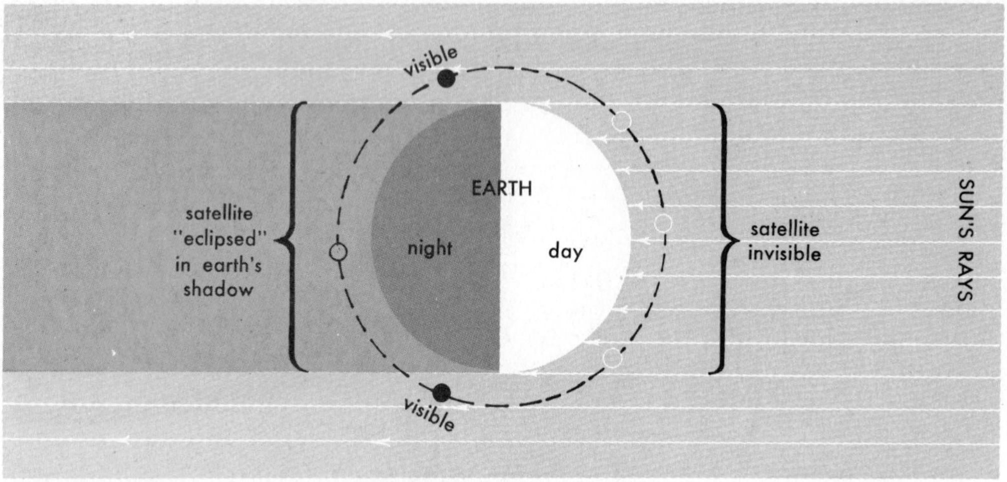

visible

satellite
"eclipsed"
in earth's
shadow

EARTH

night   day

satellite
invisible

SUN'S RAYS

visible

Fig. 28-7. Satellites can be seen only by observers on the nighttime side of the earth while the satellites are still in sunlight.

earth's revolution—the rocket will escape at a speed slightly higher than the earth's orbital speed. It will then *swing away from the sun* while going into an orbit larger than the earth's around the sun.

To send a rocket outward to Mars, then, we must launch it in the direction of the earth's revolution. (This eastward direction also makes use of the earth's rotational speed—about one-quarter of a mile per second at the Equator.) On the other hand, to send a rocket to an inferior planet such as Venus or Mercury, we would reverse our tactics. Such a rocket would be launched westward, would escape at a speed slightly lower than the earth's orbital speed, and would therefore be pulled closer to the sun while going into orbit around the sun. (See Fig. 28-8.)

9. How Many Hours to the Moon?

Suppose we launch a rocket toward the moon from a height of 300 miles at the minimum escape velocity of about 23,700 miles an hour. The moon is 240,000 miles away. Will the rocket reach the moon in 10 hours?

The answer is *no*, for two reasons. First, the rocket will have to be aimed *ahead* of the moon (because the moon is revolving around the earth at about 2,200 miles an hour) so the rocket will have to travel more than 240,000 miles. Second, the rocket does not maintain a speed of 23,700 miles an hour. Instead, it goes more and more slowly until it reaches the moon's "sphere of influence." Here the moon's

Fig. 28-8. Flight path of the Mariner IV spacecraft from earth to Mars.

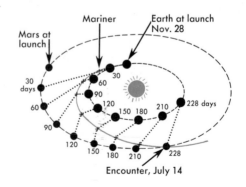

Mariner   Earth at launch
Nov. 28
Mars at
launch

30
days   30
60
90
90   120
60   150 180   210   228 days

90
120
150   180   210   228
Encounter, July 14

Fig. 28-9. Photo of the "full earth," taken by Applications Technology Satellite III from its synchronous orbit 22,300 miles above the earth. Parts of North America, South America, Africa, and Europe can be seen beneath the clouds.

gravity begins to pull the rocket downward to the moon. The rocket gains speed, finally crashing into the moon at a speed at least equal to escape velocity from the moon—about 1.5 miles a second. The time for such a one-way trip to the moon would be about 5½ days. However, this time may be reduced to half or less by giving the rocket higher initial velocity.

In the same way, trips to Mars or Venus must cover far greater distances than the minimum distance between them and the earth, and the average speed for the trip is far less than the initial speed of a rocket. When *Mariner II* was launched on August 27, 1962, Venus and the earth were 68½ million miles apart, but *Mariner* had to travel 180,000,000 miles to overtake Venus in its orbit on December 14, 1962.

Obviously the most "favorable" times for attempts to reach Mars or Venus must come when these planets are at just the "right" positions in their orbits. (See Fig. 28-8.) After landing on Mars or Venus, a spaceship might have to wait many months before Mars and the earth again come close enough together to permit the trip back.

10. Propulsion in Space

Scientists define space flight as flight that reaches beyond an altitude of 60 miles. Only *one-millionth* of the total weight of the atmosphere extends above this altitude. This near-vacuum condition of space is a great advantage for space flight. With no atmospheric drag to hold it back, a space vehicle can coast through space at high speeds with little or no power, using power only to free itself from the earth or to guide itself on its way through space. Since air is absent from

Fig. 28-10. The route of a round trip to the moon.

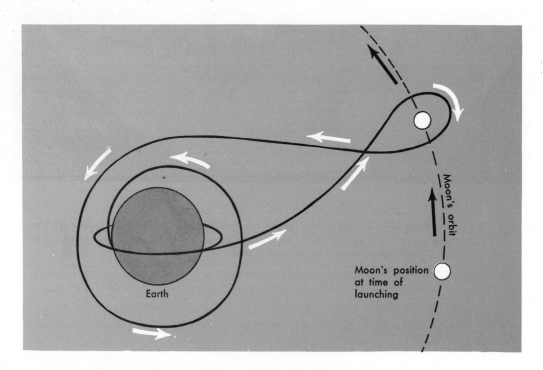

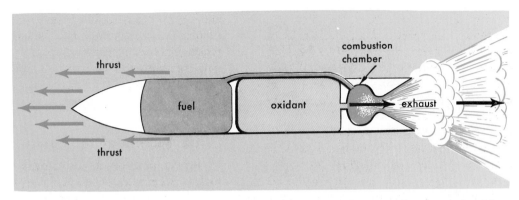

Fig. 28-11. The rocket engine operates on the action-reaction principle expressed in Newton's Third Law.

space, motive power for a space vehicle cannot be supplied by conventional engines that take oxygen from the air for the combustion of their fuels. At the present time all space vehicles are powered by rocket engines which carry their own oxygen as well as fuel, and are therefore able to operate outside the earth's atmosphere.

The rocket engine works by *jet propulsion* according to the principle expressed in Newton's Third Law of Motion. This states that "to every action, there is an equal and opposite reaction."

Here are some illustrations of this action-reaction principle: (1) As you step to shore from a rowboat or canoe, the boat or canoe is pushed *in the opposite direction*. (2) As a bullet leaves the barrel of a rifle, it "kicks back" *in the opposite direction,* causing the rifle butt to strike the shoulder. (3) Inflate a balloon. Release it into the air. As the jet of air escapes from the mouth of the balloon, the balloon moves *in the opposite direction*. The last example is a case of jet propulsion, which is how rocket motors operate.

In the rocket motor the jet is a stream of hot gases formed in the engine's combustion chamber and expelled explosively at high speed through the nozzle at the rear of the engine. As long as the rocket fuel burns, the rocket or space vehicle

is thrust forward with a force equal and opposite to the force of the escaping jet. Rocket engines can produce high speeds and enormous lifting forces. (See Fig. 28-11.)

11. Rocket Propellants

As stated before, rocket engines carry their own oxygen as well as fuel. Present-day rockets are of two types. The **liquid propellant** type usually uses a liquid fuel such as gasoline or alcohol, and a liquid oxidizer such as liquid oxygen or nitric acid. (*Liquid oxygen* is often abbreviated as LOX.) The liquids are pumped (or forced by high-pressure gas) into a combustion chamber where they are mixed and ignited. Liquid propellant rockets have rather complicated motors, but one of their advantages is that the rate of combustion can be controlled by the use of valves.

The **solid propellant** rocket uses a solid mixture of fuels and oxidizer that is packed right into the casing of the rocket, which later becomes its combustion chamber. The ordinary fireworks skyrocket is a solid propellant rocket. The fuel-oxidizer mixture is known as the *grain* or *charge*. It may be a powdery substance similar to gunpowder or a rubbery substance made of rubber

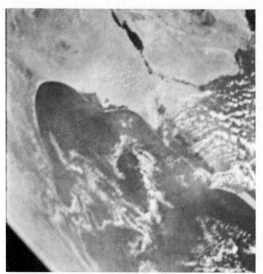

NASA

Fig. 28-12. Gemini VII photo showing area bordering the eastern Mediterranean.

Fig. 28-13. Model of a hypothetical spacecraft propelled by a nuclear rocket.

NASA

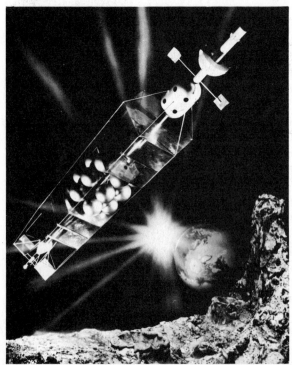

and an oxidizer. Solid propellant rockets are simpler in construction than liquid-propellant rockets, but their combustion can be stopped only by destroying the rocket. Furthermore, the ready-mixed propellant must be carefully guarded against premature explosion.

12. Rockets of the Future

Present-day rockets are classed as **chemical rockets.** Chemical rockets have two serious disadvantages. First, the weight of chemicals needed as rocket fuel is very high in proportion to the weight of the space vehicle and its "payload" of instruments and passengers. Second, the fuel is used up very rapidly. What other methods of rocket propulsion are space scientists considering for the future?

In the **nuclear rocket** scientists hope to use nuclear reactors in forming high-speed jets of gas that will power the rocket motors. The heat from the reactors will vaporize liquid hydrogen, helium, or ammonia to form the jets of gas. (See Fig. 28-13.)

In the **ion rocket** jet propulsion would be provided by streams of ions from a metal such as *cesium.* The ions would be accelerated to high speed by strong electrical fields. In the **photon rocket** intense beams of light made up of *photons* (particles of light) would exert enough pressure, because of the high speed of light rays, to move a rocket through the vacuum of interplanetary space. Neither the ion rocket nor the photon rocket would be expected to lift rockets from the earth's surface and through the earth's atmosphere. They would, however, provide the very small but continuous thrust needed to enable space vehicles to change speed and direction in their travels through space.

13. Guidance of Space Vehicles

Several kinds of guidance systems are presently possible to keep space vehicles on their chosen course. **Inertial** or **programmed guidance** makes use of gyroscopes, accelerometers, and "memory devices" like those in computing machines to guide the vehicle automatically from the inside. **Radio** or **command guidance** is guidance of the vehicle by radio signals from ground stations. The space vehicle carries a radio receiver that can operate its navigational controls. **Celestial guidance** or **infrared guidance** depends on the use of star-tracking devices to fix the vehicle's position with respect to the earth.

14. Signals from Space Vehicles

Space vehicles transmit radio signals by means of which they may be tracked by ground stations. (See Fig. 28-14.) The signals carry to earth many kinds of scientific information from scientific instruments. The radio transmitters may be powered by chemical batteries, by long-lasting solar cells that get their energy from the sun, by fuel cells (see Topic 16) or by small nuclear generators.

Very little power is needed to transmit radio signals through space on the direct "line-of-sight" from the vehicle to the earth. Besides, the world's great radio telescopes are capable of picking up even extremely weak signals. Radio signals from the Venus space probe *Mariner II* were received as it passed Venus at a distance of 36,000,000 miles from the earth. *Mariner II* had a potential radio range—both transmitting and receiving—of 64,000,000 miles.

The automatic transmission of measurements or information through space is known as **telemetry** or telemetering, which simply means "measuring at a distance." Telemetry has long been used in the **radiosonde** of the meteorologist to measure the temperature, pressure, and humidity of the upper atmosphere.

15. Landing a Space Vehicle

How is a space vehicle slowed down to the "soft landing" needed to land instruments and men safely?

Two methods have been combined thus far to slow down a returning space vehicle. Rockets

NASA

Fig. 28-14. Antenna of the deep space tracking station at Woomera, Australia.

Fig. 28-15. Imaginary moonship using retrorockets in landing on the moon.

Vision Magazine and American Museum of Natural History

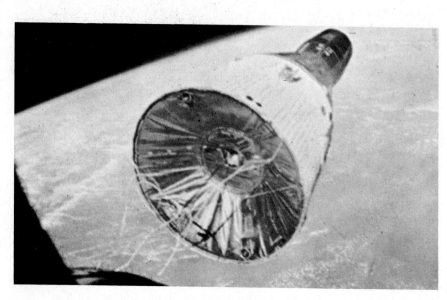

Fig. 28-16. Gemini VII photographed from Gemini VI during rendezvous and stationkeeping operations.

NASA

known as *retrorockets, braking rockets,* or *retarding rockets* are fired from the forward or nose end of the vehicle. These slow it down below orbiting speed, causing it to glide downward towards the earth and into the upper atmosphere. When the vehicle enters the atmosphere, parachutes make use of air resistance to complete the job of slowing the vehicle to a safe landing speed. Thus far all American landings have been in the ocean. Russian astronauts have come down on land.

Slow speeds are imperative in the lower atmosphere, where friction with air might otherwise heat an incoming vehicle to the melting point. In a moon landing, friction is no problem, because the moon has no atmosphere. There, however, all the slowing down must be done by retrorockets. (See Fig. 28-15.)

Even in the thin upper atmosphere through which a re-entering space vehicle plunges before its parachutes are used, enough frictional heat is produced to destroy the vehicle unless the heat can be carried off. Thus far the best way found to do this is to give the vehicle a blunt cone-shaped nose and to cover it with a *heat shield.*

The blunt *nose cone* has a broad surface from which heat can be carried off by the *shock wave* of air driven from its path. The heat shield is made of Fiberglas, which acts as an insulator for the metal nose of the vehicle. As the Fiberglas is heated, it melts or vaporizes and drops away from the nose cone, carrying the heat away with it. Even so, the nose cone is heated to a temperature of about 3,000°F.

At both take-off and landing the acceleration or deceleration of the space vehicle may be as high as 10 *g*'s. (Deceleration is *rate of slowing down.*)

16. Survival in Space: Food; Wastes; Radiations

Many *biomedical problems*—problems involving the functioning of man's mind and body —must be solved in enabling man to survive in flight through space. These problems include the provision of essential materials such as water and food, the removal of wastes, protection from harmful radiation, physiological problems such as maintenance of comfortable body temperature and effects of high acceleration and weightlessness, and psychological factors related to isolation and strangeness of the environment. Let us see briefly how some of these problems have been met in the manned space flights achieved so far.

An average-sized man breathes about 150 gallons of oxygen a day. In a spaceship this may be provided from tanks of compressed oxygen gas, from liquid oxygen, or possibly from oxygen-releasing chemicals such as hydrogen peroxide. Water may be carried in storage tanks or may be made on board. The latter is already being done in the remarkable fuel cell, which generates electricity through the union of hydrogen and oxygen and forms water as its by-product. Food is now provided as solid food in bars, as semisolid food in squeeze tubes, and as liquid in plastic bags with straws. Many of the foods are preserved by modern freeze-drying methods that retain the shape, color, and flavor of the foods almost perfectly. (See Fig. 28-17.)

For longer space flights in the future both food and oxygen may be provided by growing the simple green plants called algae in the spaceship itself. The algae, which grow very rapidly and are highly nutritious, would do the triple job of using up waste carbon dioxide, manufacturing food, and restoring oxygen to the spaceship's "atmosphere."

Wastes formed in breathing include carbon dioxide and water vapor. These can be absorbed by chemicals and possibly reused—especially the essential water.

Harmful radiations include *cosmic rays* and *ultraviolet rays*. These are much more intense in space than near the earth's surface where our atmosphere screens out most of them. The spaceship and the astronaut's space suit must provide protection from these radiations in space.

17. Survival in Space: Physiological Factors

Spaceships must be pressurized to provide normal atmospheric pressure. To keep the astronaut's body temperature normal, his ship must be air conditioned and his space suit must be thermostatically controlled.

At the very high acceleration of take-off and the deceleration of re-entry into the atmosphere (as much as 10 *g*'s) an astronaut's body

Fig. 28-17. Two Project Gemini meals, with utensils needed to open food bags and add water to freeze-dried foods.

NASA

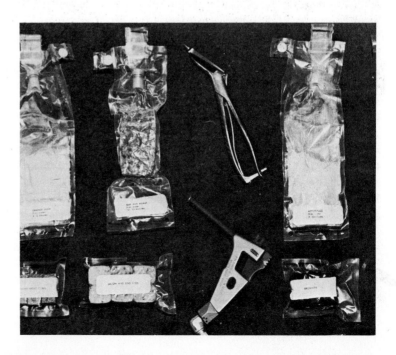

Fig. 28-18. During their training period, Mercury astronauts experienced weightlessness in aircraft flying specially calculated paths.

NASA

is subjected to strong "crushing" forces. These forces seem to present little problem as long as the astronaut remains strapped to his couch and faces backward after take-off.

Contrasting with the crushing effect of high acceleration is the weightless sensation of "zero gravity" or "free fall." This sensation is felt by the astronaut whose ship is moving in orbital flight around the earth. Gravity is then producing exactly the same acceleration on him as on his ship. When this happens, the astronaut cannot feel his weight because the ship's seat offers no resistance to his body, and he undergoes a sensation of floating in space. Everything inside a freely falling ship is then "weightless," and will "float" in the cabin unless fastened down. This is why food and drink must be taken from closed containers such as squeeze bottles. So far, astronauts have not been harmfully affected by *weightlessness*. For the longer flights of the future, however, scientists may devise a means of producing artificial gravity within a spaceship. (See Fig. 28-18.)

The following paragraphs will give brief descriptions of some of the vehicles in the United States program of manned and unmanned satellites and space probes. (A *space probe* is defined as an unmanned projectile sent into space to gather information.)

18. Unmanned Satellites

Many artificial satellites have been launched since 1957 and are now orbiting the earth. Others are still in the planning stages. Their purposes are various. Interplanetary Explorers provide information on radiation and magnetic fields between the earth and its moon. Orbiting Astronomical Observatories observe the solar system and the stars at a height of about 500 miles above the earth, thereby avoiding interference by our atmosphere. Orbiting Solar Observatories study the sun, and Orbiting Geophysical Observatories make measurements of earth-related phenomena. Pegasus satellites have a wing span of 96 feet, and are equipped to report punctures by micrometeoroids. Biosatellites carry thousands of varieties of plants and animals into space to study the biological effects of weightlessness, radiations, and other features of a space environment.

Communications satellites have made it possible to send television, telephone, teleprint, and facsimile radio signals across the oceans, and from continent to continent. The "passive" *Echo* satellites are giant balloons that merely reflect signals back to the earth. But *Relay, Syncom, Telstar,* and *Intelsat* are "active-repeater" satellites whose radio equipment repeats and strengthens the signals it transmits. *Intelsat* furnishes commercial service between Europe and North America. Its synchronous orbit (see Topic 6) keeps it in a nearly permanent location over the Atlantic Ocean.

Transits are navigation satellites designed to help ships and planes determine their positions. *Tiros, Nimbus,* and *Essa* are weather satellites that photograph the earth and its cloud cover. *ERTS* satellites make studies of the earth's natural resources. (See Fig. 28-19.)

19. Unmanned Mooncraft and Spacecraft

Ranger spacecraft to the moon begin to photograph its surface when they are still about 20 minutes away from the surface, and they continue to take pictures until they crash land. *Surveyor* spacecraft use retrorockets to make soft landings on the moon. In addition to cameras, they carry equipment for digging into and analyzing the moon's soil. *Prospector* spacecraft are also able to crawl over the lunar surface, explore it, and send soil samples back to earth by rocket. *Lunar Orbiters* orbit the moon at any desired distance. They use both wide-angle and telephoto cameras to scan the lunar surface for possible landing sites for manned mooncraft.

Fig. 28-19. A Tiros *weather satellite. From a near-polar orbit, Tiros can photograph the ocean areas where hurricanes breed.*

NASA

NASA

Fig. 28-20. Artist's drawing of Viking *spacecraft to land on Mars for exploration of the planet.*

Mariner and *Pioneer* spacecraft travel near Mercury, Venus, Mars, and Jupiter to photograph them and to study their atmospheres, temperatures, and magnetic fields. *Voyager* spacecraft will soft-land instruments on Mars to study its surface and to explore the existence of life.

20. Manned Spacecraft: Mercury, Gemini, Apollo

The first man to orbit the earth was Colonel Yuri Gagarin of the Soviet Union in the spacecraft *Vostok I* on April 12, 1961. The United States placed its first astronaut in orbit on February 20, 1962, when Colonel John Glenn was launched in the spacecraft *Friendship 7*. This was the first orbital flight in our **Project Mercury** series, which included a total of six flights, ending with Colonel L. Gordon Cooper's 22-orbit flight on May 15–16, 1963. Both the Russian and American flight programs at this stage used one-man spacecraft. Their flights showed man's ability to operate in space despite such problems as high-gravity forces at launch and re-entry, weightlessness, feeding, and temperature maintenance.

Both countries followed up their pioneer programs with two-man spacecraft programs. Ours was called **Project Gemini** (twins). When Project Gemini ended on November 15, 1966, we had completed ten successful flights, the longest of which lasted over 330 hours. These flights showed that spacecraft could be maneuvered in space, and that two spacecraft launched separately from the earth could rendezvous (meet) and even dock (link up) in space. (See Fig. 28-16.) It was also shown that an astronaut, properly clothed and equipped, could step outside of his spacecraft and "walk" and manipulate tools in space. (See Fig. 28-1.) With few exceptions, the 26 astronauts in the Mercury and Gemini programs appeared to suffer almost no harmful physical effects from their flights.

21. Project Apollo: To the Moon

From 1969 through 1972, when **Project Apollo** ended, six teams of astronauts explored the moon. Project Apollo's plan for landing man on the moon is called the **lunar-orbit rendezvous approach.** Briefly, it calls for (1) a spacecraft to be launched from earth into a lunar orbit; (2) a small lunar landing vehicle to be sent from the spacecraft to the moon; (3) the vehicle to return to the spacecraft for the trip back to earth.

Apollo spacecraft have been launched from the earth by three-stage *Saturn V* rockets with a thrust of about 7,600,000 pounds. The entire assembly is taller than a football field is long. It weighs about 3,000 tons at launch. The rocket's first two stages and part of the third stage are used to put Apollo into an earth orbit. When it reaches the correct position in this orbit, the third stage is refired to send it on its way to the moon at an initial speed of nearly 25,000 miles an hour.

The spacecraft consists of three parts: a *command section* in which the crew rides; a *service module* carrying rockets needed for navigation and the return trip; and a *lunar module*

(LM) also called the *bug* or *ferry*. At launch, the command module is on top, the service module next, and the LM last. After burnout of the rocket's third stage, the crew disconnects the command and service modules and connects the command module with the LM, so that men may transfer from one to the other. At about 100 miles from the moon, service rockets put the spacecraft in orbit around the moon's equator at about 3,400 miles an hour. From here the LM carries two of the Apollo's three-man crew into an orbit about 10 miles above the moon. The third man stays in the "parent craft." When the two men in the LM find the desired landing place, they use retro-rockets to come out of orbit for a soft landing. The LM lands on spiderlike legs that are extended as it slows down for its landing on the lunar surface. (See Fig. 28-21.)

Lunar explorers have spent up to 75 hours on the moon before rocketing back to a rendezvous with the mother ship and the return to earth in the command section. The LM's are not equipped for re-entry into the earth's atmosphere, so they are left to orbit the moon or to crash-land onto its surface.

On July 16, 1969, Apollo 11 astronauts Neil Armstrong and Edwin Aldrin made their historic first landing on the floor of the Sea of Tranquility, and with Michael Collins in the command module returned safely with about 50 pounds of lunar rock and soil. Subsequent landings were made by Apollo 12 on the floor of the Ocean of Storms; by Apollo 14 in the Fra Mauro Highlands region; by Apollo 15 in the Apennine Mountains-Hadley Rills area; by Apollo 16 in the Crater Descartes region, and finally by Apollo 17 in the Taurus-Littrow valley. Each Apollo team took photographs, conducted numerous experiments, and collected many pounds of lunar rock samples. Apollo 15, 16, and 17 were aided by the use of battery-driven automobiles called Lunar Rovers. Apollo 17 astronauts, one of whom was a trained geologist, returned to earth with 225 pounds of lunar rock samples.

22. Skylab

In the spring of 1973, NASA launched the "manned orbital research" earth-orbiting spacecraft called Skylab. Made from the remodeled third stage of a Saturn 5 rocket, Skylab is more than 100 feet long and provides a "duplex" workshop and apartment for three astronauts. The workshop is 60 feet long and nearly 13,000 cubic feet in volume. Skylab was placed in orbit about 300 miles above the earth without men aboard. The three successive Skylab astronaut teams were then launched in modified Apollo spacecraft that docked with Skylab. The Apollo spacecraft were also used for the return to Earth. The first Skylab team set a new endurance record for man in space of 28 days. The second Skylab team broke this record with a stay of 59 days. The Skylab 3 team is scheduled for 84 days.

The work done by the Skylab teams included observations of the sun and the earth, tests of the ability of people and other living things to function for extended periods in weightless space, and experiments in metallurgy. All in all, 89 different experiments were conducted.

Fig. 28-21. Astronaut Aldrin on the moon.

NASA

TOPIC QUESTIONS

Each topic question refers to the topic of the same number within this chapter.

1. (*a*) What were Goddard's contributions to the development of rocketry? (*b*) What were Oberth's contributions?

2. (*a*) What is the law of gravitation? (*b*) How is gravitational attraction affected by mass? by distance? (*c*) What is gravity? weight? (*d*) What is acceleration? How much acceleration is 1 *g*? 2 *g*'s?

3. When does a rocket escape from the earth? Why?

4. (*a*) What is escape velocity? (*b*) How can a body achieve escape velocity? Name three ways. (*c*) Describe the method we use now to achieve escape velocity.

5. (*a*) State Newton's first law of motion. (*b*) Explain how the earth's gravity and the moon's inertial motion combine to make the moon orbit the earth. (*c*) What explains the ability of planets to orbit the sun at different distances from it?

6. (*a*) What three steps are involved in putting an artificial satellite into orbit? (*b*) What is "just the right speed"? Give examples. (*c*) Why is a satellite 22,235 miles from the earth "stationary"? (*d*) Explain the motion of a satellite in terms of its rate of fall.

7. (*a*) What is a satellite's perigee? apogee? (*b*) Can a satellite have a circular orbit? Explain. (*c*) How do injection speed and angle affect its orbit? (*d*) Explain when artificial satellites are visible.

8. Explain how rockets are made to "escape" outward toward Mars or inward toward Venus.

9. Explain the factors that determine the average speed and total distance for a trip from earth to the moon, Mars, or Venus.

10. (*a*) Why is the near-vacuum of space an advantage for space flight? (*b*) Explain the principle of jet propulsion. How does it operate in a rocket motor?

11. Name and describe the two types of present-day rocket engines.

12. (*a*) What are the two disadvantages of the chemical rocket? (*b*) Explain briefly how scientists hope to operate each of the following: nuclear rocket, ion rocket, photon rocket.

13. Name and explain briefly four different kinds of rocket guidance.

14. (*a*) What sources of electricity are used by space vehicles for their radios? (*b*) How are a satellite's radio signals picked up? (*c*) What is telemetry?

15. (*a*) What two devices are used to slow a space vehicle for landing? How do they work? (*b*) Explain the construction and purpose of the nose cone and heat shield.

16. (*a*) What are the biomedical problems of space flight? List them. (*b*) How are oxygen, water, and food provided? (*c*) What use will be made of algae? (*d*) How are wastes disposed of?

17. (*a*) How is body temperature kept normal? (*b*) How does the body adapt to high acceleration? (*c*) What is weightlessness? What effect does it have?

18. Briefly name and describe some of our space research, communications, and weather and observation satellites.

19. Briefly name and describe some of our unmanned mooncraft and spacecraft.

20. Give two achievements of the Mercury and Gemini programs.

21. Give two achievements of Project Apollo.

22. Describe two kinds of work done by the Skylab program.

CHAPTER 29
Our Moon

HOW DO YOU KNOW THAT . . . ?

Until the 1960's, when American and Russian camera-carrying space ships circled the moon, we had never "seen" the "back" of the moon. To understand how the moon can revolve around the earth without showing us its far side, do the following activities. Pretend you have a printed message or sign on your back. Now walk slowly around the entire classroom in such a way that no one in the class can see the sign. What did you have to do to hide the sign? How much did you (the moon) rotate as you revolved around the class (the earth)? Now walk slowly around the classroom without rotating at all, always facing the front of the room. Do your classmates see the sign?

1. Studying the Moon

Now the Space Age has made it possible to study the moon at close range. In 1964 and 1965 "the greatest single advance in lunar knowledge since Galileo" resulted when Ranger spacecraft telecast over 17,000 closeup pictures of the moon back to the earth. Some of these pictures showed lunar features as small as 10 inches across. The Ranger spacecraft crash-landed on the moon, but they were followed in 1966 by the soft-landing Surveyors and the Lunar Orbiters. The Surveyors not only photographed their immediate surroundings but also dug into and analyzed the surface on which they rested. The Lunar Orbiters, as their name implies, went into orbit around the moon. They used telephoto and wide-angle cameras to photograph nearly the entire surface of both sides of the moon, so that choice landing spots for Project Apollo's manned exploration might be selected. In 1969 Apollo astronauts made the world's first landings on the moon. Now at last we had first-hand observations

of the lunar surface and actual samples of its rocks and soil. We had entered a new phase of space exploration.

THE SURFACE OF THE MOON

2. The Moon's Physical Characteristics

Thirty-two natural satellites circle around six planets of the solar system. Our moon is not the largest of the satellites, but it has the distinction of being closer in size to its planet than any other satellite. The moon's diameter of about 2,160 miles is more than one-fourth of the earth's average diameter of 7,913 miles. In relative size, the moon and earth compare with each other about as a baseball and basketball do.

The moon's average density is about 3.3 times that of water (the earth's is 5.5) and its total mass is about $\frac{1}{81}$ that of the earth. Although

1 Sinus Iridum
2 Plato
3 Alps
4 Aristarchus
5 Mare Imbrium
6 Apennines

12 Mare Serenitatis
13 Mare Crisium
14 Mare Tranquillitatis

7 Kepler
8 Copernicus
9 Mare Humorum
10 Mare Nubium
11 Tycho

15 Mare Foecunditatis
16 Mare Nectaris

Mount Wilson and Palomar Observatories

Fig. 29-1. This photograph of the full moon has been labeled to show some of its major features. Notice the rays (see Topic 8) that radiate from the craters Tycho, Copernicus, and Kepler.

the moon's small diameter tends to increase the force of gravity at its surface (as compared with the earth's), its mass is so much smaller than the earth's that its surface gravity is only about one-sixth that of the earth. Its velocity of escape is only 1.5 miles a second.

3. The Moon's Lack of Atmosphere

Scientists have calculated that gas molecules can easily escape from the moon because of its low escape velocity, and there is sufficient evidence to show that the moon has little or no atmosphere. When the moon moves past a star in the sky, the light of the star remains bright right to the very edge of the moon's disk before being eclipsed. If an appreciable atmosphere surrounded the moon, the star's light would gradually become redder and dimmer. Another evidence is the absence of a twilight zone, such as is caused on the earth by atmospheric dust and cloud, at the boundary between the bright and dark areas of the moon.

Again, our view of the moon's surface is never obscured by lunar haze or clouds. All of these evidences indicate that if the moon has any atmosphere at all, it must be a very thin one.

4. Erosion on the Moon?

If the moon has no atmosphere, it cannot have winds, rain, or running water. For this reason, it used to be thought that no erosion could take place on the moon. However, the pictures taken by lunar spacecraft and direct observations by the Apollo astronauts do show evidences of erosion.

Mountain peaks and crater rims that must once have been sharp are now rounded off in places. Everywhere the surface is covered by a thick powdery soil that includes many small rock fragments. There seems no doubt now that erosion of the lunar surface is the result of billions of years of bombardment by meteoroids of all sizes. Without an atmosphere the moon has no defense against this bombardment.

The lack of an atmosphere would also mean that no chemical weathering could take place on the moon. But mechanical weathering resulting from changes of temperature could certainly take place. The moon's temperature is known to rise higher than 212°F during its two-week-long day, and then to fall rapidly to −240°F or less in the two-week-long night. With such a large temperature range, exfoliation may be an important process in splitting the rock surface and shattering it into fragments of various sizes—boulders, pebbles, and sand grains.

5. Surface Features: Lunar Seas

When we look at the full moon with the unaided eye, we see a pattern of light and dark areas that seem to form a face or "man in the moon." When a good telescope is used, we can recognize five main kinds of surface features: "seas," mountains, craters, rays, and rills. Many details of these features have been revealed to us in the closeup photos taken by spacecraft and astronauts.

The **lunar seas** or **plains** are the great dark areas of the lunar surface. (See Fig. 29-1.) They are also known by the Latin word for seas, *maria* (singular, *mare;* pronounced *mah* ray), having been so named by Galileo. The lunar seas contain no water, nor is there any sign that they ever did. They appear dark compared to the other areas of the moon because their relatively smooth surfaces reflect less sunlight to the earth than do the surrounding mountainous areas. The seas are not as smooth as they look to the unaided eye. Large telescopes show their surfaces to be ridged and wrinkled, and closeup photos show they are pitted by thousands of small craters. The 14 seas have Latin names: Mare Tranquilitatis (Sea of Tranquility) where Apollo 11 landed, and Mare Imbrium (Sea of Rains). The largest is called Oceanus Procellarum (Ocean of Storms) where Apollo 12 landed. The seas are hundreds of miles in diameter, and cover about half of the front side of the moon.

The origin of the seas is not known, but many astronomers believe that the smooth floors of the seas were formed by great flows of lava.

6. Lunar Mountains

The areas of the full moon that seem so bright to observers on the earth are the lunar highlands. They include a small number of mountain ranges and a very large number of craters.

Lick Observatory

Fig. 29-2. The mountain range running diagonally across the photo is the moon's Apennine Mountains. At the right end of the mountains is the crater Eratosthenes. Below is the great crater Archimedes and the beginning of Mare Imbrium. Notice the shadows in the craters indicating the direction of the sun.

Most of the moon's mountain ranges are located at the borders of the lunar seas. The most prominent mountains form the western border of Mare Imbrium, toward which they slope steeply. (See Fig. 29-2.) Their names—the lunar Alps, Apennines, and Caucasus Mountains—were given to them in 1647. The peaks of lunar mountains rise as high as 26,000 feet above their surrounding plains. Their heights are calculated from the lengths of their shadows as shown in photographs. The angle of the sun's

rays at the times of the photographs must be known. The highest lunar mountains are the Doerfels, which do not border on a lunar sea. They are located in a region of highlands near the moon's south pole.

The origin of the lunar mountains, like that of the seas, is not known. They look as though they were just "splashed up" rather than folded or faulted into shape like so many mountains on the earth. Perhaps they were created by the smashing impact of giant meteorites.

7. Lunar Craters

In addition to thousands upon thousands of small craters like those that dot the floors of the lunar seas, the moon has more than 30,000 larger craters. These range in diameter from a few hundred feet up to the 146 miles of the great crater Clavius. (See Fig. 29-3.) Most of the craters are nearly circular in shape. Their rugged mountainous walls slope steeply into the craters and more gently away from them. The floors of the craters may extend to depths thousands of feet lower than the surrounding plains. More rarely their floors rise higher than the surrounding plains and almost up to the height of the enclosing walls. The crater floors are usually rough-surfaced and bright, but some are as dark as the seas. They may have small peaks and craterlets on their surfaces. (See Figs. 29-3 and 29-4.)

Lunar craters are named after great scholars and scientists. Thus we have the craters Plato, Aristotle, Archimedes, Kepler, and Copernicus. Copernicus is about 60 miles in diameter and two miles deep. Its floor is said to have topography as rugged as our badlands. (See Figs. 29-4 and 29-5.)

How did the lunar craters originate? The **impact hypothesis** states that they were blasted out, like meteor craters on the earth, by the impact of great meteorites. But unlike most of the craters formed this way on the earth, the lunar craters have not been destroyed by erosion

Fig. 29-3. Part of the moon at last quarter, showing many craters. Largest of the moon's craters, Clavius, about 150 miles in diameter, is near the top of the photo. Directly beneath Clavius is the crater Tycho with a small peak at its center. The dark area at the lower right is Mare Nubium.

and weathering. The **volcanic hypothesis** says that the craters are volcanic in origin. Most astronomers today favor the impact hypothesis, but agree that some of the craters probably originated by volcanic eruption.

8. Lunar Rays and Rills

Among the strange features of the lunar surface as seen in a telescope are the sets of bright streaks called **rays** that radiate in all directions from the craters Tycho, Copernicus, Kepler, and about 10 others. The rays are up to 10 miles in width, and they extend for up to hundreds of miles away from the craters, crossing mountains and plains and even other craters. The rays are seen best at the full moon phase. They cast no shadows. Closeup photos of Tycho's rays show that they include many tiny craterlets within their boundaries. What are the rays and how did they

Fig. 29-4. The light streaks radiating from the crater Copernicus are the mysterious lunar rays. To the left of Copernicus are the crater Eratosthenes and the Apennine Mountains.

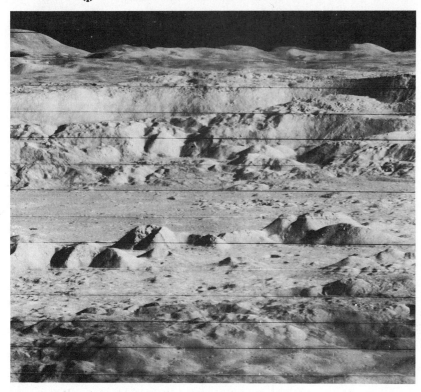

Fig. 29-5. Closeup view of part of Crater Copernicus, as photographed by Lunar Orbiter II from a height of 28 miles. Cliffs on crater rim are 1,000 feet high.

NASA

Fig. 29-6. View of eastern edge of Crater Alphonsus taken from height of 115 miles by Ranger IX. Note prominent rills and small "halo" craters.

NASA

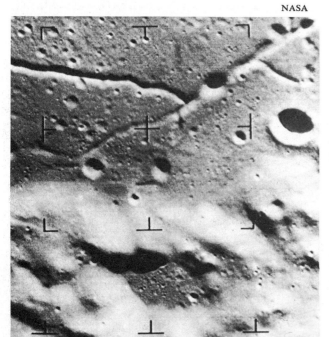

form? One suggestion is that they consist mainly of light-colored fragments of lunar rock thrown out in all directions from the central crater by the impact of the meteorite that formed the crater. Supporters of this explanation point to the fact that the rays resemble features radiating from craters formed on earth by underground nuclear explosions.

Rills are long clefts or cracks found in many parts of the lunar seas. Some of them are more than a hundred miles long and up to three miles wide. Their depth is unknown. They may have formed when the moon's crust cooled. (See Fig. 29-6.)

9. Volcanic Activity on the Moon

Until very recently, astronomers thought that the moon was a completely cold rock globe in which volcanic activity had long since ceased. Now there appears to be evidence that some vulcanism is still taking place on the moon.

In a few places, especially the crater Alphonsus, astronomers think they have seen gases being emitted as in a volcanic eruption. Other evidences of volcanic activity are the "halo" craters that appear in some of the Ranger pictures. (See Fig. 29-6.) These craters are surrounded by "halos" of dark material that astronomers think were erupted from the craters. Still a third evidence of recent volcanic activity is seen in lunar domes that resemble the volcanic domes of Oregon and northern California. They are from two to ten miles in diameter, and up to 1500 feet high.

10. Lunar Soil and Lunar Rocks

The lunar samples returned to earth by the Apollo astronauts included (1) crystalline rocks, (2) breccias, (3) soil.

There are three kinds of crystalline rocks, all believed to be of igneous origin. Most numerous are the dark, fine-grained, basalt-like rocks from the lunar seas. Like our basalts, their principal minerals are plagioclase feldspar and pyroxene, but they are richer in iron and titanium and poorer in sodium. The other two kinds of lunar rock appear to come from the highlands. These rocks are believed to be older because the highlands are thought to have formed before the seas. One kind is a lighter-colored basalt, including more feldspar and less of the dark-colored pyroxene. It is also richer in radioactive uranium and thorium. The other kind of lunar highland rock is like a rather uncommon earth rock called *anorthosite*. It is a coarse-grained rock, consisting almost entirely of light-colored plagioclase feldspar with very little dark pyroxene. It is rich in aluminum and poor in iron. On the earth, anorthosites are found in the Adirondack Mountains, the Laramie Range, and in Scandinavia.

Breccias are rocks composed of angular rock fragments mixed with fine material. Scientists think that the materials of the lunar breccias were fused together by meteorite impact. The breccias are largely gray to dark gray in color. Most of their rock fragments are less than half an inch long, and the finer materials in which they are enclosed seem to be the same as the fine materials in the lunar soil.

The *lunar soil* is a grayish-brown mixture of small rock fragments and finer materials of sand, silt, and clay size, called *fines*. The lunar soil seems to range in depth from 5 to 20 feet. Most rock fragments are the same kind of rock as the larger rocks studied, but a few fragments are entirely different and thought to come from nearby highlands. The *fines* include tiny beads of volcanic-like glass, tiny chips of such minerals as plagioclase and olivine, and bits of iron meteorites. The glass probably formed whenever high-speed meteorite impacts melted the rock and splashed droplets of molten material onto the surrounding area.

How old are these lunar materials? The youngest Apollo rocks may be about 3.1 billion years old. The oldest Apollo samples seem to be much older—about 4.25 billion years. This data suggests that the Sea of Tranquility was formed long before the Ocean of Storms. But oldest of all are the soils, with ages up to 4.6 billion years, when the solar system is thought to have originated. Why are the soils older than the rocks? One explanation is that the soils include many fragments of older rocks from the surrounding highlands and from meteorites.

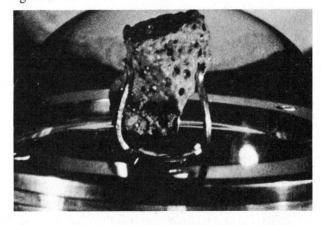

Fig. 29-7. Moon rock on display.

NASA

Fig. 29-8.
Apollo 11 Astronaut Aldrin is taking a soil sample from the lunar surface.

11. Man on the Moon

The astronauts on the moon found themselves in a harsh environment. The moon has neither water nor atmosphere. Because of its lack of atmosphere, it provides no protection against cosmic rays, ultraviolet rays, meteorites, and the blinding rays of the sun. In the two-week-long lunar day its temperature rises above 219°F, the boiling point of water. In the equally long lunar night, the absence of atmosphere permits such rapid loss of heat that the temperature falls rapidly below −240°F.

As expected, the astronauts found little difficulty in walking, lifting, running, and jumping, because of the moon's weak gravity. A 150-pound man weighs only 25 pounds on the moon. His mass and inertia, however, are the same as on earth. (See Fig. 29-8.)

12. Origin of the Moon

How did the moon originate? Many hypotheses have been suggested, but most of them are simply variations of three different ideas. The first says that the *moon was originally a part of the earth.* When the earth was first formed there was no moon. Then a great tidal bulge developed in the earth's mantle as a result of the gravitational pull of the sun. Eventually this bulging mass separated from the earth to form the moon. Supporters point out that the entire moon has about the same average density as the earth's mantle. But the great differences between earth rocks and the lunar rocks brought back by Apollo astronauts and the Russian unmanned Lunas make it seem very unlikely that the moon was ever part of the earth.

A second set of hypotheses suggests that the *earth and the moon formed at the same time by separate accumulations of material* from the original solar system dust cloud. Opponents of this idea believe that the moon could not have become a satellite under those conditions. They think it would either have fallen into the earth or escaped from it entirely.

A third set of hypotheses suggests that *the moon was captured by the earth* after having originated separately in some other part of the solar system. In this hypothesis the moon and earth did not originate at the same time. In fact, the moon's lower density would indicate that it probably was older than the earth. But just how the capture might have taken place is difficult to explain.

In a variation of the capture theory, one astronomer has proposed that the moon was once much larger than it is now. He suggests that as the moon came closer to the earth, large masses were torn away from it. These plunged onto the earth and became the continents.

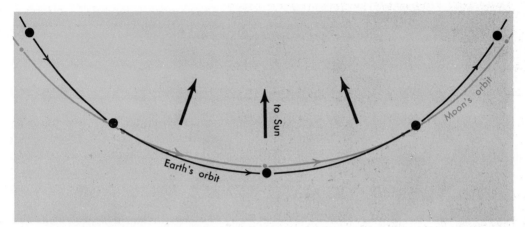

Fig. 29-9. This diagram shows how the moon revolves around the earth while moving with the earth around the sun.

Most astronomers agree that the moon was once much closer to the earth than it is now. As time passes, it gradually moves away from us, and its orbit becomes larger and larger.

THE MOON'S MOTIONS

13. The Moon's Orbit

The moon revolves around the earth from west to east in an elliptical orbit with the earth's center at one focus. The period of revolution is 27⅓ days. At perigee the distance between the centers of the moon and the earth is 221,463 miles. At apogee it is 252,710 miles. The average distance is 238,857 miles. At 186,300 miles a second, light from the moon reaches us in about 1¼ seconds.

Since the moon's revolution around the earth takes place while the earth is revolving around the sun, the moon also revolves around the sun. The actual path of the moon is like that shown in Figure 29-9. The moon's orbit is not in the same plane as the earth's orbit, but is inclined to it at an angle of about 5°. (See Fig. 29-10.) This fact is of great importance in determining how often eclipses occur. (See Topic 21.)

In our sky both moon and sun appear to be about the same size, with an angular diameter of about one-half of a degree. This is because the sun, with a diameter about 400 times that of the moon, is about 400 times as far away.

14. Moonrise and Moonset

The moon rises in the east and sets in the west every day, much as the sun does, and for the same reason. This motion through the sky is an apparent one, caused by the daily rotation of the earth from west to east on its axis. If the moon did not revolve around the earth, we would see it in the same place in the sky at a given time each day. But while the earth makes one turn on its axis, the moon revolves in the

Fig. 29-10. The moon's orbit is inclined about 5° to the plane of the earth's orbit.

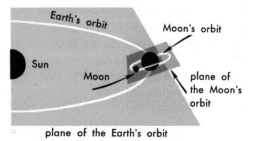

Yerkes Observatory

Fig. 29-11. The moon's librations *or "rocking" motions allow us to see a little more than one half of the moon, as can be seen by careful comparison of the features at the right edge of the moon in these two photos taken at opposite ends of the moon's orbit. Tycho's rays can be seen near the top of each photo.*

same direction, west to east, about $\frac{1}{27}$ of its path around the earth (about 13 degrees) and is no longer where it was in the sky the day before. To "catch up," the earth must now rotate the additional 13 degrees on its axis. This takes about 50 minutes (about $\frac{1}{27}$ of 24 hours). If we look for the moon on the eastern horizon where it rises, we notice that the moon appears there about 50 minutes later each day, and so we say that the moon rises about 50 minutes later each day. As it rises later, it also sets later.

Since the moon rises later each day, in the course of a month it appears at a particular place in the sky at practically all times of day as well as night. When it is on the same side of the earth as the sun, the moon appears largely in the daytime sky. When opposite the sun, it is largely in the nighttime sky.

15. The Moon's Rotation

The moon's period of rotation is exactly the same—27⅓ days—as its period of revolution. In other words, it makes just one complete turn on its axis in the same time as it revolves once around the earth. The effect of this is to have the "man-in-the-moon" side of the moon always facing the earth, leaving the back of the moon always invisible to us. Since 1959, however, orbiting mooncraft have photographed the back of the moon.

A simple experiment with a book will show you why the moon's equal periods of rotation and revolution account for our seeing only one side of the moon. Hold the book in your hand at arm's length in front of you, with its front cover facing you. Now move your arm around your head, but *keep the book's front cover facing you.*

What must you do with the book to keep from seeing the back or side of it? What would happen if the book were not "rotated" at all?

Actually, about 59 per cent of the moon's surface is directly visible to the earth in the course of a month. This is because of a number of apparent "rocking" motions or **librations** of the moon. The *6½° tilt of the moon's axis* permits us to see beyond its north pole at one end of the orbit, and beyond its south pole at the other end. A second "rocking" results from the fact that **the moon revolves faster at perigee than at apogee** (Kepler's second law), while its rotation proceeds at a uniform rate. This lets us see almost 8° more around the moon's eastern and western edges. A third reason for our seeing more than half the moon is that the earth's rotation allows us to look at the moon from different positions in the course of a day. This again lets us "look around corners." (See Fig. 29-11.)

16. The Moon's Phases

If the moon, like a star, were self-luminous, we would see a "full moon" every day, though it would be less conspicuous in the daytime than at night. But the moon has no light of its own. Like the earth, it receives its light from the sun, and being a solid rock globe, only one-half of it can be illuminated at a time. The sun lights up the half of the moon that faces it, but except for a short time each month, this is obviously not the half that is kept constantly turned toward the earth. In fact, the half facing us differs in illumination each night, changing in about two weeks from complete darkness to full light and then declining for about two weeks until it is entirely dark again. These varying amounts of the moon's illuminated half, as seen from the earth, are known as its **phases.**

Figure 29-12 shows the moon at eight evenly spaced points in its orbit. Each point is about

Fig. 29-12. Phases of the moon. The diagram at the right shows the actual illumination of the moon at eight phases with the dotted lines showing the part of the moon seen from the earth at each phase. The sketch at the left shows what the moon looks like to an observer on the earth at each phase.

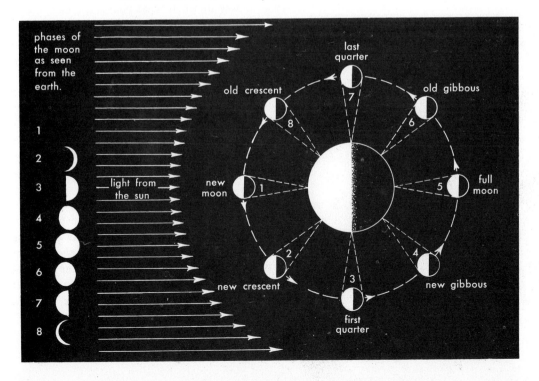

half a week away from the next. In every case the half of the moon that faces the sun is fully illuminated. Looking from the earth, however, we see different amounts of the illuminated half at each of the eight phases. What we see in the sky is shown in the sketches that are drawn in the column at the left. Remember, the whole "man in the moon" faces us at all times, but it is only at full-moon phase that he is all "lit up."

From new moon to full moon, more and more of the moon's illuminated half faces the earth, and the moon is said to be **waxing.** From full moon to new moon, less and less of the moon's illuminated half faces the earth, so it is said to be **waning.** All the phase names are self-explanatory, except *gibbous,* which might be described as "lopsided."

At new moon the entire dark side of the moon faces us and we see nothing. At the crescent phases only one edge of the side facing us is illuminated, and we see that edge as a crescent. At the quarter phases the side facing us is half light, half dark. At the gibbous phases only a dark crescent prevents our moon from being fully illuminated. At the full phase, the side facing us is fully illuminated.

17. Moonshine and Earthshine

At the crescent phases of the moon we see the brightly illuminated crescent shining in direct sunlight. The rest of the moon is also visible, although dimly. This part of the moon, though not facing the sun, is being illuminated indirectly **by sunlight that is reflected from the daytime side of the earth to the dark side of the moon.** This dim glow of the moon is known as **earthlight** or **earthshine.** (See Fig. 29-13.)

18. Daytime Moon

As explained in Topic 14, the moon is in the sky by day as much as by night, though it is less easily noticed in daylight. From Figure 29-12 it is easy to see at what phases the moon is a daytime moon, a nighttime moon, or both. If the moon is on the same side of the earth as the sun, it will be in the sky mostly in the daytime. This is true at the new and crescent phases. At the quarter phases it will be in the sky about as many daylight hours as night hours. At the full and gibbous phases the moon is on the side of the earth opposite to the sun, so it is almost entirely a nighttime spectacle.

Fig. 29-13. Earthshine or earthlight on the moon at the new crescent phase in the evening sky. The moon's bright crescent is lit up by direct sunlight. The rest of the moon is being illuminated by sunlight reflected from the earth.

Yerkes Observatory

19. Daytime Laboratory

The positions of moon, earth, and sun that produce the various phases can readily be seen outdoors. For example, Figure 29-12 shows the earth directly between the moon and the sun at full-moon phase. Standing outdoors at sunset on the day of the full moon, an observer on the earth sees the sun setting in the west, the moon rising in the east, and himself directly between them. At first-quarter phase he may see the moon in the south as the sun sets in the west, while he himself forms the corner of the right triangle on the earth. This is just what the diagram shows. The other phase positions can be observed in the same way. The observer will also notice that the lighted side of the moon always faces the sun.

20. Months

The early Roman calendar was based on the motions of the moon, from which we derive the word *month*. In our calendar a month may be either 28, 29, 30, or 31 days. To the astronomer, however, month has a somewhat different meaning.

The astronomer defines two kinds of months. The **sidereal month** (*sidereal* means "of the stars") is the moon's period of revolution, 27⅓ days. It represents the time between two successive lineups of earth, moon, and a given star. The **synodic month** or **lunar month** is the time from new moon to new moon, about 29½ days. The synodic month is longer than the moon's period of revolution because while the moon is revolving around the earth, the earth is also moving forward in its orbit around the sun, at the rate of about one degree a day. This makes it necessary for the moon to revolve about two extra days in its orbit before again lining up with earth and sun in the new-moon position. (See Fig. 29-14.)

THE MOON AND ECLIPSES

21. Earth's Shadow on the Moon

As the earth revolves around the sun, it casts its shadow off into space. This shadow, pointing away from the sun on the nighttime side of the earth, consists of two parts, an **umbra**, or total

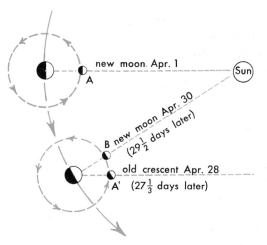

Fig. 29-14. The time taken by the moon for one full revolution from A to A' is a sidereal month. From A to B, new moon to new moon, is a synodic month.

shadow, and a **penumbra** (peh *num* bruh), or partial shadow. The umbra is an enormously long, narrowing cone which reaches its apex (tip) at a distance of about 860,000 miles from the earth. The penumbra, widening instead of narrowing, stretches endlessly off into space. When the earth's shadow falls on the moon, an **eclipse of the moon** takes place. The eclipse is **total** if the moon is entirely in the umbra, and **partial** if the moon is partly in the umbra or in the penumbra. (See Fig. 29-15.) (Penumbra shadows are hardly noticed on the moon.)

22. Time of Lunar Eclipse

The only phase at which the earth's shadow can fall on the moon is full moon. An eclipse of the moon would take place at full-moon phase every month if the moon's orbit were in the same plane as the earth's orbit. But since the moon's orbit is inclined about 5 degrees to the earth's orbit, **lunar eclipses** can take place only if full

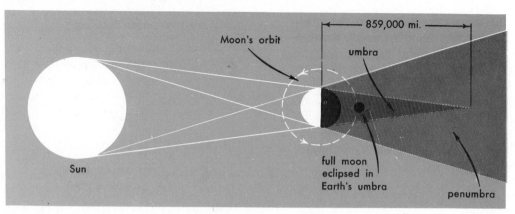

Fig. 29-15. An eclipse of the moon (lunar eclipse) can occur only at full moon.

moon comes when the moon crosses the plane of the earth's orbit, or is close to it. This happens between two and five times each year, but no more than three of these times are total eclipses.

At the moon's distance of about 240,000 miles from the earth, the earth's umbra is almost 6,000 miles in diameter, or almost three times as wide as the moon. If the moon goes through the center of the umbra, the eclipse may be total for almost two hours.

23. Seeing a Lunar Eclipse

There are many opportunities within a lifetime to see a total lunar eclipse. On the average at least one such eclipse takes place every year, and the entire nighttime half of the earth is in a position to see it. Added to this are the parts of the world that miss the beginning of the eclipse but rotate into view while the eclipse lasts. So, if the weather is good, more than half the world can see each lunar eclipse.

The earth's umbra is not completely dark, because the earth's atmosphere acts like a lens and bends some sunlight into the shadow cast by the solid earth. As a result, the moon has a dusky red color in the umbra, instead of being completely blacked out.

Eclipses can be forecast for years in advance. The times of future eclipses may be found in many astronomy publications and in the *Nautical Almanac* which is obtainable from the Government Printing Office located in Washington, D.C.

24. Moon's Shadow on the Earth

Like the earth, the moon casts a shadow into space. The moon's umbra has a maximum length of 236,000 miles, easily long enough to reach the earth at perigee but not long enough to reach it at apogee. Only the tip of the umbra touches the earth, its maximum width being just 167 miles. The penumbra is much wider, of course, since it becomes larger as it extends away from the moon. When the moon's shadow falls on the earth an **eclipse of the sun** takes place. Where the umbra falls, the eclipse is **total;** where the penumbra falls, the eclipse is **partial.** (See Fig. 29-16.)

25. Time of Solar Eclipse

An eclipse of the sun takes place when the moon "gets in the way of the sun." If the moon hides the sun completely, the sun is totally eclipsed; if the moon covers only a part of the sun, the sun is partially eclipsed. The only phase at which this can happen is new moon. An eclipse of the sun would take place at new-moon phase every month were it not for the inclination of the moon's orbit. As it is, solar eclipses occur from two to five times a year, whenever the moon crosses or comes close to the plane of the earth's orbit at new moon. Three of these eclipses may be total.

As mentioned above, the narrow tip of the umbra that reaches the earth's surface is never more than 167 miles wide; it may be much less. This means that only a very small part of the earth can see any solar eclipse as a total eclipse. (The much larger area on which the penumbra falls sees the same event as a partial eclipse.) Nor does the total solar eclipse last very long, for the moon's revolution causes the narrow shadow to race across the earth at a speed of more than 1,000 miles an hour. At any one spot a total solar eclipse can never be seen for more than 7½ minutes even under the most ideal arrangement of sun, moon, and earth. The narrow track made on the earth's surface by the eastward-moving shadow of the moon is called the **eclipse path.** It may be thousands of miles long.

26. Seeing a Solar Eclipse

While solar eclipses happen at least as often as lunar eclipses, the area covered by the umbra at each eclipse is so small that any one spot on the earth averages only one total eclipse in 300 years. It is easy to see, therefore, why a total solar eclipse is such a rare sight for any one person. Astronomers travel thousands of miles in well-planned "eclipse expeditions" to make studies of the sun's corona and other features which are best seen when the sun's photosphere is covered by the moon. The last total solar eclipse visible in a part of the United States took place March 7, 1970. At that time the path of the eclipse crossed Florida and then followed the Atlantic Coast northward. On October 12, 1977, a total solar eclipse will be visible in South America, Central America, and Hawaii.

A solar eclipse begins when the moon is first seen to come across the western edge of the sun. It ends when the moon disappears from the eastern edge. From start to finish the entire eclipse may last four hours. At totality the chromosphere and corona can be seen surrounding the blackened face of the sun, while in the darkened sky it is possible to see bright stars and planets with the naked eye.

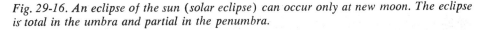

Fig. 29-16. An eclipse of the sun (solar eclipse) can occur only at new moon. The eclipse is total in the umbra and partial in the penumbra.

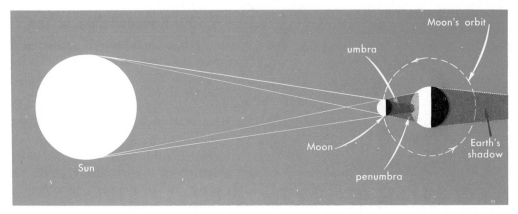

27. Annular Eclipse

Annular eclipses of the sun occur a little more often than total eclipses. In an annular eclipse the moon is in the same position as in a total solar eclipse, but its umbra does not reach the earth. The result is a **partial eclipse** with a "special feature." In those parts of the world that are directly in the center of the penumbra, the moon appears to cover all but a thin outside ring of the sun's photosphere. (The term "annular" comes from the Latin word *annulus,* which means "ring." Do not confuse "annular" with "annual," which means "yearly.") In other parts of the penumbra the eclipse is seen as an ordinary partial one.

SUN, MOON, AND TIDES

28. The Moon and the Tides Are Related

On all the seacoasts of the earth the ocean waters rise and fall daily in a rhythmic movement known as the tides. The tides are obviously related to the moon. Like the moon, they rise 50 minutes later each day on the average. The tides are unusually high at the times of new moon and full moon and unusually low at times of quarter moon. Sir Isaac Newton was the first to explain how the moon and the tides are related, using his law of gravitation.

29. How the Moon Creates Tides

Newton explained the production of tides by the moon as an effect of the *difference in its gravitational attraction* for the solid earth and its ocean waters. The ocean waters on the side of the earth facing the moon are nearest the moon and are therefore attracted most strongly. The waters on the far side of the earth, 8,000 miles farther away, are attracted least. The solid earth is attracted at its center of gravity, which is halfway between the two halves of the ocean.

According to Newton the moon attracts the ocean waters on the near side more strongly than it attracts the solid earth, causing the waters to rise or bulge under the moon in a "high tide." This is the **direct high tide**, H_D in Figure 29-17. On the far side of the earth the moon's attraction for the waters is *less* than for the solid earth. Here the waters bulge away from the surface in an **indirect** or **opposite high tide**, H_I in Figure 29-17. Halfway between the high-tide points, two areas of low tide, L and L', are formed by the withdrawal of water to the high-tide locations.

30. Rise and Fall of the Tides

Thus far Newton's explanation accounts for two high-tide locations and two low-tide locations. But as the earth rotates on its axis, it brings all parts of its surface under the moon in 24 hours and 50 minutes. (Of this, 23 hours and 56 minutes represent the earth's rotation time. The extra 54 minutes are added by the revolution of the moon around the earth in the same west-to-east direction.) In one-fourth of this time—6 hours and 13 minutes—each high-

Fig. 29-17. The moon causes high tides at H_D and H_I and low tides at L and L'. H_D is called the direct high tide, and H_I the indirect one.

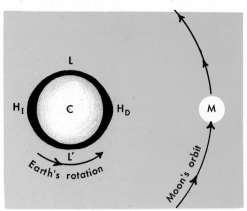

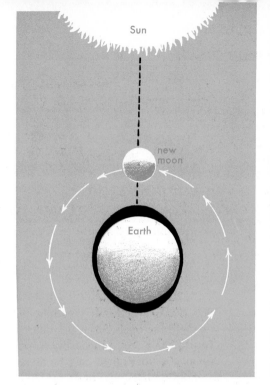 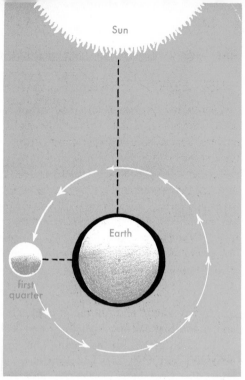

Fig. 29-18. As shown at the left spring tides occur when sun, earth, and moon are in line (at either new moon or full moon). At these times of the month high tides are highest and low tides are lowest. At the right a neap tide is shown, with sun, earth, and moon forming a right angle (at either first or last quarter). At these times the rise and fall of the tides is least for the month.

tide area has moved to low tide, and each low-tide area has moved to high tide. In 12 hours and 26 minutes the tides have changed again. As the earth rotates, the tides continue to rise and fall rhythmically in a cycle that is repeated about 50 minutes later each day.

The times given in the "model" timetable at the bottom of the page are averages. In actual observations they are much more irregular. Some coastal areas—the Gulf of Mexico, for example, and many Pacific islands—may have only one high tide and one low tide a day. On the other hand, two daily high and low tides are typical of both sides of the Atlantic Ocean.

31. Spring and Neap Tides

The sun has the same kind of effect on the earth's waters as the moon has, but because of its greater distance this effect is only about half as great as the moon's. This means that while the moon is the chief maker of tides, the sun can help or hinder the moon's effects. Tides are always high on the parts of the earth in line with the moon and low on the parts that are at right angles to the moon. But when the sun is in line with the moon, its effect is added to the moon's. When the sun-earth line is at right angles to the moon-earth line, the sun's effect is opposed to the moon's. (See Figs. 29-18 and 29-19.)

Tide	Date	Time	Interval Since First High Tide
High	July 4	1:00 AM	
Low	July 4	7:13 AM	6 hrs. 13 min.
High	July 4	1:25 PM	12 hrs. 25 min.
Low	July 4	7:38 PM	18 hrs. 38 min.
High	July 5	1:50 AM	24 hrs. 50 min.

Fig. 29-19. Tidal range is large at spring tides and small at neap tides. The sketch at the left shows the tidal range for a spring tide. The sketch at the right shows the range for a neap tide.

At new-moon and full-moon phases both sun and moon are causing high tides and low tides at the same places on the earth. This results in unusually high high-tides and unusually low low-tides. The **tidal range,** defined as the difference between the level of high tide and the level of low tide, is very large at these times. These tides are called **spring tides,** perhaps because the waters "spring so high." Remember, they occur twice every month and have nothing to do with the spring season.

At first-quarter and third-quarter phases the sun is in a position where it raises the moon's low-tide levels and lowers the moon's high-tide levels. This results in high tides that are not very high, and low tides that are not very low. The tidal range is very small at these times. These tides are called **neap tides** (*neap* means "scanty").

32. Ocean Basins, Shorelines, and Tidal Range

Tidal ranges differ greatly for reasons other than the phase of the moon. Small lakes show no tides at all. Even a great lake such as Lake Superior is raised only a couple of inches by the tides. In the open ocean the tidal range averages two to three feet, but on the shores of the same ocean the tidal range may be as large as 60 feet —as in the Bay of Fundy on the coast of Nova Scotia—or as little as two feet, as in the Gulf of Mexico.

Oceanographers believe that the size and shape of each ocean basin or gulf or bay play a large part in determining how much its waters will rise and fall under the differential pull of the moon and sun. Each basin has its own natural period of oscillation or "rocking," just as a swing or pendulum has. If the moon's tidal force is exerted in rhythm with the rocking of the water in the basin, very high tides may be produced at the margins or shorelines of the basin.

Oceanographers also believe that high tidal ranges develop through the funneling of water from the open oceans into V-shaped bays such as the Bay of Fundy. Similarly, bays that become wider from mouth to shoreline—the Gulf of Mexico, for example—spread the incoming water thin and have small tidal ranges.

Direct and indirect tides also differ in height unless the moon is in line with earth's Equator. (See Fig. 29-17.)

TOPIC QUESTIONS

Each topic question refers to the topic of the same number within this chapter.

1. Describe the great advances made recently in our ability to study the surface of the moon.

2. (*a*) Give figures and an illustration to show the relative size of the earth and the moon. (*b*) Why are the moon's surface gravity and velocity of escape smaller than the earth's?

3. What evidences tell us that the moon has little or no atmosphere?

4. (*a*) What evidences of erosion does the moon show? How are they explained? (*b*) Explain how weathering may take place on the moon, even though it has no atmosphere.

5. (*a*) What principal lunar features does a good telescope reveal? (*b*) Describe the lunar seas. Name some. (*c*) What makes the floors of the seas relatively smooth?

6. (*a*) Where are lunar mountains usually located? Name and locate some. (*b*) Where are the Doerfels? (*c*) Compare the appearance and probable origin of lunar mountains with those of mountains on the earth.

7. (*a*) Describe the lunar craters. (*b*) State two hypotheses of their origin.

8. (*a*) Describe the lunar rays and their possible origin. (*b*) What are rills?

9. Why do we think that volcanic activity may still be occurring on the moon?

10. (*a*) Describe the characteristics of lunar soil as determined from spacecraft observations. (*b*) Where are the "safe" landing areas?

11. (*a*) Why is the moon a "harsh environment" for man? (*b*) How will the moon's weak gravity be helpful to man?

12. Briefly describe three hypotheses of the moon's origin.

13. (*a*) Describe the moon's orbit as to direction, period, shape, plane, perigee, and apogee. (*b*) Why do the sun and moon look equally large in our sky?

14. (*a*) Why does the moon rise in the east and set in the west? (*b*) Why does it rise about 50 minutes later each day?

15. (*a*) Explain why one side of the moon always faces the earth. (*b*) What are librations? (*c*) Give three reasons why we can see a little more than half of the moon.

16. Why is not the moon full all the time? Explain its phases, using a diagram.

17. Explain what earthshine is and when it is seen best.

18. What phases of the moon are seen chiefly at night? in the daytime? half and half?

19. Explain how the sky may be used as a laboratory for showing how phases are caused.

20. (*a*) What is the sidereal month? (*b*) What is the synodic month? Why is it longer than the sidereal month?

21. Describe the earth's shadow. How is it related to eclipses of the moon?

22. (*a*) At what phase does a lunar eclipse occur? Why does it not occur every month? (*b*) How long may a total lunar eclipse last? (*c*) Make a diagram showing how a lunar eclipse occurs.

23. (*a*) How much of the world can see each lunar eclipse? Why? (*b*) Why is not the moon completely darkened in a total lunar eclipse?

24. Describe the moon's shadow and its relation to eclipses of the sun.

25. (*a*) At what phase does a solar eclipse occur? Why does it not occur every month? (*b*) How long can a total solar eclipse last? Why? (*c*) What is the eclipse path? (*d*) Make a diagram of a solar eclipse.

26. (*a*) Why are total solar eclipses such rare sights even though they happen almost every year? (*b*) Why do astronomers observe total solar eclipses? (*c*) Describe a total solar eclipse.

27. What is an annular eclipse? How does it happen? Where does its name come from?

28. What facts indicate a connection between the moon and the tides?

29. (*a*) Explain how the moon causes the tides. (*b*) Make a diagram showing where high and low tides are in relation to the moon's position.

30. (*a*) Explain why tides rise or fall every 6 hours and 13 minutes. (*b*) Explain why the tides come 50 minutes later each day.

31. (*a*) How does the sun affect tides? Explain. (*b*) Define tidal range. (*c*) What are spring tides? How and when do they occur? (*d*) What are neap tides? How and when do they occur? (*e*) Show spring and neap tides in diagrams.

32. (*a*) How do the size and shape of an ocean basin affect its tidal range? (*b*) How is the shape of a bay related to its tidal range?

GENERAL QUESTIONS

1. (*a*) Why is the contour interval for lunar charts so large? (See Topic 1.) (*b*) Explain why the latitude must be specified after the scale given in Topic 1.

2. Make a diagram to show that very little earthshine can strike the moon at a gibbous phase.

3. In Topic 22 it is stated that the earth's umbra is about 6,000 miles in diameter where the moon crosses it. Prove this by geometry.

4. It was once thought that there was a planet closer to the sun than Mercury. Why were observations of solar eclipses necessary to disprove this?

5. Can a solar eclipse start as an annular eclipse and then become total? Explain.

6. Direct and indirect high tides are about the same height when the moon is in the plane of the earth's Equator, but may be very unequal when the moon is above or below the Equator. Show this in a diagram.

7. (*a*) What combination of factors (moon's distance from earth, earth's distance from sun) would produce the largest spring tides? (*b*) What combination would produce the smallest neap tides?

8. Work out the approximate times of moonrise and moonset for the eight phases shown in Figure 29-12.

STUDENT ACTIVITIES

1. Observe the moon through telescopes, binoculars, and the unaided eye.

2. Observe and record the time of moonrise and moonset at various phases of the moon.

3. Collect photographs of the moon.

4. Build a model to show the inclination of the moon's orbit to the plane of the earth's orbit.

5. Observe and record the relative positions of sun, earth, and moon at various phases.

6. Demonstrate an "eclipse" of sun or moon with globes and electric lights.

7. Record and plot the time of the tides.

8. Observe the relation of tidal range to the moon's phases from actual observation or tide tables.

CHAPTER 30

The Earth's Motions

HOW DO YOU KNOW THAT . . . ?

One effect of the earth's rotation on its axis is the apparent daily movement of the sun through the sky. To see this without watching the sun itself, stand a tall slender rod in a vertical position in a sunny window. Trace its shadow every 10 minutes for at least half an hour. Why does the shadow change in length as well as in direction?

The change in the sun's height in the sky from day to day is caused by the earth's revolution around the sun. Keep a record of the length of the shadow cast by the rod at the same time each day. In which seasons does the shadow get longer? In which seasons does it get shorter?

1. The Earth's Revolution and Orbit

The motion of the earth in its orbit is called **revolution.** The earth's orbit, like those of the other planets, is an ellipse with the sun at one focus. The orbit lies in a level surface or plane called the **plane of the earth's orbit.** The earth revolves around the sun from west to east in its orbit at a speed of about 66,000 miles per hour, or 18½ miles a second. The earth's **period of revolution** is one year, or 365¼ days. Since the earth revolves 360° in 365¼ days, its **angular rate of revolution** is about 1° a day.

Because the orbit of the earth is not a circle, the distance between the earth and the sun is constantly changing. The average distance between them is about 92,900,000 miles, known as the *astronomical unit* (A.U.). The sun is about 1,500,000 miles from the orbit's center, so at *perihelion* the earth is about 91,400,000 miles from the sun. At *aphelion* the earth is about 94,400,000 miles from the sun. Perihelion comes about January 1; aphelion about July 1. (See Fig. 30-1.)

Proof of the earth's revolution is provided by the fact that the position of the nearer stars changes as the earth revolves from one end of its orbit to the other. This *parallax* effect was described in Chapter 26.

2. The Earth's Rotation

At the same time as the earth revolves around the sun, it spins around itself like a top. We call this spinning motion its **rotation.** The earth rotates around an imaginary line through its center which we call its **axis.** The ends of the axis are known as the North Pole and the South Pole. Every day the earth makes one complete rotation on its axis. This may sound like "slow

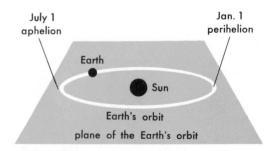

Fig. 30-1. The level surface in which the earth revolves around the sun is known as the plane of the earth's orbit.

motion" until we remember that the circumference of the earth at the Equator is nearly 25,000 miles. At the Equator, then, the earth's surface is spinning at the rate of over 1,000 miles an hour. Of course, the miles-per-hour rate of rotation gets less and less as the Poles are approached since the circumference of the earth decreases. In New York City's latitude, the rate of rotation is only about 800 miles an hour. At the Poles it is zero.

The rate of the earth's rotation may also be expressed as an angle. All points on the earth rotate one full turn or 360° in nearly 24 hours. This means an *angular rate of rotation* of about 15° an hour, or 1° in 4 minutes.

3. The Earth's Rotation and Foucault's Pendulum

How do we know that the earth is spinning? Many *effects* of rotation are known—the daily change from day to night, for example—but the first widely accepted experimental *proof* of rotation was not provided until 1851. In that year the French physicist Foucault performed his famous "pendulum" experiment at the Pantheon in Paris. (See Fig. 30-2.)

Foucault suspended a heavy iron ball from the dome of the Pantheon by a 200-foot wire; then he set it swinging along a meridian (*north-south line*). Once begun in motion, such a long, heavy pendulum has enough energy to keep it swinging for many hours. Now it is a physical fact that a freely swinging pendulum will not change its direction of vibration. Yet Foucault's pendulum steadily appeared to change direction at the rate of about 11° an hour in a clockwise direction, so that after eight hours it was swinging *from east to west*. This apparent change of the pendulum's direction was in fact caused by the *movement of the earth beneath the pendulum*. At the North Pole the earth would turn under such a pendulum 15° every hour, or completely around in one day.

Foucault pendulums, as they are known today, can be seen in operation. (See Fig. 30-3.)

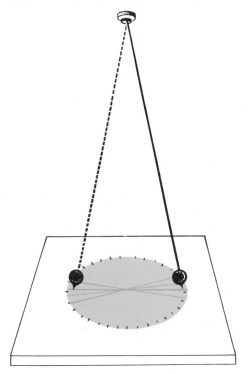

Fig. 30-2. In the Northern Hemisphere, the Foucault pendulum appears to move in a clockwise direction as the earth rotates counterclockwise under the pendulum.

Fig. 30-3. Foucault pendulum at United Nations building in New York City, proving the earth rotates.

United Nations

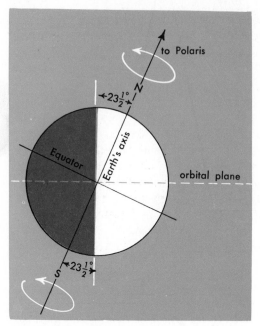

Fig. 30-4. The earth's axis is inclined 23½° from a perpendicular to the orbital plane.

4. The Direction of Rotation

The earth rotates on its axis in a west-to-east direction. Viewed from above the North Pole, the earth appears to rotate *counterclockwise*. From beneath the South Pole the direction of rotation is *clockwise*. (Try it with a globe.)

The earth's axis is not perpendicular to the plane of the earth's orbit. Instead, it leans 23½° away from the perpendicular. This angle is referred to as the **inclination of the earth's axis.** It may also be said that the axis makes an angle of 66½° (90°–23½°) with the plane of the earth's orbit. (See Fig. 30-4.)

When the axis is "extended" into the heavens, the north end comes within one degree of the North Star, also known as Polaris. Polaris, a second-magnitude star, is thus valuable to navigators as an indicator of *north*. In the Southern Hemisphere sky there is no bright star near the extension of the axis.

5. Why Day and Night Alternate and Are Unequal

Day and night exist together on the earth because the earth is a solid sphere, only half of which can be illuminated by the sun at any one moment. If the earth stood still in space, one half would be permanently in daylight, while the other half had perpetual night. But this does not happen. **The rotation of the earth on its axis causes day and night to alternate** every 24 hours for most parts of the earth. (In the "land of the midnight sun" near the North Pole and the South Pole, daylight may last several months in summer, and nighttime may last several months in winter.)

If the earth's axis were perpendicular (to the plane of its orbit), all parts of the earth would have equal day and night—about 12 hours each—on every day of the year. But the axis is inclined 23½° from the perpendicular, and on all but two days of the year one of the two hemispheres, Northern or Southern, leans toward the sun more than the other. This results in unequal distribution of sunlight on the earth. The hemisphere that leans toward the sun has longer days than nights. The hemisphere that leans away from the sun has shorter days than nights.

6. Why Day and Night Change in Length

The inclination of the earth's axis accounts for day and night being unequal in length. Again, however, if the earth stood still in space, the length of day and night would remain fixed for each part of the world. **The reason that day and night change in length is that the earth revolves around the sun.** Revolution causes a small daily change in the amount that each hemisphere leans toward or away from the sun, with a resulting gradual change in the length of day and night.

To illustrate the "change of leaning," do this simple experiment. Hold your left fist in front of you to represent the sun. Grasp a pencil in your right hand. Your right hand will represent the earth; the pencil will be its axis. Place this "earth" to the left of the "sun," with its "North Pole" pointing about 23½° to the right, toward the "sun." Now *keeping the axis parallel to its first position,* revolve the "earth" around the "sun." Notice how the *North Pole leans away from the sun at the opposite* (right) *end of the orbit.* Notice also that neither Pole leans toward the "sun" at the two points midway between the two extreme positions. Through the entire revolution the axis *remains parallel to itself,* pointing to the same direction in space, the direction of the North Star. This behavior of the earth's axis is called **parallelism.** (See Fig. 30-5.)

7. Daylight at the Solstices

The day of the year on which the North Pole leans the full 23½° into the sun is *June 21 or 22.* This day is known as the **summer solstice.** It is the longest day of the year for the Northern Hemisphere and the shortest day for the Southern Hemisphere. The day when the North Pole leans 23½° away from the sun is *December 21 or 22,* known as the **winter solstice.** It is the shortest day for the Northern Hemisphere and the longest day for the Southern Hemisphere.

Figure 30-6 (left) shows the earth at the summer solstice. Only the Equator has equal day and night. In the Northern Hemisphere the amount of daylight increases from 12 hours at

Fig. 30-5. Throughout the earth's revolution around the sun, the earth's axis continues to point in the same direction. This parallelism of the axis is an important factor in the regular change of seasons and of the length of day and night.

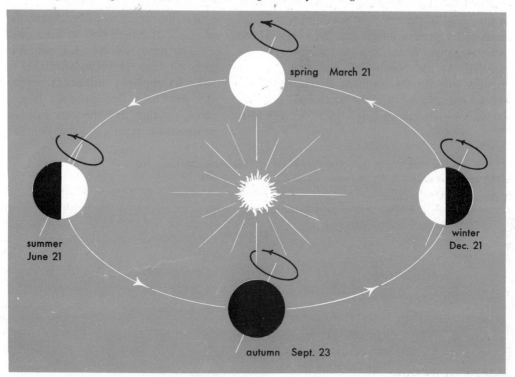

spring   March 21

summer
June 21

winter
Dec. 21

autumn   Sept. 23

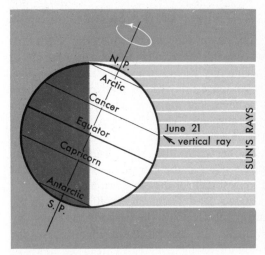
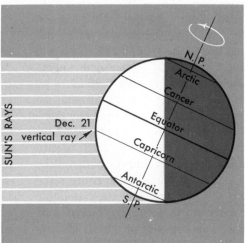

Fig. 30-6. *These drawings show how day and night are distributed on the earth from Pole to Pole on the Northern Hemisphere's longest day (June 21) and its shortest day (December 21).*

the Equator to 24 hours at the Arctic Circle (the parallel of latitude that is 23½° from the North Pole). From the Arctic Circle to the North Pole is the "land of the midnight sun." Here daylight remains for periods longer than 24 hours. These periods range from days to weeks or even months. At the North Pole the "day" is six months long. In the Southern Hemisphere conditions are reversed, and the South Pole is in the middle of a six-month long night. (See Fig. 30-7.)

Figure 30-6 (right) shows the earth at the winter solstice. Now the Northern Hemisphere has its shortest day, while the Southern Hemisphere has its longest day. Again, day and night are equal in length only at the Equator.

The name **solstice** (*sol*, sun; *stice*, stop) is given to June 21 because on that date the sun stops its apparent movement northward in our sky. Similarly, December 21 is a solstice, because on that day the sun stops its apparent southward movement in our sky. From June 21

Fig. 30-7. *The "midnight sun" photographed at 15-minute intervals from 10:45 P.M. to 1:15 A.M. on July 25. Bylot Island on Baffin Bay, Canada.*

National Film Board of Canada

to December 21, daylight decreases in the Northern Hemisphere and increases in the Southern Hemisphere. From December 21 to June 21 the reverse takes place.

The boundary between the daylight and nighttime halves of the earth at any time is called the **twilight circle.** In our diagrams this circle is seen "edge on," so it is shown as a straight vertical line.

8. Daylight at the Equinoxes

The two days of the year when neither North Pole nor South Pole leans toward the sun are *March 21 or 22,* and *September 22 or 23.* On these dates day and night are equal in length over all the world. Each date is therefore known as an **equinox** (*equi,* equal; *nox,* night). On the spring equinox, March 21 or 22, the North Pole is just about to begin its six-month day. On the fall equinox, September 22 or 23, the South Pole begins its six-month day. (See Fig. 30-8.)

9. Angle of the Sun's Rays

Figure 30-9 shows why all the rays of the sun that reach the earth are "parallel" rays. Although these rays are parallel to each other, the curved surface of the earth causes them to make angles with the surface that range from

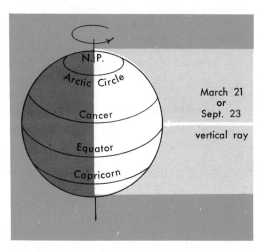

Fig. 30-8. Day and night are equal in length throughout the earth only on the two equinoxes. The view shown here is what you would see from a distant point to the right of the earth at spring or autumn in Fig. 30-5.

0° to 90° at any moment. (See Fig. 30-6.) When the sun is directly overhead (angle 90°), it is said to be in the **zenith.** The zenith is defined as the point in the sky directly above the observer. (See Fig. 30-10.)

When the sun is just rising or setting (angle 0°), it is on the **horizon.** The angle of the sun above the horizon is its **altitude.** Its angle below the zenith is its **zenith distance.**

Fig. 30-9. Even though the sun radiates energy in all directions, the only rays to reach the earth are those that lie in or close to the orbital plane. These rays are all practically parallel to one another.

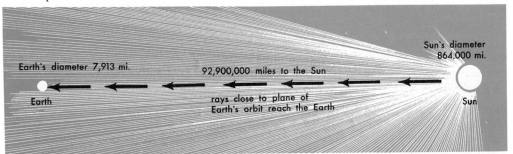

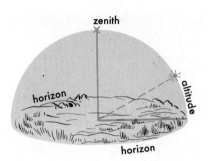

Fig. 30-10. Terms used in locating points in the sky.

The closer the sun's rays are to the vertical, the stronger and hotter they are. On any day of the year the sun's rays are strongest at noon, when the sun is highest in the sky. For continental United States the strongest sun comes on June 21, when the sun is at its highest position in our sky during the entire year.

10. The Solstices and the Seasons

Figure 30-6 shows why summer and winter occur as they do about the time of the solstices. Notice that on June 21 the Northern Hemisphere (from the Equator to the North Pole) receives far more than half of the sun's rays, including a large share of rays close to the vertical on the earth. The parallel where the sun's *vertical ray* is striking is called the **Tropic of Cancer.** It is exactly 23½° north of the Equator, because that is how far the Northern Hemisphere is tilted into the sun. The Southern Hemisphere receives a much smaller share of sunlight, most of it at a low angle.

Why is this time of the year summertime for the Northern Hemisphere? It is summer because this is the time when the Northern Hemisphere receives *strong sunshine,* while its *long days* allow ample time for heating. In the Southern Hemisphere it is winter, because the sun's rays are slanting and weak, and short days permit little time for heating.

On December 21 conditions are reversed. The sun's vertical ray is 23½° south of the Equator at the **Tropic of Capricorn.** Now the Southern Hemisphere receives the lion's share of the sunshine, both in strength of rays and length of daylight. It is summer in the Southern Hemisphere and winter in the Northern Hemisphere.

Between June 21 and December 21 the sun's vertical ray travels over a zone reaching from the Tropic of Cancer to the Tropic of Capricorn, 23½° each side of the Equator. Then from December 21 to June 21 it returns over the same area. This 47° wide belt, the **Torrid Zone,** has no true winter or summer. Its days are never far from 12 hours in length, and the sun's rays are never far from vertical, so temperatures remain high throughout the year. At the Equator, center of the Torrid Zone, the sun's rays are vertical on the equinoxes (about March 21 and September 23), roughly midway between the solstices. At the time of the equinoxes sunlight is distributed evenly over the earth, giving us our moderate spring and fall seasons. (See Fig. 30-8.)

The **sun's declination** is the distance in degrees of the sun's vertical ray from the Equator. On June 21 it is 23½° North; on December 21 it is 23½° South; on the equinoxes it is zero.

11. The Sun at Noon

In all parts of the world the sun reaches its highest position in the sky each day at noon, when it is midway between its rising and setting positions. Only in the tropics (from the Tropic of Cancer to the Tropic of Capricorn) does it reach the zenith, and even there it is in the zenith at any particular place on only two days of each year. In the United States the sun reaches the zenith only in the Hawaiian Islands, the only part of the United States south of the Tropic of Cancer.

In all other parts of the United States the sun is highest in the sky on June 21 and lowest in the sky on December 21. (See Fig. 30-11.) At noon the sun is always directly south of the zenith in this country, except in the Hawaiian Islands.

12. Summary: What Causes Seasons; Effect of Distance

We can summarize the causes of seasons as follows: (1) inclination of the earth's axis, (2) parallelism of the axis, (3) rotation of the earth on its axis, (4) revolution of the earth around the sun.

People often say that "the earth is nearest the sun in winter and farthest away in summer." It is not the whole earth, however, that has winter when the earth is nearest the sun, but only the Northern Hemisphere. At the same time the Southern Hemisphere has its summer. Six months later, the Northern Hemisphere has its summer when it is farthest from the sun, but then it is winter in the Southern Hemisphere. It is obvious from all this that *changing distance from the sun is not the cause of the seasons.* If it were, the whole earth would have the same season at the same time. For the true explanation of seasonal change we must look to the causes which have already been given.

Why is our changing distance from the sun so unimportant that we may have winter and summer with no regard to the distance? Once again the answer is a simple one. The difference between perihelion distance, where the earth's

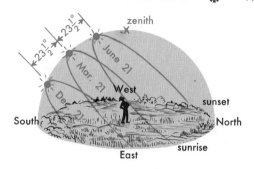

Fig. 30-11. Path of the sun in the sky at the latitude of New York City, 41°N, on the solstices and equinoxes. Total change in altitude from summer to winter is 47°.

orbit is nearest the sun, and aphelion distance, where the orbit is farthest from the sun, is 3,000,000 miles. This seems like a great distance, but proportionately it is small, for it is only about $\frac{1}{31}$ of the total distance between earth and sun. The situation is comparable to that in which a man is 31 feet from a campfire. If he felt cold, he could certainly make himself warmer by moving closer to the fire, but moving a distance of only one foot would make very little difference. So it is with the earth.

It is true, however, that the earth as a whole receives a little more heat from the sun in January than in July. If our orbit were very eccentric, like Pluto's, then change in perihelion and aphelion distance would have a tremendous seasonal effect.

TOPIC QUESTIONS

Each topic question refers to the topic of the same number within this chapter.

1. (*a*) Describe the earth's <u>orbit</u> and the <u>speed</u> and <u>direction</u> of the earth in the orbit. (*b*) What is the astronomical unit? (*c*) Give the date and distance of the earth at perihelion and aphelion. (*d*) How do we know that the earth revolves around the sun?

2. What is the earth's rotation? What is its rate?

3. Describe the experiment by which Foucault proved that the earth rotates.

4. (a) In what direction does the earth rotate? As seen from the North Pole? South Pole? (b) Describe the position of the axis.

5. (a) Why do day and night alternate? (b) Why are day and night unequal?

6. (a) Why do day and night change in length? (b) What is the axis' parallelism?

7. Describe the distribution of day and night over the earth on (a) the summer solstice, (b) the winter solstice. Give their dates.

8. (a) Why are day and night equal everywhere on the equinoxes? (b) Give the names and dates of the equinoxes.

9. (a) Explain the meaning of zenith, horizon, altitude, and zenith distance. Use a diagram. (b) How is the angle of the sun's rays related to their strength?

10. (a) What is the Tropic of Cancer? (b) Explain why June 21 is a time of warm weather in the Northern Hemisphere and cold weather in the Southern Hemisphere. (c) Why are weather conditions reversed on December 21? (d) What is the Torrid Zone? Why is it warm all year? (e) Explain why spring and fall are our "moderate" seasons. (f) What is the sun's declination? on June 21? on December 21? on March 21?

11. Why is the sun always below the zenith in continental United States at noontime? In which direction is it always seen at noon?

12. (a) State the causes of the regular change of seasons. (b) What evidence is there that our seasons are *not* caused by changing distance from the sun? (c) Why is a change in distance of 3,000,000 miles so unimportant for us?

GENERAL QUESTIONS

1. How do the earth's rotation and revolution affect conditions for life on earth?

2. How may measurements of the weight of an object be used to show the oblate shape of the earth?

3. Compare the length of day and night in New York City with that in Mexico City, Montreal, and Buenos Aires on June 21 and December 21.

4. Where would the noon sun be in the sky at the Equator on the two equinoxes and the two solstices?

5. How would increased inclination of the earth's axis change (a) the length of day and night? (b) the seasons?

6. Suppose the earth rotated from east to west at twice its present rate. What changes would be made in our day?

STUDENT ACTIVITIES

1. Figure 30-11 shows that the sun rises to the north of east and sets to the north of west on all dates from March 21 to September 23. Similarly, the sun rises south of east and sets south of west in fall and winter. This is true for all places on earth.

   Check this by actual observation of the sun in your locality for a period of several weeks in both spring and fall terms.

2. Both Figure 30-11 and Topic 11 tell us that the noon sun, in all of the United States except Hawaii, is always to the south of zenith regardless of the date. Check this by actual observation for a period of several weeks in both winter and summer.

   Measure the approximate noon zenith distance of the sun at weekly intervals for a few weeks before and after the winter solstice, when the sun's zenith distance is greatest. Do the same at the time of the summer solstice, when the zenith distance is least.

   A crude measurement of the sun's zenith distance may be made with a blackboard compass, pointing one arm of the compass at the zenith and the other at the sun. Accurate measurements can be made with a sextant. (See Chapter 31, Topic 10.)

3. Make a model of the earth at the solstices and equinoxes in its orbit.

4. Make a model to illustrate the Foucault pendulum.

CHAPTER 31

Location and Navigation

HOW DO YOU KNOW THAT . . . ?

In all of the United States (except Hawaii during part of the summer) the sun is always directly to the south at the time of day when it is highest in the sky. At that time, the shadow of a vertical post will point to the true geographical north—to the earth's North Pole. At about 11 A.M. standard time set up a long slender vertical post, outdoors or indoors, in sunlight. Stand the post on a surface on which you can mark the line of its shadow. Mark this line every five minutes. Why does it change direction? Why does it get shorter? Now watch carefully for the moment when the shadow *first gets longer*. The shadow just before this may be taken as the shortest shadow—the true north-south line. Make a permanent record of this direction for future reference.

1. Going Places

"Going places" is done in much the same way by the pilot of a river steamer, a coastwise vessel, or the short-hop airplane, for they too may follow the "roads" and watch the landmarks. But for the pilot of a transoceanic ship or airplane the problems of navigation are different. In midocean there are no streets, no marked highways, no signposts, and no landmarks. Pilots must be able to find their latitude and longitude, and locate north, south, east, and west.

2. Location Schemes

A stranger in a big city does have "navigation" problems if the city planners gave little thought to the arrangement of streets and avenues in planning their city. The simplest arrangement is usually one in which streets and avenues are laid out in north-south and east-west directions, spaced equally, and numbered consecutively. Such a scheme has been created for the entire surface of the earth, so that ship and plane pilots may determine their exact locations on the oceans or in the air and geographers may

define exact boundaries between states and countries. The north-south "streets" of the earth are called *meridians;* the east-west "streets" are called *parallels*. These "streets" have no signposts and are not paved, so special methods must be devised to identify them. We often speak of them as imaginary lines, but on maps and charts they are as real as highways, and the navigator is trained to find and use them. (See Fig. 31-1.)

Fig. 31-1. Parallels run east and west. Meridians run north and south.

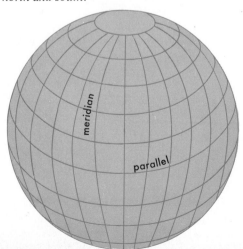

476

3. Latitude and Degrees

Our system of latitude and longitude makes use of the earth's North Pole and South Pole as reference points. To divide the earth into a Northern Hemisphere and a Southern Hemisphere, the Equator is drawn as a circle running around the earth exactly halfway between the Poles. We are now ready to define latitude. **Latitude is the distance in degrees** (angular distance) **north or south of the Equator.** To measure latitude, equal distances from the Equator are marked off by **parallels** which are imaginary **circles that go around the earth parallel to the Equator.** Like the Equator, they run in an east-west direction. (See Figs. 31-1 and 31-2.) The closer a parallel is to the North or South Pole, the smaller in circumference it is.

Latitude is expressed in degrees, not in miles. Since the Equator is the starting place from which latitude is measured, it is numbered 0°. Places north of the Equator have *north latitude;* places south of the Equator have *south latitude.* The two Poles are the points most distant from the Equator; the North Pole's latitude is 90° N and the South Pole's latitude is 90° S. (From the Equator to either Pole is one-fourth of the distance around the earth. One-fourth of 360 degrees is 90 degrees.) Each parallel is named only by its distance from the Equator, except for the Tropics of Cancer and Capricorn (23½° N and 23½° S) and the Arctic and Antarctic Circles (66½° N and 66½° S).

4. Latitude and Miles

It is easy to calculate the number of miles in a degree of latitude. The total distance around the earth through the Poles is 24,860 miles. Divided by 360, this gives an average of about 69 miles to a degree of latitude. Since the earth is not perfectly round, there is a slight variation in the length of a degree of latitude all the way from the Equator to the Poles. At the Poles, where the earth is flattest, a degree of latitude is almost a mile longer than at the Equator. (For approximate calculations we usually use 70 miles to one degree of latitude.)

Degrees alone are too large for precise locations on the earth, so they are subdivided into *minutes* and *seconds.* A degree includes 60 minutes (written as 60'); each minute includes 60 seconds (written as 60"). To find the length of

Fig. 31-2. Latitude is measured in degrees north or south of the Equator. Longitude is measured in degrees east or west of the prime meridian.

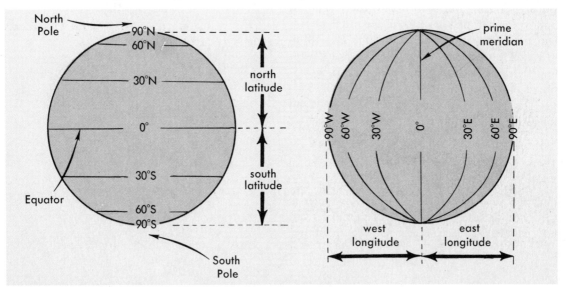

one minute (1′), we divide 70 miles (in 1°) by 60. A **minute** is therefore equal to $1\frac{1}{6}$ miles, about 6,000 feet. To find the approximate length of one second (1″) we divide 6,000 feet by 60. A **second** is therefore equal to about 100 feet.

A minute of latitude is the same as one **nautical mile,** which is therefore the equivalent of $1\frac{1}{6}$ ordinary (statute or legal) miles.

5. Longitude and Degrees

At right angles to the parallels are the **meridians,** the north-south streets of the earth. All meridians extend from the North Pole to the South Pole, and each meridian is therefore a semi-circle covering half of the earth's circumference. (See Figs. 31-1 and 31-2.) Distance between meridians is known as *longitude*. As with latitude, these distances are measured in degrees, minutes, and seconds of the earth's curved surface. There is no natural midpoint like the Equator from which longitude can be measured, but most countries have agreed to use the meridian that runs through Greenwich (near London), England, for this purpose. This meridian is called the **prime meridian** (first meridian) and is numbered 0°. **Longitude is the distance in degrees east or west of the prime meridian.** The half of the earth that lies east of the prime meridian has *east longitude* up to 180° (half of 360°); the half that lies west of the prime meridian has *west longitude* up to 180°. The 180th meridian is the same one for both east and west longitudes; it is directly opposite the prime meridian on the earth's surface. (See Fig. 31-3.)

The North Pole and South Pole have no longitude since all the meridians meet there.

6. Longitude and Miles

Being really parallel to each other, the distance between any particular pair of parallels is the same around the earth. But meridians are not parallel to each other. On the contrary,

all the meridians converge as they approach the Poles, where they meet. Because of this convergence there is no single value in miles for a degree of longitude. At the Equator a degree of longitude is about as long as a degree of latitude; that is, about 70 miles. In higher latitudes (nearer the poles) the length of a degree of longitude steadily decreases, until at the Poles it is zero. At 40° latitude a degree of longitude equals about 53 miles. (See Figs. 31-1 and 31-3.)

7. Location by Latitude and Longitude

In geometry it is said that two straight lines can intersect in only one point. The same thing is true on the face of the earth for a particular parallel and meridian. When we give the latitude and longitude of City Hall in New York City as 40°42′44″ N and 74°00′24″ W, we are saying that it lies at the intersection of those two lines on the earth's surface. Similarly, we may locate Chicago approximately 42° N and 88° W; St. Louis at 39° N and 90° W; Boston at 42° N and 71° W; London at 51° N and 0°; Paris at 49° N and 2° E; Buenos Aires at 35° S and 58° W; and Hong Kong at 21° N and 114° E.

Fig. 31-3. This view of the Northern Hemisphere shows why the 180th meridian belongs to both east and west longitude.

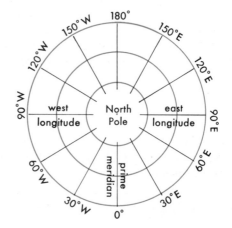

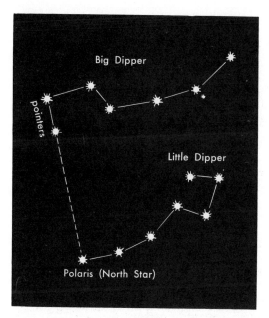

Fig. 31-4. The pointer stars in the bowl of the Big Dipper point to Polaris, the end star in the Little Dipper's handle.

found by following the pointer stars of the Big Dipper. (See Fig. 31-4.)

(2) In the daytime, north may be found by observing the sun at apparent noon, when it crosses the meridian or north-south line in the sky. At that moment, the shadow of any vertical post will run true north and south. Apparent noon can be identified by the fact that shadows are shortest at that time, since the sun is then at its highest point in the sky for that particular day. (Approximate north may be found at any time of day by pointing the hour hand of a watch directly at the sun. The point halfway between the hour hand and 12 o'clock is south; directly opposite is north. (See Fig. 31-5.)

(3) The magnetic compass gives **magnetic north.** From this, true north can be obtained by making the proper correction for **magnetic variation** or **magnetic declination. Magnetic variation is the angle by which the compass needle varies from true north.** It is caused by the fact that the

8. Navigation

In the absence of landmarks the navigator attempting to guide his ship or plane to its destination has two main problems. In order to go in the right direction he must be able to determine the "points of the compass." In order to plot his course correctly he must be able to determine his ship's position (latitude and longitude) from time to time. Determination of a ship's position by observations of the sun, moon, planets, or stars is known as **celestial navigation.**

9. Finding North

As a rule, directions are determined by finding north. If one faces north, south is to the rear, east is to the right, and west is to the left. Several different methods may be used to find north.

(1) At night, north is given almost exactly by the position of Polaris, the North Star, easily

Fig. 31-5. Using a watch to find north, as described in Topic 9. When the shadow of the vertical stick is exactly in line with the hour hand, the hour hand is pointed directly at the sun. South is then halfway to 12, and north is opposite.

north magnetic pole of the earth, toward which the compass points, is not at the earth's North Pole. The navigator carries charts which tell him the magnetic variation for all parts of the earth.

(4) Like Foucault's pendulum, a spinning gyroscope does not change its direction of vibration after it has been set in motion. This principle is used in the **gyrocompass,** which is a nonmagnetic compass. The gyroscope in this compass is pointed north (with its spin axis parallel to the earth's axis), and then is kept spinning by a small motor. Gyroscopes are used for inertial guidance in space vehicles, because they maintain a constant direction.

(5) The **radio compass** determines north from the direction of the radio signals it receives from stations whose locations are known.

10. Determining Latitude

Finding latitude by observation is based on the principle that at different latitudes the stars and the sun will appear at different altitudes in the sky. By simple geometry it can be shown that for any point in the Northern Hemisphere, *the altitude of the North Star is equal to the latitude of the observer.* For example, at the North Pole, latitude 90° N, the North Star is in the zenith, and its observed altitude is 90° (Fig. 31-6). At New York City, latitude 41° N, the

Fig. 31-7. *The North Star's altitude is always equal to the observer's latitude.*

North Star's altitude is 41° (Fig. 31-7). If the captain of a ship observes the North Star at an altitude of 46°, he knows that he is in latitude 46° N. The instrument used to observe and measure the altitude of stars, planets, and the sun is the **sextant** or **octant.**

Latitude may be determined in the daytime from the sun's noon position in the sky. Either the sextant or octant is used to "shoot the sun"; that is, to measure its altitude; the *Nautical Almanac* or *Air Almanac* is then consulted to find out in which latitude the sun has the observed noon altitude on the day of observation. (See Figs. 31-8 and 31-9.)

11. Determining Longitude

The determination of longitude—distance east or west of the prime meridian—is based on the principle that differences in time exist between the prime meridian and places east or west of it. These differences are equal to one hour for every 15 degrees of longitude. Since the sun rises in the east, places east of the prime meridian have later time, while places west of the prime meridian have earlier time. If the ship's observer can determine the difference in time between his location and Greenwich, he can calculate his longitude. For example, if sun time at his location (called *local time*) is two hours earlier than Greenwich time, his ship is at 30° W longitude.

Fig. 31-6. *At the North Pole the North Star is always in the zenith.*

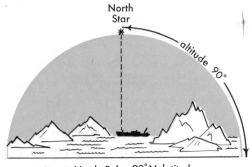

at North Pole, 90°N latitude

Greenwich time is obtained simply by carrying on the ship a very accurate clock, called a **chronometer.** This is set at Greenwich time and kept running that way, just as anyone may keep one of the clocks in his house at London time, Tokyo time, or any other time. Greenwich time signals are also transmitted over government radio stations at regular intervals. Local time is obtained most accurately at noon, when the sun crosses the meridian, as explained in Topic 9. In other words, the practice is to read the chronometer at local noon and then calculate the longitude. For example, if the ship's chronometer says 8 A.M. at local noon, it means that the ship's time (12 noon) is four hours later than Greenwich time (8 A.M.), and the ship is therefore at 60° E longitude. The chronometer is a 24-hour clock. A 12-hour clock would not show whether the time was A.M. or P.M. at Greenwich.

12. Celestial Navigation Methods

At night a navigator usually determines his ship's position by nearly simultaneous sextant

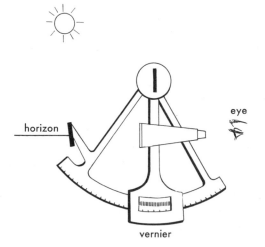

Fig. 31-8. The sextant. The two heavy vertical lines represent mirrors. The observer moves the vertical sliding arm until he sees the sun on the horizon through his telescope. He then reads the sun's altitude from the scale.

U.S. Navy Photo

Fig. 31-9. "Shooting the sun" with a sextant aboard the U.S.S. Miami.

observations of any two bright stars or planets listed in the *Nautical Almanac* or *Air Almanac.* Each observation enables him to plot a **line of position** on a chart of the earth, and the point at which the two lines of position intersect is the ship's position, or **fix.** Sirius, Rigel, and Capella are but a few of the bright stars listed in the almanacs.

In the daytime, the ship's position is usually determined at local noon, when the sun's altitude is used in calculating the latitude and the reading of the chronometer is used in calculating the longitude, as explained in Topics 10 and 11.

13. Dead Reckoning

If the navigator knows the approximate direction and speed at which he has been traveling, he can determine his position on his charts. Deducing the position of a ship in this way is known as **dead reckoning.** The reckoning can be brought up to date as often as desired.

Positions determined by dead reckoning are not entirely accurate, but they are valuable in cloudy weather and between the times of celestial observations.

The speed of a ship is measured in *knots*. A **knot is one nautical mile per hour.** The ship's *log* is the instrument used to measure the speed of the ship.

14. Great-Circle Routes

Circles drawn on the surface of a sphere may be either *great circles* or *small circles*. A **great circle is a circle whose plane passes through the center of the sphere.** Perhaps it is simpler to say that any circle that divides the sphere in half is a great circle. All other circles drawn on the sphere are smaller than the great circles and are called **small circles.** On the earth the Equator is a great circle, but all the parallels are small circles. Each meridian is half of a great circle; the meridian opposite it in the other hemisphere is the other half. Great circles may also be drawn in oblique positions between the Equator and the Poles, just as an orange may be cut in half in any direction.

The importance of a great circle in navigation is due to the fact that a **great-circle route is the shortest distance between two points on a**

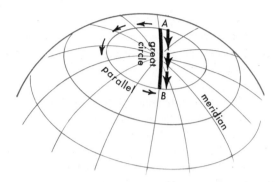

Fig. 31-10. The great-circle route from A to B is much shorter than the route along the parallel, a small circle.

sphere, just as a straight line is the shortest distance between two points on a plane. On a sphere a small circle is as indirect a route as a curved line is on a plane.

Figure 31-10 shows a great-circle route between two points, *A* and *B*, that are on the same small-circle parallel. Great-circle routes are the shortest routes but not always the most desirable for ships since winds, ocean currents, icebergs, and many other factors must also be taken into account. Airplanes are not so limited. Great-circle routes between cities in high latitudes pass over or near the Poles. To find a great-circle route between any two points on a globe, simply stretch a string between the two points.

TOPIC QUESTIONS

Each topic question refers to the topic of the same number within this chapter.

1. In what ways are the navigation problems of the transatlantic ship or plane different from those of the riverboat captain and the short-hop pilot?

2. Describe a simple street scheme for a city and explain briefly how the scheme for the earth follows this idea. Why is a location system for the earth necessary?

3. (*a*) Explain how the latitude system of the earth is set up. (*b*) Define latitude, Equator, parallels. (*c*) Explain and give examples of the manner in which latitude is expressed.

4. (*a*) How long is each of the following: (1) a degree of latitude, (2) a minute of latitude, (3) a second of latitude? (*b*) Explain why and how degrees of latitude vary in length over the earth.

5. (*a*) Explain how the longitude system of the earth is set up. (*b*) Define longitude.

(c) Explain the relation between meridians and the prime meridian. (d) Explain the division of the world into longitude degrees and give examples.

6. Explain why no single· value can be given for the number of miles in a degree of longitude.

7. (a) How do the latitude and longitude of a place indicate its exact location? (b) Give the latitude and longitude (degrees only) of three big cities.

8. (a) What are the two main problems of the navigator working without landmarks? (b) What is celestial navigation?

9. (a) Explain how to find north using (1) Polaris, (2) the sun, (3) the magnetic compass. (b) What is a gyrocompass? a radiocompass?

10. (a) Explain how the North Star is used to determine latitude. (b) How is the sun used in determining latitude? (c) What are the sextant and octant?

11. (a) How is longitude determined? Give examples. (b) What is a chronometer? (c) Why is longitude on a ship usually determined at local noon?

12. (a) Explain the celestial-navigation method used to get a fix at night. (b) How is the ship's position usually determined in the daytime?

13. (a) Describe dead reckoning and explain its uses. (b) What is a knot? ship's log?

14. (a) What are great circles? Give some examples. (b) Why are great circles important in navigation? (c) How are they found on a globe?

GENERAL QUESTIONS

1. Approximately how many miles is it to the Equator and to the North Pole from each of the following cities: New York, London, Buenos Aires, Hong Kong?

2. Explain why the rule for finding north by the use of a watch should be true.

3. At local noon on board a ship on June 21 the sun is in the zenith and the chronometer time is 3 P.M. What are the ship's latitude and longitude?

4. What is the altitude of the North Star at each of the cities listed in Topic 7?

5. In Topic 14 it is stated that airplanes are more likely than ships to be able to make use of great-circle routes. Why?

6. In Topic 13 it is stated that positions obtained by dead reckoning are not entirely accurate. Why?

STUDENT ACTIVITIES

1. Find north by the first three methods described in Topic 9. For the magnetic compass method you will need to know the magnetic variation of your locality. This may be found from any local U.S.G.S. quadrangle map or from an *isogonic map* of the United States.

2. Using the method described in Topic 14, determine the great-circle route between two selected middle-latitude cities of approximately equal latitude but differing greatly in longitude; e.g., New York City and Tokyo, Seattle and Moscow, London and Shanghai, or any other widely separated locations. Then (a) Plot the great-circle route on a Mercator outline map of the world. (This is done most easily by plotting the points where your great-circle route crosses meridians on the globe.) (b) Compare the great-circle route, with respect to both distance and direction,

with the one-directional route obtained by joining the two cities with a straight line on the Mercator map.

3. Determine your latitude and longitude at solar noon as suggested in Topics 10–12. Use a sextant to "shoot the sun" and get the sun's declination from an analemma (Chapter 32, Topic 4) or an almanac. For Greenwich time simply calculate the time in London, England, by adding the appropriate number of hours for your time belt to the clock time at the moment you make your "apparent solar noon" observation. (See Chapter 32, Topic 2.)

    To make certain that the sun's altitude is being taken when it is at its highest (noon) position in the sky, the following procedure is used: (a) The approximate time of solar noon is determined in advance. (b) A few minutes before this time observation with the sextant is begun. As the sun rises higher in the sky, continuous adjustment of the sextant arm is required to keep the sun in the sextant mirror. But when the sun reaches its highest point and then begins to go down, the observer will find that he must move the sextant arm in the opposite direction. At this moment he makes his observations.

4. Find your latitude at night from the altitude of the North Star.

CHAPTER 32
Keeping Time

HOW DO YOU KNOW THAT . . . ?

Apparent solar noon is the time when the sun actually crosses the meridian (north-south line) at a given location. Not only is your apparent solar noon unlikely to agree with noon on your watch, but it will also come at a different time each day. Why? (See Topics 2 through 6.)

To find the time when apparent solar noon occurs, observe and record the time when a vertical post casts its shortest shadow. (Use the procedure in the beginning activity of Chapter 31.) Apparent solar noon can also be calculated by dividing in half the time between sunrise and sunset (see a newspaper or almanac). How closely do the two times agree? (Remember that daylight time will make all times one hour later.) Find apparent solar noon again for several days to see how the time changes.

1. Units of Time

Because the earth's periods of rotation and revolution are so highly constant, we base our measurement of time on these motions. We define a **year** as the time taken by the earth to make one revolution around the sun. A **day** is the time taken by the earth to make one rotation on its axis. Saying that a year has 365¼ days (approximately) simply means that the earth rotates on its axis 365¼ times while it is making one revolution around the sun. (The month is not a natural unit of time, although it is close to the 29½ day period between new moons from which it originated.)

Since people require shorter units of time than the day, we have divided the day into 24 equal parts called *hours.* Each hour is divided into 60 *minutes,* and each minute is divided into 60 *seconds.*

2. Measuring a Day

Astronomers define a **day as the interval of time in which a particular heavenly body crosses the observer's meridian** (a north-south line

through the sky) **twice in succession.** It is in this way that we can tell when the earth has made exactly one rotation, just as a rider on a merry-go-round can count his rotations by noticing how often he passes a fixed object that is outside the merry-go-round. If the observer counts the time taken by a **star** to cross his meridian twice, he is measuring a **sidereal** (sy *deer* ee ul) **day.** If he counts the time taken for the **sun** to cross his meridian twice, he is measuring an **apparent solar day.**

As Figure 32-1 shows, a distant star will appear to be in exactly the same direction in space from one day to the next. Therefore the star will make two successive crossings of a given meridian in the time it takes the earth to rotate exactly 360°. In other words, a sidereal day is the time it takes the earth to rotate 360° on its axis.

To complete a solar day, however, the earth must rotate about 1° more, or a total of about 361°. This is because the earth's forward motion in its orbit changes the direction of the sun by an angle equal to the earth's daily revolution of about 1°. Since the earth takes about 4 minutes

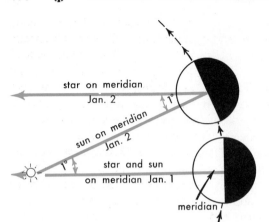

Fig. 32-1. The earth rotates 360° to complete a sidereal day, but must rotate about 1° more to complete an apparent solar day.

to rotate 1°, the sidereal day and the solar day differ in length by these four minutes. The solar day is 24 hours long; the sidereal day is about 23 hours and 56 minutes long. This also means that the stars will rise 4 minutes earlier each day.

Apparent solar noon is defined as the moment at which the *sun* crosses the meridian of the observer.

3. Mean Solar Day

Kepler's second law tells us that the angle through which the earth moves in its orbit changes very slightly from day to day as the earth's distance from the sun changes. This, in turn, means that the earth must rotate on its axis a slightly different amount each day to complete an apparent solar day. For this and other reasons (described in astronomy texts) the apparent solar day varies in length throughout the year, being longest at Christmas time and shortest in mid-September. The maximum difference is not quite a minute.

For purposes of simpler time keeping, all the apparent solar days of the year are averaged. The average is called the **mean solar day.** It is exactly 24 hours long.

4. Mean Solar Time

When we use the mean solar day as our unit of time, counting 24 hours each day from midnight to midnight, we are keeping **mean solar time** or **civil time.** Twelve o'clock noon is *mean solar noon,* the exact midpoint of the mean solar day. Except for four days a year, apparent solar noon (Topic 2) does not come at mean solar noon. The difference between apparent solar noon and mean solar noon is called the **equation of time.** On November 1 it exceeds 16 minutes. When the sun crosses the local meridian before mean solar noon (as it does on November 1, for example), it is said to be *fast.* When it crosses after mean solar noon, it is *slow.* On February 1, for example, the sun is more than 13 minutes slow.

A graph showing the equation of time and the sun's declination (distance in degrees from the Equator) is called an **analemma.** World globes usually show the analemma.

A sundial shows apparent solar time, and the equation of time must be used to convert sundial time into local time. The equation of time can be found in most almanacs. Apparent solar noon can easily be calculated for any day merely by determining the exact midpoint between sunrise and sunset. For example, if on December 3 in Philadelphia the sun rises at 7:06 A.M. and sets at 4:33 P.M., it actually crosses the meridian at 11:49½ A.M., which is apparent solar noon.

5. Local Pride and Local Time

Places that are on the same meridian have the same solar time because the sun crosses the entire meridian at the same instant. On the other hand, places that are even a short distance east or west of each other have different solar time, since the rotation of the earth from west to east brings the sun across each meridian at a different instant. The differences in solar time amount to one hour for every 15° of longitude, or 4 minutes for each 1° of longitude, or one minute for every one-quarter of a degree of longitude. For example, New York City's longitude is about 74° W; Philadelphia's is about 75° W. Because of this difference of approximately 1°, the sun reaches the meridian at New York City about 4 minutes before it reaches the meridian at Philadelphia, about 50 miles to the west.

Until 1883 most cities and other localities in the United States kept their own solar time. Fifty-three different kinds of time were used by the country's railroads, and cities through which several railroads ran had as many as five different time systems. On November 18, 1883, American railroads adopted **standard time,** which is in worldwide use today.

6. Standard Time

In standard time, meridians are marked off at intervals of 15° east and west of the prime meridian at Greenwich, England. These 24 meridians—15° E, 15° W, 30° E, 30° W, and so on, up to 180°—are called **time meridians.** Each time meridian is the center of a **standard-time zone** that is 15° wide, 7½° on each side. The entire zone has the same time; all clocks show the *mean solar time of the time meridian in that*

zone. In the zone to the east the time is exactly one hour later; in the zone to the west it is exactly one hour earlier. (See Fig. 32-2.) Thus changes of time are made only one hour at a time, and only when crossing from one zone into the next. To calculate the standard time in any part of the world, we merely add one hour for each 15-degree zone to the east, and subtract one hour for each 15-degree zone to the west. For example, when it is 10 A.M. at London, 0° longitude, it is 11 A.M. in Rome, in the 15° E zone; 5 A.M. in Philadelphia, 75° W; 3 A.M. in Denver, 105° W; and so on. A rhyme that may aid in remembering this rule is

> As you go to the east
> The time doth increase.
> As you go to the west
> The time will grow less.

7. Standard Time Belts in the United States

Theoretically each standard time zone is 15° wide. On land, however, such exactness is undesirable and unnecessary. It is undesirable because exact boundaries might cut right through a city

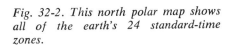

Fig. 32-2. This north polar map shows all of the earth's 24 standard-time zones.

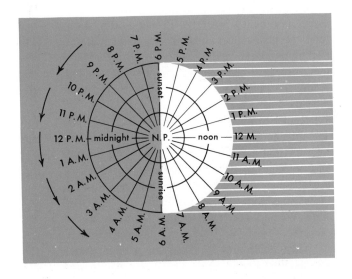

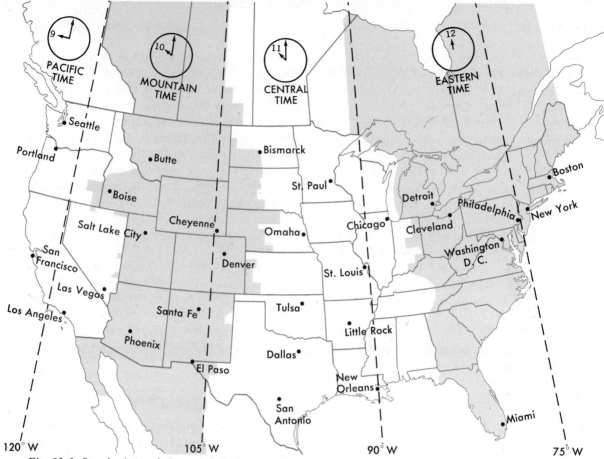

Fig. 32-3. Standard time belts and their time meridians.

or between localities that wish to keep the same time. It is unnecessary as long as the irregular zones (or belts) *average* 15° in width. Four time meridians pass through the United States, excluding Alaska and Hawaii. The United States therefore has four standard time belts, all with highly irregular boundaries. The belts and their time meridians are Eastern, 75° W; Central, 90° W; Rocky Mountain, 105° W; Pacific, 120° W. The Pacific Belt is 45° (or three belts) to the west of the Eastern Belt and is therefore 3 hours earlier. When it is 5 P.M. in New York, it is 2 P.M. in Los Angeles. (Alaska stretches through three time belts whose meridians are 135° W, 150° W, and 165° W. Hawaii is in the last of these.)

Most cities and states in the United States use **daylight-saving time** during the late spring and summer months. Clocks are set one hour ahead of standard time so that daylight will end one hour later in the evening. A sunset that would occur at 7:00 P.M. standard time takes place at 8:00 P.M. daylight time. One economy that results from daylight-saving time is the decreased use of electricity for lighting.

When in the spring we set our clocks ahead for daylight-saving time, we "lose" an hour. The hour is "returned" in the fall, for when we set our clocks back again to standard time, we "gain" an hour. (See Fig. 32-3.)

8. The International Date Line

A traveler going eastward from one time belt to another also "loses" an hour with each change of time, while a westward traveler "gains" an hour each time he sets his watch back. If either one of these travelers completes a trip around the world, he will have "lost" or "gained" 24 hours, and in his reckoning he will be either a day ahead or a day behind the calendar in the place from which he started. To prevent such confusion, the **international date line** was established. As the traveler on ship or plane crosses this line, he makes a change of date that compensates for the "losses" or "gains" of time. The *westward traveler* (who has been turning his watch back) *moves his calendar forward,* as from Sunday to Monday. The *eastward traveler* (who has been turning his watch forward) *moves his calendar back,* as from Saturday to Friday.

The international date line is located entirely in the ocean, so all changes of date are made on ship or plane, and no body of land is divided by it. For the most part it follows the 180th meridian, except for a few zigzags, or *offsets,* where the meridian runs through eastern Siberia, the Aleutian Islands, and some South Sea islands. At these places the date line swerves away from the 180th meridian and into the sea.

Since the international date line is in the interior of a time belt, no change in clock time is made when it is crossed. The change is in the date alone. The western half of this time belt is therefore always exactly one day ahead of the eastern half, and is the part of the world in which each new day has its beginning. With each passing hour, the new date moves westward, one belt at a time, around the earth. Except for the instant when the midnight line crosses the international date line, there are always two dates on the earth at any moment. For a good part of our day, we are behind the date in eastern Asia and the far Pacific islands.

9. A.M. and P.M.

A.M. means "ante meridiem"; it refers to the 12 hours from midnight to noon during which *the sun is before the meridian.* P.M. means "post meridiem"; it refers to the 12 hours from noon

to midnight during which *the sun is after the meridian.* Midnight is called 12 P.M., and noon is distinguished from it by being called 12 M., the time when *the sun is on the meridian.*

In any problems involving the determination of time in various parts of the world, *the date changes when the time becomes either later or earlier than midnight.* For example, when it is 11 P.M. *Thursday* in Los Angeles, it is 2 A.M. *Friday* in New York City, and vice versa.

10. Checking the Time

Since the entire world bases its clock time on the *mean solar time at Greenwich,* Greenwich time is called **universal time.** At Greenwich observatory clocks are checked daily by comparing their time with the exact time when the

Fig. 32-4. The international date line coincides with or runs close to the 180th meridian, always avoiding land.

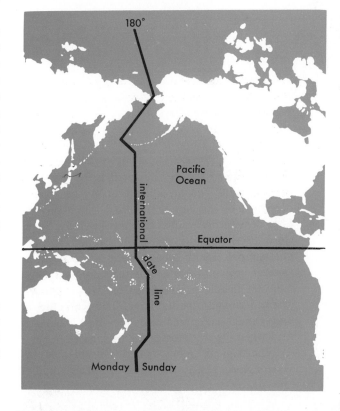

U.S. Navy Photo

Fig. 32-5. The photographic zenith tube at the Naval Observatory in Washington, D.C.

sun or a given star is calculated to be crossing the meridian. The meridian crossing or *transit* of the sun or star can be observed with a special form of telescope known as a **transit circle.** Stars close to the zenith are photographed by the **photographic zenith tube,** a telescope fixed in a vertical position. The zenith tube automatically indicates the clock time when the star is photographed crossing the meridian. Thus the clock's time can be compared with the time it should read when the star crosses the meridian.

The United States Naval Observatory in Washington, D.C., also uses a photographic

zenith tube to check the clocks on which its daily radio time signals are based. These quartz-crystal-controlled clocks keep time so precisely, even between the daily "star checks," that the average error of their time signals is less than one hundredth of a second. (The quartz crystals vibrate at a constant rate that controls the rate of the electric motors in the observatory clocks.)

Even the accuracy of a quartz-crystal-controlled clock can be improved upon. The frequency of vibration of the crystal depends upon the size and shape to which it is ground. Nowadays, scientists check the desired frequency against the frequency of vibration of the atoms in a beam of vaporized cesium metal. The *cesium beam* clock at the National Bureau of Standards is said to have an error of only one second in 300 years.

11. Our Calendar

A perfect calendar would be one in which the earth reached the same point in its orbit at exactly the same time and date each year. In such a calendar the seasons would begin at the same moment each year. A perfect calendar is almost an impossibility because the earth's rotation period (day) does not fit into its revolution period (year) an even number of times. The exact length of a year is slightly less than 365¼ days.

The early Roman calendar was based on the motions of the moon. Because it did not take into consideration the revolution of the earth around the sun, the seasons began at an earlier date each year. By 46 B.C. spring arrived in December. Julius Caesar reformed the calendar in an attempt to make the year represent the time it takes the earth to make one revolution around the sun; that is, 365¼ days. The new calendar, known as the **Julian calendar,** introduced the modern system of three years of 365 days followed by a leap year of 366 days.

But even Caesar's average year of 365¼ days was just a bit too long to match the true year, and the seasons began to "arrive early" again, but not very much too early. In 1582 the spring equinox came on March 11 instead of March 21. At this time Pope Gregory introduced an adjustment which brought the average length of the year very close to its true length. At the same time the spring equinox was dated March 21 again. This **Gregorian calendar** was adopted by Great Britain and the American colonies in 1752, and is in use in most countries of the world today.

In the Gregorian calendar the average length of the year is shortened slightly by omitting three days in every 400 years. To do this, a simple rule is used. Ordinarily every year divisible by 4 is a leap year. Under the new rule, however, *the century year is not a leap year unless its first two numbers are divisible by 4.* In any four successive centurial years, such as 1800, 1900, 2000, and 2100, there can be only one leap year. In this case it is the year 2000. By thus eliminating three leap years in each period of 400 years the rule achieves its aim of getting rid of three days in that time.

12. World Calendar

A **world calendar** has been suggested to eliminate the irregularities and difficulties of our present Gregorian calendar. In the world calendar the year is divided into four equal quarters. Each quarter begins with a 31-day month and continues with two 30-day months. The quarter also begins with a Sunday and ends on a Saturday, its 91 days totaling just 13 weeks. The four quarters add up to 364 days. To complete the year, the 365th day is added between Saturday, December 30, and Sunday, January 1. Known as December Y or *Year-End Day,* it provides a three-day weekend at the end of each year.

Leap years are taken care of by the simple device of adding a *Leap-Year Day* called June L between Saturday, June 30, and Sunday, July 1.

TOPIC QUESTIONS

Each topic question refers to the topic of the same number within this chapter.

1. (*a*) What is the origin of such units of time as the year, month, day, hour, minute, and second? (*b*) Why are only the year and the day considered to be "natural" units?

2. (*a*) Define *day*. Distinguish between a sidereal day and a solar day. (*b*) Explain why a solar day is longer than a sidereal day. (*c*) Define apparent solar noon.

3. (*a*) Why do the lengths of apparent solar days differ? (*b*) How is the mean solar day obtained?

4. (*a*) Explain what is meant by mean solar time, mean solar noon, equation of time, sun fast, sun slow, analemma. (*b*) How can the time of apparent solar noon be calculated? Illustrate.

5. (*a*) Explain, with examples, why places that are even short distances east or west of each other have different solar time. (*b*) Why was a standard time system adopted in 1883?

6. Explain the standard time system for the world.

7. (*a*) Why do standard time zones have irregular boundaries on land? (*b*) Name the standard time belts of the United States with their time meridians. (*c*) Explain what daylight time is and why it is used.

8. (*a*) Explain why we have an international date line. (*b*) Where is the date line? (*c*) How does a traveler change his calendar when crossing the date line? (*d*) Describe the start and progress of a new date.

9. Explain the meanings of A.M., P.M., and M.

10. (*a*) What is universal time? (*b*) How are observatory clocks checked for accuracy? (*c*) What is the function of the quartz crystal in these clocks?

11. (*a*) What is a "perfect calendar" and why is it "almost an impossibility"? (*b*) Why did Julius Caesar discard the old Roman calendar? (*c*) What reform did the Julian calendar introduce? (*d*) What further improvement did the Gregorian calendar introduce?

12. Briefly describe the world calendar.

GENERAL QUESTIONS

1. What is the greatest possible difference between the standard time of a zone and the local time of any place in it? (Assume that the time meridian is exactly in the middle of the zone.) Explain.

2. Name four important cities in each United States standard time belt.

3. Why do we not use daylight saving time in winter?

4. What time is it in each United States standard time belt when the new date is just beginning at the international date line?

5. Distinguish between 12:10 A.M. and 12:10 P.M.

6. What are the time and day in Manila, Tokyo, Honolulu, Melbourne, Buenos Aires, London, Moscow, and Calcutta at 10 P.M. Monday in Washington, D.C.?

7. How can an eclipse that began on Saturday end on Friday, as described in the introduction to this chapter?

8. What objection would there be to having the whole earth keep the same hour and date?

1. Measure the length of an apparent solar day by noting the time of two successive apparent solar noons (use the shortest shadow method) and computing the interval of time between them.

2. Build a sundial. Instructions may be found in a U.S. Government Printing Office leaflet on sundials, in Mayall's book on sundials, etc. (see bibliography).

BIBLIOGRAPHY

GENERAL ASTRONOMY

Asimov, I. *Universe from Flat Earth to Quasar*. Avon, N.Y., 1966.
Baker and Fredrick. *An Introduction to Astronomy*. Van Nostrand, N.Y., 1968.
Bergamini, D. *The Universe*. Time, Inc., N.Y., 1962.
Hynek and Apfel. *Astronomy One*. W. A. Benjamin, Menlo Park, Cal., 1972.
Mehlin, T. G. *Astronomy and the Origin of the Earth*. W. C. Brown, Dubuque, Iowa, 1968.
Menzel, D. H. *Astronomy*. Random House, N.Y., 1970.
Moore, P. *Atlas of the Universe*. Rand McNally, N.Y., 1970.
"Sky and Telescope" (monthly periodical). Sky Publishing Co., Cambridge, Mass.

SOLAR SYSTEM

Adler, I. *Seeing the Earth From Space*. John Day, N.Y., 1961.

Adler, I. *The Sun and Its Family*. John Day, N.Y., 1958.

Asimov, I. *The Double Planet*. Abelard-Schuman, N.Y., 1960.

Hartman, W. K. *Moons and Planets*. Bogden and Quigley, Tarrytown, N.Y., 1972.

Heuer, K. *Men of Other Planets*. Crowell-Collier, N.Y., 1963.

Kopel, D. *The Moon*. Academic Press, N.Y., 1964.

Levinson and Taylor. *Moon Rocks and Minerals*. Pergamon Press, Elmsford, N.Y., 1970.

Ley, W. *Watchers of the Skies*. Viking, N.Y., 1963.

Lyttleton, R. A. *The Modern Universe*. Harper and Row, N.Y., 1957.

Nourse, H. E. *Nine Planets*. Harper and Row, N.Y., 1970.

Ohring, G. *Weather on the Planets*. Doubleday, N.Y., 1966.

Pickering, J. S. *Captives of the Sun*. Dodd, Mead, N.Y., 1961.

Watson, F. G. *Between the Planets*. Doubleday-Anchor, N.Y., 1962.

Whipple, F. L. *Earth, Moon and Planets*. Harvard University Press, Cambridge, Mass., 1963.

Wood, J. A. *Meteorites and the Origin of Planets*. McGraw-Hill, N.Y., 1968.

NASA Booklets on Lunar Exploration by Apollo Astronauts. Available from Supt. of Documents, Washington, D.C. 20402.

TELECOPES AND AMATEUR ASTRONOMY

Branley, F. M. *Experiments in Sky Watching*. Crowell-Collier, N.Y., 1959.

Edmund and Brown. *Homebuilt Telescopes*. Edmund Scientific Co., Barrington, N.J.

Ingalls, A. G. *Amateur Telescope Making*. Scientific American, N.Y.

Mayall and Mayall. *Skyshooting: Hunting the Stars With Your Camera*. Ronald Press, N.Y., 1949.

Menzel, D. H. *Field Guide to Stars and Planets*. Houghton Mifflin, Boston, Mass., 1964.

Thompson, A. J. *Making Your Own Telescope*. Sky Publishing Co., Cambridge, Mass., 1947.

Vehrenberg, H. *Atlas of Deep Sky Splendors*. Sky Publishing Co., Cambridge, Mass., 1967.

Wilkins and Moore. *How to Make and Use a Telescope*. Norton, N.Y., 1956.

SPACE TRAVEL

Asimov, I. *The Clock We Live On*. Abelard-Schuman, N.Y., 1959.

Bell, T. and C. *The Riddle of Time*. Viking, N.Y., 1963.

Bendick, J. *Space Travel*. Franklin Watts, N.Y., 1971.

Branley, F. M. *Experiments in the Principles of Space Travel*. Crowell-Collier, N.Y., 1955.

Clarke, A. C. *Promise of Space*. Penguin Books, Baltimore, Md., 1970.

Goodwin, H. L. *Space: Frontier Unlimited*. Van Nostrand, N.Y., 1962.

Ley, W. *Satellites, Rockets, and Outer Space*. New American Library, N.Y., 1958.

Sharpe, M. R. *Satellites and Probes*. Doubleday, N.Y., 1970.

Von Braun, W. *Space Frontier*. Holt, N.Y., 1971.

Unit 7 Atmospheric Science

Do you recognize the
kind of storm illustrated on the
opposite page? What color do you think it is?
Why? What is its shape at the ground? Above the
ground? From its shape, how do you think it moves?
Spinning like a top and roaring like a hundred airplanes, this
smallest but most dangerous of all storms is a tornado. A tornado's
whirling winds of great speed are terrifying and destructive. As it twists
over the land, buildings can be blown to pieces. Walls collapse or topple
outward. Objects can be lifted up and hurled great distances.

Tornadoes occur in many parts of the world. The most favorable place for their
formation is the central part of the United States. Meteorologists, people who
study the weather, analyze and interpret many weather charts to identify the conditions and areas where a tornado may develop. Several ordinary weather conditions, happening together, may produce a tornado. In this unit you will explore some
of these weather conditions—air temperature, air pressure, moisture in the air,
the movement of air as wind. You will also see how variations in these conditions
produce different kinds of weather.

Meteorology is the study of the atmosphere and its effects on the earth's surface,
its oceans, and life in general. Its goals are explanation, prediction, and control over certain atmospheric events. Climatology is a part of atmospheric
science. Climatology focuses on the collective, long-term weather conditions in a specific area known as climate. In recent years our
concept of the atmosphere has been extended by modern
research tools such as weather balloons, earth
satellites, and space probes. Studies of the
atmosphere begin at the earth's surface but reach off into space as
far as the sun and beyond.

CHAPTER 33

The Atmosphere and Solar Radiation

HOW DO YOU KNOW THAT . . . ?

Half fill a battery jar with water. Float a piece of cork on the water to show the water level plainly. Mark the water level. Now invert an empty glass tumbler over the cork and push the tumbler straight down into the water. Hold it there. Observe the position of the cork. Was the tumbler empty? What evidence do you have that it is really filled with something (that we call air)? What evidence do you have that the air in the tumbler is compressible? Why is the air at sea level denser than the air at higher elevations?

STRUCTURE AND COMPOSITION

1. Exploring the Atmosphere

The earth's atmosphere is the cover of gases that surrounds the earth. Gases are highly compressible. The molecules of the gases in the atmosphere are squeezed close together near the earth's surface by the weight of all the molecules above them, but they thin out rapidly as distance from the surface increases. Only one per cent of the total weight of the atmosphere is found above 20 miles. The modern view is that the atmosphere gets thinner high above the earth until it meets the sun's atmosphere many thousands of miles above the earth's surface.

The atmospheric scientist is interested in such aspects of the atmosphere as its composition, its temperature, its pressure, its movements, its moisture, and its ionization. In the atmosphere close to the earth's surface, information about these things can be obtained by chemical analysis, and by direct measurement with instruments such as thermometers and barometers. Above the surface, the atmosphere can be explored to a height of about 20 miles by instrument-carrying balloons that transmit their observations by radio. For information above 20 miles, we rely on a variety of sources. Among these are rockets and satellites carrying weather instruments and cameras; observations of meteors and auroras; and the reflection of radio waves from ionized layers of the atmosphere.

2. Homosphere and Heterosphere

Direct observation of the lower atmosphere shows that it is a mixture composed largely of the gases nitrogen and oxygen, with small amounts of other gases like argon and carbon dioxide. Each gas is present in a definite percentage. Indirect studies show that the same gases are found in almost the same proportions all the way from sea level to a height of about 50 miles. Some scientists call this 50-mile layer the **homosphere** (*homo = same*) because of the uniform composition of its air mixture.

Above the homosphere the atmosphere seems to consist of almost single-gas layers in which first oxygen, then helium, and then hydrogen predominate, as shown in Figure 33-1. This part of the atmosphere is called the **heterosphere** (*hetero = different*). The gas particles in the

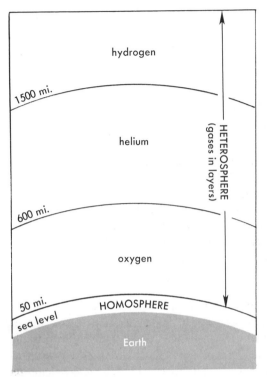

Fig. 33-1. Below 50 miles, the atmosphere is a uniform mixture of gases. From 50 miles upward, it appears to be layered as shown here.

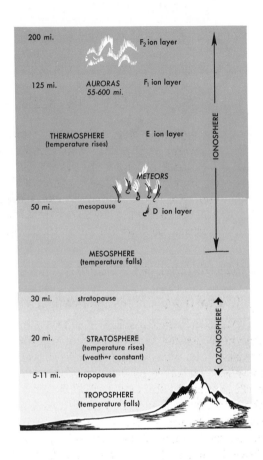

Fig. 33-2. Structure and characteristics of the atmosphere from the surface to about 200 miles.

heterosphere are very far apart and the heterosphere is actually a very high vacuum. The hydrogen layer reaches many thousands of miles into space until it probably merges with the atmosphere of the sun.

3. Temperatures in the Atmosphere

The terms *homosphere* and *heterosphere* refer to the *composition* of the atmosphere. More often, however, the atmosphere is divided into four layers according to its **thermal structure,** or temperature changes, as shown in Figure 33-2. As you will notice, these four layers alternate with respect to falling temperatures and rising temperatures. (See Fig. 33-3.)

The first layer, the **troposphere,** reaches from the earth's surface to a height ranging from 5 miles at the Poles to 11 miles at the Equator. It is the layer of clouds and changing weather and it is marked by a steady drop in temperature with increasing altitude. The level at which the temperature stops falling is called the **tropopause.** Here the temperature ranges from about −67°F at the Poles to as low as −110°F at the Equator.

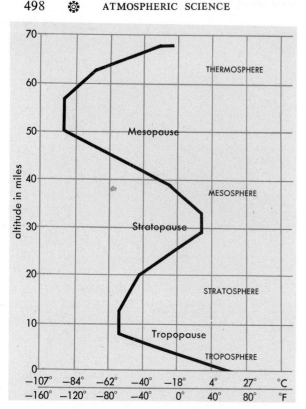

Fig. 33-3. Graph showing how the temperature of the atmosphere changes with altitude from the earth's surface through the thermosphere.

The second layer, the **stratosphere,** reaches from the tropopause to a height of about 30 miles. The stratosphere is generally clear and dry. It has strong steady winds and few sudden changes of weather. Temperatures remain constant in the lower part of the stratosphere, but then rise steadily until the **stratopause** is reached at 30 miles.

The third layer, the **mesosphere,** extends from the stratopause to the **mesopause** at about the 50-mile level. Temperatures drop steadily in the mesosphere. At the mesopause, temperatures are lower than anywhere else in the atmosphere.

The fourth layer, the **thermosphere,** extends off into space from the mesopause. Temperatures rise steadily in the thermosphere, probably reaching a maximum at about 120 miles. Although temperatures may be higher in the thermosphere, few air particles are present, and the air has little power to heat objects in space.

4. The Ionosphere

Ionized layers of air are found in the atmosphere at a number of levels reaching from about 40 miles to 300 miles above the surface. This region is known as the **ionosphere.** Here the ultraviolet rays of the sun bombard atoms of nitrogen and oxygen, knocking out electrons to form positively charged ions of oxygen and nitric oxide. These ions and the freed electrons collect in layers of different heights, known as the D, E, F_1, and F_2 layers. (See Fig. 33-2.)

The ionosphere plays a very important part in long distance radio transmission. Its various layers act like reflectors for radio waves of particular wavelengths. Without reflection, radio waves escape into space after traveling in a straight line from the transmitter and reach only a small part of the earth's surface. But when they are reflected by the ionosphere, they travel around the curved surface of the earth for much greater distances. (See Fig. 33-4).

The ionosphere does not reflect the short waves used in television transmission. However, communications satellites are now being used to do for television waves what the ionosphere does for radio waves.

5. The Magnetosphere

The **magnetosphere** is the name given to a vast doughnut-shaped zone of charged particles surrounding the earth from an altitude of about 600 miles to 40,000 miles. The particles are protons and electrons, trapped in the magnetic field of the earth, hence the name magnetosphere. The protons and electrons move back and forth between the northern and southern hemispheres, following spiral paths around the magnetic lines of force. Most of the particles are believed to come from the sun in eruptions called solar flares.

Particles are constantly escaping from the magnetosphere as they spiral close to the earth's atmosphere. When large numbers of particles enter the upper atmosphere, the atmosphere glows brilliantly to form the aurora borealis or northern lights.

The magnetosphere was discovered in 1958 by Dr. James A. Van Allen, as a result of observations made by satellites. Dr. Van Allen's early studies showed the charged particles to be concentrated in two belts which were named the Van Allen radiation belts. Further study, however, led to the present concept of a continuous zone. (See Fig. 33-5.)

Although most of the charged particles in the magnetosphere come from solar flares, there are believed to be two other minor sources of such particles. Cosmic rays form some ions when they strike the gases of the upper atmosphere. The second source is the continuous outflow of protons and electrons from the sun in a stream called the *solar wind*.

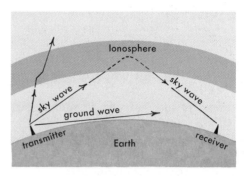

Fig. 33-4. *Reflection of radio waves by the ionosphere makes long distance reception possible.*

6. Gases of the Homosphere

The air of the earth's lower atmosphere is a mixture of many gases. With the exception of ozone and water vapor, the percentage of the various gases remains nearly uniform all the way through the 50 miles of the homosphere. The approximate percentages by volume of the principal gases in pure dry air (not including water

Fig. 33-5. *The relation of the Van Allen radiation belts to the earth.*

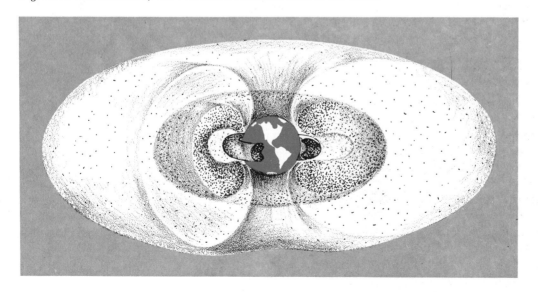

vapor) are nitrogen, 78 per cent; oxygen, 21 per cent; argon, 0.84 per cent (a little less than 1 per cent); carbon dioxide, 0.03 per cent. Other gases include neon, krypton, xenon, helium, hydrogen, and ozone, but all these together make up less than 0.01 per cent (one molecule of gas in every 10,000) of the air.

Ozone is a minute but very important part of this 0.01 per cent. It is the part of the air that is chiefly responsible for absorbing most of the powerful ultraviolet rays of the sun, thereby protecting us from excessive exposure to their strong skin-blistering action. Ozone is the chemically active form of oxygen that has three atoms instead of two in a molecule. The percentage of ozone in the air is relatively high at heights of about 10 to 30 miles, so this region is called the **ozonosphere.** Even here, there is no more than about one ozone molecule for every 100,000 molecules of air.

Carbon dioxide is another gas of small percentage but great importance. Green plants use it as one of the raw materials in making starch and it is a good absorber of heat. The percentage of carbon dioxide in the air varies somewhat. It is a bit higher near volcanoes and in industrial areas than over most of the earth. Observations over the past 100 years show a steady increase in the percentage of carbon dioxide in the air.

7. Water Vapor and Dust

In addition to the gases listed in Topic 6, the lower air always contains water vapor and dust.

The percentage of water vapor in the air varies widely from almost none to as high as 4 per cent by volume, depending on location, season, and time of day. Water vapor is of great importance, of course, for when it condenses, it forms the clouds and rain necessary for all life on the earth. The ocean is the atmosphere's principal source of water vapor.

Dust is an important part of the air, for certain kinds of dust particles act as "condensation nuclei" around which water vapor condenses to form cloud and rain droplets. Combustion products and salt particles from sea spray are the best condensation nuclei. Microscopic dust particles are also the cause of atmospheric haze.

HEATING OF THE ATMOSPHERE

Weather is the state of the atmosphere. A planet without an atmosphere can have no weather. But even with an atmosphere, energy is required to bring about the changes in temperature, movements of winds, evaporation of water, formation of clouds, and precipitation of rain and snow that constitute weather. That energy is supplied by the sun. Let us see how the sun's energy affects the earth's atmosphere.

8. Solar Radiation and the Earth

It can easily be shown by simple geometry that only one part in two billion of the sun's

Fig. 33-6. How solar energy is received by the earth.

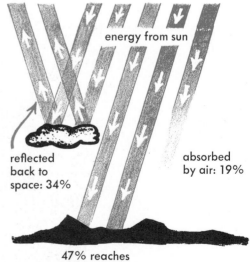

energy from sun

reflected back to space: 34%

absorbed by air: 19%

47% reaches Earth's surface

total radiation comes to the earth. Small as this amount seems, the earth makes use of only a little more than half of it. Our atmosphere with its clouds reflects about 34 per cent of our share of solar radiation back into space. (The percentage of radiant energy reflected by a surface is called its *albedo,* pronounced al *bee* doh.) About 19 per cent of the incoming radiation is absorbed directly by the atmosphere, mostly in its denser lower layers, where its chief absorbing gases, carbon dioxide and water vapor, are concentrated. The remaining 47 per cent of the solar radiation reaches the surface of the earth. The solar radiation that reaches the entire earth is sometimes called **insolation.** (See Fig. 33-6.)

9. Absorption and the Greenhouse Effect

What happens to the 47 per cent of solar radiation that reaches the earth's surface? The energy of a very hot body like the sun comes to us in the form of **short-wave radiations** such as ultraviolet rays, visible light rays, and infrared rays. Land and water can absorb these short waves far better than air can and much of the

solar radiation that strikes the earth's surface is absorbed, warming the land and water. Like the sun, land and water also radiate their energy. But at their comparatively low temperatures, the energy of warm land and water is emitted in the form of **long-wave radiations that air readily absorbs.** So instead of escaping back to space, the heat radiated from the earth warms up the air above it.

The atmosphere's transmission of the sun's short-wave radiation and its absorption of the earth's long-wave radiation is called the **greenhouse effect.** It is largely due to the carbon dioxide and water vapor of the air. In a greenhouse or hothouse the glass roof acts like the water vapor and carbon dioxide in the air, letting the sun's short waves enter the hothouse but not allowing the long waves radiated by the warm soil to escape. (See Fig. 33-7.)

10. Transfer of Heat in the Atmosphere

The transfer of heat into the atmosphere, or from one part of the atmosphere to another part, involves four different processes. (See Fig. 33-8.)

Fig. 33-7. The "greenhouse effect" shown here is duplicated by the earth's atmosphere, in which water vapor and carbon dioxide act like the glass of a greenhouse roof.

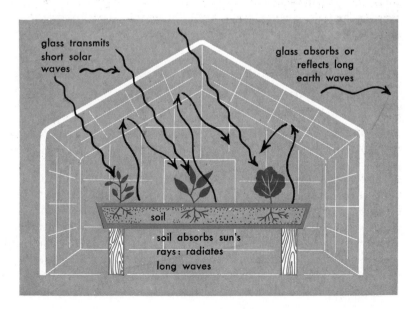

glass transmits short solar waves

glass absorbs or reflects long earth waves

soil

soil absorbs sun's rays: radiates long waves

Fig. 33-8. This diagram illustrates the four ways by which heat can be transferred into the atmosphere. See Topic 10.

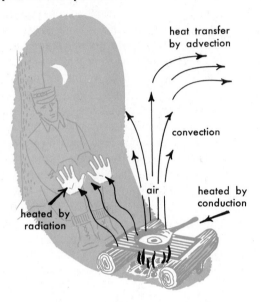

heat transfer by advection

convection

air

heated by conduction

heated by radiation

Radiation is the process by which energy is transferred through space or through transparent materials in the form of electromagnetic waves or radiations. Hot bodies like the sun radiate their energy into space largely in the form of short-wave radiations. Cooler bodies like the earth radiate energy in the form of long-wave radiations. As already explained, both help to heat our atmosphere.

Conduction is the transfer of heat from one object to another by actual contact. A kettle on a hot stove is heated by conduction. The air touching a hot radiator is heated by conduction. Similarly, the *bottom of the atmosphere* can be heated by conduction of heat from the warm surface of the earth to the air that rests upon it.

Convection is the transfer of heat by means of currents within the heated material itself. Convection can take place only in fluids (materials that can flow; liquids and gases). It represents a method by which heat is actually carried from the places in contact with the source of heat to

the more distant parts of the material being heated. Let us see, for example, how convection helps to heat a kettle of water on a hot stove. The bottom of the kettle becomes hot by conduction. The bottom water then becomes hot by conduction. But heat makes this water expand and become less dense. The denser cold water at the top of the kettle sinks, forcing the lighter warm water to the top in a continuous movement called a **convection current.** In effect, heat is carried up from the source, and the more distant material is given its chance to get close to the source of heat. Convection will not work if the heat source is at the top. Why?

Convection is a very important method of heat transfer in our atmosphere. Not only does it transfer heat but it also causes the horizontal air movements that we call winds. Winds transfer heat along the earth's surface. For example, winds may *bring* heat from the tropics into temperate latitudes. Cool ocean breezes may *remove* heat from hot beaches. This transfer of heat by winds is called **advection.** It is merely the horizontal phase of convection.

All four processes—*radiation, conduction, convection,* and *advection*—involve both gain and loss of heat, or heat transfer. Obviously, if one object gains energy in the form of heat, another object must lose an equivalent amount of energy.

11. Temperature Drops with Altitude

It might be expected that the air would become warmer as one went up and up in the troposphere. Observation shows just the opposite to be generally true. On the average, known as the *normal lapse rate,* the air temperature drops about 3.5° Fahrenheit for every 1,000 feet increase in altitude.

Why is the air warmest at the earth's surface? The answer lies in the fact that the bottom air receives more heat than the air above it. The entire troposphere is heated both by direct solar radiation and indirect earth radiation. *But the bottom air is also heated by conduction from the land and sea surfaces on which it rests.* The bottom air also has two other, though less important, advantages. Bottom air is closer to the source of earth radiations and, because of its greater density, is a somewhat better absorber of solar radiation than the less dense upper air.

At this point someone is likely to ask why the hot air from the surface does not rise by convection to the top of the troposphere, the way it does in a radiator-heated room. The answer is that *a room has a low ceiling* which traps the hot air and keeps it from escaping. Even in the heated room the *hottest* air will be found right above the radiator, not on the ceiling. In the troposphere, however, the air rises many miles to its tropopause "ceiling," and *it cools off as it rises.* To "prove" this, try heating a house without a roof! (See Fig. 33-9.)

12. Angle of Insolation

The quantity of insolation or solar energy received at a given time at any one place on the earth depends on the place's latitude, the time of day, and the day of the year. All of these factors play a part in determining the **angle of insolation,** the angle at which the sun's rays strike the earth's surface. When this angle of insolation is 90° (rays perpendicular to the surface), the maximum possible energy is available to heat the surface. The farther the angle is from the vertical (the more slanting the rays are), the larger the area which the sun's rays must cover and the less energy they bring to a given area. (See Fig. 33-10.) In other words, **vertical rays are more concentrated than slanting rays.** Another advantage of vertical rays is that their vertical path takes them through the atmosphere by the shortest possible route, so they lose less energy in the atmosphere by absorption and reflection than slanting rays do.

Places in *low latitudes* (close to the Equator, which has a latitude of 0°) *receive nearly vertical rays of the sun* throughout the year, so they get a large share of solar energy to convert into heat. Places in *middle latitudes* (like most of the United States) receive near-vertical insolation in summer but slanting rays in winter. Places in high latitudes (close to the Poles, which

Fig. 33-9. This diagram gives three reasons why the air nearest the earth's surface is warmer than the air at higher levels, and it shows the normal lapse rate.

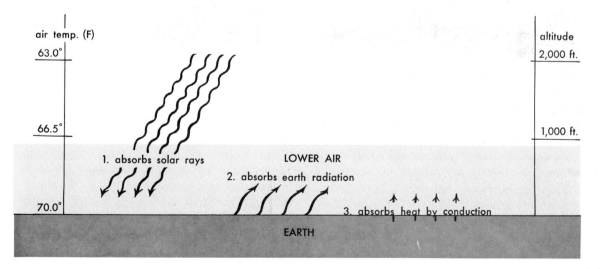

air temp. (F)

63.0°

66.5°

70.0°

1. absorbs solar rays
LOWER AIR
2. absorbs earth radiation
3. absorbs heat by conduction

EARTH

altitude
2,000 ft.

1,000 ft.

Fig. 33-10. Vertical rays concentrate more energy on a given area than do slanting rays. The two beams VV' and SS' are of equal thickness, but whereas all of VV' strikes surface AB, only a part of SS' (thickness DE) can strike the same surface. The balance of SS' (thickness EC) is spread over the surface BC.

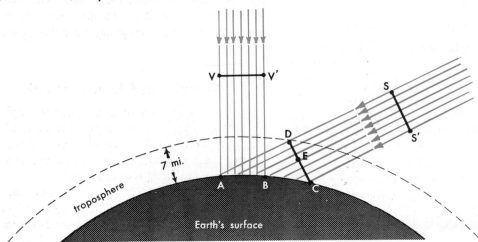

have the maximum latitude of 90°) receive slanting insolation all year, and may even have no sunshine at all during part of the winter.

The angle of insolation also varies with the time of day, being lowest at sunrise and sunset and highest at noon. *On any given date the sun's rays can be vertical at only one latitude on the earth's surface, and even there only at the instant of noon.* The sun is never vertical in latitudes higher than 23½° north or south of the Equator.

13. Heating of Land and Water

If the earth's surface were completely covered by water or some other single material, heat would be distributed uniformly in latitude zones parallel to the Equator, and temperatures would get steadily lower as the Poles were approached.

But the earth's surface is *not* uniform. Oceans surround continents and islands in a ratio of about three times as much water as land, and land and water heat up and cool off very differently. These differences have a marked effect on the world's weather.

Sunlight warms water much more slowly than land for many reasons: (1) in water the *sun's rays penetrate* to a depth of about 100 feet; on land all the heating is confined to the top few inches of soil or rock; (2) *water distributes* its heat by moving about; land cannot; (3) water has a *specific heat* about four times as great as land's (this means that it takes four times as much heat to raise the temperature of water as it does to bring about the same rise of temperature in an equal weight of land); (4) much of the radiation absorbed by water is used up in *evaporating* water instead of warming it.

Water also holds its heat longer than land does, probably mostly because its heat is spread through a large volume of water at considerable depths.

All of the above adds up to the fact that water and land in the same latitudes, exposed to the same insolation, arrive at markedly different temperatures. On a sunny day the sands of a beach are much warmer than the nearby water. At night the sands are usually colder, because they lose heat much faster than water. The same holds true on a larger scale and on a seasonal basis. Continents are warmer than adjacent oceans in summer. In winter the continents become colder than the adjacent oceans.

14. Land Heats Up Unevenly

Land heats up faster and cools off faster than water. But unlike water, land has a great variety of surface materials, each of which differs somewhat from the others in its ability to absorb solar radiation. Dark soils and rock are better absorbers than light-colored ones. Dry ground warms up faster than wet ground. Meadows warm up more quickly than forests. Pavements warm up faster than grassy lawns. And in every case the surfaces that warm up faster also cool off faster and are likely to be colder at night.

15. Warmest and Coldest Hours

The warmest hour of the day usually comes in the afternoon. From sunrise to noontime the angle of insolation gets higher and higher, and the air warms up steadily. Then the sun begins to decline, but for several hours after noon the air usually still receives more heat from the sun and the earth than it radiates, so its temperature continues to rise. The warmest hour is usually later in summer than in winter. Why?

The coldest hour of the night usually comes just before sunrise, because the air continues to radiate heat and cool off all through the night. Not until the first rays of the sun arrive at sunrise, does the warming process begin again. The coldest hour is usually later in winter than in summer. Why?

The difference between the highest temperature and lowest temperature of a day is the **daily temperature range.** For example, a high of 70°F and a low of 45°F give a range of 25°F. The daily temperature range is usually largest when skies are clear. The clear skies permit strong heating by day and rapid loss of heat by radiation to space at night.

The daily temperature range is small on cloudy days. The clouds keep out solar radiation by day, preventing the air from warming up. At night the clouds prevent the earth's heat from escaping into space. This "blanket" effect keeps the temperature from dropping much during the night.

16. Warmest and Coldest Months

For reasons similar to those given in Topic 15, the warmest month of the year (in our north temperate latitudes) is usually July, even though the sun's rays are most nearly vertical and daylight hours are longest about June 21.

The coldest month of the year is usually January, even though days are shortest and sunlight is weakest about December 21. In the Southern Hemisphere, where seasons are reversed, January is the warmest month and July is the coldest month.

The difference between the average temperatures of the year's warmest and coldest months is the **annual temperature range.** Oceans have a small annual temperature range, since they are relatively cool in summer and warm in winter. Large land masses and continents have a large annual temperature range, since they are relatively hot during the summer and cold during the winter.

17. Temperature Inversions

Normally the air becomes colder as one goes up in the troposphere. Occasionally, however, the air becomes warmer with altitude, sometimes warming up for several thousand feet, before the normal cooling-with-altitude situation is resumed. This "upside down" condition is called a **temperature inversion.** The term "inversion" is also used for the layer of air in which temperature rises with altitude. Temperature inversions may occur by *advection* (horizontal movements) of warm winds blowing into a region on top of

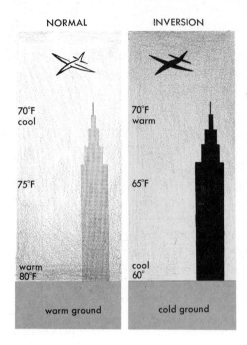

NORMAL   INVERSION

70°F
cool

70°F
warm

75°F

65°F

warm
80°F

cool
60°

warm ground   cold ground

Fig. 33-11. Normally the air is warmest near the surface and cooler at higher elevations (left diagram). In an inversion, however, the opposite is true (right diagram).

colder air already present at the surface. Temperature inversions also occur even more frequently through *conduction and radiation* on nights when the sky is clear and the air is dry. The ground loses heat rapidly by radiation on clear dry nights, and it soon becomes very cold. (Campers who sleep on the ground are well aware of this.) The air close to the ground is cooled by conduction to a temperature that may be considerably lower than that of the air at higher levels, which is cooling much more slowly

by radiation. The result is an inversion—cold air below, warmer air above. As a rule, this type of inversion ends at relatively small heights of a few hundred feet or less. (See Fig. 33-11.)

Inversions are important in the formation of fog, smog, and sleet, as will be seen in Chapters 36 and 37.

18. Measuring Air Temperature

Thermometers are instruments used to measure temperature. For measuring air temperature two types are commonly used, both operating on the principle that a rise in temperature will cause expansion. **Liquid thermometers** use mercury or alcohol as the expanding material. (See Fig. 33-12.) Mercury is naturally silver-colored; alcohol is colorless but is usually dyed red or blue so that it can be seen more easily. The liquid fills the broadened *bulb* part of a long tube. When exposed to higher temperatures, the alcohol or mercury expands into the almost invisibly narrow stem of the thermometer tube, which has had all air removed from it and is sealed at the top. The thermometer is made so that the glass through which the stem is viewed acts as a magnifier when held at the proper angle. On good thermometers the scale of temperatures is etched on the glass. Mercury thermometers are more accurate than alcohol thermometers because mercury expands more evenly, but mercury cannot be used in very low temperatures because it freezes at −39°F. Alcohol does not freeze until −200°F. (See Fig. 33-12.)

In **metal thermometers,** two equally long strips of different metals—brass and iron, for example—are bonded together, one on top of the

Fig. 33-12. In this type of thermometer, the expansion of a liquid is proportional to the rise in temperature.

bulb   magnifying glass   stem

mercury or alcohol   vacuum

other, to form a "bimetal." Since the metals expand at different rates, a change in temperature will make the bimetal bend into a curve in which the longer bar is on the outside. A rise in temperature bends it one way; a drop in temperature bends it in the opposite direction. As a rule the bimetal is shaped into a coil and fastened at one end of the thermometer case. (See Fig. 33-13.) A pointer is attached to the free end. When the temperature changes, the coil winds or unwinds, and the pointer moves in a circular arc over the thermometer scale.

If a pen is put at the end of the pointer, and a sheet of paper marked with the temperature scale is used instead of an ordinary scale, the temperature may be recorded by the instrument. Furthermore, if this graph paper is mounted on a cylinder that is turned by clockwork at a uniform speed, the pen will write a continuous temperature record for the period of time during which the cylinder turns. Such a device is called a **thermograph,** a self-recording metal thermometer. (See Fig. 33-13.) Usually the record is for one week, and the graph paper is divided into days and 2-hour periods. The ink used in the thermograph is a special kind, made with glycerine instead of water, to prevent freezing and evaporation. A few drops of this ink are enough for a week's record.

A **maximum thermometer** records the highest temperature to which it has been exposed. A **minimum thermometer** records the lowest temperature to which it has been exposed. Like ordinary thermometers, these thermometers show the temperature of the air that surrounds them at any particular instant, but they also contain special devices for showing the highest (or lowest) temperature that has occurred. The clinical thermometer used by a doctor is a maximum thermometer.

Figure 33-14 shows the Weather Bureau types of maximum and minimum thermometer and explains how they work. Figure 33-15 shows a combination instrument.

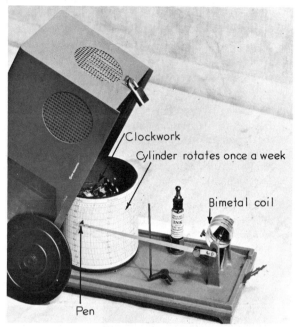

Taylor Instrument Co.

Fig. 33-13. A thermograph is a self-recording thermometer.

19. Temperature Scales

Temperatures are measured and recorded in *degrees*. A **degree** is a definite fraction of the difference between the temperature of *melting ice* (also called the freezing point) and the temperature of *boiling water*. (Both the ice and the water must be pure and at standard sea-level air pressure.) These two temperatures are known as the *fixed points* of the thermometer. The **Celsius scale,** formerly call the **centigrade scale,** is used throughout continental Europe and in our upper-air observations. Its fixed points are 0° and 100° respectively, and one degree Celsius is therefore 1/100th of their difference. On the less convenient **Fahrenheit scale,** which we still use in our surface weather observations, the fixed points are marked 32° and 212° respectively, and one degree Fahrenheit is therefore 1/180th of the difference, since $212 - 32 = 180$.

Friez Instrument Div., Bendix Aviation Corp.

Fig. 33-14. *Maximum and minimum thermometers of the Weather Bureau type. The maximum thermometer has a constriction or narrow part in the stem just above the bulb. When air temperatures rise, the expanding mercury forces its way up past the constriction, but when temperatures fall, the mercury thread cannot fall back unless it is shaken. The minimum thermometer has a small dumbbell-shaped glass index fitting snugly in the stem. (In the photo it can be seen just above the word MINIMUM.) When the thermometer is placed with the bulb slightly lower than the top, as in the photo, the pin is dragged down whenever the alcohol column goes down. When temperatures rise, the alcohol forces its way past the pin without moving it. To reset the thermometer, it is merely held upside down, allowing the pin to slide to the top of the tube.*

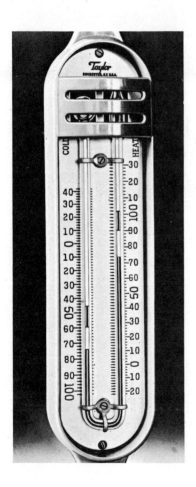

Fig. 33-15. *Six's type of maximum and minimum thermometer. The spherical bulb at the left top is filled with a non-freezing liquid such as alcohol. The tapered bulb at the right top contains compressed air. Joining the two bulbs is a U-shaped glass stem containing a thread of mercury. Fitting snugly above the mercury on each side of the U-tube is a dumbbell-shaped steel-in-glass index. When the temperature rises the alcohol expands, forcing the mercury thread to rise on the right, lifting its index and also compressing the air in the bulb above it. When the temperature falls the alcohol contracts, allowing the compressed air to force the mercury thread back and up on the left, raising that index. Thus the bottom of the right index always shows the highest temperature it has reached, and the left index shows the lowest temperature. The indexes are reset by using a magnet to draw them down to the tops of the mercury thread. Note that the minimum scale on the left is an inverted scale. Note also that the mercury thread always gives the current temperature on both left and right sides.*

Taylor Instrument Co.

Any thermometer may be marked with either or both scales, as long as the fixed points are properly indicated to begin with and the degrees properly scaled. And, of course, the thermometer need not show the entire scale from freezing point to boiling point; any part of the scale may be used, depending on its purpose. A thermometer used for measuring outdoor air temperatures, for example, may have a range of from −40°F to 120°F, whereas a clinical thermometer may range from 94°F to 108°F. Figure 33-16 shows a comparison of Fahrenheit and Celsius scales. Note that a Celsius degree is almost twice as large as a Fahrenheit degree. To be exact, 1°C = 1.8°F, or 1°C = 9/5°F. To convert Fahrenheit temperatures into Celsius or vice versa, these formulas are used:

$$F = 9/5C + 32° \qquad\qquad C = 5/9(F − 32°)$$

20. Air Temperatures on Maps

On weather maps the air temperature for a particular city is shown as a number next to the **station circle** marking that city's location. The number is placed to the left of the circle and a little above it, about where 10 o'clock is on a clock face.

Temperatures are also shown on United States Weather Bureau maps and on climatic maps by using solid or broken lines called *isotherms*. The word **isotherm** means "equal heat." Isotherms are lines drawn through places which have the same temperature at a given time. They are usually drawn for intervals of 5 or 10 degrees Fahrenheit on weather maps and climatic maps, although special isotherms, such as those of 32°F (the freezing line) and 0°F may also be shown. Ordinary weather maps show temperatures at the surface, but upper-air maps also use isotherms to show temperatures at any specified height above the surface. Figures 33-17 and 33-18 show isothermal maps that indicate average temperatures for July and January for the entire world. In mountainous areas, where the

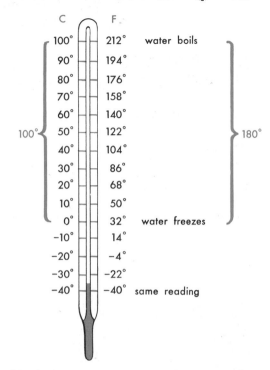

Fig. 33-16. A comparison of the Celsius and Fahrenheit temperature scales.

temperature changes very quickly with height, an actual isotherm map becomes very complicated. The temperatures are often then "reduced to sea level" by adding the normal lapse rate of about 1°F for every 300 feet of elevation; the isotherms are simplified in this way.

The **heat equator** is sometimes shown on isothermal maps. Much as the Equator is the geographic center of the earth, so the heat equator is the "heat center." It is a line that connects the hottest places in the world on the various meridians at any particular time. These points do not have the same temperature; the heat equator is therefore not an isotherm. Each point is simply the hottest, regardless of its temperature, for its own meridian at a given time. Thus we may have a heat equator for January, for July, for the year, or for any specified period.

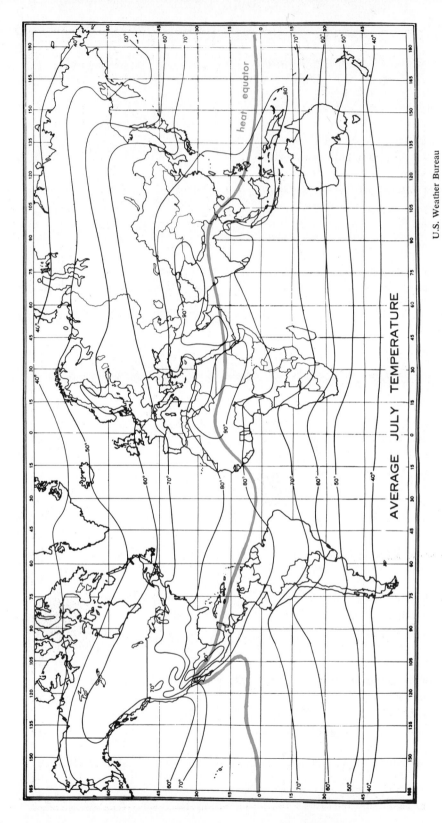

U.S. Weather Bureau

Fig. 33-17. Isothermal map of the world for July, showing the July heat equator. Temperatures are in degrees Fahrenheit.

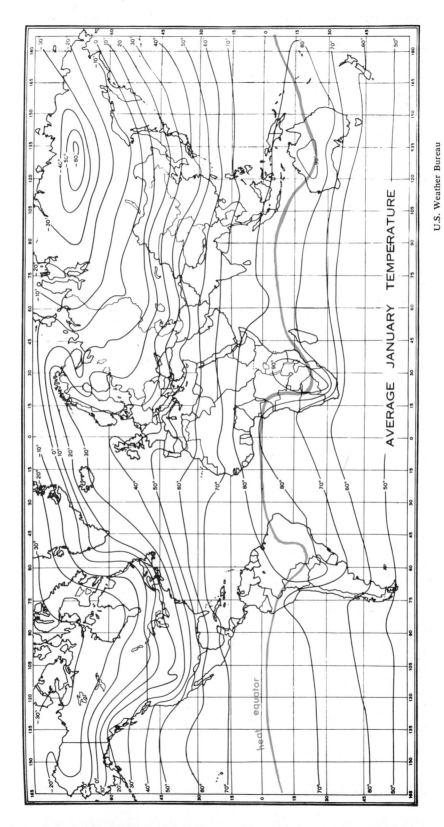

U.S. Weather Bureau

Fig. 33-18. Isothermal map of the world for January, showing the January heat equator. Temperatures are in degrees Fahrenheit.

21. Why World Isotherms Are Irregular

Since the amount of insolation depends on latitude, it might be expected that isotherms, which join points of equal temperature, would follow the parallels of latitude right around the world, with the highest temperatures closest to the Equator. This would be the case if the earth's surface were absolutely uniform. The Southern Hemisphere, which is largely water, has much more regular isotherms than does the Northern Hemisphere. The chief causes of irregularity in the isotherms are (1) the fact that land is hotter in summer and colder in winter than oceans in the same latitude and (2) the existence of ocean currents of contrasting temperatures along the shores of the continents, as in the case of the warm Gulf Stream and the cold Labrador Current off the coasts of northeastern North America.

The "bending" of an isotherm always means that at least one part of a parallel of latitude does not have the same temperature as the rest. When an isotherm *bends toward the Pole,* the part of the parallel from which it swerves is *warmer* than the rest. Conversely, when an isotherm *bends toward the Equator,* the part of the parallel from which it swerves is *colder* than the rest.

22. Why the Isotherms Shift

From June 21 to December 21, the sun's vertical rays are moving southward. From December 21 to June 21, they return northward. As they move, the heating of the earth changes and the isotherms and heat equator may also be said to "shift with the sun." But, as explained in Topic 16, the warmest weather "lags behind the sun" by about a month, and so the heat equator and the isotherms are farthest north of the Equa-

tor in July and farthest south in January rather than in June and December. Usually July is the warmest month and January the coldest.

Looking at the isothermal maps of Figures 33-17 and 33-18, we see, in addition to the irregularities noted in Topic 21, that (1) the isotherms have shifted more over the Northern Hemisphere than over the Southern Hemisphere, (2) the shift is greater over the continents than over the oceans, (3) the hottest and coldest regions are always land areas, (4) the North Pole is not the coldest place in the Northern Hemisphere in winter. All these facts are easily explained on the basis of the principles studied in this chapter.

23. Heat Balance of the Atmosphere

Scientists have made many measurements of the amount of solar radiation reaching the earth's surface. From these, they have determined the **solar constant.** This tells us the rate at which solar energy is received by the earth at the top of the atmosphere. It is approximately two calories per minute on a square centimeter surface that is perpendicular to the sun's rays. (A calorie is the amount of heat needed to raise the temperature of one gram of water 1°C.) This means that for every minute of every single day the earth is receiving enough energy from the sun to provide the United States with electricity for a whole year.

The heat absorbed by the atmosphere differs from place to place and from time to time. Nevertheless, scientists have concluded that the atmosphere as a whole is neither gaining nor losing heat. Apparently at the present time there is an exact balance between the heat energy absorbed from the sun and the heat radiated back into space.

TOPIC QUESTIONS

Each topic question refers to the topic of the same number within this chapter.

1. (*a*) What is the modern view about where the atmosphere ends? (*b*) How does the scientist get his information about the various parts of the atmosphere?

2. (*a*) What is the homosphere? (*b*) What is the heterosphere?

3. (*a*) On what basis is the atmosphere divided into the four layers described in this Topic? (*b*) Give a brief description of the extent and characteristics of the four layers.

4. (*a*) Describe the ionosphere with respect to its location, the kind and origin of its ions, and its layers. (*b*) How does it help radio transmission?

5. Locate and describe the magnetosphere.

6. (*a*) Give the name and percentage of the four most abundant atmospheric gases. (*b*) What is ozone? What is the ozonosphere? What is its importance? (*c*) Describe the importance and variations in amount of the carbon dioxide in the air.

7. (*a*) What is the air's percentage of water vapor? (*b*) What are condensation nuclei? Give examples.

8. (*a*) Describe the three things that happen to the solar radiation that comes to the earth. (*b*) Define albedo.

9. Explain what is meant by the greenhouse effect as it applies to solar radiation reaching the earth's surface.

10. Define or explain how heat is transferred by radiation, conduction, convection, and advection.

11. (*a*) What is the normal lapse rate? (*b*) Explain why the atmosphere is usually warmest at the earth's surface.

12. (*a*) What factors determine the angle of insolation at a particular location? (*b*) What is the relation between the angle of insolation and the heating effect of the sun's rays? How is this related to low, middle, and high latitudes?

13. (*a*) Why does sunlight warm water more slowly than land? (*b*) Why does water hold its heat longer than land? (*c*) Compare the temperatures of water and adjacent land during daytime and nighttime. (*d*) Compare them in summer and winter.

14. Why does land warm up unevenly?

15. (*a*) Explain why the warmest hour of the day is usually in the afternoon. (*b*) Why is the coldest hour just before sunrise? (*c*) Define temperature range.

16. (*a*) Which are usually the warmest and coldest months in the Northern Hemisphere? Southern Hemisphere? (*b*) Define annual temperature range.

17. (*a*) Explain what a temperature inversion is. (*b*) How do temperature inversions occur?

18. (*a*) How does a liquid thermometer work? (*b*) How does a metal thermometer work? (*c*) What is a thermograph? (*d*) What is a maximum thermometer? a minimum thermometer?

19. (a) What are the fixed points of any thermometer? (b) What are the fixed-point temperatures on the Fahrenheit and Celsius scales?

20. (a) How is a city's temperature shown on the weather map? (b) What is an isotherm? (c) What is the heat equator? Explain how it differs from an isotherm.

21. (a) Why are isotherms so regular in the Southern Hemisphere? (b) Name two factors that cause irregularity in isotherms. (c) What is the meaning of poleward bending of an isotherm? of equatorward bending?

22. (a) Why do the world's isotherms and heat equator shift? (b) When are they farthest from the Equator? Why? (c) Where do isotherms and the heat equator show the greatest shifts? (d) Where are the hottest and coldest regions (1) in July? (2) in January?

23. (a) What is the solar constant? (b) Explain the heat balance of the atmosphere.

GENERAL QUESTIONS

1. Make a diagram showing the convection currents in the air of a room heated by (1) a central stove, (2) a radiator against one wall.

2. Why is a lake not heated by convection (see Topic 10)?

3. How do convection currents help to cool the waters of a lake in autumn?

4. Why does the stratosphere contain very little dust or water vapor?

5. Why is there very little variation in the time of the warmest and coldest hours of the day at the Equator?

6. Even though you hold your face vertically to the rays of the sun in December, you will not sunburn as much in the same time as you would in June. Why?

7. Why are temperature inversions unlikely on cloudy nights?

8. Why is the stratopause colder at the Equator than at the Poles?

STUDENT ACTIVITIES

1. Check the fixed points of a thermometer in boiling water and melting ice.

2. Expose equal areas of water (in a beaker or other suitable container) and sand to the rays of the sun, or to an electric light bulb, or to a radiant heater equidistant from both the water and sand. Note the temperature of the upper layers at regular intervals as the water and sand warm up. Remove the source of heat and again note the temperatures as the materials cool off. Do the observations bear out the discussion in Topic 13?

3. Study the records of a thermograph to determine the warmest and coldest hour of each day of the week. See if these agree with the "predictions" of Topic 15. Where there are exceptions, try to explain them.

CHAPTER 34

Atmospheric Pressure and Winds

HOW DO YOU KNOW THAT . . . ?

An aneroid barometer is an instrument that measures atmospheric pressure. Use one to tell you the atmospheric pressure at the street level of your school building. Record this number. Now carry the barometer to the top floor of the building. Again read and record the atmospheric pressure. Explain why the two readings are different.

To find out how much atmospheric pressure changes for a given altitude, measure the difference in elevation between the two levels at which you made your observations. Probably the easiest way to do this is to count the number of steps and multiply by the height of each step.

1. Cause of Atmospheric Pressure

In a sense our atmosphere is an "ocean of air," and man is a "deep-air animal" who lives at the bottom of the air ocean. Like deep-sea animals who are adapted to the crushing weight of all the water above them, man is subjected to the pressure of all the air that extends from the earth's surface to the very top of the atmosphere. The *air pressure*, caused by the air's own weight, is about 14.7 pounds of air for every square inch of the earth's surface at sea level. It is less, of course, at higher levels. (See Fig. 34-1.)

Like water pressure, air pressure is transmitted equally in all directions, so it is exerted on all surfaces of the human body or on any other surfaces. It also exists within any object containing air—a building, the human body, "empty" bottles and cans. Since inside and outside pressures are normally equal, neither we nor our buildings nor our "empty" bottles and cans are crushed by air pressure.

2. Measuring Air Pressure

A **barometer** is an instrument that measures

atmospheric pressure. In 1643 the Italian physicist Torricelli (tor rih *chel* ee) invented the first

Fig. 34-1. The pressure of the air is caused by its weight. Every square inch of the whole air column weighs nearly 15 pounds.

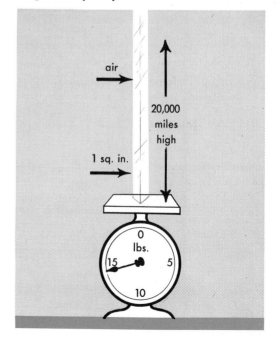

air

20,000
miles
high

1 sq. in.

0
lbs.
15   5
10

such instrument, a *mercury barometer* that balanced the weight of the atmosphere against the weight of a column of the heavy liquid metal *mercury*. A Torricellian barometer is made by filling a strong glass tube, about 36 inches long and closed at one end, with mercury. With the mercury held in at the top by the thumb, the tube is inverted into a dish of mercury, as shown in Figure 34-2. When the thumb is removed, the mercury in the tube drops, but only to a level at which its weight is balanced by the air pressure on the mercury surface in the dish. The space above the mercury column in the tube is a vacuum, known as "Torricelli's vacuum." Mercury vapor is poisonous, so care should be taken not to inhale it.

At sea level, air pressure will support a mercury column about 30 inches long in the barometer. (That is why we use a tube longer than 30 inches. If we used water instead of mercury to make a barometer, we would require a much longer tube, because water is less than one-thirteenth as heavy as mercury.) At higher altitudes where air pressure is less, the length of the

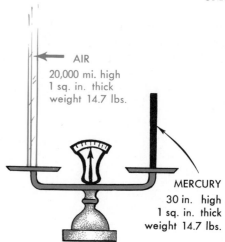

Fig. 34-3. Thirty inches of mercury and 22,000 miles of atmosphere weigh the same, thickness for thickness.

mercury column is correspondingly less. To find out how much *sea-level air pressure* is in *pounds per square inch*, we can weigh the 30-inch long column of mercury contained in a tube one square inch in cross-section. We find this weight to be about 14.7 pounds. Therefore the air pressure at sea level is about 14.7 pounds per square inch. (See Fig. 34-3.)

3. Air Pressure Decreases as Altitude Increases

Since air pressure is due to the weight of the overlying atmosphere, air pressure decreases as altitude increases. But at what rate? From sea level a rise of 1,000 feet reduces the air pressure by about one-thirtieth, making a mercury barometer read only 29 inches instead of 30. If the atmosphere were of uniform density and this rate continued, the air pressure would become zero at 30,000 feet altitude (about six miles), above which there would be no air at all. We know, however, that this is not so. Because air is highly compressible, the atmosphere is compressed by its own weight, and it is not uniformly dense. The air is densest at the earth's surface, becomes rarer and rarer as altitude increases, and extends

Fig. 34-2. Making a mercury barometer.

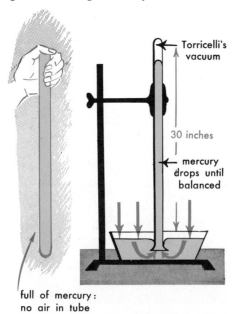

full of mercury: no air in tube

thousands of miles into space. But most of its weight lies comparatively close to the earth's surface. Ninety-nine per cent of the total weight of the atmosphere lies within 20 miles of the surface. Fifty per cent of its total weight lies within 3.5 miles, or about 18,000 feet. At this height the barometer reads about 15 inches.

If the lower 3.5 miles of the atmosphere weighs as much as all of the atmosphere in the thousands of miles above, the rate of pressure change is obviously not uniform. However, if we take any small section of the atmosphere, the variation will not be very large, and we may calculate its average rate. The average rate for the lowest 5,000 feet or so of the atmosphere, as shown in Figure 34-4, is about one inch of mercury per 1,000 feet change in altitude. The higher the altitude, the lower the air pressure.

4. Atmospheric Pressure Units

Since air pressure is measured by the mercury barometer, it is customary to express the pressure in terms of the *length of the mercury column,* which is easily measured, rather than in pounds per square inch. Normal sea-level air pressure is usually given as about 30 inches, which is a short way of saying that the air pressure is suporting a 30-inch column of mercury. Normal sea-level air pressure, expressed as a *pressure,* is nearly 15 pounds per square inch, as previously explained. Dividing 30 by 15, we see that each 2 inches of the mercury column represent, roughly, 1 pound of pressure.

In recent years meteorologists over all the world have adopted a metric pressure unit for expressing air pressure. This unit is called the **millibar** (abbreviated as mb.). It is equal to about one-thousandth of sea-level air pressure. The table above shows how *inch units* and *millibars* are related. The number **29.92 inches of mercury** is given because it is the official **standard atmospheric pressure at sea level** averaged for the entire world; 31.00 is about as high as the barometer ordinarily reads at sea level; 29.00 is about as low as it ordinarily reads.

Inches of Mercury	Millibars of Pressure	
31.00	1050.0	(approx.)
30.00	1015.9	
29.92	1013.2	
29.53	1000.0	
29.00	982.1	
1.00*	34.0	(approx.)
0.10	3.4	(approx.)
0.12	4.0**	(approx.)
0.03	1.0†	(approx.)

* Use this value to convert inches of mercury into millibars.
** Pressure interval used on United States weather maps.
† Use this value to convert millibars into inches of mercury.

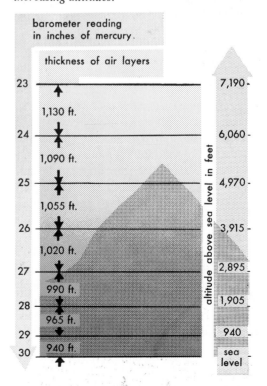

Fig. 34-4. The greater the altitude, the less dense the air. This diagram shows the approximate thickness of equal-weight layers of the atmosphere at increasing altitudes.

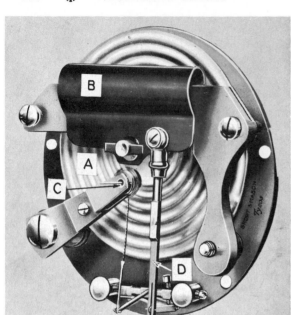

Taylor Instrument Co.

Fig. 34-5. An aneroid barometer removed from its case. A is the "vacuum can." B is the spring that supports the can. D is one of the levers that transmits the movement of the can and spring to the pointer (not shown) pivoted at C.

5. Aneroid Barometer; Barograph

The mercury barometer is a very accurate instrument and is generally used by a weather bureau as its standard barometer. The **aneroid barometer** is less accurate but more compact and more rugged. *Aneroid* means "without liquid"; an aneroid barometer contains no liquid. Its chief part is a flexible metal can which has had almost all the air pumped out of it and has then been sealed airtight. This can is therefore "sensitive" to air pressure, and will collapse if not supported by a strong spring. When air pressure increases, the top of the can is forced down a bit. When air pressure decreases, the top of the can is pulled up a bit more by the spring. This slight movement is passed on to a pointer and enlarged.

The pointer moves over a scale which is "calibrated" so that it reads the same as a mercury barometer in the same place at the same time. When calibrated to read *height above sea level* instead of air pressure, an aneroid barometer is called an **altimeter.** (See Fig. 34-5.)

The **barograph** is an aneroid barometer with a pen at the end of a pointer and a rotating scale sheet instead of an ordinary scale. It bears the same relation to the aneroid barometer as the thermograph bears to the metal thermometer. The barograph is a *recording barometer.* (See Fig. 34-6.)

6. Air Pressure on Maps

Air pressure is usually shown in two ways on United States Weather Bureau maps. The exact air pressure reading for a particular station (converted to sea level; see Topic 9) expressed *in millibars* is written at the upper right of the station circle showing the city's location, as shown in Figure 34-7. Suppose we wish to show readings of 1013.2 mb. and 984.6 mb. On the map these will be written as 132 and 846. Notice that the 10, the 9, and the decimal point are left out to save space. This can be done because the pressure readings always begin with a 9 or a 10, and always have one decimal place, so we need not write those parts of the readings on the map. Furthermore, practically all ordinary readings lie in the *low thousands* or *the high nine hundreds* (see table in Topic 4), so when we see a number like 13.2 we know a 10 must precede it; when we see an 84.6, we know a 9 must precede it.

The second way of showing air pressure is by *isobars* (*eye* so barz). **Isobars** are solid lines that join points having the same air pressure at the time shown by the map. (The idea is the same as for isotherms, which join points of equal temperature.) On United States Weather Bureau maps isobars are marked in millibars. An isobar will pass *through* a station circle only if the city's

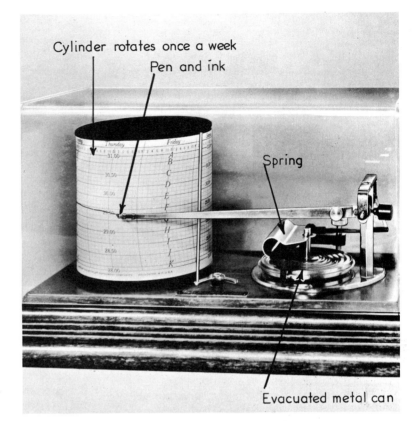

Cylinder rotates once a week
Pen and ink
Spring
Evacuated metal can

Fig. 34-6. The baragraph is a self-recording barometer.

Taylor Instrument Co.

reading is *exactly* that of the isobar. A new isobar is drawn at specified changes of air pressure on the map; for example, for changes of 2, 3, 4, or 5 millibars. The interval that is chosen is known as the **pressure interval.** At the present time, maps of the United States Weather Bureau use a 4-millibar pressure interval. A new isobar is drawn for each change of 4 millibars in air pressure on the map, and the millibar reading is always one that is divisible by 4. For example, consecutive isobars might be numbered 996, 1000, and 1004. See the table in Topic 4 again for the relation between inches and millibars. A difference of 4 millibars is equal to a difference of about 0.12 inches of mercury.

Climatic maps use isobars to show *average air pressures* for an entire month, an entire

Fig. 34-7. A weather map "station model" showing that the temperature is 51°F and the air pressure is 1013.2 millibars.

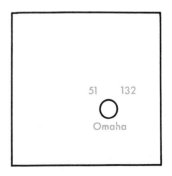

51   132
O
Omaha

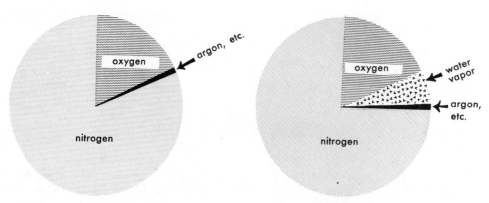

dry air: 1.20 oz. per cu. ft.   humid air: 1.18 oz. per cu. ft.

Fig. 34-8. Humid air weighs less than dry air because its water vapor weighs less than the oxygen and nitrogen it displaces.

season, or an entire year. Any suitable pressure interval may be used in such maps. (See Fig. 34-11.)

7. Air Pressure, Temperature, and Humidity

We have already seen that air pressure depends on the height of the air column resting on the observer. But even when the height of the air column is the same, the air pressure may be different. For example, though both New York and Philadelphia are approximately at sea level, they usually have different barometer readings. There are two principal reasons for this. First, *warm air is lighter than cold air,* so a column of warm air exerts less pressure than an equally large column of cold air. Secondly, *air containing water vapor* is lighter than dry air; the more water vapor, the lighter the air. This sounds contradictory, but it is easily explained. In the atmosphere water vapor is not simply *added* to dry air. If it were, it would, of course, make the air heavier. The water vapor in humid air *displaces* an equal volume of dry air. For example, a cubic foot of dry air is about 99 per cent nitrogen and oxygen; but a cubic foot of humid air with 4 per cent water vapor in it

contains only 95 per cent nitrogen and oxygen. But *water vapor is much lighter than either the nitrogen or oxygen whose place it took,* so the humid air is lighter than the dry air. (See Fig. 34-8.)

8. Importance of Barometer Readings

Air pressure is always rising or falling at any one place in the temperate zone. Meteorologists have learned that these pressure changes are closely connected with changes in weather. We already know that low air pressure may be due to high temperature and large water-vapor content, and that high air pressure may be due to low temperature and low water-vapor content. This agrees with observed weather changes, for, generally speaking, a falling barometer (decreasing air pressure) has been found to accompany warmer, more humid weather; a rising barometer usually accompanies colder and drier weather.

9. Reducing Barometer Readings to Sea Level

Normal air pressure for any location depends on its altitude. In New York City 30 inches is a

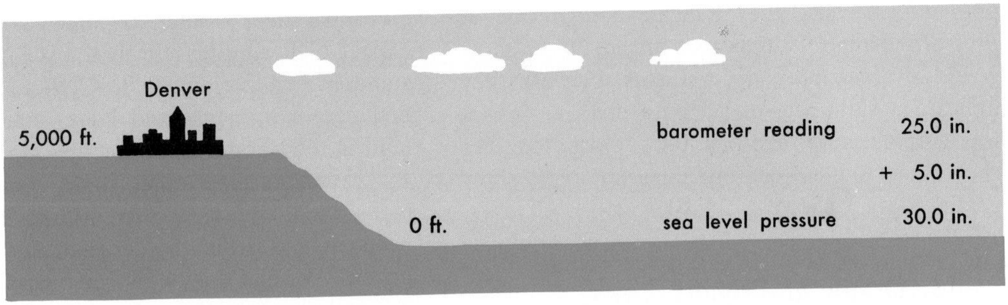

Fig. 34-9. A barometer reading of 25 inches at Denver is equivalent to a reading of 30 inches at sea level. Approximately one inch is added for each 1,000 feet above sea level.

normal reading. In Denver, Colorado, at 5,280 feet above sea level the normal barometer reading is about 25 inches. But if air pressures are to be compared on a weather map and used in drawing isobars, they must all be reduced to sea-level pressure. Denver's pressure of 25 inches is the equivalent of New York City's pressure of 30 inches; in other words, if Denver's atmosphere continued all the way down to sea level, its pressure at that time would be 30 inches. To determine sea-level pressures, the weather bureau uses very accurate tables, instead of the rough figure of one inch to 1,000 feet. These tables take the air temperature at the station into account, as well as its altitude. (See Fig. 34-9.)

10. Highs, Lows, and Pressure Gradients

On almost any weather map, the isobars will be seen to form systems of concentric ovals or circles that strongly resemble the contour lines of hills and depressions on a topographic map. When the pressure numbers on the isobars are read, it is found that the systems of isobars fall into two classes. In one class **the center isobar has the highest pressure reading,** and the pressure becomes lower with each outward isobar. These isobar systems are called **highs,** and they represent regions of the atmosphere in which the air pressure is higher than in surrounding air. Highs are like hills in the atmosphere.

In the second class **the center isobar has the lowest pressure reading,** and pressure increases with each outward isobar. These systems are **lows,** and they represent regions of the atmosphere in which the air pressure is lower than in surrounding air. Lows are like basins or depressions in the atmosphere.

The rate at which air pressure changes on the shortest path between any two isobars is called the **pressure gradient.** Isobars that are *close together* show *steep or strong* pressure

Fig. 34-10. The two classes of pressure systems as seen on weather maps.

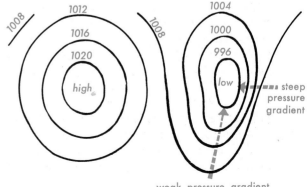

1008
1012
1016
1020
high

1008
1004
1000
996
low

steep pressure gradient

weak pressure gradient

gradients, because they indicate a high rate of pressure change. Isobars that are *far apart* show *gentle or weak* pressure gradients, because they indicate a slow rate of pressure change. (On a topographic map contour lines close together show steep slopes; contour lines far apart show gentle slopes.) (See Fig. 34-10.)

11. Origin of Primary Lows and Highs

Pressure maps of the world show a number of lows and highs that cover large areas of the earth's surface for the entire year or a good part of it. (See Fig. 34-11.) These lows and highs are known as **primary** or **semipermanent lows and highs.** They result from movements of air caused by unequal heating of the earth's surface. Lows are likely to form where air rises over warmer regions. Thus we may expect a world-wide belt of low air pressure in the very warm equatorial region. Highs are likely to form where air sinks over cooler regions. Thus we may expect high air pressure in the polar regions. In summer, semipermanent lows should be intensified over continents and large islands, because land is then hotter than the surrounding oceans. In winter, on the other hand, semipermanent highs should be strong over large land masses, because land is then colder than the surrounding oceans. We find this to be true over North America and the Eurasian (Europe and Asia) land mass.

Primary high pressure areas in the Northern Hemisphere include the Siberian High and the Canadian High over land areas, and the Pacific High and the Bermuda High (east of Florida) over oceans. Primary lows include the Aleutian Low (southwest of Alaska), and the Icelandic Low, both over ocean areas. (See Fig. 34-11.) Because of their great importance in "making the weather" these semipermanent highs and lows are known as **centers of action.**

Secondary lows and highs that *travel* over

Fig. 34-11. Isobaric map of the world for January. In the Northern Hemisphere primary highs include the Siberian, Canadian, Pacific, and Bermuda Highs. Primary lows include the Aleutian and Icelandic Lows.

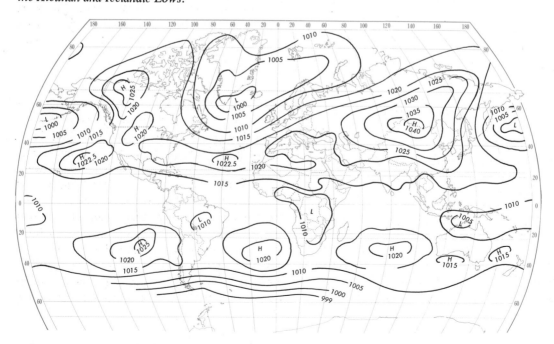

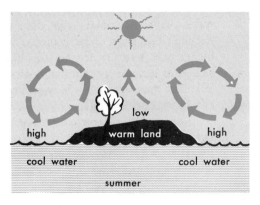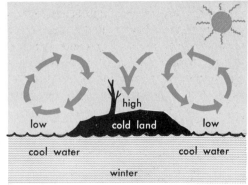

Fig. 34-12. In summer warm land surrounded by cooler water becomes a region of lower air pressure, and winds blow into the land. In winter the reverse takes place. In both cases, winds blow from higher pressure to lower pressure.

continents and oceans, principally in middle latitudes, have an origin that is different from that of the primary lows and highs. Their origin and characteristics will be discussed in Chapter 39.

WINDS

The air of the earth's atmosphere travels about under many names and in a variety of characters. As a *calm,* it stands so still that it barely disturbs a column of smoke rising from a chimney. It blows in from the ocean to break the sultry heat of a summer's day, and we welcome it as a *breeze.* Its speed increases, and it becomes a *wind,* a *gale,* a *hurricane.*

The wind blows into every corner of the earth's surface. What makes it blow? What makes it blow hot, blow cold, blow gently, blow violently? Where does it start? Where does it go to? How high does it reach?

12. How Winds Originate

We have already seen how unequal heating of the earth's surface by the sun causes convectional rising of air in the more highly heated areas. These areas become regions of low air pressure. Cooler areas become regions of high air pressure, where air descends and then moves into the low-pressure areas. At the surface **air moves from regions of higher pressure toward regions of lower pressure.** Movements of air more or less parallel to the surface are called **winds,** while up or down movements, such as those that exist at the center of a convectional system, are usually called **currents.** (See Fig. 34-12.)

Winds differ in strength. When pressure gradients are steep, winds are strong; when pressure gradients are gentle, winds are weak.

13. The Coriolis Force

If the earth did not rotate on its axis, winds would move from high to low pressure in a direction perpendicular to the isobars. (This direction is called the pressure gradient direction.) But the earth's rotation produces an effect called the **Coriolis** (kor ee *oh* lis) **force** which is at right angles to the direction of motion of all moving bodies—rivers, ocean currents, streams of air, and even projectiles. The Coriolis force causes winds in the Northern Hemisphere to be deflected to the right of the pressure gradient direction. (See Fig. 34-13.) In the Southern Hemisphere the deflection is to the left of the

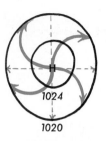
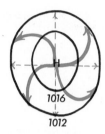

Northern Hemisphere
deflection to right

Southern Hemisphere
deflection to left

Fig. 34-13. This diagram shows how the Coriolis force deflects winds from the pressure gradient direction (shown by the dotted lines) in both hemispheres.

pressure gradient direction. (This statement of the effect of the Coriolis force is also known as Ferrel's Law.)

The Coriolis effect is greatest at the Poles and decreases to zero at the Equator. It also varies directly with wind speed. The stronger the wind, the greater the Coriolis effect. The Coriolis force affects the direction of all winds on the earth's surface, except those moving along the Equator.

14. Wind Direction and Speed; Effect of Surface Friction

As explained in Topics 12 and 13, the direction in which a wind blows depends upon *two* main factors: (1) the pressure gradient direction and (2) the Coriolis force. These two factors combine to make winds *at the earth's surface blow diagonally across the isobars.* The angle they make with the isobars is usually about 10° over water and about 30° over land. The rougher the surface is, the larger the angle.

The speed of the wind is proportional to the steepness of the pressure gradient, but it is also affected by friction with the earth's surface. Since friction is greatest at the surface and decreases upward, wind speeds are usually lowest at the surface, and increase with altitude up to about 3,000 feet over smooth land, and sooner over

water. At these levels the effects of surface friction disappear. Wind speeds are generally higher over water than over land because of the smoother surface. They are also generally higher in winter than in summer because pressure gradients are steeper in winter.

As wind speeds increase, the Coriolis effect increases. Above 3,000 feet, where friction no longer slows down the wind, the Coriolis effect is so large that the wind blows *along the isobars,* not across them. (See Fig. 34-14.) A law known as Buys-Ballot's Law states that if your back is to the wind (in the Northern Hemisphere), low pressure is to your left. Try it with Figure 34-14.

15. Gusts

Winds are rarely steady. Instead they often blow in spurts called **gusts,** die down briefly, and then blow gustily again. Even the direction of the wind varies from moment to moment, although maintaining one general course. These variations in speed and direction are due principally to the irregularities and obstacles of the

Fig. 34-14. At the earth's surface, winds blow at angles to the isobars. At altitudes of 3,000 feet or higher, they blow along the isobars.

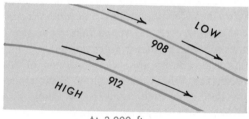

At 3,000 ft.

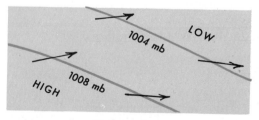

At the surface

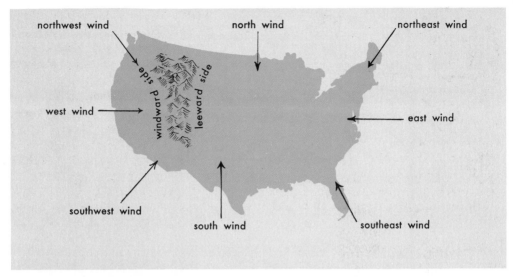

Fig. 34-15. Winds are named for the direction from *which they blow. The windward side of a mountain is the side the winds reach first. The leeward side is the sheltered side.*

surface over which the wind travels. Over a smooth surface, such as an ocean, winds are much steadier than over rough land surfaces.

16. Wind Names, Directions, and Weather

How are winds named? The answer can easily be derived by considering a few familiar illustrations. *North winds* in our hemisphere are usually cold winds because they come from the cold north. *South winds* are warm because they come from the warm south. A *sea breeze* is damp and salty because it comes from the sea. Obviously, then, *winds are named for the direction from which they come.* (See Fig. 34-15.)

There is usually a very definite relation between the direction of the wind and the weather. Winds from a northerly direction (north, northeast, or northwest) are coming from generally cooler latitudes and are likely to bring cool or cold weather. Winds from a southerly direction come from warmer latitudes and bring warm or hot weather. The reverse is true in the Southern Hemisphere, where south winds are cold and

north winds are warm. Winds from the sea carry large amounts of water vapor and may therefore bring clouds and rain. Winds from the interior, on the other hand, are much drier and usually bring relatively clear weather.

17. Observing the Wind

The direction of the wind is usually determined by the use of the familiar **wind vane.** This instrument points *into the wind* or *to windward*—the direction from which the wind is blowing. For example, a wind vane pointing to the south shows a south wind. The wind vane has a broad "tail" which offers much more resistance to the wind than the slender arrowhead end. A south wind swings the tail toward the north, causing the arrowhead to point to the south. Wind vanes may be connected to electrical indicators. The **wind socks** which can be seen at airports serve pilots as very large indicators of the wind's direction.

Wind speed near the earth's surface is measured by the **anemometer.** The cup anemometer (*anemo,* wind; *meter,* measure) is used by many

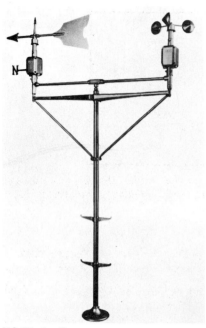

Fig. 34-16. A 3-cup anemometer and a wind vane. The wind vane shows a north wind.

Fig. 34-17. The observer is about to release a pilot balloon and follow its flight with the theodolite.

weather bureaus. The cups of the anemometer are hollow cones or hemispheres, all mounted to face the same way. The cups catch the wind on their open sides, no matter what the wind direction. The stronger the wind, the faster the cups turn, and the higher the reading of the instrument. The speed is given in miles per hour. (See Fig. 34-16.)

18. Winds Aloft

The speed and direction of *upper-air winds* may be determined by tracking the flight of special weather balloons either by telescope or by radar. In the telescope method, a **pilot balloon** is inflated with helium to a diameter of two to three feet and then released into the air. (See Fig. 34-17.) The flight of the balloon is followed through a special telescope called a theodolite (thee *odd* oh lyte), which resembles a surveyor's transit. The balloon rises at a fairly constant

speed of about 600 feet per minute, and from its angle of flight both the direction and the speed of the upper winds can be calculated by trigonometry. The record of these observations is called a **pibal** (from *pilot balloon*). About 80 selected stations in the United States make *pibal* observations every 6 hours (at night a small lantern is hung from the pilot balloon). Because the balloon must actually be seen, the theodolite method can be used in fair weather only.

In the *rawin* (radio winds-aloft) method, a special weather balloon carries a radio transmitter aloft. The balloon can then be tracked by special radio receivers on the ground that pick up the signals sent out by the transmitter. This method has three great advantages over the theodolite method. Balloons can be tracked to much higher altitudes (about 20 miles), bad weather is no obstacle, and tracking may be made automatic. (See Fig. 38-7.)

19. Winds on Maps

Wind directions are shown on maps by arrows that "fly with the wind." **Wind speeds** are shown by *feathers* and *flags* on the left side of the shaft of the arrow. Each full "feather" roughly represents a speed of 10 knots (about 12 miles per hour). Each half feather represents about 5 knots. A "flag" represents a speed of 50 knots. To save space the head of the arrow is not shown on weather maps, the direction of the wind being inferred from the position of the shaft. Figure 34-18 shows a station model with 2½ feathers on the shaft of the arrow. This represents a speed of about 25 knots. More specifically, the Weather Bureau table gives this a speed of 23 to 27 knots, or 26 to 31 miles per hour. (See Fig. 34-19.) A speed of one knot is a speed of

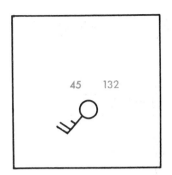

Fig. 34-18. Station model showing temperature 45°F, pressure 1013.2 millibars, southwest wind of 25 knots.

one *nautical mile per hour.* (A nautical mile is equal to 1⅙ statute or ordinary miles. To convert knots to miles per hour, multiply by 1⅙.)

Fig. 34-19. U.S. Weather Bureau symbols for wind speed on the weather map.

Symbol	Miles (Statute) Per Hour	Knots	Symbol	Miles (Statute) Per Hour	Knots
 ◎	Calm	Calm	 ||||	44 – 49	38 – 42
 —	1–2	1–2	 |||||	50 – 54	43 – 47
⟍	3 – 8	3 – 7	◣	55 – 60	48 – 52
⟍	9 –14	8 –12	◣|	61 – 66	53 – 57
⟍|	15–20	13 –17	◣||	67 – 71	58 – 62
⟍||	21 –25	18 –22	◣|||	72 – 77	63 – 67
⟍|||	26 –31	23 –27	◣||||	78 – 83	68 – 72
⟍||||	32 –37	28 –32	◣|||||	84 – 89	73 – 77
 ⟍|||||	38 –43	33 –37	 ◣◣◣	119 –123	103 –107

TOPIC QUESTIONS

Each topic question refers to the topic of the same number within this chapter.

1. (*a*) What causes air pressure? How much is it at sea level? (*b*) Why is an empty can or bottle not crushed by air pressure?

2. (*a*) Define barometer. (*b*) What is the principle of Torricelli's barometer? (*c*) How can the mercury barometer be used to prove that sea-level air pressure is 14.7 pounds per square inch?

3. (*a*) At what rate does air pressure drop with altitude? (*b*) Why is the rate not constant?

4. (*a*) What does "air pressure 30 inches" actually mean? (*b*) What is the relation of "inches of mercury" to "pounds of pressure"? (*c*) What is a millibar? (*d*) express standard sea-level pressure in inches and in millibars.

5. What is an aneroid barometer? an altimeter? a barograph?

6. (*a*) With the aid of a diagram explain how the air pressure at a Weather Bureau station is shown on the weather map. (*b*) What are isobars? How are they drawn? (*c*) What is the pressure interval?

7. (*a*) How does the temperature of the atmosphere affect its pressure? (*b*) Why is humid air lighter than dry air?

8. What is the relation between changing air pressure and weather?

9. Why must barometer readings be reduced to sea level?

10. (*a*) Explain what a high is. (*b*) What is a low? (*c*) Define pressure gradient. (*d*) How do isobars show pressure gradients?

11. (*a*) What are the primary or semipermanent lows and highs? (*b*) How and where do they form? (*c*) How do summer and winter affect them? (*d*) Name and locate 6 "centers of action."

12. (*a*) Explain how winds originate. (*b*) What "rule" describes their direction? (*c*) What determines their strength?

13. (*a*) What is the pressure gradient direction? (*b*) What is the Coriolis force? What is its effect on winds? (*c*) How is the Coriolis force related to latitude? To wind speed?

14. (*a*) What two main factors determine wind direction? (*b*) In what direction do they make the wind blow? (*c*) How does wind speed change with altitude? With the type of surface? With the season? Explain why in each case. (*d*) In what direction does the wind blow above 3,000 feet? Why?

15. What are gusts? What causes them?

16. (*a*) Explain, with examples, how winds are named. (*b*) How is weather related to wind direction?

17. (*a*) How does a wind vane work? (*b*) How does an anemometer work?

18. (*a*) What is a theodolite? How is it used in observing upper-air winds? What is a pibal? (*b*) In what way are *rawin* observations superior to *pibal* observations?

19. Explain how wind direction and speed are shown on weather maps.

GENERAL QUESTIONS

1. What is the air pressure in pounds per square inch (approximate) at 2,000 feet? 6,000 feet? 3.5 miles?

2. If the 1020 mb. isobar is marked 30.12 inches, what is the inch reading on the 1016 mb. isobar and the 1024 mb. isobar?

3. How high would the atmosphere be if its density throughout were the same as at sea level? Explain.

4. Verify the statement that air at sea level weighs about 1/800 as much as fresh water. (Fresh water weighs 62.5 pounds per cubic foot. Air at sea level weighs 1.25 ounces per cubic foot.)

5. Why does the low near Iceland persist even in summer when the ocean should be cooler than the adjoining land?

6. State Buys-Ballot's Law for the Southern Hemisphere.

STUDENT ACTIVITIES

1. To show that air pressure drops with altitude, carry an aneroid barometer from the basement to the roof of your school building or of any tall building, or to the top of a hill or mountain. Record the reading of the barometer at both levels.

   This "experiment" may also serve to give a rough measure of the height climbed, using an equivalence of 1 inch (barometer) = 1,000 feet (altitude).

2. Keep daily records of barometer readings, wind direction, cloudiness, and precipitation. Study them for any relation between the rise or fall of the barometer, the wind direction, and the weather.

3. Make a wind vane and an anemometer. (See *Weather for a Hobby* by R. F. Yates.)

CHAPTER 35

General Circulation of the Atmosphere

HOW DO YOU KNOW THAT . . . ?

Set up a two-hole convection box with a sliding window on one side. Place glass chimneys or wide tubing over the two openings in the top. Place a short lighted candle directly beneath one hole. Close the window. Observe the movement of air at each chimney by holding over it a piece of burning "smoke paper" or a match flame. Also note the movement of the air inside the box. Explain the wind pattern you observed. How is this pattern related to winds in the atmosphere? Now cover the hole over the "cold chimney," and open the window a few centimeters. Observe and explain the new air movements.

The "wind pattern" of your classroom may be observed in winter if there are radiators. Clap a chalk-filled eraser just above a hot radiator, Watch the movement of the chalk powder as high and as far as you can follow it. Now clap the eraser near the floor just below the radiator. Describe and explain the "wind pattern."

1. If the Earth Did Not Rotate

When all the winds and pressure belts of the earth's surface are plotted on a map of the world—whether it be for a single day, for a month, for a season, or for the entire year—both winds and pressure belts are seen to form distinct world-wide patterns or systems. The winds and pressures are related, just as theory tells us. Winds blow out of high-pressure areas and into low-pressure areas. But the locations of the pressure belts, and the winds they produce, are not exactly what we might expect. Let us see why.

Since the earth is heated most strongly in equatorial regions and least in polar regions, we might expect a very simple circulation to result. Warm air rising at the Equator would make this a low-pressure belt. Cold air sinking at the Poles would produce high-pressure belts. Winds would blow along the meridians from the Poles to the

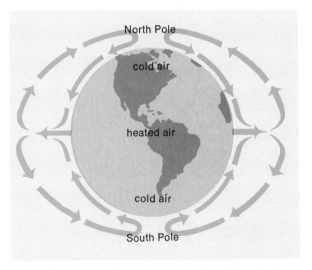

Fig. 35-1. *If the earth's surface were all water, and if it did not rotate on its axis, it would probably have this simple circulation.*

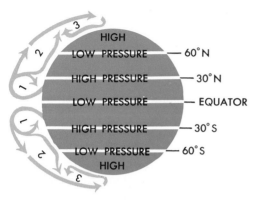

Fig. 35-2. Because the earth rotates on its axis, three pairs of circulation "cells" develop in the atmosphere.

Equator at the earth's surface, and air would move from the Equator to the Poles in the upper atmosphere.

A study of the map of world winds shows no such simple pattern. Meteorologists think that such a pattern might exist if the earth did not rotate on its axis and it had a uniform surface. (See Fig. 35-1.)

2. Three-Cell Theory: Equator-to-30° Cells

To explain the more complicated pattern of world pressure belts and winds that actually exists, meteorologists offer this explanation. Heated air rises at the Equator, creating a belt of low air pressure. (See Fig. 35-2.) The rising air flows toward both Poles in the *upper troposphere.* But the Coriolis force of the earth's rotation—to the right (eastward) in the north and to the left (also eastward) in the south—deflects the moving air strongly. By the time it reaches 30°N and 30°S latitudes (still in the upper troposphere) its direction in both hemispheres is almost due east. The air therefore piles up at 30° latitude, creating a belt of high pressure in each hemisphere. Some of the upper air forms a descending current here, but the rest continues

aloft toward the Poles. As the descending current approaches the surface, part of it flows back to the Equator and part flows poleward. Meteorologists call these two regions of the atmosphere (from the Equator to 30° in each hemisphere) "cells of circulation," because each includes within itself a complete and simple convection pattern. These twin cells may be called the **Equator-to-30° cells.** They lie entirely within the part of the world we call the tropics.

A second twin set of cells forms between 30° and 60° in each hemisphere, and a third set forms between 60° and the Pole in each hemisphere. Let us describe the 60°-to-Pole cells next.

3. Three-Cell Theory: 60°-to-Pole Cells

In the **60°-to-Pole cell** the cold polar air has its pressure increased by the descent from the upper atmosphere of some of the overflow from the Equator. A high pressure area is created at the Pole. Air then blows from the Pole toward the Equator along the surface. At about 60° it meets the air flowing poleward from the 30° high pressure belt described above. This coming together, or *convergence,* at 60° causes both streams of air to rise, making a low-pressure belt at this latitude. (The air from the 30° belt is warm, while that from the Pole is cold. The contact surface between them is known as the **polar front.** It is of great importance in producing frequent weather changes in middle latitudes.) When the rising air reaches the upper atmosphere, it turns poleward with the upper flow from the Equator, thus completing the circulation in this cell.

4. Three-Cell Theory: 30°-to-60° Cells

Now we can return to the middle cells of the three-cell circulation. At 30°, descending air from the high-pressure belt reaches the surface and flows poleward to 60°, where it meets the air from the Poles in the polar front. Here it rises in the 60° low-pressure belt until it meets and joins the poleward flow of the upper air coming from the Equator.

5. The Pressure Belts and Their Winds

The pressure belts and air movements described in the three-cell theory actually exist, though not quite as neatly as thus far described, and they have been given names. The equatorial low-pressure belt is called the **doldrums** or **doldrum belt.** The 30° high-pressure belts are called the **subtropical highs** or **horse latitudes.**

The 60° low-pressure belts are known as the **subpolar lows,** while the high-pressure belts at the Poles are called the **polar highs.** Notice how low- and high-pressure belts alternate: low at 0°, high at 30°, low at 60°, high at 90°.

When we examine the wind belts that lie between the pressure belts, we find their directions in the lower troposphere to be just about what we would expect. The winds blow from high pressure to low pressure, and they are deflected to the right in the Northern Hemisphere and to the left in the Southern Hemisphere. (See Fig. 35-3.) Thus in the Northern Hemisphere we have the polar northeasterlies blowing from the polar high to the subpolar low; the prevailing southwesterlies blowing from the horse latitudes high to the subpolar low; and the northeast

Fig. 35-3. Generalized map of the pressure and wind belts of the earth.

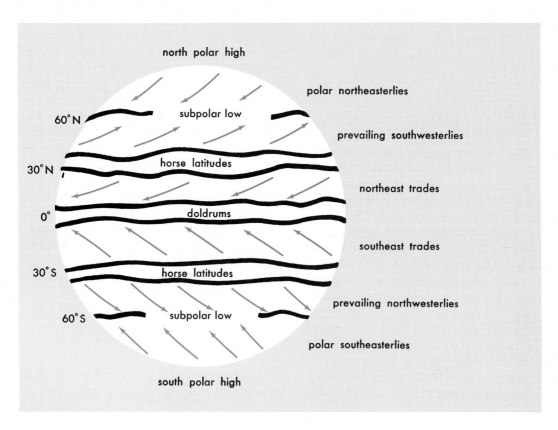

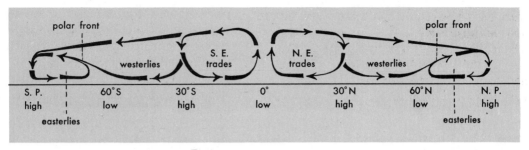

Fig. 35-4. A vertical cross section through the troposphere from the Equator to the Poles, showing air movement at and above the earth's surface.

trades blowing from the horse latitudes to the doldrums low. The Southern Hemisphere has a similar set of winds.

Since winds blow into the doldrums from both sides of the Equator, this region is also called the **intertropical convergence zone.** Unlike the winds of the polar front convergence zone at 60° latitude, the intertropical zone's winds are alike in temperature and density.

6. Direction of the Upper-Air Winds

The winds of the upper troposphere do not, of course, blow in the same direction as do those at the earth's surface. (See Fig. 35-4.) Most of the upper-air winds blow almost due west to east, except in the trades winds belts and in occasional equatorward outbursts of polar air. In the trades, the surface winds reach upward to a height of about 25,000 feet, blowing from east to west. (See Fig. 35-5.) Above this level they gradually change direction, finally becoming west-to-east like the upper-air winds of the higher latitudes. Wind speeds are very high in the upper troposphere, and it is here that we find the spectacular jet stream.

7. The Jet Stream

The **jet stream** was discovered by American planes flying toward Japan in World War II.

Since they were flying westward in the prevailing westerlies, they expected headwinds. But they were hardly prepared for headwinds as high as 300 miles per hour which they met at their flying level of 30,000 feet. The jet stream is a narrow tubelike stream of air that moves eastward at high speed through the upper troposphere, usually in the temperate zone. Sometimes the stream forms a continuous but meandering

Fig. 35-5. Upper-air winds. This diagram shows the direction of air flow at a height of 20,000 feet in the troposphere. At this height the winds are all westerlies except in the tropics, where they are easterlies. Above 25,000 feet all winds are westerlies. See Topic 5.

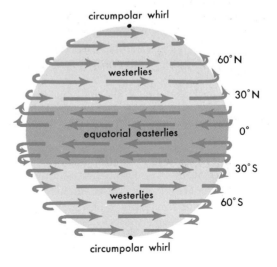

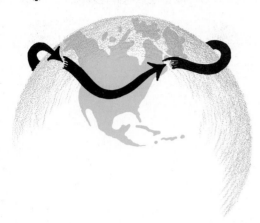

Fig. 35-6. A typical position of the Northern Hemisphere's jet stream over North America.

band around the entire earth. More often, it consists of two or more disconnected segments. The position of the jet stream shifts with the seasons. It moves north in summer and south in winter, but is found most often at about 40°N latitude. Its height ranges from about 20,000 to 40,000 feet, with its strongest winds at about 35,000 feet. Individual segments range in length from about 1,000 to 3,000 miles, in width from 100 to 400 miles, and in depth from one-half to one and one-half miles. Wind speeds are commonly about 150 miles per hour, but they may exceed 300 miles per hour. (See Figs. 35-6 and 35-7.) Two or even more jet streams may be found over a continent at the same time, with the more southerly one as far south as 20°N. Such a stream is usually known as a **subtropical jet stream.**

Pilots can make use of the jet streams on eastward flights, and they do well to avoid them on westward flights. But the jet streams appear to be important in controlling weather in the lower troposphere. The snakelike course of the jet streams, particularly during their southward shifting in winter, is believed to create great waves in the polar front at high elevations. As a result of these waves, massive outbreaks of polar air may penetrate far to the south, and tropical air may reach far north. Such outbreaks appear to bring cold waves, warm spells, stormy weather, and heavy precipitation.

Meteorologists are convinced that the jet streams may hold the key to improved weather forecasting.

8. Description of Wind and Calm Belts

Here are brief descriptions of the major wind and pressure belts of the three-cell theory:

The doldrums. This is a hot belt of low pressure, rising air, light breezes, and frequent calms. In the days of the sailing vessel it was a misfortune to be becalmed in the doldrums, where "the wind blew up the mast" instead of horizontally.

The horse latitudes. Part of the air that rises in the doldrums comes down in the two belts of the horse latitudes, north and south, to make them belts of high pressure. Air movement is largely vertical but downward, so these belts are calm belts too. The air is warm but not as warm as in the doldrums.

The name "horse latitudes" is derived from the belief that when sailing vessels carrying horses to America from Europe were becalmed here, horses were thrown overboard to conserve drinking water.

The trade winds. From the high pressures of the horse latitudes winds blow in both directions, toward and away from the Equator, to make two of the great wind belts of each hemisphere. The winds blowing toward the Equator are known as the **trade winds.** In the Northern Hemisphere, deflected to their right by the earth's rotation, they become the *northeast trades.* In the Southern Hemisphere, deflected to their left, they are the *southeast trades.* The trade winds are remarkably constant in both direction and velocity (10 to 15 knots), and derive their

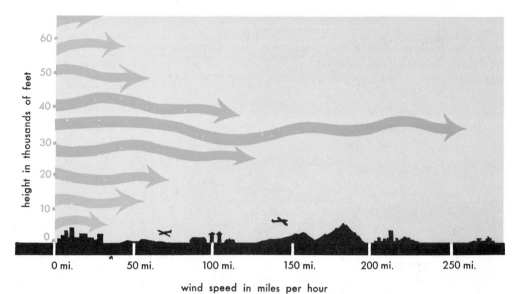

Fig. 35-7. This diagram shows how wind speed changed with height in going from the surface to 60,000 feet in central United States. The very high speed layer at about 35,-000 feet marks the position of the jet stream on the day of the observation.

name from the trade routes charted through them by sailing vessels in earlier times.

The prevailing westerlies. These winds also originate in the high-pressure belts of the horse latitudes and *blow poleward* as far as the subpolar lows. Deflected by the earth's rotation, they are *southwesterlies* in the Northern Hemisphere and *northwesterlies* in the Southern Hemisphere. Unlike the trades, they are highly variable in both strength and direction, and the term "prevailing" merely indicates that they blow from that direction more often than from any other. The strength of the westerlies increases with latitude, and it is greater over the ocean than over the land. In the almost unbroken ocean area of the Southern Hemisphere beyond South America the violently stormy westerlies are known as the "roaring forties."

The polar easterlies. From the polar highs fiercely cold winds blow into the subpolar low-pressure regions in both hemispheres. These *polar northeasterlies* and *polar southeasterlies* have the same general direction as the trades. Traveling storms occur frequently in both the prevailing westerlies and the polar easterlies. The *polar highs* and the *subpolar lows* are also stormy regions.

9. Shifting of Pressure and Wind Belts

The location of the doldrums belt changes with the seasons, as the sun's hottest rays move back and forth across the Equator. The shift in position of the doldrums is far greater over the great land masses of the continents than over the oceans, and greatest over the largest land mass, Asia. The most northerly position is reached in late summer; the most southerly position in late winter. But as the doldrums belt shifts, all the other pressure and wind belts shift along with it. The average shift is about 5°

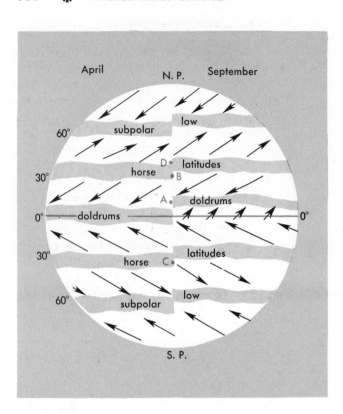

Fig. 35-8. This diagram shows how the wind and pressure belts shift with the seasons. At the left is shown the "average" position in spring. At the right, the belts are shown after having shifted northward in northern summer. A similar shift, not shown, would take place southward in northern winter. See Topic 9.

latitude, but it is much larger over the continents.

Shifting of the belts causes marked weather changes in places so located as to be in more than one belt during the year. There are two important cases of this kind. Places near the Equator (such as A in Fig. 35-8) may have both doldrums and trades over them during the year. Places in or near the horse latitudes may have both trades and westerlies over them during the year. See B, C, and D in Fig. 35-8.

Hooked trade winds develop when the doldrums belt into which the trades blow is entirely north or south of the Equator. As the trades cross the Equator, they are subjected to a deflection opposite to that in the hemisphere of their origin; they then become "hooked." For example, when the doldrums belt is entirely north of the Equator, the southeast trades from the Southern

Hemisphere must cross the Equator as they go north. When they cross, they are deflected to the right and become southwest trades. (See Fig. 35-8.) Similarly, if the northeast trades cross the Equator, they become hooked northwest trades.

10. Monsoon Winds, Especially India's

In winter the continents are colder than their neighboring ocean waters, and they become regions of sinking air and high pressure *from which* winds tend to blow outward to the sea. In summer the continents are warmer than their neighboring ocean waters, and they become regions of rising air and low pressure *toward which* winds tend to blow from the sea. This seasonal change of wind direction is known as the **monsoon effect,** and its changing winds are called **monsoons.** The best-developed monsoon winds in the world are found over India, southeast Asia, and the Indian Ocean, where a complete reversal of wind direction takes place between summer and winter.

In winter a great high-pressure area forms over the cold lands of Central Asia. From here winds blow southward over India and southeast Asia to form the **winter monsoon.** Coming from the interior, the winter monsoon is **dry** as well as cold. (See Figs. 35-9 and 35-11.)

In summer the situation is reversed. The hot continent becomes a region of low air pressure, and the direction of air flow is northward toward the land from the Indian Ocean. The winds from the ocean are warm and humid, and when they rise over the high plateaus and mountains of India and southeast Asia, heavy rains result. Thus the **summer monsoon** is also the **wet monsoon.** (Figs. 35-9 and 35-12.)

Other regions that have monsoons, though not nearly so complete a reversal as in India, are northern Australia, Spain, South Africa, and southeastern United States.

11. Land and Sea Breezes

These breezes may be called the "daily monsoons." During the daytime, coastal regions warm up more than the adjoining waters. The land becomes an area of rising air, the water becomes an area of sinking air, and a cool onshore breeze blows from water to land. Along seacoasts this **sea breeze** usually begins gently about 11 A.M., increases in velocity until 2 P.M. or 3 P.M., and dies down toward sunset. It is felt inland not more than 10 or 15 miles and extends upward about 1,000 feet into the atmosphere.

At night the land usually becomes cooler than the adjoining waters. The land is then an area of sinking air, the water is an area of rising air, and an *offshore* breeze blows from land to sea. This **land breeze** may start long before midnight and die down toward sunrise. Sea breezes are usually better developed than land breezes; at least they are more noticeable, particularly on hot summer days when they provide a most welcome cooling effect on the near-coastal areas. Similar water and land breezes may develop along lake shores, especially those of large lakes such as our Great Lakes. (See Fig. 35-10.)

Fig. 35-9. India's winter monsoon is shown as the left. Its summer monsoon is at the right.

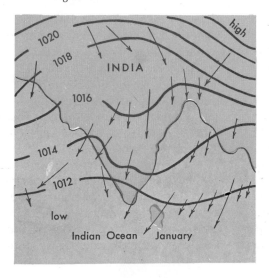

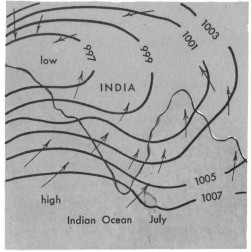

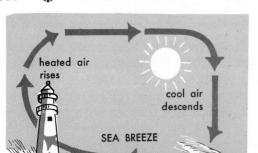

Fig. 35-10. Sea and land breezes, like small-scale monsoons, originate through unequal heating of land and adjacent water.

12. Mountain and Valley Breezes

Mountainous regions also have their "daily monsoons." At· night cold, heavy air drains down from the mountain tops into the valleys below. The narrower the valley, the stronger the breeze is likely to be. Coming from the mountains, it is called the **mountain breeze.** During the daytime warm air rises convectionally along the sunny mountain slopes from which the air receives most of its heat, and a **valley breeze** blows upslope from the valley. Its velocity is generally much less than that of the downhill mountain breeze.

13. Actual World Circulation

Topics 2–6 considered the wind belts as if they were uniformly extended across the entire world in their particular latitudes. Figures 35-11 and 35-12 show the world wind and pressure belts as they are actually observed for the months of January and July.

The *doldrums* (into which the trades blow) are seen as a series of lows rather than as a single low-pressure belt. In January these lows

are centered over the three continental areas south of the Equator, where the vertical sun is then located. In July the doldrums are mostly north of the Equator, with one great low extending far north into India.

The *trades* are easily identified. On the January map northeast trades and southeast trades blow into the doldrums, and only near the west coast of Africa and near Australia do the northeast trades cross the Equator to become *hooked northwest trades.* In July hooking is conspicuous where the southeast trades cross the Equator to form the southwest monsoon of India and Africa.

The *horse latitude* belts, 30° to 35° latitude, are seen to consist of a series of highs. These highs are very definite in the Southern Hemisphere, which is mostly ocean. They are less distinct in the Northern Hemisphere than in the Southern Hemisphere.

The *prevailing westerlies,* from the horse latitudes through the temperate zone, are plainly seen in the Southern Hemisphere over the great ocean areas. In the Northern Hemisphere's great land masses of North America and Eurasia however, the strong monsoon circulation due to

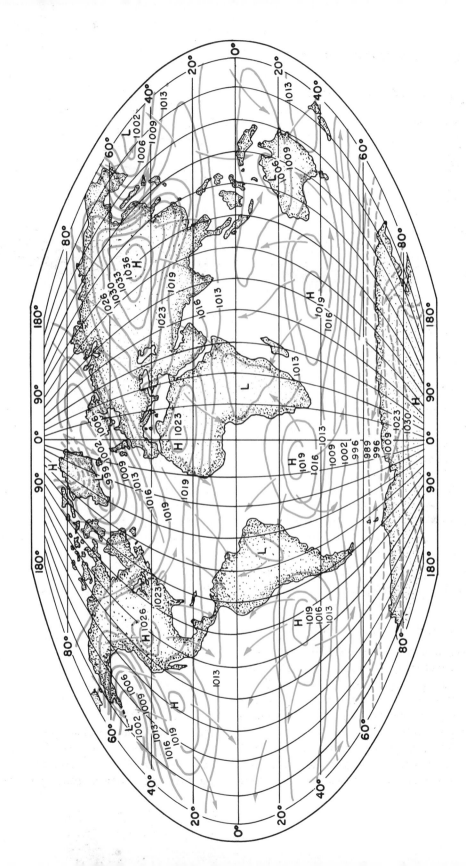

Fig. 35-11. Map of world pressure belts and winds for January.

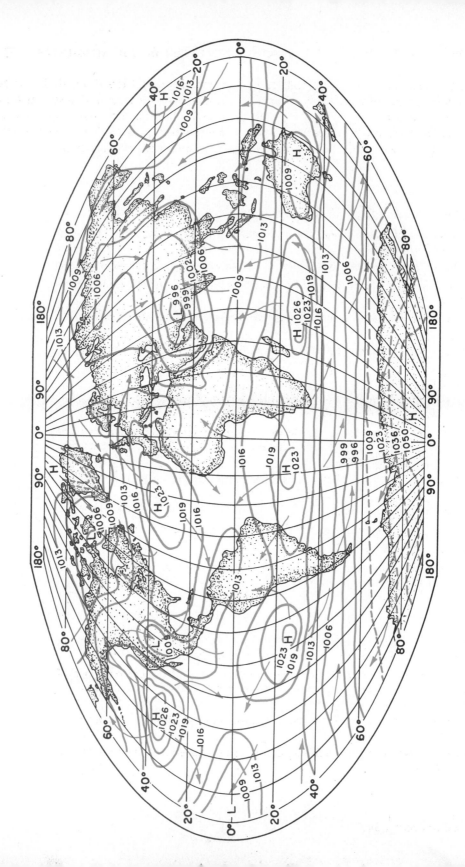

Fig. 35-12. Map of world pressure belts and winds for July.

continental low pressure in July and high pressure in January makes this belt very different from the idealized picture.

The *subpolar lows* can be identified as a single belt in latitude 60° to 65° in the Southern Hemisphere, and less distinctly in the Northern Hemisphere in the form of lows near Iceland and Alaska. Blowing into these lows are seen the *polar easterlies* that originate in the *polar highs* over Greenland and Antarctica.

TOPIC QUESTIONS

Each topic question refers to the topic of the same number within this chapter.

1. What kind of circulation would the atmosphere probably have if the earth did not rotate? Describe it.

2. With the aid of a diagram describe the air circulation in the Equator-to-30° cells.

3. (*a*) With the aid of a diagram describe the air circulation in the 60°-to-Pole cells. (*b*) What is the polar front?

4. With the aid of a diagram describe the air circulation in the 30°-to-60° cells.

5. (*a*) What are the doldrums, the horse latitudes, the subpolar lows, and the polar highs? (*b*) Name and locate the three sets of winds at the earth's surface. (*c*) What is the intertropical convergence zone?

6. Describe the directions of the upper air winds.

7. (*a*) Describe the location and characteristics of the jet stream. (*b*) How are jet streams believed to affect the weather?

8. (*a*) Work out and reproduce the simple diagram of the earth's planetary wind and calm belts. Learn it. (*b*) Give a brief description of each wind and calm belt.

9. (*a*) Why and how much do the wind belts shift? (*b*) Where do shifting wind belts cause weather changes? (*c*) Explain how hooked trade winds develop.

10. (*a*) What is the monsoon effect? How does it develop? (*b*) Describe the summer and winter monsoons of India.

11. Describe the origin and characteristics of sea breezes and land breezes.

12. Explain the origin of mountain and valley breezes.

13. Explain the actual appearance of the world pressure and wind belts as shown on the maps of Figures 35-11 and 35-12.

GENERAL QUESTIONS

1. Make a diagram (similar to that in Figure 33-8) showing how hooked northwest trade winds develop when the doldrums are south of the Equator in February.

2. Make a diagram to show the probable summer and winter monsoon winds of Australia. Compare your diagram with actual conditions shown in the maps of Figures 35-11 and 35-12.

3. What parts of the United States show marked seasonal changes of winds? See Figures 35-11 and 35-12.

4. On what time schedule might a fishing fleet of sailing vessels make best use of land and sea breezes?

STUDENT ACTIVITIES

See list at end of Chapter 34.

CHAPTER 36

Evaporation and Condensation

HOW DO YOU KNOW THAT . . . ?

It takes energy to evaporate a liquid, and heat is the form of energy that usually makes evaporation take place (Topic 3). To illustrate this, put a drop of water and a drop of alcohol about 3 cm apart on your wrist. Which one evaporates first? Which one makes your wrist feel cooler? Why?

The water that evaporated is present in the atmosphere as water vapor. Some of this water vapor can be returned to the liquid state by reversing the process that made it water vapor—by cooling it. To do this, fill a dry glass or metal cup with a mixture of ice and water. After a minute or two, observe the mist that forms on the outside of the glass. Where does this water come from? What makes it form?

1. The Three States of Water

Water exists in the atmosphere in all of the three states of matter: solid, as snow and hail and cloud particles; liquid, as rain or cloud droplets; gas, as invisible water vapor.

Water may change from any one state into any other. The meteorologist is most interested in changes involving water vapor. The change from solid ice to liquid water is **melting;** the reverse process is **freezing.** The change from liquid water to water vapor is **evaporation;** the reverse change from water vapor to liquid water is **condensation.** Solid ice or snow may also evaporate directly to form water vapor without first melting. The direct solid-to-gas change is given the special name of **sublimation,** although it is still a form of evaporation. Sublimation explains how snow can disappear without melting in below-

freezing weather. The term "sublimation" is also used for the reverse gas-to-solid change that takes place when water vapor forms frost or snow crystals. Sublimation takes place only when temperatures are below freezing. (See Fig. 36-1.)

2. Sources of Water Vapor

Water vapor enters the air from anyplace on the earth's surface where water exists either as a liquid or as ice. Most of the water vapor in the atmosphere comes from the oceans, lakes, marshes, and glaciers that comprise about three-fourths of the earth's surface, but additional amounts are supplied by moist ground, by **transpiration** from the leaves of plants, and in the gases of erupting volcanoes. Water vapor is most abundant near the surfaces from which it arises, although it is distributed throughout the troposphere by convection and winds, and may be carried a thousand miles inland from the oceans. Since convection ends at the tropopause, there is very little water vapor in the stratosphere.

3. Energy for Evaporation

When liquid water evaporates, water vapor enters the atmosphere. The molecules of liquid water are in constant motion. Molecules that reach the water surface and escape into the atmosphere are said to "evaporate." At ordinary temperatures evaporation is slow because the molecules are not moving very fast. As energy in the form of heat enters the water, the molecules speed up their motion and escape more rapidly. **The higher the temperature, the higher the rate of evaporation.**

Physicists have observed that definite amounts of heat are required to evaporate water by imparting rapid motion to its molecules. Careful measurements show that about 540 calories of heat will evaporate one gram of water at the normal 100°C boiling point. (A calorie is the heat needed to raise the temperature of one gram of water 1°C.) As one might expect, more energy is required when the water is colder to begin with. The heat required to evaporate water is called the **latent heat of vaporization.**

Since water absorbs heat from its surroundings when it evaporates, *evaporation is a cooling process.* For example, a fevered patient is cooled by the rapid evaporation of alcohol from his skin. An electric refrigerator is chilled by the rapid evaporation of liquid ammonia or other coolants in its coils.

Water molecules evaporate more rapidly into dry air than into air already containing many water molecules. For this reason *evaporation is faster on a windy day,* when the wind keeps changing the layer of air touching the water.

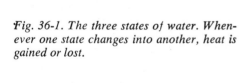

Fig. 36-1. The three states of water. Whenever one state changes into another, heat is gained or lost.

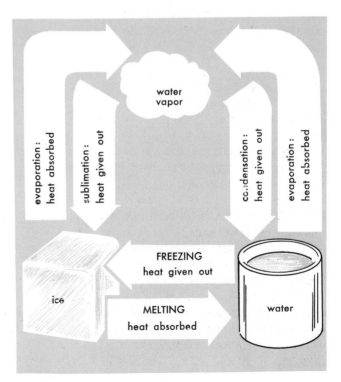

4. Specific Humidity and Capacity

The **capacity** of air for holding water vapor depends entirely on its temperature. The higher its temperature, the more water vapor air can hold. The meteorologist calls the amount of water vapor in the air the **specific humidity,** and defines it as the **number of grams of water vapor in one kilogram of air.** (A gram is one-thousandth of a kilogram. A kilogram weighs about 2.2 pounds.) When the specific humidity of the air equals its capacity, the air is **saturated.** The air between the water surface and the glass cover of a fish tank is likely to be saturated. Here the drops of water suspended from the underside of the cover show that while water may continue to evaporate from the warm tank, an equal amount of water must leave the already saturated air.

The capacity of air for holding water vapor is roughly doubled for every rise in temperature of about 20°F. For example, a kilogram of air at 60°F has a capacity of about 11 grams of water vapor. A kilogram at 80°F has a capacity of about 22 grams. (See Fig. 36-2.)

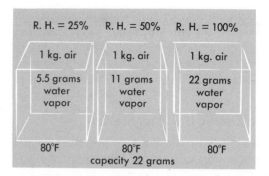

Fig. 36-3. The meaning of relative humidity. Each cube represents a kilogram of air at 80°F, which therefore has a capacity of 22 grams of water vapor. In each case, however, the specific humidity is different. The relative humidity is the ratio of the specific humidity to the capacity.

5. Relative Humidity

The meteorologist is interested in knowing to what extent of its capacity the air is filled with water vapor. To express this information he uses the **relative humidity,** which he defines as the **ratio of the amount of water vapor in the air to the amount that the air would contain if saturated at the same temperature.** Relative humidity is usually stated as a percentage, and can be calculated from the following expression:

$$\% \text{ Rel. Hum.} = \frac{\text{Spec. Hum.}}{\text{Capacity}} \times 100$$

For example, air at a temperature of 80°F has a *capacity* of 22 grams. If its *specific humidity* at a particular time is 11 grams, its *relative humidity* is 50 per cent.

$$\% \text{ R.H.} = \frac{11}{22} \times 100 = 50\%$$

Saturated air (specific humidity equals capacity) has a relative humidity of 100 per cent. (See Fig. 36-3.)

Fig. 36-2. The relation of capacity to temperature. Each cube in this diagram represents a kilogram of saturated air—air that is filled to capacity with water vapor. As the temperature rises, the capacity increases.

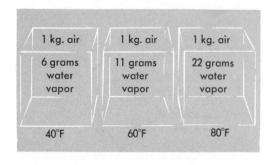

6. Finding Relative Humidity

Instruments used to measure relative humidity are called **hygrometers** (hy *grom* uh ter). In the *hair hygrometer* (*hygro,* moisture; *meter,* measure) changes in the length of a bundle of human hairs cause a pointer to move over a scale from which the relative humidity is read directly in per cent. Human hair is very sensitive to changes in the moisture content of the air, contracting in dry air and lengthening in humid air. The *hygrograph* is merely a hygrometer, a pen, and a rotating record sheet, as in the barograph and thermograph. It makes a continuous record of the relative humidity.

Another form of hygrometer is the **psychrometer** (sy *krom* uh ter) or **wet-bulb and dry-bulb thermometer**. It works on the principle that evaporation causes cooling, and dry air causes more rapid evaporation than moist air, as explained in Topic 3. The instrument, shown in Figure 36-4, consists of two identical thermometers, one of which has a water-soaked wick wrapped around its bulb. The air is forced past the two bulbs by fanning or whirling the thermometers. The dry-bulb thermometer simply shows the air temperature; the wet-bulb thermometer usually shows a lower temperature because as water evaporates from its wick, heat is taken from its bulb. *The drier the air, the faster the rate of evaporation and the lower the reading of the wet bulb.* So far the instrument shows nothing but two thermometer readings which give some indication of how dry the air is, but no actual relative humidity readings. With the observed thermometer readings, the *relative humidity* can be found from a table derived from the relationship between the wet- and dry-bulb readings. These percentages are more accurate than those of a hair hygrometer.

A section of a table used with the psychrometer appears on page 546. Assume the dry-

bulb reading is 70°F and the wet-bulb reading is 63°F—seven degrees lower. First find 70°F in the "Air Temperature" column. Then find 7 in the "Wet-bulb Depression" line. At the intersection of 70° and 7 the number 68 is the relative humidity in per cent. If both wet-bulb and dry-bulb thermometers read the same, it means that no evaporation has taken place because the air is saturated. The relative humidity at saturation is 100 per cent, since the air is filled to capacity with water vapor.

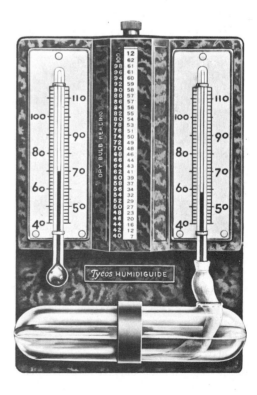

Fig. 36-4. *The wet-bulb and dry-bulb thermometer shown here includes a revolving relative humidity table that can be turned to the desired column by the knob above it. The instrument now indicates a relative humidity of 48 per cent. Do you see how?*

Taylor Instrument Co.

TABLE: FINDING RELATIVE HUMIDITY IN PER CENT

Difference in degrees between wet-bulb and dry-bulb thermometers.

Air Temperature (reading of dry-bulb thermometer) in degrees Fahrenheit

	1	2	3	4	5	6	7	8	9	10	11	12	13	14	15	16	17	18	19	20	21	22	23	24	25	26	27	28	29	30
30°	89	78	68	57	47	37	27	17	8																					
32°	90	79	69	60	50	41	31	22	13	4																				
34°	90	81	72	62	53	44	35	27	18	9	1																			
36°	91	82	73	65	56	48	39	31	23	14	6																			
38°	91	83	75	67	59	51	43	35	27	19	12	4																		
40°	92	84	76	68	61	53	46	38	31	23	16	9	2																	
42°	92	85	77	70	62	55	48	41	34	28	21	14	7																	
44°	93	85	78	71	64	57	51	44	37	31	24	18	12	5																
46°	93	86	79	72	65	59	53	46	40	34	28	22	16	10	4															
48°	93	87	80	73	67	60	54	48	42	36	31	25	19	14	8	3														
50°	93	87	81	74	68	62	56	50	44	39	33	28	22	17	12	7	2													
52°	94	88	81	75	69	63	58	52	46	41	36	30	25	20	15	10	6													
54°	94	88	82	76	70	65	59	54	48	43	38	33	28	23	18	14	9	5												
56°	94	88	82	77	71	66	61	55	50	45	40	35	31	26	21	17	12	8	4											
58°	94	89	83	77	72	67	62	57	52	47	42	38	33	28	24	20	15	11	7	3										
60°	94	89	84	78	73	68	63	58	53	49	44	40	35	31	27	22	18	14	10	6	2									
62°	94	89	84	79	74	69	64	60	55	50	46	41	37	33	29	25	21	17	13	9	6	2								
64°	95	90	85	79	75	70	66	61	56	52	48	43	39	35	31	27	23	20	16	12	9	5	2							
66°	95	90	85	80	76	71	66	62	58	53	49	45	41	37	33	29	26	22	18	15	11	8	5	1						
68°	95	90	85	81	76	72	67	63	59	55	51	47	43	39	35	31	28	24	21	17	14	11	8	4	1					
70°	95	90	86	81	77	72	68	64	60	56	52	48	44	40	37	33	30	26	23	20	17	13	10	7	4	1				
72°	95	91	86	82	78	73	69	65	61	57	53	49	46	42	39	35	32	28	25	22	19	16	13	10	7	4	1			
74°	95	91	86	82	78	74	70	66	62	58	54	51	47	44	40	37	34	30	27	24	21	18	15	12	9	7	4	1		
76°	96	91	87	83	78	74	70	67	63	59	55	52	48	45	42	38	35	32	29	26	23	20	17	14	12	9	6	4	1	
78°	96	91	87	83	79	75	71	67	64	60	57	53	50	46	43	40	37	34	31	28	25	22	19	16	14	11	9	6	4	1
80°	96	91	87	83	79	76	72	68	64	61	57	54	51	47	44	41	38	35	32	29	27	24	21	18	16	13	11	8	6	4
82°	96	91	87	83	79	76	72	69	65	62	58	55	52	49	46	43	40	37	34	31	28	25	23	20	18	15	13	10	8	6
84°	96	92	88	84	80	77	73	70	66	63	59	56	53	50	47	44	41	38	35	32	30	27	25	22	20	17	15	12	10	8
86°	95	92	88	84	80	77	73	70	66	63	60	57	54	51	48	45	42	39	37	34	31	29	26	24	21	19	17	14	12	10
88°	96	92	88	85	81	78	74	71	67	64	61	58	55	52	49	46	43	41	38	35	33	30	28	25	23	21	18	16	14	12
90°	96	92	88	85	81	78	74	71	68	64	61	58	56	53	50	47	44	42	39	37	34	32	29	27	24	22	20	18	16	14

7. Condensation and Dew Point

The change from invisible water vapor to visible water or ice is called **condensation.** It is the opposite of evaporation. When water evaporates, it removes heat from its surroundings, as explained in Topic 3. When water vapor condenses, it returns an equivalent amount of heat to its surroundings. This heat is known as the **latent heat of condensation.** (See Fig. 36-1.)

Theoretically, condensation of water vapor in the atmosphere may take place because of continuing evaporation, as in the fish tank re-ferred to in Topic 4. But the atmosphere rarely has a "cover" over it, so condensation rarely occurs in this way. How condensation usually comes about is best explained by an illustration. Suppose that on a sunny spring afternoon the air temperature is 60°F and the specific humidity is 8 grams. The capacity for a kilogram of air at 60°F is 11 grams of water vapor, so the air is not saturated. But at night, under clear skies, the air cools rapidly. When it reaches 50°F, it will be saturated, for at 50°F it can hold just what it already has—8 grams. If the temperature

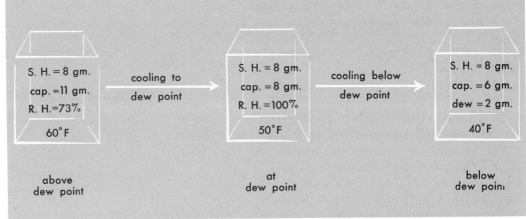

Fig. 36-5. How condensation takes place. When the kilogram of unsaturated air at the left is cooled to 50°F, it becomes saturated. Its dew point is therefore 50°F. When further cooling takes place, excess water vapor is condensed (S.H. means specific humidity; cap. means capacity; R.H. is relative humidity.) See Topic 7.

goes below 50°F, the air will have to release all the water vapor in excess of its capacity. For example, if at 40°F its capacity is 6 grams, each kilogram of this air would have to release 2 grams of water vapor at 40°F. This released water vapor condenses into visible water, perhaps as dew on the grass, mist over the ground, or droplets in a cloud. (See Fig. 36-5.)

The temperature at which saturation occurs is the dew point. In the illustration given above, the dew point is 50°F, but it may be any temperature, and it depends on one factor alone—the specific humidity. The more water vapor present in the air, the higher the dew point; the less water vapor, the lower the dew point. For example, a specific humidity of 8 grams means a 50°F dew point; 22 grams, an 80°F dew point. **Condensation of water vapor takes place when air is cooled below its dew point.**

The **dew point** may also be defined as the temperature to which the air must be cooled before condensation can begin. A simple method for finding the dew point by cooling is described in Student Activity 2 and shown in Figure 36-6.

On weather maps the dew point is shown beneath the temperature.

8. Condensation Requires Cooling and Nuclei

In order for water vapor to condense, the air must be cooled below its dew point. But this cooling may take place in a number of different ways in the atmosphere. In each case, the form in which the water vapor condenses—dew, frost,

Fig. 36-6. Finding the dew point. When the surrounding air is cooled to its dew point, its condensed water vapor appears as mist on the outside of the glass. The temperature of the water at that moment is the dew point.

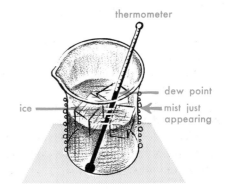

cloud droplets, or snow crystals—may depend on the way in which the cooling of the air takes place. A part of the atmosphere may lose heat by (1) radiation, (2) contact with a colder surface, (3) mixing with colder air, (4) its own expansion when it rises. The last process is the most important one in bringing about rain and snow. It will be explained fully in Topic 15.

Even when air is cooled below its dew point, condensation does not occur unless tiny particles called *condensation nuclei* are present to provide places for the water vapor to condense on. Examination of droplets of cloud and fog shows that most of them contain tiny amounts of either common salt or sulfur trioxide—about one ten-thousandth (0.0001) of the droplet by weight. Apparently, microscopic particles of these highly *hygroscopic* substances are the principal condensation nuclei in the atmosphere. (*Hygroscopic* means having an attraction for water.) The bits of salt enter the atmosphere from the ocean when fine sea spray evaporates in the air. The sulfur trioxide is a product of the burning of fuels. Condensation nuclei are so tiny that even a handful of smoke may contain millions of them.

Ionized particles of air are also believed to act as condensation nuclei, as they do in the scientist's "cloud chamber." Some scientists think that meteorite dust raining down from the upper atmosphere may be an important source of condensation nuclei.

9. Dew and Frost

When the air is cooled below its dew point by contact with a colder surface, water vapor condenses directly on that surface. If the temperature at which condensation is taking place is above 32°F or 0°C, drops of water called **dew** will form on the colder surface. (See Fig. 36-7.) Dew may form on the ground, on blades of grass, on leaves of shrubs, on auto tops, on garage roofs, or in fact on anything that has a temperature which is lower than the dew point

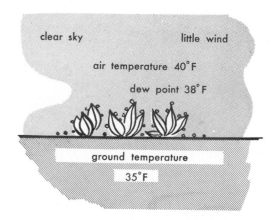

Fig. 36-7. Dew forms on a cold surface when its temperature falls below the dew point of the air in contact with it, but not below 32°F.

of the air that touches it. The objects just mentioned become cooler than the air at night because they consist of materials that radiate heat more rapidly than air does. When dew forms on a surface, it means that the air has reached its dew point only where it is touching that surface. The clearer the night, the greater the cooling by radiation and the heavier the dew.

If the temperature at condensation is below 32°F or 0°C, feathery white crystals of **frost** will form, since the water vapor sublimes directly into the solid form. When temperatures near the ground drop below 28°F, plant cell liquids may freeze, bursting the cell walls and killing the plants. Such occurrences, called *killing frosts,* have nothing to do with atmospheric moisture. (See Fig. 36-8.)

10. Fogs

It often happens that the cooling of the air extends through a considerable thickness of the bottom air, so that anywhere from a few feet to a few hundred feet are cooled below the dew point, and water vapor condenses throughout the entire layer. When this happens, tiny droplets of water or crystals of ice, depending on the

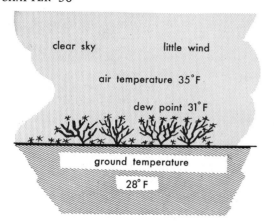

clear sky   little wind

air temperature 35°F

dew point 31°F

ground temperature

28° F

Fig. 36-8. Frost forms on a cold surface when the temperature at condensation is below 32°F.

temperature of condensation, fill the air and form a **fog.** The average size of the droplets is about 0.001 inch in diameter, and each one is centered about a condensation nucleus. The droplets are heavier than air, but they are so small and they fall so slowly that the lightest air movement is sufficient to keep them suspended.

Radiation fogs, or **ground fogs,** form under conditions very similar to those which favor the formation of dew or frost. Again the nighttime sky is clear and the ground loses heat rapidly by radiation. But instead of a dead calm, there are often light winds which mix the cold bottom air with the air a short distance above the surface. As a result, a thicker layer of air is cooled below dew point, and fog forms in this layer. Radiation fogs are especially common in humid valleys near rivers or lakes and are most frequent in the fall of the year. These fogs form in the cool of night, are thickest in the early morning, and are "burnt away" by the morning rays of the sun. Since the bottom air in this fog is colder than the air above it, a radiation fog is always associated with a temperature inversion.

Advection fogs are fogs that result from the horizontal movement of warm, moist air over a cool surface. In northern United States or southern Canada advection fogs may form in winter when warm, moist southerly winds blow over snow-covered ground or over ice-covered lakes or seacoasts. They may also form, as in the famous fogs of Newfoundland, when warm, moist Gulf Stream air blows over the cold Labrador Current or over great icebergs. Summer fogs in coastal California result when warm ocean air strikes upwelling cold coastal waters. Winter fogs along the Gulf coast occur when cold Mississippi River waters, flowing from the north, chill the warm Gulf air at the mouth of the river.

Upslope fogs often form on the eastern side of the Rocky Mountains as warm, moist winds from a high-pressure area blow westward over the mountains and are cooled as they rise. **Steam fogs** are important only in polar regions, where they are known as "arctic sea smoke." They occur when a water surface evaporates into much colder air blowing over it.

11. The Origin of Clouds

A cloud brought down to the ground would look exactly like a fog. Conversely, a fog raised above the surface would appear to be a cloud. Clouds, like fogs, consist of billions of tiny water droplets or ice crystals suspended in the air. Fogs touch the ground; clouds do not.

Clouds are produced when air *above the surface* is cooled below its dew point. The cooling may come about through any one of the processes listed in Topic 8 or through combinations of these processes. But since clouds form above the earth's surface, *rising air* is usually involved in their formation. The shapes of clouds are determined by their manner of formation. If the movement of the cooling air is largely horizontal, the clouds will form in layers and are said to be **stratiform.** If the air movement is largely vertical, the clouds will grow upward in great billowy mounds called **cumuliform.** (See Fig. 36-9.)

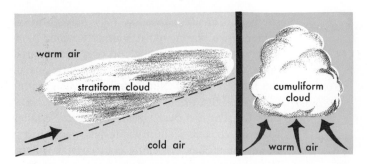

Fig. 36-9. Air movements that are largely horizontal make stratiform clouds. Vertical movements make cumuliform clouds.

At temperatures above freezing, clouds are composed entirely of water droplets. At temperatures below freezing, down to about 0°F, clouds are mixtures of *solid* snow or ice crystals and *liquid* droplets of *supercooled water*. (Supercooled water is water that has cooled below 32°F without freezing. Supercooled water is found in air as cold as −40°F. When supercooled droplets are disturbed, as by the passage of an airplane, they freeze instantly.) Below 0°F, clouds consist almost entirely of snow and ice crystals.

12. Classification of Clouds

Figure 36-10 and the cloud classification chart show the four families of clouds. The "average height range" given in the chart is for middle latitudes. The heights are measured above

the surface where they occur, not above sea level. Cloud heights are greater in equatorial regions and less in polar regions.

13. Cloud Names and Their Meaning

The ten cloud names listed in the classification show three simple names—cirrus, stratus, and cumulus—and seven compound names. The three simple names represent the three basic cloud types. All the others are combinations or variations. **Cirrus** (meaning "curl") clouds are thin, feathery, or tufted, and so high that they are always composed of tiny ice crystals. All of the "high" family of clouds are of the cirrus type. **Stratus** (meaning "spread") clouds are low uniform sheets or layers of cloud. **Cumulus**

CLASSIFICATION OF CLOUDS

Family	Average Height Range	Types	Symbols
High clouds	20,000 to 40,000 feet	Cirrus	Ci
		Cirrostratus	Cs
		Cirrocumulus	Cc
Middle clouds	6,500 to 20,000 feet	Altostratus	As
		Altocumulus	Ac
Low clouds	1,600 to 6,500 feet	Stratocumulus	Sc
		Stratus	St
		Nimbostratus	Ns
Vertical development	1,600 to 40,000 feet	Cumulus	Cu
		Cumulonimbus	Cb

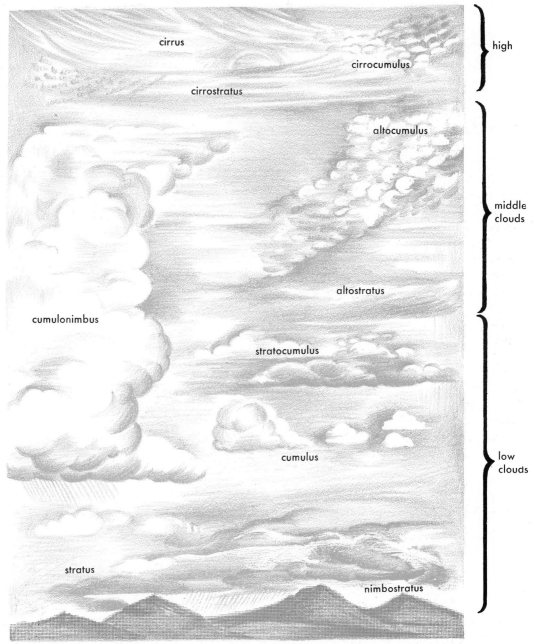

Fig. 36-10. Cloud families and cloud types. Cumulus and cumulonimbus belong to the family of "clouds of vertical development."

U.S. Weather Bureau

Fig. 36-11. Cirrus clouds.

U.S. Weather Bureau

Fig. 36-13. Altocumulus clouds.

Fig. 36-12. Cirrostratus showing halo.

U.S. Weather Bureau

(meaning "heap") clouds are formed by vertically rising air currents and are piled high in thick, fleecy masses.

When two of these words are combined, it implies that the cloud so named has some characteristics of each main type. For example, **cirrostratus** clouds are high, thin, feathery sheets or "veils" of ice-crystal clouds. They sometimes produce halos, or "rings," around the moon and sun, and may indicate the approach of rain or snow. **Stratocumulus** clouds are layers composed of globular masses or rolls, often covering the whole sky, especially in winter. **Cirrocumulus** clouds are patches of small globular ice-crystal clouds heaped up from cirrus or cirrostratus clouds.

The prefix *alto,* meaning "high," and the word *nimbus,* meaning "rain cloud," are also used in forming compound cloud names. **Altocumulus** clouds look like higher, thinner stratocumulus clouds in smaller masses. **Altostratus** clouds look like thick cirrostratus at lower altitudes, gray or bluish in color, through which the sun or moon shows vaguely as through ground glass or not at all. **Nimbostratus** clouds are dark gray low layers, uniformly dense and threatening, from which steady rain or snow may develop. The prefix *fracto,* which means "broken," is often used to describe clouds that have been torn apart by strong winds. An example is **fractostratus,** often seen below rain clouds.

U.S. Weather Bureau

Fig. 36-14. Altostratus clouds.

U.S. Weather Bureau

Fig. 36-16. Cumulus clouds.

14. Cumulus and Cumulonimbus

When convection takes place to a height sufficient to reach the dew point of the vertically rising air, cumulus clouds are formed. These clouds often appear in the late morning or early afternoon of bright sunny days, the products of

Fig. 36-17. Cumulonimbus or thunderhead.

U.S. Weather Bureau

Fig. 36-15. Stratocumulus clouds.

U.S. Weather Bureau

unequal heating of the surface, and are regarded as fair-weather clouds. Flat-based with dome-shaped tops, they always indicate rising air currents. The flat base represents the level at which the rising air has cooled to its dew point, for it is there that the water vapor begins its condensation. (See Fig. 36-18.) The billowy tops indicate the height which the rising air currents reach before condensation dies out. The stronger the convection, the thicker the cloud. On hot summer days when humidity is high, or in other circumstances favoring strong convection, cumulus clouds may grow very rapidly to mountainous heights, forming cumulonimbus, or thunderhead, clouds. **Cumulonimbus** clouds are characterized by heavy showers of rain, snow, or hail, often accompanied by thunder and lightning.

15. Rising Air Cools Itself; Descending Air Becomes Warmer

As stated in Topic 8, the cooling that takes place in rising air is the most important cause of condensation. When air *rises* in the troposphere, it comes into levels where the air pressure is less; it therefore *expands*. When a gas expands by itself, as happens here, it uses some of its own heat energy to push aside the surrounding air, and its temperature drops. **For every 1,000 feet that dry air rises in the troposphere its expansion causes cooling of 5.5°F.** This is known as the **dry-adiabatic** (add ee a *bat* ik) **lapse rate.** It is considerably more than the normal lapse rate of 3.5°F per 1,000 feet. (Chapter 33, Topic 11.)

The word *adiabatic* is used to describe a temperature change within the substance itself, caused by its own expansion or compression. No heat is taken from it or added to it by anything on the outside. Adiabatic cooling can be felt in the expanding air escaping from an automobile tire or a football bladder.

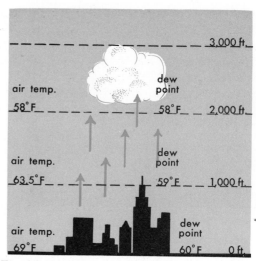

Fig. 36-18. The condensation level of rising air can be determined if the dew point is known. Rising air cools at the rate of 5.5°F per 1,000 feet, but dew point also falls 1°F in the same distance.

As air *descends* in the troposphere, it comes into levels of greater air pressure and is *compressed*. Energy is thus added to it, showing itself as a rise in temperature. As with rising dry air, the change is at the rate of 5.5°F per 1,000 feet. This warming by compression can be felt in the air that has just been pumped into a basketball bladder or a bicycle tire. In nature, air warmed by compression often causes excessive evaporation and dryness.

16. Condensation Level

When the temperature and the dew point of the air at the ground are known, the height at which cumulus clouds will begin to form in rising air can be calculated. (See Fig. 36-18.) The rate of cooling by expansion is 5.5°F per 1,000 foot rise. As air rises, however, its dew point is also dropping at the rate of 1°F per 1,000 feet, because the expanding air contains less water vapor per unit volume than it had at the surface. The net result is that the dew point is approached at the rate of 4.5°F for each 1,000 foot rise. As an illustration: at the surface air temperature is 69°F, dew point is 60°F; the difference between them is 9°F. Nine is divided by 4.5, giving 2 as the number of thousands of feet rise necessary for the beginning of condensation. This level is known as the **lifting condensation level;** it is of considerable importance in weather forecasting.

$$\text{L.C.L.} = \frac{T_A - T_D}{4.5} \times 1,000 \text{ feet}$$

(L.C.L. is the lifting condensation level; T_A is the surface temperature; T_D is the surface dew point.)

17. Moist-Adiabatic Lapse Rate

In Figure 36-18 the air temperature at the base of the cloud is calculated by using the dry-adiabatic lapse rate of 5.5°F per 1,000 feet. Above the cloud base, however, air does not cool at the same rate because as water vapor condenses, heat is released. The amount of heat released depends on the amount of water vapor condensed. An average situation is one in which the heating effect of condensation in a 1,000 foot rise is about 2.5°F. This reduces the net cooling by expansion in the same distance from 5.5°F to about 3°F. To illustrate, at 3,000 feet the air in Fig. 36-18 would be approximately 3° (not 5.5°) cooler than at 2,000 feet. Thus its temperature would drop to 55°F rather than to 52.5°F. This cooling rate in rising *saturated* air

is called the **moist-adiabatic lapse rate.** Unlike the dry-adiabatic lapse rate, it is not a fixed quantity.

18. Clouds on the Weather Map

The station models on United States Weather Bureau maps give very detailed information about the clouds in the sky. The total amount of sky covered by clouds is estimated by the weather observer, reported in tenths, and shown by shading in the station circle. The Weather Bureau uses as many as ten symbols to show **sky coverage,** as it is called. Newspaper weather maps go into less detail, showing only three different symbols. (See Fig. 36-19.) The following terms are also used: sky cover 0.1 to 0.5 = scattered clouds, 0.6 to 0.9 = broken clouds, more than 0.9 = overcast.

By means of codes and symbols explained on the back of the weather map, the station model also shows the *type of cloud*—low, middle, and high—that is present at each level; the *height of the cloud base;* and the *amount of sky covered by the low clouds.* Arrows are used to show the directions in which the clouds are moving.

19. Smog

In recent years large cities such as Los Angeles, New York, and London, as well as small industrial cities and communities, have

Fig. 36-19. Symbols used to show how cloudy the sky is.

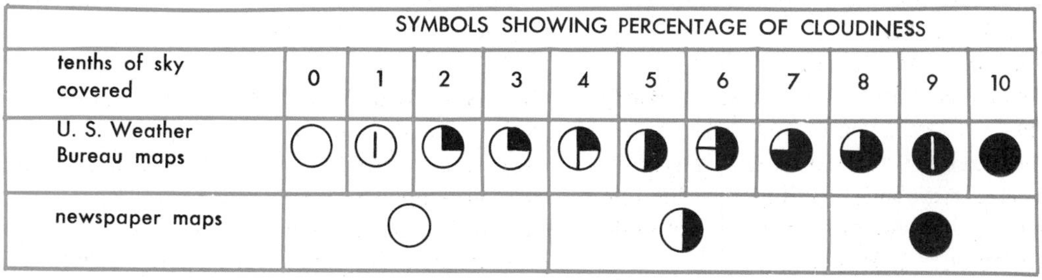

SYMBOLS SHOWING PERCENTAGE OF CLOUDINESS											
tenths of sky covered	0	1	2	3	4	5	6	7	8	9	10
U. S. Weather Bureau maps	○	◉	◔	◔	◑	◐	◑	◕	◕	◉	●
newspaper maps		○				◑				●	

been plagued by a combination of smoke and fog to which the name **smog** has been given. Smog is most likely to form during times when little or no convection is taking place in the atmosphere over these areas. Without rising air currents to carry them away, the smoke and chemical fumes from home and factory chimneys and from automobile exhausts combine with fog particles in the air to form a dense cloud that is often harmful to health. Many deaths have been attributed to the poisonous industrial gases, normally escaping from chimneys into the upper atmosphere, that smog has kept close to the earth's surface. In England such deadly smogs are known as "killer fogs."

Smogs, like fogs, are often connected with or caused by the presence in the atmosphere of a temperature inversion. The warm air layer at the top of the inversion acts like a lid on the lower atmosphere, sealing in the cool air at the surface. The cool air is unable to escape by convection until it becomes warmer and less dense than the "lid" layer. In the Los Angeles area in particular smogs may persist for many days, and sharp changes in wind direction are needed to disperse them. The mountains surrounding Los Angeles are also a factor in keeping its smogs from escaping.

Wide World Photo

Fig. 36-19. At this steelmaking plant, stacks spew thick smoke (top) during normal operations, but cut back (bottom) during an air pollution crisis.

TOPIC QUESTIONS

Each topic question refers to the topic of the same number within this chapter.

1. (*a*) In what forms does water exist in the atmosphere? Give examples. (*b*) Explain the terms melting, freezing, evaporation, condensation, and sublimation.

2. (*a*) What are the sources of water vapor in the atmosphere? (*b*) How is water vapor spread throughout the troposphere? Why is there very little in the stratosphere?

3. (*a*) Why does water evaporate more rapidly as temperature rises? (*b*) Explain what the latent heat of vaporization is. (*c*) Why is evaporation a cooling process?

4. (*a*) How are capacity and temperature related? (*b*) What is specific humidity? (*c*) When is air saturated?

5. Define relative humidity and explain how it can be calculated.

6. (*a*) What is a hygrometer? How does the hair hygrometer work? (*b*) What is the psychrometer? What is the principle of its operation? (*c*) How is the psychrometer used in finding relative humidity?

7. (a) Define condensation. What is the latent heat of condensation? (b) Explain how condensation usually occurs in the atmosphere. (c) Define dew point. (d) When does condensation occur? (e) Figure 36-6 shows how to find the dew point. Explain it.

8. (a) Name four ways by which the atmosphere may lose heat. (b) What are condensation nuclei? What are they made of? How do they originate?

9. Explain the formation of dew and frost.

10. (a) Explain the formation and composition of fog. (b) How do radiation fogs form? (c) How do advection fogs form? (d) What are upslope fogs? steam fogs?

11. (a) How are clouds formed? (b) When are clouds stratiform? cumuliform? (c) When do clouds consist only of water? only of snow and ice? a mixture of both? (d) What is supercooled water?

12. Briefly classify clouds into four families.

13. Explain the meanings of cloud names.

14. (a) How is a cumulus cloud formed? (b) What is a cumulonimbus cloud?

15. (a) Why does rising air become cooler? At what rate? What is this rate called? (b) Why does descending air become warmer?

16. (a) What is meant by the "lifting condensation level"? (b) Give the formula for finding it.

17. What is the moist-adiabatic lapse rate? Why is it less than the dry-adiabatic lapse rate?

18. What information about clouds is shown on the weather map?

19. (a) What is smog? (b) When is smog most likely to form? (c) Why is it dangerous? Where does it come from? (d) What is being done to eliminate smog gases from industry? from automobiles?

GENERAL QUESTIONS

1. Which contains more water vapor, air at 80°F with a relative humidity of 50 per cent or saturated air at 40°F? Why? (See Topics 4 and 5.)

2. Why should a psychrometer be fanned or whirled to get an accurate reading?

3. How can a single thermometer be used to obtain the relative humidity?

4. How many degrees must the air be cooled in order that dew may form if its temperature is 80°F and its relative humidity is 50 per cent?

5. The dry bulb reads 50°F, the wet bulb 40°F. What is the relative humidity? (See Topic 6.)

6. How may spraying an orchard with water help to prevent frost formation?

7. In distance and altitude contests glider pilots always try to go beneath cumulus clouds. Why?

8. At what height will condensation occur in rising air that starts out with a temperature of 60°F and a dew point of 42°F? What will the temperature be at the base of the cloud formed?

STUDENT ACTIVITIES

1. Make a simple chemical hygrometer by soaking a piece of filter paper in a strong solution of cobalt chloride and letting it dry. The paper will be blue in dry air but will turn pink in humid air.

2. Find the dew point of the air in your room by the method shown in Figure 36-6: (*a*) Half fill a shiny metal container (or a clean glass tumbler) with water at room temperature. (*b*) Place a thermometer in the water. (*c*) Add cracked ice or ice cubes, a little at a time, while stirring. Watch the outside surface of the container closely for the first appearance of mist. Read the temperature immediately. (*d*) Wait until the mist just disappears. Note the temperature again. (*e*) Average the temperatures noted in *c* and *d*. This is the dew point.

3. Find the relative humidity with a psychrometer, as explained in Topic 6. Do this for both indoors and outdoors and compare your results.

4. Make a simple cloud chamber with which you can demonstrate the effects of condensation nuclei.

CHAPTER 37

Precipitation

HOW DO YOU KNOW THAT . . . ?

1. Raindrops grow from cloud droplets by *coalescence* (Topic 1). To demonstrate coalescence, try this experiment. Take a piece of wax paper about 20 cm square. Using a medicine dropper, glass rod, or even your fingertip, place about 10 drops of water at different points on the paper. Now wiggle the paper until all the drops merge into one drop. What forces would cause this coalescence of cloud droplets?

2. Make a rain gauge (Topic 4). Match a funnel with a clear container of the same diameter. Fill it with water to a height of 1 cm. Set the funnel in a 15 cm (6″) test tube. Pour the "1-cm rain" from the container into the tube. Measure the height of the water in the tube. By what number must you divide to get the "true rainfall" reading? What is the advantage of this funnel-and-tube arrangement over a direct reading of rainfall?

1. From Condensation to Precipitation

Precipitation is the throwing down of moisture from the clouds to the surface of the earth. Tiny suspended cloud droplets grow into larger raindrops heavy enough to fall to earth. (See Fig. 37-1.) Meteorologists believe this process may occur in two different ways.

In an ordinary cloud composed of tiny cloud droplets of uniform size, all the droplets fall through the cloud or are carried up by rising air currents at about the same speed. This means that there are relatively few collisions among the droplets, and there is little chance for them to grow larger by joining or *coalescence*. But if occasional extra-large droplets were present among the billions of smaller ones, they would fall much more rapidly, would collide with and capture many small droplets, and would soon grow to raindrop size. If enough such large droplets were scattered throughout a thick cloud, rain would result. Do such large droplets exist?

The first source is found in warm water clouds, especially cumulus clouds, in which occasional extra-large water droplets form around unusually large *giant salt nuclei*. These large droplets grow rapidly by coalescence as shown

Fig. 37-1. Relative sizes of cloud and rain droplets. The average cloud droplet has a diameter of about one-thousandth of an inch, a raindrop (in a drizzle) about one-fiftieth of an inch, a raindrop (in heavy showers) about one-tenth of an inch.

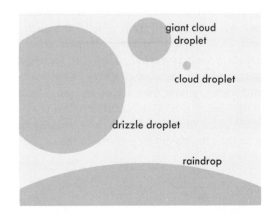
giant cloud droplet

cloud droplet

drizzle droplet

raindrop

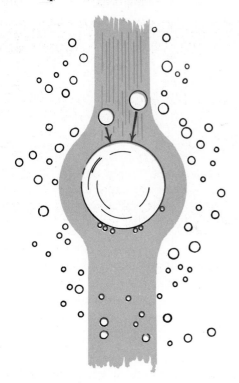

Fig. 37-2. A falling raindrop captures smaller droplets by collision and by suction.

in Figure 37-2, not only by collision, but also by sucking other droplets into the partial vacuum that results from their rapid fall through the cloud.

The second source of large droplets is quite different. In the very cold upper levels of thick tall clouds, the cloud may consist entirely of small supercooled *water* droplets. But if condensation nuclei such as clay particles are present, *ice crystals* will form around the nuclei and will grow rapidly to large droplet size. Their rapid growth is explained by the fact that the surrounding supercooled water droplets evaporate more rapidly than ice at the same temperature. (See Fig. 37-3.) As the droplets evaporate, their water vapor condenses onto the ice crystals, and the crystals get larger. When the crystals fall

through the clouds, they also grow by coalescence, just as water droplets do. As they fall to lower and warmer levels, they may melt and reach the ground as rain. In winter or on high mountains, they are likely to reach the surface as snow.

2. Rainmaking

In recent years atmospheric scientists have given increasing thought to the possibility of modifying the weather, especially in producing or increasing rainfall. Many experiments have been conducted, and many observations have been made, but there is still no conclusive proof that rainfall has been appreciably increased by the techniques now known to us.

What are these techniques? They simply represent applications of the knowledge we have acquired about the causes of precipitation. We know that the presence of ice crystals will cause precipitation in supercooled clouds, so we look for a way of *seeding* the cloud with such crystals artificially. One way is to drop pellets of Dry Ice (solid carbon dioxide) into the cloud from an airplane. The Dry Ice has a temperature of $-79°C$ ($-110°F$), and its effect is to create numerous ice crystals that quickly remove the

Fig. 37-3. Ice crystals in clouds grow larger as nearby supercooled water droplets evaporate.

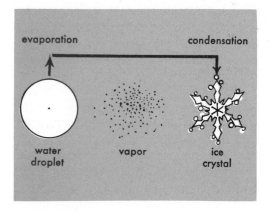

supercooled droplets from their part of the cloud, leaving a clear "hole" where the Dry Ice was sprayed. But this process seems more effective in clearing fog than in producing rain. A second way of seeding a supercooled cloud is with chemicals whose crystals are similar in structure to ice crystals. The substance most frequently used is *silver iodide*. Billions of microscopic crystals of silver iodide are sent into selected clouds from special smoke generators either on the ground or in airplanes. Ice crystals usually form on the silver iodide crystals, and these, in turn, may cause some precipitation.

In clouds that are not supercooled, scientists have attempted to produce rain by adding the giant salt nuclei that are known to form large water droplets. Even more directly, they have sprayed large water droplets into the clouds. Both salt particles and water droplets are added from airplanes. These methods have produced some rain, but so far not enough to indicate that we can effectively modify the weather. Nature is still withholding some of its rainmaking secrets from us.

3. Forms of Precipitation

Precipitation occurs in a variety of forms. **Drizzle** consists of extremely fine drops very close together falling very slowly. **Raindrops** are larger and farther apart than drizzle, ranging in diameter up to 0.1 inch. Larger raindrops may form in clouds, but they are torn apart as they fall. **Snow** consists of branched hexagonal (six-sided) crystals or stars except at very low temperatures, when very fine ice needles are formed. (See Fig. 37-4.) Snowflakes falling into warm air melt together to form large clots of wet, sticky snow, or they may melt completely and reach the surface as rain.

In winter temperature inversions, below-freezing layers of air may lie at or near the ground while rain clouds lie above them. Rain-

American Museum of Natural History

Fig. 37-4. Six principal forms of snowflakes. All are hexagonal except the ice needles formed at very low temperatures.

drops falling through the freezing layers become pellets of clear ice. This *frozen rain* is called **sleet.** (See Fig. 37-5.)

Frequently during the winter in the northern United States, supercooled rain freezes when it strikes below-freezing surfaces at or near ground

Fig. 37-5. Sleet is frozen rain. It can form only if a temperature inversion exists.

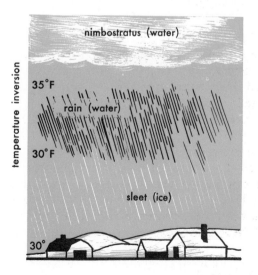

Fig. 37-6. The destructive effects of an ice storm result from the great weight of accumulated ice.

level. It then forms *sheet ice* or *glaze* on everything it touches. If this continues for some time, it is called an **ice storm.** When the weight of the accumulated ice becomes considerable, the ice storm may cause great damage to trees and power lines. (See Fig. 37-6.)

Fig. 37-7. The structure of this hailstone clearly shows the concentric layers of ice and snow from which it grew.

Hail is formed exclusively in thunderstorms. A hailstone may be as small as a buckshot or as large as a baseball. Its shape is usually more or less spherical. Large hailstones have an onion-like structure, with an icy center surrounded by alternating layers of clear ice and milky ice. (See Fig. 37-7.) Meteorologists believe that these layers develop as a result of the very strong updrafts that rise to heights of many miles in thunderstorms. It is thought that hailstones rise and fall many times in these updrafts, accumulating new layers of ice with each rise and fall in the freezing levels of the cloud, until eventually they become so heavy that they fall to the ground. The hailstone first forms when a large raindrop is carried upward until it freezes. Layers of *milky ice* are believed to be added when the falling hailstone picks up only a small number of supercooled droplets which freeze almost instantly, trapping air bubbles within the ice layer. Layers of clear ice form when the rising hailstone picks up so much supercooled water that freezing takes place slowly, and air bubbles can escape.

The more violent the thunderstorm and the more sustained the updrafts, the larger are the hailstones. The worst hailstorms in the world occur on the Great Plains of North America, where hailstones often severely damage crops and buildings. The largest single hailstone on record (17.5 inches around, 1.67 pounds) fell at Coffeyville, Kansas, on September 3, 1970.

4. Measuring Precipitation

Rainfall is measured in inches and hundredths of an inch by means of an instrument called a **rain gauge.** The measurement is supposed to represent the thickness of the water layer that the rain would leave on a perfectly level surface if no rain were lost. Any cylindrical container placed in the open may serve as a rain gauge. In the standard observatory rain gauge a brass funnel directs the rain into a narrow cylindrical tube. (See Fig. 37-8.) The mouth of the funnel has ten times the area of the mouth of the tube. The tube therefore receives ten times as much rain, standing ten times as high, as it would receive if exposed alone. This larger amount is easier to read, but of course it must be divided by ten to give the actual rainfall. A marked stick is dipped into the tube to get the

Fig. 37-8. Parts of a standard rain gauge.

U.S. Weather Bureau

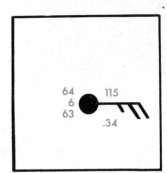

Fig. 37-9. The weather map station model shows that 0.34 inches of rain fell in the last six hours. The station model tells seven other facts about the weather at this location. Can you read them?

reading. The *tipping bucket rain gauge* and the *weighing rain gauge* can automatically record both the time and the amount of the rainfall.

Snowfall, like rainfall, is measured in inches and tenths of an inch. A simple measuring stick is used. The measurement is usually taken in as open and average a location as is possible. The water or rain equivalent of the snowfall is determined by melting a definite depth of the snow. Dry snows pile up much higher than equal weights of wet snow. On the average, ten inches of snow equal one inch of rain, but this may range from as little as five inches of snow to as much as thirty inches. Why?

5. Precipitation on the Weather Map

Shading is used on Weather Bureau maps to show large areas in which *precipitation is occurring.* Total precipitation for the last six hours is given in hundredths of an inch below and to the right of the station circle, as shown in Fig. 37-9.

The *form* of precipitation is shown to the left of the station circle by symbols listed by the Weather Bureau in a detailed table called "Present Weather." This table contains a hundred symbols, but they include various arrangements and combinations of just a few basic symbols that show drizzle, rain, snow, sleet, hail, thunder-

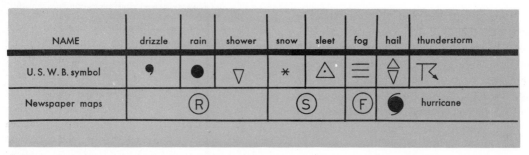

NAME	drizzle	rain	shower	snow	sleet	fog	hail	thunderstorm
U. S. W. B. symbol	❟	●	▽	✳	△	☰	⧨	⤬
Newspaper maps		Ⓡ			Ⓢ	Ⓕ	⬤	hurricane

Fig. 37-10. Precipitation symbols used on official and newspaper weather maps.

storms, showers, and fog. The arrangements merely show how hard or how steady the precipitation is. The basic symbols are shown in Fig. 37-10.

6. Where Does It Rain?

Precipitation—rain, sleet, hail, or snow—can and does occur in every part of the world. But in some locations, such as parts of the desert of Peru, it does not rain for years at a time; in other places, as in the Amazon Valley, it may rain almost every day. Parts of Death Valley, California, average about one inch of rain a year, whereas Cherrapunji in India averages 457 inches a year. What accounts for such differences?

In general, condensation that is vigorous enough to lead to precipitation takes place only in rising currents, where air in large quantities is being cooled below its dew point by expansion. Wherever air rises high enough and in large enough quantities, precipitation will occur. The warmer the air, the more moisture it may contain, although that will also depend upon where it comes from. Within limits, the higher the air rises, the more moisture it can drop. It follows, therefore, that the **rainy regions of the earth will be the regions where air often rises in large quantities.** The more often this happens, the more frequently will it rain. Such regions are the following: (1) the entire *dol-*

drums belt of warm, humid, convectionally rising air that reaches up to the stratosphere to form gigantic cumulonimbus clouds and almost daily thunderstorms; included here are the dense tropical forests of the Amazon, the Congo, and Indonesia; (2) the *windward sides of mountain ranges,* where prevailing winds are forced to climb to great heights; examples are the rainy western slopes of the Cascade Mountains in northwestern United States and the rainy eastern slopes of the mountains of Central America in the trade-wind belt (Fig. 37-11); (3) *storm areas* of all kinds, such as hurricanes, typhoons, cyclones, fronts, thunderstorms, and tornadoes, for in all of these there are great masses of moist rising air. Storm areas will be described in Chapters 38 and 39.

Places over which the doldrums pass have almost daily rains while the doldrums are over them. Places windward of mountains have heavy rains whenever the winds blow from a moist source. Other locations have rain only when they have storms of one kind or another. ("Rain" here means any form of precipitation.)

7. Where Does It Not Rain?

The answer to this question is almost the exact opposite of the answer to "Where does it rain?" **In regions of descending air the air is being warmed by compression, and no precipitation can occur.** Descending air may become so warm and dry that it causes excessive evaporation and creates desert conditions. Large masses of descending air are found (1) in the *two horse-latitude* belts, (2) on the *leeward sides of mountains,* (3) in middle-latitude *highs* (described in Chapter 39), and (4) in the great *polar highs.* Now let us examine briefly the rainfall patterns of low, middle, and high latitudes of the world.

8. Precipitation in the Tropics

Precipitation follows a fairly simple pattern in the tropics. Rising air in the moist, hot doldrums or equatorial low-pressure belt brings almost daily thundershowers and heavy annual precipitation to the entire equatorial belt around the world. Just the reverse is true in the horse-latitude high-pressure belts, where dry descending air brings desert conditions to the latitudes of 30° to 35° around the world in both hemispheres. Lands lying between the rainy doldrums and the arid horse latitudes have alternate rainy and dry seasons caused by the shifting of the wind belts with the seasons.

For most regions in the tropics rains come almost entirely with the arrival of the doldrums belt. In addition, however, heavy rains fall on the windward slopes of coastal mountains when the normally dry trade winds blow from the oceans onto the east coasts of Africa and South and Central America. The heavy monsoon rains of India and southeast Asia are similarly due to warm ocean winds rising over the great Himalayan mountain range of India and Burma.

Storms play little part in bringing precipitation to the tropics, except for the occasional hurricane or typhoon that may strike island or coastal areas.

9. Precipitation in Middle Latitudes

The middle latitudes from 35° to about 65° in both hemispheres are covered for most of the year by the prevailing westerly winds. There are no world-circling belts such as the "all wet" doldrums or the "all dry" subtropical high-pressure belts. Instead, the chief causes of raininess or dryness are mountain ranges, distance from the ocean, and storms. The rainiest regions are the windward slopes of high coastal mountains, such as the western slopes of the Olympic Mountains in northwest Washington. The driest regions are the lands lying in the leeward "rain shadow" of high mountain ranges such as the Sierra Nevadas in western United States or the Himalayas in Asia.

Fig. 37-11. Precipitation is usually heavy on the windward side of a mountain and very light on the leeward side.

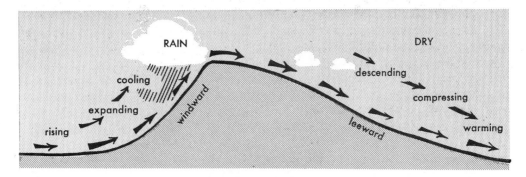

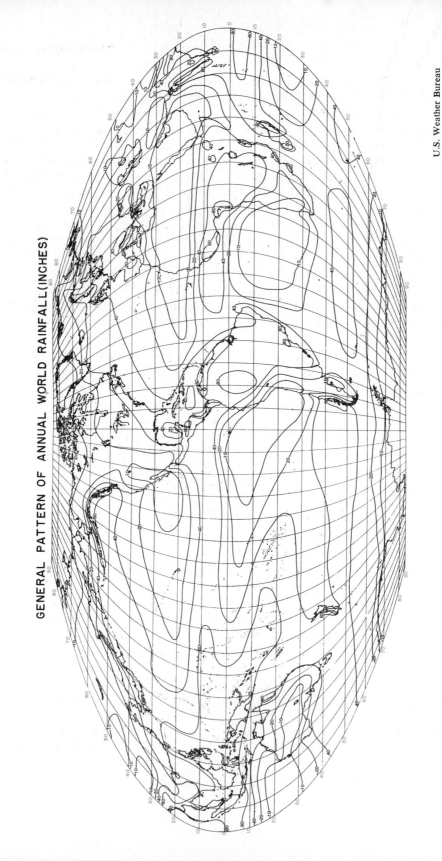

GENERAL PATTERN OF ANNUAL WORLD RAINFALL (INCHES)

U.S. Weather Bureau

Fig. 37-12. Average annual rainfall of the world.

The western interior of North America and the eastern interior of Asia are arid regions because of both distance from the ocean and the effect of high mountains in keeping out moist ocean air. They are saved from total dryness, however, by the occasional occurrence of the rain-bearing storms of middle latitudes, particularly in summer. As the east and south coasts of both North America and Asia are approached, precipitation increases until semi-arid conditions give way to abundant rainfall, as in eastern United States and southeastern China. The increase in rainfall is due to the larger number of storms and the higher moisture content of the air blowing into the storms from the oceans to the east. In summer the "monsoon effect" helps to bring moist air from the cool oceans to the heated land.

10. Precipitation in High Latitudes

The high latitudes from about 60° to the Poles in both hemispheres are covered for most of the year by either the polar easterlies or the cold, dry polar highs. The extremely cold air has little capacity for holding water vapor, and precipitation is light in all seasons, falling almost entirely from cyclonic storms. Total yearly precipitation is rarely more than 10 or 15 inches, but very little water evaporates from the soil or from the surface because of the consistently low temperatures.

TOPIC QUESTIONS

Each topic question refers to the topic of the same number within this chapter.

1. (*a*) Compare the size of cloud droplets and raindrops. (*b*) What is coalescence? Explain why droplets of uniform size are unlikely to grow larger by coalescence. (*c*) Explain how large droplets grow into raindrops. (*d*) How do large droplets form in warm water clouds? (*e*) How do large droplets form in supercooled clouds?

2. Describe the techniques used for rainmaking: (*a*) in supercooled clouds; (*b*) in warm water clouds.

3. (*a*) Describe drizzle, raindrops, and snow. (*b*) How does sleet form? sheet ice? (*c*) How do hailstones form?

4. (*a*) What is a rain gauge? Describe one. (*b*) In what units are snow and rain measured? Explain.

5. Make a labeled diagram showing the symbols used for different forms of precipitation.

6. (*a*) When does condensation usually lead to precipitation? (*b*) Name the three kinds of regions in which rising air causes rain. Explain why the air rises in two of these regions. Name some places located in them.

7. (*a*) Why are regions of descending air dry? (*b*) Name four regions of descending air and explain why the air descends in two of them.

8. (*a*) Describe the rainfall pattern of (1) the doldrums, (2) the horse latitudes, (3) regions between them. (*b*) When do the trade winds and monsoons bring rainfall to the tropics?

9. (*a*) What factors are important in determining raininess or dryness in middle latitudes? (*b*) Which are our rainiest regions? our driest regions? (*c*) How does any rain come to the dry interiors of North America and Asia?

10. Describe the rainfall pattern of high latitudes.

GENERAL QUESTIONS

1. How may Dry-Ice seeding be of value at airports?

2. Why are winter hailstorms rather rare?

3. Why should average annual precipitation be greater in Mississippi than in Maine?

4. Why should average annual precipitation be greater in Massachusetts than in Minnesota?

5. Read the eight items of weather information given in the station model of Figure 37-9.

STUDENT ACTIVITIES

Make a rain gauge similar to the standard weather bureau type described in Topic 3. To calibrate it, simply fill the larger container with water to a depth of 1 inch; then pour this water into the long narrow tube. Now dip a slender measuring stick or ruler into the tube, mark the height reached by the water, and label it "1 inch." Use this as a scale for further calibration of the "gauge."

CHAPTER 38
Air Masses and Fronts

HOW DO YOU KNOW THAT . . . ?

Air masses and fronts (Topics 1, 10) are like currents. Set up a model to visualize them. Get a rectangular aquarium tank. Place a fairly watertight, rigid partition of wood or plastic across the shorter dimension of the tank. The partition divides the tank into two halves, but is easily removable. Prepare enough cold, concentrated salt water to nearly fill one side of the tank. This dense solution will represent a mass of cold air. Add food color, red ink, or other dye to make this clearly visible. Fill one half of the aquarium with warm tap water. This represents the mass of warm air. Pour the colored salt water into the other half. Now slide out the partition smoothly and observe carefully how the two "masses" mix. Describe and explain what happens.

AIR MASSES

1. What an Air Mass Is

Careful examination of any daily weather map usually shows remarkable uniformity of *temperature* and *humidity* conditions over broad areas, two or three of which usually cover all of continental United States. This uniformity of temperature and humidity within each area exists not only in the air at the surface but also in the upper air to a height of several miles. Each of these tremendous masses of air, hundreds or even thousands of miles in diameter and several miles high, is known as an **air mass.** More specifically, an air mass is a huge section of the lower troposphere in which temperature and humidity are fairly uniform at any given level.

2. Origin of an Air Mass

Where do air masses come from? How do they originate? Why are there several different kinds over the United States at one time? Why are they different? These are questions that arise

as soon as we recognize that there are air masses. Part of the answer can be supplied by looking at the weather maps for several days back to see when and where the uniform masses of air first appear. The maps must go beyond the United States into northern Canada, into the Pacific Ocean, into the Atlantic Ocean and the Gulf of Mexico. And there it is found that great sections of the troposphere are "stagnant" or remain more or less stationary over one kind of surface, either continent or ocean, for many days or even weeks at a time. Contact with a uniformly warm or cold surface gives the air *uniform temperature*. Contact with a uniformly wet or dry surface gives the air *uniform humidity*. These characteristics make it an "air mass." (See Fig. 38-1.)

Air masses originate chiefly in the more stagnant parts of the terrestrial wind belts on both sides of the prevailing westerlies. Air masses on the poleward sides of the westerlies consist of cold polar air. Air masses on the equatorial side of the westerlies consist of warm

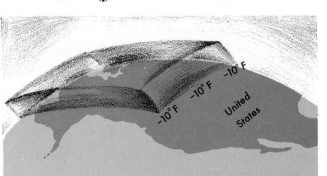

Fig. 38-1. A mass of cold dry air originating over Canada in winter brings uniformly cold weather with it as it moves south.

tropical air. These air masses give their own polar and tropical regions fairly uniform weather. The middle latitudes, however, are really "caught in the middle" when the air masses on both sides of them begin to move. Invading polar air masses bring cold weather to the middle latitudes. Tropical air masses bring warm weather. When polar and tropical masses meet, stormy weather is a likely result, as we shall see later in this chapter when we study *fronts*.

3. Kinds of Air Masses

Basically, air masses owe their characteristics to the surfaces over which they originate. Those that originate in the tropics have temperatures that are higher than the normal for northern United States and Canada. They are called **tropical,** abbreviated *T*. Those that originate in

high latitudes have relatively low temperatures. They are called **polar,** abbreviated *P*. Besides being polar or tropical, the "source region" is either a continental area or an ocean (maritime) area. Air masses from continents are called **continental,** abbreviated *c,* while air masses from oceans are called **maritime,** abbreviated *m*. Continental air is relatively dry; maritime air is humid. Together these make four main kinds of air masses, as listed below.

These symbols are used on United States Weather Bureau maps to label air masses.

The term **Arctic,** *A,* is also used to designate an air mass from extremely cold, ice-covered arctic regions. **Equatorial,** *E,* refers to moist, hot doldrums air, which never affects the United States.

4. Source Regions, Movement, Paths

The place where an air mass originates is called its **source region** or **source.** cP air masses develop over central and northern Canada; mP masses come from the North Atlantic and North Pacific oceans; mT masses come from the Gulf of Mexico, the Caribbean Sea, the middle Atlantic Ocean, and the Pacific Ocean south of California. cT air masses are not common but may originate in the southwestern desert region of the United States in summer. In general, the polar air masses move southward with the polar easterly winds; the tropical air masses move northward and eastward with the prevailing southwesterly winds. Figure 38-2 shows further details of their seasonal occurrence and paths.

Abbreviation	Name	Characteristics
cP	continental polar	dry, cold
mP	maritime polar	moist, cold
cT	continental tropical	dry, warm
mT	maritime tropical	moist, warm

5. Weather in an Air Mass

Air masses are usually very extensive and may take many days to pass a given locality. During all this time the weather of the locality is determined largely by the original characteristics of the air mass. When a mass of cold, dry cP air from central Canada invades the United States, it is as if, temporarily, part of the United States had a Canadian climate. If it is winter, the cP air is usually felt as an icy, clear, cold wave that may last for many days and may extend as far south as Florida; in summer cP air is felt as a cool spell. When mP air comes in from the northern oceans, it brings cool, humid weather. The mT air masses from the Gulf of Mexico or from the Atlantic or Pacific Ocean may bring mild, humid weather in winter; in summer they are responsible for the oppressively hot, humid spells that often continue for weeks in central and eastern United States. Maritime tropical air also brings frequent thunderstorms and occasional tornadoes. As one air mass after another passes over a locality, its weather may change from polar to tropical, from humid to dry, over and over again. Such changes explain the great variability of the weather in most of the United States.

6. Air Masses Undergo Changes

An air mass that starts out from its source region in Canada and moves southward will obviously not stay cold indefinitely; it will warm up more and more the farther south it goes and the longer it is away from its source. Air masses that move from south to north become colder; those that move from ocean to continent become drier; those that move from land to water become more humid. The first days of a winter cold wave are the most frigid; then the cold wave slowly moderates and eventually the weather returns to "normal." That is, air masses alter gradually to become more characteristic of the surfaces over which they pass.

7. A Warm Air Mass

An air mass that is warmer (in its lower layers) than the surface over which it is passing is defined as a **warm air mass.** This term must not be confused with the term "tropical." A tropical (T) air mass comes from a tropical source and consists of warm air. On the other hand, a "warm air mass" may consist of either warm or cold air; the term "warm" in this case is simply a comparison; it says that the air mass, whatever its temperature, *is warmer than the surface it rests upon.* "Warm" is abbreviated as *w,* and the w is placed after the original air-mass name. For example, an air mass originating over the Gulf of Mexico in winter is warmer

Fig. 38-2. Source regions and paths of air masses in North America.

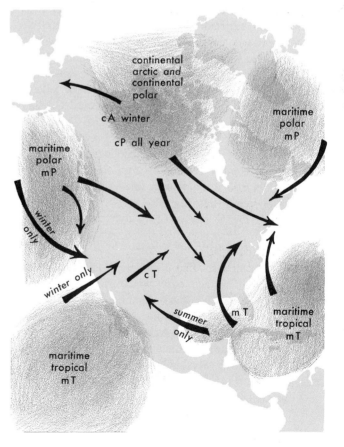

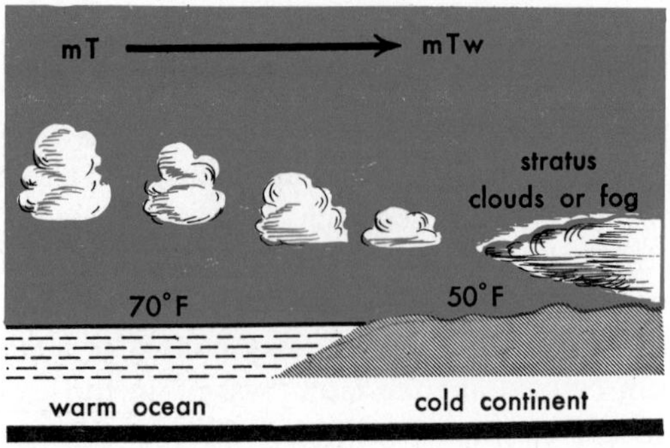

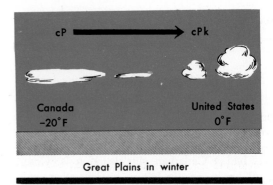

Fig. 38-3. The mT air mass becomes mTw when it moves over the land because its 70°F air is warmer than the 50°F surface onto which it moves. See Topic 7.

Fig. 38-4. The cP air mass becomes cPk when it moves south because its −20°F air is colder than the 0°F surface onto which it moves. See Topic 8.

than the land areas of southern United States which it invades. Such a mass is designated as mTw, meaning "maritime, tropical, warmer than the surface over which it is passing." Other possible "warm" masses are mPw, cPw, and cTw.

The colder land or water surface on which a warm air mass rests produces certain important weather effects, regardless of the source of the air mass, and it is in these general effects that the value of this classification lies. Cooling of an air mass at the bottom tends to form dew, fogs, stratiform clouds, drizzle, or even light rain. There is little or no tendency for convection. Visibility is poor because smoke and dust do not rise. If fogs form, the visibility may become zero. (See Fig. 38-3.)

8. A Cold Air Mass

An air mass that is colder in its lower layers than the surface over which it is passing is called a **cold air mass.** Again, the term "cold" is comparative and is not to be confused with "polar." Cold cannot be abbreviated as *c*, which already means "continental," so *k* is used, from the German word *kalt,* which means "cold." When an air mass from Canada is called cPk, it indicates that it is "continental, polar, and

colder than the surface over which it is passing."

All cold air masses, regardless of their source, are being warmed at the bottom and possess certain common characteristics. Warming causes convection. This produces cumulus clouds, windiness, and generally good visibility. If the warming is considerable and enough moisture is present, as when the warm surface beneath is a lake or ocean, the cumulus clouds may grow into cumulonimbus, and showers or thunderstorms may result. Otherwise fair weather is likely. A dry cPk air mass (winter) usually brings fair weather (see Fig. 38-4), whereas the

Fig. 38-5. Heating of the humid mTk air mass by the warm ground it rests on causes the formation of cumulonimbus clouds and showers.

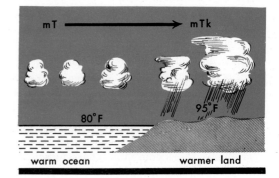

more humid mTk air mass (summer) causes showery precipitation. (See Fig. 38-5.)

9. Radiosonde Observations

Information about the upper levels of an air mass is obtained in many ways, some of which have already been described in the chapters on winds and water vapor. In addition, *radiosonde* observations are taken twice daily at the same time at weather stations all over the world.

The **radiosonde** (Fig. 38-6) is a tiny combination of thermometer, barometer, hygrometer, and radio transmitter. The transmitter automatically emits signals that indicate the temperature, pressure, and relative humidity of the air through which the radiosonde is passing. The radiosonde is carried to heights of from 15 to 20 miles by a large helium-filled balloon. An automatic radio receiver at the weather station records the signals.

Figure 38-7 shows *rawin* equipment used at weather stations to track the flight of the radiosonde automatically. This tracking gives information about the direction and velocity of the upper winds that would otherwise require the use of a pilot balloon and theodolite. Observations made by rawin are called *rawinsondes*.

FRONTS

10. What a Front Is

Air masses travel across the country in a generally eastward direction. At any given moment there may be several different air masses on the surface of the United States, one behind the other, usually moving from west to east. The *surface* that marks the rear of one mass and the front of the one following it is called a **frontal surface**. The *line* along which that surface meets the ground is called a **front**. It is common practice to use the word "front" for either the surface or the line, so a front is usually defined as

Friez Instrument Div., Bendix Aviation Corp.

Fig. 38-6. A radiosonde.

Fig. 38-7. Rawin (radio wind) equipment includes a radiosonde and radio tracking equipment.

U.S. Army Photo

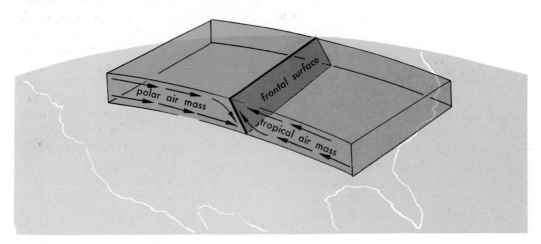

Fig. 38-8. A front is a boundary between two air masses. At the front, the warmer air is always forced to rise over the colder air.

that line representing the **boundary between two air masses.**

A frontal surface would be vertical if two air masses of different temperature could stand side by side, like heaps of sand and cement, without mixing. But cold air is denser and heavier than warm air, and air can flow. The cold air flows under the warm air, forcing the lighter warm air up and over it. (See Fig. 38-8.) This is just what would happen with water and oil, or with any two liquids of different density. Were it not for the earth's rotation, the frontal surface would become perfectly horizontal, and the warm air would simply lie on top of the cold air. Actually, the frontal surface has a very gentle slope that averages about one mile in 100 miles, but may be as steep as one mile in 40 or as gentle as one mile in 200. The cold air slides in under the warmer air like a gigantic thin wedge. Figure 38-9 shows a frontal surface of average slope. In diagrams of frontal surfaces the vertical scale is always exaggerated; otherwise the very gentle slopes of these surfaces would hardly show.

11. The Importance of Fronts

Since a front is the boundary between two air masses, **when a front passes a particular place, it invariably means a change of weather.** The greater the difference between the air masses, the greater the change in weather. For example, if mT air is replaced by cP air, it will mean the end of a warm, humid spell and the beginning of a cool or cold, dry spell. Another feature of great importance is that **fronts are almost always accompanied by precipitation.** The reason is that at a frontal surface warm air is rising in great quantities and to great heights, and rising air means precipitation. As will be seen, this precipitation sometimes

Fig. 38-9. A frontal surface of average slope.

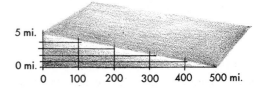

precedes and sometimes follows the actual passing of the front on the ground.

12. Locating a Front

To locate a front, all that is necessary is to find where one air mass ends and the next one begins. An airplane pilot flying through a front may not actually see it, but he can hardly escape the fact that the weather undergoes certain definite changes as he leaves one air mass and enters the next. In similar fashion, a meteorologist in his office can deduce the position of a front on a weather map by noticing where sharp changes of weather occur. The most noticeable changes, all of which are illustrated in Figure 38-10, are as follows:

(1) Temperatures are usually distinctly lower on one side of a front than on the other.

(2) Wind directions are sharply different on opposite sides of a front.

(3) Wind velocities are usually higher on one side of the front than on the other.

(4) Dew points differ greatly from one side to the other.

(5) The barometer shows a falling *pressure tendency* as the front approaches and a rising pressure tendency as the front passes. (The pressure tendency or change for the three-hour period preceding observation is shown on the weather map station model just below the pressure. See Fig. 39-16.)

Since air pressure usually changes abruptly as the front is crossed, the isobars of the weather map make sharp bends or kinks at the front. These kinks represent the easiest and surest features for locating the front on the weather map. They always point toward higher pressure or away from low pressure.

13. Kinds of Fronts; Symbols; Direction

Meteorologists classify fronts into three different kinds according to the motion of the air

masses involved. If cold air is displacing warmer air the front is called a **cold front.** If warm air is displacing colder air, the front is a **warm front.** If neither air mass is being displaced, the front is said to be **stationary.** Fronts may also be defined as follows: (1) a cold front is the leading edge of an advancing mass of cold air; (2) a warm front is the leading edge of an advancing mass of warm air; (3) a stationary front is the boundary line between two air masses that

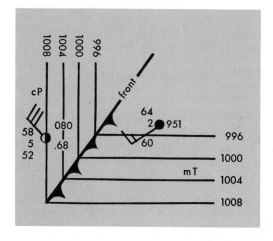

Fig. 38-10. On a weather map a front is marked by sharp bends in the isobars. Weather differs greatly on opposite sides of the front.

are not moving. Since masses of cold polar air usually invade from the northwest, cold fronts usually move to the southeast. Similarly, since masses of warm, tropical air usually come from the southwest, warm fronts generally move northeastward.

A fourth kind of front, the **occluded front,** is really a combination of cold and warm fronts. It will be fully explained in Chapter 39, but may now be defined as the front that results when a cold front overtakes a warm front. Figure 38-11 shows the weather-map symbols for fronts. In each case the solid half-circles (for warm fronts)

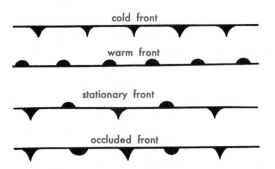

cold front

warm front

stationary front

occluded front

Fig. 38-11. Symbols for fronts.

and the solid triangles (for cold fronts) point in the direction of the front's movement.

14. Warm-Front Weather

Warm fronts, along which warm air is displacing colder air, have comparatively gentle slopes. The average slope is about one mile in 100, but in some cases it is as little as one mile in 200. This means that the warm air must travel from 500 to 1,000 miles in order to rise five miles. (See Fig. 38-12.) The gently rising air, unless it is very dry, soon reaches its dew point as it cools by expansion, and a vast system of clouds forms in the warm air above almost the entire frontal surface. The clouds are largely *stratiform,* and they may extend for 1,000 miles ahead of the front on the ground. Thin, icy cirrus clouds lead the procession at the highest level. Behind them comes a veil of cirrostratus clouds which may cause halos around the sun or moon and make it possible for an observer to forecast the coming of the warm front 24 to 36 hours in advance. As the warm air increases in quantity, the thick, middle-height altostratus clouds appear, almost screening out the sun or moon, and precipitation is near. Finally, heavy, low nimbostratus cloud masses turn the sky gray and steady precipitation sets in, extending for hundreds of miles *ahead of the front on the ground,* and at least 100 miles along the front. Thunderstorms may occur on occasion, but they are not typical of the weather of warm fronts.

Figure 38-12 shows the cloud system of a warm front in cross section. When the front passes, the mass of warm air arrives, and many weather elements change. The temperature rises, the wind shifts, the pressure falls and rises again, the rain ends, and the sky undergoes partial clearing. Until the next front comes along, air-mass weather prevails.

Fig. 38-12. Vertical section through the cloud system and air masses of a warm front.

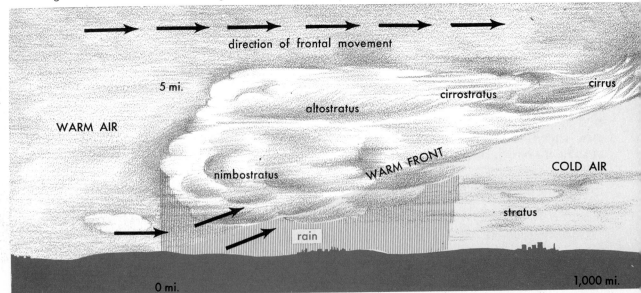

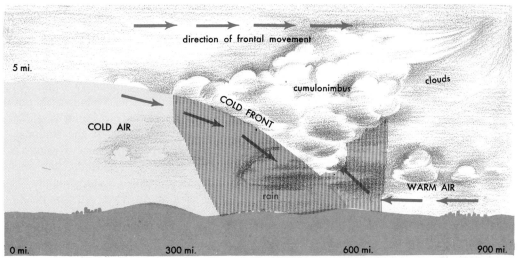

Fig. 38-13. Vertical section through the cloud system and air masses of a cold front.

15. Weather of a Cold Front

Cold fronts are steeper than warm fronts. This is because the advancing cold-air winds move faster at higher altitudes because of less friction, so the top of the frontal surface tends to catch up to the bottom and become more nearly vertical. Even so, the slope is small, averaging about one mile in 80. Cold fronts move faster than warm fronts. The direction of movement of cold fronts, like that of the polar air masses which they lead, is likely to be from northwest to southeast, or from west to east.

Again, it is the rising warm air which is cooled to its dew point and forms clouds. This time, however, the slope is often steep enough to cause convection and *cumuliform* clouds, and the cloud system *extends behind the ground front as well as ahead of it.* Since most of the rising warm air is found within a rather short distance of the steep front, the cloud system is much less extensive than in the warm front, usually covering between 200 and 300 miles. There is no long warning sequence of approaching precipitation as in the warm front. The cumulonimbus clouds arrive rather suddenly, and precipitation is showery, heavy, and of comparatively short duration. Thunderstorms are common.

When the front passes on the ground, the changes of weather which occur are usually much more striking and abrupt than those that accompany the passage of the warm front. Temperatures fall rapidly as the cold air arrives.

Fig. 38-14. This dust storm at Manteer, Kansas was produced by a cold front moving rapidly from left to right in the photograph.

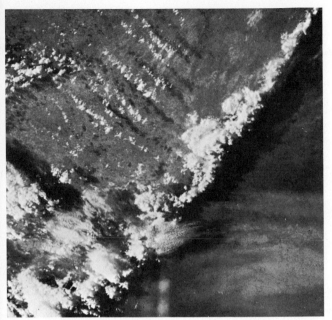

Fig. 38-15 Squall line over Great Indian Desert west of New Delhi, India, as seen from spacecraft.

The wind rises in velocity, often becoming gale-like, and usually shifts sharply from a southerly direction to a northerly one. Air pressure rises. *The rain continues for a short time after the front passes.* When the rain ends, partial clearing occurs, and once again air-mass weather prevails until the next front arrives.

Because of the sharp changes in wind direction that take place along them, cold fronts are sometimes called **wind-shift lines.** When extremely humid mT air is being pushed forward by the cold front, a pressure wave may be generated which will form a line of thunderstorms at or some distance ahead of the front. This line of storms is known as a **squall line.** It may be hundreds of miles long. (See Fig. 38-15.)

16. Stationary Fronts

Frequently a cold front or a warm front slows down until it stops moving entirely. The air masses on either side are then said to be separated by a *stationary front.* Although the air masses are not changing their positions relative to the ground, warm air is still rising above cold air. The slope of the stationary air-mass boundary tends to become as gentle as that of a warm front. Consequently, the weather of a stationary front is approximately the same as that of a warm front. After remaining stagnant for a time, all or part of a stationary front may resume motion in either direction. Where the warm air advances, it is again a warm front. Where the cold air advances, it becomes a cold front.

17. Summary

In all Temperate Zone climates, in both the Northern and the Southern Hemisphere, the most important changes of weather, other than those due to seasons, are the ones brought about by the passage of fronts. All fronts—warm, cold, stationary, or occluded—are almost certain to bring rain with them. Warm-front rains are steady and extensive and are usually associated with stratiform clouds. They precede the ground position of the front. Cold-front rains are showery, are of short duration, and are usually associated with cumuliform clouds. Cold-front rains come both before and after the passage of the front at the ground. Cold fronts move more rapidly than warm fronts and cause sharper changes of weather.

TOPIC QUESTIONS

Each topic question refers to the topic of the same number within this chapter.

1. (*a*) Define air mass and explain your definition. (*b*) Explain how air masses can be "discovered" on a weather map.

2. (*a*) How does an air mass originate? (*b*) How does an air mass acquire uniform temperature? uniform humidity?

3. Name each of the following air masses, state its characteristics, and explain why it has these characteristics: cP, mP, cT, mT.

4. (*a*) What is a source region? (*b*) In which source region does each of these air masses originate: cP, mP, mT, cT? (*c*) In what directions do air masses move? Why?

5. Give a brief description of weather in each of the following air masses in summer or winter: cP, mP, mT.

6. What changes do air masses undergo as they move away from their source regions?

7. (*a*) Define and explain what a warm air mass is. (*b*) Explain what kind of air mass each of the following is: mPw, cPw, cTw. (*c*) Explain why certain weather phenomena are true of all warm air masses. List these phenomena.

8. (*a*) Define and explain what a cold air mass is. (*b*) What do the following symbols mean: cPk, mTk, mPk? (*c*) Explain why certain weather phenomena are true of all cold air masses. List these phenomena. (*d*) How is the weather in cPk air likely to differ from that in mTk air?

9. (*a*) Describe the radiosonde. What three weather elements does it measure? (*b*) What does *rawin* equipment do?

10. (*a*) Explain what a frontal surface is. (*b*) Explain what a front is. (*c*) Describe the average slopes and relative positions of warm and cold air in any front.

11. (*a*) Explain why precipitation is almost always associated with a front. (*b*) Why does the passing of a front mean changes in weather?

12. (*a*) What differences in weather can be seen on opposite sides of a front? (*b*) How do isobars show the location of a front?

13. (*a*) Define or explain the four kinds of fronts and draw the symbol for each. (*b*) How do the symbols indicate the direction in which fronts move? (*c*) In what direction do cold fronts move? Why? (*d*) In what direction do warm fronts move? Why?

14. Using a diagram as part of your explanation, describe the slope, cloud system, precipitation, and weather changes associated with a warm front and its passage.

15. Using a diagram as part of your explanation, describe the slope, cloud system, precipitation, and weather changes associated with a cold front and its passage.

16. How does a stationary front originate? What kind of weather does it have?

17. Summarize the importance of fronts in the Temperate Zone. Briefly contrast warm fronts with cold fronts.

GENERAL QUESTIONS

1. In what directions would polar and tropical air masses move in the Southern Hemisphere? Why?

2. How will weather in an mPw air mass differ from that in a cPw air mass?

3. How will mTw weather differ from cPw weather?

4. How may mPk weather differ from mTk weather?

5. What kind of thermometer is the radiosonde likely to carry? what kind of barometer? hygrometer? Why?

6. Why should the radiosonde balloon burst at very high altitudes? What determines how high it goes before bursting?

7. Can you tell from a weather map which way an occluded front is moving? Explain.

8. What kind of air-mass weather is likely to follow the passing of a warm front? of a cold front?

9. Why should there be small cumulus clouds in the cold air in Figure 38-13?

10. Why should there be stratus clouds in the warm air behind the warm front in Figure 38-12?

11. Item by item, compare the weather data of the two stations on opposite sides of the front in Figure 38-10.

STUDENT ACTIVITIES

1. Make a three-dimensional model of a warm-frontal or a cold-frontal cloud system, using a framework of wire or other material and hospital cotton, etc. for clouds.

2. Observe the temperature, barometer reading, relative humidity, wind direction, and wind speed during a period of cool, dry weather apparently caused by a continental polar air mass. Make the same observations during a warm, humid period caused by a maritime tropical air mass. Compare the two sets of observations.

CHAPTER 39

Storms and Weather Forecasts

HOW DO YOU KNOW THAT . . . ?

Falling pressure brings cloudy skies with rain or snow, and rising pressure brings fair weather. Test these generalizations for yourself. Keep a record of the atmospheric pressure and the state of the sky each day for several weeks. Atmospheric pressure is most conveniently recorded with a barograph, which writes its own record for every hour of the day. But if a barograph is not available, you and classmates can take turns reading the barometer several times able, you and your classmates can take turns reading the barometer several times a day. The class can plot its own atmospheric pressure curve on graph paper.

After recording your observations over a period of several weeks, go over them. Does it seem that daily changes in atmospheric pressure, taken alone, seem to provide a sufficient basis for accurate weather forecasting? What other information does the National Weather Service use in making its forecasts?

1. Waves on the Polar Front: Cyclone Formation

The **polar front** separates the prevailing westerlies from the polar easterlies. The polar front frequently separates polar air masses on the north from tropical air masses to the south. From time to time wave motion develops along this front. The wave travels from west to east like a wave passing from left to right through a stage curtain that is shaken at one end. The wave moving through the air masses resembles an ocean swell

The effect of the wave is to create a *cold front* where the polar air bulges southward and

a *warm front* where the tropical air bulges northward. As the wave passes along the polar front, both the cold front and the warm front move eastward. Between the two fronts, the warm, light tropical air that bulges into the cold polar air mass forms *a region of low air pressure* known as a **cyclone** or **low.** The isobars of the cyclone form a roughly oval or circular pattern, and winds whirl about the center in a counterclockwise direction in the Northern Hemisphere. Figure 39-1 illustrates this *wave theory of cyclone development,* with stage c representing a typical full-grown middle-latitude cyclone and its two fronts.

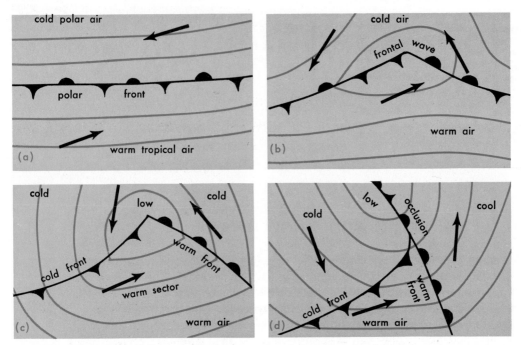

Fig. 39-1. Four stages in the growth and occlusion of a cyclone developed as a wave on the polar front. Arrows show wind directions. See Topic 1.

As the wave continues to move eastward, it behaves very much like a sea swell approaching shore and scraping bottom. As the faster moving cold front overtakes the slower warm front, the wave becomes unstable, like a sea wave forming breakers. The front that is formed where the cold front and warm front merge is called an **occluded front.** Occlusion (meaning "closing in") begins at the apex that separates the cold and warm fronts, and continues until both fronts merge completely to lift the "warm sector" completely off the ground. When the warm air and cold air are thoroughly mixed, the low dies out and disappears, and the polar front becomes stationary again until a new wave develops. Stage *d* illustrates the start of the occlusion process.

The development from stage *a* to *c* takes only 12 to 24 hours. From *c* to complete occlusion usually takes three days or more.

2. The "Typical" Cyclone of Middle Latitudes

Figure 39-2, center, shows a detailed diagram of a typical cyclone of middle latitudes like that of stage *c* in Figure 39-1. The lower part of Figure 39-2 shows a vertical section south of the cyclone center along line *CD,* where the warm sector is on the ground between the two fronts, with cold air ahead of and behind it. Here the passage of a cyclone consists of (1) the rainy passage of a warm front, (2) passage of a clearing mass of warm air, (3) the rainy passage of a cold front.

The upper part of Figure 39-2 shows a vertical section through the cyclone along the line *AB,* north of the cyclone center. Here the warm air is above the surface. Rain from the upper air fronts is continuous, and there is no change from cold to warm air at the ground.

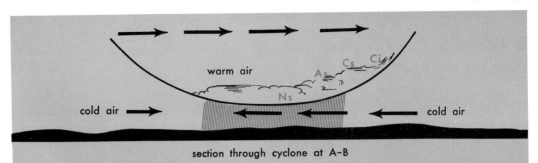

section through cyclone at A–B

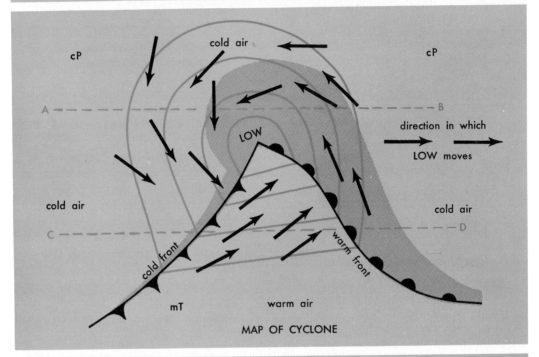

MAP OF CYCLONE

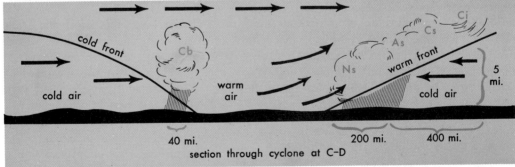

section through cyclone at C–D

Fig. 39-2. *The middle drawing shows how a typical cyclone of middle latitudes might appear on a weather map. The lower drawing is a vertical section through the cyclone at CD. The upper drawing is a vertical section at AB. The shading represents precipitation. See Topic 2.*

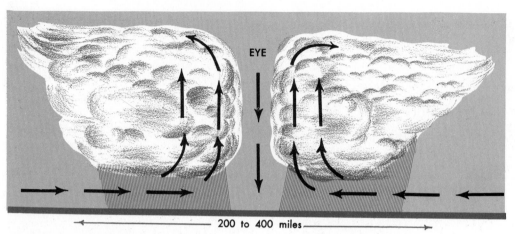

Fig. 39-3. Vertical cross section through a hurricane or tropical cyclone.

The word "cyclone" means "whirl," and the cyclone is so named because of the whirling pattern made by the winds that circulate around its center. These winds blow to the right in the Northern Hemisphere, producing a *counterclockwise* whirl. In the Southern Hemisphere, where deflection is to the left, cyclones have a *clockwise* whirl.

3. Occluded Front Weather

As explained in Topic 1, an occluded front is formed when a cold front (and the body of cold air behind it) overtakes a warm front (and the body of cold air ahead of it), lifting the intervening warm sector off the ground. When an occluded front approaches a locality, the weather it brings is a combination of the warm front weather that precedes the front and the cold front weather that follows the front. However, the passing of the front on the ground does not usually bring as great a change of weather as with ordinary cold fronts and warm fronts.

4. Energy Released in Cyclones

The energy that starts the formation of cyclone waves is probably derived from the winds blowing at the polar front. However, as soon as condensation begins at the cyclone's two fronts, a vast new source of energy becomes available—the latent heat of condensation. As explained in Chapter 36, nearly 600 calories of heat energy are released to the atmosphere for every gram of water formed by condensation in clouds. This energy heats the air in the cyclone, intensifies its low pressure, and increases the strength of its spiraling winds. Thus cyclones—and in fact all bodies of air in which condensation occurs—are "heat engines" that grow and sustain themselves as long as large-scale condensation continues to provide them with energy.

5. Cyclones in the United States

The cyclones that cross the United States originate chiefly in three places: the northwest, the southwest, and the southeast. Almost all cyclones eventually move toward the northeast and New England, causing great variability of weather in this part of the country. In winter cyclones are better developed, move faster, and are more frequent than in summer. Their rate of movement across the country in winter is about 700 miles a day. In summer it is about 500 miles a day. Cyclones have diameters of from

500 to 1,000 miles, and a single large cyclone may cover nearly half of the country.

6. Hurricanes: Tropical Cyclones

A **hurricane** is a *tropical cyclone*. A Weather Bureau pamphlet describes hurricanes as "large revolving storms accompanied by violent destructive winds, heavy rains, and high waves and tides." In some ways a tropical cyclone resembles our own middle-latitude cyclones. Both of them are storm areas of low air pressure. Winds spiral into their centers in the same general pattern: counterclockwise in the Northern Hemisphere, clockwise in the Southern Hemisphere. As a rule there are areas of heavy precipitation in both of them.

In many ways, however, the hurricane differs from the middle-latitude cyclone. A hurricane is a much more intense storm with an average diameter of only 200 to 400 miles. (See Fig. 39-3.) Its pressure gradients are very steep, and its central air pressure may go as low as 26.35 inches (recorded at Key West, Florida, in 1935). A hurricane has no fronts, and it has a strange central area of descending air currents, known as the "eye of the storm." The eye is usually from 10 to 30 miles in diameter. Here the sun shines, the sky is clear, there is no rain, and there are almost no winds. But all around the eye the winds whirl violently, with their highest speeds produced in a circular band reaching 20 to 30 miles outward from the eye. Within this band wind speeds may exceed 150 miles an hour. Beyond it wind speeds decrease, but nevertheless the area of destructive winds may have a diameter as high as 500 miles, and may travel over a path more than 1,000 miles long during the storm's complete life history. While the hurricane's whirling winds are violent, the entire storm area moves very slowly through the tropics and speeds up only when it enters middle latitudes. (See Fig. 39-4.)

The rains of a hurricane are almost always very heavy. They increase in amount toward the center, where the rain comes down in torrents, except in the dry eye. The world's record for a 24-hour rainfall is the 46 inches that fell during a tropical cyclone in the Philippines in 1911.

Tropical cyclones are known by various names. (See Fig. 39-5.) In the West Indies they are called **hurricanes,** in the Indian Ocean **cyclones,** in the China Sea **typhoons,** in the Philippine Islands **baguios** (bah gee *ohs*) and in the Pacific near Australia **willy-willies.** Much of the damage done by these great storms is the result

Fig. 39-4. Normal track of a West Indian hurricane and its wind system.

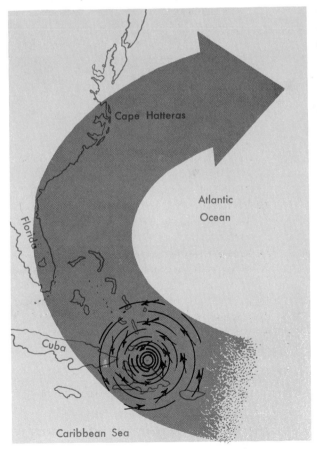

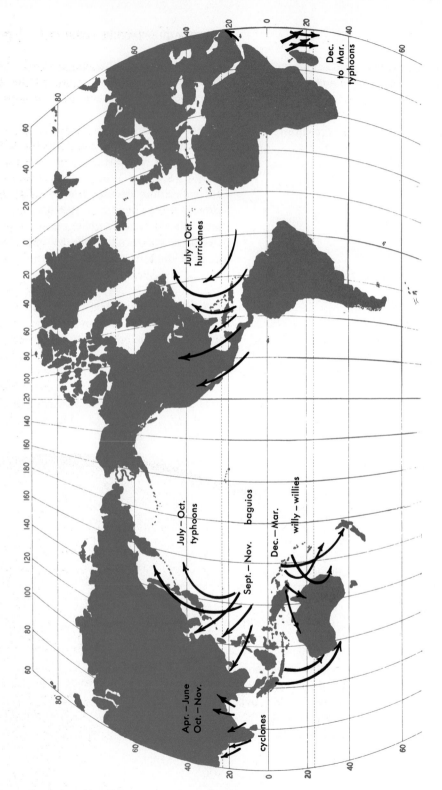

Fig. 39-5. Names, tracks, and seasons of tropical cyclones throughout the world.

of the gigantic sea waves generated by them along coastal areas, especially when they coincide with the arrival of high tides. The famous Galveston, Texas, hurricane of September 8, 1900, took the lives of over 6,000 people, many of whom were drowned by great waves that rolled over the offshore bar on which Galveston is built.

7. Sources and Tracks of Tropical Cyclones

All tropical cyclones originate on the western sides of the oceans in the doldrums, between 6° and 20° latitude in both hemispheres. This includes the West Indies and Caribbean area, the China Seas of East Asia, the southern Indian Ocean, and the ocean areas adjacent to east Australia and east Africa. The only part of the doldrums in which tropical cyclones do not occur is the South Atlantic area. They are most likely to develop when the doldrums are farthest north or south of the Equator. In fact, the absence of tropical cyclones from the areas which are located very close to the Equator indicates that the Coriolis force is important in their development.

The tracks of most tropical cyclones are shaped like parabolas. After forming in the doldrums, these cyclones move westward and away from the Equator through the tradewind belts at a slow, drifting pace of from 6 to 12 miles an hour. Still moving slowly, they pass through the horse latitudes and into the belt of prevailing westerlies. (This holds true for either Northern or Southern Hemispheres.) Here they speed up and turn eastward, while continuing to move away from the Equator. Helped by the prevailing westerly winds, they may now move at a rate of 30, 40 or even 50 miles an hour. But as their rate of movement increases, their wind speeds usually decrease, and eventually the hurricanes "blow themselves out" at sea and vanish.

West Indian hurricanes are most frequent in late summer and early fall. Hurricanes developing at this time, when the doldrums are farthest

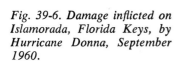

Fig. 39-6. Damage inflicted on Islamorada, Florida Keys, by Hurricane Donna, September 1960.

north, are the ones most likely to reach the United States. Many of them strike Florida and southeastern United States before blowing out past Cape Hatteras, North Carolina, to the Atlantic Ocean on the normal hurricane track. (See Fig. 39-4.)

8. Hurricanes in the Northeast

Occasionally a hurricane fails to follow the "regular track" which would take it curving out into the Atlantic Ocean at Cape Hatteras. Instead, it may continue northward along the coast or even invade the interior, sometimes penetrating as far north as New England and southern Canada. Although such a storm becomes greatly modified as it travels through the prevailing westerlies, it may still be far more violent than any ordinary middle-latitude cyclone.

In 1960 Hurricane Donna struck Florida and the Atlantic Coast as far north as the Gulf of St. Lawrence, destroying more than one billion dollars worth of property. Fierce winds, torrential rains, high waves, and floods combined to cause great devastation.

9. Naming and Forecasting Hurricanes

The practice of identifying hurricanes by giving them feminine names began in 1953. In 1960 the Weather Bureau introduced the use of four semipermanent lists of names. Each list is alphabetical. One list is used each year and the entire set is to be used over again at the end of a four-year cycle. Because of the tremendous importance of early forecasts in protecting life and property, the closest watch is kept on each hurricane as it grows and moves. *Weather reconnaisance planes* fly around and even inside hurricanes to observe their locations, extent, wind strengths, and direction and speed of movement.

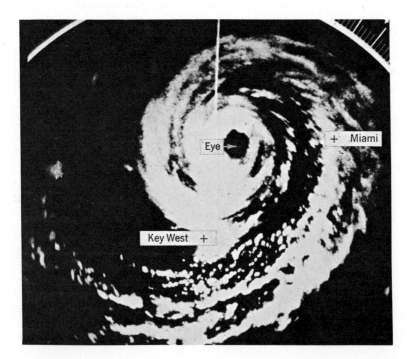

Fig. 39-7. Hurricane Donna on the radarscope at Key West, Florida. September 10, 1960.

U.S. Weather Bureau

Fig. 39-8. The approach and arrival of a tornado at Gothenburg, Nebraska. In its 30-mile path across the plains it caused six casualties and property loss of $200,000.

Weather detection radar equipment can determine the location of rain areas in storms within the range of the radar set. Weather satellites discover hurricanes and other storms by transmitting television pictures of the atmosphere to stations at the earth's surface. (See Fig. 39-7.)

10. Tornadoes: Occurrence and Characteristics

Tornadoes are the smallest, briefest, and most violent of all storms. Tornadoes occur in many parts of the world, but they are much more frequent in the United States than anywhere else. Every one of our 50 states has experienced tornadoes, but most of our tornadoes occur in the Mississippi Valley and the eastern half of the Great Plains, where they are also called *twisters* or *cyclones.*

Tornadoes are narrow, funnel-shaped, spiral whirls whose diameters average about one-fourth of a mile, but may on occasion exceed a mile. Their paths are twisting and unpredictable. They usually travel at rates of from 25 to 40 miles an hour, passing any particular point with a thunderous roar in but a few seconds. Their life spans are measured in hours. The path of destruction of a single tornado has been known to reach 300 miles, but in most cases it is less than 16 miles. (See Fig. 39-8.)

The violence and erratic path of a tornado makes it almost impossible to measure its wind speeds and air pressure directly. When tornadoes pass over places equipped with weather instruments, the anemometers and other instruments are almost always destroyed. From their destructive effects, however, it is estimated that the air pressure of a tornado may be as much as one-third lower than normal atmospheric pressure, its wind speeds may reach 500 miles an hour, and its updrafts may exceed 150 miles an hour. Air rushing into the low-pressure funnel of a tornado cools by expansion to form a dense water cloud that is blackened by the dust and debris that blows into it. The tornado cloud hangs low from the thundercloud with which it is always associated, and every now and then it dips onto the ground as it moves along its twisting path. Where it touches the ground, its effects are destructive. Lightning and thunder, hail, and heavy rains from the thundercloud almost always accompany the tornado. When a tornado passes over a body of water, it causes one kind of **waterspout.**

11. Tornado Destructiveness

Many of the destructive effects of a tornado are unique. Straws have been driven into wooden utility poles; chickens have been plucked of their feathers; roofs of buildings have been blown away and walls have exploded outward; heavy objects such as automobiles and farm animals have been lifted and carried many feet, sometimes being set down unharmed. Perhaps the most awesome example of the tornado's power occurred in 1931 in Minnesota, where a tornado carried an 83-ton railroad coach and 117 passengers 80 feet through the air before dropping them in a ditch.

How does a tornado pluck feathers from a chicken and make the walls of a building explode outward? Much of a tornado's destructiveness results from its violent winds, but its powerful updrafts and the partial vacuum in its funnel account for the effects different from those of other wind storms. When the tornado funnel envelops a barn or house, the air pressure outside the building is suddenly reduced so much that the air inside literally explodes. If 300-mile-an-hour winds are swirling around the building at almost the same time, it is not surprising that the roof flies away, the walls collapse, and the chickens lose their feathers as if they were vacuum-cleaned.

Fig. 39-9. Number of days each month on which tornadoes are reported.

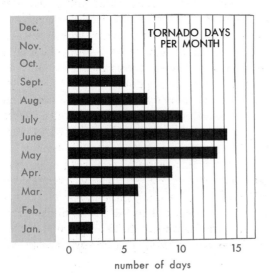

In areas where tornadoes are strong possibilities, many people provide themselves with storm cellars for use in tornado emergencies. These are located close enough to the home to be reached in just a few seconds, but not so close that falling walls or other debris might block their exits.

12. Tornadoes: Origin and Warnings

How do tornadoes originate? The answer to this question is by no means settled, and weather scientists are continuing their research into this question and the related one of the source of a tornado's energy. But scientists are fairly well agreed as to the atmospheric conditions that are likely to bring about the formation of tornadoes. Warm, moist air from the Gulf of Mexico moves northward into the Mississippi Valley and Great Plains, reaching upward into the atmosphere to a height of about two miles. At the same time cool, dry air moves eastward over the Rocky Mountains and rides over the air from the Gulf. When the cold air sinks under the warm air and causes it to rise, a line of thunderstorms—a line squall—is likely to be formed, and tornadoes may be born with the thunderstorms.

Experts in the analysis of tornado conditions are constantly at work in the National Severe Storms Forecast Center at Kansas City, Missouri, ready to issue a *tornado watch* or *tornado warning* whenever necessary. A tornado watch specifies the area covered by the watch, and the period in which tornado probabilities will be dangerously high. A tornado warning is issued when a tornado has actually been sighted in an area or has been detected by radar. It gives the location of the tornado when detected, the area in which it is likely to move, and the period of time during which it is expected to move. Tornado watches and warnings are broadcast by radio and television.

13. Frequency of Tornadoes

Tornadoes are most frequent during spring and early summer, and are most likely to occur in the late afternoon. (See Fig. 39-9.) For the period 1953–1965, the average number of tornadoes reported in the United States was 628, of which about half occurred in April, May, and June. The greatest tornado disaster in 49 years occurred on April 3, 1974, when 100 tornadoes struck 11 states (Georgia, Alabama, Oklahoma, Tennessee, North Carolina, Kentucky, Michigan, West Virginia, Illinois, Indiana, Ohio), and a Canadian border city. Over 300 people were killed, thousands were injured, and many thousands were made homeless. Damage was estimated at $1 billion. Tornadoes in the United States have killed an average of about 120 persons yearly since 1953.

14. Where Thunderstorms Originate

Thunderstorms are local, relatively small-area storms generated by the strong upward movement of warm, moist air. It is estimated that 44,000 thunderstorms occur every day across the surface of the earth. Thunderstorms are usually classified into two types according to their origin. **Air-mass thunderstorms** occur within an air mass when warm, moist air is heated strongly at the earth's surface and powerful convection currents are developed. These thunderstorms, also called *thermal* or *convective thunderstorms,* are usually widely scattered. They may form over either land or water, being most likely to occur in summer over land by day and over water at night. Air-mass thunderstorms may also develop on the *windward side of a mountain range.* Such storms are common in the northern Rockies when winds from the Pacific blow eastward over the mountains.

Frontal thunderstorms occur when warm, moist air is forced to rise over upward sloping frontal surfaces. Although most likely to occur in summer, they may occur in any season, and at night as well as in the daytime. In warm fronts, with their gentle slopes, thunderstorms are usually scattered and few. In steep cold fronts, on the other hand, a line of thunderstorms may stretch several hundred miles along the front.

15. Inside the Thunderstorm

A good deal of observation and research has been done by meteorologists to determine the internal structure of a thunderstorm. One theory, known as the **bubble theory,** pictures the thunderstorm as a series of great "bubbles" or separate spheres of air rising one under the other from the lower air to form the thundercloud. A second theory, known as the **columnar theory,** pictures the thunderstorm as made up of one or more "cells" in each of which great columns of air move vertically in directions that change during the cell's life history. The columnar theory is based to a large extent on observations made by the Thunderstorm Project group led by meteorologist H. R. Byers of the University of Chicago from 1945 to 1950. Although research on thunderstorms continues, no one theory is yet able to explain the thunderstorm fully, but the columnar theory is referred to most frequently.

The life history of a thunderstorm includes its growth from the small harmless cumulus cloud to the gigantic cumulonimbus cloud with its violent gusts and updrafts, its heavy precipitation, and its lightning and thunder. The columnar theory describes the life cycle of a cell in three stages as described below and shown in Figure 39-10. The entire life cycle of a cell lasts about an hour, but a thunderstorm consisting of several cells may last for several hours. Each cell is believed to have a diameter of a few miles, and to rise to a height of from 40,000 to 60,000 feet.

1. Cumulus stage. In this building stage of the thunderstorm *strong updrafts of warm air are*

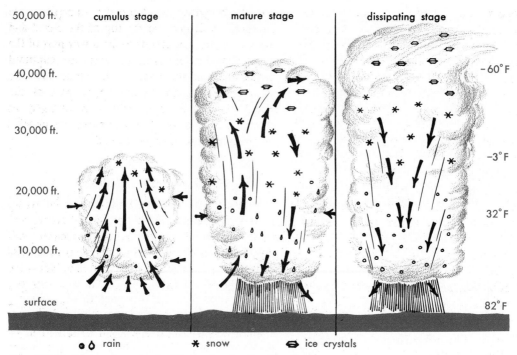

Fig. 39-10. Three stages in the life cycle of a thunderstorm.

found throughout the "convective cell" reaching from the ground to the top of the cloud. (See Fig. 39-10.) As convection continues, usually to heights above 25,000 feet, the cloud grows *above the freezing level,* ice crystals and snow form in its upper levels, and raindrops form. The cumulus stage usually ends about 10 or 15 minutes after the cloud top rises above the freezing level.

2. Mature stage. The arrival of precipitation at the earth's surface marks the beginning of the mature stage. The falling rain drags the air down with it to begin a downward motion which results in *strong downdrafts in the lower forward half of the cell, while strong updrafts continue in the rear half of the cell* and at all upper levels, building the cloud to heights of 40,000 feet or higher and often forming hail. Strong turbulence occurs in the violent updrafts and downdrafts, which reach maximum speeds of about 100 feet

per second and 40 feet per second respectively. At the surface the downdraft spreads out in fierce gusts of wind. As heavy rainfall continues, the *downdraft area spreads over the entire lower part of the cell, ending the mature stage* about 15 to 30 minutes after it began.

3. Dissipating or anvil stage. *Downdrafts spread through the entire cell* until even at upper levels there is no upward motion, so condensation stops, the rain soon ends, and the storm *dissipates* or dies out. During this stage, strong winds in the highest levels of the cloud tilt its top into an *anvil* shape, hence the name *anvil stage.*

16. Electricity in the Thunderstorm

A thunderstorm is also, of course, a lightning storm. And lightning is the result of the discharge of vast quantities of electricity from the thundercloud to the ground or to another cloud. But where do the great quantities of electricity come from? How are the positive and negative charges separated from each other and concentrated in the different parts of the cloud as shown in Figure 39-11? Observations of thunderclouds show the upper part to be charged mostly positively, and the lower part to be charged mostly negatively. (After rain begins, a small area of positive charge may form in the lower part of the cloud.) Nevertheless, meteorologists are as yet unable to explain fully either the source or the separation of the thundercloud's electricity.

It used to be thought that the cloud's electricity resulted from friction between rising air currents and falling raindrops in the cloud. Unfortunately for this hypothesis, the rising air acquires a negative charge and the falling rain acquires a positive charge, which would give the thundercloud a charge nearly the reverse of what is actually observed. (See Fig. 39-11.) Experiments do show, however, that when water begins to freeze, the ice crystals become charged negatively and the water is left with a positive charge. In a thundercloud, rising currents might carry the lighter water droplets to the upper half of the cloud, giving it the observed positive (+) charge, while falling snow and ice carry negative (−) charge to the lower half.

Many meteorologists now favor some such explanation of thundercloud electricity, which requires that the *cloud have ice crystals in it and that precipitation be occurring*. As supporting evidence, they point to the fact that lightning appears to begin *after* the thundercloud grows to ice crystal levels and precipitation has begun.

Other meteorologists dispute the ice crystal-precipitation hypothesis. They cite examples—rare though they may be—of lightning in "warm" clouds in which no ice particles have formed. They believe that the thundercloud acquires its electricity by *ion capture*. In this process, the cloud droplets become charged by "capturing" tiny charged particles or ions already present in the air. Negative ions from the ionosphere are captured by droplets at the top of the cloud and are carried by downdrafts to the lower part of the cloud. Positive ions from the earth are captured by droplets at the base of the cloud and are carried by updrafts to the upper part of the cloud. Thus the thundercloud is charged as shown in Figure 39-11 before either ice crystals or precipitation have developed.

17. Lightning and Thunder

As more and more electric charge builds up in the thundercloud, the voltage difference between the cloud and the ground increases until the air between them can no longer prevent discharge. It is then that lightning occurs. The voltage required for this is about 25,000 volts per inch.

Lightning appears to the eye as a single brilliant flash, usually zigzagged or forked in its

Fig. 39-11. Distribution of electric charges in a cumulonimbus cloud.

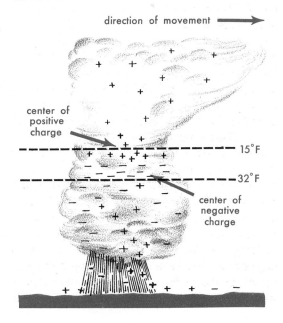

direction of movement ➡

center of positive charge

center of negative charge

15°F

32°F

ESSA

Fig. 39-12. The many-branched pattern of a flash of "forked lightning."

path, resembling a giant electric spark. Special high-speed cameras, however, show that the main lightning flash is preceded by a barely visible discharge called the *stepped leader*. The stepped leader moves from the base of the cloud to the ground in a series of interrupted steps, each 200 to 300 feet long, that reaches the ground in about one hundredth of a second. The stepped leader ionizes the air and prepares a conducting path for the main discharge. This takes place when the stepped leader is within a few hundred feet of the ground, and a spark seems to leap from the ground to complete the path. Vast quantities of charge surge from the cloud to the ground, causing a brilliant lightning flash visible to the eye. Meteorologists call this the *return stroke* because it seems to streak from the ground to the cloud, traveling in a *channel* only a few inches wide. The sequence of leader and return stroke may be repeated in this channel several times within hundredths of a second. The more return strokes, the longer the lightning flash seems to last.

Lightning may also strike from cloud to cloud, or within a single cloud. *Forked lightning* results when the stepped leader branches as it nears the ground, so that more than one return stroke path is formed. *Heat lightning* is the glow of a distant lightning flash so far off that its thunder cannot be heard.

The temperature inside the channel of a lightning flash is believed to reach about 50,-000°F. At this high temperature, the air expands almost explosively to produce the tremendous sound wave we call thunder. Light travels at a speed of 186,000 miles a second, so lightning is seen almost instantaneously. But the sound waves from the lightning take about five seconds to travel a mile in the lower air. By counting the seconds between the lightning flash and the thunder, therefore, it is possible to calculate the approximate distance to the lightning stroke. If the stroke covers a long distance horizontally, sound waves will arrive continuously for several seconds from different parts of the channel, and the thunder will "rumble." Rumbling also results when thunder echoes from mountainsides or when the sound waves from a number of different lightning strokes arrive in rapid succession. The greatest distance at which it is possible for thunder to be ordinarily heard is about 10 miles.

18. Lightning Danger and Protection

Lightning is awesome and beautiful, but it is potentially dangerous and must be treated with the greatest respect. Every year lightning in the United States causes thousands of forest fires and electrocutes about 200 people.

When lightning strikes, it is likely to go from the cloud base to the nearest point projecting from the ground; hence it often strikes tall objects such as trees, church steeples, and the tops of city skyscrapers. Benjamin Franklin's invention of the lightning rod was based on this fact. The lightning rod projects above the house roof and is connected to the ground by a good conductor. When lightning strikes the rod, the electricity is conducted harmlessly to the ground, instead of striking some part of the house which it might set on fire.

Where should one take shelter in a lightning storm? The best shelter is a house. If you are driving and visibility is poor, it may be advisable to pull off the road, but stay in the car. It, too, will protect you from lightning. Bathers and boaters should seek shelter as soon as a storm threatens. A tree or group of trees in an open field should be avoided, for they "attract" lightning. If no other shelter is nearby, it is better to stay in the open and get wet than to take refuge under a tree.

19. Weather in an Anticyclone

Highs, or *anticyclones,* usually appear on weather maps as a series of smooth circular isobars, in contrast with the kinked oval isobars of lows or middle-latitude cyclones. Unlike a low, *a high represents a single air mass.* Since the air pressure in a high is highest at the center, winds blow outward to form a whirl that is clockwise in the Northern Hemisphere and counterclockwise in the Southern Hemisphere. Isobars are generally farther apart than in lows, and pressure gradients and wind velocities are correspondingly smaller. Bright, clear weather is usually present throughout an anticyclone, which may have a diameter in excess of 1,000 miles. Descending dry air at the anticyclone center is believed to account for its fair weather. As a rule the only important forms of condensation are the heavy dew, frost, and radiation fogs that may form at night in the still, clear air near the surface. Occasionally, however, rain, drizzle, and cloudy skies do develop in the southwestern and western sectors of anticyclones.

20. Making the Weather Map

Weather map data is gathered by observers in about 600 official Weather Service stations in the United States. Additional reports are received from countries in all parts of the Northern Hemisphere and from about 150 ships at sea each day. **Synoptic maps** are prepared at the National Weather Service every three hours, starting with 1 A.M. (*A synoptic map* gives a *synopsis* or summary of the weather *at the surface* over a large area. Our regular weather map is therefore a synoptic map.) Observations are also transmitted immediately by teletype, telegraph, telephone, or radio to other forecast centers where weather maps can be drawn up and local forecasts made. Official maps and general forecasts are drawn up at the National Meteorological Center at Suitland, Maryland (near Washington, D.C.), and are then sent by wire to all forecast centers and by radio to ships at sea. Only the map showing 7 A.M. weather is distributed in printed form, although maps for other times may be reproduced in modified form in newspapers.

From July 1, 1878, until April 14, 1968, the Weather Service printed a daily weather map that was mailed to subscribers each day. On April 15, 1968, it discontinued this service for economic reasons and substituted a "weekly series" in the form of a booklet of maps mailed to subscribers each Monday. The booklet includes a page of maps for each day of the preceding week from Monday through Sunday. There are four maps on each page: (1) an 8″ × 6″ map showing *surface weather* at 7:00 A.M. Eastern Standard Time; (2) a 5″ × 4″ map showing *upper-atmosphere* temperature, pressure, and winds at 7:00 A.M. E.S.T.; (3)

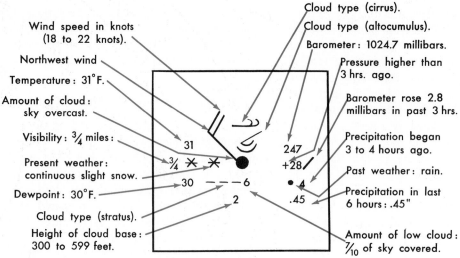

Wind speed in knots (18 to 22 knots).

Northwest wind

Temperature: 31°F.

Amount of cloud: sky overcast.

Visibility: ¾ miles:

Present weather: continuous slight snow.

Dewpoint: 30°F.

Cloud type (stratus).

Height of cloud base: 300 to 599 feet.

Cloud type (cirrus).

Cloud type (altocumulus).

Barometer: 1024.7 millibars.

Pressure higher than 3 hrs. ago.

Barometer rose 2.8 millibars in past 3 hrs.

Precipitation began 3 to 4 hours ago.

Past weather: rain.

Precipitation in last 6 hours: .45"

Amount of low cloud: ⁷⁄₁₀ of sky covered.

Fig. 39-13. Explanation of the complete station model used by the Weather Service.

a 2″ × 3″ map of *highest and lowest temperatures* for the 24-hour period ending at 1:00 A.M. E.S.T.; (4) a 2″ × 3″ map of *precipitation areas and amounts* in the 24 hours ending at 1:00 A.M. E.S.T.

The symbols on the weather map are explained on a sheet available from the Weather Service's Publications Section.

21. The Station Model

About 20 different weather observations may be plotted next to each station on the weather map. To show this information concisely, the Weather Service arranges it around the station in a form called the **station model.** (See Fig. 39-13.) Where possible, direct readings are given. In all other cases codes are used. Both station model and codes are based on those of the World Meteorological Organization, and can be read by meteorologists of any country, as can the coded information sent by wire or radio. (Figure 39-14 is part of a weather map on which the reading of the station model may be practiced. Figure 39-15 shows a simplified form of a daily weather map.)

22. Weather Forecasts and Services

Forecasters at each forecasting center may prepare daily weather forecasts for their own regions. These are forecasts for 36 hours in advance and are issued at about 10 A.M. through radio, television, telephone, and the press. They are revised at about 5 P.M., 11 P.M., and 5 A.M. the next day, if such revisions are found necessary in the light of the day's later weather maps.

The Weather Service's Extended Forecast Branch prepares "forecasts and outlooks" for intervals of from 5 to 30 days. A weekly weather and crop bulletin, a daily Mississippi River stages and forecast bulletin, and a daily weather and river bulletin are published throughout the year. All of these are available by subscription.

The National Severe Storms Forecast Center in Kansas City, Missouri, prepares special forecasts of severe thunderstorms and tornadoes. The Hurricane Warning Service in Miami, Florida, coordinates all services relating to hurricanes. Other services include the River and Flood Forecasting Service, the Fire-Weather Warning Serv-

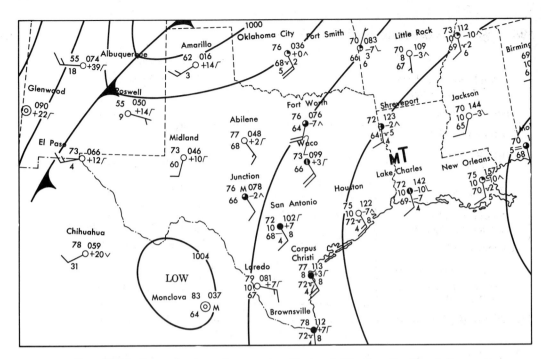

Fig. 39-14. Reproduction of part of a National Weather Service daily weather map.

Fig. 39-15. The modified form of weather map that appears in the New York Times. *Isobars are marked in inches at one end, in millibars at the other.*

The New York Times

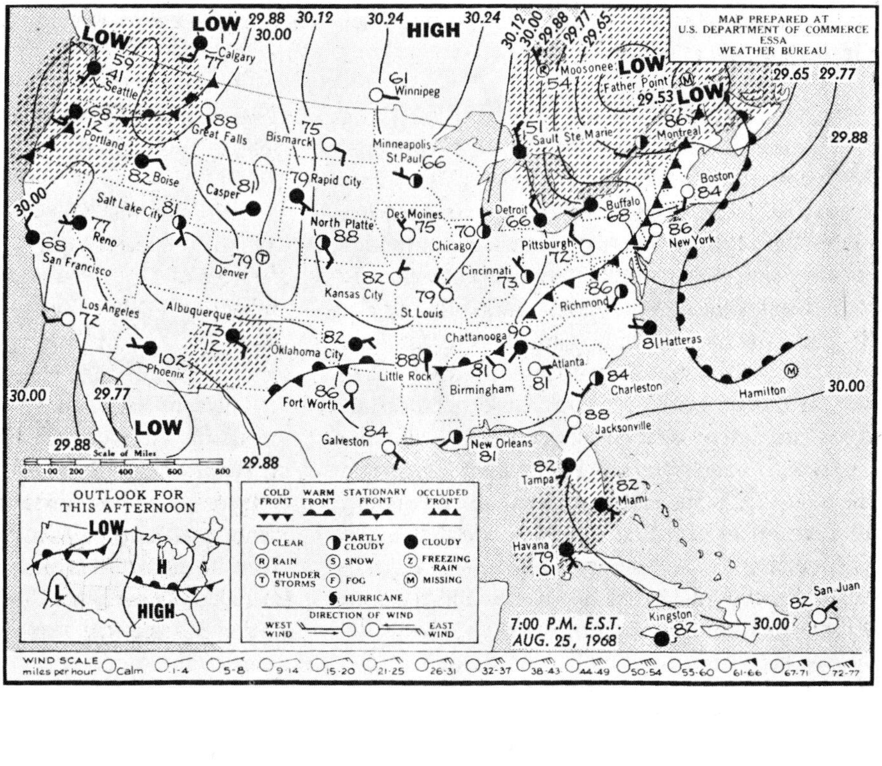

Fig. 39-16. *Meteorological technicians tuning in picture signals from an ESSA Weather Satellite.*

ice, the Fruit-Frost Service, the Marine Meteorological Service, and Aviation Forecasts.

All of the Armed Forces have their own weather services.

23. Modern Weather Forecasting

Before World War I the daily weather map showed only the weather at the earth's surface. Very little was known about the upper atmosphere, and weather forecasts were based almost entirely on the synoptic map. Forecasts were made by individual "experts," and little use was made of mathematics.

Today's weather forecasts are made by teams of forecast specialists. Mathematical formulae and computing machines assist in evaluating upper air data obtained by modern equipment such as the radiosonde, radar, weather balloons, and weather satellites. Together with the data still collected at the surface by the weather observer, the upper air data gives a three-dimensional picture of the atmosphere from which highly accurate forecasts can be made.

Surface weather maps show the locations and surface characteristics of air masses, highs and lows, fronts, potential hurricanes, and numerous other features. Upper air observations are plotted on **constant-pressure charts** that show the elevations of the surface at which air pressure is equal to some specific quantity such as 700 millibars or 500 millibars. Such maps also show wind speeds, wind directions, and temperatures at the indicated elevations. The 500-millibar map, especially valuable to the weather forecaster, normally includes elevations from about 15,000 to 20,000 feet.

Before making a weather forecast, the meteorologist consults prognostic charts prepared by the Analysis and Forecast Branch of the National Meteorological Center. These **prognostic charts** (forecasting charts) are of two kinds. One kind shows the probable future *surface* locations of lows, highs, and fronts in the next 24 to 48 hours. The second kind shows the probable future *upper-air* conditions at the 500-millibar surface or others. The prognostic charts are sent by teletype and facsimile networks to all continental United States weather stations. (*Facsimile* machines transmit and receive printed pictures and symbols by wire or radio. Newspapers use these machines to send pictures from city to city.) These two powerful "tools"—the prognostic charts for both the surface and the upper air—give the meteorologist a basis for accurate forecasts.

24. Radar and Satellites in Weather Observation

The use of radar in weather observation depends on the fact that radar waves are reflected as **radar echoes** from the water droplets and ice crystals in clouds, rain, and other forms of precipitation. Like television signals, radar echoes form images on the radarscope that represent the surfaces from which they are reflected. Thus "pictures" may be seen of thunderstorms, hurricanes, and other areas of heavy precipitation.

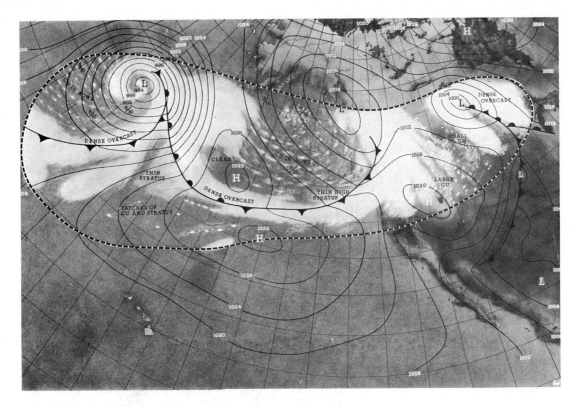

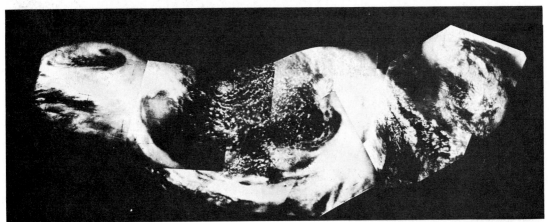

U.S. Weather Bureau

Fig. 39-17. The lower panel shows photographs taken by Tiros I of storms reaching from north of Japan to the eastern United States on May 20, 1960. The upper panel shows the weather map of the same area, with the cloud cover sketched in.

Ground-based radar can detect and track such storms within a radius of 200 miles. U.S. Navy "hurricane hunter" planes also use radar in their search for hurricanes.

Radar echoes are sometimes useful in measuring the rate of rainfall and in distinguishing between snow and rain or between ice clouds and water clouds.

Tiros (*T*elevision and *I*nfra*R*ed *O*bservation *S*atellite) is the weather satellite that revolves around the earth in nearly circular orbits every 100 minutes at an altitude of about 450 miles. Two television cameras take pictures of the earth on command from the earth during each daytime orbit, store them on magnetic tape, and then transmit them automatically or on command to ground "readout" stations. The cloud map made from these pictures is called a **nephanalysis.** It provides valuable information about the location and origin of storms, especially in ocean areas not easily observed. *Nimbus* and *ESSA* are other weather satellites.

TOPIC QUESTIONS

Each topic question refers to the topic of the same number within this chapter.

1. (*a*) Explain how waves on the polar front are related to warm fronts and cold fronts. (*b*) What is a cyclone? (*c*) What is an occluded front? How does it form?

2. (*a*) What weather changes take place (along line CD) as the full-grown cyclone passes a station? (*b*) Describe the direction of cyclone winds in each hemisphere.

3. What kind of weather does the passage of an occluded front bring?

4. (*a*) Explain how condensation provides a cyclone with energy. (*b*) What is the effect of this energy on the cyclone?

5. (*a*) Where do our cyclones originate? (*b*) Where do they move to? (*c*) How fast do they move? (*d*) How large are they?

6. (*a*) How do tropical cyclones resemble cyclones in middle latitudes? (*b*) How do tropical cyclones differ from those in middle latitudes? (*c*) What is the "eye of the storm"? (*d*) What are the various names given to tropical cyclones?

7. (*a*) Where do tropical cyclones originate? (*b*) What general path do they follow? At what speeds do they travel? (*c*) When are hurricanes most likely to reach the United States? Why?

8. (*a*) What paths are followed by hurricanes that go north of the regular track? (*b*) In what ways are hurricanes destructive?

9. Describe the "forecasting" of hurricanes by our National Weather Service.

10. (*a*) Where do tornadoes occur? (*b*) Describe the appearance and weather elements of a tornado.

11. (*a*) What are some of the strange effects of a tornado? (*b*) Explain how a tornado can make a building "explode." (*c*) What is a storm cellar?

12. (*a*) Describe the atmospheric conditions that favor the formation of tornadoes. (*b*) Who issues tornado watches and tornado warnings? How do they differ?

13. (*a*) Discuss the frequency of tornadoes in the United States. (*b*) How did the Severe Storms Forecast Center help reduce casualties in the great disaster of April 11, 1965?

14. Explain the difference in origin between air-mass thunderstorms and frontal thunderstorms.

15. (*a*) How does the bubble theory picture the structure of a thunderstorm? (*b*) How does the columnar theory picture it? (*c*) Briefly describe the three stages in the life cycle of a thunderstorm.

16. (*a*) Describe the distribution of electricity in a thundercloud. (*b*) How does the ice crystal-precipitation theory explain the origin and concentration of a thundercloud's electricity? (*c*) How does the ion capture theory explain the same things?

17. (*a*) What is the *stepped leader* of a lightning stroke? (*b*) What is the *return stroke?* (*c*) How is thunder explained? (*d*) How can the distance to a lightning flash be calculated? (*e*) What causes thunder to rumble?

18. (*a*) How does a lightning rod protect a building from lightning? (*b*) Where should shelter be sought during a lightning storm?

19. (*a*) Describe the direction and strength of winds in an anticyclone. (*b*) What kind of weather characterizes an anticyclone? Why?

20. Why is our regular Weather Service map a *synoptic map?* Where is it drawn up?

21. What is the station model? List 10 weather items it shows.

22. (*a*) Where is the daily weather forecast prepared? How is it publicized? (*b*) Where are tornadoes forecast? hurricanes?

23. (*a*) Compare modern weather observations and forecasting with that of pre-World War I. (*b*) What are the two kinds of prognostic charts so important to the weather forecaster?

24. (*a*) What does the use of radar for weather observation depend on? (*b*) How do Tiros satellites provide useful weather information?

GENERAL QUESTIONS

1. What is the meaning, in terms of air masses, of the fact that hurricanes have no fronts?

2. What accounts for the heavy precipitation in tropical cyclones?

3. How does a tornado pluck a chicken's feathers?

4. If thunder is heard 10 seconds after lightning is seen, how far away is the storm?

5. Why should heavy frosts, dew, and fogs be associated with highs?

6. In what kind of air mass are air-mass thunderstorms most likely to develop? Why?

7. In what ways may state or federal forest services plan for protection against forest fires, as suggested in Topic 22?

STUDENT ACTIVITIES

1. Form a school weather bureau. Build an instrument shelter to house maximum and minimum thermometers and a psychrometer. Set up a standard rain gauge, an anemometer, and a wind vane. Make daily observations of temperature, pressure, relative humidity, wind direction, wind speed, state of sky, types of clouds, and any precipitation. Record your observations daily on prepared mimeographed forms, and post them on school bulletin boards.

(Write to the Superintendent of Documents, Washington, D.C. 20402, for a free price list of Weather Bureau publications. Get the "Instructions for Cooperative Observers," "Cloud Chart," and other helpful publications. Also consult Yate's *Weather for a Hobby* and Middleton's *Meteorological Instruments*. See Bibliography.)

2. Keep an individual daily record, in columnar form, of weather observations you can easily make by yourself at home or in school. These include temperature, state of sky, cloud types, wind direction, present weather. Make your observations at the same time each day. See what relations you can establish among the weather elements you observe.

CHAPTER 40
Light in the Sky

HOW DO YOU KNOW THAT . . . ?

Light bends through certain materials (Topic 3). Stand a pencil in a tall jar of water, with most of the pencil submerged. Observe it through the side of the jar. Does it seem bent? Why? Place a coin in a small cup or bowl. Set the cup at a level high enough so that its edge just keeps you from seeing the coin. While you stay put, have your partner pour water into the cup very slowly. What happens to the coin? Try to explain why (see Fig. 40-1).

1. Seeing Things

When light from any object comes to the eye, that object is "seen." If the light is produced by the object itself, as with the sun, a star, a gas flame, or a hot electric-light wire, the object is described as **self-luminous.** If the light is supplied by some other source, as when sunlight lights up the earth's surface, the planets, the moon, or the interior of a schoolroom, the objects thus seen are said to be **illuminated.**

2. Apparent Position

To be seen, an object need not send light rays directly to the eye, even though light does travel in straight lines. Objects that are behind us, for example, may be seen in a mirror. In this case, the light rays go from the object to the mirror, then from the mirror to the eye. A periscope enables a submarine observer to see over the ocean surface, and arrangements of mirrors enable drivers to see rear exit doors in crowded buses. But whenever we "see," the human eye places the object it sees *in the straight-line direction from which the last rays of light came,* and it is only familiarity with the mirror or periscope that teaches us to interpret the position of the viewed object correctly.

3. Bending of Light

When light rays pass from air into water or vice versa, they change direction and are said to be *bent.* This bending of rays of light in passing from one transparent material to another of different density is called **refraction,** and its effect is to change the apparent position of an object, since the eye sees the object in the direction of the rays of light that strike the eye. A familiar illustration of this effect is the apparent bending of a stick held partly in water. The eye sees the rays from the water part of the stick in a different line from those of the part in the air, and the stick appears to be broken. (See Fig. 40-1.)

4. Bending of Light in the Atmosphere

In the atmosphere light rays change direction when passing through air layers of different density. *Normally, the layers of air nearest the ground are denser than the upper layers,* although on very hot surfaces the lower layers may be less dense than those immediately above them. As a result of the bending that light rays undergo in layers of different density, four very interesting effects of changed apparent position occur.

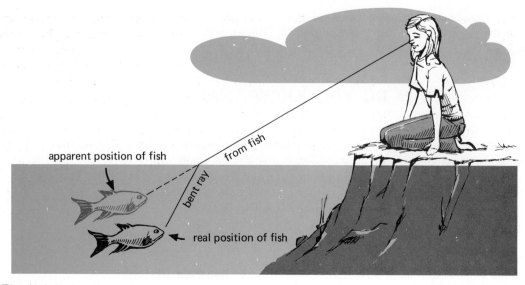

apparent position of fish

bent ray from fish

real position of fish

Fig. 40-1. Refraction of light causes objects in water to appear to be nearer to the surface than they really are.

(a) Sunrise and sunset.   For from two to four minutes (in middle latitudes) before the sun appears above the horizon, its light rays reach the observer because they are bent downward toward the curved surface of the earth. Consequently the sun is "seen" before it actually rises.

In the same way it is "seen" for the same length of time after it sets. The effect is the same for the moon (See Fig. 40-2).

(b) The sun's shape.   The closer that light rays come to the horizon, the more they are bent. Because of this, the lower parts of the sun and

Fig. 40-2. Refraction of the sun's rays by the denser layers of air in the lower atmosphere causes the sun to appear higher than it really is at sunrise and sunset.

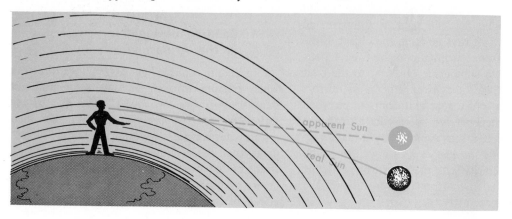

apparent Sun

real Sun

moon disks appear to be raised more than the upper portions, making them appear flattened when they are very low in the sky.

(c) Twinkling of stars. A star appears in the sky as a single "point source" of light. This light, too, is continuously bent as it passes through the atmosphere. Any stirring of atmospheric layers by the wind changes the amount of bending. This, in turn, changes the apparent position of the star at each moment, and makes the star seem to dance up and down in the sky, or "twinkle." The closer the star is to the horizon, the greater is the thickness of air through which its light passes and the more it twinkles. Planets do not twinkle except when they are close to the horizon. Being much closer to the earth, they appear as sizable round disks which give off many rays of light at once, and the changes of position of individual rays are not conspicuous.

(d) Mirages. In the three illustrations just considered the denser air layers were near the earth, and the effect of bending was to create an apparent position higher than the object's real one. In mirages the reverse is true. In hot, desert regions or on hot, concrete highways the *lower air layers* may become so highly heated by contact with the hot surface that they *become much less dense than the upper air layers.* The light rays from distant high objects may bend upward from the lower hot air, and reach the observer's eye as if they came from below the surface. (See Fig. 40-3.) A distant tree or building is then seen upside down as if by reflection, and the illusion of a body of water is created. On a concrete highway such mirage effects make the road look wet. In a desert they may create the illusion of an oasis.

5. Color

Just as an object's apparent position depends on the direction from which its light rays come, so its color depends on the color of the light it sends to the eye. Sunlight, or white light, is a mixture of light of different wavelengths, and each wavelength is a different color. In passing

Fig. 40-3. Over hot surfaces the layers of air nearest the ground are less dense than overlying layers, causing rays of light from tall objects to bend upward, as if being reflected from water.

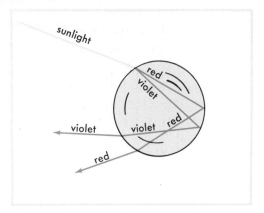

Fig. 40-4. Raindrops refract and reflect sunlight in forming the rainbow.

through layers of different densities the shorter waves are bent more than the longer waves. Consequently, when sunlight passes through a thick triangular glass prism, the different wavelengths are separated sufficiently to produce a band of colors called the *spectrum,* ranging through red, orange, yellow, green, blue, and violet. The red, longest wavelength, is bent least; the violet, shortest wavelength, is bent most. (See Fig. 26-9.)

When white light strikes an object, the object will look white if it reflects all the wavelengths equally well. If it absorbs some of the wavelengths and reflects the rest, it will look colored. If it absorbs *all* the light and reflects none, it will look black. The apparent color of an object also depends on the color of the light that strikes it. If a white object is illuminated by red light alone, it can reflect only red, and it will look red. A red object reflects only red light and absorbs every other color of light. If red light illuminates the red object, it will look red. If green light strikes the red object, the green light is absorbed, nothing is reflected, and the red object looks black.

6. Color in the Sky

(a) The rainbow. During "sun showers" one part of the sky is clear and the sun is visible, while in another part of the sky there are clouds and it is raining. If the sun and the rain are opposite each other, and the sun is low in the sky, an observer with his back to the sun may see a rainbow. The raindrops in the air act like prisms, splitting the sunlight that strikes them into the colors of the spectrum, and reflecting

Fig. 40-5. Rainbow with secondary bow at the right.

Clarke, U.S. Weather Bureau

and refracting this light to the eye of the observer. Because the sun must be low in the sky, rainbows cannot be seen around midday. They are most frequent in late summer afternoons after thundershowers. (See Figs. 40-4 and 40-5.)

(b) Halos. Halos, or "rings," around the moon and sun are produced when rays of light pass through the ice crystals of thin cirrostratus clouds. Here the crystals act like prisms, splitting the light into colors and causing the observer to see a ring that is reddish on the inside and blue on the outside, as in the spectrum. The halo of the moon is fainter than the halo of the sun, and its colors are hardly noticeable. Cirrostratus clouds are usually part of an approaching warm-front cloud system, so seeing a halo may mean that rain or snow will soon follow.

(c) Blue sky and yellow sun. The daytime sky looks blue because blue light is coming from it to the eye of the observer. This is because of "selective scattering." The atmosphere's billions and billions of air molecules scatter light rays. But air molecules interfere more with the passage of the short violet, blue, and green waves than they do with the longer red, orange, and yellow waves. (See Fig. 40-6.) Looking toward the sun, an observer sees a yellow sun because much of the blue light has been screened out by the air molecules. The nearer the sun comes to the horizon, the more air its rays must pass through and the redder it looks. *Looking at the sky away from the sun,* the observer's eye receives the blue waves which have been "scattered" out of the sun's white light, and the sky appears blue. High in the stratosphere, where there are relatively few air molecules to scatter or reflect the sun's light to the eye, the sky looks black, and the stars can be seen in the daytime.

(c) Cloud colors and sunsets. The color of a cloud is that of the light which it sends to the eye. Clouds reflect all colors equally well. During most of the day ordinary sunlight strikes the clouds, causing them to appear white. In early morning or late afternoon, however, the sun is close to the horizon and its light appears to be

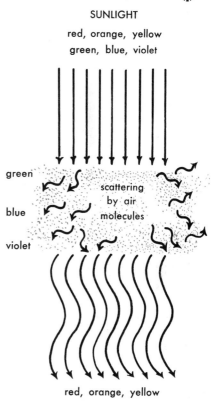

SUNLIGHT

red, orange, yellow
green, blue, violet

green

blue

violet

scattering
by air
molecules

red, orange, yellow

Fig. 40-6. Selective scattering of sunlight by air molecules makes the sky look blue and the sun look orange or yellow.

largely red or orange in color, as explained above. The clouds then reflect these colors and produce varying appearances that depend on their positions, composition, and shapes. At the same time patches of green, blue, or violet sky may be seen through and around the clouds to produce the magnificent patterns so often seen at sunrise or sunset.

7. Twilight

Long after the sun has disappeared below the horizon and day has ended, daylight continues and only gradually fades away into night. This period of fading daylight is known as **twilight.** Similarly, in early morning before sunrise

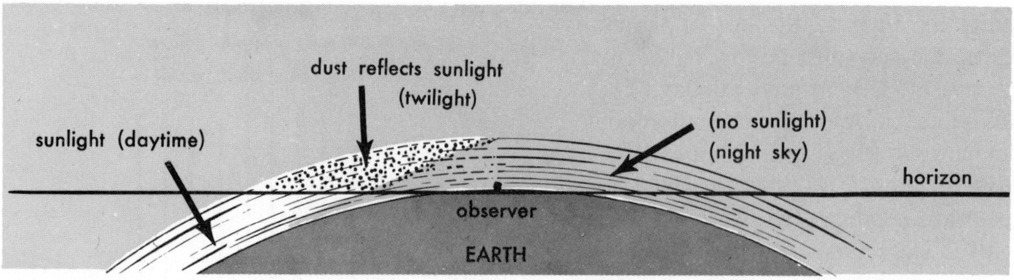

Fig. 40-7. When the sun is a short distance below the observer's horizon, as it is after sunset, its rays still illuminate dust and clouds in the observer's western sky, causing twilight. In similar fashion, twilight is seen in the eastern sky before sunrise.

twilight arrives to break the dark of night, gradually increasing in illumination until the sun appears over the horizon. These periods of evening **dusk** and morning **dawn** are the result of the reflection of sunlight from the dust and clouds in the atmosphere. (See Fig. 40-7.)

TOPIC QUESTIONS

Each topic question refers to the topic of the same number within this chapter.

1. (*a*) Explain what "seeing an object" consists of. (*b*) Distinguish between self-luminous and illuminated objects. Give examples.

2. (*a*) Give an illustration to prove that an object may be seen, even though light rays do not go directly from it to the eye. (*b*) Where does the eye place the object it sees?

3. (*a*) What is the refraction of light? (*b*) What effect does refraction have on apparent position? Explain and illustrate.

4. (*a*) What causes light rays to bend in the atmosphere? Explain how the sun can be seen for a few minutes before it rises and after it sets. (*b*) Why does the sun look flattened when it is low in the sky? (*c*) Why do stars twinkle? Why do planets not twinkle? (*d*) Explain formation of a mirage. In what way is the formation of a mirage different from the other refraction effects of this topic?

5. (*a*) What is the spectrum? (*b*) What determines the color of an object that is illuminated by white light? (*c*) How can a white object look colored? (*d*) How can a colored object look black?

6. (*a*) What causes rainbows? Why are they commonest in late summer afternoons? (*b*) What causes halos? Why do they often mean that precipitation will soon occur? (*c*) Explain how selective scattering makes the sun look yellow, orange, or even red, while making the sky look blue. Why is the sky black at very high altitudes? (*d*) Explain how cloud colors may vary with time of day.

7. What is twilight? What causes it?

GENERAL QUESTIONS

1. Even planets may twinkle when near the horizon. Why?

2. Why does the sun look redder as it approaches the horizon?

3. Why are rainbows unlikely in winter?

4. Sunset colors can be seen in the eastern sky as well as in the west. Why?

5. Twilight lasts longer in high latitudes than in low latitudes. Why?

STUDENT ACTIVITIES

To form the spectrum of sunlight, allow a beam of sunlight to pass through a triangular glass prism. Hold the prism in your hand and rotate it very slowly until you see the spectrum formed clearly on a screen or wall. Observe and note the colors in the spectrum and the order in which they appear. Draw it with pencil on paper and label it. Better yet, color it with crayons.

CHAPTER 41

Factors That Control Climate

HOW DO YOU KNOW THAT . . . ?

Temperature is not the only factor in determining climate. Figure 41-1 is a graph showing the average temperature for each month of the year in Peking, China, and Valdivia, Chile. Which month is warmest in Peking? What is its average temperature? Which month is coldest? What is its temperature? How much is the range of temperature for Peking? Which month is warmest in Valdivia? What is its average temperature? Which month is coldest? What is its temperature? How much is its temperature range? Why does Peking have its warmest weather when Valdivia is having its coldest weather and vice versa? Why are their temperature ranges so different? (See Topics 6, 7.)

1. Average Temperature and Temperature Range

Average temperatures are obtained, like any averages, by adding together two or more observations and dividing the sum by the number of observations. The **average daily temperature** is usually obtained by averaging the highest and lowest temperatures of a day. (For example, a day with a high of 85°F and a low of 65°F has an average of 75°F.) The **average monthly temperature** is the average of all the daily averages of the month. The **average yearly temperature** is usually obtained by averaging the twelve monthly averages.

The **daily temperature range** is the difference between the highest and lowest temperatures of the day. The **yearly temperature range** is the difference between the average of the warmest month and that of the coldest month.

2. Is Climate Average Weather?

We might define climate in simple fashion by calling it "average weather." It is true that the climate of a region is made up of its temperature, moisture, winds, storms, cloudiness, and other weather elements. But averages or totals of these elements, taken by themselves without informative details, give an incomplete and often misleading picture of a place's climate. Let us look at two examples that illustrate this point.

Peking, China, and Valdivia, Chile, have almost identical yearly average temperatures of 53°F, which might lead one to believe that their climates were very much alike. Far from it! A year in Peking includes an icy January averaging 24°F and a hot July averaging 79°F, as compared with Valdivia's mild 46°F and 62°F averages for its coldest and warmest months. In Peking the annual range in temperature is therefore 55°F; in Valdivia it is only 16°F. Certainly their climates are not the same, yet their yearly temperature averages would give such an impression. Similar contrasts exist in the United States between east-coast and west-coast cities, such as New York City and Portland, Oregon, though the differences are not quite as large as in Peking and Valdivia. (See Fig. 41-1.)

Bombay, India, has a yearly rainfall of about 74 inches. Mobile, Alabama, has almost as much rain, about 68 inches. But almost all of Bombay's rain falls in a monsoon season of four summer months, and the rest of the year is practically rainless. In Mobile the rain is distributed through the year, and no month averages less than 3 inches of rain.

In these illustrations climate can hardly be defined accurately as average weather. Perhaps a better definition would be "composite weather." In any event, no climate can be described accurately without going into considerable detail.

3. Climatic Controls

The climate of any region depends on factors called climatic controls. The principal climatic controls include latitude, altitude, prevailing winds, topography, distance from the sea or large lakes, and ocean currents. In this chapter we shall explain how climatic controls determine the two principal elements of climate, temperature and rainfall. In the next chapter we shall describe the principal types of climate that exist on the earth's surface.

FACTORS THAT CONTROL TEMPERATURE

4. How Latitude Controls Temperature

The latitude of a place—its distance from the Equator—has more to do with its temperature characteristics than any other single factor. Latitude helps to determine not only the average yearly temperature of a place but also its daily and yearly ranges of temperature. Let us take a few illustrations.

Suppose you live within 5 degrees or 10 degrees of the Equator—perhaps in Panama or the Congo or northern Brazil. Every day of the year the sun shines for about 12 hours; every night is about 12 hours long. At noontime the sun is never very far from vertical, whether the month is July or January. Your climate is uniformly hot throughout the year, and your average temperature is very high, perhaps about 80°F. There is no summer and no winter; there are only rainy seasons and dry seasons. Your yearly range of temperature is but 3 or 4 degrees. Afternoons are, of course, very hot. Surprisingly, though, the rather long 12-hour nights may become cool by contrast, and the daily temperature range is large enough to make nighttime "the winter of the tropics."

Now move to a middle latitude—40 degrees or 45 degrees from the Equator and almost halfway to the North Pole, perhaps to Chicago or New York City or Montreal. In July you enjoy 15 or 16 hours of strong sunshine daily, and

Fig. 41-1. Although the average yearly temperature of Peking, China, and Valdivia, Chile, are the same, their climates are quite different. Both cities are about the same distance from the Equator.

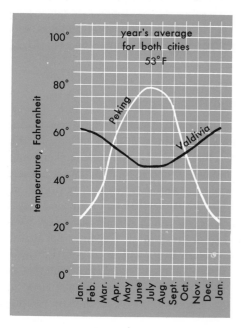

nights are only 8 or 9 hours long. But six months later a weak sun shines only 8 or 9 hours a day. For 15 or 16 hours each night no heat is received, while heat continues to be radiated into space. On the average your yearly temperature is far lower than that of the equatorial latitudes. The annual range of temperature is very large, perhaps as much as 50 degrees.

Now move to the polar regions—to Greenland or Baffinland or Antarctica. Here most of your sunshine comes in a "day" that lasts for many months. Your winter includes an equally long night. The weak sun is never high in the sky, but as it goes completely around the sky each summer day, it stays at nearly the same height all day, and temperatures hardly change for days at a time. The summer is comparatively mild, but the long winter night becomes fearfully cold. In these high latitudes, then, the average annual temperature is very low, the annual temperature range is very large, but the daily temperature range is very small.

Summarizing the relation between latitude and temperature: **the higher the latitude, the lower the average yearly temperature and the larger the yearly temperature range.**

5. Altitude and Temperature

Altitude is height above sea level. Its effect on temperature is similar to that of latitude. Increased altitude means lower temperatures at the average rate of 3½ °F per 1,000 feet. The **higher the altitude, the lower the average yearly temperature.** Mexico City, in the tropics but almost 7,500 feet above sea level, has a cool pleasant climate that is in delightful contrast to the steaming atmosphere of Vera Cruz, at the same latitude but located at sea level. At still higher altitudes, even at the Equator, temperatures can be so low that snow always covers the mountain tops, and glaciers are formed. Mount Chimborazo, more than 20,000 feet high in the Andes Mountains of Ecuador, is only one of many mountain peaks located almost on the Equator, yet in a land of perpetual frost.

6. Land, Sea, and Temperature

Since land gains and loses heat much more quickly than water, land areas tend to have hot summers and cold winters, while sea areas have cooler summers and milder winters. Small islands have climates like those of their surrounding waters, these climates being known as **equable marine climates** (equable means "even" or "uniform.") The interiors of continents, on the other hand, experience greater extremes of temperature, especially in middle latitudes, and are said to have extreme or **continental climates.** Reykjavik, Iceland, 64°N, and Verkhoyansk, Siberia, 68°N, are in nearly the same latitude. Reykjavik is on the south coast of Iceland, and its marine climate has an annual temperature range of only 20°F; Verkhoyansk, deep in the interior of the great Asian land mass, has a continental climate with an annual range of almost 120°F.

Summarizing, **ocean areas have marine climates with a small yearly temperature range; continental interiors have continental climates with a large yearly temperature range.** (See Fig. 41-2.)

7. Prevailing Winds and Temperature

While only small islands can have true marine climates, many continental locations have what is known as a **marine west-coast climate.** This near-marine climate is found in middle latitudes, where the prevailing westerlies carry maritime air masses from the Pacific Ocean to the *west coasts* of North America, South America, and New Zealand, and from the Atlantic Ocean to the British Isles and western Europe. The cities of Portland, Oregon, and London, England, are examples of places with a marine west-coast climate. How far inland does a marine west-coast climate extend?

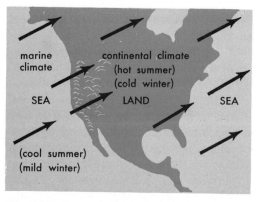

Fig. 41-2. In our belt of prevailing westerlies ocean winds bring marine climates to west coast areas, whereas most of the interior and the east coast have continental climates.

This depends chiefly on the topography. It is usually no farther than the first high mountain range. Beyond the mountains, the continental interiors will have continental climates.

East coasts in middle latitudes do not have marine climates. Because of the prevailing westerlies, most air masses come to the east coasts from the continental interiors to the west of them rather than from the oceans to the east of them. (See Fig. 41-2.) So even though cities like New York and Boston are on the ocean, their climate is continental rather than marine.

To summarize: **in the belts of prevailing westerlies, west coasts have marine climates with cool summers and mild winters; east coasts have continental climates with hot summers and cold winters.**

8. Topography and Temperature

High mountain ranges often keep out winds that might otherwise affect the temperature of a region. For example, the marine climate of the Pacific coast of the United States extends no farther than the west side of the Coast Ranges. On the east side of these mountains, only a short distance from the sea, the Sacramento Valley

and other interior regions have intensely hot summers, with temperatures often going as high as 115°F. Southern Italy owes its balmy climate partly to the fact that cold north winds are kept out by the Alps. In contrast, the level Great Plains of North America allow icy winds to sweep all the way from the Arctic Ocean to the Gulf of Mexico during many a cold wave of winter.

9. Ocean Currents and Temperature

The temperatures of some islands and coastal regions are greatly affected by ocean currents that are considerably warmer or colder than the normal for their latitudes. The effect of such currents is greatest when the prevailing winds blow from them to the land. In one famous example, the prevailing westerlies blow from the warm Gulf Stream to the shores of Iceland, the British Isles, and Scandinavia, making these regions as warm as places many hundreds of miles closer to the Equator. London, England, is about 700 miles nearer the North Pole than Cleveland, Ohio, but its average annual temperature is higher than Cleveland's. As an example of the effect of a cold current, northern Labrador, chilled by the Labrador Current, has a yearly average more than 20 degrees lower than Stockholm, Sweden, in the same latitude! (See the isothermal maps of the world in Chapter 33 for many more illustrations of the effects of ocean currents on temperature.)

10. Summary of Temperature Factors

The factors that control the temperature characteristics of a region may be summarized as follows: (1) In general, the higher the *latitude,* the lower the average annual temperature and the larger the annual temperature range. (2) The higher the *altitude,* the colder the climate.

(3) *Sea or land locations* affect temperature ranges; sea areas have marine climates with small ranges, while land areas have continental climates with large ranges. (4) *The direction of prevailing winds* also affects temperature ranges. When winds blow from large bodies of water, temperature ranges are small; when they blow from large land areas, temperature ranges are larger. (5) *Topography* of the land determines whether winds from distant regions may affect the climate. (6) *Ocean currents* may make the climate of a region warmer or colder than the normal for its latitude.

FACTORS THAT CONTROL RAINFALL

11. Latitude and Rainfall

The climatologist, like the baseball fan, wants to know not only the "final score" or total rainfall for the year but also the "score by innings," or the monthly distribution of the rainfall. Latitude is as important in determining both these features of climate as it is in determining the an-

nual and monthly temperatures. The latitude of a place determines the wind belt it is in, and these belts are largely responsible for the wetness or dryness of the climate. However, wind belts shift during the year. If a place is in a rainy belt such as the doldrums all year, then its rains will fall fairly evenly throughout the year. If it is in a dry belt such as the horse latitudes all year, its lack of rain will persist throughout the year. But places over which both wet and dry belts pass during the year will have wet seasons and dry seasons. The longer the wet belts remain, the longer the rainy season will be. Places nearer the centers of wet belts will have long rainy seasons and short dry ones; places nearer the centers of dry belts will have short rainy seasons and long dry ones.

12. Mountains and Rainfall

It was explained in the chapter on precipitation why the windward sides of high mountains are rainy and the leeward sides are dry. In the belt of trade winds, heavy rains fall on eastern and northern slopes in the Northern Hemisphere, on eastern and southern slopes in the Southern

Fig. 41-3. Windward sides of mountains are rainy; leeward sides are dry. This diagram shows how both the position of the mountain and the direction of the prevailing winds are involved.

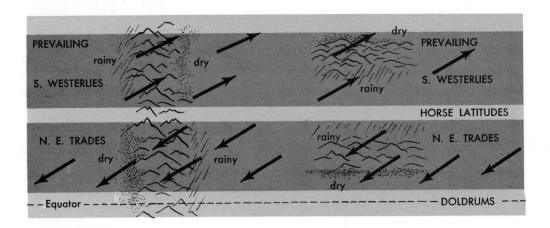

Hemisphere, and on southern and western slopes of the Himalaya Mountains in India at the time of the summer southwest monsoon. These rains are usually seasonal. (See Fig. 41-3.)

In the prevailing westerlies, western slopes will be rainy, but eastern slopes and land extending beyond them will be dry. Dry leeward slopes are said to be in the "rain shadow" of the mountain. Just as an object that casts a shadow is keeping out light, so a mountain that casts a rain shadow is keeping out rain. Great deserts in Nevada, Arizona, and southern California are east of and in the rain shadow of the Sierra Nevada Mountains. On the other hand, the heaviest rains of the United States fall on the windward western slopes of the Coast and Cascade ranges of Washington and Oregon.

Winds descending the leeward slopes of mountains become heated by compression and warm up at the dry-adiabatic rate of 5½ °F per 1,000 feet. (See Fig. 37–11.) A descent of 5,500 feet will produce a temperature rise of about 30°F. When the resulting warm, dry winds blow down the eastern slopes of the Rockies or the northern slopes of the Alps in Switzerland, they cause rapid melting and evaporation of the snows in the valleys at the base of the mountains. These winds are called **chinooks** (chih *nooks*) in the Rockies and **foehns** (ferns) in the Alps and other parts of the world. The sudden arrival of the foehn has been known to raise the temperature as much as 40°F in 15 minutes. The chinook and the foehn are usually welcome because they make winters milder and springs earlier. They clear pastures for cattle grazing and fields for planting many weeks before this happens in comparable locations on the opposite side of the mountains. On the other hand, when the foehn blows steadily for several days, houses and fields become so dry that special precautions must be taken against the threat of widespread fire, and mountain snows may melt so rapidly as to cause great avalanches.

13. Distance from the Sea

Nearness to the sea is no guarantee of sufficient rainfall. The desert of Chile and Peru, for example, is located next to the Pacific Ocean, yet it is one of the driest regions in the world. Its southeast trade winds come from the dry interior, and to make matters worse, it is located on the leeward western side of the great Andes Mountains. But where winds do blow from the sea, rains are likely to be heavier nearer the ocean than farther inland and heavier near warmer parts of the oceans. In eastern United States total yearly rainfall is greatest along the Gulf and Atlantic coasts and decreases inland and northward. (See Fig. 41-4.) Continental interiors are likely to have more rain in summer than in winter. The warm summer winds can carry more moisture, and convectional showers occur more often in summer.

14. Ocean Currents and Fogs

The most striking moisture effect of ocean currents is the production of *advection fogs* (see Chapter 36) along coastal regions. The frequent winter fogs of England and Scotland can be attributed largely to the fact that warm, moist Gulf Stream air, carried over the British Isles by the prevailing westerlies, is cooled over the land. The summer fogs of the New England coast are formed when warm winds from the south are cooled over New England's cold coastal waters. The fogs of Newfoundland occur when warm Gulf Stream air blows over the cold Labrador Current. The summer fogs of the Pacific coasts of the United States, Peru, and northern Chile are caused by the blowing of warm ocean winds over cold, upwelling coastal waters.

15. Summary of Rainfall Factors

The factors that control the rainfall features of climate may be summarized as follows: (1)

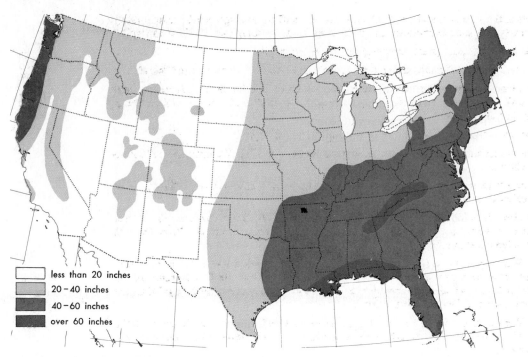

Fig. 41-4. Generalized map showing average annual precipitation of the United States. In the Far West, distribution of rainfall is controlled largely by mountain ranges. In the interior and eastern parts of the country, rainfall increases with nearness to the Atlantic Ocean and the Gulf of Mexico.

less than 20 inches
20 – 40 inches
40 – 60 inches
over 60 inches

The *latitude* of a place determines its wind belts and air masses, which are of primary importance in determining total rainfall and its seasonal occurrence. (2) *Location on the windward or leeward side of a mountain* will mean either more or less rain than the normal for the place's latitude. (3) Where prevailing winds blow from the sea, the *areas closest to the sea* generally receive the most rain. (4) Where *ocean currents* are much warmer or colder than adjoining land or water a high percentage of cloudiness and fog is likely to be found.

TOPIC QUESTIONS

Each topic question refers to the topic of the same number within this chapter.

1. (*a*) Explain how a city's average daily temperature, average monthly temperature, and average yearly temperature are calculated. (*b*) Define daily temperature range. (*c*) Define yearly temperature range.

2. (*a*) Show that two cities may have the same average temperature but markedly different climates. (*b*) Show that two cities may have nearly the same yearly rainfall but markedly different climates.

3. Name six important climatic controls.

4. Explain the relation between a place's latitude and its average yearly temperature, its yearly range in temperature, and its daily range in temperature. Give examples.

5. How does altitude affect temperature? Give examples.

6. How do marine climates differ from continental ones in temperature? Why?

7. (a) How do prevailing winds determine whether a climate is marine or continental? (b) How do the climates of the east and west coasts of the United States differ in temperature?

8. How may topography affect temperature? Give examples.

9. Give examples to show the temperature effects of the Gulf Stream and the Labrador Current.

10. Name six factors that may affect the temperature characteristics of a climate. State the effect of each.

11. (a) How does latitude determine a place's rainfall? (b) Why do some places have rains throughout the year? (c) Why are some places dry all year? (d) Why do some places have wet and dry seasons?

12. (a) Which are the rainy sides of mountains in the trade-wind belts? in the westerlies? (Use compass directions.) (b) Which are the dry sides? (Use compass directions.) (c) What is meant by the rain shadow of a mountain? (d) What are chinook winds? Describe their effects.

13. (a) Why is closeness to the sea no guarantee of rain? (b) How is closeness to the sea related to rainfall? (c) Why do interiors usually have more rain in summer than in winter?

14. What is the principal moisture effect of ocean currents? Illustrate.

15. Name the four factors that are most important in controlling the rainfall features of a climate and summarize the effect of each.

GENERAL QUESTIONS

1. Why is the daily temperature range likely to be greater in mountain regions than at sea level?

2. How does the climate of an equatorial mountain differ from that of a mountain in middle latitudes? Use Mount Chimborazo in Ecuador and Pike's Peak in Colorado as specific examples.

3. In the doldrums belt temperature ranges are small in the interior as well as in coastal areas. Why is the effect of land or sea less important here than in higher latitudes?

4. Why does the Gulf Stream have little effect on the temperatures of eastern United States? Why does the Labrador Current have so great an effect on the temperatures of Labrador?

5. Why should the rains of the western slopes of the Coast and Cascade ranges be so much heavier than those of the Rocky and Appalachian mountains?

6. Why does the chinook come down so much warmer than it was when it started? (Look up the moist-adiabatic lapse rate in Chapter 36, Topic 17.)

CHAPTER 42

Climates of the World

HOW DO YOU KNOW THAT . . . ?

Your locality has certain climatic characteristics. Examine Fig. 42-1. Which of these broad climatic zones do you live in? How is this zone defined in Topic 2? Do you agree that your locality meets the temperature limits given for this zone? Now examine Fig. 42-3 and again try to locate the specific zone in which you live. Topic 5 will tell you what name the symbol stands for. When you have obtained the name of your zone, find the Topic in which the zone is described and read it carefully. Does the description fit your climate? In which respects is it accurate for your climate? What specific differences or details of your climate can you point out that are not covered by the description in the text?

1. Classifying Climates

There are no two places that have exactly the same climate. But many places in different parts of the world have similar climates. Because of these similarities, climatologists find it useful and efficient to classify climates.

2. Isotherms as Boundaries of Climatic Zones

The two most important features of a climate are its temperature and its precipitation. Modern classifications of climates usually begin by dividing the world into three climatic zones on the basis of average temperatures. To do this, isotherms are used as boundary lines. (Isotherms, you recall, are lines joining points having the same temperature for any specified period of time.) The three zones of climate defined by the isotherms usually include *tropical climates* that are hot or warm all year long, *middle latitude climates* that have both summer and winter seasons, and *polar climates* with no real summer at all. (See Fig. 42-1.)

The **zone of tropical climates** is defined as the part of the earth in which **even the coldest month** has an average temperature of at least 64°F. It therefore extends from the Equator in both directions, north and south, until it reaches the 64°F isotherm for each hemisphere's coldest month (January for the Northern Hemisphere, July for the Southern Hemisphere). The Equator's average temperature for the year (at sea level) is about 80°F.

The **zone of middle latitude climates** is defined as the part of the earth in which the **coldest month's average is below 64°F** and the **warmest month's average is at least 50°F.** It extends in each hemisphere from the zone of tropical climates toward the Poles, as far as the 50°F isotherm for the warmest month (July in the north, January in the south).

The **zone of polar climates** is defined as the part of the earth in which **even the warmest month's average is below 50°F.** It extends in each hemisphere from the zone of middle latitude climates to the Pole. The 50°F warmest-month isotherm roughly indicates the poleward limit of tree growth, so trees are rare in the zone of polar climates.

High mountains and high plateaus in any region may be so much colder than surrounding

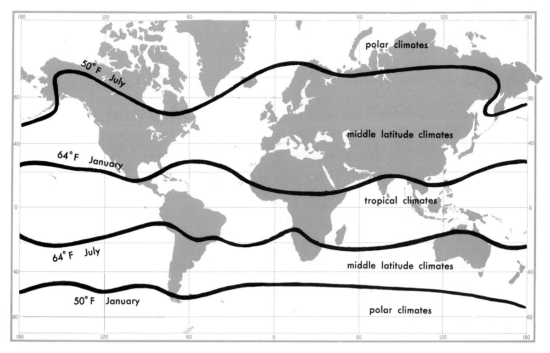

Fig. 42-1. Dividing the world into three kinds of climatic zones on the basis of temperature.

lowlands as to have markedly different climates. For this reason climatologists usually provide a fourth classification of **highland climates.**

3. Subdividing the Three Climatic Zones

Although all parts of the zone of tropical climates share the characteristic of high average temperatures throughout the year, their climates are far from the same. In one place the rainfall may be 100 inches a year, with every month rainy. In another place there may be only 40 inches of rain, and half the year may be dry. In still a third place it may not rain at all for two or three years. Each of these places represents a different type of climate, though they are all tropical. Such differences are also found in the middle latitude and polar zones. To provide for them in this classification, the climatologists

subdivide the three principal zones, largely on the basis of *total yearly precipitation* and the *distribution of the precipitation through the year.*

4. Climate and Natural Vegetation

The kind of natural vegetation found in any part of the earth's surface is closely related to the climate. In fact, some climatic subdivisions are named for their natural vegetation. Examples are *equatorial rainforest, tropical savanna, middle latitude grassland,* and *arctic tundra.*

Temperature and rainfall are obviously important in determining whether the natural vegetation of a region will be *tropical forest, middle latitude forest, grassland, desert scrub,* or *arctic tundra.* Climatologists have learned that the kind of natural vegetation depends a good deal on the *balance of rainfall over evaporation,* not

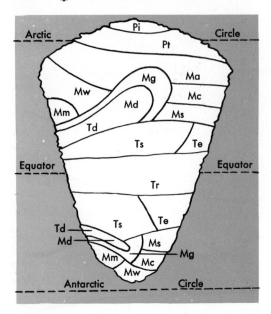

Fig. 42-2. Location of most of the climatic types on an "ideal" continent. See Topic 5 for meaning of abbreviations.

simply on the total rainfall. Evaporation, of course, varies with temperature. In a cool climate only half as much rain may be needed to grow trees as in a tropical climate. Heavy rainfall with little evaporation, for example, is largely responsible for the great forests of our Pacific Northwest.

In forests more rain falls than evaporates. In grasslands and deserts the reverse is true—evaporation equals or exceeds precipitation and trees cannot grow because of insufficient water. In the arctic regions trees cannot grow because the temperatures are too low, even where there may be sufficient water. Mosses, lichens, and sedges grow in the arctic tundra wherever poor drainage keeps the ground wet, but trees will not grow.

5. Outline of Our Classification of Climates

The following outline shows the climatic subdivisions into which we shall divide the principal climatic zones we defined in Topic 3. Figure 42-2 shows where each type of climate might be located on an "ideal" continent with a large land mass north of the Equator (like Eurasia or North America) and a smaller area south of the Equator (like South America). Figure 42-3 is a map of the world that shows the approximate locations of the different climatic types. Abbreviations are used on both maps.

Zone of Tropical Climates

T_R Equatorial rainforest
T_E Tropical east coast
T_M Tropical monsoon
T_S Tropical savanna
T_D Tropical desert

Zone of Middle Latitude Climates

M_M Mediterranean (dry subtropical)
M_W Marine west coast
M_S Humid subtropical
M_C Humid continental
M_G Middle latitude grassland
M_D Middle latitude desert
M_A Subarctic

Zone of Polar Climates

P_T Tundra
P_I Icecap

Highland Climates H

TROPICAL CLIMATES

6. The Tropical Rainy Climates

Three of the subdivisions of tropical climates are rainy climates in which the year's rainfall may range from about 40 to more than 400 inches. Warm, moist air masses from the tropical oceans carry the moisture over the lands. In areas that are close to the Equator and in the doldrums all year, every month may be rainy. Farther from the Equator rains may come only in summer when the doldrums arrive or when the summer monsoon winds bring moist air from the oceans over the lands. The tropical

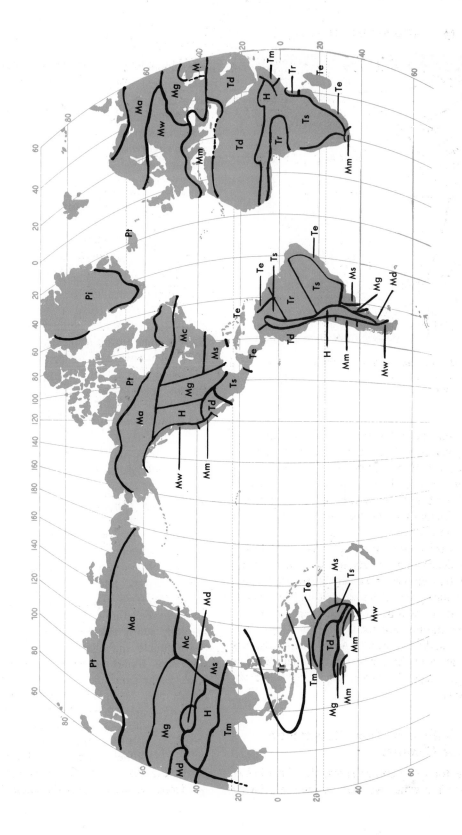

Fig. 42-3. Approximate location of climatic regions of the world, as classified in Topic 5.

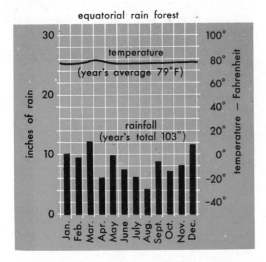

Fig. 42-4. This graph shows both average temperature and average rainfall for each month in Iquitos, Peru, in the Amazon Valley. The scale for the temperature line graph is at the right. The scale for the rainfall bar graph is at the left. The graphs show the equatorial rainforest climate to be uniformly hot and rainy.

Fig. 42-5. Tropical rainforest in Ecuador.

rainy climates include the equatorial rainforest, the tropical east coast, and the tropical monsoon climates.

In the descriptions that follow, all temperatures refer to elevations fairly close to sea level, unless otherwise specified. Higher elevations are colder.

7. Equatorial Rainforest

The equatorial rainforest climate is found in the Amazon Valley of South America, the Congo Basin and Guinea coast of Africa, and in Malaya and the islands of Indonesia. All of these regions straddle the Equator, thereby receiving nearly vertical rays of the sun and nearly equal day and night throughout the year. Daily temperatures range from about 70°F to 90°F. The average temperature for the year is close to 80°F, and the warmest and coldest months may differ by only a few degrees. Rain falls almost daily in afternoon thundershowers, and annual precipitation may total 100 inches. Rainfall in the Congo, however, is lighter than in Indonesia and the Amazon Valley, because the lofty East Africa Plateau acts as a partial barrier to winds from the Indian Ocean.

Tropical rainforest vegetation is known as the **selva.** Here tall, broadleaf evergreen trees and heavy vines form a dense foliage that almost completely shades the floor of the forest. In the absence of sunlight few shrubs and grasses grow, and the undergrowth consists chiefly of ferns. Dense **jungle** undergrowth is likely to develop only in abandoned clearings or along sunny river banks.

Valuable mahogany, rosewood, and ebony trees are found scattered through the selva. Rice, sugar cane, cacao (cocoa), bananas, and rubber may be grown on cultivated land. (See Figs. 42-4 and 42-5.)

8. Tropical East Coast

Increasing distance from the Equator leads to regions over which the rainy doldrums and the trade winds alternate during the year. On the east coasts of the continents there is no dry season, because the trades blow from the east and bring moist, tropical air from the oceans to these coasts. Included are the east coasts of Brazil, Central America, the West Indies, southern Florida, British, French, and Dutch Guiana, and Madagascar and Mozambique in Africa.

Because of the greater distance from the Equator, the average annual temperature is lower, and the yearly temperature range is larger. Rainfall is usually heavier during the summer doldrums period, but all months are rainy. Total annual rainfall is much less than in the equatorial rainforest, with most areas averaging about 40 inches. Natural vegetation is like that of the rainforest, except that with less rainfall trees are likely to be smaller and farther apart, and jungle undergrowth is more likely to develop on the sunnier forest floor. Coffee, cacao, and sugar cane are cultivated. (See Fig. 42-6.)

9. Tropical Monsoon

The principal regions of tropical monsoon climate include India, Ceylon, Pakistan, and southeast Asia, including Burma, Thailand, Laos, Cambodia, Vietnam, and south China. Here in summer the warm, wet monsoon brings heavy rains from the Indian Ocean and the South China Sea from June through September or October. From November to April the winter monsoon brings cool, dry air from the cold north Asian interior. In spring the temperatures rise steadily, reaching their peak in May, just before the wet monsoon begins.

The tropical monsoon climate differs from the tropical east coast climate in having distinct wet and dry seasons and a somewhat larger annual temperature range. Yearly rainfall averages about 50 inches, and may go as high as the world record—457 inches at Cherrapunji in northern India. (See Fig. 42-7.)

The natural vegetation of the monsoon areas depends largely upon the total rainfall and

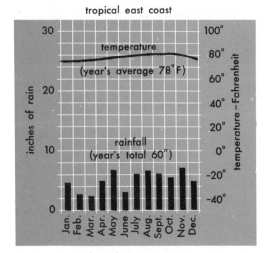

Fig. 42-6. *The tropical east coast climate of San Juan, Puerto Rico. See Topic 8.*

ranges from grassland to dense forest. In most areas of average rainfall the surface is covered by forests similar to those of the tropical east coast regions, in which a dense undergrowth of shrubs and grasses covers the forest floor between the uncrowded trees.

Fig. 42-7. *The tropical monsoon climate of Calcutta, India. See Topic 9.*

Unit IX THE EARTH AND ITS CLIMATES

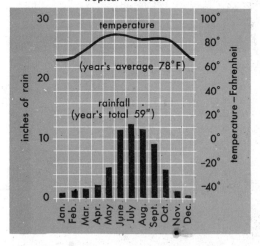

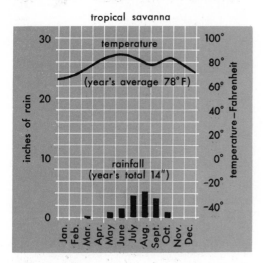

Fig. 42-8. The tropical savanna climate with a short rainy season is found in El Obeid, about 13°N latitude in Sudan, Africa. See Topic 10.

Fig. 42-9. Rhinoceroses in the tropical savanna region of South Africa.

South African Railways

Cultivated crops include rice, millet, and jute. Tea is grown in the highlands of Ceylon and of Assam in India.

10. Tropical Savanna

The tropical savanna climate is found in the same latitudes as the tropical east coast climate, but it includes the interiors and west coasts of these latitudes. Here, too, the rainy doldrums and the trade winds alternate, but the trades come from interior deserts rather than from the oceans, and they bring no rain. The result is a climate with rainy summers and dry winters, similar to that of the tropical monsoon, but with much less rainfall. Places close to the Equator are in the doldrums a good part of the year. They have a long rainy season and a small annual temperature range. As distance from the Equator increases, the rainy season becomes shorter, the total rainfall decreases, and the annual temperature range becomes much larger. Average temperature for the year, however, is still nearly as high as in equatorial regions. (See Fig. 42-8.)

Savannas are tropical grasslands in which occasional thickets of small trees grow among great expanses of thick, tall tropical grasses. Forests are found only along river banks where sufficient water is available for tree growth. Regions of savanna climates include the interiors of Brazil and Venezuela in South America, the interior of Africa between the Sahara and the Congo and south of the Congo, and the north interior of Australia. The African savanna is famous for its elephants, lions, antelopes, giraffes, and other game animals. (See Fig. 42-9.)

Cattle ranching is the principal industry of the savannas of Brazil, Venezuela, and Australia.

11. Tropical Deserts

The tropical deserts lie on the poleward sides of the zone of tropical climates. They are always covered by either the dry descending air of the horse latitudes or by trade winds blowing from dry continental interiors. The result is a climate with almost no rainfall and with exceedingly high summer and daytime temperatures. (The world's high temperature of 136°F was recorded at Azizia in Libya in September, 1922.) Daily temperature ranges are high, however, because of the clear skies which permit rapid loss of heat by radiation at night. A nighttime low of 70°F may follow a daytime high of 120°F. Yearly temperature ranges are also large, and may exceed 40°F. (See Figs. 42-10 and 42-11.)

Tropical deserts include the great desert belt of North Africa (Sahara Desert, Libyan Desert), the Arabian Desert, deserts in Iran and Iraq, the Sonora Desert of northwest Mexico, the Mojave Desert of southwestern United States, the Kalahari Desert of southwest Africa, the desert of central Australia, and the coastal Atacama Desert of Peru and northern Chile. In the Atacama Desert cool winds from the upwelling cold ocean waters of the Peru Current create a cool marine climate without rain, although fogs are common.

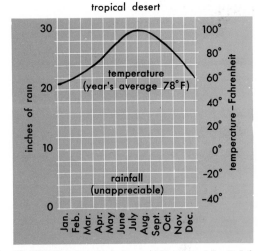

Fig. 42-10. The tropical desert climate of In-Salah in the Sahara Desert of Algeria at about 27°N latitude. See Topic 11.

Tropical deserts may go without rain for years. Iquique, Chile, has a record of 14 years without measurable rainfall. The rare rains of tropical deserts usually come in violent thundershowers that may send flash floods racing down

Fig. 42-11. Tropical desert in Morocco, North Africa.

Fig. 42-12. Oasis de Gabes, in the desert of Tunisia, North Africa.

dry stream courses within a matter of minutes.

Desert vegetation usually includes a variety of cacti, shrubs, and coarse grasses that grow in widely separated clumps. In some deserts shifting sand dunes or rocky pavements support almost no vegetation, except around the rare gardenlike spots known as oases. An oasis is either a spring which receives its water from an artesian formation or a river running through the desert. In both cases the source of the water is heavy rainfall in distant mountains. (See Fig. 42-12.)

MIDDLE LATITUDE CLIMATES

12. Middle Latitude Climates in General

These climates have been defined as having average temperatures of *at least 50°F* in their warmest month and *less than 64°F* in their coldest month. The zone of middle latitude climates

lies principally in the belt of the prevailing westerly winds. Its weather is highly changeable as it is invaded periodically by both tropical air masses and polar air masses. Annual temperature ranges are generally much larger than in the tropics, and precipitation is largely the result of the passage of fronts and cyclones.

Topic 5 and Figure 42-2 show seven types of middle latitude climate. The western sides of the continents have *Mediterranean climates* nearer the Equator and *marine west coast climates* farther from the Equator. The eastern halves of the continents have *humid subtropical climates in the south* and *humid continental climates in the north*. In the interiors of the continents the *middle latitude deserts* appear as poleward extensions of the tropical deserts, and the *middle latitude grasslands* lie between the deserts and more humid types of climate. Moving poleward, we find a broad belt of *subarctic climate* making up the northernmost part of the Northern Hemisphere zone of middle latitude climates. In the Southern Hemisphere there is no such zone, because no continental land mass is found in subarctic latitudes.

Fig. 42-13. The Mediterranean climate of Los Angeles, California. See Topic 13.

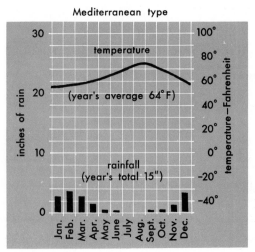

Fig. 42-14. Gathering dates in Saudi Arabia. Dates are a typical fruit of Mediterranean climates.

Standard Oil Co. (N.J.)

13. Mediterranean Climate

The Mediterranean climate type, also known as the *dry-summer subtropical* type, is marked by warm or hot, dry summers and by mild, rainy winters. The nearly rainless summer weather is explained largely by the presence of the horse latitudes with their warm, dry descending air masses. In winter the prevailing westerlies carry maritime air masses over these regions, bringing rains in their fronts and cyclonic storms. Annual rainfall may be as low as 10 inches nearest the Equator, but it increases poleward to more than 25 inches. (See Fig. 42-13.)

The world's principal regions of Mediterranean climate lie approximately between latitudes 30° and 40°. They include southern California, central Chile, the southwestern corner of South Africa, southwestern and southeastern Australia, and the Mediterranean Sea margins of southern Europe and North Africa. In Chile and California the Mediterranean climate extends inland only as far as the high Andes and Sierra Nevada mountains, but in the Mediterranean Sea region it reaches to the easternmost shores of the Mediterranean. Coastal areas of Mediterranean climate are decidedly cooler in summer than areas even a short distance inland, where tropical desert temperatures are likely to be found.

The natural vegetation of Mediterranean regions takes two forms. One is a forest of scattered low trees, shrubs, and bunch grass. The other is a dense growth of shrubs and grasses with few trees or none at all. In California this dense growth is called **chaparral.** With the aid of irrigation, great wine, fruit, and vegetable industries thrive in southern California, Mediterranean Europe, and other areas of Mediterranean climate. Grapes, olives, figs, and dates are typical Mediterranean fruits. (See Fig. 42-14.)

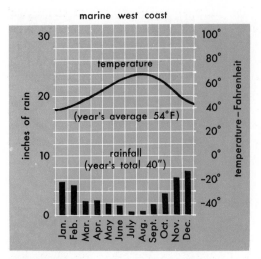

marine west coast

Fig. 42-15. The marine west coast climate of Portland, Oregon. See Topic 14.

Fig. 42-16. Giant redwood trees flourish in the cool rainy forest of northern coastal California, a region of marine west coast climate. (Bull Creek Flat State Park, Humboldt County.)

U.S. Forest Service

14. Marine West Coast Climate

Continuing away from the Equator along the west coasts of the continents, we find the Mediterranean climate gradually changing until it passes into the marine west coast type. Here the horse latitude highs do not reach even in summer, and the climate is controlled for most of the year by moist air masses carried in from the oceans by the prevailing westerlies. The result is an equable marine climate, with mild winters and cool summers, though heat waves may occur with the invasion of occasional tropical air masses.

Precipitation results from the passage of middle latitude cyclones, and occurs in all months of the year, with a distinct peak in fall and winter when cyclones are stronger and more frequent. Winter skies are almost always foggy or overcast. The heaviest rainfall occurs on the windward western slopes of coastal mountain ranges such as the Olympic Mountains of Washington. Here the heaviest precipitation in the United States may exceed 100 inches of rain annually. (See Fig. 42-15.)

Marine west coast climates are found in the coastal regions of northern California, Oregon, Washington, British Columbia, and the Alaskan panhandle; in northwestern Europe, including the British Isles and Norway; in southern Iceland; and in southern Chile and southern New Zealand. Vast coniferous evergreen forests of giant redwoods, Douglas fir, cedar, and spruce grow in the North Pacific coastal areas of North America, making one of the great lumbering regions of the world. (See Fig. 42-16.) Where forests have been cleared away, it is possible to grow potatoes, sugar beets, truck vegetables, apples, and grains. In northwestern Europe grass is grown for the raising of dairy cattle.

15. Humid Subtropical Climate

Except in the Mediterranean Sea region itself, the lands that have Mediterranean climates

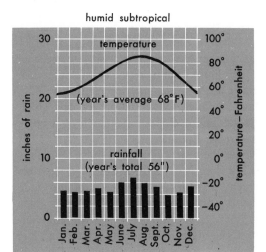

humid subtropical

Fig. 42-17. The humid subtropical climate of New Orleans, Louisiana. See Topic 15.

The principal regions of humid subtropical climate are southeastern and southcentral United States, southern Brazil, northeastern Argentina, Uruguay, southeastern China, southern Japan, and part of Australia's east coast. Forests are abundant in this warm, rainy climate, and pine forests are common in southeastern United States. (See Fig. 42-18.) Cotton, tobacco, corn, and rice are important crops grown in the humid subtropics.

16. Humid Continental Climate

North of the humid subtropical regions, to about 50°N latitude, large areas of North America, Europe, and Asia have humid continental climates. These climates are marked by cold winters and hot summers, sharp cyclonic weather

are found almost exclusively on the western sides of the continents. In generally the same latitudes, but *mainly on the eastern sides of the continents,* lie the lands of wet subtropical climate. In the United States they extend from the Atlantic Ocean westward to about the 100th meridian and northward from the Gulf of Mexico to about 38°N.

The humid subtropical climate differs from the Mediterranean climate in several important respects. It has *no dry season, and more rain falls in summer than in winter. Total yearly rainfall is usually between 30 and 60 inches,* with rainfall decreasing inland and westward. Skies are not quite so sunny, the weather is often oppressively humid, and summers are hot. Although winters are generally mild, cold waves and killing frosts are frequent. (See Fig. 42-17.)

Summer rainfall comes largely from thunderstorms that develop in maritime tropical air masses. Hurricanes or typhoons are occasional visitors in late summer and early fall. Winter precipitation is caused mainly by fronts and cyclones.

Fig. 42-18. Pine forest in the wet subtropical climate of southern Arkansas.

U.S. Forest Service

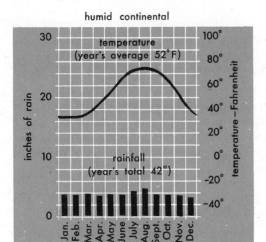

humid continental

Fig. 42-19. The humid continental climate of New York City. See Topic 16.

changes, winter blizzards and cold waves, sultry summer heat waves, and large annual temperature ranges that increase inland and poleward.

Annual precipitation ranges from about 20 inches in the drier, interior sections to about 45 inches in coastal areas. More rain falls in summer than in winter. Summer rains are largely due to thundershowers in maritime tropical air, as in the humid subtropics. Tornadoes occur, especially in the hotter interior regions of North America. Winter precipitation comes chiefly with fronts and cyclones, and much of it comes as snow. (See Fig. 42-19.)

Where the yearly rainfall is more than about 30 inches, forests of both broadleaved trees and evergreens are found. Where the rainfall is under 30 inches, prairie grass grows. Corn, wheat, barley, oats, and rye are important cultivated crops. (See Fig. 42-20.) Beef cattle and pigs are raised in some areas. Elsewhere the dairy industry may predominate.

Most of the United States east of the 100th meridian and north of the 38th parallel has this climate, with broad variations from south to north and from interior to seacoast. Here are much of the Prairies, the North Central States, the Middle Atlantic States, and New England. Southeastern Canada, northern China, northern Japan, southeastern Siberia, and the great plains

Fig. 42-20. A cornfield on the prairies of Iowa, in the drier phase of humid continental climate.

Iowa Development Commission

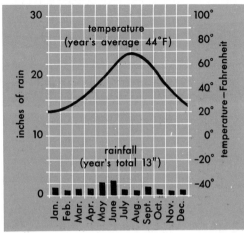

Fig. 42-21. The middle latitude grassland climate of Helena, Montana. See Topic 17.

U.S. Forest Service

Fig. 42-22. Bluebunch wheatgrass on the Sheep Station Range in Idaho.

of central Europe also have this climate. Chicago, St. Louis, and St. Paul are typical of its more extreme interior phase. Although New York City and Boston represent the slightly modified phase typical of the east coast, their climate too is largely controlled by air masses from the western interior because of the prevailing westerly circulation in these latitudes.

17. Middle Latitude Grassland and Desert

Between the Mediterranean and marine west coast regions to the west, and the humid subtropical and humid continental regions to the east, lie the middle latitude grasslands and deserts. The grasslands have an annual rainfall of about 10 to 20 inches. The desert rainfall is less than 10 inches, averaging 5 inches or less in most places. In both grassland and desert the climate is controlled largely by continental tropical air masses in summer and by continental polar or arctic air masses in winter. The aridity of these regions is due to their great distance from the oceans and their position leeward of

mountain ranges. Most of the precipitation falls in late spring and summer. (See Fig. 42-21.)

Grasslands are found in the Great Plains of the United States, the western prairies of Canada, the steppes of central Siberia, the steppes of the Ukraine, the pampas of Argentina, and in southern Australia. The Northern Hemisphere grasslands have cold winters and warm to hot summers typical of the continental interiors in which they lie. (See Fig. 42-22.) The Southern Hemisphere grasslands, however, are relatively close to the ocean because of the narrowness of South America in their latitudes. This gives them a marine climate with cool summers and mild, frost-free winters. Middle latitude grasslands support great herds of beef cattle on the Great Plains of North America and the *pampas* of Argentina and sheep on the *downs* of Australia. Wheat is grown on cleared grasslands.

Middle latitude deserts are found in the Great Basin of the United States, in Patagonia in South America, and in the great Gobi Desert of Mongolia and China. As in the middle latitude grasslands, winters are cold and summers are warm to hot, except in Patagonia's marine

Fig. 42-23. Sagebrush desert in Nevada.

climate. Natural vegetation consists chiefly of bunch grasses and widely scattered shrubs such as the sagebrush and creosote bush of the United States. (See Fig. 42-23.) Great bare sand dune areas may also be found in parts of middle latitude deserts.

18. Subarctic Climate

Most of Alaska and northern Canada, most of Europe north of 60°, and almost all of Siberia lie in this region of most extreme continental climate. North of 66½° (the Arctic Circle) is the "land of the midnight sun" in summer and of no sun at all for weeks or even months in winter. Phenomenal temperature ranges result from this great seasonal difference in solar radiation. Deep in the northeastern interior of the earth's greatest land mass, the city of Verkhoyansk, 68°N latitude in Siberia, holds the world record for annual temperature range, with a difference of about 120°F between the *averages* of July and January! Winters are fiercely cold and very long. Summers are warm but very brief. (See Fig. 42-24.)

Annual precipitation is less than 20 inches, most of it coming during summer in fronts and

cyclones. Winter precipitation is very light, for at this time the great Canadian and Siberian highs control the weather with their masses of dry descending air. Stunted evergreen forests are the principal plant growth. The principal occupations are lumbering for pulpwood, mining, and trapping.

Fig. 42-24. The subarctic climate of Verkhoyansk, Siberia, holds the world record for annual temperature range. See Topic 18.

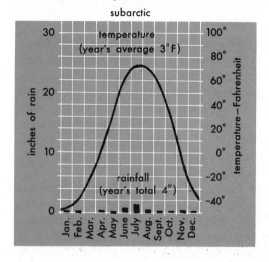

POLAR AND HIGHLAND CLIMATES

19. Polar Climates in General; Tundra Climate

The polar climates cover those parts of the world in which not even the warmest month averages 50°F, and trees do not grow. For the most part they include areas beyond the Arctic and Antarctic Circles, subdivided into **tundra** and **icecap** according to whether the warmest month is above or below 32°F.

Broad northern strips of North America and Siberia and narrow coastal strips of Greenland and Antarctica form the lands of *tundra* climate. Winters are dark and long and bitterly cold, but in summer the sun is warm enough to melt the frost in a few upper feet of the otherwise frozen ground. Slight summer rains combine with the melted frost to support a tundra vegetation of sedges, mosses, and lichens on a wet and muddy surface. The tundra is the home of the reindeer, the musk ox, and the Eskimo. (See Figs. 42-25 and 42-26.)

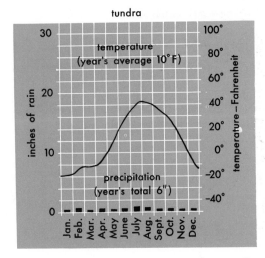

Fig. 42-25. The tundra climate of Point Barrow, Alaska. See Topic 19.

20. Icecap Climate

Most of Greenland and Antarctica are always covered by the ice and snow of great icecaps or continental glaciers. Even in the warmest month the average temperature is below 32°F,

Fig. 42-26. Aerial photograph of tundra in northwestern Canada.

Royal Canadian Air Force Photo

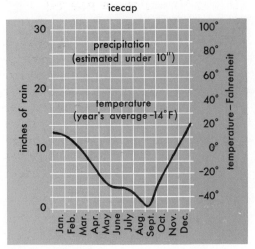

Fig. 42-27. *The icecap climate of interior Antarctica. See Topic 20.*

and the snow never melts enough to expose the earth beneath it. Precipitation, always in the form of fine dry snow, is very light. Its origin is cyclonic. The icecaps, completely uninhabited, are deserts even more desolate than those in the tropics. (See Figs. 42-27 and 42-28.)

For the entire winter of 1957 the United States South Pole station, 9,200 feet high on the Antarctic Plateau, recorded an average temperature of 73° *below zero Fahrenheit.* On August 24, 1960, Soviet scientists stationed at Vostok, 11,500 feet above sea level, recorded a temperature of −127°F. It was the lowest temperature ever recorded at the earth's surface. But not all of Antarctica is either so high or so cold. Little America, 100 feet above sea level, has an average yearly temperature of about −10°F. Wilkes

Fig. 42-28. *Crevassed surface of the Greenland icecap.*

French Embassy Press and Information Service

Fig. 42-29. *The highland climate of Quito, Ecuador, resembles the tropical equatorial climate of its lowland neighbors in uniformity of temperature and precipitation, but it is much cooler and somewhat less rainy. Quito is 9,350 feet above sea level. See Topic 21.*

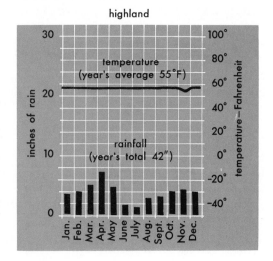

Station on the coast of Antarctica's most northerly location (farthest from the South Pole) is "moderated" by the ocean into a comparatively mild marine climate. Its average yearly temperature is +17°F, and its winters are milder than Nebraska's!

21. Highland Climates

Increase in altitude causes a drop in temperature at an average rate of 1°F for 300 feet. In the hot tropics such modifications of climate are usually very desirable, and the highlands of India, Mexico, and Central America, for example, are favored habitations. (See Fig. 42-29.) In middle latitudes the cooler mountain regions with their clearer air and brighter sunshine are very popular as summer resorts, but they are generally too cold for all-year living. In recent years, however, the growing popularity of snow sports has extended the resort season into winter as well.

On their lower slopes mountains usually receive more precipitation than adjacent lowlands, at least on the windward side. Mountains are therefore often areas of fertile growth in otherwise arid regions. But climates within a mountain area are so varied, and they change within such short distances, that climatic maps cannot show them all accurately. Generally the area is shown on the map simply as one in which a mountain range, and therefore a variety of climates, exists. The climate of any part of a mountain or plateau area depends not only on its height and latitude but also on its topography, the direction of its prevailing winds, and the extent to which it faces the sun. Because of these factors, local differences may be considerable.

22. How Have People Altered Local Climates?

Although we seem to have had no effect on world climates, we have changed the **microclimates** ("small climates") of smaller areas. Large reservoirs bring the effects of a lake climate to their immediate surroundings. These may include milder winters and cooler summers, higher humidity, and lake and land breezes. The clearing of forested land to make field or pasture usually results in greater temperature extremes and stronger winds near ground level.

Our most striking climatic effects are seen in large cities, especially in industrial areas. Since city buildings stand in the way of the wind, there are lower wind speeds at low levels. On the other hand, the maze of structures breaks up the wind patterns and creates a good deal of turbulence.

Other effects are even more marked. Cities become warmer than their surrounding areas. Climatologists call cities *heat islands* for three reasons. First, their pavements absorb more sunshine than did the soils they now cover. Second, since nearly all the rain that falls on pavements runs off, there is very little evaporation of water to remove heat energy, as would happen on soil. Third, the city itself adds great quantities of heat (and water vapor) from automobiles, factories, furnaces, and people. So we have a heat island in a "sea" of cooler ground, and rising air currents form easily over the city. Since condensation nuclei from combustion are plentiful, clouds develop frequently, and rain increases in amount. With runoff high, nearby streams are more likely to be flooded than formerly. Air pollution from autos and chimneys causes haze, more frequent fogs, poor visibility, and fewer hours of sunshine.

TOPIC QUESTIONS

Each topic question refers to the topic of the same number within this chapter.

1. Why do we classify climates?
2. Define the three principal climatic zones described in this topic.

3. On what basis are the principal climatic zones usually subdivided?

4. (*a*) Name a few climatic subdivisions whose names show the relation between climate and natural vegetation. (*b*) Explain how the form of natural vegetation is related to rainfall and evaporation.

5. (*a*) What does the outline in this topic show? (*b*) What does Figure 42-2 show?

6. (*a*) Briefly describe the tropical rainy climates. (*b*) Which three climates are included in this category?

7. (*a*) Briefly describe the equatorial rainforest climate. (*b*) Name the regions where it is found.

8. Describe the tropical east coast climate. Where does it occur?

9. Describe the tropical monsoon climate. List its principal regions.

10. Locate and describe the tropical savanna climate.

11. Locate and describe the regions of tropical desert climate.

12. (*a*) Describe the general features of middle latitude climates. (*b*) Give the general locations of the seven types of middle latitude climate.

13. Describe the principal features of the Mediterranean climate and locate its chief regions.

14. Locate and describe the marine west coast climate.

15. Locate and describe the humid subtropical climate.

16. Locate and describe the humid continental climate.

17. Locate and describe (*a*) the middle latitude grassland climate, (*b*) the middle latitude desert climate.

18. Locate and describe the subarctic climate.

19. (*a*) How are tundra and icecap climates differentiated? (*b*) Describe and locate the tundra climate.

20. Locate and describe the icecap climate.

21. Compare the climate of highlands with that of adjacent lowlands.

22. How may local climate be altered by (*a*) a large reservoir nearby (*b*) the cutting down of surrounding forest areas (*c*) the growth of a city?

STUDENT ACTIVITIES

1. To obtain data for the making of climatic graphs similar to those used as illustrations in this chapter, consult the references listed in the Bibliography under climatology. Rainfall and temperature data for the principal cities of the United States may also be found in the *World Almanac*.

2. Use an outline map of the United States as a base for making a climate map of the country.

CHAPTER 43
The Earth in Balance

HOW DO YOU KNOW THAT . . . ?

1. Look through recent issues of your local newspaper for articles related to pollution of air, soil, rivers, lakes, or the ocean. Clip the articles and use them to start a scrapbook on people's effects on the environment. Make a list of the pollutants mentioned in each case, and of any remedial measures suggested in the articles.

2. Try the following simple technique for collecting some of the dust particles blown about in your local atmosphere. Get a roll of masking tape at least 5 cm (2 in.) wide. Fasten a strip of this tape—sticky side out—completely around the outside of a glass jar or tin can. Expose the jar outdoors to the air and wind for about a week, preferably on a pole or other support above the ground and away from building walls. At the end of the week, remove the strip and study it. From which direction did most dust come? Why? Examine the strip with a hand magnifier or low power microscope. Can you identify any of the dust particles as to material and source? Are most of the particles about the same size? Why?

1. Dead Lakes, Poisoned Air, and Fouled Beaches

Lake Erie, one of our five Great Lakes, has an area of nearly 10,000 square miles, and a maximum depth of 210 feet. It is considerably larger than the state of Massachusetts. In 1956, Lake Erie's thriving fishing industry recorded a catch of nearly 7 million pounds of blue pike alone. Seven years later the catch of blue pike totaled 200 pounds! Today the lake's once-prized commercial species of whitefish, wall-eyed pike, and blue pike have all but disappeared.

Lake Onondaga is a small lake near Syracuse,

New York. A center of recreational activities, it is used for rowing and sailing, but contact sports such as swimming and water skiing are no longer permitted because of the hazard of disease. Much of its 5 square miles of surface is covered with growths of slimy algae. Its fish, generally undesirable mudfish, are dangerously contaminated with mercury. Like Lake Erie, Onandaga is a lake that is dying before its time. Why?

In 1965, 18,000 people in the city of Riverside, California, became sick with gastroenteritis, a bacterial disease of the stomach. The disease was traced to the artesian wells that supply the city with its water. How did the wells become polluted?

For six days in October 1948, a thick smog formed and hung over the industrial city of Donora, Pennsylvania. Six thousand people became ill of respiratory diseases and 19 died. In London, England, in the winter of 1952–1953, periods of thick smog were followed by an increase of 4,000 in the death rate for the months of December, January, and February. In New York City, an increase of 647 in the death rate for January and February of 1963 coincided with a period in which persistent smog blanketed the city.

In 1967 the tanker *Torrey Canyon* ran aground and sprang a leak in the English Channel. Eighteen million gallons of oil poured out onto the sea and fouled miles of beaches in southern England and northern France. And in February 1969, a leak in an offshore oil well poured more millions of gallons of oil onto the sea and the beaches of Santa Barbara, California.

Occurrences such as these are among the best publicized incidents of our pollution of the environment in recent years. Unfortunately these are but a few of the thousands of cases, many of them chronic and perhaps no longer curable, of damage to the environment in all parts of the world. How does this happen? What are the harmful effects? What can we do to prevent or control it?

2. Ecology and Ecosystems

Ecology is an old word with a new-found fame. It is defined as "the relations between

Fig. 43-1. High school students examine this oil-covered duck, victim of an oil slick that blackened parts of the shore along the Atlantic Ocean. The sea bird on the right is covered with oil that seeped from an accident off the Pacific coast.

Wide World Photo

organisms and their environment." The ecologist also speaks of *ecosystems*. An **ecosystem** is any "unit consisting of all the living organisms in a given area interacting with the physical environment." Lake Erie, the human and animal population surrounding it, and all the organisms in its waters make up an ecosystem. Similarly, Lake Onondaga and its shores is an ecosystem. And each one of us is part of a "local ecosystem" consisting of his own community and its environment.

The interaction of a "community" of living things with its environment need not be harmful to the environment. In a balanced aquarium, for example, the fish, the snails, and the water plants thrive in almost perfect harmony with their water environment. For most of human existence, people have managed to inhabit this planet without serious damage to its essential life-giving resources. More recently, however, this has been less and less true. The expansion of chemical industries, the growth of large cities, and the tremendous increase in the use of the automobile, have combined to do serious damage to our air, our waters, and our soil. Let us see what some of this damage is.

3. Parts of the Hydrosphere

The hydrosphere is defined as the water part of the earth. There are four "parts" of the hydrosphere—ground water, running water, lakes, and oceans. They are all intimately connected by what we call the *water cycle*. The ground water seeps into streams and rivers and lakes. Streams and rivers drain into lakes, inland seas, and the ocean. So it is possible, and even probable, that pollutants entering the ground water will reach rivers and lakes. Pollutants entering rivers will reach lakes and seas, and may seep into ground water in regions where the water table is low. And pollutants may be dumped directly into the ocean.

4. What Pollutes the Hydrosphere?

What are the pollutants that may find their way into the waters of the hydrosphere? Raw or inadequately treated sewage is discharged by city sewage systems into rivers, lakes, and the sea. Sewage from inefficient cesspools drains into the ground and enters the ground water. Insecticides, pesticides, and excess fertilizers are washed by rains from the soils and vegetation on which they were used. Poisonous chemical wastes and residues from industrial plants are dumped into the rivers, the lakes, and the sea. Cool water is taken from rivers and lakes for cooling processes in power generating plants, steel mills, oil refineries, and other industrial plants. This water is

Fig. 43-2. Cutting down trees can destroy plant and animal habitats, increase stored ground water, and change ground temperatures and ground winds.

Grant Heilman

Fig. 43-3. A river barge passing through a lock of a polluted river in France is completely buried under a layer of foam. Foam like this comes from dumping detergents and other chemical wastes into the river upstream.

UPI

often returned to its source at a higher temperature. Oil sometimes pours into the sea in unwanted but tragic accidents when tankers run aground or offshore oil wells leak, or when waste oil is deliberately dumped from ships at sea. Radioactive wastes come from uranium mining and milling, from nuclear plants, and sometimes from the testing of nuclear weapons.

5. How is the Hydrosphere Harmed?

Some of the poisons poured into rivers and lakes—and even the ocean—may become concentrated in fish in percentages that make the fish unfit to eat, and may even kill waterfowl that feed upon the fish. These poisons include DDT, lead, and mercury. DDT has been responsible for fish kills in rivers.

Mercury, for example, has been concentrated in some swordfish and tuna. The concentration probably takes place through a "food chain" that begins when bacteria convert metallic mercury into an inorganic substance called methyl mercury. This substance is absorbed by tiny sea plants and animals called plankton. Small fish feed on the plankton, and the plankton, in turn, are eaten by larger fish such as tuna and swordfish.

Harmful germs from sewage may contaminate shellfish beds and cause such diseases as typhoid and hepatitis. The presence of contaminants may make it necessary to restrict swimming at beach resorts, and may even spoil a water supply.

Untreated sewage may also contain quantities of laundry detergents. Some of the latter, especially the phosphate detergents, are not "biodegradable"; this means that, unlike soap, they are not broken down by bacteria into simpler substances which are not harmful. In communities where the sewage goes into cesspools, the phosphates may find their way back into the wells, and reappear in the kitchen as foam in the drinking water.

Thermal pollution—heating caused by hot water wastes—may destroy fish both by making the river or lake water too warm for them and by depleting the oxygen supply of the water. As already indicated, oil on the sea may foul beaches and destroy sea birds by depriving them of their ability to swim and fly.

6. Eutrophication: How a Lake Dies

In Chapter 16, Topic 10, we point out that lakes are "temporary features" that disappear from the landscape in relatively short geological time. The natural destruction of a lake usually occurs through filling with sediment and the growth of vegetation that turns a lake into a swamp. This process is called **eutrophication**, and ordinarily it takes thousands of years for its completion.

But pollution can kill a lake—a small one like Lake Onondaga, or a large one like Lake Erie—in dozens rather than in thousands of years. Somewhat surprisingly, the pollutants responsible for the acceleration of eutrophication are not poisons. They are nutrients from organic wastes, from fertilizers, and especially from phosphate laundry detergents. These nutrients drain through sewers into rivers and lakes. In warm weather, the simple plants called *algae* grow rapidly in these nutrient-fed lakes. Large parts of the lake surface become covered with mats of foul-smelling green slime. When the algae die, decay bacteria attack them, using up the oxygen in the lake's waters. It is this depletion of oxygen which causes the lake to "die," because oxygen-deficient water will not support a food chain.

7. Controlling Water Pollution

The cure for pollution of the hydrosphere is obvious but expensive. Municipal and community sewage treatment plants must eliminate harmful solid, bacteriological, and chemical wastes from sewage before returning it to streams, lakes, and the sea. Similarly, industrial wastes must be purged of their poisons before they are released into bodies of water. Heated liquids must be allowed to cool, and radioactive wastes must be carefully disposed of, away from bodies of water if necessary.

Measures are already being taken to reduce pollution from persistent insecticides and pesticides. The use of DDT and other long-lasting poisons has been greatly curtailed by federal, state, and local regulation. As a result, fewer fish and birds are dying from these poisons.

The use of phosphates in detergents has been greatly reduced. There are signs that this measure

Fig. 43-4. What could be some ways in which the earth is polluted in a scene like the one below?

Grant Heilman

UPI

Fig. 43-5. Aircraft leave a trail of fumes as they fly over this city. Large jet planes create noise pollution, which also may upset the environment.

may eventually result in the revival of such bodies of water as Lake Onondaga and Lake Erie. It should also reduce pollution of such heavily polluted rivers as the Hudson, the lower Mississippi, the lower Missouri, the middle Ohio, and the Red River of Louisiana. In some areas such as Sulfolk County, Long Island, the sale of almost all detergents has been banned to keep phosphates out of the county's artesian wells and from its drinking water.

The prevention of oil spills is another difficult problem. Federal regulation of offshore oil drilling procedures can be and has been tightened, but the policing of ships that discharge oil wastes at sea requires international cooperation. Accidents to tankers may never be entirely eliminated, but improved construction of these giant ships can reduce the risk of spillage. Oil spills can be partly cleaned up by chemical foams and absorbent materials.

8. What Pollutes the Atmosphere?

Most atmospheric pollutants are either solids or gases. Air pollution scientists call the solid particles *particulates*. The main particulates found suspended in the air are soot, dust from soil, and plant pollens. Soot gets into the air mainly from the smoke of coal-burning or oil burning furnaces in power plants, factories, and homes. Additional soot may come from the burning of garbage in municipal and apartment house incinerators, and from the burning of leaves and trash. Most of the "dust" that plagues the housewife is a mixture of soot and dust blown up from the soil. Because soot is greasy and smudges easily, it is by far the more annoying part of household dust. Plant pollens are, of course, disturbing to hay fever sufferers, of whom there are said to be 8,000,000 in the United States alone. Ragweed is probably the principal cause of hay fever.

The principal gas pollutants in the air are sulfur dioxide, carbon monoxide, oxides of nitrogen, and hydrocarbons. Sulfur dioxide comes mainly from the burning of coal and fuel oil. It is a very poisonous gas that is highly irritating to the nose and throat. When it combines with droplets of water in the air it forms a corrosive acid. The other gas pollutants come mainly from the burning of gasoline in automobile engines, although some are found in industrial smoke as well. (In addition, poisonous lead compounds enter the air when leaded gasoline is burned.) All of the gasoline exhaust gases are poisonous. In a closed garage, or in a closed car with defective exhaust pipes, they can cause death. The nitrogen oxides and hydrocarbon gases are also smog formers. They are largely responsible for the smogs of Los Angeles.

9. Air Pollution: Dangers and Controls

Even though air pollutants are generally present in the air in less than toxic concentrations they are a serious menace to health. The death tolls described in the first topic of this chapter resulted principally from the effects of poisonous pollutants. Most of the deaths were among older people, but people of all ages were affected. Air pollution is believed to be a factor in causing such respiratory diseases as pneumonia, bronchitis, emphysema, tuberculosis, and lung cancer. Scientists say that on the average a resident of New York City inhales daily as much benzopyrene (a cancer-producing substance formed in the burning of coal, oil, and gasoline) as if he smoked two packs of cigarettes a day. Pollution is generally worse in areas centered around chemical industries and power plants.

Many measures must be adopted to control air pollution. Pollution from sulfur dioxide may be reduced by burning low sulfur fuels. These are less common and are more expensive than those types of coal and oil which are high in sulfur. Pollution by chemical plants can be reduced by requiring the use of both mechanical and chemical devices to eliminate soot and poisonous gases from the smoke. Very tall smokestacks help by sending the smoke high into the air where it can "disperse" into the upper atmosphere. The emission of soot may be reduced by burning oil instead of coal. An example of a city where industry and government worked together to clean up its air is Pittsburgh. Once known as the Smoky City, it is now a model of the successful use of air pollution controls.

Control of automobile pollution is more difficult. By 1967, Los Angeles had done an excellent job of eliminating soot and sulfur dioxide from its daily load of air pollutants. But 14,000 tons of pollutants were still entering the air each day, and nearly 90% of these were automobile exhaust products. Lead compounds

Fig. 43-6. Pittsburgh found ways to decrease smog. Views of downtown Pittsburgh are shown (left) before smoke control and (right) afterward.

UPI

Fig. 43-7. The Wankel engine is smaller than a conventional engine and has 40% fewer moving parts. Below are two devices to reduce a car's exhaust pollutants: left, a catalytic reactor; right, an afterburner that replaces a car's muffler.

Wide World Photo

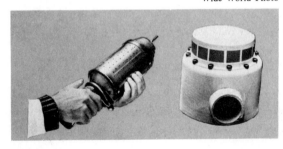

can be eliminated if non-leaded gasolines are used exclusively. But substitutes would have to be found to perform lead's anti-knock function. Pollution by nitrogen oxides, hydrocarbons, and carbon monoxide can be reduced by improving engine combustion, or by using devices to burn or convert these pollutants to harmless substances. New engines that promise improved combustion include the rotary (Wankel) engine, the stratified charge (Honda) engine, and the gas turbine engine. Steam engines and battery-powered engines are also being tried. After-

burners, blowby devices to recycle exhaust gases into the engine, and catalytic devices to convert exhaust gases into harmless substances are being used.

Local concentrations of pollutants are periodically removed from the air by natural processes. They are washed out by rains, blown away by winds, and carried into the upper air by convection. Until relatively recent times, these processes were generally enough to keep the air of our cities fit to breathe. But sometimes, they were not enough, as we have seen in the smog-produced tragedies of London and Donora. As the use of the automobile increased and as great centers of chemical industry grew up in many parts of the country, we learned that natural cleansing processes alone could not keep pace with pollution of the atmosphere. The result of this awareness is seen today in the concerted effort being made worldwide to solve the problems of air pollution.

10. Pollution Control and the Energy Crisis

The appearance in late 1973 of an "energy crisis" has created new problems in our battle against pollution of the environment. The United States, with the highest living standard in the world, has been using about 30% of the world's energy production for only 6% of the world's population. Most of our "energy" has come to us in the form of gasoline and fuel oil from the refining of petroleum, part of which we import from Arabia, Iran, Venezuela, and Canada. Part of this source may not be available to us, and what is available will be sharply increased in price.

Aside from price, what are the new problems? For years we have been converting home and industrial furnaces from coal to oil, and from high sulfur oil to low sulfur oil, as we switch over to the use of "cleaner" fuels. But now we are faced with a shortage of heating oil, especially low sulfur oil, much of which we import. Power plants and chemical plants are demanding that regulations forbidding the use of coal or high sulfur oils be relaxed. Oil companies are asking that strict rules governing the drilling and operation of offshore oil wells be eased to reduce the cost of new oil production. Pressure is put on Congress to permit quick construction of the Alaska pipeline opposed by environmentalists. Operators of coal mines want to be allowed to mine coal by strip mining without being required to make expensive restoration of the mined areas. On the positive side, however, reduced gasoline supply has curtailed the use of the automobile, thereby decreasing air pollution from exhaust gases.

What are the answers to these problems? Obviously compromises must be made. Wise local, state, and federal environmental protection agencies are making allowances such as the use of higher sulfur fuels. But they are not relaxing regulations any more than necessary, and they are not giving up all environmental safeguards.

TOPIC QUESTIONS

Each topic question refers to the topic of the same number within the chapter.

1. Describe briefly how pollution has harmed each of the following: the waters of Lake Erie or Lake Onondaga; the air of Donora, Pennsylvania, or Riverside, California; the beaches of Santa Barbara, California.

2. What is ecology? What is an ecosystem? What are the main parts of your local ecosystem?

3. What are the parts of the hydrosphere? How are they connected?

4. Give examples showing how each part of the hydrosphere may become polluted.

5. Give examples of the harm done by pollutants to (*a*) the sea (*b*) local water supply. What is thermal pollution? What are its harmful effects?

6. What is eutrophication? Explain how certain pollutants hasten eutrophication. Why is eutrophication harmful to a lake?

7. How can water pollution be controlled? How can oil spills be prevented or reduced?

8. What are the particulates that pollute the atmosphere? What gases pollute the atmosphere? Where do such gases come from?

9. What are the harmful effects of air pollution? How can air pollution from factories be controlled? How can air pollution from automobiles be reduced? What natural processes help to remove pollutants from the air?

10. What new problems in environmental protection have been created by the "energy crisis"?

BIBLIOGRAPHY

WEATHER

American Meteorological Society. *Weatherwise* (a bimonthly periodical). A.M.S., 45 Beacon St., Boston, Mass. 02108.
Battan, L. J. *The Unclean Sky.* Doubleday, Garden City, N.Y., 1966.

Battan, L. J. *The Nature of Violent Storms*. Doubleday, Garden City, N.Y., 1961.
Battan, L. J. *Radar Observes the Weather*. Doubleday, Garden City, N.Y., 1962.
Blair, T. A. *Weather Elements*. Prentice-Hall, Englewood Cliffs, N.J., 1957.
Blumenstock, D. I. *Ocean of Air*. Rutgers University Press, New Brunswick, N.J., 1959.
Cole, J. W. *Introduction to Meteorology*. Wiley, N.Y., 1970.
Dobson, G. M. B. *Exploring the Atmosphere*. Oxford University Press, Fairlawn, N.J., 1968.
Fisher, R. M. *How About The Weather?* Harper and Row, N.Y., 1958.
Forrester, F. H. *1001 Questions Answered About the Weather*. Dodd, Mead; N.Y., 1957.
Hare, F. K. *The Restless Atmosphere*. Harper, N.Y., 1963.
Laird, C. *Weathercasting*. Prentice-Hall, Englewood Cliffs, N.J., 1955.
Lehr, Burnett, and Zim. *Weather*. Golden Press, N.Y., 1965.
Loebsack, T. *Our Atmosphere*. New American Library, N.Y., 1961.
Miller, A. *Meteorology*. Merrill Publishing Co., Columbus, Ohio, 1971.
Reiter, E. R. *Jet Streams*. Doubleday, Garden City, N.Y., 1967.
Spar, J. *Earth, Sea and Air*. Addison-Wesley, Reading, Mass., 1962.
Spilhaus, A. F. *Weathercraft*. Viking, N.Y., 1951.
Sutton, O. G. *Challenge of the Atmosphere*. Harper and Row, N.Y., 1961.
U.S. Weather Bureau. *Weather Science Study Kit*. Govt. Printing Office, Washington, D.C. 20402.
Yates, R. F. *Weather for a Hobby*. Dodd, Mead; N.Y., 1956.

CLIMATE

Barry, R. G. and Chorley, R. J. *Atmosphere, Weather, and Climate*. Holt, N.Y., 1970.
Kendrew, W. G. *Climates of the Continents*. Oxford University Press, N.Y., 1961.
Kimble, G. H. T. *Our American Weather*. McGraw-Hill, N.Y., 1955.
Shapley, H. *Climatic Change*. Harvard University Press, Cambridge, Mass., 1954.
Trewartha, G. T. *Introduction to Climate*. McGraw-Hill, N.Y., 1954.

ECOLOGY

Battan, L. J. *The Unclean Sky*. Doubleday, Garden City, N.Y., 1966.
Carson, R. L. *Silent Spring*. Houghton Mifflin, Boston, 1968.
Colinvaux, P. A. *Introduction to Ecology*. Wiley, N.Y., 1973.
De Bell, G. (ed.) *Environmental Handbook*. Ballantine Books, N.Y., 1970.
Goldman, M. I. (ed.) *Controlling Pollution*. Prentice-Hall, Englewood Cliffs, N.J., 1967.
Hellman-Evans, H. *Energy in the World of the Future*. Lippincott, Philadelphia, 1973.
Jennings, G. *The Shrinking Outdoors*. Lippincott, Philadelphia, 1972.
Jones, T. C. Ed. and Ferguson. *The Environment of America: Present/Future/Past*. Doubleday, Garden City, N.Y., 1972.
Turk, et al. *Environmental Science*. W. B. Saunders Company, Philadelphia, 1974.
Ward, B. and Dubos René. *Only One Earth*. Norton, N.Y., 1972.
Ecology Society of America *Ecology* (periodical). Duke University Press, Durham, North Carolina.

APPENDIX

THE METRIC SYSTEM AND SI UNITS

Some Basic Units of Measurement in the SI (International System of Units)

Quantity	Name	Symbol
length	meter	m
mass	kilogram	kg
time	second	s

Metric System Prefixes

Prefix	Symbol	Multiples
kilo	k	1000
hecto	h	100
deka	da	10
		Divisions
deci	d	0.1 $(\frac{1}{10})$
centi	c	0.01 $(\frac{1}{100})$
milli	m	0.001 $(\frac{1}{1000})$

Examples Using the Meter

Name	Symbol	Equivalent
kilometer	km	1000 m
hectometer	hm	100 m
dekameter	dam	10 m
meter	m	1 m
decimeter	dm	0.1 m
centimeter	cm	0.01 m
millimeter	mm	0.001 m

Metric and English Equivalents in the SI (International System)

Length

1 meter = 39.37 in.
     = 3.280 ft
     = 1.093 yd
     = 0.00062 mi

1 cm = 0.393 in.
1 km = 0.62 mi

1 inch = 0.0254 m or 2.54 cm
1 foot = 0.3048 m or 30.48 cm
1 yard = 0.9144 m or 91.44 cm
1 mile = 1,609 m or 1.609 km

Area

1 square meter = 1550.0 sq in.
     = 10.76 sq ft
     = 1.19 sq yd

1 sq in. = 0.000645 sq m or 6.45 sq cm
1 sq ft = 0.09290 sq m
1 sq yd = 0.8361 sq m
1 sq mi = 2,589,900 sq m or 2.589 sq km

Volume

1 cubic meter = 61,023 cu in.
     = 35.314 cu ft
     = 1.308 cu yd

1 cu in. = 0.000016 cu m or 16.38 cu cm
1 cu ft = 0.02832 cu m
1 cu yd = 0.7646 cu m

Capacity

1 liter = 1.06 qt
     = 33.9 oz
1 kiloliter = 265 gal

1 quart = 0.95 l
1 pint = 0.47 l
1 gallon = 3.8 l

1 cu meter = 265 gal
     = 113.51 pecks
     = 28.38 bushels

Mass

1 kilogram = 2.204 lb
     = 35.274 oz

1 pound = 0.4536 kg
     = 453.6 g

1 ounce = 0.2845 kg
     = 28.35 g

Table 1: THE CHEMICAL ELEMENTS

ELEMENT	SYMBOL	ATOMIC NUMBER	ATOMIC WEIGHT	ELEMENT	SYMBOL	ATOMIC NUMBER	ATOMIC WEIGHT
Hydrogen	H	1	1.0079	Iodine	I	53	126.90
Helium	He	2	4.003	Xenon	Xe	54	131.30
Lithium	Li	3	6.939	Cesium	Cs	55	132.91
Beryllium	Be	4	9.012	Barium	Ba	56	137.34
Boron	B	5	10.811	Lanthanum	La	57	138.91
Carbon	C	6	12.01	Cerium	Ce	58	140.12
Nitrogen	N	7	14.007	Praseodymium	Pr	59	140.91
Oxygen	O	8	15.999	Neodymium	Nd	60	144.24
Fluorine	F	9	18.999	Promethium	Pm	61	(147)
Neon	Ne	10	20.183	Samarium	Sm	62	150.35
Sodium	Na	11	22.99	Europium	Eu	63	151.96
Magnesium	Mg	12	24.32	Gadolinium	Gd	64	157.25
Aluminium	Al	13	26.98	Terbium	Tb	65	158.92
Silicon	Si	14	28.01	Dysprosium	Dy	66	162.50
Phosphorus	P	15	30.97	Holmium	Ho	67	164.93
Sulfur	S	16	32.064	Erbium	Er	68	167.26
Chlorine	Cl	17	35.453	Thulium	Tm	69	168.93
Argon	Ar	18	39.948	Ytterbium	Yb	70	173.04
Potassium	K	19	39.102	Lutetium	Lu	71	174.97
Calcium	Ca	20	40.08	Hafnium	Hf	72	178.49
Scandium	Sc	21	44.96	Tantalum	Ta	73	180.95
Titanium	Ti	22	47.90	Tungsten	W	74	183.85
Vanadium	V	23	50.94	Rhenium	Re	75	186.2
Chromium	Cr	24	52.00	Osmium	Os	76	190.2
Manganese	Mn	25	54.94	Iridium	Ir	77	192.2
Iron	Fe	26	55.85	Platinum	Pt	78	195.09
Cobalt	Co	27	58.93	Gold	Au	79	196.97
Nickel	Ni	28	58.71	Mercury	Hg	80	200.59
Copper	Cu	29	63.54	Thallium	Tl	81	204.37
Zinc	Zn	30	65.37	Lead	Pb	82	207.19
Gallium	Ga	31	69.72	Bismuth	Bi	83	208.98
Germanium	Ge	32	72.59	Polonium	Po	84	(210)
Arsenic	As	33	74.92	Astatine	At	85	(210)
Selenium	Se	34	78.96	Radon	Rn	86	(222)
Bromine	Br	35	79.91	Francium	Fa	87	(223)
Krypton	Kr	36	83.80	Radium	Ra	88	(226)
Rubidium	Rb	37	85.47	Actinium	Ac	89	(227)
Strontium	Sr	38	87.62	Thorium	Th	90	232.04
Yttrium	Y	39	88.91	Protactinium	Pa	91	(231)
Zirconium	Zr	40	91.22	Uranium	U	92	238.03
Niobium	Nb	41	92.91	Neptunium	Np	93	(237)
Molybdenum	Mo	42	95.94	Plutonium	Pu	94	(242)
Technetium	Tc	43	(99)	Americium	Am	95	(243)
Ruthenium	Ru	44	101.1	Curium	Cm	96	(247)
Rhodium	Rh	45	102.90	Berkelium	Bk	97	(247)
Palladium	Pd	46	106.4	Californium	Cf	98	(249)
Silver	Ag	47	107.87	Einsteinium	Es	99	(254)
Cadmium	Cd	48	112.40	Fermium	Fm	100	(253)
Indium	In	49	114.82	Mendelevium	Md	101	(256)
Tin	Sn	50	118.69	Nobelium	No	102	(256)
Antimony	Sb	51	121.75	Lawrencium	Lw	103	(257)
Tellurium	Te	52	127.60	Kurchatovium	Ku	104	(not known)

Table 2: SIMPLIFIED MINERAL IDENTIFICATION KEY

The minerals are subdivided into three main groups on the basis of luster (metallic or nonmetallic) and color (light or dark). Further subdivision is based upon the presence or absence of cleavage. In the last column on the right, the minerals are arranged in order of decreasing hardness. See Table 3 for a list of some of the physical properties of a number of the more common minerals. A few minerals are listed in more than one place: e.g., some specimens of a certain mineral may be light, whereas others are dark colored; some specimens of another mineral may have a metallic luster, whereas others do not. You should not expect to detect relatively small differences in hardness: e.g., the difference between 3.5 and 4; but you should easily distinguish between 5 and 7 or 2 and 4.

Nonmetallic, light-colored minerals

- Scratch glass
  - Show cleavage
    - Sodium plagioclase feldspar (6–6.5)
    - Potassium feldspar (6)
  - Show fracture only
    - Beryl (8)
    - Quartz (7)
    - Olivine (6.5–7)
    - Opal (5–6.5)
- Do not scratch glass
  - Show cleavage
    - Fluorite (4)
    - Dolomite (3.5–4)
    - Calcite (3)
    - Biotite mica (2.5–3)
    - Muscovite mica (2–2.5)
    - Halite (2–2.5)
    - Gypsum (2)
    - Talc (1+)
  - Show fracture only
    - Kaolinite (2–2.5)
    - Sulfur (1.5–2.5)
    - Talc (1+)

Nonmetallic dark-colored minerals

- Scratch glass
  - Show cleavage
    - Corundum (9) has parting which looks like cleavage
    - Calcium plagioclase feldspar (6–6.5)
    - Amphibole (5–6)
    - Pyroxene (5–6)
  - Show fracture only
    - Corundum (9)
    - Tourmaline (7–7.5)
    - Garnet (6.5–7.5)
    - Quartz (7)
- Do not scratch glass
  - Show cleavage
    - Fluorite (4)
    - Sphalerite (3.5–4)
    - Biotite mica (2.5–3)
    - Chlorite (2–2.5)
    - Graphite (1–2)
  - Do not show cleavage
    - Hematite (5–6, but may appear softer)
    - Apatite (5)
    - Limonite (1–5.5)
    - Serpentine (2.5–5)

Minerals with metallic luster

- Streak black, greenish black, or gray
  - Pyrite (6–6.5)
  - Magnetite (5.5–6.5)
  - Chalcopyrite (3.5–4)
  - Galena (2+)
  - Graphite (1–2)
- Streak red or red brown
  - Hematite (5–6, but may appear softer)
  - Copper (2.5–3)
- Yellow, yellowish-brown, or white streak
  - Limonite (1–5.5)
  - Sphalerite (3.5–4)

Table 3: PROPERTIES OF SOME COMMON MINERALS

The minerals are arranged alphabetically, and the most useful properties in identification are printed in italic type. Most minerals can be identified by means of two or three of the properties listed below. In some minerals, color is important; in others, cleavage is characteristic; and in others, the crystal shape identifies the mineral.

NAME AND CHEMICAL COMPOSITION	HARD-NESS	COLOR	STREAK	TYPE OF CLEAVAGE	REMARKS
Amphibole (complex ferromagnesian silicate)	5–6	*Dark green to black*	Greenish black	Two directions at angles of 56° and 124°	Vitreous luster. Hornblende is the common variety. Long, slender, six-sided crystals. *Black with shiny cleavage surfaces at 56° and 124°.*
Apatite (calcium fluophosphate)	5	Green, brown, red, variegated	White	Indistinct	Crystals are common as are granular masses; vitreous luster.
Beryl (beryllium silicate)	8	*Greenish*	Colorless	None	*Hardness, greenish color, six-sided crystals.* Aquamarine and emerald are gem varieties. Nonmetallic luster.
Biotite mica (complex silicate)	2.5–3	Black, brown, dark green	Colorless	*Excellent in one direction*	*Thin elastic films peel off easily.* Nonmetallic luster.
Calcite (CaCO₃)	3	Varies	Colorless	*Excellent, three directions, not at 90° angles*	*Fizzes in dilute hydrochloric acid. Hardness.* Nonmetallic luster.
Chalcopyrite (CuFeS₂)	3.5–4	*Golden yellow*	Greenish black	None	*Hardness and color distinguish from pyrite.* Metallic luster.
Copper (Cu)	2.5–3	*Copper red*	Red	None	*Metallic luster on fresh surface. Ductile and malleable. Sp. gr. 8.5 to 9.*
Corundum (Al₂O₃)	8	Dark grays or browns common	Colorless	Parting resembles cleavage	*Barrel-shaped, six-sided crystals with flat ends.*
Diamond (C)	10	Colorless to black	Colorless	Excellent, four directions	Hardest of all minerals.
Chlorite (complex silicate)	1–2.5	*Greenish*	Colorless	Excellent, one direction	*Nonelastic flakes, scaly, micaceous.*
Dolomite (CaMg(CO₃)₂)	3.5–4	Varies	Colorless	*Good, three directions, not at 90°*	*Scratched surface fizzes in dilute hydrochloric acid. Cleavage surfaces curved.*
Feldspar (Potassium variety) (silicate)	6	*Flesh, pink, and red are diagnostic;* may be white and light gray	Colorless	*Good, two directions 90° intersection*	*Hardness, color, and cleavage.*
Feldspar (sodium plagioclase variety) (silicate)	6	*White to light gray*	Colorless	*Good, two directions, about 90°*	*If striations are visible, they are diagnostic.* Nonmetallic luster.
Feldspar (calcium plagioclase variety) (silicate)	6	*Gray to dark gray*	Colorless	*Good, two directions, about 90°*	*Striations commonly visible;* may show iridescence. Associated with augite, whereas other feldspars are associated with hornblende. Nonmetallic luster.
Fluorite (CaF₂)	4	Varies	Colorless	*Excellent, four directions*	Nonmetallic luster. In cubes or octahedrons as crystals and in cleavable masses.
Galena (PbS)	2+	*Bluish lead gray*	Lead gray	*Excellent, three directions, intersect 90°*	*Metallic luster.* Occurs as crystals and cleavable masses. *Very heavy.*
Gold (Au)	2.5-3	*Gold*	Gold	None	Malleable, ductile, *heavy.* Metallic luster.

Table 3: PROPERTIES OF SOME COMMON MINERALS (cont.)

NAME AND CHEMICAL COMPOSITION	HARDNESS	COLOR	STREAK	TYPE OF CLEAVAGE	REMARKS
Graphite (C)	1–2	*Silver gray to black*	Grayısn black	Good, one direction	Metallic or earthy luster. *Foliated, scaly masses co. mon. Greasy feel, marks paper.* This is the "lead" in a pencil (mixed with clay).
Gypsum (hydrous calcium sulfate)	2	White, yellowish, reddish	Colorless	*Very good in one direction*	Vitreous luster. *Can be scratched easily by fingernail.*
Halite (NaCl)	2–2.5	Colorless and various colors	Colorless	*Excellent, three directions intersect at 90°*	*Taste, cleavage, hardness.*
Hematite (Fe_2O_3)	5–6 (may appear softer)	*Reddish*	*Reddish*	None	Sp. gr. 5.3. Metallic luster (also earthy).
Kaolinite (hydrous aluminum silicate)	2–2.5	White	Colorless	None (without a microscope)	Dull, earthy luster. Claylike masses.
Limonite (group of hydrous iron oxides)	1–5.5	*Yellowish brown*	*Yellowish brown*	None	Earthy, granular. Rust stains.
Magnetite (Fe_3O_4)	5.5–6.5	*Black*	Black	None	Metallic luster. Occurs in eight-sided crystals and granular masses. *Magnetic. Sp. gr. 5.2.*
Muscovite mica (complex silicate)	2–2.5	Colorless in thin films; yellow, red, green, and brown in thicker pieces	Colorless	*Excellent, one direction*	*Thin elastic films peel off readily.* Nonmetallic luster.
Olivine (iron-magnesium silicate)	6.5–7	*Yellowish and greenish*	White to light green	None	*Green, glassy, granular.*
Opal (hydrous silica)	5–6.5	Varies	Colorless	None	*Glassy and pearly lusters, conchoidal fracture.*
Pyrite (FeS_2)	6–6.5	*Brass yellow*	Greenish black	None	*Cubic crystals* and granular masses. Metallic *luster.* Crystals may be striated. *Hardness important.*
Pyroxene (complex silicate)	5–6	Greenish black	Greenish gray	*Two, nearly at 90°*	*Stubby eight-sided crystals and cleavable masses. Augite* is common variety. Non-metallic.
Quartz (SiO_2)	7	Varies from white to black	Colorless	None	Vitreous luster. *Conchoidal fracture. Six-sided crystals common.* Many varieties. Very common mineral. *Hardness.*
Serpentine (hydrous magnesium silicate)	2.5–4	*Greenish (variegated)*	Colorless	Indistinct	*Luster resinous to greasy. Conchoidal fracture.* The most common kind of asbestos is a variety of serpentine.
Sphalerite (ZnS)	3.5–4	Yellowish brown to black	White to yellow	*Good, six directions*	*Color, hardness, cleavage, and resinous luster.*
Sulfur (S)	1.5–2.5	*Yellow*	White to yellow	Indistinct	Granular, earthy.
Talc (hydrous magnesium silicate)	1+	White, green, gray	Colorless	Good, one direction	Nonelastic flakes, *greasy feel. Soft.* Nonmetallic luster.
Topaz (complex silicate)	8	Varies	Colorless	*One distinct (basal)*	Vitreous. *Crystals commonly striated lengthwise.*
Tourmaline (complex silicate)	7–7.5	Varies; *black* is common	Colorless	Indistinct	*Elongated, striated crystals with triangular-shaped cross sections are common.*

GLOSSARY

Aa. Hawaiian name for lava flows with a rough, jagged surface.

Abrasion. Wearing away of rock by grinding action.

Abyssal plains. Flat, nearly level areas in the deepest portions of the ocean basins.

Acceleration. Rate at which velocity changes.

Adiabatic change. A temperature change within a substance caused only by its own expansion or compression.

Advection fog. Type of fog formed when warm, moist air moves horizontally over a cooler surface.

Aerolite. A stony meteorite.

Air mass. Large section of the troposphere in which temperature and humidity are fairly uniform at any given level.

Albedo. The percentage of radiant energy reflected by a surface.

Alluvial fan. Deposit of a stream where it emerges from a steep mountain valley upon open level land.

Altimeter. An instrument used to measure altitude.

Altitude. Height above sea level.

Altitude of a star. Angle between the star and the horizon.

Amber. Fossil resin from ancient conifers.

Ammonites. Extinct shell animals resembling today's chambered pearly nautilus.

Amorphous. Without shape or form. Applied to minerals having no crystalline structure.

Amphibian. Land-and-water animal like present-day frogs and salamanders.

Analemma. Graph showing equation of time and Sun's declination for each day of the year.

Anemometer. An instrument that measures the speed of the wind.

Aneroid barometer. A nonliquid barometer.

Annular eclipse. A partial eclipse of the Sun, in which the Sun is seen as a ring.

Antarctic circle. The parallel of latitude 66½°S of the Equator.

Anticline. Upfold of rock layers.

Anticyclone (high). Area of high air pressure in which winds spiral away from the center— clockwise in Northern Hemisphere, counterclockwise in Southern Hemisphere.

Aphelion. Point in orbit farthest from the Sun.

Apogee. Point farthest from the earth in the orbit of an earth satellite.

Apparent solar day. Time required for the Sun to cross a given meridian twice.

Apparent solar noon. Moment when the Sun crosses observer's meridian.

Aquifer. Water-bearing layer of rock.

Archeopteryx. First bird, closely resembling a reptile. Appeared in Jurassic period.

Archeozoic era. The oldest era in earth history for which there is a rock record. Early Precambrian time.

Arctic circle. The parallel of latitude 66½°N of the Equator.

Arête. Narrow, sharp divide between two glacial cirques.

Artesian well. Well in which the water comes from an aquifer below an impervious layer.

Asteroids (planetoids). "Minor planets" revolving around the Sun, mainly between Mars and Jupiter.

Astronomical unit. Average distance between Earth and Sun: about 92,900,000 miles.

Atoll. Ring-shaped island, usually of coral limestone, nearly encircling a lagoon.

Atomic number. Number of protons in the nucleus of an atom.

Atomic weight. Number of protons and neutrons in an atom.

Aurora. Luminous glow in nighttime sky, produced in the upper atmosphere by solar radiations.

Axial plane. A plane through a rock fold which divides the fold symmetrically.

Axis of fold. The line following the apex or trough of a fold.

Badlands. Areas of deeply gullied clay deposits.

Baguio. A tropical cyclone in the Philippines.

Barchan. Crescent-shaped sand dune.

Barograph. A recording barometer.

Barometer. An instrument that measures atmospheric pressure.

Barrier beach. Beach separated from the mainland by a lagoon or marsh.

Base level. Level of the body of water into which a stream flows.

Batholith. Great mass of intrusive igneous rock of unknown depth.

Bathyscaphe. Deep-sea ballasted diving apparatus with observation cabin which is lowered and raised by those aboard.

Baymouth bar. Bar extending across the mouth of a bay.

Beach. Part of shoreline that lies between high tide and low tide.

Bedding plane. The surface which separates one rock layer from another.

Bedrock. The solid rock of the unbroken crust of the earth.

Belemnite. Mesozoic shell animal with a cone-shaped chambered shell. Related to present-day squids.

Bench mark. Marker in the ground indicating exact elevation above sea level.

Benthoscope. Deep-sea exploration sphere lowered by cable.

Binary star. A pair of stars that revolve around a common center of gravity.

Block mountains. Mountains formed by faulting and tilting.

Blowout. A deflation basin, especially on a sand dune.

Brachiopods. Small marine shellfish abundant in Paleozoic seas, also known as "lamp-shells."

Braided (stream). Overloaded stream that winds in and out among sandbars.

Butte. In western United States, a flat-topped steep-sided hill smaller than a mesa.

Calcareous. Containing calcium carbonate.

Caldera. A volcanic crater several miles in diameter.

Calving. Blocks of ice breaking off from glaciers to form icebergs.

Cancer (Tropic of). Parallel which marks the farthest north position of the vertical rays of the Sun, 23½ °N.

Capacity. Maximum weight of water vapor a given quantity of air can hold at a given temperature.

Capricorn (Tropic of). Parallel that marks the farthest south position of the Sun's vertical rays, 23½ °S.

Carbonation. Chemical weathering in which minerals are altered to carbonates by carbonic acid.

Ceiling. Height of lowest layer of clouds that obscures more than half the sky.

Celestial navigation. Determining position from observations of the Sun, Moon, planets, or stars.

Celsius scale. Scale on which the fixed points of

freezing and boiling of water are 0° and 100° respectively.

Cenozoic. Most recent of the eras of earth history.

Cepheid variable. Pulsating star whose distance can be determined from its period of pulsation.

Chaparral. Dense growth of shrubs and grasses in California.

Chemical weathering. Weathering in which a change in composition occurs.

Chemosphere. The ozone layer.

Chernozem. A dark brown or black soil rich in humus and lime.

Chinook wind. Warm, dry wind resulting from compressional movement of air down the eastern slope of the Rocky Mountains.

Chromosphere. The layer of the Sun's atmosphere just above the photosphere.

Chronometer. Very accurate ship's clock used in determining longitude.

Cinder cone. Steep-sided volcanic cone composed largely of loose volcanic cinder or ash.

Cirque. Steep-walled basin at the head of a glacial valley.

Cirrus clouds. Feathery, wispy clouds of ice crystals at high altitudes.

Cleavage. Tendency of a mineral to split easily along planes parallel to the crystal faces, leaving smooth flat surfaces in one or more directions.

Clinometer. An instrument used to measure vertical angles, such as degree of dip.

Coal sacks. Two very dark areas in the Milky Way.

Coastal plain. Any plain that has its margin on the shore of a large body of water, particularly the sea.

Col. Gap or pass through an arête.

Cold air mass. Air mass that is colder than the surface over which it passes. Indicated on a weather map by *k*.

Cold front. Leading edge of mass of relatively cold air.

Comet. A mass of rock, ice, dust, and gas re-

volving around the Sun in a highly eccentric orbit.

Complex mountains. Those formed by complex combinations of diastrophism (folding and faulting) and vulcanism (volcanic action).

Composite cone. Large volcanic cone built of alternating layers of lava and cinders.

Conchoidal fracture. The shell-like surface produced in some minerals when they break.

Condensation. Process by which water vapor changes into liquid water or solid ice crystals.

Condensation nuclei. Microscopic chemical particles on which water vapor condenses in forming cloud droplets.

Connate water. The water trapped in sedimentary rocks at the time they were formed.

Constellation. Group of stars that form a pattern to which a name has been given.

Constructional forces. Forces (vulcanism and diastrophism) that build up or raise portions of the continents.

Contact metamorphism. Metamorphism caused by contact with hot lava.

Continental air mass. Air mass that originates over a continental (land) area and in general is relatively dry.

Continental climate. One of great extremes of temperature; hot summers, cold winters.

Continental shelf. Comparatively shallow ocean floor bordering a sea coast.

Continental slope. Relatively steep slope leading from the outer edge of the continental shelf to the deep ocean basin.

Contour interval. Difference in elevation between two consecutive contour lines.

Contour line. Line drawn through points at the same height above sea level.

Contour plowing. Plowing around a hill at uniform levels rather than up and down it.

Cordaites. Primitive conifers of the Paleozoic era, resembling modern cone-bearing pines and firs.

Core (inner). Zone of Earth's interior, extending over 800 miles from outer core to Earth's center. Very dense nickel-iron, probably solid.

Core (outer). Zone of Earth's interior extending 1,400 miles from mantle to inner core. Dense nickel-iron, probably liquid.

Coriolis force. An effect of the Earth's rotation that causes deflection of moving objects everywhere except at the Equator.

Corona. The Sun's outer atmosphere above the chromosphere.

Cosmic rays. Radiations coming to the Earth from outer space.

Countercurrent. One flowing in a direction opposite to that of a particular current.

Crater. Cuplike depression, as at the top of a volcano or on the lunar surface.

Crevasse. (1) Deep crevice, or fissure, especially in a glacier. (2) A break in a levee or other stream embankment.

Crinoids. Marine animals known as "sea lilies," related to starfish. Prominent during Mississippian period.

Crust. Layer of granite or basalt rock forming outer part of Earth's bedrock.

Crystal. Geometric solid bounded by regularly arranged plane faces meeting at definite angles.

Crystalline structure. Regular patternlike arrangement of atoms in a mineral.

Cumuliform clouds. Clouds having dome-shaped upper surfaces with horizontal bases.

Cyclone (low). Area of low air pressure in which winds spiral into the center—counterclockwise in Northern Hemisphere, clockwise in Southern Hemisphere. Also, a tropical storm in the China Sea.

Daylight saving time. Standard time advanced one hour.

Dead reckoning. Determining position by knowing speed, time, and direction of travel.

Deceleration. Rate at which velocity decreases.

Declination of the Sun. Number of degrees the Sun's vertical ray is north or south of the Equator.

Deflation basin. Shallow basin formed by wind erosion.

Delta. Level, fan-shaped deposit formed at the mouth of stream entering quiet body of water.

Density current. A subsurface current heavier (denser) than the surrounding water.

Depression contour. Contour line joining points of equal elevation within a depression.

Desert pavement. Pebble and boulder surface resulting from removal of sand and clay by wind.

Destructional forces. Forces that wear down the Earth's surface (weathering and erosion).

Dew point. Temperature at which air becomes saturated.

Diastrophism. Movement of the Earth's solid rock crust.

Diatom. Single-celled water plant that forms tiny shell of white silica.

Diatomite or diatomaceous earth. Lightweight white rock formed of diatom shells.

Diffuse nebula. A cloud of cosmic dust and gas.

Dike. Intrusion of magna into vertical or nearly vertical fissures in bedrock.

Dip. The angle a rock layer makes with the horizontal.

Distributaries (passes). Branches into which a stream divides as it flows across a delta.

Divide. Higher land separating two adjacent drainage basins.

Doldrums. Rainy equatorial belt of low air pressure and rising air.

Dome. Oval or circular elevation of rocks.

Doppler effect. An apparent change in the wavelength of a radiation where there is relative motion between the source of radiation and the receiver.

Dormant (volcano). A volcano that has not erupted in modern times, but appears to be alive.

Drainage basin. Land drained by a river system.

Drift. (1) Material deposited by a glacier. (2) One of the slower movements of oceanic circulation.

Drift bottles. Dated floats which drift with ocean currents.

Drizzle. Precipitation in the form of very fine drops of water falling very slowly.

Drumlin. Smooth, oval, or elongated hill or ridge of glacial drift.

Dry-adiabatic lapse rate. The rate—5½ °F per 1,000 feet—at which rising air cools by expansion.

Dune. Hill or ridge formed by the wind from sand or other granular material.

Dune migration. Movement of a sand dune.

Dwarf stars. Stars of absolute magnitude +1 or less.

Earthshine. Light reflected on the Moon from the Earth. Best seen at new and old crescent.

Ebb tide. Outgoing or falling tide.

Echo sounder. Device for measuring depth of water by means of sound waves.

Ecliptic plane. Plane in which the Earth moves around the Sun.

Ecology. The study of the relations between organisms and their environment.

Ecosystem. Any unit made up of all the organisms in a given area interacting with the physical environment.

Electron. Negatively charged particle which spins around the nucleus of an atom.

Element. A substance of atoms of one type which cannot be broken down or subdivided by simple chemical means.

Emergence. Process by which part of a sea or lake floor becomes dry land.

Entrenched meander. Canyon with meandering form, resulting from uplift or rejuvenation of a meandering river.

Epicenter. Point on the Earth's surface vertically above the origin (focus) of an earthquake.

Epoch. Subdivision of a geological period of earth history.

Equation of time. Difference in time between apparent solar noon and mean solar noon.

Equinox. Time of year (usually March 21, September 23) when day and night are everywhere equal on the Earth, and Sun's vertical rays are on the Equator.

Era. A major division of geological time.

Erosion. Process of breaking up and removing rock materials by such moving forces as streams, wind, glacier, waves, and ground water.

Erratic. Glacially transported boulder, different from the bedrock on which it rests.

Escape velocity. Minimum speed needed for an object to escape from any other body to which it is held by gravitation.

Escarpment. Extended line of cliffs or bluffs; high, steep face of a mountain or ridge.

Esker. Long, winding ridge of sand and gravel, deposited by a stream flowing beneath a glacier.

Estuary. That portion of drowned river valley which is entered by ocean tides.

Eutrophication. The process of a lake becoming a swamp as sediments and plants fill it in.

Exfoliation. Peeling of outer layers of bare rock.

Exfoliation domes. Mountain tops rounded by large-scale exfoliation.

Exosphere. Region of atmosphere above the ionosphere.

Extrusive (eruptive) rocks. Igneous rocks formed by hardening of magma after it reaches the Earth's surface.

Eye of storm. Calm, clear center of a tropical cyclone.

Fahrenheit scale. Scale on which the fixed points of freezing and boiling of water are 32° and 212° respectively.

Fall equinox. The beginning of fall, about September 23.

Fall zone. Series of falls and rapids occurring where streams flow from harder rock of the Piedmont Upland to softer sediments of the Atlantic Coastal Plain.

Fault. Deep fracture in rock, along which vertical or horizontal displacement has occurred.

Faulting. Movement of bedrock along a fault.

Fault scarp. Cliff that forms along a fault as a result of vertical faulting.

Ferrel's Law. Winds are deflected to their right in the Northern Hemisphere, and to their left in the Southern Hemisphere, because of the earth's rotation.

Fetch. Extent of water over which the wind blows with nearly constant direction and speed.

Finger lake. Lake occupying long, narrow rock basin or dammed river valley.

Fiord. Narrow, deep, steep-walled inlet of the sea formed by the partial submergence of a glaciated mountainous coast.

Fireball. An unusually bright meteor.

Firn (névé). The granular snow or ice of a glacier.

Fix. Position of a plane or ship as determined from lines of position.

Flash floods. Floods occurring suddenly in narrow valleys as a result of heavy downpours or "cloudbursts."

Flood plain. Any plain that borders a stream and is covered by its waters in time of flood.

Flood tide. Incoming or rising tide.

Fluorescence. Ability to glow when exposed to ultraviolet rays.

Focus. (1) Point within the Earth at which an earthquake originates. (2) Position of the Sun inside the Earth's elliptical orbit.

Foehn wind. *See* Chinook.

Fog. A cloud resting on the Earth's surface.

Folded mountains. Mountains formed as a result of lateral or sidewise pressure which folds the Earth's crust.

Foliated. Refers to the arrangement of minerals in layerlike parallel bands, as in schist and gneiss.

Foot wall. The face of the faulted block below the fault surface.

Foraminifera. Tiny protozoans that form shells of lime.

Fossil. Remains, impressions, or any evidence of the former existence of life, as found in the rocks.

Fracture. Appearance of a mineral surface where it breaks along other than cleavage planes.

Fringing reef. A coral reef attached to the shore in places.

Front. Boundary between two adjacent air masses.

Frontal thunderstorm. Thunderstorm that occurs along a well-developed or fast-moving front, usually a cold front.

Fumarole. Hole or vent in volcanic region, from which steam or hot gases are emitted.

g. The acceleration due to gravity at the earth's surface.

Galaxy. (1) A system of billions of stars, cosmic dust, and gas held together by gravitation. (2) Our own Milky Way galaxy.

Gangue. The waste rock in an ore.

Gap. Deep notch in a ridge or mountain chain.

Gastropods. Snails.

Geosyncline. Great elongated downfold in the Earth's crust, in which deposition and subsidence occur.

Geyser. Hot spring that erupts hot water and steam from time to time.

Geyserite. Deposits of silica formed around the openings of hot springs and geysers.

Glacial trough. U-shaped valley formed by glacier.

Glaze. Smooth transparent or translucent ice. *See* Sheet ice.

Globigerina. One-celled animals whose shells form calcareous deep-sea ooze.

Gradient (stream). Slope of a stream bed, usually expressed in feet per mile.

Granitization. The formation of granites by the metamorphism of other rocks.

Graptolite. Extinct marine invertebrate abundant in the Ordovician period.

Great circle. Circle whose plane passes through the center of a sphere, or divides the sphere into halves.

Great-circle route. Shortest distance between two points on a sphere, following the great circle that joins them.

Greenhouse effect. Ability of the air to absorb long heat waves from the Earth after allowing the Sun's short waves to pass through it.

Greenwich time. Mean solar time at the prime meridian.

Gregorian calendar. Calendar of Pope Gregory XII, in use by most countries today.

Gully. Miniature valley formed on a hillside by heavy rains.

Guyot. Deeply submerged volcanic cone with broad flat top. Common in Pacific Ocean. Also known as *tablemount*.

Gyrocompass. A gyroscopic device for showing north.

Hail. Precipitation in the form of irregular balls or lumps made of concentric layers of ice and snow.

Half-life. Time required for a radioactive substance to lose half of its activity. Half-lives range from fractions of seconds to billions of years.

Hanging trough. A hanging valley formed by glacial erosion.

Hanging valley. Tributary valley which enters the main valley some distance above the main valley floor.

Hanging wall. The face of the faulted block above the fault surface.

Hard water. Water which contains dissolved compounds of calcium, magnesium, or iron.

Hardness. Resistance to scratching.

Haze. Fine particles of moisture, smoke, or dust in the air, which decrease visibility.

Heat equator. A line on a world map connecting the hottest places in the world on the various meridians at any given time.

Heterosphere. That part of the atmosphere, from about 50 miles to several thousand miles above the earth's surface, in which the gases are arranged in layers.

High. *See* Anticyclone.

Homosphere. That part of the atmosphere, from the surface to about 50 miles up, which is a uniform mixture of gases.

Hook. Spit with a curved end.

Hooked trades. Winds that change their direction as they cross the Equator.

Horn (matterhorn). Sharp, hornlike or pyramid-shaped mountain peak.

Horse latitudes. Belts of high air pressure and very dry descending air, located at about 30°–35° latitudes both north and south of the Equator.

Humidity. Moisture content of the air.

Hurricanes. Tropical cyclones that develop over the oceans near the West Indies.

Hydration. Chemical union of water with a substance.

Hydrosphere. Water sphere of the Earth, including surface and subsurface waters.

Hygrometer. Instrument that measures relative humidity.

Humus. Decayed organic remains in soil.

Ichthyosaurs. Sea-going fishlike reptiles of the Mesozoic era, now extinct.

Igneous rocks. Those formed by the solidification of hot molten rock material called magma.

Index (guide) fossils. Those that are typical of a particular period or epoch of earth history.

Inertia. Tendency of all matter to resist any change in its state of rest or motion.

Inertial guidance. Automatic navigational system inside a space vehicle.

Insolation. The solar energy that reaches the Earth.

Intermittent stream. Stream whose bed is dry part of the year.

International date line. Imaginary line through the Pacific Ocean, roughly following the 180th meridian. Ships crossing westward advance the date. Ships crossing eastward set the date back.

Intrusive (plutonic) rocks. Igneous rocks formed

by hardening of magma below the Earth's surface.

Ion. Electrically charged particle.

Ionosphere. The part of the Earth's atmosphere, from about 40 miles to 300 miles above the surface, in which layers rich in electrified particles exist.

Isobar. Line on a map connecting places of the same atmospheric pressure at the same time.

Isoseismals. Lines drawn on a map between points of equal earthquake intensity.

Isostasy. A condition of balance within the earth's crust.

Isotherm. Line draw on a map through places having the same atmospheric temperature at a given time.

Jet stream. A narrow band of very strong westerly winds at high levels in middle latitudes. Usually at heights of 30,000 to 40,000 feet.

Juvenile water. Water from magma.

Kame. Small cone-shaped hill of partly stratified sand and gravel deposited by glacial streams.

Kame terrace. Long, narrow deposit formed between glacier and valley wall.

Karst topography. Surface of area containing sinks, sink hole lakes, disappearing streams and streamless valleys underlain by limestone.

Kepler's Law of Equal Areas. Each planet revolves so that the line joining it to the sun sweeps over equal areas in equal intervals of time.

Kettle (kettle hole). Depression in the terminal moraine or outwash plain formed when buried blocks of ice melted.

Knot. Speed of one nautical mile per hour.

Laccolith. Dome-shaped intruded mass of igneous rock.

Lagoon. Area of quiet, shallow water between a bar and the mainland.

Lapse rate. Rate at which atmospheric temperasure changes with altitude.

Laterite. A hard red or yellow soil rich in hydrous iron and aluminum oxides.

Latitude. Distance in degrees north or south of the Equator.

Lava. (1) Molten rock that reaches the Earth's surface. (2) The same material after it has solidified.

Lava cone. Broad, gently sloping volcanic cone composed chiefly of solidified lava.

Law of Equal Areas. *See* Kepler.

Leeward side. Side opposite to that from which the wind blows. The sheltered side.

Levee. Bank confining a stream channel, either natural or artificial.

Libration. Rocking motion of a rotating or revolving object.

Light-year. Distance light travels in one year: about 6 million million miles.

Line squall. *See* Squall line.

Lithosphere. Solid part of the Earth.

Lead. Material carried by geologic agents such as winds, rivers, and glaciers.

Local noon. Moment when the sun crosses the meridian of a particular locality.

Longitude. Distance in degrees east or west of the prime meridian.

Longshore current. A current which flows parallel to the shore.

Loran. Long range navigation that uses radio beams.

Low. *See* Cyclone.

Lunar month. Time from new moon to new moon—29½ days.

Luster. Shine of a mineral surface.

Mach number. Speed expressed as a multiple of the speed of sound. Near the Earth's surface "Mach 1" means about 750 miles per hour.

Magma. Hot liquid rock beneath the Earth's surface.

Magnetic variation or declination. Angle by

which the compass needle varies from true north.

Magnetosphere. The Van Allen radiation belts.

Magnitude (absolute). Apparent magnitude at a distance of 10 parsecs (32.6 light-years).

Magnitude (apparent). Brightness of a star as observed by the eye or telescope.

Mantle. Zone of rock extending from crust downward 1,800 miles.

Map scale. Ratio of distance on the map to distance on the Earth.

Mare. Latin word for *sea.* An extensive dark area on the Moon.

Marine climate. Oceanic or equable type of climate, with small temperature range.

Maritime air mass. Air mass that originates over water areas and is relatively moist.

Massive rocks. Unstratified rocks.

Mesopause. Boundary zone between the mesosphere and the ionosphere.

Mesosphere. The layer of the Earth's atmosphere between the stratosphere and the heterosphere.

Mass wasting. Downslope movement of large masses of rock material.

Meander. One of a series of somewhat regular winding or looping bends in a stream.

Mean solar day. Average of all the apparent solar days—24 hours.

Mechanical weathering. Weathering in which no change of chemical composition occurs.

Mediterranean climate. Warm, dry summers and mild, rainy winters.

Meridian. (1) Line on the Earth extending from N Pole to S Pole. (2) North-south line on a map. (3) A north-south line on the ground or through the sky.

Mesa. Isolated, broad, flat-topped hill with steep sides.

Mesozoic era. The second most recent era in earth history. Also known as the Age of Reptiles.

Metamorphic rocks. Those formed by the effect of heat, pressure, and chemical action on other rocks.

Meteor (meteoroid). Particle of rock flying through space. Friction with Earth's atmosphere heats it to incandescence.

Meteor shower. A fall of many meteors.

Meteor swarm. A family of billions of meteors.

Meteoric water. Water derived from precipitation.

Meteorite. A meteor that reaches the Earth's surface.

Meteorology. Science of the atmosphere.

Micrometeor. A tiny meteor or bit of meteoric dust.

Milky Way. The galaxy to which our Sun belongs.

Millibar. Unit used by meteorologists to measure air pressure; 34 millibars equal 1 inch of mercury.

Mineraloid. Noncrystalline mineral-like substance.

Mohorovicic discontinuity (Moho). Boundary between the Earth's crust and the mantle.

Moist-adiabatic lapse rate. Rate at which *saturated* air cools when it rises (usually 2°F to 3°F per 1,000 feet).

Molecule. The smallest part of a substance that retains the composition and properties of the substance and can exist free.

Monadnock. Hill or mountain left standing above the eroded surface of a peneplane.

Monocline. A rock fold consisting of one limb.

Monsoon. Wind that changes its direction with a change of season, particularly in Asia.

Moraine. (1) Rock material carried by a glacier. (2) Rock material deposited directly by glacial melting, therefore unassorted and unstratified.

Mosasaur. Extinct giant sea reptile of the Cretaceous period.

Mudflow. Rapid movement of large masses of mud and other rock debris.

Nansen bottle. Bottle used to get samples of sea water at different depths.

Native metal. Metal which occurs as a mineral uncombined with other elements.

Nautical mile. One minute of latitude; about $1\frac{1}{16}$ ordinary miles.

Neap tide. A tide of small range occurring at quarter phase of the Moon.

Nebula. Great cloud of interstellar dust and gas.

Neck. Land separating the ends of a stream meander. Also, the core of a volcano.

Neutron. One of the three basic atomic particles; weighs slightly more than the proton and has no electric charge.

Névé. Granular snow and ice. *See* Firn.

Newton's Third Law of Motion. To every action there is an equal and opposite reaction.

Nimbus cloud. Any rain cloud.

Normal fault. A fault in which the hanging wall has moved down.

Normal lapse rate. Average rate of change of temperature with elevation in the troposphere. It is equal to a drop of $3\frac{1}{2}°F$ for a rise in elevation of 1,000 feet.

Nose cone. Cone-shaped forward end of a space vehicle.

Nucleus. Inner core of the atom consisting of neutrons and protons tightly locked together.

Nuclide. Atoms of the same chemical element that have different atomic weights.

Nunatak. Mountain peak which projects through a continental glacier.

Oasis. Fertile spot in a desert, resulting from a spring or stream.

Oblate spheroid. A sphere which is flattened at its poles and bulges at its equator.

Occluded front. Front formed when a cold front overtakes a warm front.

Oceanography. Science dealing with the oceans and ocean basins.

Offshore bar. Sand bar running parallel to coast line.

Oil shale. Type of shale from which oil can be extracted.

Ooze. Fine lime or silica mud, found on deep ocean floor.

Orbit. Path of a revolving body, like that of the earth around the sun.

Ore. A natural mixture of minerals from which an element or compound can be extracted profitably.

Ostracoderms. Primitive fishes believed to be the first vertebrate animals.

Outwash plain. Broad, stratified, gently sloping deposit formed beyond the terminal moraine by streams from a melting glacier.

Overloaded stream. A stream so heavily loaded with sediment that it deposits material all along its course.

Oxbow lake. Crescent-shaped lake remaining after a meandering river has formed a cut-off and the ends of the original bend have been silted up.

Oxidation. Union of oxygen with other elements.

Ozonosphere or ozone layer. The part of the Earth's atmosphere richest in ozone, reaching from 10 to 30 miles above the surface.

Pahoehoe. Hawaiian name for lava flows with a smooth and ropelike surface.

Paleontology. The science that deals with prehistoric life and fossil remains as found in rocks.

Paleozoic era. The era of earth history which followed Precambrian time.

Parallax of a star. Angle formed by the two lines from the star to the Sun and to one end of the Earth's orbit.

Parallelism of axis. Each position of the Earth's axis is parallel to every other position during revolution.

Parallels. East-west circles around the Earth parallel to the Equator.

Parasitic cone. Small cone formed on the side of a volcano.

Parsec. Distance at which a star would have a parallax of one second of arc; 3.26 light-years.

Peat. Dark brown decomposed plant material representing first stage in coal formation.

Pedalfers. Soils whose B-horizon is rich in iron oxides and clays.

Pedocal. Soils rich in lime, especially in the B-horizon.

Pegmatite. Very coarse-grained igneous rock, usually found in dikes. Contains large crystals of quartz, feldspar, mica, and other minerals.

Peneplane. Low, rolling, nearly level region formed by erosion.

Penumbra. Part of shadow that is partly illuminated. Partial shadow.

Perched boulders. Glacier deposited boulder lying in an unstable position.

Perigee. Point nearest the Earth in the orbit of an earth satellite.

Perihelion. Point in orbit nearest the Sun.

Period. Subdivision of a geological era of earth history.

Period (of a revolving body). Time taken to complete one orbit or revolution.

Period (of a wave). The time needed for one full wavelength to pass a given point.

Permeable rock. Rock which transmits fluids, such as ground water.

Phenocrysts. The large mineral grains or crystals in porphyritic rocks.

Photosphere. The visible "surface" layer of the Sun.

Pibal. A record of observations made by a pilot balloon.

Pillow lava. Basaltic lava that has a pillowlike structure.

Pitch. Up-and-down motion.

Placer. A rich concentration of a heavy mineral (like gold) in the gravels of ocean beaches or river sand bars.

Plain. Region of horizontal rock structure and low relief.

Plankton. Microscopic sea plants and animals.

Plateau. Region of horizontal rock structure and high relief.

Plate tectonics. A hypothesis suggesting that the surface of the earth is covered by a number of thick blocks, or plates, of rock that move with respect to one another.

Playa. Temporary broad, shallow lake characteristic of desert areas.

Plesiosaurs. Giant sea-going reptiles of the Mesozoic era.

Plunge. Angle the axis of a fold makes with the horizontal.

Plunge pool. Large depression formed at the base of a waterfall.

Podsol. The light gray soil of a pine forest.

Polar creep. Slow movement of cold water along the ocean bottom from the Poles to the Equator.

Polar easterlies. Winds that blow out of the polar highs toward the subpolar lows.

Polar front. Permanent front between the prevailing westerlies and the polar easterlies.

Porphyry. Rock containing large crystals embedded in a fine-grained groundmass.

Pothole. Circular hole in the bed of a stream, formed by the grinding action of rock material.

Prairie. Treeless and grassy plain.

Precambrian. Time preceding the Cambrian, such as the Archeozoic and Proterozoic eras.

Pressure gradient. Rate at which air pressure changes on the shortest path between two isobars.

Pressure gradient direction. The direction at right angles to the isobars.

Prevailing westerlies. Winds that originate in the horse latitude highs and blow toward the subpolar lows.

Primary lows and highs. Areas of air pressure that result from movements of air caused by unequal heating. Also called semipermanent lows and highs.

Prime meridian. Zero meridian, which passes through Greenwich, England, and from which longitude is measured.

Prominence. A flamelike cloud of gas above the Sun's chromosphere.

Promontory (headland). A long, narrow projection of a coastline.

Propellant. Fuel and oxidizer for a rocket engine.

Proper motion. Rate at which a star changes position among the other stars.

Proterozoic era. The second and later era of Precambrian time.

Protocontinent. In the theory of continental drift, a single continent that preceded all our present continents.

Proton. A positively charged particle in the nucleus of an atom.

Psychrometer. An instrument that measures relative humidity by using wet-bulb and dry-bulb thermometers.

Pterosaur. Flying reptile of the Mesozoic era.

Pyroclastic. Blown out of a volcano during an eruption.

Quasars. Very distant intense radio sources that resemble stars, but are far larger, more luminous, and more massive. Also called *quasistellar radio sources*.

Radarscope. A screen, similar to a television screen, on which objects located by radar are pictured.

Radial velocity. Rate at which a star is moving toward or away from us.

Radiation (ground) fog. Fog that occurs during calm, clear nights when moist air near the surface is cooled by radiation.

Radioactivity. Emission of very fast atomic particles or rays from the nucleus of an atom.

Radiocarbon. Radioactive isotope of carbon; atomic weight, 14.

Radio compass. A device for determining north from the direction of radio waves from known sources.

Radiolaria. One-celled animals whose shells form siliceous deep-sea ooze.

Radiosonde. Weather radio carried aloft by balloon to determine relative humidity, temperature, and pressure of the upper air.

Radio telescope. An instrument that picks up radio waves emitted by bodies in space.

Radius vector. An imaginary line joining an orbiting body to the object around which it revolves.

Rain gauge. Instrument for measuring amount of precipitation.

Rays (lunar). Bright streaks of unknown origin radiating from lunar craters.

Red shift. Doppler shift toward the red end of the spectrum, caused by relative motion of source and receiver away from each other.

Reflector or reflecting telescope. Telescope that uses a concave mirror as its objective.

Refraction. Bending of light rays when passing from one transparent substance to another of different density.

Refraction (of water wave). The bending effect that causes obliquely approaching waves to turn parallel to the shoreline they are about to strike.

Refractor or refracting telescope. Telescope that uses a convex lens as its objective.

Regolith. Loose rock material that covers the bedrock.

Rejuvenated stream. One which has become more active in erosion because of an uplift in the land.

Relative humidity. The extent to which air is saturated with water vapor. Expressed in per cent.

Relief. Difference in height between the highest and lowest points in a given area.

Residual soil. Soil that remains where it was formed.

Retrorocket. Rocket fired from a forward end of a space vehicle to slow it down, usually for a landing.

Reverse fault. A fault in which the hanging wall is raised relative to the footwall.

Rill. A long crack in the Moon's surface.

Rip current. A strong surface current that flows away from the beach in a narrow channel through incoming breakers.

Roches moutonnées. Outcrops of bedrock, smoothed and striated by glacial action and resembling sheep's backs.

Rock flour. Mixture of fine sand and silt formed by the crushing of unweathered rock under a glacier.

Rock glacier. A ridge of loose rock material that moves slowly downslope in a mountain valley.

Roll. Rolling motion around an axis.

Rotation. Turning of an object on its axis.

Saltation. Moving in short jumps and bounces.

Satellite. Smaller body revolving around a larger body.

Savanna. Tropical grassland.

Schmidt telescope. A reflecting telescope with a wide field of view, especially suited to photography.

Seamount. A submerged, steep-sloped peak rising from the ocean floor. Flat-topped peaks are called guyots.

Seismograph. Instrument that detects and records earthquake shocks.

Selva. Tropical rainforest vegetation.

Sextant. Instrument used to measure the altitude of the sun, stars, and other heavenly bodies.

Shield. Large area of Precambrian rock.

Shore current. Movement of water parallel to the shoreline.

Shoreline of emergence. Shoreline formed by the emergence of a sea or lake floor.

Shoreline of submergence. Shoreline formed by the partial submergence of a land mass.

Sidereal day. Day whose length is measured between two successive appearances of a star on a given meridian.

Sidereal month. About 27⅓ days.

Siderite. A nickel-iron meteorite. Also the mineral iron carbonate.

Sill. Sheet of igneous rock forced between sedimentary rock layers.

Silver iodide. Chemical used as condensation nucleus for water vapor in rainmaking.

Sink (sinkhole). A surface depression in a region of soluble bedrock such as limestone.

Slack water. Short period of time in which there is no movement of the water between changing tides.

Sleet. Frozen raindrops.

Slickensides. Polished rock surfaces along a fault plane.

Slip face. Leeward side of a sand dune.

Smog. Mixture of smoke (or other chemical fumes) and fog.

Snow line. Level above which snow exists all the year.

Solar day. A day whose length is measured between two successive appearances of the Sun on a given meridian.

Solar flare. A great eruption of glowing gas into the photosphere.

Solar wind. Streams of protons and electrons that are blown out from the sun in all directions.

Solstice. The time of year when the Sun's vertical rays reach farthest north (June 21) or south (Dec. 21) of the Equator.

Sounding. Method of determining depth of water.

Specific gravity. Ratio of the weight of a substance to the weight of an equal volume of water.

Specific humidity. Number of grams of water vapor in one kilogram of air.

Spectrograph. A spectroscope used as a camera.

Spectroscope. An instrument that can disperse a beam of light into a spectrum of its component wavelengths.

Spectrum. The band of colors formed when light is split into its separate wavelengths.

Spit. Bar built across a bay with one end attached to the land.

Spring equinox. Beginning of spring, about March 21.

Spring tide. A tide of large range occurring at new moon and full moon.

Squall line. A line of thunderstorms at or ahead of a fast-moving cold front.

Stalactite. Iciclelike deposit of mineral (usually calcite) hanging from a cavern roof.

Stalagmite. Blunt, rounded deposit of mineral (usually calcite) grown upward from the floor of a cavern.

Standard atmospheric pressure. Equals 29.92 inches of mercury or 1013.2 millibars at sea level.

Standard time. Time based on one particular meridian but used over a belt of about 15 degrees longitude.

Star cluster. Group of stars within our galaxy. Example, star cluster in Hercules.

Stationary front. Boundary between two air masses that are not moving.

Steppe. Semiarid grasslands or brushlands in middle latitudes.

Stock. A large igneous intrusion similar to a batholith, but with smaller exposed surface area.

Stratification. Arrangement of rock beds in visible layers.

Stratiform clouds. Those which are arranged in unbroken, horizontal layers or sheets.

Stratopause. Boundary between the stratosphere and the mesosphere.

Stratosphere. The layer of the Earth's atmosphere that extends from the troposphere to the mesosphere.

Streak. Color of a mineral when powdered or rubbed on a streak plate.

Streak plate. Unglazed piece of porcelain or tile used to obtain the streak of a mineral.

Stream piracy (capture). Diversion of the upper part of one stream by the headward growth of another stream.

Striations. (1) Fine parallel lines common on plagioclase feldspars. (2) Scratches on rocks and bedrock due to glacier movement.

Strike. Compass direction of a line formed where a rock layer intersects an imaginary horizontal plane.

Stike-slip fault. Displacement of rock in a horizontal direction only.

Subglacial steam. Stream which flows in a tunnel beneath a glacier.

Sublimation. The change of state in which ice and snow change directly into water vapor without melting. Also the reverse change, in which water vapor changes directly to snow or ice crystals.

Submergence. The covering of all or part of a land form by a sea or lake.

Subpolar lows. Stormy belts of low air pressure located at about 60°–65° latitudes in both hemispheres.

Subtropical highs. The horse latitudes.

Summer solstice. Beginning of summer, about June 21.

Sunspot. A dark area on the Sun's photosphere.

Superposition, Law of. In historical geology the general rule that younger rocks lie on top of older rocks.

Synchronous satellite. An artificial satellite which revolves in its orbit in the same time and in the same direction as the earth rotates, so constantly stays above the same place on the earth.

Syncline. Downfold of rock strata.

Synodic month. About 29½ days.

Talus. Fallen rock material at the foot of a steep hillside or cliff.

Tarn. Small mountain lake formed in the rock basin of a cirque.

Telemetering. Method by which coded readings are sent from radiosondes and artificial satellites carrying automatic transmitters.

Temperature gradient. Rate of change of temperature between two places.

Temperature inversion. Increase in temperature with increase in altitude.

Terrigenous sediments. The ocean sediments derived from land areas.

Theodolite. Instrument used to observe pilot balloons in determining direction and speed of winds aloft.

Thermocline. Transitional layer between warm

surface waters and cold bottom waters in oceans or lakes.

Thermograph. A recording thermometer.

Thrust fault. A reverse fault with dip of less than 45°.

Tidal range. Vertical distance between low and high tide.

Till. Unstratified glacial deposits, chiefly clay, gravel, and boulders.

Tillite. Consolidated glacial till of ancient ice ages.

Time meridians. The 24 meridians, each of which is the approximate center of a standard time zone. They begin at the prime meridian, and are 15 degrees apart.

Tombolo. Sand bar which ties an island to the mainland.

Tornado. Small, violent, twisting storm occurring over level land areas.

Torrid Zone. Forty-seven-degree wide belt between the Tropics over which the vertical rays of the Sun pass.

Trade winds. Winds that originate in the horse latitudes and blow toward the doldrums.

Transit. Passage of Mercury or Venus across the face of the Sun. Also, the passage of a celestial body across the meridian.

Travertine. Ground water deposit composed of calcite.

Trenches. Long, narrow depressions forming the deepest parts of the ocean floor.

Triboluminescence. Property of glowing when scratched or crushed.

Trilobites. Crablike marine animals, now extinct. They were abundant all through the Paleozoic era.

Tropopause. Boundary between the troposphere and the stratosphere.

Troposphere. Convective region of the atmosphere that extends from the Earth's surface to the stratosphere. Its height ranges from 5 miles at the poles to 11 miles at the Equator.

Tsunami. Gigantic waves that result from earthquakes or landslides on the sea floor.

Tuff. Rock formed of volcanic fragments.

Tundra. Continuously cold, damp, treeless plain of arctic regions, characterized by mosses, lichens, and small shrubs.

Turbidity current. Currents carrying mud down continental slopes. Believed to have carved out some submarine canyons.

Twilight circle. Boundary line around the earth between its day and night halves.

Typhoon. A tropical cyclone in the Indian Ocean.

Ultraviolet rays. Rays of shorter wavelength than visible light but longer than X rays.

Umbra. Darkest part of the shadow of the Moon or Earth.

Unconformity. A surface that separates the rocks of two different ages of earth history.

Uniformitarianism. The concept that the present is the key to the past.

Universal time. Mean solar time at Greenwich, England.

Upslope fog. Fog formed when moist air cools as it rises along hillsides or mountain slopes.

Valley train. A long narrow body of sediment deposited by the stream flowing out of a valley glacier.

Van Allen belts. Doughnut-shaped zones of intense radiation surrounding the earth between 800 miles and 40,000 miles above the surface. Also called the magnetosphere.

Varve. Pair of layers of clay deposited in a glacial lake in one year.

Vein. Crack or fissure filled with mineral matter formed from underground solutions.

Velocity of escape. Speed required for an object to escape gravitational pull.

Ventifact. Wind abraded pebble with one or more flat sides.

Vertical temperature gradient. *See* Normal lapse rate.

Visibility. Greatest distance toward the horizon

at which prominent objects can be recognized by the unaided eye.

Vitreous. The luster of broken glass.

Volcanic cone. Cone-shaped mound built up through volcanic eruptions.

Volcanic neck. The solidified lava filling the central vent of an extinct volcano.

Volcano. Opening in the Earth's crust through which an eruption takes place.

Vulcanism. Movements of liquid rock inside or outside of the Earth's crust.

Waning. The decreasing of the Moon's visible illuminated surface, from full moon to new moon.

Warm air mass. Air mass that is warmer than the surface over which it passes. Indicated on a weather map by *w*.

Warm front. Leading edge of a mass of relatively warm air.

Water gap. Pass in a mountain ridge through which a stream flows.

Watershed. The entire area drained by a stream and its tributaries.

Water table. Surface below which the ground is saturated with water.

Wave height. Vertical distance from trough to crest.

Wave period. Time between two successive wave crests at a given point.

Wavelength. Distance between two successive wave crests.

Waxing. The increasing of the Moon's visible illuminated surface, from new moon to full moon.

Weathering. Process in which rocks are broken up by the action of the atmosphere and organisms.

Willy-willy. A tropical cyclone in the Pacific near Australia.

Wind gap. Water gap no longer occupied by a stream.

Windward side. Side from which the wind blows.

Winter solstice. Beginning of winter, about December 21.

Yaw. Side-to-side motion.

Yazoo stream. Tributary stream which flows parallel to the main stream for some distance through its flood plain.

Zenith. Point in the sky directly above the observer.

Zenith distance. Angle between the sun or star and the zenith.

Zone of aeration. Unsaturated area above the water table.

Zone of saturation. The area beneath the earth's surface which is saturated with water.

INDEX

An italicized page number indicates that the entry is illustrated on that page.